Economic Harmonies

ECONOMIC HARMONIES

ECONOMIC HARMONIES

by

Frederic Bastiat

Translated from the French by
W. HAYDEN BOYERS

Edited by GEORGE B. de HUSZAR

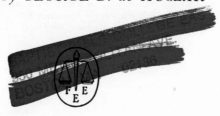

THE FOUNDATION FOR
ECONOMIC EDUCATION, INC.
IRVINGTON-ON-HUDSON, NEW YORK 10533

THE PUBLISHER

The Foundation for Economic Education is a nonpolitical, nonprofit, educational institution. Its Senior Staff and numerous writers are students as well as teachers of the free market, private ownership, limited government rationale. Sample copies of the Foundation's monthly study journal, *The Freeman,* are available on request.

First printed in cloth edition by
D. Van Nostrand Company, Inc., 1964

Second printing of this paperback edition in 1968
by The Foundation for Economic Education, Inc.
Irvington-on-Hudson, New York   10533

LC# 64-5729

PRINTED IN THE UNITED STATES OF AMERICA

This volume is dedicated to the memory of

LOREN BARKER MILLER

in whose endeavors in behalf of human freedom while he was directing governmental research in Newark, Kansas City, and Detroit, Frédéric Bastiat was an inspiration and a challenge, both in the finding of better answers to immediate problems and in the influencing of many keen young minds to a new dedication to integrity and leadership in public affairs.

WILLIAM VOLKER FUND

Preface to the English-Language Edition

Frédéric Bastiat has said that the *Harmonies* is a counterpart to *Economic Sophisms,* and, while the latter pulls down, the *Harmonies* builds up. Charles Gide and Charles Rist in a standard treatise, *A History of Economic Doctrines,* have referred to "the beautiful unity of conception of the *Harmonies,*" and added, "we are by no means certain that the *Harmonies* and the *Pamphlets* are not still the best books that a young student of political economy can possibly read."

Unfortunately the *Harmonies* after chapter 10 are unfinished fragments and therefore are filled with repetitions which Bastiat would have corrected had he lived. It is also important to keep in mind that parts of the *Harmonies* were first given as speeches.

This translation follows as faithfully as possible the original French standard edition of the complete works of Bastiat. Cross references have been included among the three volumes of the present translation.

Three types of notes are included: Translator's notes are directed at the general reader and are mainly about persons and terms. Editor's notes refer to notes by the editor of the French edition; Bastiat's notes stand without such notations. Only the Translator's notes are at the bottom of the page; the Editor's notes and Bastiat's notes are at the end of the volume. The latter two are more important but were put in the back to avoid cluttering the pages and to promote readability. Where the French editor has indicated a cross reference to a chapter or passage in *Economic Sophisms* or to any of the pamphlets or speeches included in *Selected Essays on Political Economy,* the original reference to the

French edition has been replaced by one directing the reader to the English translation.

Although these three volumes of English translations of Bastiat are published simultaneously, there is some repetition of the Translator's notes and the editorial Prefaces. This is necessary because some may obtain only one volume of this three-volume series, and therefore each volume has been made as self-sufficient as possible.

The Editor wishes to express his appreciation to W. Hayden Boyers, to Dean Russell for writing the Introduction, to Arthur Goddard, and to the William Volker Fund.

GEORGE B. DE HUSZAR

Bibliographical Notice

Les Harmonies économiques, par Frédéric Bastiat, Paris, Guillaumin, 1850, 463 pp.
This was the first edition. It was published just a few months
before Bastiat died, and was incomplete, containing only the
first ten chapters.

*Les Harmonies économiques, par Frédéric Bastiat, 2ème édition
augmentée des manuscrits laissés par l'auteur, publiée par la
Société des Amis de Bastiat (sous la direction de P. Paillottet
et R. de Fontenay),* Paris, Guillaumin, 1851, xi, 567 pp.
This was the first complete edition, and no changes of any
importance were subsequently made in it. Paillottet brought
back from Rome (where Bastiat had died) the manuscript of
the *Harmonies* and had Bastiat's commission to edit and
publish the entire work.

*Oeuvres complètes de Frédéric Bastiat, mises en ordre, revues et
annotées d'après les manuscrits de l'auteur (par P. Paillottet
et R. de Fontenay),* Paris, Guillaumin, 1854–55, 6 vols.
The *Harmonies* were incorporated into this as Volume VI.

Oeuvres complètes, etc., *2ème édition,* in the series "La Biblio-
thèque des sciences morales et politiques," Paris, Guillaumin,
1862–64, 7 vols.
The *Harmonies* remains the sixth volume, and a seventh
(*Mélanges*) is added. This has remained the standard edition.
Reprints of various volumes, given special "edition" numbers,
and sometimes with slight differences in pagination, appeared
at various times through 1893.

The edition of the *Harmonies* used by the translator is *Les
Harmonies économiques, par Frédéric Bastiat, 6ème édition,*

Paris, Guillaumin, 1870. It is still listed as Volume VI in the *Oeuvres complètes, 2ème edition*. The translator also consulted the 1862 and 1884 editions of the *Harmonies* and found no significant variants. The Appendix letter, entitled "A Tentative Preface to the *Harmonies*," was consulted in the *Oeuvres complètes, 2ème edition*, Vol. VII, 1861, pp. 303 ff.

W. HAYDEN BOYERS

Introduction

Frédéric Bastiat, 1801–1850, is generally classified as an economist. But, as I showed in my book on his life, works, and influence, his real claim to fame properly belongs in the field of government—both in its organization and in its philosophy.* Even so, his contribution to the field of economics was considerable, especially in the area of free trade.

Bastiat was a contemporary of Richard Cobden, the man most responsible for bringing free trade to Great Britain in 1846. The two men became close friends when Bastiat attempted to do in France what Cobden had accomplished in England. While Bastiat was unsuccessful in bringing free trade to France during his lifetime, his disciple, Michel Chevalier, was the co-author with Cobden of the Anglo-French Treaty of Commerce that finally accomplished the objective in 1860.

Bastiat's interest in free trade, however, was still incidental to his passion for freedom in general. As he wrote in one of his numerous letters to Cobden, "Rather than the fact of free trade alone, I desire for my country the general philosophy of free trade. While free trade itself will bring more wealth to us, the acceptance of the general philosophy that underlies free trade will inspire all needed reforms."

Bastiat spelled out that philosophy in considerable detail in his major work, *Principles of Political Economy*. In the Introduction to that book, he made the statement, "It would be nonsense for me to say that socialists have never advanced a truth, and that economists [those who advocate a free market] have never supported an error." † As we shall see, one of Bastiat's major ideas

* *Frédéric Bastiat: Ideas and Influence* (Foundation for Economic Education, 1963).
† All translations in this Introduction are from the original French. Thus, my selection of words will doubtless differ somewhat from those chosen by the translator of the text. That, of course, is of no consequence.

in his *Harmonies*—his theory and definition of *value,* of which he was especially proud—is now generally held to be somewhat pointless. That fact, of course, does not deny the soundness of his fundamental principle that the interests of mankind are essentially harmonious and can best be realized in a free society where government confines its actions merely to suppressing the robbers, murderers, falsifiers, and others who wish to live at the expense of their fellow men.

The first economic harmony that Bastiat illustrated was the idea that, as the capital employed in a nation increases, the share of the resulting production going to the workers tends to increase both in percentage and in total amount. The share going to the owners of the capital tends to increase in total amount but to decrease percentagewise. Bastiat used hypothetical figures merely to *indicate the direction* of this relationship that occurs when capital accumulation increases, with its resulting increase in production.

DISTRIBUTION OF SHARES OF INCREASED PRODUCTION

	Total Units	To Owners		To Employees	
		Per Cent	Units	Per Cent	Units
When total national product is	50	20	10	80	40
When total national product is	75	15	12	85	63
When total national product is	100	14	14	86	86

That theory was offered to refute the gloomy "iron law of wages" advanced by Ricardo, as well as Malthus' equally horrible prediction that an increasing population must necessarily face starvation. Bastiat recognized the fact that, in this division of national income, the amounts and percentages going to capital and labor would, for a variety of reasons, vary widely from industry to industry, from country to country, and from time to time. But he was quite positive that the tendency would be in the direction indicated by his figures for the nation that encourages the private accumulation of capital.

This trend that Bastiat predicted in the division of the total production of the nation is just what did happen under increased capital formation in the United States and other countries that more or less follow the concepts of a market economy.

Bastiat arrived at his theory by observing that new tools and new methods are more productive than older tools and former methods, and that competition tends to cause most of the resulting benefits to be passed along in higher wages or lower prices, or both. In either instance, real wages are thereby increased. Like many of his predecessors, Bastiat also noted that interest on capital is likely to decline as capital becomes more plentiful. (History does not record the first person who discovered this primary law of supply and demand.) At any rate, the verdict of the Twentieth Century to date refutes the gloomy predictions of Ricardo, who argued that wages always tend toward the lowest level needed to sustain the required working force at a minimum standard of health. Bastiat's optimistic theory that real wages tend to rise constantly in a free market is more in accord with reality.

Thus, according to Bastiat, the interests of capital and labor are harmonious, not antagonistic. Each is dependent on the other. Both gain by working harmoniously together to increase both capital and production, even though the employees tend to get the lion's share of the increased production. Government interference *in the long run* will injure the interests of both owners and workers, but most especially the workers.

In his major work, Bastiat discussed the "harmony of capital" in almost every chapter, and from various viewpoints. His treatment of the subject is, by far, the most convincing part of his book. While it is doubtless correct to observe that Bastiat contributed nothing new to the actual *theory* of capital, it is perhaps equally correct to suggest that his presentation and development of several facets of the subject are superior to those of his predecessors and teachers—Smith, Say, and others.

We have already noted one of his "harmonies of capital" above. Here is another. If the market is free, said Bastiat, no one can accumulate capital (excluding gifts) unless he renders a service to someone else. The people who have the capital (including the person who has only one dollar) won't part with it unless they are offered a product or service that they value as highly as the capital. In reality, said Bastiat, capital is always put at the service of other people who do not own it, and it is always used to satisfy a desire (good or bad) that other people want satisfied. In that important sense, all capital is truly owned in common by the entire community—and the greater the accumulation of capital, the more its benefits are shared in common.

"Here is a worker whose daily wages is four francs. With two of them, he can purchase a pair of stockings. If he alone had to manufacture those stockings completely—from the growing of the cotton to the transporting of it to the factory and to the spinning of the threads into material of the proper quality and shape—I suspect that he would never accomplish the task in a lifetime." Bastiat offered several other similar stories and parables based on that same idea of the benefits that come to all from the increasing division of labor that automatically follows the accumulation of capital.

Contrary to most of his classical predecessors, Bastiat was almost totally concerned with the interests of the consumer. While he wished to render justice to the producer (the capitalist and the entrepreneur), he seemed concerned with him only in passing. Perhaps that can be explained by the fact that the socialists of Bastiat's day were in the ascendancy—and Bastiat desired to beat them at their own game by showing that the workers and consumers (rather than the owners of capital) are the chief beneficiaries of private ownership, competition, free trade, interest, profits, rent, capital accumulation, and so on.

The harmony that Bastiat found in all this was the same as that demonstrated by Adam Smith and the physiocrats: In serving his own selfish interests, the producer has no choice but to serve first the interests of the consumer, if the market is free. Each person may be working only to benefit himself but, doubtless unknown to himself, he is really working primarily to satisfy the needs and desires of others.

By both observation and reason, Bastiat was led to the conclusion that man tends to satisfy his wants with the least possible effort. That would seem self-evident, but Bastiat used that simple axiom to show that a popular way to satisfy one's wants with minimum effort is to vote for subsidies and protection. Bastiat pointed out the awkward fact that such a solution is contrary to the wants and actions of the persons who must pay the resulting higher taxes and higher prices. This government path to satisfying one's wants is antagonistic, rather than harmonious, and is thus self-defeating in the long run. It will result in less than maximum production by both those who must pay the subsidy and those who receive it. When the government interferes, said Bastiat, the natural harmony of the free and productive market is destroyed, and the people waste their energies in attempting to win political power in order to exploit each other. "Everybody wishes to live at the expense of the state, but they forget that the state lives at the expense of everybody." In another book, Bastiat also stated that idea in this way: "The state is the great fiction by which everybody tries to live at the expense of everybody else."

In his *Harmonies*, Bastiat felt that he had made a major contribution to political economy by his definition of *value*. He felt that his concept should reconcile the conflicting opinions of all economists—including even the socialists and communists! He introduced the subject by making a sharp distinction between *utility* and value. Under utility, he listed the sun, water, and undeveloped land. According to him, none of the gifts of Nature have any *value*—until human effort has been applied to them. While he specifically rejected the labor theory of value, he may well have endorsed it unknowingly under another name—service.

According to Bastiat, service is the source of all value, and any exchange implies equal value. Water has no value in its native state. But the building of a well and the hauling of the water to the consumers (services) have value. And the purchaser pays for it with equal services, even though it may be in the intermediate form of money that facilitates the transferring of past, present, and future services.

Bastiat felt compelled to defend the rightness and justice of every voluntary exchange. Thus, he was most happy with his idea that the *service* supplied by the man who accidentally discovers a valuable diamond is worth a large price (other services) because it saves the purchaser from the effort that is usually connected with the securing of such a gem.

Bastiat just ignored the fact that the value to the purchaser would be the same, whether the seller had found the diamond, inherited it, or worked for several years digging it out of the ground. Thus, the value of an article is clearly not directly related to the "service" supplied by the seller himself, and Bastiat's effort to reconcile that fact with his general theory led him completely astray in this area.

In his chapters on "Exchange" and "Value," Bastiat quoted two men who clearly (and perhaps first) saw the true relationship between exchange and value—and he then scoffed at both of them. The first was Étienne Bonnot de Condillac, 1714–1780: "From the very fact that an exchange is made, it follows that there must be a profit for each of the contracting parties; otherwise the exchange would not take place. Thus, each exchange represents two gains for humanity."

The second quotation cited by Bastiat was by Heinrich Friedrich von Storch, 1766–1835: "Our judgment enables us to discover the relation that exists between our wants and the utility of things. The determination that our judgment forms upon the utility of things also determines their value."

These two statements combined are perhaps the basic concepts of exchange and value later developed so brilliantly by the Austrian school of economists. That is, the value of a product or service is purely subjective on the part of the purchaser; neither seller nor buyer will make the exchange unless each values what he receives more than what he gives up; there is no automatic relationship between value and the labor or capital that goes into the product or service; no one can determine the value of any product or service for another person.

Thus, Bastiat had full opportunity to make a vital contribution to economic thought by developing these two ideas, with which he was obviously familiar. Most unfortunately, he missed the opportunity.

Even so, perhaps Bastiat supplies the connecting link between the English classicists, with their objective theory of value, and the Austrians, with their subjective theory based on the universal actions of men in real life. At least, the following series of quotations extracted from various pages of his *Harmonies* indicates

clearly that he had advanced far beyond the former and was
making excellent progress toward the latter.

"The subject of political economy is MAN. . . . [who is]
endowed with the ability to compare, judge, choose, and act;
which implies that men may form right and wrong judgments,
and make good and bad choices. . . . . This faculty, given to men
and to men alone, to work for each other, to transmit their efforts,
and to exchange their services through time and space, with all
the infinite and varied combinations thereby involved, is precisely what constitutes economic science, identifies its origin, and
determines its limits. . . . . The objects of political economy [the
actions of men in the exchange of their goods and services] cannot
be weighed or measured. . . . . Exchange is necessary in order to
determine value. . . . . Owing to ignorance, what one man values
may be despised by another. . . . . A man's happiness and well-being
are not measured by his efforts, but by his satisfactions, and this
also holds true for society at large. . . . . It may happen, and frequently does, that the service we esteem highly is in reality harmful to us; value depends on the judgment we form of it. . . . . In an
exchange society, man seeks to realize value irrespective of utility.
The commodity he produces is not intended to satisfy his own
wants, and he has little interest in how useful it may be. It is for
the purchaser to judge that. What concerns the producer is that it
should have maximum value in the market. . . . . It is in vain that
we attempt to separate choice and responsibility."

In addition to the ideas expressed above, Bastiat also developed
in great detail the theory that competition will cause all of the
gifts of Nature to become widespread—including, of course, land
and all other natural resources.

Like almost all economists of his time, Bastiat was obsessed
with this problem of rent on land. If it could not be justified and
harmonized, he said, then the question asked by the socialist
Proudhon was correct: "Who is entitled to the rent on land? Why,
of course, the one who made the land. Then who made it? God.
In that case, would-be owner, get off."

Bastiat's defense of rent covers many pages, but it adds up to
this: Land rent is justified because the owners of the land (current

and past) have rendered a valuable service. They have cleared the land, drained it, and made it suitable for planting. They have paid taxes to have roads built to it. If the amount of labor and capital that has been expended on the agricultural lands of France were capitalized, Bastiat contended, the current return in the form of rent would be considered a most unattractive investment today. Therefore, the owners of land do not enjoy an unearned income—or, at least, they would not if the market were free. Bastiat argued that any "unearned" rent was, like protected prices for manufactured products, the result of government interference with domestic and foreign trade. On the subject of rent, Bastiat was a physiocrat, pure and simple. He also used this same idea to defend the necessity and justice of a return on capital in general; all current capital, he said, merely represents past labor that has been saved and is rendering a service today.

While Bastiat's arguments on land rent are most persuasive—and were doubtless true in the context presented—they were too carefully selected to prove any over-all principle. For it is undeniably true that land (like other products and services) can and does vary widely in price for a variety of reasons, and that the owner of the land can reap a profit (or suffer a loss) even though he has done no work at all on it. But, once again, it does not follow that Bastiat was wrong in imagining that harmony can be found in the private ownership of land and the charging of a *free-market rent* for its use.

Bastiat was particularly anxious to refute the gloomy theories of Ricardo and Malthus in regard to wages, rent, population, and starvation. He felt that his theory that labor receives an *increasing* share from additional capital accumulation was an answer to Ricardo on wages and to Malthus on starvation. He answered Ricardo directly on the subject of land and rent. Finally, he offered the *opinion* that if man were free—truly free—with God's help he would discover harmonious ways to keep the population from increasing beyond the ability of science to discover new ways to feed it.

Bastiat has no great standing among leading economists as an innovator or an original thinker in the field of economic theory. That verdict may be justified. But his development of his central idea of a universal harmony in all areas of human relationships led Gide and Rist to write, "The fundamental doctrines of [the liberal or optimistic school] were definitely formulated about the same time, though in very different fashion of course, in the *Principles* of Stuart Mill in England and the *Harmonies* of Bastiat in France."

DEAN RUSSELL

To the Youth of France

Eagerness to learn, the need to believe in something, minds still immune to age-old prejudices, hearts untouched by hatred, zeal for worthy causes, ardent affections, unselfishness, loyalty, good faith, enthusiasm for all that is good, beautiful, sincere, great, wholesome, and spiritual—such are the priceless gifts of youth. That is why I dedicate this book to the youth of France. The seed that I now propose to sow must be sterile indeed if it fails to quicken into life upon soil as propitious as this.

My young friends, I had intended to present you with a finished painting; I give you instead only a rough sketch. Forgive me. For who in these times can complete a work of any great scope? Here is the outline. Seeing it, may some one of you exclaim, like the great artist: *Anch'io son pittore,** and, taking up the brush, impart to my unfinished canvas color and flesh, light and shade, feeling and life.

You will think that the title of this work, *Economic Harmonies,* is very ambitious. Have I been presumptuous enough to propose to reveal the providential plan within the social order and the mechanism of all the forces with which Providence has endowed humanity to assure its progress?

Certainly not; but I have proposed to put you on the road to this truth: *All men's impulses, when motivated by legitimate self-interest, fall into a harmonious social pattern.* This is the central idea of this work, and its importance cannot be overemphasized.

It was fashionable, at one time, to laugh at what is called the *social problem;* and, it must be admitted, certain of the proposed solutions were only too deserving of derision. But there is surely nothing laughable about the problem itself; it haunts us like Banquo's ghost at Macbeth's banquet, except that, far from being silent, it cries aloud to terror-stricken society: Find a solution or die!

---

* ["I, too, am a painter," supposedly the young Correggio's words when he first saw Raphael's painting of Saint Cecilia.—Translator.]

Now the nature of this solution, as you readily understand, will depend greatly upon whether men's interests are, in fact, harmonious or antagonistic to one another.

If they are harmonious, the answer to our problem is to be found in liberty; if they are antagonistic, in coercion. In the first case, it is enough not to interfere; in the second, we must, inevitably, interfere.

But liberty can assume only one form. When we are certain that each one of the molecules composing a liquid has within it everything that is needed to determine the general level, we conclude that the simplest and surest way to obtain this level is not to interfere with the molecules. All those who accept as their starting point the thesis that *men's interests are harmonious* will agree that the practical solution to the social problem is simply not to thwart these interests or to try to redirect them.

Coercion, on the other hand, can assume countless forms in response to countless points of view. Therefore, those schools of thought that start with the assumption that *men's interests are antagonistic to one another* have never yet done anything to solve the problem except to eliminate liberty. They are still trying to ascertain which, out of all the infinite forms that coercion can assume, is the right one, or indeed if there is any right one. And, if they ever do reach any agreement as to which form of coercion they prefer, there will still remain the final difficulty of getting all men everywhere to accept it freely.

But, if we accept the hypothesis that men's interests are by their very nature inevitably bound to clash, that this conflict can be averted only by the capricious invention of an artificial social order, then the condition of mankind is indeed precarious, and we must fearfully ask ourselves:

1. Shall we be able to find someone who has invented a satisfactory form of coercion?

2. Will this man be able to win over to his plan the countless schools of thought that have conceived of other forms?

3. Will mankind submit to this form, which, according to our hypothesis, must run counter to every man's self-interest?

4. Assuming that humanity will consent to being trigged out in this garment, what will happen if another inventor arrives

with a better garment? Are men to preserve a bad social order, knowing that it is bad; or are they to change their social order every morning, according to the whims of fashion and the ingeniousness of the inventors?

5. Will not all the inventors whose plans have been rejected now unite against the accepted plan with all the better chance of destroying it because, by its very nature and design, it runs counter to every man's self-interest?

6. And, in the last analysis, is there any one human force capable of overcoming the fundamental antagonism which is assumed to be characteristic of all human forces?

I could go on indefinitely asking such questions and could, for example, bring up this difficulty: If you consider individual self-interest as antagonistic to the general interest, where do you propose to establish the acting principle of coercion? Where will you put its fulcrum? Will it be outside of humanity? It would have to be, in order to escape the consequences of your law. For if you entrust men with arbitrary power, you must first prove that these men are molded of a different clay from the rest of us; that they, unlike us, will never be moved by the inevitable principle of self-interest; and that when they are placed in a situation where there can be no possible restraint upon them or any resistance to them, their minds will be exempt from error, their hands from greed, and their hearts from covetousness.

What makes the various socialist schools (I mean here those schools that look to an artificial social order for the solution of the social problem) radically different from the economist* school is not some minor detail in viewpoint or in preferred form of government; it is to be found in their respective points of departure, in their answers to this primary and central question: Are men's interests, when left to themselves, harmonious or antagonistic?

* [As the ensuing pages of this book make clear, Bastiat uses the words "political economy" and the "economists" to designate in a general way the "classical" school of economists to which he himself gave allegiance. These include the eighteenth-century "physiocrats": Quesnay (*Tableau économique*, 1759), Mercier de la Rivière, Dupont de Nemours, Le Trôsne, Mirabeau, Condorcet, and Turgot; the "English School": Adam Smith, Malthus, John Stuart Mill, Senior, Scrope, and Ricardo; and his own French contemporaries: Jean-Baptiste Say, Pellegrino Rossi, Garnier, and others less well known who held similar views on wealth and free exchange. See also Bastiat's comments in chapter 9.—TRANSLATOR.]

It is evident that the socialists set out in quest of an artificial social order only because they deemed the natural order to be either bad or inadequate; and they deemed it bad or inadequate only because they felt that men's interests are fundamentally antagonistic, for otherwise they would not have had recourse to coercion. It is not necesary to force into harmony things that are inherently harmonious.

Therefore they have found fundamental antagonisms everywhere:

Between the property owner and the worker.

Between capital and labor.

Between the common people and the bourgeoisie.

Between agriculture and industry.

Between the farmer and the city-dweller.

Between the native-born and the foreigner.

Between the producer and the consumer.

Between civilization and the social order.

And, to sum it all up in a single phrase:

Between personal liberty and a harmonious social order.

And this explains how it happens that, although they have a kind of sentimental love for humanity in their hearts, hate flows from their lips. Each of them reserves all his love for the society that he has dreamed up; but the natural society in which it is our lot to live cannot be destroyed soon enough to suit them, so that from its ruins may rise the New Jerusalem.

I have already stated that the economist school, on the contrary, starting from the assumption that there is a natural harmony among men's interests, reaches a conclusion in favor of personal liberty.

Still, I must admit, if economists, generally speaking, do advocate personal liberty, it is not, unfortunately, equally true that their principles firmly establish their initial premise that men's interests are harmonious.

Before going further, and in order to forewarn you against the conclusions that will inevitably be drawn from this admission, I must say a word regarding the respective positions of the socialists and the political economists.

It would be senseless for me to say that the socialists have never discovered truth, and that the political economists have never fallen into error.

What makes the great division between the two schools is the difference in their methods. Socialism, like astrology and alchemy, proceeds by way of the imagination; political economy, like astronomy and chemistry, proceeds by way of observation.

Two astronomers observing the same phenomenon may not reach the same conclusion. Despite this temporary disagreement they feel the bond of a common method that sooner or later will bring them together. They recognize that they belong to the same communion. But between the astronomer who observes and the astrologer who imagines, there stretches an unbridgeable gulf, although at times some common understanding may perchance be reached.

The same is true of political economy and socialism.

The economists observe man, the laws of his nature and the social relations that derive from these laws. The socialists conjure up a society out of their imagination and then conceive of a human heart to fit this society.

Now, if science cannot be wrong, scientists can be. I therefore do not deny that the economists can make faulty observations, and I shall even add that in the beginning they inevitably did.

But note what happens. If men's interests are actually harmonious, it follows that any observation that would lead *logically* to the opposite conclusion—namely, that they are antagonistic—has been faulty. What then are the socialists' tactics? They collect a few faulty observations from the economists' works, deduce all the conclusions to be derived from them, and then prove that they are disastrous. Up to this point they are within their rights. Next, they raise their voices in protest against the observer— Malthus * or Ricardo,† for example. They are still within their rights. But they do not stop here. They turn against the science of political economy itself; they accuse it of being heartless and of

---

* [Thomas Robert Malthus (1766–1834), English economist. Cf. chapter 16 for Bastiat's discussion of his *Essay on the Principle of Population.*—TRANSLATOR.]
† [David Ricardo (1772–1823), English economist of the classical school.— TRANSLATOR.]

desiring evil. In so doing, they go against reason and justice; for science is not responsible for the scientist's faulty observations. Finally, they go even farther yet. They even accuse society itself and threaten to destroy it and remake it. And why? Because, they say, science proves that our present society is on the road to disaster. In this they outrage good sense; for, either science is not mistaken—and in that case why attack it?—or else it is mistaken, and in that case they had best leave society alone, since it is in no danger.

But these tactics, however illogical, can nonetheless be most harmful to the science of poltical economy, particularly should those who espouse it give way to the understandable but unfortunate impulse of blindly supporting the opinions of one another and of their predecessors on all points. Science is a queen whose court etiquette should be based on a free and easy give-and-take. An atmosphere of bias and partisanship is fatal to it.

As I have already said, in political economy every erroneous proposition unfailingly leads to the conclusion that there are antagonistic elements in the social order. On the other hand, the numerous writings of the economists, including even the most eminent, cannot fail to contain a few false propositions. In the interest of our science and of society it is our duty to point these out and to correct them. To continue obstinately to defend them for the sake of preserving the prestige of the whole school would mean exposing not only ourselves, which is unimportant, but the truth itself, which is of greater consequence, to the attacks of the socialists.

To continue, then: I state that the political economists advocate liberty. But for the idea of liberty to win men's minds and hearts, it must be firmly based on the premise that men's interests, when left to themselves, tend to form harmonious combinations and to work together for progress and the general good.

Now, some of the economists, and among them some who carry considerable authority, have advanced propositions that step by step lead logically to the opposite conclusion, that *absolute evil* exists, that injustice is inevitable, that inequality will necessarily increase, that pauperism is unavoidable, etc.

For example, there are, to my knowledge, very few political

economists who have not attributed *value* to natural resources, to the gifts that God has lavished *without cost* on his creature, man. The word "value" implies that we surrender the things possessing it only in return for payment. Therefore, we see men, especially the landowners, selling God's bounty in return for other men's toil, and receiving payment for *utilities,* that is, for the means of satisfying human wants, without contributing any of their own labor in return—an obvious, but necessary, injustice, say these writers.

Then there is the famous theory of Ricardo. It can be summarized in this fashion: The price of foodstuffs is based on the amount of labor required to produce them on the poorest soils under cultivation. Now, as population increases, it is necessary to turn to less and less fertile soils. Hence, all humanity (except the landowner) is forced to exchange a constantly increasing amount of labor for the same quantity of foodstuffs; or, what comes to the same thing, to receive a constantly decreasing quantity of foodstuffs for the same amount of labor; whereas the owners of the soil see their income rising with each new acre of inferior land that is put into cultivation. Conclusion: increasing wealth for the leisure classes; increasing poverty for the laborers: or, inevitable inequality.

Then there is the even more famous theory of Malthus. Population tends to increase more rapidly than the means of subsistence, and this trend is to be observed at any given moment in the history of mankind. Now, men cannot live in peace and happiness unless they have enough to eat. There are only two checks to this constant threat of excess population: a decrease in the birth rate or an increase in the mortality rate, with all its attendant horrors. Moral restraint, in order to be effective, must be observed everywhere, which is more than can be expected. There remains, then, only the positive check of vice, poverty, war, pestilence, famine, and death; that is, inevitable pauperism.

I shall not mention other systems of less general import that also lead to desperately discouraging conclusions. For example, M. de Tocqueville * and many others like him declare that

* [Alexis Charles Henri Clérel de Tocqueville (1805–1859), statesman and author of numerous significant books.—TRANSLATOR.]

if we admit the right of primogeniture, we end with a very small
and rigid aristocracy; if we do not admit it, we end with the country divided into tiny, unproductive individual holdings.

And the remarkable thing is that these four melancholy theories
do not in any way come into direct conflict with one another.
If they did, we could find consolation in the fact that they are
mutually destructive. But such is not the case; they agree, they
fit into the same general theory, which, supported by numerous
and plausible facts, apparently explains the convulsive state of
modern society and, since it is endorsed by a number of eminent
authorities, presents itself to our discouraged and bewildered
minds with terrifying conviction.

It remains to be seen how the exponents of this gloomy theory
have at the same time been able to maintain the harmony of
men's interests as their premise and deduce personal liberty as
their conclusion. For certainly, if humanity is inevitably impelled
toward injustice by the laws of value, toward inequality by the laws
of rent, toward poverty by the laws of population, and toward steri-
lization by the laws of heredity, we cannot say that God's handiwork is harmonious in the social order, as it is in the physical
universe; we must instead admit, with heads bowed in grief, that
He has seen fit to establish His social order on revolting and irremediable discord.

You must not believe, my young friends, that the socialists
have refuted and rejected the theory that, in order to avoid
offending anyone, I shall call the theory of discord. On the contrary: despite their protests, they have accepted it as true; and, for
the very reason that they accept it as true, they propose to substitute coercion for freedom, an artificial social order for the natural
social order, and a work of their own contrivance for the handiwork of God. They say to their opponents (than whom, in this
respect, I am not sure that they are not more logical): If, as you
have declared, men's interests when left to themselves did tend
to combine harmoniously, we could only welcome and extol
freedom as you do. But you have proved irrefutably that these
interests, if allowed to develop freely, lead mankind toward
injustice, inequality, pauperism, and sterility. Therefore, we
react against your theory precisely because it is true. We wish
to destroy society as it now is precisely because it does obey the

inevitable laws that you have described; we wish to try what we can do, since God's power has failed.

Thus, there is agreement in regard to the premises. Only in regard to the conclusion is there disagreement.

The economists to whom I have referred say: *The great laws of Providence are hastening society along the road to disaster;* but we must be careful not to interfere with their action, for they are fortunately counteracted by other secondary laws that postpone the final catastrophe, and any arbitrary interference on our part would only weaken the dike without lowering the great tidal wave that will eventually engulf us.

The socialists say: *The great laws of Providence are hastening society along the road to disaster;* we must abolish them and choose in their place other laws from our inexhaustible arsenal.

The Catholics say: *The great laws of Providence are hastening society along the road to disaster;* we must escape them by renouncing worldly desires, taking refuge in self-abnegation, sacrifice, asceticism, and resignation.

And, amid the tumult, the cries of anguish and distress, the appeals to revolt or to the resignation of despair, I raise my voice to make men hear these words, which, if true, must silence all protesting voices: *It is not true that the great laws of Providence are hastening society along the road to disaster.*

Thus, while all schools stand divided on the conclusions they draw from their common premise, I deny their premise. Is not this the best means of ending the division and the controversy?

The central idea of this work, the harmony of men's interests, is a *simple* one. And is not simplicity the touchstone of truth? The laws governing light, sound, motion, seem to us all the more true because they are simple. Why should the same thing not be true of the law of men's interests?

It is *conciliatory.* For what can be more conciliatory than to point out the ties that bind together industries, classes, nations, and even doctrines?

It is *reassuring,* since it exposes what is false in those systems that would have us believe that evil must spread and increase.

It is *religious,* for it tells us that it is not only the celestial but also the social mechanism that reveals the wisdom and declares the glory of God.

It is *practical,* for certainly no maxim is easier to put into practice than this: Let men labor, exchange, learn, band together, act, and react upon one another, since in this way, according to the laws of Providence, there can result from their free and intelligent activity only order, harmony, progress, and all things that are good, and increasingly good, and still better, and better yet, to infinite degree.

Now there, you will say, is the optimism of the economists for you! They are so completely the slaves of their own systems that they shut their eyes to the facts for fear of seeing them. In the face of all the poverty, injustice, and oppression that desolate the human race, they go on imperturbably denying the existence of evil. The smell of the gunpowder burned in insurrections does not reach their indifferent senses; for them the barricades in the streets are mute; and though society should crumble and fall, they will continue to repeat: "All is for the best in the best of all possible worlds."

Certainly not. We do not think that all is for the best.

I have complete faith in the wisdom of the laws of Providence, and for that reason I have faith in liberty.

The question is whether or not we have liberty.

The question to determine is whether these laws act with full force, or whether their action is not profoundly disrupted by the contrary action of institutions of human origin.

Deny evil! Deny pain! Who could? We should have to forget that we are talking about mankind. We should have to forget that we ourselves are men. For the laws of Providence to be considered as *harmonious,* it is not necessary that they exclude evil. It is enough that evil have its explanation and purpose, that it be self-limiting, and that every pain be the means of preventing greater pain by eliminating whatever causes it.

Society is composed of men, and every man is a *free* agent. Since man is free, he can choose; since he can choose, he can err; since he can err, he can suffer.

I go further: He must err and he must suffer; for his starting point is ignorance, and in his ignorance he sees before him an infinite number of unknown roads, all of which save one lead to error.

Now, all error breeds suffering. And this suffering either falls upon the one who has erred, in which case it sets in operation the law of responsibility; or else it strikes innocent parties, in which case it sets in motion the marvelous reagent that is the law of solidarity.

The action of these laws, combined with the ability that has been given us of seeing the connection between cause and effect, must bring us back, by the very fact of suffering, to the path of righteousness and truth.

Thus, we not only do not deny that evil exists; we recognize that it has its purpose in the social order even as in the physical universe.

But if evil is to fulfill this purpose, the law of solidarity must not be made to encroach artificially upon the law of responsibility; in other words, the freedom of the individual must be respected.

Now, if man-made institutions intervene in these matters to nullify divine law, evil nonetheless follows upon error, but it falls upon the wrong person. It strikes him whom it should not strike; it no longer serves as a warning or a lesson; it is no longer self-limiting; it is no longer destroyed by its own action; it persists, it grows worse, as would happen in the biological world if the imprudent acts and excesses committed by the inhabitants of one hemisphere took their toll only upon the inhabitants of the other hemisphere.

Now, this is exactly the tendency not only of most of our governmental institutions but also and to an even greater degree of those institutions that are designed to serve as remedies for the evils that afflict us. Under the philanthropic pretext of fostering among men an artificial kind of solidarity, the individual's sense of responsibility becomes more and more apathetic and ineffectual. Through improper use of the public apparatus of law enforcement, the relation between labor and wages is impaired, the operation of the laws of industry and exchange is disturbed, the natural development of education is distorted, capital and manpower are misdirected, minds are warped, absurd demands are inflamed, wild hopes are dangled before men's eyes, unheard of quantities of human energy are wasted, centers of population are relocated, experience itself is made ineffective; in brief, all interests are given artificial foundations, they clash, and the people cry: You see, all men's interests are antagonistic. Personal liberty causes all the trouble. Let us execrate and stifle personal liberty.

And so, since liberty is still a sacred word and still has the power to stir men's hearts, her enemies would strip her of her name and her prestige and, rechristening her *competition,* would lead her forth to sacrifice while the applauding multitudes extend their hands to receive their chains of slavery.

It is not enough, then, to set forth the natural laws of the social order in all their majestic harmony; it is also necessary to show the disturbing factors that nullify their action. That is the task I have undertaken in the second part of this work.

I have tried to avoid controversy. In so doing, I have undoubtedly missed the opportunity of presenting my principles with the comprehensiveness that comes from thorough discussion. But by drawing the reader's attention to the many details of my digressions, would I not have run the risk of confusing his view of the whole? If I present the edifice as it actually is, what does it matter how it has appeared to others, even to those who taught me how to view it?

And now I confidently appeal to those men of all persuasions who place justice, truth, and the general welfare above their own particular systems.

Economists, my conclusion, like yours, is in favor of individual liberty; and if I undermine some of the premises that have saddened your generous hearts, yet you will perhaps discover in my work additional reason for loving and serving our sacred cause.

Socialists,* you place your faith in *association.* I call upon you,

---

* ["Socialists," "egalitarians," "communists": In France, before the time of Karl Marx, of course, these terms were used, as Bastiat uses them, to refer generally to those political theorists advocating collectivism primarily as a means to advance equality. Before and during the Revolution they included Morelly (*Code de la nature,* 1755); Mably (*Doutes. . . . sur l'ordre naturel et essentiel des sociétés politiques,* 1768); Babeuf, founder of the society of "the Equals" (executed in 1797), and his later followers: Philippe Buonarroti, Armand Barbès, Martin Bernard, and Louis Auguste Blanqui. Bastiat also includes as sharers of these ideas his contemporary "planners of artificial social orders": Fourier, Louis Blanc, Considérant, Cabet, Owen, and Saint-Simon. (Cf. notes on Fourier, Louis Blanc, Owen, and Cabet, chapter 1, p. 11; on Proudhon, chapter 5, p. 128; on Considérant, p. 550.) —TRANSLATOR.]

after you have read this work, to say whether the present social order, freed from its abuses and the obstacles that have been put in its way—enjoying, in other words, the condition of freedom—is not the most admirable, the most complete, the most lasting, the most universal, and the most equitable of all associations.

Egalitarians,* you recognize only one principle, the *reciprocity of services*. Let human transactions once be free, and I declare that they are, or can be, nothing more nor less than a reciprocal exchange of *services*, constantly decreasing in cost, or value, constantly increasing in *utility*.

Communists,† you desire that men, as brothers, may enjoy in common the benefits that Providence has lavished upon them all. I propose to demonstrate that the present social order has only to achieve freedom in order to realize and go beyond your fondest hopes and prayers; for in this social order all things are common to all, provided only that every man either himself go to the trouble to gather in God's gifts (which is only natural), or else that he render equivalent service to those who go to this trouble for him (which is only just).

Christians of all communions, unless you alone of all mankind doubt the divine wisdom as manifested in the most magnificent of God's works that it is given us to know, you will not find one word in this book that contravenes the strictest tenet of your moral code or the most mystical of your dogmas.

Property owners, however vast may be your possessions, if I prove that your rights, which people today so vehemently contest, are confined, as are those of the simplest manual worker, to receiving services in return for real services performed by you or your forefathers, then these rights of yours will henceforth be beyond challenge.

Workers, I promise to prove that you do enjoy the fruits of the land that you do not own, and with less pain and effort on your part than you could cultivate them by your own labor on land given you in its original state, unimproved by other men's labor.

Capitalists and laborers, I believe that I can establish this law: "In proportion as capital accumulates, the *absolute* share of

* See preceding footnote.
† See footnote *supra* on "socialists."

capital in the total returns of production increases, and its *relative* share decreases; labor also finds that its *relative* share increases and that its *absolute* share increases even more sharply. The opposite effect is observed when capital is frittered away." [1] If this law can be established, it is clear that we may conclude that the interests of workers and employers are harmonious.

Disciples of Malthus, sincere but misjudged lovers of your fellow man, you whose only fault is your desire to protect humanity against the fatal effects of a law that you consider inevitable, I have a more reassuring law to offer you in its place: "Other things being equal, increased population means increased efficiency in the means of production." If such is the case, you will certainly not be the ones to complain that the crown of thorns has dropped from the brow of our beloved science.

Predatory men, you who, by force or fraud, in spite of the law or through the agency of the law, grow fat on the people's substance; you who live by the errors you disseminate, by the ignorance you foster, by the wars you foment, by the restraints you impose on trade; you who tax the labor you have made unproductive, making it lose even more than you snatch away; you who charge for the obstacles you set up, so as to charge again for those you subsequently take down; you who are the living embodiment of selfishness in its bad sense; parasitical excrescences of faulty policies, prepare the corrosive ink of your critique: to you alone I can make no appeal, for the purpose of this book is to eliminate you, or rather to eliminate your unjust claims. However much we may admire compromise, there are two principles between which there can be no compromise: liberty and coercion.

If the laws of Providence are harmonious, they can be so only when they operate under conditions of freedom, for otherwise harmony is lacking. Therefore, when we perceive something inharmonious in the world, it cannot fail to correspond to some lack of freedom or justice. Oppressors, plunderers, you who hold justice in contempt, you cannot take your place in the universal harmony, for you are the ones who disrupt it.

Does this mean that the effect of this book would be to weaken the power of government, endanger its stability, lessen its authority? The goal I have in view is precisely the opposite. But let us understand one another.

The function of political science is to determine what should and what should not fall under government control; and in making this important distinction, we must not lose sight of the fact that the state always acts through the instrumentality of force. Both the services it renders us and those it makes us render in return are imposed upon us in the form of taxes.

The question then amounts to this: What are the things that men have the right to impose upon one another *by force?* Now, I know of only one, and that is *justice.* I have no right to force anyone to be religious, charitable, well educated, or industrious; but I have the right to *force* him to be *just:* this is a case of legitimate self-defense.

Now, there cannot exist for a group of individuals any new rights over and above those that they already possessed as individuals. If, therefore, the use of force by the individual is justified solely on grounds of legitimate self-defense, we need only recognize that government action always takes the form of force to conclude that by its very nature it can be exerted solely for the maintenance of order, security, and justice.

All government action beyond this limit is an encroachment upon the individual's conscience, intelligence, and industry—in a word, upon human liberty.

Accordingly, we must set ourselves unceasingly and relentlessly to the task of freeing the whole domain of private activity from the encroachments of government. Only on this condition shall we succeed in winning our liberty or assuring the free play of the harmonious laws that God has decreed for the development and progress of the human race.

Will the power of government be weakened by these restrictions? Will it lose stability as it loses some of its vastness? Will it have less authority because it will have fewer functions? Will it be the object of less respect because it will be the object of fewer grievances? Will it become more the puppet of special interests when it has reduced the enormous budgets and the coveted patronage that are the special interests' lure? Will it be exposed to greater dangers when it has less responsibility?

On the contrary: it seems evident to me that to restrict the public police force to its one and only rightful function, but a function that is essential, unchallenged, constructive, desired

and accepted by all, is the way to win it universal respect and
co-operation. Once this is accomplished, I cannot see from what
source could come all our present ills of systematic obstruction-
ism, parliamentary bickering, street insurrections, revolutions,
crises, factions, wild notions, demands advanced by all men to
govern under all possible forms, new systems, as dangerous as they
are absurd, which teach the people to look to the government for
everything. We should have an end also to compromising diplomacy, to the constant threat of war, and the armed peace that is
nearly as disastrous, to crushing and inevitably inequitable taxation, to the ever increasing and unnatural meddling of politics
in all things, and to that large-scale and wholly artificial redistribution of capital and labor which is the source of needless irrita-
tion, of constant ups and downs, of economic crises and setbacks.
All these and a thousand other causes of disturbances, friction,
disaffection, envy, and disorder would no longer exist; and those
entrusted with the responsibility of governing would work
together for, and not against, the universal harmony. Harmony
does not exclude evil, but it reduces evil to the smaller and
smaller area left open to it by the ignorance and perversity of
our human frailty, which it is the function of harmony to prevent
or chastise.

Young men, in these times when a lamentable skepticism
appears to be the effect and the punishment of our intellectual
anarchy, I should deem myself happy if the reading of this book
would stir you to utter those reassuring words, so sweet to the
lips, which are not only a refuge from despair but a positive
force, strong enough, we are told, to remove mountains, those
words that begin the Christian's profession of faith: *I believe.* I
believe, not with blind and submissive faith, for we are not here
concerned with the mysteries of revelation; but with reasoned
scientific faith, as is proper in matters left to man's own inquiry
and investigation. I believe that He who designed the physical
world has not seen fit to remain a stranger to the social world. I
believe that His wisdom extends to human agents possessed of
free will, that He has been able to bring them together and cause
them to move in harmony, even as He has done with inert molecules. I believe that His providence shines forth at least as clearly

in the laws to which men's wills and men's interests are subject as in the laws that He has decreed for mass or velocity. I believe that everything in society, even that which inflicts pain, is a source of improvement and progress. I believe that evil ends in good and hastens its coming, whereas the good can never end in evil, and therefore must eventually triumph. I believe that the inevitable trend of society is toward a constantly rising physical, intellectual, and moral level shared by all mankind. I believe, if only man can win back his freedom of action and be allowed to follow his natural bent without interference, that his gradual, peaceful development is assured. I believe these things, not because I desire them or because they satisfy the longings of my heart, but because after mature reflection my intellect gives them its full consent.

Ah! if ever you utter these words, *I believe,* you will be eager to carry them to others, and the social problem will soon be solved, for despite all that is said, its solution is simple. Men's interests are harmonious; therefore, the answer lies entirely in this one word: *freedom.*

Table of Contents

Contents

1

Natural and Artificial Social Order[1]

Are we really certain that the mechanism of society, like the mechanism of the heavenly bodies or the mechanism of the human body, is subject to general laws? Are we really certain that it is a harmoniously *organized* whole? Or is it not true that what is most notable in society is the *absence* of all order? And is it not true that a social order is the very thing that all men of good will and concern for the future are searching for most avidly, the thing most in the minds of all forward-looking commentators on public affairs, and of all the pioneers of the intellectual world? Are we not but a mere confused aggregation of individuals acting disconcertedly in response to the caprices of our anarchical liberty? Are our countless masses, now that they have painfully recovered their liberties one by one, not expecting some great genius to come and arrange them into a harmonious whole? Now that we have torn down, must we not begin to build anew? *

If the import of these questions were simply whether society can dispense with written laws, with regulations, with repressive measures, whether each man can make unlimited use of his faculties, even when he might infringe on another's liberties or do damage to the community as a whole—whether, in a word,

* [The reader is reminded that this introduction was written in the days immediately following the Revolution of 1848, when the "bourgeois king," Louis Philippe, had been overthrown and a Constitutional Convention (of which Bastiat was a member) was engaged in drafting a constitution for the newly formed Second Republic. Bastiat did not live to see the sorry aftermath—the *coup d'état* of 1852, which turned the idealistic Second Republic into the Second Empire under Napoleon III.—TRANSLATOR.]

1

we must see in the doctrine of *laissez faire, laissez passer,** the absolute formula of political economy; the answer could be doubtful to no one. Political economists do not say that a man may kill, pillage, burn, that society has only to let him alone; they say that society's resistance to such acts would manifest itself in fact even if specific laws against them were lacking; that, consequently, this resistance is a general law of humanity. They say that civil or criminal laws must regularize, not contravene, these general laws on which they are predicated. It is a far cry from a social order founded on the general laws of humanity to an artificial, contrived, and invented order that does not take these laws into account or denies them or scorns them—an order, in a word, such as some of our modern schools of thought would, it seems, impose upon us.

For if there are general laws that act independently of written laws, and whose action needs merely to be regularized by the latter, we must study these *general laws;* they can be the object of scientific investigation, and therefore there is such a thing as the science of political economy. If, on the contrary, society is a human invention, if men are only inert matter to which a great genius, as Rousseau says, must impart feeling and will, movement and life, then there is no such science as political economy: there is only an indefinite number of possible and contingent arrangements, and the fate of nations depends on *the founding father* to whom chance has entrusted their destiny.

I shall not indulge in lengthy dissertations to prove that society is subject to general laws. I shall confine myself to pointing out certain facts that, though somewhat commonplace, are nonetheless important.

Rousseau said, "It requires a great deal of scientific insight to discern the facts that are close to us." †

* [*Laissez passer:* "allow to pass," only slightly different from *laissez faire,* which of course does not require translation. These phrases are associated with Quesnay and the other physiocrats.—Translator.]

† [This quotation, which so impressed Bastiat that he refers to it five times in the course of the *Harmonies,* is to be found in Part One of the *Discourse on Inequality.* The original passage reads as follows: "It is not to him (the savage) that we must look for the scientific insight man needs in order to observe carefully even once what he has seen every day."—Translator.]

Such is the case with the social phenomena in the midst of which we live and move. Habit has so familiarized us with these phenomena that we never notice them until, so to speak, something sharply discordant and abnormal about them forces them to our attention.

Let us take a man belonging to a modest class in society, a village cabinetmaker, for example, and let us observe the services he renders to society and receives in return. This man spends his day planing boards, making tables and cabinets; he complains of his status in society, and yet what, in fact, does he receive from this society in exchange for his labor? The disproportion between the two is tremendous.

Every day, when he gets up, he dresses; and he has not himself made any of the numerous articles he puts on. Now, for all these articles of clothing, simple as they are, to be available to him, an enormous amount of labor, industry, transportation, and ingenious invention has been necessary. Americans have had to produce the cotton; Indians, the dye; Frenchmen, the wool and the flax; Brazilians, the leather; and all these materials have had to be shipped to various cities to be processed, spun, woven, dyed, etc.

Next, he breakfasts. For his bread to arrive every morning, farm lands have had to be cleared, fenced in, ploughed, fertilized, planted; the crops have had to be protected from theft; a certain degree of law and order has had to reign over a vast multitude of people; wheat has had to be harvested, ground, kneaded, and prepared; iron, steel, wood, stone have had to be converted by industry into tools of production; certain men have had to exploit the strength of animals, others the power of a waterfall, etc.—all things of which each one by itself alone presupposes an incalculable output of labor not only in space, but in time as well.

In the course of the day this man consumes a little sugar and a little olive oil, and uses a few utensils.

He sends his son to school to receive instruction, which, though limited, still presupposes on the part of his teachers research, previous study, and a store of knowledge that startles one's imagination.

He leaves his house: he finds his street paved and lighted.

His ownership of a piece of property is contested: he finds lawyers to plead his rights, judges to reaffirm them, officers of the law to execute the judgment. These men, too, have had to acquire extensive and costly knowledge in order to defend and protect him.

He goes to church: it is a prodigious monument, and the book that he brings with him is perhaps an even more prodigious monument of human intelligence. He is taught morals, his mind is enlightened, his soul is elevated; and for all this to be done, still another man has had to have professional training, to have frequented libraries and seminaries, to have drawn knowledge from all the sources of human tradition, and to have lived the while without concerning himself directly with his bodily needs.

If our artisan takes a trip, he finds that, to save him time and lessen his discomfort, other men have smoothed and leveled the ground, filled in the valleys, lowered the mountains, spanned the rivers, and, to reduce their friction, placed wheeled cars on blocks of sandstone or iron rails, tamed horses or steam, etc.

It is impossible not to be struck by the disproportion, truly incommensurable, that exists between the satisfactions this man derives from society and the satisfactions that he could provide for himself if he were reduced to his own resources. I make bold to say that in one day he consumes more things than he could produce himself in ten centuries.

What makes the phenomenon stranger still is that the same thing holds true for all other men. Every one of the members of society has consumed a million times more than he could have produced; yet no one has robbed anyone else. If we examine matters closely, we perceive that our cabinetmaker has paid in services for all the services he has received. He has, in fact, received nothing that he did not pay for out of his modest industry; all those ever employed in serving him, at any time or in any place, have received or will receive their remuneration.

So ingenious, so powerful, then, is the social mechanism that every man, even the humblest, obtains in one day more satisfactions than he could produce for himself in several centuries.

Nor is this all. This social mechanism will seem still more ingenious if the reader will consider his own case.

I shall assume that he is simply a student. What is he doing in Paris? How does he live? No one can deny that society puts at his disposal food, clothing, lodging, amusements, books, instruction —such a host of things, in a word, that it would take a long time just to tell how they were produced, to say nothing of actually producing them. And in return for all these things that have demanded so much work, the sweat of so many brows, so much painful toil, so much physical or mental effort, such prodigies of transportation, so many inventions, transactions, what services has our student rendered society? None; but he is getting ready to render them. How, then, can these millions of men who are engaged in positive, effective, and productive work turn over to him the fruit of their labor? Here is the explanation: This student's father, who was a doctor or a lawyer or a businessman, had already rendered services—perhaps to Chinese society—and had received in return, not immediate services, but certificates for services due him on which he could demand payment at the time and place and in the form that he saw fit. Today society is paying for those distant and past services; and, amazingly, if we were to follow in our minds the chain of endless transactions that had to take place before the final result was reached, we should see that each one was paid for his pains; that these certificates passed from hand to hand, sometimes split up into fractions, sometimes combined into larger sums, until by our student's consumption the full account was balanced. Is not this indeed a most remarkable phenomenon?

We should be shutting our eyes to the facts if we refused to recognize that society cannot present such complicated combinations in which civil and criminal law play so little part without being subject to a prodigiously ingenious mechanism. This mechanism is the object of study of political economy.

One other thing worthy of notice is that in this really incalculable number of transactions that have resulted in maintaining a student for a day, not one millionth part, perhaps, was done directly. The things he has enjoyed today, and they are innumerable, are the work of men many of whom have long since disappeared from the face of the earth. And yet they have been paid as they intended to be, although the one who profits from their work today did nothing for them. He did not know them; he will never know them. The person who is reading this page, at the very moment he reads it, has the power, though perhaps he is unaware of it, to set in motion men of all lands, all races, and, I could almost say, of all times, whites, blacks, redskins, men of the yellow race; he makes generations dead and gone and generations still unborn work for his present satisfactions; and this extraordinary power he owes to the fact that his father once rendered services to other men who apparently have nothing in common with those whose labor is being performed today. Yet such balance was effected in time and space that each was remunerated, and each received what he had calculated he should receive.

In truth, could all this have happened, could such extraordinary phenomena have occurred, unless there were in society a natural and wise *order* that operates without our knowledge?

In our day people talk a great deal about inventing a new order. Is it certain that any thinker, regardless of the genius we grant him and the authority we give him, could invent and operate successfully an order superior to the one whose results I have just described?

What would it be in terms of its moving parts, its springs, and its motive forces?

The moving parts are men, that is, beings capable of learning, reflecting, reasoning, of making errors and of correcting them, and consequently of making the mechanism itself better or worse. They are capable of pain and pleasure, and in that respect they are not only the wheels, but the springs of the machine. They are also the motive forces, for the source of the power is in them. They are more than that, for they are the ultimate object and *raison d'être* of the mechanism, since in the last analysis the problems of its operation must be solved in terms of their individual pain or pleasure.

Now, it has been observed, and, alas, the observation has not been a difficult one to make, that in the operation, the evolution, and even the progress (by those who accept the idea that there has been progress) of this powerful mechanism, many moving parts were inevitably, fatally, crushed; that, for a great number of human beings, the sum of unmerited sufferings far exceeded the sum of enjoyments.

Faced with this fact, many sincere and generous-hearted men have lost faith in the mechanism itself. They have repudiated it; they have refused to study it; they have attacked, often violently, those who have investigated and expounded its laws; they have risen up against the nature of things; and, in a word, they have proposed to *organize* society according to a new plan in which injustice, suffering, and error could have no place.

Heaven forbid that I should raise my voice against intentions so manifestly philanthropic and pure! But I should be going back on my own convictions, I should be turning a deaf ear to the voice of my own conscience, if I did not say that, in my opinion, they are on the wrong track.

In the first place, they are reduced by the very nature of their propaganda to the unfortunate necessity of underestimating the good that society has produced, of denying its progress, of imputing every evil to it, and of almost avidly seeking out evils and exaggerating them beyond measure.

When a man feels that he has discovered a social order different from the one that has come into being through the natural tendencies of mankind, he must, perforce, in order to have his invention accepted, paint in the most somber colors the results of the order he seeks to abolish. Therefore, the political theorists to whom I refer, while enthusiastically and perhaps exaggeratedly proclaiming the perfectibility of mankind, fall into the strange contradiction of saying that society is constantly deteriorating. According to them, men are today a thousand times more wretched than they were in ancient times, under the feudal system and the yoke of slavery; the world has become a hell. If it were possible to conjure up the Paris of the tenth century, I confidently believe that such a thesis would prove untenable.

Secondly, they are led to condemn even the basic motive power of human actions—I mean *self-interest*—since it has brought about such a state of affairs. Let us note that man is made in such a way that he seeks pleasure and shuns pain. From this source, I agree, come all the evils of society: war, slavery, monopoly, privilege; but from this source also come all the good things of life, since the satisfaction of wants and the avoidance of suffering are the motives of human action. The question, then, is to determine whether this motivating force which, though individual, is so universal that it becomes a social phenomenon, is not in itself a basic principle of progress.

In any case, do not the social planners realize that this principle, inherent in man's very nature, will follow them into their new orders, and that, once there, it will wreak more serious havoc than in our natural order, in which one individual's excessive claims and self-interest are at least held in bounds by the resistance of all the others? These writers always assume two inadmissible premises: that society, as they conceive it, will be led by infallible men completely immune to the motive of self-interest; and that the masses will allow such men to lead them.

Finally, our social planners do not seem in the least concerned about the implementation of their program. How will they gain acceptance for their systems? How will they persuade all other men simultaneously to give up the basic motive for all their actions: the impulse to satisfy their wants and to avoid suffering? To do so it would be necessary, as Rousseau said, *to change the moral and physical nature of man.*

To induce all men, simultaneously, to cast off, like an ill-fitting garment, the present social order in which mankind has evolved since its beginning and adopt, instead, a contrived system, becoming docile cogs in the new machine, only two means, it seems to me, are available: force or universal consent.

Either the social planner must have at his disposal force capable of crushing all resistance, so that human beings become mere wax between his fingers to be molded and fashioned to his whim; or he must gain by persuasion consent so complete, so exclusive, so blind even, that the use of force is made unnecessary.

I defy anyone to show me a third means of setting up and putting into operation a phalanstery* or any other artificial social order.

Now, if there are only two means, and we demonstrate that they are both equally impracticable, we have proved by that very fact that the social planners are wasting their time and trouble.

Visionaries though they are, they have never dreamed of having at their disposal the necessary material force to subjugate to their bidding all the kings and all the peoples of the earth. King Alfonso had the presumption to say, "If God had taken me into His confidence, the solar system would have been better arranged." † But if he set his wisdom above the Creator's, he was not mad enough to challenge God's power; and history does not record that he tried to make the stars turn in accord with the laws of his own invention. Descartes likewise was content to construct a little world of dice and strings,‡ recognizing that he was not *strong* enough to move the universe. We know of no one but Xerxes who was so intoxicated with his power as to say to the waves, "Thus far shall ye come, and no farther." The waves, however, did not retreat from Xerxes, but Xerxes from the waves, and, if not for this wise but humiliating precaution, he would have been drowned.

The social planners, therefore, lack the force to subject humanity to their experiments. Even though they should win over to their cause the Czar of Russia, the Shah of Persia, and the Khan of the Tartars, and all the rulers who hold absolute power over their subjects, they still would not have sufficient force to

* [Allusion to *Le Phalanstère ou la réforme industrielle,* the newspaper started by François Marie Charles Fourier in 1832. Fourier proposed a division of society into "phalanges" or large groups, each numbering about 1600 persons and occupying a common building, or *phalanstère.*—TRANSLATOR.]

† [This observation, attributed to Alfonso X, "The Learned" (1221–1284), is better known in English in the form given by Bartlett's *Familiar Quotations:* "Had I been present at the Creation, I would have given some useful hints for the better ordering of the universe."—TRANSLATOR.]

‡ [In Rule XIII of his *Rules for the Direction of the Mind* (1629), Descartes suggests such an experiment with strings and weights.—TRANSLATOR.]

distribute mankind into groups and categories * and abolish the general laws of property, exchange, heredity and family, for even in Russia, even in Persia and Tartary, men must to some extent be taken into account. If the Czar of Russia took it into his head to *alter the moral and physical nature* of his subjects, he probably would soon have a successor, and the successor would not be tempted to continue the experiment.

Since *force* is a means quite beyond the reach of our numerous social planners, they have no other resource open to them than to try to win *universal consent*.

This can be done in two ways: by persuasion or by imposture.

Persuasion! But not even two minds have ever been known to reach perfect agreement on every point within even a single field of knowledge. How, then, can all mankind, diverse in language, race, customs, spread over the face of the whole earth, for the most part illiterate, destined to die without ever hearing the reformer's name, be expected to accept unanimously the new universal science? What is involved? Changing the pattern of work, trade, of domestic, civil, religious relations—in a word, altering man's physical and moral nature; and people talk of rallying all humanity to the cause by conviction!

Truly, the task appears an arduous one.

When a man comes and says to his fellow men:

"For five thousand years there has been a misunderstanding between God and man. From Adam's time until now the human race has been on the wrong road, and if it will but listen to me, I shall put it back on the right track. God intended mankind to take a different route; mankind refused, and that is why evil entered the world. Let mankind hearken to my voice, and turn about; let it proceed in the opposite direction; then will the light of happiness shine upon all men."

When, I say, a man begins like this, he is doing well if he gets five or six disciples to believe him; and from five or six to a billion men is a far, far cry, so far in fact that the distance is incalculable!

* [In the original French, *groupes* and *séries*, a reference to Fourier's *phalanges* and his proposed divisions according to occupation.—TRANSLATOR.]

And then, reflect that the number of social inventions is as limitless as man's own imagination; that there is not a single planner who, after a few hours alone in his study, cannot think up a new scheme; that the inventions of Fourier, Saint-Simon, Owen, Cabet, Blanc,* etc., bear no resemblance whatsoever to one another; that not a day passes without still others burgeoning forth; that, indeed, humanity has some reason for drawing back and hesitating before rejecting the order God has given it in favor of deciding definitely and irrevocably on one of the countless social inventions available. For what would happen if, after one of these schemes had been selected, a better one should present itself? Can the human race establish a new basis for property, family, labor, and exchange every day in the year? Can it risk changing the social order every morning?

"Thus," as Rousseau says, "since the lawgiver cannot use either force or reason, he must have recourse to a different manner of authority that can win support without violence and persuade without convincing."

What is that authority? Imposture. Rousseau does not dare utter the word; but, as is his invariable custom in such cases, he puts it behind the transparent veil of a purple passage:

"This," he says, "is what, in all times, forced the founding fathers of nations to have recourse to the intervention of Heaven and to give credit to the gods for their own wisdom, so that the people, submitting to the laws of the state as if to the laws of

* [François Marie Charles Fourier (1772–1837), French socialist and advocate of experimental societies, of which the best known in America was the famous Brook Farm. In addition to his newspaper, *Le Phalanstère ou la réforme industrielle* (cf. p. 9), he wrote other works.

Claude Henri de Rouvroy, Comte de Saint-Simon (1760–1825), historic founder of French socialism, advocate of an industrial state directed by modern science. His works greatly influenced all socialist thought of his and the next generation.

Robert Owen (1771–1858), British reformer and socialist, active in efforts to improve factory workers' conditions.

Étienne Cabet (1788–1856), French socialist theorist and experimenter. He founded associations in France, Texas, and Illinois.

Louis Blanc (1811–1882), French politician and historian, creator of the "social workshop," which combined elements of the co-operative and the trade-union, attributed the evils of society to the pressures of competition, proposing instead "to each according to his needs, from each according to his abilities."—TRANSLATOR.]

Nature, and recognizing the selfsame power as the creator of men and as the creator of their commonwealth, might obey *with liberty* and bear docilely the yoke of their public felicity. The decrees of *sublime* reason, which is above the reach of the common herd, are *imputed* by the lawgiver *to the immortal gods,* so as to win by divine authority the support of those whom human wisdom could not move. But it is not for every man to make *the gods* speak. . . ."

And so, lest anyone be deceived, he completes his thought in the words of Machiavelli: *Mai non fu alcuno ordinatore di leggi STRAORDINARIE in un popolo che non ricorresse a Dio.**

Why does Machiavelli recommend invoking *God's* authority, and Rousseau the authority of *the gods,* and *the immortals?* I leave the answer to the reader.

Certainly I do not accuse the modern founding fathers of stooping to such unworthy subterfuge. Yet, considering the problem from their point of view, we readily appreciate how easily they can be carried away by their desire for success. When a sincere and philanthropic man is firmly convinced that he possesses a social secret by means of which his fellow men may enjoy boundless bliss in this world; when he clearly sees that he cannot win acceptance of his idea either by force or by reason, and that guile is his only recourse; his temptation is bound to be great. We know that even the ministers of the religion that professes the greatest horror of untruth have not recoiled from the use of *pious fraud;* and we observe (witness the case of Rousseau, that austere writer who inscribed at the head of all his works the motto: *Vitam impendere vero*) † that even proud philosophy herself can be seduced by the enticements of a very different motto: *The end justifies the means.* Why, then, be surprised if the modern social planners should likewise think in terms of "giving credit to the gods for their own wisdom, of putting their own decrees in the mouths of the immortal gods,

---

* ["Never was there a promulgator of *extraordinary* laws in a nation who did not invoke God's authority."—Translator.]

† ["Stake life on truth." The quotation comes from Juvenal, Satire IV, line 91 Rousseau used it as Bastiat indicates.—Translator.]

of winning support without violence and persuading without convincing"?

We know that, like Moses, Fourier had his Deuteronomy following his Genesis. Saint-Simon and his disciples had gone even further in their apostolic nonsense. Others, more shrewd, lay hold of religion in its broadest sense, modifying it to their views under the name of neo-Christianity. No one can fail to be struck by the tone of mystic affectation that nearly all the modern reformers put into their preachings.

But the efforts in this direction have proved only one thing, which has, to be sure, its importance, namely, that in our day not everyone who wills may become a prophet. In vain he proclaims himself God; nobody believes him, not the public, not his peers, not even he himself.

Since I have mentioned Rousseau,* I shall venture to make a few observations about this social planner, particularly as they will be helpful in showing in what respects artificial social orders differ from the natural order. This digression, moreover, is not inopportune, since for some time now the *Social Contract* has been hailed as a miraculous prophecy of things to come.

Rousseau was convinced that isolation was man's *natural state*, and, consequently, that *society* was a human invention. *"The social order,"* he says at the outset, *"does not come from Nature; it is therefore founded on convention."*

Furthermore, our philosopher, though loving liberty passionately, had a low opinion of men. He considered them completely incapable of creating for themselves the institutions of good government. The intervention of a lawgiver, a founding father, was therefore indispensable.

"The people being subject to the law should be the authors of the law," he says. "Only those who associate together have the right to regulate the conditions of their association. But how shall they regulate them? Shall it be by common agreement or by

* [While Bastiat was thoroughly familiar with all Rousseau's main political writings *(The Social Contract, Discourse on the Arts and Sciences, Discourse on the Origin of Inequality, Discourse on Political Economy)*, the quotations and paraphrases he uses here come from the *Social Contract*: Book I, chap. iv; Book II, chaps. vi and vii; and Book III, chap. xv.—TRANSLATOR.]

a sudden inspiration? How is a blind multitude of men, who often do not know what they want, since they rarely know what is good for them, to accomplish of themselves such a vast and difficult enterprise as that of devising a system of legislation? . . . . Individuals see the good and reject it; the public seeks the good and cannot find it: both are equally in need of guides. . . . . Hence the necessity of a lawgiver."

This lawgiver, as we have seen, "being unable to use either force or reason, must of necessity have recourse to a different manner of authority," namely, in plain words, to guile and duplicity.

Nothing can adequately convey the idea of the dizzy heights above other men on which Rousseau places his lawgiver:

"We should have gods to give laws to men. . . . . He who dares to institute a society must feel himself capable, so to speak, of changing human nature itself. . . . of altering man's essential constitution, so that he may strengthen it. . . . . He must deprive man of his own powers that he may give him others that are alien to him. . . . . The lawgiver is, in every respect, an extraordinary man in the state. . . . his function is a unique and superior one, which has nothing in common with the ordinary human status. . . . . If it is true that the great prince is a very special man, what should one say of the great lawgiver? The former has only to follow the ideal, whereas it is the latter's role to create it. The lawgiver is the inventor of the machine; the prince, merely the operator."

And what, then, is mankind in all this? The mere raw material out of which the machine is constructed.

Truly, what is this but arrogance raised to the point of monomania? Men, then, are the raw materials of a machine that the prince operates and the lawgiver designs; and the philosopher rules the lawgiver, placing himself immeasurably above the common herd, the prince, and the lawgiver himself; he soars above the human race, stirs it to action, transforms it, molds it, or rather teaches the founding fathers how to go about the task of stirring, transforming, and molding it.

However, the founder of a nation must set a goal for himself. He has human raw material to put to work, and he must shape it to a purpose. Since the people are without initiative and every-thing depends on the lawgiver, he must decide whether his nation is to be commercial or agricultural, or a society of barbarians and fisheaters, etc.; but it is to be hoped that the lawgiver makes no mistake and does not do too much violence to the nature of things.

The people, by *agreeing* to form an association, or rather by forming an association at the will of the lawgiver, have, then, a very definite end and purpose. "Thus it is," says Rousseau, "that the Hebrews and more recently the Arabs, had religion as their principal object; the Athenians, letters; Carthage and Tyre, com-merce; Rhodes, shipping; Sparta, war; and Rome, civic virtue."

What will be the national objective that will persuade us French to abandon the isolation of the *state of nature* in order to form a new society? Or rather (for we are only inert matter, the raw material for the machine), toward what end shall our great lawgiver direct us?

According to the ideas of Rousseau, it could hardly be toward letters, commerce, or shipping. War is a nobler goal, and civic virtue is nobler still. Yet there is one goal above all others, one which "should be the end and purpose of all systems of legisla-tion, and that is *liberty and equality.*"

But we must know what Rousseau meant by liberty. To enjoy liberty, according to him, is not to be free, but to *cast our vote,* even in case we should be "swept along without violence and persuaded without being *convinced,* for then we obey with liberty and bear docilely the yoke of public felicity."

"Among the Greeks," he said, "all that the populace had to do it did for itself; the people were constantly assembled in the market place, their climate was mild, they were not avaricious, *slaves did all their work, and their great concern was their liberty.*"

"The English people," he says elsewhere, "believe that they are free. They are very much mistaken. They are free only while they are electing their members of parliament. Once they have elected them, they are slaves, they are nothing."

The people, then, must do for themselves everything that

relates to the public service if they are to be free, for it is in this that liberty consists. They must be constantly carrying on elections, constantly in the market place. Woe to them if they think of working for their livelihood! The instant a single citizen decides to take care of his own affairs, that very instant (to use a favorite phrase of Rousseau) everything is lost.

But surely this is no minor difficulty. What is to be done? For, obviously, in order to practice virtue, even to enjoy the right to liberty, we must first stay alive.

We have already noted the rhetorical verbiage that Rousseau uses to conceal the word "imposture." Now we see him resort to flights of oratory to gloss over the logical conclusion of his whole work, which is *slavery*.

"Your harsh climate imposes special wants. For six months in the year your market place cannot be frequented, your muted tongues cannot make themselves heard in the open air, and you fear slavery less than poverty.

"Truly you see that you cannot be free.

"What! Liberty can be preserved only if supported by slavery? Perhaps."

If Rousseau had ended with this horrible word, the reader would have been revolted. Recourse to impressive declamation is in order. Rousseau responds nobly.

"Everything that is unnatural [he is speaking of society] has its inconveniences, and civil society even more than anything else. There are unfortunate situations in which one man's liberty can be preserved only at the expense of another's, and where the citizen can be perfectly free only on condition that the slave be abjectly a slave. You nations of the modern world have no slaves, but you yourselves are slaves; you purchase their freedom at the price of your own. . . . . I am unmoved by the noble motives you attribute to your choice; I find you more cowardly than humane."

Does not this simply mean: Modern nations, you would do better not to be slaves yourselves but, instead, to own slaves?

I beg the reader to forgive this long digression, which, I trust, has not been without value. For some time we have had Rousseau and his disciples of the Convention * held up to us as the apostles of the doctrine of the brotherhood of man. Men as the raw material, the prince as the operator of a machine, the founding father as the designer, the philosopher high and mighty above them all, fraud as the means, and slavery as the end—is this the brotherhood of man that was promised?

It also seemed to me that this analysis of the *Social Contract* was useful in showing what characterizes artificial social orders. Start with the idea that society is contrary to Nature; devise contrivances to which humanity can be subjected; lose sight of the fact that humanity has its motive force within itself; consider men as base raw materials; propose to impart to them movement and will, feeling and life; set oneself up apart, immeasurably above the human race—these are the common practices of the social planners. The plans differ; the planners are all alike.

Among the new arrangements that poor weak mortals are invited to consider, there is one that is presented in terms worthy of our attention. Its formula is: *progressive and voluntary association.*

But *political economy* is based on this very assumption, that *society* is purely an *association* of the kind described in the foregoing formula; a very imperfect association, to be sure, because man is imperfect, but capable of improvement as man himself improves; in other words, *progressive.* Is it a question of a closer association among labor, capital, and talent, which should result in more wealth for the human family and its better distribution? Provided the association remains voluntary, that force and constraint do not intervene, that the parties to the association do not propose to make others who refuse to enter foot the bill, in what way are these associations contrary to the idea of political economy? Is not political economy, as a science, committed to the examination of the various forms under which men see fit to join

* [The national assembly formed during the Revolution (1792) to frame a constitution for France. It ruled the nation until October, 1795. The theories of Rousseau, particularly on equality, civic virtue, and religion, influenced profoundly many of the seven hundred eighty-two members.—TRANSLATOR.]

their forces and to apportion their tasks, with a view to greater and more widely diffused prosperity? Does not the business world frequently furnish us with examples of two, three, four persons forming such associations? It not the *métayage*,* for all its imperfections, a kind of association of capital and labor? Have we not recently seen stock companies formed that permit even the smallest investors to participate in the largest enterprises? Are there not in our country some factories that have established profit-sharing associations for their workers? Does political economy condemn these efforts of men to receive a better return for their labor? Does it declare anywhere that mankind has gone as far as it can? Quite the contrary, for I am convinced that no science proves more clearly that society is in its infancy.

But, whatever hopes we may entertain for the future, whatever ideas we may have of the forms man may discover for the improvement of his relations with his fellow man, for the more equitable distribution of wealth, and for the dissemination of knowledge and morality, we must nonetheless recognize that the social order is composed of elements that are endowed with intelligence, morality, free will, and perfectibility. If you deprive them of liberty, you have nothing left but a crude and sorry piece of machinery.

Liberty! Today, apparently, we are no longer interested. In this land of ours, this France, where fashion reigns as queen, liberty seems to have gone out of style. Yet, for myself, I say: Whoever rejects liberty has no faith in mankind. Recently, it is alleged, the distressing discovery has been made that liberty leads inevitably to monopoly.[2] No, this monstrous linking, this unnatural joining together of freedom and monopoly is nonexistent; it is a figment of the imagination that the clear light of political economy quickly dissipates. Liberty begets monopoly! Oppression is born of freedom! But, make no mistake about it, to affirm this is to affirm that man's tendencies are inherently evil, evil in their nature, evil in their essence; it is to affirm that his natural bent is toward his deterioration and that his mind is attracted

* [The *métayage:* a system of share-cropping established in the South of France. —TRANSLATOR.]

irresistibly toward error. What good, then, are our schools, our study, our research, our discussions, except to add momentum to our descent down the fatal slope; since, for man, to learn to choose is to learn to commit suicide? And if man's tendencies are perverse, where will the social planners seek to place their fulcrum? According to their premises, it will have to be outside of humanity. Will they seek it within themselves, in their own intelligence, in their own hearts? But they are not yet gods: they too are men and hence, along with all humanity, careening down toward the fatal abyss. Will they call upon the state to intervene? But the state is composed of men; and we should have to prove that the men who form the state constitute a class apart, to whom the general laws of society are not applicable, since they are called upon to make the laws. Unless this be proved, the facing of the dilemma is not even postponed.

Let us not thus condemn mankind until we have studied its laws, forces, energies, and tendencies. Newton, after he had discovered the law of gravity, never spoke the name of God without uncovering his head. As far as intellect is above matter, so far is the social world above the physical universe that Newton revered; for the celestial mechanism is unaware of the laws it obeys. How much more reason, then, do we have to bow before the Eternal Wisdom as we contemplate the mechanism of the social world in which the universal mind of God also resides (*mens agitat molem*),* but with the difference that the social world presents an additional and stupendous phenomenon: its every atom is an animate, thinking being endowed with that marvelous energy, that source of all morality, of all dignity, of all progress, that exclusive attribute of man—*freedom!*

---

* ["Mind moves matter" (Virgil, *Aeneid*, VI, 727).—Translator.]

2

Wants, Efforts, Satisfactions[1]

What a profoundly appalling spectacle France presents! It would be difficult to say whether anarchy has passed from a theory to a fact or from a fact to a theory, but it is certain that it has spread everywhere.

The poor have risen against the rich; the proletariat against the capitalists; agriculture against industry; the country against the city; the provinces against the capital; the native-born against the foreigners.

And now the theorists who seek to build a system out of all this division and conflict step forward. "It is the *inevitable* result," they say, "of the nature of things, that is, of freedom. Man is possessed of *self-love,* and this is the cause of all the evil; for, since he is possessed of self-love, he strives for his own well-being and can find it only at the expense of his brothers' misfortune. Let us, then, prevent him from following his impulses; let us stifle liberty; let us change the human heart; let us find another motivating force to replace the one that God gave him; let us invent an artificial society and direct it as it should go!"

When the theorist reaches this point, he sees an endless vista arising to challenge his logic or his imagination. If his mind runs to dialectics and his temperament to melancholy, he devotes himself wholly to the analysis of evil; he dissects it, he puts it in the test tube, he probes it, he goes back to its very beginnings, he follows it forward to its ultimate consequences; and since, in

20

view of our innate imperfection, there is nothing in which evil is not present, there is nothing at which he fails to carp bitterly. He presents only one side of the question when he examines property, the family, capital, industry, competition, freedom, self-interest—the damaging and destructive side. He reduces human biology, so to speak, to a clinical post-mortem. He defies God to reconcile what has been said of His infinite goodness with the existence of evil. He defiles everything, he makes everything distasteful, he denies everything; nevertheless, he does succeed in winning a certain sullen and dangerous following among those classes whose suffering has made them only too vulnerable to despair.

If, on the other hand, our theorist has a heart open to benevolence and a mind that delights in illusions, he takes off for the happy land of dreams. He dreams of Oceanas, Atlantises, Salentes, Spensones, Icarias, Utopias, and Phalansteries;* he peoples them with docile, loving, devoted beings who would never impede the dreamer's flights of fancy. He complacently sets himself up in his role of Providence. He arranges, he disposes, he creates men to his own taste. Nothing stops him; no disappointment overtakes him. He is like the Roman preacher who, pretending that his square cap was Rousseau, refuted vigorously the *Social Contract* and then triumphantly declared that he had reduced his adversary to silence. In just this way the reformer dangles before the eyes of people in misery a seductive picture of ideal bliss well fitted to make them lose their taste for the harsh necessities of real life.

But the utopian is rarely content to stop at these innocent dreams. As soon as he tries to win mankind over to them, he discovers that people do not readily lend themselves to transformation. Men resist; they grow bitter. In order to win them over, he speaks not merely of the good things that they are rejecting; he

---

* [Reference to various utopias, classic and contemporary: *Oceana,* by James Harrington (1656); *The New Atlantis* (unfinished), by Francis Bacon; *Salente* (or *Salentum*), the imaginary site of an imaginary government in *Télémaque* (1699), by Fénelon (see note to chap. 3, p. 37); *Spensone, the Millennium or Happy World,* by Thomas Spense (1750–1814); *Voyage to Icaria,* by Étienne Cabet; *Phalanstère* (or phalanstery, housing), the model society of Fourier (see note to chap. 1, p. 9). —TRANSLATOR.]

speaks especially of the evils from which he proposes to deliver them. He cannot paint these too strikingly. He grows accustomed to increasing the intensity of the colors on his palette. He seeks out the evil in present-day society as passionately as another would seek out the good. He sees only suffering, rags, emaciated bodies, starvation, pain, oppression. He is amazed, he is exasperated, by the fact that society is not sufficiently aware of all its misery. He neglects nothing as he tries to make it shake off its apathy, and, after beginning with benevolence, he, too, ends with misanthropy.[2]

God forbid that I should question any man's sincerity! But I really cannot understand how those political theorists who see a fundamental antagonism at the foundation of the natural order of society can enjoy a moment's calm and repose. It seems to me that discouragement and despair must be their unhappy lot. For if nature erred in making *self-interest* the mainspring of human society (and her error is evident as soon as we admit that men's interests are inherently antagonistic), how can they fail to see that the evil is beyond repair? Not being able to go beyond men, for we are men ourselves, where shall we find a fulcrum for our lever with which to change human tendencies? Shall we call upon law and order, the magistrates, the state, the legislator? But to do so is to appeal to men, that is, to beings subject to the common infirmity. Shall we resort to universal suffrage? But this is only giving the freest rein of all to the universal tendency.

Only one recourse, then, remains open to these social planners. They must pass themselves off as the possessors of a special revelation, as prophets, molded from a different clay, drawing their inspiration from a different source from that of the rest of mankind; and this is doubtless the reason that we often see them enveloping their systems and their admonitions in mystical phraseology. But if they are sent from God, let them prove their high calling. In the last analysis, what they desire is supreme authority, the most absolute, despotic power that ever existed. They not only desire to control our actions; they even go so far as to propose to alter the very nature of our feelings. The least that can be asked is that they show their credentials. Do they expect that humanity will take them at their word, especially when they can come to no agreement among themselves?

But, before we examine their blueprints for artificial societies, is there not something we should make sure of, namely: Are they not on the wrong track from the very outset? Is it, indeed, certain that *men's interests are inherently antagonistic,* that inequality develops inevitably and irremediably in the natural order of human society, under the influence of self-interest, and that God, therefore, was obviously wrong when He told man to pursue his own happiness?

This is what I propose to investigate.

Taking man as God saw fit to make him, capable of anticipating the future and of learning from the past, hence perfectible, given to self-love admittedly, but kindly disposed toward others and invariably quick to respond to their kindly affections, I seek to learn what social order necessarily results from the combination of these elements if their free play is not interfered with.

If we find that the resulting order leads progressively toward the general welfare, improvement and equality; toward the physical, intellectual, and moral leveling of all classes, and that this level is constantly raised; then God's ways will be vindicated. We shall learn to our joy that there are no gaps in the creation, and that the social order, like all the others, bears witness to the existence of the *harmonious laws* before which Newton bowed in reverence, and which moved the psalmist to cry out: *Coeli enarrant gloriam Dei.**

Rousseau said: "If I were a prince or a lawgiver, I should not waste my time saying what must be done; I should do it, or hold my tongue." †

I am not a *prince,* but the confidence of my fellow citizens in me has made me a *lawgiver.*‡ Perhaps they will tell me that it is time for me to act and not to write.

---

* ["The heavens declare the glory of God." Psalm XIX.—TRANSLATOR.]
† [*The Social Contract,* Preamble to Book I.—TRANSLATOR.]
‡ [Bastiat had just been elected a Deputy to the National Assembly.—TRANSLATOR.]

I ask their pardon. Whether it is the truth itself that urges me on, or whether I am the victim of an illusion, the fact remains that I feel the need of putting together into a single volume ideas for which, to date, I have failed to win acceptance because I have presented them separately, as scattered fragments. It seems to me that I perceive in the interplay of the natural laws of society sublime and reassuring *harmonies*. What I see, or think I see, must I not try to show to others, in order to rally together around an ideal of peace and brotherhood men whose minds have been misled, whose hearts have become embittered? If, when our beloved ship of state is tossed by the storm, I appear sometimes to withdraw, in order to get my bearings, from the post to which I have been called, the reason is that my feeble hands are unavailing at the helm. And besides, am I betraying my trust when I reflect on the causes of the storm and strive to act accordingly? And who knows whether it would be granted to me to do tomorrow what I should fail to do today?

I shall begin by setting down a few general ideas about economics. Using the works of my predecessors, I shall try to sum up the science of political economy in a single, simple, true, and constructive principle, one that political economists from the very beginning have been dimly aware of and have come closer and closer to comprehending. Perhaps the time has now come to give it expression in a definitive formula. Then, in the light of this clear knowledge, I shall try to resolve a few of the problems still controversial, such as competition, the role of the machine, foreign trade, luxury, capital, income from investments, etc. I shall point out some of the relationships, or rather, the harmonies, that exist between political economy and the other moral and social sciences, with a glance at the important topics designated by the words "self-interest," "property," "public ownership," "liberty," "equality," "responsibility," "solidarity," "brotherhood," "unity." Finally, I shall call the reader's attention to the artificial obstacles that beset the peaceful, orderly, and progressive development of human society. From these two ideas—natural, harmonious laws, on the one hand, and artificial, disruptive elements on the other—will be deduced the solution of the social problem.

It would be difficult to fail to see the pitfalls that threaten this undertaking from two sides. In the midst of the hurricane that is sweeping us along, if our book is too abstruse, it will not be read; if it succeeds in winning readers, it will be because the questions it poses have been touched upon only lightly. How can we reconcile scientific integrity with the demands of the reader? To satisfy all the requirements of form and content, we should have to weigh each word and study its context. It is thus that the crystal is formed drop by drop in silence and obscurity. Silence, retirement, time, peace of mind—I have none of these: and I am compelled to appeal to the good sense of the public and to beg its indulgence.

The subject of political economy is man.

But it does not embrace the whole man. Religious sentiment, paternal and maternal affection, filial devotion, love, friendship, patriotism, charity, politeness—these belong to the moral realm, which embraces all the appealing regions of human sympathy, leaving for the sister science of political economy only the cold domain of self-interest. This fact is unfairly forgotten when we reproach political economy with lacking the charm and grace of moral philosophy. How could it be otherwise? Let us challenge the right of political economy to exist as a science, but let us not force it to pretend to be what it is not. If human transactions whose object is wealth are vast enough and complicated enough to constitute a special science, let us grant it its own special appeal, and not reduce it to talking of self-interest in the language of sentiment. I am personally convinced that recently we have done it no service by demanding from it a tone of enthusiastic sentimentality that from its lips can sound only like hollow declamation. What does it deal with? With transactions carried on between people who do not know each other, who owe each other nothing beyond simple justice, who are defending and seeking to advance their own self-interest. It deals with claims that are restricted and limited by other claims, where self-sacrifice and unselfish dedication have no place. Take up the poet's lyre, then, to speak of these things. I would as soon see Lamartine * consult a table of logarithms to sing his odes.[3]

This is not to say that political economy does not have its own special poetry. Whenever there is order and harmony, there is poetry. But it is to be found in the results, not in the demonstrations. It is revealed; it is not created by the demonstrator. Kepler did not set himself up as a poet; yet certainly the laws he discovered are the true poetry of the mind.

Thus, political economy regards man from one side only, and our first concern must be to study him from this point of view. For this reason we cannot avoid going back to the primary phenomena of human sensation and activity. Let me reassure the reader, however. Our stay in the cloudy regions of metaphysics will not be a long one, and we shall borrow from this science only a few simple, clear, and, if possible, incontestable ideas.

The soul (or, not to become involved in spiritual questions, man) is endowed with the faculty of *sense perception*. Whether sense perception resides in the body or in the soul, the fact remains that as a *passive* being he experiences *sensations* that are painful or pleasurable. As an *active* being he strives to banish the former and multiply the latter. The result, which affects him again as a *passive* being, can be called *satisfaction*.

From the general idea of *sensation* come the more definite ideas of pain, wants, desires, tastes, appetites, on the one hand; and, on the other, of pleasure, enjoyment, fulfillment, and well-being.

Between these extremes is interposed a mean, and from the general idea of *activity* come the more definite ideas of pain, effort, fatigue, labor, and production.

An analysis of *sensation* and *activity* shows one word common

---

* [Alphonse Marie Louis de Lamartine (1790–1869), one of the great poets of French romanticism and subsequently a distinguished statesman. First elected Deputy in 1834, he knew his greatest glory at the time of the Revolution of 1848, when he was a prime mover in the establishment of the Second Republic. By his eloquence he calmed the Paris mobs which threatened to destroy it, and became the head of the provisional government. More an idealist than practical politician, however, he soon lost influence and retired to private life in 1851.—TRANSLATOR.]

to both domains, the word *pain*. It is *painful* to experience certain sensations, and we can stop them only by an effort that we call *taking pains*. Thus, we are apprised that here below we have little else than the choice of two evils.

Everything in this complex of phenomena is on the *personal* level, the sensation that precedes the effort as well as the satisfaction that follows it.

We cannot doubt that *self-interest* is the mainspring of human nature. It must be clearly understood that this word is used here to designate a universal, incontestable fact, resulting from the nature of man, and not an adverse judgment, as would be the word *selfishness*. The moral sciences would be impossible if we perverted at the outset the terms that the subject demands.

Human effort does not always and inevitably intervene between sensation and satisfaction. Sometimes satisfaction is obtained by itself. More often effort is exerted on *material objects,* through the agency of *forces* that Nature has without cost placed at man's disposal.

If we give the name of *utility* to everything that effects the satisfaction of wants, then there are two kinds of utility. One kind is given us by Providence without cost to ourselves; the other kind insists, so to speak, on being purchased through *effort*.

Thus, the complete cycle embraces, or can embrace, these four ideas:

$$\text{Want} \left\{ \begin{array}{c} \text{Gratuitous Utility} \\ \text{Onerous Utility} \end{array} \right\} \text{Satisfaction}$$

Man is endowed with a faculty for improvement. He compares, he looks ahead, he learns, he profits by experience. If want is a *pain,* and effort too entails *pains,* there is no reason for him not to seek to reduce the pains of the effort if he can do so without impairing the satisfaction that is its goal. This is what he accomplishes when he succeeds in replacing *onerous utility* by *gratuitous utility*, which is the constant object of his search.

Our *self-interest* is such that we constantly seek to increase the sum of our satisfactions in relation to our efforts; and our intelligence is such—in the cases where our attempt is successful—that we reach our goal through increasing the amount of gratuitous utility in relation to onerous utility.

Every time progress of this type is achieved, a part of our efforts is freed to be placed on the available list, so to speak; and we have the option either of enjoying more rest or of working for the satisfaction of new desires if these are keen enough to stir us to action.

Such is the source of all progress in the economic order. It is also, as we easily comprehend, the source of all miscalculations, for progress and miscalculation both have their roots in that marvelous and special gift that God has bestowed upon man: *free will*.

We are endowed with the faculty of comparing, of judging, of choosing, and of acting accordingly. This implies that we can arrive at a good or a bad judgment, make a good or a bad choice— a fact that it is never idle to remind men of when we speak to them of liberty.

We are not, to be sure, mistaken about our own sensations, and we discern with an infallible instinct whether they are painful or pleasurable. But how many different forms our errors of judgment can take! We can mistake the cause and pursue eagerly, as something sure to give us pleasure, what can give us only pain; or we can fail to see the relation of cause and effect and be unaware that an immediate pleasure will be followed ultimately by greater pain; or again, we can be mistaken as to the relative importance of our wants and our desires.

We can give a wrong direction to our efforts not only through ignorance, but also through the perversity of our will. "Man," said de Bonald,* is an intellect served by bodily organs." Indeed! Do we have nothing else? Do we not have passions?

When we speak, then, of harmony, we do not mean that the natural arrangement of the social world is such that error and

---

* [Louis Gabriel Ambroise, Vicomte de Bonald (1754–1840), French *moraliste* and political reactionary, author of various treatises on religious, social, and philosophical questions.—Translator.]

vice have been excluded. To advance such a thesis in the face of the facts would be carrying the love of system to the point of madness. For this harmony to be without any discordant note, man would have to be without free will, or else infallible. We say only this: Man's principal social tendencies are harmonious in that, as every error leads to disillusionment and every vice to punishment, the discords tend constantly to disappear.

A first and vague notion of the nature of property can be deduced from these premises. Since it is the individual who experiences the sensation, the desire, the want; since it is the individual who exerts the *effort;* the satisfactions also must have their end in him, for otherwise the effort would be meaningless.

The same holds true of *inheritance.* No theory, no flights of oratory can succeed in keeping fathers from loving their children. The people who delight in setting up imaginary societies may consider this regrettable, but it is a fact. A father will expend as much *effort,* perhaps more, for his children's *satisfactions* as for his own. If, then, a new law contrary to Nature should forbid the bequest of private property, it would not only in itself do violence to the rights of private property, but it would also prevent the creation of new private property by paralyzing a full half of human *effort.*

Self-interest, private property, inheritance—we shall have occasion to come back to these topics. Let us first, however, try to establish the limits of the science with which we are concerned.

I am not one of those who believe that a science has *inherently* its own natural and immutable boundaries. In the realm of ideas, as in the realm of material objects, everything is linked together, everything is connected; all truths merge into one another, and every science, to be complete, must embrace all others. It has been well said that for an infinite intelligence there would be only one single truth. It is only our human frailty, therefore, that reduces us to study a certain order of phenomena as though isolated, and the resulting classifications cannot avoid a certain arbitrariness.

The true merit consists in the exact exposition of the facts, their causes and their effects. There is also merit, but a purely minor and relative one, in determining, not rigorously, which is impossible, but rationally, the type of facts to be considered.

I say this so that it may not be supposed that I wish to criticize my predecessors if I happen to give to political economy somewhat different limits from those that they have assigned to it.

In recent years economists have frequently been reproached for too great a preoccupation with the question of *wealth*. It has been felt that they should have included as part of political economy everything that contributes, directly or indirectly, to human happiness or suffering; and it has even been alleged that they denied the existence of everything that they did not discuss, for example, the manifestations of altruism, as natural to the heart of man as self-interest. This is like accusing the mineralogist of denying the existence of the animal kingdom. Is not wealth—i.e., the laws of its production, distribution, and consumption—sufficiently vast and important a subject to constitute a special field of science? If the conclusions of the economist were in contradiction to those in the fields of government or ethics, I could understand the accusation. We could say to him, "By limiting yourself, you have lost your way, for it is not possible for two truths to be in conflict." Perhaps one result of the work that I am submitting to the public may be that the science of wealth will be seen to be in perfect harmony with all the other sciences.

Of the three *terms* that encompass the human condition—sensation, effort, satisfaction—the first and the last are always, and inevitably, merged in the same individual. It is impossible to think of them as separated. We can conceive of a sensation that is not satisfied, a want that is not fulfilled, but never can we conceive of a *want* felt by one man and its *satisfaction* experienced by another.

If the same held true of the middle term, *effort*, man would be a completely solitary creature. The economic phenomenon would occur in its entirety within an isolated individual. There could be a juxtaposition of persons; there could not be a society. There could be a *personal* economy; there could not be a *political* economy.

But such is not the case. It is quite possible, and indeed it frequently happens, that one person's *want* owes its *satisfaction* to another person's *effort.* The fact is that if we think of all the satisfactions that come to us, we shall all recognize that we derive most of them from efforts we have not made; and likewise, that the labor that we perform, each in our own calling, almost always goes to satisfy desires that are not ours.

Thus, we realize that it is not in wants or in satisfactions, which are essentially personal and intransmissible phenomena, but in the nature of the middle term, *human effort,* that we must seek the social principle, the origin of political economy. It is, in fact, precisely this faculty of *working for one another,* which is given to mankind and only to mankind, this transfer of efforts, this exchange of services, with all the infinitely complicated combinations of which it is susceptible in time and space, that constitutes the science of economics, demonstrates its origins, and determines its limits.

I therefore say: *Political economy has as its special field all those efforts of men that are capable of satisfying, subject to services in return, the wants of persons other than the one making the effort, and, consequently, those wants and satisfactions that are related to efforts of this kind.*

Thus, to cite an example, the act of breathing, although containing the three elements that make up the economic phenomenon, does not belong to the science of economics, and the reason is apparent: we are concerned here with a set of facts in which not only the two extremes—want and satisfaction—are nontransferable (as they always are), but the middle element, *effort,* as well. We ask no one's help in order to breathe; no giving or receiving is involved. By its very nature it is an individual act and a nonsocial one, which cannot be included in a science that, as its very name implies, deals entirely with interrelations.

But let special circumstances arise that require men to help one another to breathe, as when a workman goes down in a diving bell, or a doctor operates a pulmotor, or the police take steps to purify the air; then we have a want satisfied by a person other than the one experiencing it, we have a service rendered, and breathing itself, at least on the score of assistance and remuneration, comes within the scope of political economy.

It is not necessary that the transaction be actually completed.

Provided only a transaction is possible, the *labor* involved becomes economic in character. The farmer who raises wheat for his own use performs an economic act in that the wheat is exchangeable.

To make an effort in order to satisfy another person's want is to perform a *service* for him. If a service is stipulated in return, there is an exchange of *services;* and, since this is the most common situation, political economy may be defined as *the theory of exchange.*

However keen may be the want of one of the contracting parties, however great the effort of the other, if the exchange is freely made, the two services *are of equal value.* Value, then, consists in the comparative estimation of reciprocal services, and political economy may also be defined as the *theory of value.*

I have just defined political economy and marked out the area it covers, without mentioning one essential element: *gratuitous utility,* or *utility without effort.*

All authors have commented on the fact that we derive countless satisfactions from this source. They have termed these utilities, such as air, water, sunlight, etc., *natural wealth,* in contrast to *social wealth,* and then dismissed them; and, in fact, since they lead to no effort, no exchange, no service, and, being without value, figure in no inventory, it would seem that they should not be included within the scope of political economy.

This exclusion would be logical if *gratuitous* utility were a fixed, invariable quantity always distinct from *onerous* utility, that is, utility created by *effort;* but the two are constantly intermingled and in inverse ratio. Man strives ceaselessly to substitute the one for the other, that is, to obtain, with the help of natural and gratuitous utilities, the same results with less effort. He makes wind, gravity, heat, gas do for him what originally he accomplished only by the strength of his own muscles.

Now, what happens? Although the result is the same, the effort is less. Less effort implies less service, and less service implies less value. All progress, therefore, destroys some degree of value, but how? Not at all by impairing the usefulness of the result, but by substituting gratuitous utility for onerous utility, natural wealth for social wealth. From one point of view, the part of value thus destroyed no longer belongs in the field of political economy, since it does not figure in our inventories; for it can no longer be exchanged, i.e., bought or sold, and humanity enjoys it without effort, almost without being aware of it. It can no longer be counted as relative wealth; it takes its place among the blessings of God. But, on the other hand, political economy would certainly be in error in not taking account of it. To fail to do so would be to lose sight of the essential, the main consideration of all: the final outcome, the *useful result;* it would be to misunderstand the strongest forces working for sharing in common and equality; it would be to see everything in the social order except the existing harmony. If this book is destined to advance political economy a single step, it will be through keeping constantly before the reader's eyes that part of value which is successively destroyed and then reclaimed in the form of *gratuitous utility* for all humanity.

I shall here make an observation that will prove how much the various sciences overlap and how close they are to merging into one.

I have just defined *service*. It is *effort* on the part of one man, whereas the *want* and the *satisfaction* are another's. Sometimes the service is rendered gratis, without payment, without any service exacted in return. It springs from altruism rather than from self-interest. It constitutes a gift and not an exchange. Consequently, it seems to belong, not to political economy (which is the theory of exchange), but to moral philosophy. In fact, acts of this nature are, because of their motivation, moral rather than economic phenomena. Nevertheless, we shall see that, by reason of their results, they pertain to the science with which we are here concerned. On the other hand, services rendered in return for effort, requiring payment, and, for this reason, essentially economic, do not on that account remain, in their results, outside the realm of ethics.

Accordingly, these two fields of knowledge have countless points in common; and, since two truths cannot be contradictory, when the economist views with alarm a phenomenon that the moralist hails as beneficial, we can be sure that one or the other is wrong. Thus do the various sciences hold one another to the path of truth.

3

Man's Wants

It is perhaps impossible and, in any case, not very useful to present a complete and methodical catalogue of all of man's wants. Almost all those of real importance are included in the following list:

Breathing (I keep this want here as marking the absolute limit where the transfer of labor or the exchange of services begins), food, clothing, housing, the preservation or recovery of health, transportation, security, education, amusement, enjoyment of the beautiful.

Wants exist. This is a fact. It would be childish to inquire whether it would be better if they did not exist and why God has made us subject to them.

It is certain that man *suffers* and even dies when he cannot satisfy the wants that it is his nature as a human being to feel. It is certain that he *suffers* and can die when he satisfies certain of them overmuch.

We can satisfy most of our wants only by taking pains, which can themselves be considered *suffering*. The same is true of the act by which, exercising a noble restraint over our appetites, we deprive ourselves of something.

Thus, *suffering* is unavoidable, and we have little more than a choice of evils. Furthermore, suffering is the most personal, intimate thing in the world; consequently, *self-interest,* the impulse that today is branded as selfish and individualistic, is indestructible. Nature has placed *feeling* at the ends of our nerves, at all the approaches to our hearts and our minds, like an outpost, to warn us where there is a lack or an excess of satisfaction. Pain, then, has a purpose, a mission. It has often been asked if the existence of evil can be reconciled with the infinite goodness of the Creator—an awesome problem that philosophy will always grapple with and will probably never solve. As far as political economy is concerned, man must be taken as he is, inasmuch as it has not been vouchsafed to the imagination to picture—and to reason even less to conceive of—an animate and mortal being exempt from pain. All our efforts to understand feeling without pain or man without feeling would be vain.

Today, some sentimentalist schools reject as false any social science that has not succeeded in devising a system by means of which pain will disappear from the world. They pass a harsh judgment on political economy because it recognizes what cannot be denied: the existence of suffering. They go further; they hold political economy responsible for it. This is like attributing the frailty of our organs to the physiologist who studies them.

Of course, a man can make himself momentarily popular, can attract to himself men who are suffering, and can arouse them against the natural order of society by telling them that he has in mind a plan for the artificial arrangement of society that will exclude pain in any form. He can even say that he has stolen God's secret and has interpreted His supposed will by banishing evil from the face of the earth. And yet the sentimentalist schools call irreverent the science that refuses to make such claims, accusing it of misunderstanding or denying the foresight or omnipotence of the Author of all things!

At the same time, these schools paint a frightening picture of present-day society, and they do not perceive that, if it is *irreverent* to predict suffering for the future, it is no less irreverent to note its existence in the past or in the present. For the Infinite admits of no limits; and if, since Creation, even one man has suffered in this world, that is reason enough to admit, without *irreverence,* that pain has entered into the plan of Providence.

It is certainly more scientific and more manly to recognize

the existence of the great facts of Nature, which not only do exist, but without which mankind could not be imagined.

Thus, man is subject to suffering, and, consequently, society is also.

Suffering has a role to play in the life of the individual and, consequently, in that of society as well.

The study of the natural laws of society will reveal that the role of suffering is gradually to destroy its own causes, to restrict itself to narrower and narrower limits, and, finally, to guarantee us, by making us earn and deserve it, a preponderance of the good and the beautiful over the evil.

The catalogue presented above puts material needs first.

We live in times that force me to warn the reader once again against the sentimental affectation so very much in vogue.

There are people who hold very cheap what they disdainfully call *material needs, material satisfactions.* They will doubtless say to me, as Bélise says to Chrysale:

> Is the body, this rag, of sufficient importance,
> Of sufficient worth, that we should give it the
> slightest heed? *

And these people, though generally well provided for in every respect (on which I sincerely congratulate them), will blame me for having listed *food,* for example, as coming first.

Certainly I recognize that moral improvement belongs to a higher order of things than the preservation of the body. But, after all, are we so beset by this mania for cant and affectation that we are no longer permitted to say that in order to attain moral improvement we must keep soul and body together? Let us avoid these childish attitudes, which stand in the way of science. By trying to pass ourselves off as philanthropic, we cease to be truthful; for it is contrary to logic and to the facts that moral progress, the concern for personal dignity, the cultivation of refined sentiments should have priority over the simple needs of preserving

---

* [Quoted from *Les Femmes savantes (The Learned Ladies)* of Molière.— TRANSLATOR.]

the body. This type of prudery is quite recent. Rousseau, that enthusiastic panegyrist of the *state of nature,* did not indulge in it; and a man endowed with exquisite delicacy, with appealing gentleness of heart, with a spirituality that led him to embrace quietism, and withal a stoic in his own mode of life, Fénelon, said, "In the final analysis, soundness of mind consists in seeking to learn how those things are done that are the basis of human life. All the matters of great importance turn upon them." *

Without professing, then, to classify human wants in a rigorously methodical order, we may say that man cannot direct his efforts toward the satisfaction of his highest and noblest moral wants until he has provided for those that concern the preservation of his life. Hence, we can already conclude that any legislative measure that makes material life difficult is harmful to the moral life of nations, a *harmony* that I call to the reader's attention in passing.

And, since the opportunity has arisen, I shall point out another one.

Since the inexorable necessities of material life are an obstacle to moral and intellectual development, it follows that more virtue will be found in the more affluent nations and classes. Good Heavens! What have I said, and what an uproar assails my ears! Today there is a veritable mania for attributing to the poorer classes a monopoly of all the devotion, all the self-sacrifice, all the noble qualities that constitute in man moral grandeur and beauty; and this mania has recently spread further under the influence of a revolution † that, by bringing these classes to the surface of society, has not failed to raise up about them a horde of adulators.

I do not deny that wealth, and especially opulence, particularly when unjustly distributed, tends to develop certain special vices.

* [François de Salignac de La Mothe-Fénelon (1651-1715), Archbishop of Cambrai, preceptor to the grandson of Louis XIV, author of a collection of *Fables, the Dialogues of the Dead,* and *Télémaque.*—TRANSLATOR.]

† [The February Revolution, of 1848, which ousted the "bourgeois king," Louis Philippe, and established the short-lived Second Republic, of which the poet-statesman Lamartine was the provisional head. Bastiat served in the Legislative Assembly and was a member of the Committee of Finance. This government, however, was subject to communist and socialist pressures, the object of Bastiat's relentless criticism, and adopted many measures that he deplored.—TRANSLATOR.]

But is it possible to admit as a general proposition that virtue is the privilege of the poverty-stricken, and that vice is the unlovely and unfailing companion of the well-to-do? This would be to affirm that moral and intellectual development, which is compatible only with a certain degree of leisure and comfort, works to the detriment of intelligence and morality.

And I appeal to the honest judgment of the unfortunate classes themselves. To what horrible *discords* would such a paradox not lead?

We should therefore have to say that humanity is faced with the terrible alternatives of either remaining eternally poverty-stricken or of moving toward ever increasing immorality. In accordance with this logic, all the forces that lead to wealth, such as enterprise, thrift, orderliness, skill, honesty, are the seeds of vice; whereas those that hold us back in poverty, like improvidence, idleness, dissipation, negligence, are the precious buds of virtue. Could a more discouraging discord be imagined in the moral world? And if such were the case, who would dare speak to the people or proffer any advice? You complain of your sufferings, we should have to say, and you are anxious to see them end. You groan under the yoke of the most pressing material wants, and you long for the hour of deliverance; for you, too, desire a measure of leisure to develop your intellectual and emotional capacities. For this reason you seek to make your voice heard in the political arena and to protect your interests. But learn the nature of what you desire, and realize that the granting of your wishes would be fatal to you. Solvency, easy circumstances, wealth engender vice. Cling lovingly, then, to your poverty and your virtue.

The flatterers of the people thus fall into an obvious contradiction when they point to wealth as a vile cesspool of selfishness and vice, and at the same time urge the people—and often, in their haste, by the most illegal of means—toward that region which they consider so abominable.

No, such discord is not to be found in the natural order of society. It is not possible that all men should aspire to live in comfortable circumstances, that the natural way to attain it should be through the exercise of the strictest virtue, and that on reaching it, they should, nevertheless, fall again under the yoke of vice. Such rantings are fit only to kindle and keep alive the fires of class hatred. Were they true, they would give humanity only the choice between dire poverty and immorality. Being false, they make lies serve the cause of disorder, and, by their deceit, set against each other classes that should mutually love and assist each other.

Yes, unnatural inequality, inequality that the law creates by disturbing the natural and orderly development of the various classes of society, is, for all, a prolific source of resentments, jealousies, and vices. For this reason we must make sure whether or not this natural order leads to the progressive equalization and improvement of all classes; and we should be stopped short in this study by what is known in law as a peremptory exception if this twofold material progress inevitably entailed a twofold moral deterioration.

On the subject of human wants I have an observation to make that is important, even fundamental, for political economy: they are not a fixed, immutable quantity. By nature they are not static, but progressive.

This characteristic is to be noted even in the most material of our wants; it becomes more marked as we advance to those intellectual tastes and yearnings that distinguish man from beast.

It would seem that, if there is any one thing in which men must resemble one another, it is in their need for food; for, except for abnormalities, all stomachs are about the same. Nevertheless, foods that would have been a delicacy in one era have become coarse fare for another, and the diet which suits a lazzarone would cause a Dutchman anguish. Thus, this want, the most immediate, the most elemental, and, consequently, the most uniform of all, still varies according to age, sex, temperament, climate, and habit.

The same is true of all other wants. Hardly has man got himself a shelter when he wants a house; hardly has he clothed himself when he wants adornment; hardly has he satisfied the needs of his body when study, knowledge, art open to his desires a new and endless vista.

It is quite worth while to note the speed with which, through continued satisfaction, what was only a vague desire becomes a taste, and what was only a taste becomes a want and even a want that will not be denied.

Take, for example, a rough and industrious artisan. Accustomed to coarse fare, humble clothing, mediocre lodging, he thinks that he would be the happiest of men, that he would want nothing more, if he could mount to the rung of the ladder that he sees immediately above him. He is amazed that those who have got there are still tormenting themselves. Let the modest fortune he has dreamed of come his way, and he is happy; happy—alas! for a few days.

For soon he becomes familiar with his new position, and little by little he ceases to be aware of his longed-for good fortune. He dons with indifference the garment he had once coveted. He has created a new environment for himself, he associates with different people, from time to time he touches his lips to a different goblet, he aspires to climb another rung; and, if he will but look into his own heart, he will be well aware that, if his fortune has changed, his soul has remained what it was, an inexhaustible well of desires.

It would appear that Nature has given *habit* this peculiar power in order that it should be in us what the ratchet wheel is in mechanics, and that humanity, ever urged on toward higher and higher regions, should never stop at any level of civilization.

The *sense of one's own worth* acts, perhaps, even more powerfully in the same direction. The Stoic philosopher has often blamed man for wanting to *appear* rather than to *be*. But, if he take a broader view of things, is it quite certain that *appearing* is not for mankind one of the forms of *being?*

When, through industry, orderliness, and thrift, a family rises step by step toward those social regions where tastes are more and more refined, relations more polite, sentiments more delicate, minds more cultivated, who does not know the poignant grief that accompanies a reversal of fortune? In that case it is not the body alone that suffers. The descent breaks habits that have become, as we say, second nature; it impairs the sense of one's own worth and with it all the faculties of the soul. Therefore, it is not unusual, in such cases, to see the victim give way to despair and fall at once into a state of brutish degradation. As with the air we breathe, so with the social milieu. The mountaineer, accustomed to his pure air, soon wastes away in the narrow streets of our cities.

I hear a voice crying: Economist, already you falter. You had announced that your science was in harmony with ethics, and here you are justifying sybarite luxury.

Philosopher, I shall say in my turn, divest yourself of those garments you wear, which were never those of primitive man, break your furniture, burn your books, feed yourself on the raw meat of animals, and I shall reply to your objection. It is too easy to challenge the force of habit while readily consenting to be the living proof of what it can do.

It is possible to criticize this inclination that Nature has given the organs of our body, but criticism will not prevent it from being universal. We note its presence among all peoples, ancient and modern, savage and civilized, in the antipodes as in France. Without it, it is impossible to account for civilization. Now, when an inclination of the human heart is universal and indestructible, has social science the right not to take it into account?

Objection will be raised by the political theorists who claim the honor of being disciples of Rousseau. But Rousseau never denied the phenomenon of which I speak. He comments positively on the elasticity of our wants, on the force of habit, and even on the role that I assign to it of preventing humanity from taking any backward step. But what I admire, he deplores, and it could not be otherwise. Rousseau conjectures that there was a time when men had neither rights nor duties nor contacts with other men nor affections nor language, and that was the time when they were happy and perfect. He could not fail to abhor, therefore, the complicated social machinery that is ceaselessly moving mankind away from its earlier perfection. Those who believe, on the contrary, that perfection is to be found, not at the beginning, but at the end, of the evolutionary cycle, marvel at the driving force that impels us forward. But in regard to the existence of this driving force and the way it works, we are in agreement.

"Men," he said, "enjoying much leisure, used it to procure for themselves various types of commodities unknown to their fathers, and this was the first yoke that they unconsciously placed about their necks and the beginning of the woes that they prepared for their descendants; for, in addition to the fact that they thus softened their bodies and their minds, these commodities having, *through habit,* lost nearly all their charm, and having at the same time degenerated into *real wants,* their loss became much more cruel than their possession had been sweet, and men were miserable at losing them without ever being happy at possessing them." *

Rousseau was convinced that God, nature, and man were wrong. I know that this opinion still sways many minds, but mine is not one of them.

After all, God forbid that I should attack man's noblest portion, his fairest virtue, dominion over himself, control over his passions, moderation in his desires, scorn of ostentatious luxury! I do not say that he should let himself become the slave of any artificial want. I do say that, generally speaking, his wants, such as both his physical and his immaterial nature makes them, combined with force of habit and his sense of his own worth, are capable of being indefinitely multiplied, because they stem from an inexhaustible source—desire. Who will censure a man merely because he is wealthy, if he is sober, restrained in his dress, not given to ostentation and soft living? But are there not loftier desires that he is permitted to gratify? Are there any limits to his longing for knowledge? Are his efforts to serve his country, to encourage the arts, to disseminate valuable information, to aid his less fortunate brethren, in any way incompatible with the proper use of wealth?

Furthermore, whether or not the philosopher approves, human

---

* [From Part Two of the *Discourse on the Origin of Inequality.* Nearly all the arguments that Bastiat attempts to refute in this chapter can be found either in the *Discourse on Inequality* or in the *Discourse on the Arts and Sciences,*—TRANSLATOR.]

wants are not a fixed and unchangeable quantity. This is a fact, certain, not to be gainsaid, universal. In no category, whether food, lodging, or education, were the wants of the fourteenth century as great as ours, and we may well predict that ours do not equal those to which our descendants will become accustomed.

This is an observation that holds good for all the elements that have a place in political economy: wealth, labor, value, services, etc., all of which share the extreme variability of their source, man. Political economy does not have, like geometry or physics, the advantage of speculating about objects that can be weighed or measured; and this is one of its initial difficulties and, subsequently, a perpetual source of error; for, when the human mind applies itself to a certain order of phenomena, it is naturally disposed to seek a *criterion,* a common measure to which it may refer everything, in order to give to the particular field of knowledge the character of an *exact science.* Thus, we note that most authors seek fixity, some in *value,* others in *money,* another in *grain,* still another in *labor,* that is to say, in measures exhibiting the very fluctuation they seek to avoid.

Many economic errors are due to the fact that human wants are considered as a fixed quantity; and for that reason I have felt obliged to enlarge on this subject. At the risk of anticipating what I shall say later I shall now describe briefly this mode of reasoning. All the chief satisfactions of the age in which one happens to live are taken into account, and it is presumed that humanity admits of no others. Then, if the bounty of Nature or the productivity of machinery or habits of temperance and moderation result for a time in rendering idle a certain part of human labor, this progress is viewed with alarm, it is considered a disaster, and the theorists take refuge behind absurd but plausible formulas, like: *We are suffering from overproduction; we are dying of a surfeit; production has outstripped consumer buying power,* etc.

It is impossible to find a good solution to the problem of *the machine, foreign competition, and luxury,* as long as *wants* are considered as an invariable quantity, or their capacity for indefinite multiplication is not taken into account.

But if man's wants are not fixed quantities, but progressive, capable of *growth* like the inexhaustible desires on which they constantly feed, we must conclude, granting that a balance between the means and the end is the first law of all harmony, that Nature has placed in man and about him unlimited and constantly increasing means of *satisfaction*. This is what we shall now examine.

I said, at the beginning of this work, that political economy has for its subject *man,* considered from the point of view of his wants and the means whereby he is able to satisfy them.

It is thus natural to have begun by studying man and his nature.

But we have also seen that he is not a solitary being. If his *wants* and his *satisfactions*—in virtue of the nature of his senses—are inseparable from his being, the same is not true of his *efforts,* which are part of his dynamic constitution. These are transferable. In a word, men work for one another.

Now a very strange thing happens.

When we consider man from a general and, so to speak, abstract point of view—his wants, his efforts, his satisfactions, his constitution, his inclinations, his tendencies—we arrive at a series of observations that seem clear beyond all doubt and strikingly self-evident, for each one of us finds their proof within himself. So obvious and commonplace are these truths that the writer fears the public's derision if he presents them. He feels, with some reason, that he can see the angry reader throwing away the book and crying out, "I will not waste my time learning anything so trivial."

Nevertheless, these truths, held to be so incontestable—as long as they are presented in a general way—that we can hardly bear to be reminded of them, are no longer regarded as anything but ridiculous errors, absurd theories, as soon as we view man in his social surroundings. Who, contemplating man in his isolated state, would ever think of saying: *We have overproduction; consumption cannot keep pace with production; luxury and artificial tastes are the source of wealth; mechanical inventions destroy labor;* and other aphorisms of the same import, which, when applied to the mass of mankind, are nevertheless accepted as so axiomatic that they are made the foundation of our industrial and commercial laws? *Exchange* produces in this respect an illusion capable of beguiling even the best minds, and I affirm that *political economy* will have gained its objective and fulfilled its mission when it has conclusively proved this fact: *What holds true for one man holds true for society.* Man in a state of isolation is at once producer and consumer, inventor and entrepreneur, capitalist and worker; all the economic phenomena are performed in him, and he is, as it were, a society in miniature. In the same way, humanity, viewed in its totality, is like a single man, immense, composite, many-sided, to whom are applicable exactly the same truths observable in a single individual.

I felt the need to make this remark, which, I hope, will be better justified later, before continuing my studies on man. Had I not made it, I should have feared that the reader would reject as superfluous the deductions, the veritable *truisms,* that are to follow.

I have just spoken of man's *wants,* and, after an approximate enumeration of them, I have observed that they are not static, but progressive. This is true whether they are considered by themselves alone or included altogether in the physical, intellectual, or moral order. How could it be otherwise? There are certain wants of our bodies that must be satisfied, or we die; and, up to a certain point, we could maintain that these wants are fixed quantities, though this statement is not strictly accurate. For, however little we may desire to overlook an essential element —the force of habit—and to condescend to subject ourselves to honest self-examination, we are constrained to admit that our wants, even the most elemental, like eating, are unquestionably modified by habit. Anyone who would take exception to this remark, as smacking of materialism or epicureanism, would be most unhappy if we took him at his word and reduced him to the black broth of the Spartans or to the pittance of an anchorite. But, in any case, when these wants are satisfied once and for all, there are others that spring from the most elastic of all our faculties— desire. Can we imagine a moment in man's life when he is incapable of new desires, even reasonable desires? Let us not forget that a desire that is unreasonable at a certain point in civilization, when all human resources are absorbed in the satisfaction of lesser desires, ceases to be unreasonable when the improvement of these resources has cleared the way. Thus, a desire to go thirty miles an hour would have been unreasonable two centuries ago but is not so today. To assert that the wants and desires of man are fixed and static quantities is to misunderstand the nature of the soul, to deny the facts, to make civilization inexplicable.

It would be still more inexplicable if the unlimited formation of new wants were not accompanied by the potentially unlimited development of new means to satisfy them. As far as progress is concerned, what good would the indefinitely elastic nature of our wants do us if, at a certain definite point, our faculties could advance no further, if they encountered an immovable barrier? Therefore, unless Nature, Providence, or whatever may be the power that rules our fate, has fallen into the most cruel and shocking contradiction, we must presume, since our desires are without limit, that our means of satisfying them are likewise without limit.

I say "without limit," and not "infinite," for nothing that relates to man is infinite. Because our desires and our faculties go on developing endlessly, they have no assignable limits, although they do have absolute limits. We can mention countless points above and beyond humanity that humanity can never reach, yet we cannot for that reason determine an exact instant when progress toward them will come to a halt.[1]

I do not mean that desire and the means of satisfying it keep pace with one another. *Desire* runs ahead, while the *means* limps along behind. The nature of our desire, so quick and adventurous compared with the slowness of our faculties, reminds us that at every step of civilization, on every rung of the ladder of progress, a certain degree of suffering is and always will be man's lot. But it teaches us also that suffering has a mission, since it would be impossible to comprehend the role of desire as a goad to our faculties if it lagged behind them, instead of rushing along ahead, as it does. Yet let us not accuse Nature of cruelty for having built this mechanism, for it is to be noted that desire does not become a real want, that is, a painful desire, unless habit has turned it into a permanent satisfaction; in other words, unless the *means* of gratifying it has been discovered and placed permanently and irrevocably within our reach.[2]

We must now consider this question: What means are available to us to satisfy our wants?

It seems clear to me that there are two: Nature and labor, the gifts of God and the fruits of our efforts, or, if you will, the application of our faculties to the things that Nature has placed at our disposal.

No school of thought, as far as I know, has attributed to Nature *alone* the satisfaction of our wants. Such an assertion is obviously refuted by experience, and we do not have to study political economy to perceive that the intervention of our *faculties* is necessary.

But there are schools that have attributed this distinction to labor alone. Their axiom is: *All weath comes from labor; labor is wealth.*

I cannot refrain from observing here that these formulas, taken literally, have led to gross errors of principle and, consequently, to deplorable legislative measures. I shall speak of this subject elsewhere.

I confine myself here to maintaining that, in point of fact, *Nature* and *labor* function together for the satisfaction of our wants and our desires.

Let us look at the facts.

The first want, which we have placed at the head of our list, is that of *breathing*. On this score we have already noted that, generally, Nature foots the whole bill, and that human *labor* intervenes only in certain exceptional cases as, for example, when it is necessary to purify the air.

The want of *quenching our thirst* is satisfied by Nature, to a greater or lesser degree, according to the availability and quality of the water provided; and the role of labor is to compensate by wells and cisterns for Nature's deficiencies.

Nature is no more uniformly liberal toward us in the matter of *food;* for who will say that the amount of labor we must perform is always the same whether the land is fertile or barren, the forest filled with game, the river with fish, or the contrary is the case?

As for *lighting,* there is certainly less for human labor to do in places where the night is short than where it has pleased the sun to run a briefer course.

I dare not state this as an absolute rule, but it seems to me that as we rise on the scale of our wants, Nature's co-operation diminishes, and more is left to our own faculties. The painter, the sculptor, even the writer, are forced to use materials and instruments that Nature alone furnishes; but we must admit that they must draw upon their own genius for the qualities that make for the charm, the merit, the usefulness, and the value of their works. *Learning* is a want that is satisfied almost entirely by the use of our intellectual faculties. Nevertheless, could we not say that here too *Nature* aids us by offering to us, in different degrees, objects for observation and comparison? For an equal amount of work can an equal amount of progress in botany, geology, or biology be made everywhere in the world?

It would be superfluous to cite other examples. We can already state as a fact that Nature gives us means of satisfaction that have greater or lesser degrees of *utility.* (This word is used in its etymological sense, i.e., the property of rendering a service.) In many cases, in almost every case, something remains for labor to do before this *utility* is complete; and we recognize that this contribution by labor will be greater or less, in each individual case, in accordance with the extent to which Nature herself has furthered the operation.

We can therefore lay down these two formulas:

1. *Utility is transmitted sometimes by Nature, sometimes by labor alone, almost always by the conjunction of Nature and labor.*

2. *To bring a thing to its complete state of utility, the contribution of labor is in inverse ratio to the contribution of Nature.*

From these two propositions, combined with what we have said about the indefinite elasticity of our wants, allow me to draw a conclusion whose importance will be demonstrated later. If we imagine two men without means of mutual communication placed in unequal situations, with Nature generous to one and parsimonious to the other, the first one will obviously have less work to do for each given satisfaction. Does it follow that that part of his energies thus left, so to speak, *available,* will necessarily be stricken with inertia, and that this man, because of Nature's liberality, will be reduced to enforced idleness? No, what happens is that he will be able, if he so desires, to employ his energies to enlarge the circle of his enjoyments; that for an equal amount of labor he will obtain two satisfactions instead of one; in a word, progress will be easier for him.

Perhaps I am deluding myself, but it does not seem to me that any science, not even geometry, presents, at its outset, truths more unassailable. If, nevertheless, someone were to prove to me that all these truths are so many errors, he would have destroyed in me not only the confidence that they inspire, but the bases of all certainty and all faith in evidence of any kind whatsoever, for what logic could be more convincing than the logic that he would thus have overturned? On the day when an axiom will be found to contradict the axiom that a straight line is the shortest distance between two points, the human mind will have no other refuge than absolute skepticism, if that can be called a refuge.

Therefore, I feel a real embarrassment in insisting on primary truths so clear that they seem childish. Nevertheless, I must say, in the midst of the complications of human transactions, these truths have been misunderstood; and, to justify myself in the eyes of the reader for delaying him so long on what the English call *truisms,* I shall point out the singular aberration that has misled some very excellent minds. Setting aside, neglecting entirely, the *co-operation of Nature,* in relation to the satisfaction of our wants, they have laid down this absolute principle: *All wealth comes from labor.* On this premise they have constructed the following syllogism:

"All wealth comes from labor.

"Hence, wealth is in proportion to labor.

"But labor is in inverse ratio to the bounty of Nature.

"Hence, wealth is in inverse ratio to the bounty of Nature."

And, whether we like it or not, many of our economic laws have been inspired by this singular logic. These laws can be only detrimental to the creation and distribution of wealth. For this reason I am justified in setting down these apparently very trivial truths as a preliminary step toward refuting the errors and deplorable misconceptions under which present-day society is laboring.

Let us now analyze this question of the contribution of Nature.

Nature puts two things at our disposal: *materials* and *forces*.

Most material objects that contribute to the satisfaction of our wants and our desires are brought to the state of *utility*, which adapts them to our use through the intervention of labor, by the application of human faculties. But, in any case, the elements, the atoms, if you wish, of which these objects are composed, are gifts, and I add, *gratuitous* gifts, of Nature. This observation is of the greatest importance, and, I am convinced, will shed a new light on the theory of wealth.

I beg the reader to be good enough to remember that I am studying here in a general way the physical and moral constitution of man, his wants, his faculties, and his relations with Nature, with the exception of exchange, which I shall take up in the next chapter; we shall then see in what areas and in what way social transactions modify the phenomena.

It is obvious that if man in the state of isolation must, so to speak, *purchase* most of his satisfactions by labor, by effort, it is strictly accurate to say that before any labor, any effort, of his has come into play, the materials he finds available are the *gratuitous* gifts of Nature. After the first effort, however slight, they cease to be *gratuitous;* and if the terminology of political economy had always been exact, the name *raw materials* would have been reserved for material objects in this state, prior to any human activity.

I say again at this point that the *gratuitousness* of these gifts of Nature, before the intervention of labor, is of the highest importance. In fact, I said in the second chapter that political economy was the *theory of value*. I add now, anticipating, that things begin to have *value* only when labor gives it to them. I propose to demonstrate, later, that all that is *gratis* to man in the state of isolation remains gratis to man in society, and that the gratuitous gifts of Nature, *however great their utility*, have no value. I say that a man receiving directly and without effort a benefit from Nature cannot be considered as having rendered himself an *onerous service*, and that, consequently, he cannot render any service to another in regard to things that are common to all. So, when there are no services rendered or received, there is no value.

All that I say of *materials* applies also to the forces supplied us by Nature. Gravitation, volatile gases, the power of the wind, the laws of equilibrium, plant and animal life—these are so many forces that we learn to turn to our advantage. The pains, the mental energy, we expend to accomplish this are subject to payment, for we cannot be required to devote our efforts gratis to another's advantage. But these natural forces, considered in themselves alone, and without reference to any intellectual or physical labor, are *gratuitous* gifts from Providence; and, as such, remain without *value* through all the complications of human transactions. Such is the central idea of this work.

This observation, I admit, would have little importance if the co-operation of Nature were entirely uniform, if every man, at all times, in all places, under all circumstances, invariably received exactly the same assistance from Nature. In that case science could be excused for not taking into account an element that, remaining always and everywhere the same, would affect the exchange of services to the same extent in all areas. Just as in geometry the segments of lines common to two figures under comparison are eliminated, so in political economy we could disregard this ever-present co-operation and be content to say, as has been said until now: Natural wealth does exist; political economy notes the fact once and for all and is no longer concerned with it.

But this is not the way things happen. The irresistible tendency of the human intellect, stimulated by self-interest and aided by previous discoveries, is to substitute the gratuitous contribution of Nature for the onerous contribution of man; so that any given utility, although remaining the same in its result, in the satisfaction it gives, represents a continually decreasing amount of labor. Certainly we cannot fail to see the tremendous influence of this marvelous phenomenon on our idea of value. For what is the result? In every product the tendency is for *gratuitous* utility to replace *onerous* utility. Since *utility* is the result of two contributions, one requiring payment in terms of effort, the other not, value that is determined only by the former decreases for an identical amount of utility from both sources in proportion as Nature's share is made more effective. Thus, we can say that humanity enjoys greater *satisfactions,* or *wealth,* in proportion as *value* decreases. Now, since most authors have given a kind of synonymous meaning to the three expressions—"utility," "wealth," "value"—they have formulated a theory that is not only incorrect, but the exact opposite of the truth. I sincerely believe that a more exact description of this combination of natural and human forces in the work of production or, putting it another way, a more accurate definition of *value,* will put an end to inextricable theoretical confusions and will reconcile schools of thought now divergent; and if I anticipate here some of the findings of this inquiry, I do so to justify myself to the reader for dwelling on notions whose importance would otherwise be difficult to appreciate.

After this digression I resume my study of man considered solely from the economic point of view.

Another observation by Jean-Baptiste Say* which is obvious enough, although too often neglected by other authors, is that man creates neither the *materials* nor the *forces* of Nature, if we understand the word "create" in its strict sense. These materials, these forces, exist independently of man. Man can only combine them, move them about for his own or others' advantage. If he does so for his own advantage, *he renders a service to himself;* if for the advantage of others, *he renders a service to his fellow men,* and it is his right to exact an *equivalent* service in return.

---

* [Jean-Baptiste Say (1767–1832), French professor of political economy, champion of free trade. His views influenced Bastiat greatly. His son, Horace (1794–1860), and his grandson, Léon (1826–1896), were also economists.—TRANSLATOR.]

Hence, it follows also that *value* is in proportion to the service rendered, and not at all in proportion to the absolute *utility* of the thing. For this utility can be, in large part, the result of a *gratuitous* act of Nature, in which case the human service, the service involving labor and remuneration, is of little value. This results from the axiom stated above: *In bringing a thing to the highest degree of utility, man's share in the action is in inverse ratio to Nature's.*

This observation overturns the doctrine that places value in the *materiality* of things. The contrary is true. Materiality is a quality that is given by Nature and is, therefore, *gratuitous,* possessing no value, although of incontestable utility. Human action, which can never succeed in *creating* matter, alone constitutes the service that man in a state of isolation renders to himself or that men in society render one another, and it is the free appraisal of these *services* that is the basis of *value.* Value cannot be thought of as residing only in matter, as Adam Smith would have put it; rather, between matter and value there is no possible connection.

From this erroneous doctrine, rigorously adhered to, came the conclusion that those classes alone are *productive* that work directly with matter. Smith thus prepared the way for the error of the modern *socialists,* who always represent as unproductive parasites those whom they call the *middlemen* between the producer and the consumer, such as the businessman, the merchant, etc. Do they render services? Do they spare us pains by taking pains for us? In that case, they create value, even though they do not create matter. And, indeed, since nobody creates matter, since we are all limited to rendering reciprocal services, it is altogether accurate to say that all of us, including farmers and artisans, are middlemen in our relations with one another.

For the moment, this is what I have to say about the contribution of Nature. Nature places at our disposal, in varying amounts according to climate, seasons, and our own degree of enlightenment, but always gratis, materials and forces. Therefore, these materials and these forces do not have *value;* it would be very strange if they did. In accordance with what criterion would we estimate it? How can we understand Nature being paid, recompensed, remunerated? We shall see later that exchange is necessary to determine *value*. We do not buy Nature's goods; we gather them in, and if, to gather them in, an effort of some sort has to be made, it is in this *effort*, not in the gift of Nature, that the value consists.

Let us pass, now, to man's action, designated in a general way under the name of *labor*.

The word "labor," like nearly all those used in political economy, is very vague; the breadth of its connotations varies from author to author. Political economy has not had, like most sciences —chemistry for example—the advantage of being able to create its own vocabulary. Dealing with things with which men have been occupied since the beginning of the world, and which they have made the habitual subject of their conversation, political economists have found their terms ready-made and have been forced to use them. The sense of the word "labor" is frequently restricted to the muscular activity of men working with material things. Thus, we speak of the "working classes" when we mean those who carry out the mechanical part of production.

The reader will understand that I give this a broader sense. By *labor* I mean the use of our faculties for the satisfaction of our wants. *Want, effort, satisfaction*—this is the orbit of political economy. *Effort* can be physical, intellectual, or even moral, as we shall see.

It is unnecessary to demonstrate here that all our powers, all or nearly all our faculties, can and in fact do contribute to production. Concentration, sagacity, intelligence, imagination have their part to play in it.

M. Dunoyer, in his admirable book on *The Freedom of Labor*,* has included, and with full scientific accuracy, our moral faculties among the factors to which we owe our wealth. This is a new idea and as stimulating as it is sound; it is destined to add scope and luster to the field of political economy.

I shall dwell on this idea here only in so far as it gives me the opportunity to shed a little light on the origin of a powerful

* [Barthélemy Charles Pierre Joseph Dunoyer (1786–1862), French economist and administrator.—TRANSLATOR.]

agent of production about which I have not yet spoken: *capital*.

If we examine successively the material objects that serve to satisfy our wants, we shall recognize that all or nearly all of them require for their production more time, a greater part of our lives, than we can expend without renewing our strength, that is to say, without satisfying our wants. Hence, the men who produced such things were first required, presumably, to reserve, to set aside, to accumulate, their means of livelihood during the operation.

The same is true for satisfactions of a nonmaterial order. A priest could not devote himself to his preaching, a professor to his teaching, a magistrate to the maintenance of law and order, unless by their own devices or with the help of others they had at their disposal previously produced means of subsistence.

Let us go back and imagine a man in the state of isolation reduced to earning a living by hunting. It is easy to see that if, every evening, he ate all the game he had caught during the day, he would never be able to undertake any other type of work, such as building a hut or repairing his weapons; all progress would be out of the question for him.

This is not the place to define the nature and function of capital. My only purpose is to show how, even if we do not go beyond mere considerations of wealth, certain moral virtues such as orderliness, foresight, self-control, thrift, contribute directly to the improvement of our way of life.

Foresight is one of man's noblest privileges, and it is hardly necessary to say that, in almost all the circumstances of life, the odds are all in favor of the man who best knows the consequences of his decisions and his acts.

Restraint of one's appetites, control of one's passions, acceptance of present privation for the sake of future, though distant, gain—these are the essential conditions for the building up of capital; and capital, as we have seen, is itself the essential prerequisite for all undertakings that are at all complicated or extensive. All the evidence suggests that if two men were placed in completely identical situations, if we supposed them to possess the same degree of intelligence and initiative, the one making the greater progress would be he who, by storing up his resources, would be able to carry on long-range operations, improve his tools, and thus enlist the forces of Nature in accomplishing his ends.

I shall not dwell on this. We need only look about us to realize that all our strength, all our faculties, all our virtues, work together for the advancement of man and society.

By the same token there is not one of our vices that does not contribute directly or indirectly to poverty. Idleness paralyzes the very sinews of production. Ignorance and error give it false direction. Lack of foresight opens the way to miscalculations. Yielding to the appetites of the moment prevents the building up of capital. Vanity leads to dissipating our energies on illusory satisfactions, at the expense of real ones. Violence, fraud, provoking violence and fraud in return, force us to surround ourselves with burdensome protective measures, to the great depletion of our energies.

I shall end this preliminary study of man with an observation that I have already made concerning wants. The factors enumerated in this chapter that enter into the science of economics and constitute it are essentially variable and diverse. Wants, desires, materials and forces supplied by Nature, muscular strength, bodily organs, intellectual faculties, moral qualities—all vary according to the individual, the time, and the place. No two men are alike in any one of these respects and even less alike in all of them taken together. Furthermore, no man is exactly like himself for two hours running. What one man knows, another does not; what one man treasures, another despises; here Nature has been lavish, there miserly; a virtue that is difficult to practice at one degree of temperature becomes easy in a different climate. The science of economics, therefore, does not have the advantage, as do the so-called exact sciences, of possessing a measure, a yardstick, enabling it to determine the precise intensity of desires, efforts, and satisfactions. If we were called upon to work in solitude, like certain animals, our circumstances would differ to some degree, and even if these outside circumstances were similar, and our milieu identical, we should still differ in our desires, our wants, our ideas, our judgment, our energy, our values, our foresight, our activity; so that a great and inevitable inequality would be manifested among men. Certainly, absolute isolation, the absence of all contacts among men, is only a flight of fancy born in the imagination of Rousseau. But, supposing that this antisocial state, the so-called *state of nature,* ever existed, I woulder how Rousseau and his faithful followers ever managed to attribute equality to it. We shall see later that equality, like wealth, like liberty, like brotherhood, like unity, is an end, and not a point of departure. It arises from the natural and orderly development of society. Humanity does not move away from equality, but toward it. This thought is more reassuring than what Rousseau would have us believe, and far truer.

Having spoken of our *wants* and the *means* we possess to satisfy them, I have a word to say about our *satisfactions.* They are the result of the whole mechanism. According to the degree of physical, moral, and intellectual *satisfactions* enjoyed by humanity, we know whether the machine is functioning well or badly. Hence, the word *consommation* (taken over in French by the economists to mean *consumption)* would have profound meaning, if, keeping its etymological sense, it were used as a synonym of *end, achievement.* Unfortunately, in common usage and even in the scientific language, it suggests to the mind a coarse and material connotation, accurate undoubtedly for physical wants, but not for wants of a higher order. The raising of wheat, the spinning of wool are concluded by an act of *consumption.* Can the word *consumption* be also applied to the works of the artist, the songs of the poet, the deliberations of the jurist, the sermons of the priest? Here again we encounter the difficulties of the basic error that led Adam Smith to confine political economy to material values; and the reader will pardon me if I often use the word *satisfaction* to apply to all our wants and to all our desires, since I think it better corresponds to the wider scope that I feel justified in giving to political economy.

Economists have often been reproached for concerning themselves exclusively with the *interests of the consumer.* "You forget the producer," people say. But satisfaction being the goal, the end of all efforts, and, as it were, the final *consummation* of economic phenomena, is it not evident that it is the touchstone of all progress? A man's well-being is not measured by his *efforts*, but by his *satisfactions*. This observation also holds true for men taken collectively. This again is one of those truths accepted by everybody when it is applied to the individual, but disputed endlessly when applied to society as a whole. The expression so much attacked means only this: The value of every economic activity is determined, not by the labor it entails, but by the positive effect it produces, which in turn results in increasing or decreasing the general welfare.

We have said, apropos of wants and desires, that no two men are alike. The same is true of our satisfactions. They are not equally esteemed by all; which is tantamount to the trite observation: tastes differ. But it is the intensity of our desires and the variety of our tastes that determine the direction of our efforts. Here the influence of morality on habits of work becomes clear. We can imagine an individual man as a slave to idle, childish, immoral tastes. In that case, it is obvious that his strength, which is limited, will satisfy his depraved desires only at the expense of more intelligent and reasonable desires. But when society as a whole is considered, this obvious axiom appears erroneous. We tend to believe that idle tastes, illusory satisfactions, which we recognize as a cause of poverty for the individual, are nevertheless a source of national wealth because they create an outlet for a multitude of industries. If such were the case, we should arrive at a very distressing conclusion: Man in the social state has the choice of poverty or immorality. Once again, it is political economy that can resolve these seeming contradictions in the most satisfactory and conclusive way.

4

Exchange

Exchange *is* political economy. It is society itself, for it is impossible to conceive of society without exchange, or exchange without society. Therefore, I do not expect to exhaust in this one chapter so vast a subject. The whole book will hardly present more than a rough outline of it.

If men, like snails, lived in complete isolation from one another, if they did not exchange their work and their ideas, if they did not engage in transactions with one another, there could be multitudes, human units, juxtapositions of individuals, but there could not be a society.

Indeed, there would not even be individuals. For man, isolation means death. Now, if he cannot live outside society, it is strictly logical to conclude that his natural state is the social state.

All sciences arrive at this same truth, so much misunderstood in the eighteenth century, which founded its moral and political systems on the contrary assumption. Men of that time, not content with merely contrasting the state of nature with the social state, gave the former marked superiority over the latter. "Happy are men," said Montaigne,* "when they live without ties, without laws, without language, without religion!" We know that Rousseau's system, which once had, as it still has, so great an influence over men's opinions and actions, rests entirely on the hypothesis that one day men, to their undoing, *agreed* to abandon the innocent *state of nature* for the stormy *state of society.*

* [Michel de Montaigne (1533–1592), famous humanistic essayist of the Renaissance. —TRANSLATOR.]

It is not the intent of this chapter to assemble all the refutations that could be made against this fundamental error, the most virulent that ever infected the social sciences; for, if society is simply contrived and artificially agreed upon, it follows that every man may invent a new social order, and such has been, since Rousseau, the direction taken by many minds. I could easily prove, I feel sure, that isolation precludes language, just as the absence of language precludes thought. And certainly man without thought, far from being man in the state of nature, is not even man.

But an unanswerable refutation of the idea on which Rousseau's doctrine rests will come directly, without our seeking it, from a few considerations on the subject of exchange.

Want, effort, satisfaction: such is man, from the point of view of economics.

We have seen that the two extremes are essentially nontransferable, for they occur in the realm of sensation; they are themselves sensation, which is the most personal thing in the world: the want that precedes the effort and calls it forth is a sensation, as is the satisfaction that follows the effort and rewards it.

Effort, then, is the element that is exchanged; and it cannot be otherwise, since exchange implies activity, and our activity displays itself only in terms of effort. We cannot suffer or enjoy for one another, however sensitive we may be to others' pains and pleasures. But we can help one another, work for one another, render reciprocal *services,* put our faculties, or the product of our faculties, at the *service* of others, subject to payment in return. This is society. The causes, the effects, the laws of these exchanges constitute political and social economy.

We not only can aid one another in all these ways, but we do so of necessity. What I affirm is this: We are so constituted that we are obliged to work for one another under penalty of immediate death. If this is true, society is our natural state, since it is the only state in which we can live at all.

There is one observation that I have to make concerning the equilibrium between our wants and our productive capacities, an observation that has always filled me with admiration for the providential plan that rules our destiny.

In the state of isolation, our wants exceed our productive capacities.

In society, our productive capacities exceed our wants.

Hence, man in the state of isolation cannot survive; whereas, with man in society, the most elemental wants give way to desires of a higher order, and this process, tending always toward a more perfect condition, goes on without interruption or assignable limits.

This is not mere oratory, but a statement that can be fully proved by reason and analogy, if not by experience. And why not by experience, by direct observation? Simply because the statement is true; simply because, since man cannot live in a state of isolation, it is impossible to demonstrate the effects of absolute solitude on living human nature. Our senses cannot grasp something that does not exist. You can prove to my mind that a triangle never has four sides; you cannot, in support of your argument, place before my eyes a tetragonal triangle. If you did, you would destroy your assertion by your own evidence. Similarly, to ask me for a proof based on experiment, to demand that I study the effects of isolation on living human nature, would be to force upon me a logical contradiction, since, isolation and life being mutually incompatible for man, no one has ever seen, no one will ever see, men without human contacts.

There may be animals, for all I know, destined by their bodily structure to live out their span of life in absolute isolation; if so, it is very clear that Nature must have established an exact balance between their wants and their productive capacities. We could also conceive of their productive capacities as superior to their wants, in which case they would be perfectible and capable of progress. Exact balance makes them static creatures, but a preponderance of wants cannot be conceived of: from their birth on, from their first appearance on the scene of life, their productive capacities would have to be fully adequate to satisfy the wants for which they would have to provide, or, at least, the two would have to develop side by side at the same rate. Otherwise the species would die at birth and would not be available for observation.

Of all the species of living creatures about us, not one, certainly, is subject to as many wants as man. In not one is the period of immaturity so long and so helpless, maturity so loaded with responsibility, old age so feeble and ailing. And, as if his wants were not enough for him, man also has tastes whose satisfaction taxes his faculties quite as much as his wants. Hardly has he learned to satisfy his hunger when he seeks to tickle his palate; to cover his nakedness, when he seeks adornment; to shelter himself from the elements, when he dreams of beautifying his dwelling. His mind is as restless as his body is demanding. He seeks to penetrate the mysteries of Nature, to tame the animals, to harness the elements, to delve into the bowels of the earth, to cross the boundless oceans, to soar above the winds, to annihilate time and space; he seeks to know the inner workings, the springs, the laws, of his own will and heart, to rule over his passions, to achieve immortality, to merge his being in his Creator, to place everything under his dominion—Nature, his fellows, himself; in a word, his desires reach out endlessly toward the infinite.

Hence, in no other species are faculties to be found capable of such great development as in man. He alone appears able to compare and to judge; he alone reasons and speaks; he alone looks ahead; he alone sacrifices the present for the future; he alone transmits from one generation to another his works, his thoughts, the treasures of his experience; he alone, in a word, is capable of forging the countless links of a chain of progress seemingly stretching beyond the limits of this earth.

Let us make a purely economic observation here. However extensive our productive capacities may be, they cannot go so far as to enable us to *create*. It is not given to man, in fact, to add to or subtract from the existing number of molecules. His role is confined to modifying or combining for his use the substances he finds everywhere about him. (J. B. Say.)

To modify substances in such a way as to increase their utility for us is to *produce,* or rather it is one way of producing. I conclude that value, as we shall see later, can never reside in these substances themselves, but in the effort which is exerted in order to modify them and to which exchange gives a relative appraisal based on other comparable efforts. For this reason, value is merely the appraisal of the services exchanged, whether a material commodity is or is not involved in the transaction. As regards the notion of value, it is a matter of complete indifference whether I render my fellow man a direct service—for example, by performing a surgical operation—or an indirect service by making him some medicinal preparation; in the latter case the *utility* is in the substance, but the *value* is in the service, in the intellectual and material effort made by one man for the benefit of another. It is pure metonymy to attribute value to the material commodity itself, and in this case, as in so many others, the metaphor leads science astray.

I return to the subject of the way man is constituted. If we stopped at the notions we have already presented, man would be different from other animals only in the greater range of his wants and the superiority of his capacities. All are subject to the former and endowed with the latter. Birds undertake long migrations in search of the proper temperature; beavers cross streams on dams that they have built; hawks attack their prey in full view; cats stalk theirs patiently; spiders set up snares; all work in order to live and increase.

But, while Nature has set up an exact balance between the wants of animals and their productive capacities, she has treated man more grandly and munificently. If, in order to force him to be *sociable,* she has decreed that in the state of isolation his wants should exceed his productive capacities, whereas in society his productive capacities, superior to his wants, should open up boundless vistas for his nobler enjoyments; we must also recognize that, even as man in his relation to his Creator is raised above the beasts by his religious feeling, in his dealings with his fellow men by his sense of justice, in his dealings with himself by his morality, so, in finding his means of survival and increase, he is distinguished from them by a remarkable phenomenon, namely, *exchange*.

Shall I try to portray the state of poverty, barrenness, and ignorance in which, without the faculty of exchange, the human species would have wallowed eternally, if indeed, it would not have disappeared altogether from the face of the earth?

One of the most popular of philosophers, in a novel that has had the good fortune to charm generation after generation of children, shows us how a man can rise above the hardships of absolute solitude by his energy, his initiative, and his intelligence. Desiring to show all the resources possessed by this noble creature, our author imagines him accidentally cut off, so to speak, from civilization. It was, therefore, Daniel Defoe's original plan to cast Robinson Crusoe ashore on the Isle of Despair alone, naked, deprived of all that can be added to one man's strength by united effort, specialized skills, exchange, and society.

Nevertheless, and despite the fact that the obstacles are purely fictitious, Defoe would have deprived his novel of every trace of verisimilitude if, overfaithful to the thought he wished to develop, he had not made necessary social concessions by allowing his hero to save from the shipwreck a few indispensable objects, such as provisions, gunpowder, a rifle, an ax, a knife, rope, boards, iron, etc.—decisive evidence that society is man's necessary milieu, since even a novelist cannot make him live outside it.

And note that Robinson Crusoe took with him into solitude another *social* treasure worth a thousand times more, one that the waves could not swallow up: I mean his ideas, his memories, his experience, and especially his language, without which he could not have communicated with himself or formed his thoughts.

We have the distressing and unreasonable habit of attributing to *society* the suffering that we see about us. Up to a point we are right, if we mean to compare society with itself, taken at two different stages of its progress; but we are wrong, if we compare the social state, even in its imperfection, with the state of isolation. To be able to assert that even the most unfortunate of men are worse off in society than out of it, we should have to begin by proving that the poorest of our fellow men has to bear, in the social state, a heavier burden of privations and suffering than would have been his lot in solitude. Now, consider the life of the humblest day laborer. Consider, in all their detail, the articles of his daily consumption. He wears a few coarse pieces of clothing; he eats a little black bread; at night he has a roof over his head and at the very worst some bare planks to sleep on. Now, ask yourself whether this man in isolation, without the resources of exchange, would have the remotest possibility of obtaining this coarse clothing, this black bread, this crude cot, this humble shelter. The most impassioned advocate of the *state of nature,* Rousseau himself, admitted that this was completely impossible. Men did without everything, he said; they went naked, they slept in the open air. Thus, Rousseau himself, in order to present the state of nature favorably, was obliged to make happiness consist in privation. But I affirm that even this negative happiness is a delusion, and that man in the state of isolation would surely die in a very few hours. Perhaps Rousseau would have gone so far as to say that that would be the true perfection. He would have been consistent, for if happiness lies in privation, then perfection lies in annihilation.

I trust that the reader will not conclude from the preceding remarks that we are insensible to the social suffering of our fellow men. Although the suffering is less in the present imperfect state of our society than in the state of isolation, it does not follow that we do not seek wholeheartedly for further progress to make it less and less; but if the state of isolation is worse than the worst in the social state, then I was right in saying that isolation makes our wants, to mention only the most elemental of them, far exceed our productive capacities.

How does exchange reverse this order to our advantage and make our productive capacities exceed our wants?

First of all, this is proved by the very fact of civilization. If our wants exceeded our productive capacities, we should be irremediably retrogressive creatures; if the two were in complete balance, we should be irremediably static. However, we advance; hence, every period in the life of society, compared to a previous period, frees for other purposes, in relation to a given number of satisfactions, a certain part of our productive capacities.

Let us try to explain this marvelous phenomenon.

The explanation we owe to Condillac* seems to me entirely insufficient and empirical, or rather it fails to explain anything at all. "The very fact that an exchange takes place," he says, "is proof that there must necessarily be profit in it for both the contracting parties; otherwise it would not be made. Hence, every exchange represents two gains for humanity."

Even granting that the proposition is true, we see in it only a statement of fact, not an explanation. It was thus that the hypochondriac explained the narcotic power of opium:

> *Quia est in eo*
> *Virtus dormitiva*
> *Quae facit dormire.*†

The exchange represents two gains, you say. The question is: Why and how? It results from the very fact that it takes place. But why does it take place? What motives have induced the two men to make it take place? Does the exchange have in it a mysterious virtue, inherently beneficial and incapable of explanation?

Others attribute the benefit to the fact that we give from what we have in excess to receive what we lack. Exchange, they say, is *the barter of the surplus for the necessary*. Aside from the fact that this is contrary to what we see happening before our own eyes— who would dare say that the peasant, who parts with the grain he has grown and will never eat, is giving from his surplus?—I see from it how two men happen to strike a bargain, but I do not see any explanation of progress.

* [Étienne Bonnot de Condillac (1714–1780), philosopher of the French Enlightenment. His main ideas on political economy are presented in *Le Commerce et le gouvernement.*—Translator.]

† ["Because there is in it a soporific virtue that induces sleep." Argan, the "imaginary invalid," gives this answer in his doctor's examination, in Latin, at the end of Molière's comedy, *Le Malade imaginaire.*—Translator.]

Observation will give us a more satisfactory explanation of the power of exchange.

Exchange produces two phenomena: the joining of men's forces and the diversification of their occupations, or the division of labor.

It is very clear that in many cases the combined force of several men is superior to the sum of their individual separate forces. In moving a heavy object, for example, a thousand men taking successive turns would fail where four men by uniting their efforts could succeed. Try to imagine the things that would never have been done in the world without this kind of joint action.

And yet the co-operative use of muscle power for a common goal is a mere nothing. Nature has given us highly varied physical, moral, and intellectual faculties. There are inexhaustible combinations in the co-operative union of these faculties. Do we need to carry out a useful project, like building a road or defending our country? One places his strength at the disposal of the community; another, his agility; another, his daring; still another, his experience, his foresight, his imagination, even his renown. It is easy to understand that the same men, working separately, could never have accomplished, or even contemplated, such an undertaking.

Now, the joining of men's forces implies exchange. To gain their co-operation, they must have good reason to anticipate sharing in the satisfaction to be obtained. Each one by his efforts benefits the others and in turn benefits by their efforts according to the terms of the bargain, which is exchange.

We see how exchange, in this form, adds to our satisfactions. By the mere fact of their union, efforts equal in intensity produce superior results. Here there is no trace of the so-called *barter of the superfluous for the necessary,* nor of the double and empirical profit alleged by Condillac.

We may make the same observation concerning the division of labor. Indeed, if we look closely at the matter, we see that the diversification of occupations is only another, more permanent, way of joining forces, of co-operating, of *forming an association;* and it is altogether accurate to say, as will be shown later, that the present social organization, provided the principle of free exchange is recognized, is the most beautiful, most stupendous of associations—a marvelous association, but very different from the associations dreamed up by the socialists, since in it, by an admirable arrangement, the principle of individual liberty is recognized. All men, at all times, may join or leave it at their pleasure. They contribute what they will; they receive in return a constantly increasing degree of satisfaction, which is determined, according to the laws of justice, by the nature of things, not by the arbitrary will of a chief. But I should not anticipate what I shall say later. All that I have to do at the moment is to explain how the division of labor adds to our strength.

Without dwelling on this subject, one of the few that has not provoked controversy, I do have something to say that is not without value. Perhaps, indeed, its importance has been minimized. To demonstrate the power of *the division of labor,* writers have been content to point out the marvelous things it accomplishes in certain industries, pin manufacture, for example. The question can be given broader and more philosophical significance. Moreover, habit has the peculiar power of making us shut our eyes and lose sight of the things around us. There is no truer word than that of Rousseau: "It takes a great deal of scientific insight to observe what we see every day." * It is not superfluous, then, to call to men's attention what they owe to exchange without being aware of it.

How has the power of exchange raised humanity to its present heights? By its influence on *labor,* on the harnessing of the *forces of Nature,* on the *capacities* of man, and on *capital.*

Adam Smith has well shown this influence on labor.

"The increase in the quantity of labor that can be performed by the same number of men as a result of the division of labor is due to three factors," said the celebrated economist: "(1) the level of skill acquired by each worker; (2) the saving of time normally lost by moving from one occupation to another; (3) the increased opportunity each man has of discovering easy and efficient ways

---

* [Already quoted by Bastiat in chap. 1. (See p. 2.)—TRANSLATOR.]

of attaining an object when his attention is centered on it, rather than diverted to many other things." *

Those who, like Adam Smith, see in labor the sole source of wealth, confine themselves to the question of how division improves its efficiency. But we have seen in the preceding chapter that labor is not the only agent for procuring our satisfactions. *Natural forces* also contribute. This is not open to question.

Thus, in agriculture, the action of the sun and the rain, the moisture in the soil, the gases in the atmosphere, are certainly resources that co-operate with human labor in the growing of vegetables.

Industry owes similar services to the chemical qualities of certain substances: to the power generated by waterfalls, to the pressure of steam, to gravitation, to electricity.

Commerce has learned to turn to man's profit the strength and instincts of certain animals, the power of the wind for sailing boats, the laws of magnetism, which, acting on the compass, guide ships over great oceans.

There are two great incontrovertible truths. The first is: *The better man exploits the forces of Nature, the better he provides himself with all that he needs.*

It is self-evident that we get more wheat, for the same amount of effort, from good, rich soil than from dry sand or barren rocks.

The second truth is: *The resources of Nature are unequally distributed over the earth.*

Who would dare maintain that all lands are equally favorable

* [In his third point Bastiat has taken certain liberties with the original text of Adam Smith: "This great increase of the quantity of work, which, in consequence of the division of labour, the same number of people are capable of performing, is owing to three different circumstances: first, to the increase of dexterity in every particular workman; secondly, to the saving of the time which is commonly lost in passing from one species of work to another; and last, to the invention of a great number of machines which facilitate and abridge labour, and enable one man to do the work of many." (*The Wealth of Nations*, Oxford, I, 9.)

Bastiat substitutes for "the invention of a great number of machines, etc.," a remark Smith makes subsequently on this subject: "Men are much more likely to discover easier and readier methods of attaining any object, when the whole attention of their minds is directed towards that single object, than when it is dissipated among a great variety of things." (*Op. cit.*, p. 11.)—TRANSLATOR.]

for growing the same crops, all countries for producing the same goods?

Now, if it is true that natural resources vary from one part of the globe to another, and if, on the other hand, the more men use them, the richer they are, it follows that the power of exchange increases immeasurably the usefulness of these resources.

Here once again we encounter gratuitous utility and onerous utility, the first replacing the second by virtue of exchange. Is it not clear, in fact, that if, deprived of the power of exchange, men were reduced to producing ice at the equator and sugar at the poles, they would have to do with great effort what heat and cold today do for them gratis, and that, as far as they were concerned, a great percentage of natural resources would remain idle? Thanks to exchange, these resources are put to use wherever they are found. Wheat land is sown with wheat; land suitable for the production of grapes is planted with vineyards; there are fishermen on the sea coasts, and woodcutters in the mountains. Here water, there wind, is directed against a wheel, replacing ten men. Nature becomes a slave whom we neither have to clothe nor feed, whose services require no payment, who costs neither our purse nor our conscience anything.[1] The same sum of human efforts, that is to say, the same service—the same value—produces a constantly increasing sum of utility. For every project completed, only a part of human activity is expended; the rest, through the instrumentality of Nature, is made available and is turned to new problems, satisfies new desires, creates new utilities.

The effects of exchange on our intellectual faculties are such that even the most ingenious imagination would be unable to gauge their extent.

"Our knowledge," says M. de Tracy * "is our most precious possession, since it is knowledge, in proportion to its soundness and breadth, which guides our efforts and makes them productive. Now, no man is in a position to see everything, and it is much easier to learn than to invent. But when several men are in com-

* [Antoine-Louis-Claude Destutt de Tracy (1754–1836), disciple of Condillac and chief of the so-called "ideologue" school of philosophy.—TRANSLATOR.]

munication, what one observes is soon known by all, and only one of them needs to be especially ingenious for all of them soon to be in possession of valuable discoveries. The sum total of knowledge, therefore, grows much more rapidly than in the state of isolation, not to mention that it can be preserved and, therefore, passed on from generation to generation."

If Nature has distributed unequally the resources she places at man's disposal, she has been no more uniform in her distribution of human endowments. We are not all blessed with the same degree of strength, courage, intelligence, patience, or artistic, literary, and industrial talents. If it were not for exchange, this diversity, far from being turned to our well-being, would contribute to our wretchedness, each one being more aware of the talents he lacked than of the advantages of the talents he had. Thanks to exchange, the strong man can, up to a point, do without genius; the intelligent man, without brawn; for, by the admirable pooling of gifts that exchange establishes among men, each one shares in the distinctive talents of his fellows.

To satisfy our wants and our tastes, it is not enough to work, to use our faculties on or through the resources of Nature. We also need tools, instruments, machines, provisions—in a word, capital. Let us imagine a tiny community of ten families, each one of which, working solely for itself, is obliged to engage in ten different occupations. Each head of a family would need the equipment for ten different industrial units. There would be, then, in the community ten plows, ten teams of oxen, ten forges, ten carpenter's shops, ten looms, etc.; with exchange a single plow, a single team of oxen, a single forge, a single loom would suffice. The capital savings due to exchange surpass one's imagination.

The reader can now well perceive the true power of exchange. It does not imply, as Condillac says, *two gains,* because each of the contracting parties sets more store by what he receives than by what he gives. No more is it a matter of each giving from his surplus to acquire what is necessary. It is simply that, when one man says to another, "You do only this, and I will do only that, and we'll share," there is better employment of labor, talents, natural resources, capital, and, consequently, there is *more* to share. So much the better if three, ten, a hundred, a thousand, a million men join the association.

The two propositions that I have advanced are therefore strictly correct, namely:

In the state of isolation, our wants exceed our productive capacities.

In society, our productive capacities exceed our wants.

The first is true because the entire area of France could not for long keep alive a single man in the state of absolute isolation.

The second is true because, in fact, the population of this same area is growing in numbers and prosperity.

Progress in Exchange

The primitive form of exchange is *barter*. Two persons, each of whom feels a want and possesses the object that can satisfy the other's want, either exchange objects or agree to work separately at different things and share, to the extent stipulated, in the finished product. This is *barter,* which is, as the socialists would say, exchange, business, commerce *in embryo.* We note here two wants as the motivating force, two efforts as the means, two satisfactions as the result, or as the termination of the entire process, and nothing in it differs essentially from the same process as carried out in the state of isolation, except that only the wants and satisfactions have remained nontransferable, as is their nature, while the efforts have been exchanged; in other words, two persons have worked for each other and have rendered reciprocal *services.*

It is at this point, therefore, that political economy really begins, for it is here that we can first observe the appearance of *value.* Barter occurs only after an agreement, a discussion. Each of the contracting parties makes his decision after considering his self-interest. Each one calculates in this fashion: "I shall barter if the trade brings me the *satisfaction* of my *want* with less *effort* on my part." It is certainly a striking phenomenon that exchange makes it possible to give men's wants the same satisfaction at the cost of less effort, and it is explained by the considerations I presented in the first paragraph of this chapter. When two products or two services are *bartered,* we may say that they are of *equal* value. Later we shall have occasion to go more deeply into the question of value. For the moment this vague definition will suffice.

We can conceive of *roundabout barter,* involving three contracting parties. *Paul* renders a service to *Peter,* who renders an equivalent service to *James,* who in turn renders an equivalent service to *Paul,* thereby completing the cycle. I need not say that this rotation does not take place unless it satisfies all parties, and it changes in no wise either the nature or the result of a simple barter.

The fundamental character of barter would not in any way be affected if the number of contracting parties should be further increased. In my parish the winegrower uses his wine to pay for the services of the blacksmith, the barber, the tailor, the beadle, the vicar, the grocer. The blacksmith, the barber, the tailor, in turn, deliver to the grocer the wine they receive from the winegrower as payment for the commodities they consume during the year.

This roundabout barter, I cannot repeat too often, does not in any way alter the original concepts set forth in the preceding chapter. When the process is completed, each participant has presented this triple phenomenon: *want, effort, satisfaction.* Only one thing has been added: the exchange of efforts, which means the transfer of services and the division of labor. The results are advantageous to all parties; for otherwise the bargain would not have been agreed to, and each would have preferred his own isolated, individual effort, which is always a possible alternative.

It is easy to understand that roundabout barter in kind cannot be greatly expanded, and there is no need to dwell on the obstacles that prevent its further development. If a man wished to barter his house for the thousand and one items he would use in the course of the year, how would he go about it? In any case, barter cannot go beyond a small circle of persons acquainted with one another. Humanity would soon have reached the limits of the division of labor, the limits of progress, if a means of facilitating exchange had not been found.

That is why, since the beginnings of society, men have employed in their transactions some intermediate article, such as grain, wine, animals, and, almost always, metals. These articles perform their function as a medium of exchange, some more, some less satisfactorily; but all are acceptable, provided they represent effort in terms of *value,* which is the thing to be transmitted.

When this type of intermediate commodity is resorted to, two economic phenomena appear, which are called *sale* and *purchase.* It is clear that the idea of *sale* and *purchase* is not included in simple barter or even in roundabout barter. When one man gives another something to drink in return for something to eat, we have a simple act that cannot be further broken down into component parts. Now, at the outset of our study of political economy, we must notice that the exchange that is transacted through an intermediate commodity loses nothing of the nature, essence, or character of barter; it is simply a form of indirect barter. As Jean-Baptiste Say very wisely and profoundly observed, it is barter with two factors added, one called *sale,* the other *purchase,* which together are indispensable to complete a barter transaction.

In fact, the appearance in the world of a convenient medium of barter does not change the nature of men or of things. There remain for every man the *want* that prompts the *effort,* and the *satisfaction* that rewards it. Exchange is not complete until the man who has made an *effort* for another man receives in return an equivalent service, that is, a *satisfaction.* For this purpose, he *sells* his service for the intermediate commodity; then with it he *buys* equivalent services, and thus the two factors reconstitute for him a simple barter transaction.

Take the case of a doctor, for example. For some years he has devoted his time and his faculties to the study of diseases and their cure. He has called on his patients, he has given them medical care—in a word, he has rendered *services.* Instead of receiving from his patients, in payment, direct *services,* which would have constituted simple barter, he has received an intermediate commodity, pieces of metal, with which he has procured the satisfactions that were his objective. His patients have not supplied him with bread, wine, or furniture, but they have supplied him with value to that amount. They have been able to give him pieces of money because they themselves had rendered *services*. There is, therefore, a balance of *services* for them as well as for the doctor; and, if it were possible to trace this circulation of money in our imaginations to its very end, we should see that exchange through the medium of money breaks down into a multitude of simple acts of barter.

Under the system of simple barter, value is the appraisal of the worth of the two services exchanged, arrived at through direct comparison. Under the system of *indirect exchange,* the two services are also appraised, but in comparison with the middle factor, the intermediate commodity, which is called money. We shall see elsewhere what difficulties, what errors, have arisen from this complication. It is enough to observe here that the presence of this intermediate commodity does not in any way alter the fundamental notion of *value.*

Once it is admitted that exchange is both the cause and the effect of the division of labor, once it is admitted that the division of labor multiplies *satisfactions* in relation to *effort,* for the reasons presented at the beginning of this chapter, the reader will readily understand the services money has rendered humanity by the mere fact that it facilitates the act of making an exchange. Thanks to money, exchange has truly been able to expand indefinitely. Each one turns his services over to society, without knowing who will receive the satisfactions they are intended to give. Likewise each one receives from society, not immediate services, but pieces of money, with which he will buy particular services where, when, and how he wills. In this way the ultimate transactions are carried on across time and space between persons unknown to one another, and no one knows, at least in most instances, by whose *effort* his *wants* will be *satisfied,* or to whose wants his own *efforts* will bring *satisfaction.* Exchange, through the intermediary of money, breaks down into countless acts of barter between parties unacquainted with each other.

Yet exchange is so great a benefit to society (indeed, is it not society itself?) that society, to encourage and expand it, has done more than introduce money. In logical order, after want and satisfaction brought together in the same individual by isolated effort, after direct barter, after indirect barter, in which the exchange consists of *purchase* and *sale,* come other transactions, extended over time and space by credit: mortgages, bills of exchange, bank notes, etc. Thanks to this marvelous device, which is the result of civilization, which perfects civilization, and which at the same time is perfected along with civilization, an effort exerted in Paris today will cross the oceans and the centuries to satisfy a person unknown; and the one making the effort nevertheless receives his remuneration now, through persons who advance it and are willing to go to distant lands to ask for their compensation, or to await it from the far-off future—an amazingly intricate piece of machinery, which, when submitted to exact analysis, shows us, after all, the soundness of the economic process, *want, effort, satisfaction,* functioning for each individual in keeping with the laws of justice.

Limits of Exchange

The general nature of exchange is to *lessen the amount of effort in relation to the satisfaction.* Between our wants and our satisfactions there are interposed *obstacles* that we succeed in lessening by joining our forces or dividing our labor, that is, by *exchange.* But exchange too encounters obstacles and demands effort. Proof of this is to be found in the great mass of human labor that exchange brings into play. Precious metals, roads, canals, railways, coaches, ships—all these things absorb a considerable part of human activity. And just think of how many men are employed solely in expediting acts of exchange, how many bankers, businessmen, shopkeepers, brokers, coachmen, sailors! This vast and costly assemblage of men and things proves better than any argument the tremendous power in the faculty of exchange; otherwise, why would humanity have consented to burden itself with it?

Since it is in the nature of exchange both to *save* effort and to *demand* effort, it is easy to understand what its natural limitations are. By virtue of that force within man that always impels him to choose the lesser of two evils, exchange will expand indefinitely as long as the effort it requires is less than the effort it saves. And it will halt, naturally, when, in the aggregate, the sum total of satisfactions obtained by the division of labor reaches the point where it is less, by reason of the difficulties of exchange, than the satisfactions that could be procured by direct, individual action.

Consider a small community, for example. If it desires a certain satisfaction, it will have to make the necessary effort. It can say to another such community: "Make this effort for us, and we shall make another one for you." The arrangement can satisfy everybody, if, for example, the second community is able, through its situation, to bring to bear on the task a larger proportion of gratuitous natural resources than the first. In that case it will accomplish what it wants with an effort equal to, say, eight, while the first community could not do so for an effort of less than twelve. Since only eight is required, there is a saving of four for the first community. But then come the cost of transportation, the remuneration of middlemen—in short, the effort required by the machinery of the exchange. Evidently the figure of eight will have to be added to. The exchange will continue in effect as long as it itself does not cost four. Once that figure is reached, the exchange comes to a halt. It is not necessary to legislate on this matter. For either the law intervenes before this level has been reached, and then the law is harmful, since it thwarts the economizing of effort; or it comes afterwards, and then it is superfluous, like a law forbidding the lighting of lamps at noonday.

When exchange thus comes to a halt because it ceases to be advantageous, the least improvement in the *commercial machinery* gives it a new impetus. A certain number of transactions are carried on between Orléans and Angoulême. These two towns exchange whenever this procedure brings more satisfactions than direct production could. They stop exchanging when production by exchange, aggravated by the costs of the exchange itself, reaches or exceeds the level of effort required by direct production. Under these circumstances, if the machinery of exchange is improved, if the middlemen lower their costs, if a mountain is tunneled, if a bridge is thrown over a river, if a road is paved, if obstacles are reduced, exchange will increase, because the inhabitants wish to avail themselves of all the advantages we have noted in exchange, because they desire to obtain gratuitous utility. The improvement of the *commercial machinery*, therefore, is equivalent to moving the two towns closer together. Hence, it follows that bringing men closer together is equivalent to improving the machinery of exchange. And this is very important, for it is the solution of the problem of population; here in this great problem is the element that Malthus has neglected. Where Malthus saw discord, this element will enable us to see *harmony*.

By means of exchange, men attain the same *satisfaction* with less *effort,* because the mutual services they render one another yield them a larger proportion of gratuitous utility.

Therefore, the fewer obstacles an exchange encounters, the less effort it requires, the more readily men exchange.

And the closer men are together, the fewer the obstacles, the smaller the effort. A greater density of population is, therefore, necessarily accompanied by a greater proportion of gratuitous utility. It transmits greater power to the machinery of exchange; it makes available a greater part of human effort; it is a source of progress.

And now let us, if you please, leave off generalities and look at the facts.

Does not a street of equal length render more service in Paris than in a small town? Does not a railroad a kilometer long in the Department of the Seine render more service than one in the Department of Landes? * Cannot a merchant in London be satisfied with a smaller profit per sale because of his volume? In everything we shall see that two mechanisms of exchange, though

* [The Department of the Seine is an administrative district of France which includes Paris and the rich countryside around it. The Department of Landes, in southwestern France, along the Atlantic coast, is, on the contrary, sandy, marshy, and relatively barren. Bastiat himself was from this department, and was elected by it to the national Chamber of Deputies.—'TRANSLATOR.]

identical, render very different services according to their location, depending on whether they function in areas with a dense or a sparse population.

Density of population enables us not only to get a better return from the apparatus of exchange but also to enlarge and perfect this apparatus itself. Certain improvements that are desirable in a densely populated area, because they will save more effort than they will cost, are not feasible in a sparsely populated area, because they would require more effort than they would save.

When one leaves Paris for a short stay in a little town in the provinces, one is astonished at the number of occasions when certain little *services* can be secured only at excessive cost of time and money and with great difficulty.

It is not only the physical side of the commercial mechanism that is put to use and improved by the mere fact of the density of the population, but the moral and cultural side as well. Men living in close proximity are better able to divide their labor, join forces, work together to found schools and museums, build churches, provide for their security, establish banks and insurance companies—in a word, to enjoy mutual advantages with the expenditure of much less effort per person.

These considerations will again become apparent when we reach the question of population. Let us confine ourselves here to this observation: Exchange is a means given to men to enable them to make better use of their productive capacities, to economize their capital, to exploit more effectively the gratuitous resources of Nature, to increase the ratio of gratuitous utility to onerous utility, to decrease, therefore, the ratio of effort to result, to free more and more of their energy from the business of providing for their more urgent and elemental wants, in order to use it instead for enjoyments of a higher and higher order.

If exchange saves effort, it also requires effort. It expands, increases, multiplies to the point where the effort it requires equals the effort it saves, and then it comes to a halt until, through improvement in the commercial machinery, through the mere fact of increased population, of more men living closer together, it encounters the conditions necessary to resume its forward march.

Consequently, laws that limit exchange are always either harmful or unnecessary.

Governments, which are always disposed to believe that nothing can be done without them, refuse to understand this law of harmony.

Exchange develops naturally to the point where further development would be more onerous than useful, and stops of its own accord at this limit.

Consequently, we see governments everywhere greatly preoccupied either with giving exchange special favors or with restricting it. To carry it *beyond* its natural limits, they seek after new outlets and colonies. To hold it *within* these limits, they think up all kinds of restrictions and checks.

This intervention of *force* in human transactions is always accompanied by countless evils.

The very increase in its size is already a primary evil; for it is very evident that a state cannot make conquests, place distant countries under its domination, divert the natural flow of commerce by means of tariffs, without multiplying greatly the number of its agents.

The diverting of the agencies of law and order from their natural function is an even greater evil than adding unduly to their size. Their rational function was to protect all liberty and all property, and instead we see them bent on doing violence to the liberty and the property of the citizens. Thus, governments seem to be dedicated to the task of removing from men's minds all notions of equity and principle. As soon as it is admitted that oppression and plunder are legitimate provided they are legal, provided they are practiced on the people only through the authority of the law and its powers of enforcement, we see each class little by little demanding that all other classes be sacrificed to it.

Whether this intervention of force in the process of exchange creates exchanges that otherwise would not be made or prevents others from being made, it cannot fail to result in the waste and misuse of labor and capital, and consequently in the disturbance of the natural distribution of population. Natural interests disappear at one point, artificial interests are created at another, and men are compelled to follow the course of these interests. Thus, great industries are established where they have no right to be. France makes sugar; England spins cotton brought from the plains of India. It took centuries of war, torrents of spilled blood, the frittering away of immense treasure, to arrive at this result: substituting in Europe precarious industries for vigorous ones, and thus opening the door to panics, unemployment, instability, and, in the last analysis, pauperism.

But I see that I am anticipating. We must first know the laws of the free and natural development of human society. We may then study the disturbances.

The Moral Force of Exchange

We must repeat, at the risk of distressing modern sentimentalists: Political economy is restricted to the area that we call *business,* and business is under the influence of *self-interest.* Let the puritans of socialism cry out as much as they will: "This is horrible; we shall change all this"; their rantings on this subject constitute their own conclusive refutation. Try to buy a printed copy of their publications on the Quai Voltaire,* using brotherly love as payment!

It would be falling into another kind of empty oratory to attribute morality to acts determined and governed by *self-interest.* But surely Nature, in her ingenuity, has been able so to arrange the social order that these same acts, though they have no moral motivation, nevertheless achieve moral results. Is this not true of labor? So I say that exchange, whether in the form of direct barter or grown into a vast industry, develops in society tendencies more noble than its motives.

God forbid that I should try to attribute to but a single aspect of human energy all the grandeur, glory, and charm of our existence. As there are two forces in the physical universe, centripetal force and centrifugal force, so there are two principles in the

* [The Quai Voltaire, an area along the Seine in Paris, where there are many booksellers' shops and stalls.—TRANSLATOR.]

social world: self-interest and altruism. Who is unfortunate enough not to know the benefits and the joys that come from altruistic impulses, manifested by love, filial devotion, parental affection, charity, patriotism, religion, enthusiasm for the good and the beautiful? There are those who say that altruism is only a glorified form of self-love, and that, in reality, loving others is only an intelligent way of loving oneself. This is not the place to delve into the profundities of this question. Whether our two motivating forces be distinct or merged, it is enough to know that, far from clashing, as is so often said, they combine and work together for the same common end: the general welfare.

I have established these two propositions:

In the state of isolation, our wants exceed our productive capacities.

By virtue of exchange, our productive capacities exceed our wants.

They explain the reason for the existence of society. Here are two others that assure unlimited progress:

In the state of isolation, one man's prosperity is inimical to that of all others.

By virtue of exchange, one man's prosperity is beneficial to all others.

Is there need to prove that, if Nature had destined men for a solitary existence, the prosperity of one would be an obstacle to the prosperity of another? The more numerous they were, the less chance they would have of attaining well-being. In any case, we can well see how their numbers could be harmful to them; we cannot see how they could be beneficial. And then, I ask, under what form would altruism manifest itself? What would bring it into being? How could we even conceive of it?

But men exchange. Implicit in exchange, as we have seen, is the division of labor. It gives rise to the professions and trades. Each one applies himself to conquering one set of obstacles for the benefit of the community. Each one devotes himself to rendering one kind of service. Now, a complete analysis of value demonstrates that the *worth* of every service is dependent first on its intrinsic utility, and then on the fact that it is offered for sale in a richer locality, that is, in a community more inclined to demand it, more able to pay for it. Actual experience—which shows us the artisan, the doctor, the lawyer, the businessman, the coach-maker, the teacher, the scholar, receiving a better return for their services in Paris, London, or New York, than in the moors of Gascony, the mountains of Wales, or the prairies of the Far West—confirms us in this truth:

The more prosperous the place in which he is situated, the better the chances a man has to prosper.

Of all the harmonies about which I have written, this one is certainly the most important, the finest, the most decisive, the most productive. It implies and sums up all the others. For this reason I can give it here only a very incomplete demonstration. I should consider it fortunate, indeed, if it emanates from the spirit of this book and more fortunate still if it appears sufficiently probable to induce the reader to proceed on his own from probability to certainty!

For, beyond all shadow of doubt, this is the reason why we must decide between the natural social order and all artificial social orders; here, and here alone, is the solution to the social problem. If the prosperity of all is requisite for the prosperity of one, we may place our trust not only in the economic power of free exchange, but also in its moral force. Once men know what their true interests are, then all the restrictions, all the industrial jealousies, the commercial wars, the monopolies, will fall before the protest of public opinion; then they will ask, before demanding the passage of any legislation, not: "What good will it do me?" but: "What good will it do the community?" I admit that we sometimes ask ourselves this second question at the prompting of our altruism; but as the light of understanding comes to prevail, we shall ask it also out of self-interest. Then, indeed, it will be possible to say that the two motive forces of our nature work together for the same result—the general good; and it will be impossible to deny that in self-interest, and likewise in the transactions that stem from it, at least as far as their results are concerned, there resides a source of moral power.

Whether we consider the relations of man to man, family to

family, province to province, nation to nation, hemisphere to hemisphere, capitalist to worker, or property owner to proletarian, it is evident, I believe, that we cannot solve or even approach the social problem from any of these points of view without first choosing between these two maxims:

The profit of the one is the loss of the other.

The profit of the one is the profit of the other.

For, if Nature has arranged things in such a way that antagonism is the law of free transactions, our only recourse is to conquer Nature and to stifle liberty. If, on the contrary, these free transactions are harmonious, that is, if they tend to improve and equalize conditions, we must confine our efforts to allowing Nature to act and to maintaining the rights of human liberty.

And that is why I urge the young men to whom this book is dedicated to scrutinize carefully the doctrines it contains and to analyze the inner nature and the results of exchange. Yes, I am confident that there will be one among them who will finally adduce a rigorously logical demonstration of this proposition: *The good of each is favorable to the good of all, even as the good of all is favorable to the good of each;* who will be able to plant this truth deeply in all minds, making it simple, crystal-clear, irrefutable. This young man will have solved the social problem; he will be the benefactor of the human race.

Let us, then, bear this in mind: According to the truth or falsity of this axiom, the natural laws of society are harmonious or antagonistic; and according to their harmony or antagonism, it is to our interest to conform to them or to deviate from them. If, then, it were once clearly demonstrated that, under liberty, each man's self-interest is in accord with that of every other, and those of all are mutually favorable, all the efforts that we now see governments making to disrupt the action of these natural laws of society would better be devoted to leaving to them their full power; or rather no effort would be needed at all, except the effort it takes not to interfere. In what does the interference by governments consist? This can be deduced from the end they have in view. What is that? To remedy the inequality that is thought to spring from liberty. Now there is only one way to re-establish the balance: *to take from some to give to others.* Such is, in fact, the mandate that governments have given themselves or have received, and it is the logical deduction from the proposition: *The profit of the one is the loss of the other.* This axiom being held as true, force must indeed repair the damage done by liberty. Thus, governments, which we thought were instituted to guarantee every man his liberty and his property, have taken it upon themselves to violate all liberty and all property rights, and with good reason, if in liberty and property resides the very principle of evil. Thus, everywhere we see them busy changing artificially the existing distribution of labor, capital, and responsibility.

On the other hand, a truly incalculable amount of intellectual energy is being wasted in the pursuit of contrived social organizations. *To take from some to give to others,* to violate both liberty and property rights—this is a very simple objective; but the ways of going about it can vary to infinity. Hence these multitudes of systems, which throw all classes of workers into consternation, since, by the very nature of their goal, they menace all existing interests.

Therefore, arbitrary and complicated governments, the denial of liberty and property rights, the antagonism of classes and nations—all this is the logical outgrowth of the axiom: *The profit of the one is the loss of the other.* And, for the same reason, simplicity in government administration, respect for individual dignity, freedom of labor and exchange, peace among nations, protection of person and property—all this is the outgrowth of this truth: All interests are harmonious, provided, however, only that this truth be generally accepted.

Such is far from the case. Many persons, reading the above, are prompted to say to me: You are breaking down an open door. Who has ever thought seriously of challenging the superiority of exchange over isolation? In what book, except perhaps Rousseau's, have you encountered this strange paradox?

Those who stop me with this observation forget only two things, two symptoms, or rather two aspects, of our modern society: the doctrines with which the theorists flood us, and the practices that governments foist upon us. No, it must indeed be that the harmony of interests is not universally recognized, since, on the one hand, the force of government is constantly intervening to disrupt their natural combinations; and, on the other, the reproach is everywhere made that government does not intervene enough.

This is the question: Is evil (it is clear that I here refer to evil that is not the necessary consequence of our original infirmity) traceable to the action of the natural laws of society or to our penchant for disturbing this action?

Now, two facts are coexistent: evil, and the force of government directed against the natural laws of society. Is the first of these two facts the consequence of the second? Personally, I believe it is; I will even say that I am sure of it. But at the same time I attest to this: as evil spreads, governments seek the remedy in new interferences with the action of these laws; and the theorists complain that they still do not interfere enough. Am I not, then, justified in concluding that there is little confidence in the natural laws of society?

Yes, without a doubt, if the question is posed as a choice between isolation or exchange, there is agreement. But if the choice is between free exchange and forced exchange, is there likewise agreement? Is there nothing artificial, forced, restrained or constrained, in France, in the exchange of services relative to commerce, credit, transportation, arts, education, religion? Are labor and capital naturally distributed between agriculture and industry? When men are moved out of their normal channels, are they still allowed to follow the natural direction of their own self-interest? Do we not find obstructions everywhere? Are there not a hundred vocations that are closed to most of us? Is the Catholic not *obliged* to pay for the services of the Jewish rabbi, and the Jew for the services of the Catholic priest? * Is there one man in France who has had the education his parents would have given him if they had been free? Are not our minds, our way of life, our ideas, our industry, fashioned under the rule of the arbitrary or at least of the artificial? Now, I ask, is not such disturbing

* [Reference to the system established by Napoleon I providing government subsidies for the leading religious denominations.—TRANSLATOR.]

of the free exchange of services a way of denying the harmony of interests? On what pretext am I deprived of my liberty if not that my liberty is judged to be harmful to others? It can hardly be said to be harmful to me, for that would be adding but one antagonism the more. And where on earth are we, in Heaven's name, if Nature has placed in every man's heart a permanent, indomitable drive that impels him to harm both others and himself?

We have tried so many things; when shall we try the simplest of all: freedom? Freedom in all our acts that do not offend justice; freedom to live, to develop, to improve; the free exercise of our faculties; the free exchange of our services. What a fine and solemn spectacle it would have been had the government brought to power by the February Revolution * spoken thus to the citizens:

"You have invested me with the power of authority. I shall use it only in cases where the intervention of force is permissible. But there is only one such case, and that is for the cause of justice. I shall require every man to remain within the limits set by his rights. Every one of you may work in freedom by day and sleep in peace at night. I take upon myself the safety of your persons and property. That is my mandate; I shall fulfill it, *but I accept no other.* Let there be no misunderstanding between us. Henceforth you will pay only the slight assessment indispensable for the maintenance of order and the enforcement of justice. But also, please note, each one of you is responsible to himself for his own subsistence and advancement. Turn your eyes toward me no longer. Do not ask me to give you wealth, work, credit, education, religion, morality. Do not forget that the motive power by which you advance is within yourselves; that I myself can act only through the instrumentality of force. All that I have, absolutely all, comes from you; consequently, I cannot grant the slightest advantage to one except at the expense of others. Cultivate your fields, then, manufacture and export your products, conduct your business affairs, make your credit arrangements, give and receive your services freely, educate your children, find them a calling, cultivate the arts, improve your minds, refine your sentiments,

* [Cf. note, chap. 3, p. 37.—TRANSLATOR.]

strengthen your bonds with one another, establish industrial or charitable associations, unite your efforts for your individual good as well as for the general good; follow your inclinations, fulfill your individual destinies according to your endowments, your values, your foresight. Expect from me only two things: freedom and security, and know that you cannot ask for a third without losing these two."

Yes, I am convinced, if the February Revolution had proclaimed these principles, we should not have had another revolution. Can we imagine citizens, otherwise completely free, moving to overthrow their government when its activity is limited to satisfying the most vital, the most keenly felt of all social wants, the need for justice?

But, unfortunately, it was impossible for the National Assembly to follow this course or to speak these words. These utterances were not in accord with the Assembly's thinking or with the public's expectations. They would have spread as much consternation throughout society, perhaps, as would the proclaiming of a socialist state. Be responsible for ourselves! they would have said. Look to the state for nothing beyond law and order! Count on it for no wealth, no enlightenment! No more holding it responsible for our faults, our negligence, our improvidence! Count only on ourselves for our subsistence, our physical, intellectual, and moral progress! Merciful heavens! What is going to become of us? Won't society give way to poverty, ignorance, error, irreligion, and perversity?

Such, you will agree, would have been the fears, voiced on all sides, if the February Revolution had proclaimed liberty, that is, the reign of the natural laws of society. Hence, either we do not know these laws, or we do not trust them. We cannot help thinking that the motive forces that God implanted in man are essentially perverse; that there is integrity only in the intentions and designs of government; that the tendencies of mankind lead to disorder, to anarchy; in a word, we believe in the inevitable mutual antagonism of men's interests.

Therefore, French society during the February Revolution, far from showing the slightest desire for a natural organization, never, perhaps, turned its thoughts and its hopes so ardently toward artificial contrivances. What were they? We know only too well. It was proposed, according to the language of the time, *to give it a try*: *Faciamus experimentum in corpore vili.** And the social planners seemed to have such contempt for human personality, to identify man so completely with inert matter, that they spoke of conducting social experiments with mankind as one would speak of making chemical experiments with alkalis or acids. An initial experiment was begun at the Luxembourg,† we know with what success. Soon the Constituent Assembly formed a Committee on Labor which was deluged with a thousand social plans. A Fourier spokesman, in all seriousness, asked for land and money (he undoubtedly would not have been slow to ask for men as well) to implement his model society. Another spokesman, an egalitarian, offered his recipe, which was rejected. The manufacturers, more fortunate, succeeded in having theirs accepted. Finally, at this juncture, the legislative assembly named a commission to set up a public relief program.

What is surprising in all this is that those in power, simply to stay in power, did not now and then protest: "You are leading thirty-six million citizens to imagine that we are responsible for everything, good or bad, that happens to them in this world. On these terms, no government is possible."

In any case, however much these various proposals, glorified as social planning, may differ from one another in their methods, they are all predicated on the same proposition: Take from some to give to others. Now, it is very clear that such a proposition could meet with so sympathetic a response from the whole nation only because of the general conviction that men's interests are naturally antagonistic and human inclinations are essentially perverse.

* ["Let us make the experiment on a worthless body." Quoted by Antoine Teissier, *Éloges des hommes sçavans* (1585). Cf. Thomas Benfield Harbottle, *Dictionary of Quotations* (Classical) (London, 1906).—TRANSLATOR.]

† [The Luxembourg Palace, the seat of the French Senate. The references in this paragraph are to the government's efforts to end unemployment, which resulted in the establishment of the relief measure known as the National Workshops. —TRANSLATOR.]

Take from some to give to others! I know that this is the way
things have been going for a long time. But, before contriving, in
our effort to banish poverty, various means of putting this outlandish principle into effect, ought we not rather to ask ourselves whether
poverty is not due to the very fact that this principle has already
been put into effect in one way or another? Before seeking the
remedy in the further disturbance of the natural law of society,
ought we not first to make sure that these disturbances are
not themselves the very cause of the social ills that we wish to
cure?

Take from some to give to others! Permit me to point out
the danger and the absurdity of the economic thinking in this
so-called social aspiration, which welled up in the hearts of the
masses and finally burst forth so violently during the February
Revolution.

When there are a number of strata in society, it is understandable that the uppermost one should enjoy privileges at the expense
of the others. This is hateful, but it is not illogical.

Then the second stratum from the top will not fail to batter
down these privileges; and, with the help of the masses, will
sooner or later stage a revolution. In that case, as power passes
into its hands, we can understand that it too creates privileges for
itself. This is always detestable, but it is not illogical; at least it is
not unfeasible, for privilege is possible so long as it has the great
mass of the people under it to support it. If the third and the
fourth strata also stage their revolutions, they too will arrange,
if they can, to exploit the masses through carefully contrived
privileges. But now the great masses of the people, downtrodden,
oppressed, exhausted, stage their revolution too. Why? What do
they propose to do? You think perhaps they are going to abolish
all privilege, inaugurate the reign of universal justice? Do you
think that they are going to say: "An end to restrictions; an end
to restraints; an end to monopoly; an end to government interference for the benefit of one class; an end to heavy taxation; an
end to diplomatic and political intrigue"? No, their aim is very
different. They become a pressure group; they too insist on
becoming *privileged*. They, the masses of the people, imitating

the upper classes, cry in their turn for privileges. They demand their right to employment, their right to credit, their right to education, their right to pensions. But at whose expense? That is a question they never stop to ask. They know only that being assured of employment, credit, education, security for their old age, would be very pleasant indeed, and no one would deny it. But is it possible? Alas, no, and at this point, I say, it is no longer detestable, but illogical to the highest degree.

Privileges for the masses! People of the lower classes, think of the vicious circle you are placing yourselves in. Privilege implies someone to profit from it and someone to pay for it. We can conceive of a privileged man or a privileged class; but can we conceive of a whole nation of privileged people? Is there another social stratum under you that you can make carry the load? Will you never understand the weird hocus pocus of which you are the dupes? Will you never understand that the state cannot give you something with one hand without taking that something, and a little more, away from you with the other? Do you not see that, far from there being any possible increase of well-being in this process for you, its end result is bound to be an arbitrary government, more galling, more meddling, more extravagant, more precarious, with heavier taxes, more frequent injustices, more shocking cases of favoritism, less liberty, more lost effort, with interests, labor, and capital all misdirected, greed stimulated, discontent fomented, and individual initiative stifled?

The upper classes become alarmed, and not without reason, at this disturbing attitude on the part of the masses. They sense in it the germ of constant revolution, for what government can endure when it has had the misfortune to say: "I have the force, and I shall use it to make everybody live at the expense of everybody else. I take upon myself the responsibility for the happiness of all"? But is not the consternation these classes feel a just punishment? Have they themselves not set the baneful example of the attitude of mind of which they now complain? Have they not always had their eyes fixed on favors from the state? Have they ever failed to bestow any privilege, great or small, on industry, banking, mining, landed property, the arts, and even their means of relaxation and amusement, like dancing and music—everything, indeed, except on the toil of the people and the work of their hands? Have they not endlessly multiplied public services in order to increase, at the people's expense, their means of livelihood; and is there today the father of a family among them who is not taking steps to assure his son a *government job?* Have they ever voluntarily taken a single step to correct the admitted inequalities of taxation? Have they not for a long time even exploited their electoral privileges? And now they are amazed and distressed that the people follow in the same direction! But when the spirit of mendicancy has prevailed for so long among the rich, how can we expect it not to have penetrated to the less privileged classes?

However, a great revolution has taken place. Political power, the law-making ability, the enforcement of the law, have all passed, virtually, if not yet completely in fact, into the hands of the people, along with universal suffrage.* Thus, the people, who raise the problem, will be called upon to resolve it; and woe to the nation if, following the example that has been given them, they seek the solution in privilege, which is always the violation of the rights of others! Certainly it will result in great disillusionment, and also in a great lesson; for, though it is possible to violate the rights of the many for the benefit of the few, how can we violate the rights of all for the benefit of all? But at what price will this lesson be bought? What should the upper classes do to warn against this frightful danger? Two things: give up their privileges of their own accord, and enlighten the masses; for there are but two things that can save society: justice and enlightenment. They should examine carefully whether they are not enjoying some monopoly—if so, let them renounce it; whether they are not benefiting by some artificial inequities—if so, let them eradicate them; whether pauperism is not due, in part at least, to their disturbance of the natural law of society—if so, let them make an end of it in order that they may show their hands to the people and say: These hands are not empty,

* [Universal suffrage had just been adopted by the Second Republic.—TRANSLATOR.]

but they are clean. Is this what they actually do? Unless I am completely blind, they do the exact opposite. They begin by keeping their monopolies and have even been seen to take advantage of the Revolution to increase them. After thus putting themselves in the position where they cannot tell the truth and cannot invoke any principles without appearing inconsistent, they promise to treat the people as the people would treat themselves, and dangle before their eyes the lure of privilege. But they feel that they are being very wily in that today they grant the people only a small privilege—the right to pensions—in the hope that they may avoid any request for a great privilege—the right to employment. And they do not see that by extending and systematizing more and more the axiom: Take from some to give to others, they are encouraging the error that creates the difficulties of the present and dangers for the future.

Let us not exaggerate, however. When the upper classes seek in the extension of privilege the remedy for the ills that privilege has caused, they act in good faith, and, I feel sure, more through ignorance than from a desire to commit injustice. The fact that successive governments in France have always blocked the teaching of political economy has done irreparable harm. Even greater is the harm done by our university system, which fills all our heads with Roman prejudices, that is, with everything most incompatible with social truth. This is what leads the upper classes astray. It is fashionable today to declaim against them. For my part, I believe that their intentions have never been more benevolent in any age. I believe that they earnestly desire to solve the problems of society. I believe that they would go further than give up their privileges and would willingly turn over to charitable works a part of the property they have acquired, if, by so doing, they felt that they could definitely end the hardships of the working classes. People will say, doubtless, that they are motivated by self-interest or fear, and that there is no great generosity in giving up a part of one's goods in order to save the rest. It is the commonplace prudence of a man who keeps a fire within bounds. Let us not thus abuse human nature. Why refuse to admit any less selfish motive? Is it not quite natural for the democratic attitudes that prevail in our country to make men sensitive to the suffering of their fellows? But, whatever may be the motive, what cannot be denied is that everything that reveals public opinion—philosophy, literature, poetry, the drama, the pulpit, parliamentary debate, the press—indicates in the wealthy class more than a desire, an ardent longing, to solve the great problem. Why, then, does nothing come from our legislative assemblies? Because of their ignorance. Political economy offers them this solution: *Legal justice, private charity.* But they are off on a wrong scent and, without realizing it, follow the socialist influence; they want to incorporate charity into the law, that is, to banish justice from the law, a course likely to destroy private charity, which is always quick to give way before legal charity.

Why do our legislators thus contravene all sound notions of political economy? Why do they not leave things in their proper place: altruism in its natural realm, which is liberty; and justice in its, which is law? Why do they not use the law exclusively to further justice? It is not that they do not love justice, but that they have no confidence in it. Justice is liberty and property. But they are socialists without knowing it; for achieving the progressive reduction of poverty and the progressive increase in wealth, they have no faith, whatever they may say, in liberty or in property or, consequently, in justice. And that is why we see them in all good faith seeking to achieve the good by the constant violation of the right.

We can call the *natural laws of society* that body of phenomena, considered from the standpoint of their motivations and their results, which govern the free transactions of men.

Once this is postulated, the question is: Must we permit these laws to function, or must we prevent them from functioning?

This question is tantamount to asking:

Must we recognize the right of every man to his property, his freedom to work and to exchange on his own responsibility, whether to his profit or his loss, invoking the law, which is force, only for the protection of his rights; or can we reach a higher plane of social well-being by violating property rights and liberty, regulating labor, disrupting exchange, and shifting responsibility away from the individual?

In other words:

Must the law enforce strict justice, or be the instrument of organized confiscation administered more or less intelligently?

It is quite evident that the answer to these questions is dependent on the study and knowledge of the laws of society. We cannot make any reasonable pronouncement until we know whether property, liberty, the varied pattern of services freely exchanged, lead men forward toward their improvement, as economists assert, or backward toward their debasement, as the socialists affirm. In the first case, the ills of society must be attributed to interference with the operation of natural laws, to the legalized violation of the right to liberty and property. It is this interference and violation, then, that must be stopped, and the political economists are right. In the second case, we do not yet have enough government interference. Forced and artificial patterns of exchange have not yet sufficiently replaced the free and natural pattern; too much respect is still paid to justice, property, and liberty. Our lawmakers have not yet attacked them violently enough. We are not yet taking enough from some to give to others. So far we have taken only from the many to give to the few. Now we must take from all to give to all. In a word, we must organize confiscation, and from socialism will come our salvation.[2]

Disastrous Fallacies Derived from Exchange

Exchange is society. Consequently economic truth is the complete view, and economic error is the partial view, of exchange.

If man did not exchange, every part of the economic process would take place in the individual, and it would be very easy for us to set down from observation its good and bad effects.

But exchange has brought about a division of labor, or, to

speak less learnedly, the establishment of professions and trades. Every service (or every product) involves two persons, the one who provides it, and the one who receives it.

Undoubtedly, at the end of the evolutionary process, man in society, like man in isolation, is at once producer and consumer. But the difference must be clearly noted. Man in isolation is always the producer of what he consumes. This is almost never true of man in society. It is an incontestable point of fact that everyone can verify from his own experience. This is so because society is simply an exchange of services.

We are all producers and consumers, not of the thing, but of the value that we have produced. While we exchange things, we always remain the owners of their value.

From this circumstance are derived all economic misconceptions and fallacies. It is certainly not superfluous to indicate here the course of men's thinking on this subject.

We can give the general name of *obstacle* to everything that, coming between our wants and our satisfactions, calls forth our efforts.

The interrelations of these four elements—want, obstacle, effort, satisfaction—are perfectly evident and understandable in the case of man in a state of isolation. Never, never in the world, would it occur to us to say:

"It is too bad that Robinson Crusoe does not encounter more obstacles; for, in that case, he would have more outlets for his efforts; he would be richer.

"It is too bad that the sea has cast up on the shore of the Isle of Despair useful articles, boards, provisions, arms, books; for it deprives Robinson Crusoe of an outlet for his efforts; he is poorer.

"It is too bad that Robinson Crusoe has invented nets to catch fish or game; for it lessens by that much the efforts he exerts for a given result; he is less rich.

"It is too bad that Robinson Crusoe is not sick oftener. It would give him the chance to practice medicine on himself, which is a form of labor; and, since all wealth comes from labor, he would be richer.

"It is too bad that Robinson Crusoe succeeded in putting out the fire that endangered his cabin. He has lost an invaluable opportunity for labor; he is less rich.

"It is too bad that the land on the Isle of Despair is not more barren, the spring not farther away, the sun not below the horizon more of the time. Robinson Crusoe would have more trouble providing himself with food, drink, light; he would be richer."

Never, I say, would people advance such absurd propositions as oracles of truth. It would be too completely evident that wealth does not consist in the amount of effort required for each satisfaction obtained, but that the exact opposite is true. We should understand that value does not consist in the want or the obstacle or the effort, but in the satisfaction; and we should readily admit that although Robinson Crusoe is both producer and consumer, in order to gauge his progress, we must look, not at his labor, but at its results. In brief, in stating the axiom that the paramount interest is that of the consumer, we should feel that we were simply stating a veritable *truism*.

How happy will nations be when they see clearly how and why what we find false and what we find true of man in isolation continue to be false or true of man in society!

Yet it is certainly a fact that the five or six propositions that appeared so absurd when we applied them to the Isle of Despair seem so incontestably true when applied to France that they serve as the basis of all our economic legislation. And, on the contrary, the axiom that seemed truth itself when applied to the individual is never mentioned without provoking a disdainful smile.

Could it be true, then, that exchange so alters us that what makes for the poverty of the individual makes for the wealth of society?

No, this is not true. But, it must be said, it is plausible, very plausible indeed, since it is generally believed.

Society consists in the fact that we work for one another. We receive more services either as we give more or as those we give are assigned greater value, are more in demand, that is to say, are better paid. On the other hand, the division of labor causes each one of us to apply his efforts to conquering obstacles that block the satisfactions of others. The farmer attacks the obstacle called hunger; the doctor, the obstacle called illness; the priest, the obstacle called vice; the writer, the obstacle called ignorance; the miner, the obstacle called cold; etc., etc.

And, since the more keenly all those about us are aware of the obstacles that stand in their way, the more generously they are inclined to remunerate our efforts, it follows that we are all disposed, from this point of view, as producers, to dedicate ourselves almost religiously to exaggerating the importance of the obstacles that it is our business to combat. We consider ourselves richer if these obstacles are increased, and we immediately conclude that what is to our personal gain is for the general good.[3]

5

On Value

A long discourse is always boring, and a long discourse on value must be doubly so.

Therefore, naturally enough, every inexperienced writer, when confronted with a problem in economics, tries to solve it without involving himself in a definition of value.

But inevitably it does not take him long to discover how very inadequate such a procedure is. The theory of value is to political economy what a numerical system is to arithmetic. How hopelessly confusing Bezout * would have become if, to spare his students tedium, he had tried to teach them the four fundamental operations of arithmetic—addition, subtraction, multiplication, and division—and the theory of proportions without first explaining to them how the ten digits by their shape and position represent numerical values!

If only the reader could foresee the fascinating conclusions to be deduced from the theory of value, he would accept the tiresome explanation of the basic principles, just as he resigns himself to the dull chore of learning the elementary principles of geometry by keeping in mind the exciting prospect of things to come.

But in the field of political economy one does not intuitively anticipate anything of this sort. The more pains I shall take to make clear the distinctions between value and utility, and between value and labor, in order to explain how natural it was for early economic theory to have run aground on these treacherous shoals,

* [Étienne Bezout (1730–1783), French naval inspector and mathematician.— Translator.]

the more surely the reader will find in my careful analysis mere sterile and idle subtleties, of no possible interest to anyone, except perhaps professionals in the field.

You are laboriously considering, he will say to me, whether wealth resides in the utility of things or in their value or in their scarcity. Is not this like the question asked by the Scholastics: Does form reside in the substance or in the accident? Are you not afraid of being parodied in a vaudeville skit by some would-be Molière?

And yet I must say: From the viewpoint of political economy society is exchange. The primary element of exchange is the notion of value, and consequently the connotations that we give to this word, whether true or erroneous, lead us to truth or error in all our social thinking.

I have undertaken in this work to show the harmony of the providential laws that govern human society. These laws are harmonious rather than discordant because all the elements, all the motive forces, all the springs of action, all the self-regarding impulses within man, work together toward attaining a great final result that he will never completely reach, because of his innate *imperfection,* but which he will constantly approach because of his indomitable *capacity for improvement;* and this result will be the progressive merging of all classes at a higher and higher level —in other words, the *equalizing* of all individuals in the general enjoyment of a *higher standard of living.*

But, to succeed in my effort, I must explain two things, namely:

1) *Utility*—that is, the service a thing renders tends to cost less and less, to become more generally available, as it gradually passes outside the domain of individual ownership.

2) *Value,* on the contrary, which alone can be claimed as a possession, which alone, in law and in fact, constitutes property, tends to decrease in proportion to the amount of utility it represents.

Consequently, if I base my demonstration both on private ownership, but exclusively on private ownership of value, and on public ownership, but exclusively on public ownership of utility, I should be able, provided my reasoning is valid, to satisfy and reconcile all schools, since I recognize that all have had a glimmering of the truth, but only of a part of the truth seen from different points of view.

Economists, you defend private ownership. In the social order no private ownership exists save the ownership of value, and it cannot be called into question.

Socialists, you dream of public ownership. You have it. The social order makes all *utilities* common to all, provided the exchange of privately owned values remains free.

You are like architects arguing over a building of which each one has seen only one side. They do not see *poorly*, but they do not see *all*. To reach an agreement, they need only to walk around the entire edifice.

But how can I reconstruct this social edifice and present it to the public in all its beautiful harmony if I reject its twin cornerstones—utility and value? How could I effect the much-to-be-desired reconciliation of all schools of thought on the common ground of truth if I should yield to my reluctance to analyze these two ideas, whose confused interpretations have unfortunately given rise to so much disagreement?

A preamble of this kind has been necessary to persuade the reader, if possible, to arm himself for a short while with the concentration and the patience to endure some degree of tiresomeness, and alas! of boredom. Unless I am much mistaken, the beauty of the conclusions will richly compensate for the dullness of the premises. If Newton had allowed himself, in the beginning, to be deterred from the study of mathematics by his distaste for its elementary principles, his heart would never have quickened with admiration at the vision of the harmonies of the celestial universe; and I insist that we have only to work our way manfully through a few elementary notions of political economy to realize that God has not been less lavish in bestowing touching goodness, admirable simplicity, and magnificent splendor upon the social universe.

In the first chapter we saw that man is both *passive* and *active;* that *wants* and *satisfactions,* being concerned exclusively with *sensation,* are, by their nature, personal, intimate, and nontransferable; that *effort,* on the contrary, the link between want and satisfaction, the mean between the extremes of motive cause and end result, stemming as it does from our *activity,* our impulse, our will, can be transmitted by mutual agreement from one individual to another. I know that this assertion could be challenged on metaphysical grounds, and that it could be maintained that effort also is personal and individual. I have no desire to become involved in any such ideological debate, and I hope that my thought will be accepted without controversy when expressed in this nontechnical form: We cannot *feel* another persons' wants; we cannot feel another person's satisfactions; but we can *render services* to one another.

This transmission of effort, this exchange of services, forms the subject matter of political economy; and since, on the other hand, political economy can be summed up in the word *value,* which is the thing it seeks to explain in all its detail, it follows that our notion of *value* will be an imperfect one, an erroneous one, if, neglecting the mean, we base it on the extremes, which are phenomena of our sensations—*wants* and *satisfactions,* which are intimate, nontransferable, not subject to measurement from one individual to another—instead of founding it on our *activity,* our *effort,* our exchange of reciprocal *services,* since these are capable of comparison, appraisal, *evaluation,* and can indeed be *evaluated* for the very reason that they are exchanged.

In the same chapter we arrived at these conclusions:

Utility (the ability of certain acts or things to serve us), is composite, one part of it being due to the action of Nature, the other part to the action of man. The more Nature has done to effect a given result, the less there is for human labor to do. Nature's contribution is essentially *gratuitous;* man's contribution, whether intellectual or physical, exchanged or not exchanged, collective or individual, is essentially *onerous,* as is implied by the very word "effort."

And since what is *gratuitous* cannot have *value,* the notion of *value* implying acquisition through *effort,* it follows that value too will be misunderstood if we extend its meaning to include, in whole or in part, those things that are received as gifts from

Nature, instead of restricting its meaning to the human contribution only.

Thus, from two points of view, from two different approaches, we reach the conclusion that *value* must have reference to the *efforts* made by men in order to secure the *satisfaction* of their *wants*.

In chapter 3 we noted that man cannot live in the state of isolation. But if, in our thinking, we conjure up this imaginary case, this state *contrary to nature,* to which the eighteenth century paid homage under the name of the *state of nature,* we realize at once that, although it exhibits the active phenomenon that we have named effort, it still does not reveal the notion of value. The reason is simple: value implies comparison, a rating, an evaluation, a measure. For two things to be measured, they must be commensurate; and to be commensurate, they must be of the same kind. In the state of isolation, to what can effort be compared? To wants? To satisfactions? This can lead us only to grant to effort a greater or a lesser degree of timeliness, of appropriateness. In the social state we compare the effort of one man with the effort of another man (and from this comparison arises the idea of value), two phenomena of the same kind, and hence *measurable*.

Thus, the definition of the word "value," to be accurate, must have reference not only to human efforts, but also to efforts that are exchanged or exchangeable. Exchange does more than take note of values or measure them; it creates them. I do not mean that it creates the acts or the things that are exchanged, but it imparts the idea of *value* to them.

So, when two men exchange their present effort, or the fruits of their past effort, they are *serving* each other; they are rendering each other mutual *service*.

I therefore say: *Value is the relationship existing between two services that have been exchanged.*

The idea of value first entered the world when a man said to his brother, "Do this for me, and I will do that for you," and the brother agreed; for then, for the first time, men were able to say, "Two *services* that are exchanged *are equal* to each other."

It is curious to note that the true theory of value, which is to be sought in vain in many a thick volume, is found in the delightful little fable of Florian, the *Blind Man and the Paralytic*:

> *Aidons-nous mutuellement,*
> *La charge des malheurs en sera plus légère.*
> *. . . . . À nous deux*
> *Nous possédons le bien à chacun nécessaire.*
> *J'ai des jambes, et vous des yeux.*
> *Moi, je vais vous porter; vous, vous serez mon guide:*
> *Ainsi, sans que jamais notre amitié décide*
> *Qui de nous deux remplit le plus utile emploi,*
> *Je marcherai pour vous, vous y verrez pour moi.**

This is *value* identified and defined with rigorous economic accuracy, except for the touching reference to friendship, which takes us into another realm. We can well understand how two handicapped persons can render each other mutual *service* without undue concern as to which one performs the more useful function. The special circumstances invented by the fabler produce a strong sense of sympathy that prevents the two men from trying to assess the relative importance of the services they exchange, although this assessment is indispensable in order to bring completely into focus the notion of value in this transaction. This idea would become fully apparent if all men, or most men, were stricken with paralysis or blindness; for then the inexorable law of supply and demand would take over, and, eliminating the

---

* [Jean-Pierre Claris de Florian (1755–1794), great-nephew of Voltaire, and author of plays and tales of some merit, but better known for his fables, which are generally recognized in France as second only to those of the great La Fontaine.

        Let us aid each other . . . .
        The burden of our ills will be the lighter . . . .
        Together we have all that fate to each denies.
         I have legs, and you have eyes.
        I shall carry you, and you will be my guide.
        Thus, without our friendship ever having to decide
        Which of us of greater use can be,
        I shall walk for you, and you will see for me.—TRANSLATOR.]

element of voluntary sacrifice on the part of the one performing the more useful function, would re-establish the transaction on the solid ground of justice.

We are all halt or blind in some respect; and we readily understand that by mutual aid *the burden of our ills will be the lighter.* Hence *exchange.* We work to provide food, clothing, lodging, light, health, defense, education for one another. Hence reciprocity of *services.* These services we compare, we discuss, we evaluate. Hence *value.*

A host of circumstances can increase the relative importance of a service. We find it greater or less in proportion to its usefulness to us; to the number of persons ready to perform it for us; to the amount of labor, pains, skill, time, preparation it requires, to the degree to which it relieves us of the necessity of providing these same things for ourselves. Value depends not only on these circumstances but also on the estimate we make of them; for it can happen, and often does, that we rate a given service very highly, because we judge it to be very useful, whereas in reality it is detrimental. For this reason, vanity, ignorance, error play their part in influencing this essentially elastic and fluctuating relationship that we call "value"; and one could say that the evaluation of services tends to come closer to absolute truth and justice as men progress in knowledge and morality.

Up to now the principle of value has been sought in those circumstances that increase or lessen it, in material quality, wear, usefulness, scarcity, labor, inaccessibility, subjective judgment, etc. —things that from the very beginning have given the science of political economy a wrong direction, for the accident that modifies the phenomenon is not the phenomenon itself. Moreover, every writer has set himself up as the godfather, so to speak, of the particular one of these circumstances that he considered the most significant—the inevitable outcome of the tendency to generalize; for the whole universe is in everything, and there is nothing that a word cannot be made to include if only its meaning is sufficiently broadened. Thus, the principle of value for Adam Smith is in material quality and wear (durability); for Say, in utility;

for Ricardo, in labor; for Senior, in scarcity; for Storch, in subjective judgment; etc.*

What happened, inevitably, was that these writers in all innocence weakened the authority and dignity of the science of political economy by giving the impression of contradicting one another, whereas in reality each one was correct from his own point of view. Furthermore, they enmeshed the primary notion of political economy in a maze of inextricable difficulties, since the same words did not connote for all of them the same meaning; and, although one set of circumstances might be declared fundamental, they also noted other factors at work that were too important to be neglected, and thus their definitions became more and more involved.

This book is not designed to add to the controversy, but to be an exposition of principles. I point out what I see, not what others have seen. I cannot, however, refrain from calling the reader's attention to the circumstances on which the idea of value has been based. But before proceeding with this topic, I shall turn to a series of concrete illustrations of the nature of value, for it is through different applications of it that we grasp the meaning of a theory.

I shall show how every transaction can be reduced to a bartering of services. But the reader must keep in mind what was said about barter in the previous chapter. It is rarely a simple transaction; sometimes it is accomplished through products or commodities circulated among several contracting parties; more often it is accomplished by means of money, in which case it can be broken down into two factors, *sale* and *purchase;* but, since this complicating feature does not in any way alter the nature of the transaction, let me assume, for the sake of simplicity, an immediate and direct barter between two parties. In this way we may avoid any misconception as to the nature of value.

* [Nassau William Senior (1790–1864), English economist. First professor of political economy at Oxford.

Heinrich Friedrich von Storch (1766–1835), German economist, instructor to the imperial children.—Translator.]

We are all born with one overwhelming physical want, which must be satisfied on pain of death: the need to breathe. On the other hand, we are all placed in an environment that provides for this want, generally speaking, without requiring any effort from us. Air, then, has utility, but no *value*. It has no value, because, since it occasions no effort, it calls for no service. Rendering a service implies sparing someone pains; and when no pains are required to achieve a satisfaction, there are none to be spared.

But if a man goes down to the bottom of a river in a diving bell, a foreign body is introduced between the air and his lungs; to re-establish connections, the pump must be set in motion; then there is effort to be exerted, pains to be taken; and certainly the man will be ready to co-operate, for his life is at stake, and no service to him could be greater.

Instead of making this effort himself, he requests me to make it; and, in order to induce me to do so, he promises in his turn to take pains that will procure me satisfaction. We discuss the matter, and we come to an agreement. What do we have here? Two wants, two satisfactions, that are not mutually exclusive; two efforts that are the subject of a voluntary transaction; two *services* that are exchanged—and value makes its appearance.

Now, it is said that utility is the basis of value; and as utility is inherent in air, we are to assume that this is likewise true of value. There is obvious confusion here. Air, by its composition, has physical properties that are adapted to one of our bodily organs, the lungs. What I take out of the atmosphere to fill the diving bell is not changed in any way; it is still oxygen and nitrogen. There is no combining to form a new physical quality; no reagent brings forth a new element called *value*. The fact is that value comes only from the service that has been rendered.

When someone states the axiom that utility is the basis of value, I have no quarrel with him if he means that service has value because it is useful to the one who receives it and pays for it. This is a truism that adds nothing new to the idea of the word "service."

But we must not confuse utility of the type provided by the air with the utility of a service. These two are distinct, of different orders and natures, and do not necessarily have any common denominator or relationship. Under certain conditions, I can do someone a service that is trifling, as far as the effort it costs me or saves him is concerned, and yet, by so doing, I can place at his disposal something of very great intrinsic *utility*.

Let us see how the two contracting parties would go about evaluating the *service* that the one renders the other in sending air down to him. There must be a common ground for comparison, and it can only be in the *service* that the diver has promised to give in return. What they demand will depend on their respective situations, the urgency of their wants, the relative ease with which one can get along without the other, and many other circumstances that demonstrate that value is in the service, since both increase in the same ratio.

If the reader so desires, he can easily think up for himself other examples of this kind that will convince him that value is not necessarily commensurate with the amount of effort expended. This is a remark that I throw out here in anticipation of later discussion, for I expect to prove that value no more resides in labor than it does in utility.

Nature has seeen fit to make me in such a way that I should die if I did not quench my thirst from time to time; and the spring to which I must go for water is two miles from my village. Therefore, every morning I must take the trouble of going after my little supply of water, for I find in water those *useful* qualities that have the power to assuage that type of suffering known as thirst. Want, effort, satisfaction—they are all there. I am familiar with the utility I derive from this act; I do not yet know its value.

However, suppose my neighbor also goes to the spring, and I say to him, "*Spare me the trouble* of making this trip; *do me the service* of bringing me some water. While you are so engaged, I will do something for you; I will teach your child to spell." It happens that this suits both of us. This is the exchange of two services, and we can say that the one *is equal* to the other. Note that what is compared here are the two efforts, not the two wants or the two satisfactions; for on what basis can we compare the relative merits of having a drink of water and learning how to spell?

Soon I say to my neighbor, "Teaching your child is becoming a bore; I prefer to do something else for you. You will continue to bring me water, and I will give you five sous." If the offer is accepted, the economist may say without fear of error: *The service is worth five sous.*

After a while my neighbor no longer waits for me to ask him. He knows, by experience, that I need to drink every day. He anticipates my want. And while he is at it, he provides water for other villagers. In a word, he becomes a water-seller. Then we begin to put it this way: *Water is worth five sous.*

But has the water really changed? Has the value, which so recently was in the service, now become a material thing, a new chemical element added to the water? Has a slight change that my neighbor and I made in our arrangements been powerful enough to upset the principle of *value* and alter its nature? I am not so pedantic as to object to saying that *water is worth five sous,* any more than to saying that *the sun sets.* But we must realize that both are examples of metonymy; that metaphors do not alter facts; that scientifically, since, after all, we are dealing with a science, it is no more true that value is contained in water than that the sun sets in the sea.

Let us therefore assign to things the qualities that are proper to them: to water, to air, *utility;* to services, *value.* Let us say: Water has *utility* because it has the property of quenching thirst; the service is the thing that has *value,* because it is the subject of the agreement. This truth is apparent when we reflect that whatever may be our distance from the spring, the utility of the water remains constant, but its value varies. Why? Because the *service* becomes greater or smaller. *Value,* then, is in the service, since value changes as the service does and in the same degree.

The diamond plays an important role in the books written by economists. They use it to elucidate the laws of value or to indicate the so-called disturbances of these laws. It is a shining weapon that all schools use in their combat. The English school says: "Value consists in labor." The French school produces a diamond and says: "Here is a product that requires no labor and is yet of immense value." Then, if the French school affirms that value resides in utility, the English school cites the diamond, along with air, light, and water, as proof to the contrary. "Air is very useful and has no value; the diamond's *utility* is highly questionable, and yet it is *worth* more than the whole atmosphere." And the reader can only say with Henry IV, "On my word, they're both right." * Eventually they reach common agreement in the following error, which is worse than the other two: We must admit that the handiwork of God has *value,* and that value, then, is *material.*

These anomalies disappear, it seems to me, on the basis of my definition, which is corroborated rather than invalidated by the example in question.

I take a stroll along the seashore. A stroke of good luck puts a superb diamond into my hand. I have come into possession of a considerable amount of *value.* Why? Am I going to contribute something great to humanity? Have I toiled long and arduously? Neither the one nor the other. Why, then, does the diamond have such value? Because the person to whom I give it believes that I am rendering him a great *service,* all the greater because many rich people would like to have it, and I alone can render it. Their judgment is open to question, granted. It is based on vanity and love of display, granted again. But the judgment exists in the mind of a man ready to act in accordance with it, and that is enough.

We could say that this judgment is far from being based on a reasonable evaluation of the diamond's *utility;* indeed, it is quite the contrary. But making great sacrifices for the *useless* is the very nature and purpose of ostentation.

* [A remark concerning Protestants and Catholics attributed to Henry when he became King of France in 1589. Himself a Protestant, he became a Catholic in order to win the crown. His Edict of Nantes, providing religious tolerance for the entire nation, put an end to France's bloody Wars of Religion.—TRANSLATOR.]

Value, far from having any necessary relation to the labor *performed* by the person rendering the service, is more likely to be proportionate, we may say, to the amount of labor *spared* the person receiving the service; and this is the law of values. It is a general law and universally accepted in practice, although, as far as I know, not taken into account by the theorists. We shall describe later the admirable mechanism that tends to keep value and labor in balance when the latter is free; but it is nonetheless true that value is determined less by the effort expended by the person *serving* than by the effort spared the person *served*.

The transaction relating to the diamond may be supposed to give rise to a dialogue of this nature:

"Let me have your diamond, please."

"I am quite willing; give me your whole year's labor in exchange."

"But, my dear sir, getting it didn't cost you a minute's time."

"Well, then, the way is open to you to find that kind of minute."

"But, in all justice, we ought to exchange on terms of *equal labor.*"

"No, in all justice, you set a price on your services, and I set one on mine. I am not forcing you; why should you force me? Give me a whole year's labor, or go find your own diamond."

"But that would entail ten years of painful search, and probable disappointment at the end. I find it wiser and more profitable to spend ten years in some other way."

"And that is just why I feel that I am still doing you a *service* when I ask only for one year. I am saving you nine years, and for that reason I consider this *service* of great *value*. If I appear demanding to you, it is because you consider only the labor I have performed; but consider also the labor that I save you, and you will find that I am almost too easy."

"Nevertheless, you are making a profit from what is a work of Nature."

"And if I let you have my lucky find for nothing or next to nothing, you would be the one to make the profit. Besides, if this diamond has great value, it is not because Nature has been toiling away on it since the beginning of time; Nature does as much for a dewdrop."

"Yes, but if diamonds were as plentiful as dewdrops, you would not be laying down the law to me."

"Certainly, because in that case you would not be appealing to me, or you would not be disposed to pay me a high price for a service that you could easily perform for yourself."

We see from this dialogue that value resides no more in the diamond than it does in water or in air; it resides entirely in the *services* performed and received in connection with these things and is determined after free discussion by the contracting parties.

Go through what the economists have to say; read, compare their definitions. If any one of them can account for air and the diamond, two cases apparently so opposite, then throw this book of mine into the fire. But if my definition, simple as it is, resolves the difficulty, or rather, eliminates it, then, reader, in all good conscience, you are bound to read me through to the end; for so good an introduction to the science we are studying cannot fail to hold promise for the rest.

I ask indulgence to cite other examples, in order both to clarify my thought and to familiarize the reader with a new definition. Besides, this attention to the principle of value, showing it in all its aspects, will pave the way for my conclusions, which will prove to be, I venture to predict, no less important than unexpected.

Among the wants to which we are subject because of our physical nature is the need for food; and one of the best commodities for satisfying it is bread.

Naturally, since it is I who experience the need to eat, it is I who should perform all the operations that will produce the amount of bread I require. I cannot ask my fellow men to perform this service for me gratis, since they too are subject to the same want and are obliged to make the same effort.

If I were to make my own bread, I should have to perform a series of tasks much like those involved in getting water from the well, but much more complicated. The elements of which bread is composed exist, of course, everywhere in Nature. As Jean-Baptiste Say so wisely observed, man has neither the need nor the ability to create anything. Gases, minerals, electricity, plant life all exist about me; I need only bring them together, help them along, combine and transport them, with the aid of that great laboratory which we call the earth, so full of mysterious things that science has barely begun to discover. Even though the sum total of all the operations I must go through in pursuit of my objective is quite complicated, each individual operation is as simple as drawing water from the spring where Nature has placed it. Each one of my efforts, therefore, is merely a service that I perform for myself; and if, through an agreement freely arrived at, other persons spare me some or all of these efforts, I have received that amount of *services*. The sum of these services, in comparison with those that I perform in return, constitutes and determines the value of my bread.

A convenient intermediate agent is introduced to facilitate this exchange of services and to measure their relative importance, viz., money. But the fundamental nature of things remains the same, even as in mechanics power is transmitted in accordance with the same laws, whether it be passed through one or several sets of gears.

We can see the truth of all this in the following illustration. If a good accountant were to analyze the elements entering into the *value* of my loaf of bread costing, say, four sous, he would eventually identify, in the course of searching through many complicated transactions, all the individuals whose *services* had contributed to determining this value, all who had saved trouble for the person who, in the last analysis, pays for the bread because he is the consumer. First, there would be the baker, who keeps a twentieth part, and out of his twentieth pays the mason who built his oven, the woodcutter who prepared his firewood, etc.; then, there would be the miller, who would receive not only enough to pay for his own labor but also something for the quarryman who made his millstone, the workman who built the banks for his millrace, etc. Other parts of the total value would go to the thresher, the harvester, the cultivator, the planter, until the account was complete to the last centime. But no part of it, none whatsoever, would go to pay God or Nature. Such an assumption is absurd, on the face of it, and yet logically it is implicit in the theories of those economists who attribute to matter or the forces of Nature any part of the *value* of a product. No, once again, what has *value* here is not the loaf of bread, but the series of *services* that made the bread available to me.

It is quite true that, among the constituent parts of the loaf's value, our bookkeeper will find one part that he will have trouble itemizing as a *service*, at least as a service requiring effort. He will find that out of his twenty centimes, which make up his total of four sous, one or two go to the owner of the land, to the possessor of the field of operations. This small part of the bread's value constitutes what is called the *land rent;* and, confused by the expression, by the metonymy that we again encounter here, our accountant will perhaps be tempted to list this as the share due the forces of Nature, due, that is, to the land itself.

I maintain, however, that if he is a good accountant, he will realize that even this item is actually the cost of true *services* like all the others. This fact will be conclusively demonstrated when we study *real property*. For the moment, I shall simply remind the reader that here I am dealing, not with property, but with *value*. I am not inquiring whether all services are valid and legitimate, or whether some men have succeeded in receiving payment for services they did not render. After all, the world is full of injustices of this sort, but *rent* should not be included among them.

All that I am seeking to demonstrate here is that the so-called value of *things* is, in fact, only the value of the *services,* real or fancied, that are transmitted through the medium of things; that value does not reside in the things themselves, and is no more to be found in bread than in diamonds, in water, or in air; that Nature receives no payment for value; that the entire amount, paid by the ultimate consumer, is distributed among men; and that the consumer is willing to make them this payment only because they have rendered him services, cases of fraud and violence excepted.

Two men think that ice is a good thing in summer, and that coal is a better thing in winter. The one cools us, and the other warms us, both thus answering to two of our wants. I cannot insist too much that the utility of these objects consists in certain physical properties that are adapted to our *physical organs*. Let us note that neither *value* nor anything like it is included among these properties, which physics or chemistry could isolate. How, then, could anyone have reached the conclusion that value resides in matter and is itself material?

If these two men wish to satisfy their wants independently, each one will have to labor at storing up his own supply of both ice and coal. If they come to an understanding, one will go to the mines to get enough coal for both of them, the other to the mountains for enough ice for both. But in that case an agreement has to be reached. The two services exchanged must be carefully evaluated and compared. All the circumstances must be taken into account: the difficulties to be overcome, the dangers to be faced, the time to be lost, the pains to be taken, the skill required, the risks to be run, the possibility of satisfying the want in some other way, etc., etc. When the two men reach agreement, the economist will say that the two *services* that are exchanged *are equivalent;* but the common way of putting it, by metonymy, will be: So much coal *is worth* so much ice, as though value has passed physically into these objects. Though it is easy to realize that the common expression indicates the result well enough, only the scientific statement gives a true idea of the cause.

Instead of two services and two persons, the agreement may include a great number of services and persons, substituting indirect or roundabout exchange for direct barter. In that case money will be introduced to facilitate the act of exchange. Need I say that the principle of value will not be displaced or altered in the process?

But I do need to add a comment about the coal. It might well be that there is only one mine in the region, and that one man has got possession of it. In that case, this man will make his own terms, that is to say, he will set a high price on his *services* or his so-called *services*.

We have not yet come to the question of law and justice, of distinguishing between real services and fraudulent services. For the moment, what concerns us is to elucidate the true theory of value and rid it of the error from which the science of economics has suffered. When we say, "What Nature has done, or given, it has done, or given, gratis; consequently these things have no value," people answer by giving us a cost analysis of coal or any other natural product. They admit readily enough that the price, in most cases, includes human services. One man has dug the earth; another has drained off the water; this man has brought the coal up from the mine; another one has delivered it; and the sum total of all these actions constitutes, they say, *almost all* the value of the coal. Yet there still remains a part of the *value* that does not correspond to any labor, to any *service*. That is the price of the coal lying underground, still untouched, as they say, by human labor. This is the owner's share; and since this part of the value is not created by man, it must indeed be created by Nature.

I reject this conclusion, and I warn the reader that if he accepts it in any guise whatsoever, he will make no further progress in the science of political economy. No, value is no more created by an act of Nature than matter is created by the action of man. One of two things must be true: either the owner has contributed to the final result and has performed real services, in which case the part of the value that he has set on the coal falls rightly within my definition; or else he has entered the transaction as a parasite and, in that case, has been sharp enough to receive payment for services that he did not perform; the price of the coal is improperly raised. This situation proves that injustice has crept in; but it cannot upset the theory to the point of warranting the assertion that that portion of value is material, that it has combined, like a physical element, with the gratuitous gifts of Providence. And here is the proof: Put an end to the injustice, if there is injustice, and the corresponding amount of value will disappear. Such would not be the case, certainly, if value were inherent in matter and created by Nature.

Let us now pass to the second of our most elemental wants: security.

A certain number of men land on an inhospitable shore. They set to work. But not one of them ever knows at what moment he will have to stop his work to defend himself against savage beasts or men more savage still. Beyond the time and effort spent directly in defending themselves, more is required to provide arms and munitions. They finally realize that the total loss in effort would be infinitely less if some of them gave up their other work and devoted themselves entirely to this *service*. They would assign to it those with the most skill, courage, and strength. These latter would perfect themselves in an art that would be their constant occupation; and while they watched over the safety of the community, the others would bring in from their labors more *satisfactions for everybody* than would have been possible if ten of their number had not been removed from the general working force. Consequently, the arrangement is carried out. What can we see in this except more progress in the direction of the division of labor, introducing and requiring an exchange of services?

Are the services of these troops, soldiers, militiamen, guards—call them what you will—productive? Undoubtedly, since the arrangement is made solely in order to increase the ratio of total satisfactions to the general effort.

Do these services have value? They do indeed, since they are appraised, assigned a price, evaluated, and, after all, paid for by other *services* against which they are compared.

The form under which the remuneration is stipulated, the manner of assessment, the procedure whereby the terms of the arrangement are discussed and agreed upon, all this in no wise alters the principle. Do some save the others effort? Do some procure satisfactions for the others? If so, then there is exchange, comparison, *evaluation* of services, and there is *value*.

Services of this type, in a complex society, often lead to terrible consequences. Since the very nature of the services demanded from this class of workers requires that force be placed in their hands, and enough force to overcome all resistance, those to whom it has been entrusted may abuse it and turn it against the community itself. It can also happen, since they receive from the community services that are proportionate to the community's need for *security*, that they foment a sense of insecurity and, through overcunning diplomacy, involve their fellow citizens in continual warfare.

All this has been known to happen and still happens. It results, I admit, in upsetting frightfully the just balance of reciprocal services. But it does not result in altering in any way the fundamental principle or the scientific theory of value.

One or two more examples. I beg the reader to believe that I am just as aware as he is of the wearisomeness and dullness of this series of hypothetical cases, all presenting the same proofs, all reaching the same conclusions, all couched in the same terms. I am sure that it will be realized that this procedure, if not the most entertaining in the world, is the surest way to establish the true theory of value and thus open the road that we must travel.

We are in Paris. This vast metropolis seethes with countless desires; it also abounds with the means of satisfying them. A host of men, wealthy or well-off, turn their energies to industry, the arts, politics; and, when evening comes, they are eager for an hour's diversion and relaxation. First among the pleasures so avidly sought after is that of hearing Mme. Malibran * sing Rossini's beautiful music or Rachel interpret Racine's admirable poetry.† Only two women in all the world can provide such noble and exquisite pleasure; and, unless recourse could be had to violence or torture, which probably would not succeed, they will perform only on their own terms. Thus, the services requested from Malibran and Rachel will have great *value*. This explanation is prosaic enough, but nonetheless true.

Let a wealthy banker decide that, to gratify his vanity, he will have one of these great artists appear at his home, and he will discover, through personal experience, that my theory is correct in all respects. He seeks a great satisfaction; he desires it keenly; a single person in the world can provide it. The only means of

---

* [Maria-Felicia Garcia Malibran (1808–1836), a most celebrated soprano-contralto of her day, best known, as Bastiat indicates, for her interpretations of Rossini's operas.—TRANSLATOR.]

† [Elisa Felix Rachel (1820–1858), whose tremendous popularity at the Paris Théâtre Français in leading roles of Racine's tragedies was responsible for a revival of these seventeenth-century classics.—TRANSLATOR.]

inducing the person to accept is by offering a very considerable remuneration.

What are the extreme limits within which the transaction will be conducted? The banker will go to the point of preferring to do without the satisfaction rather than pay the price demanded for it; the diva, to the point of preferring the price offered to not being paid at all. The point of balance between these two extremes will determine the value of this special service, as it does all others. In many cases it happens that usage may have fixed this delicate point. People in high society have too much good taste to *haggle* over certain services. It may even happen that the remuneration will be gallantly disguised to mitigate the crassness of economic law. Yet economic law presides over this transaction just as surely as it does over the most commonplace transactions, and the nature of value is not changed because the experience or urbanity of the contracting parties enables them to dispense with certain details of the bargaining.

Thus are explained the vast fortunes earned by great artists of exceptional talent. Another circumstance favors them. The nature of their services is such that they can be rendered, for the same effort, before a great multitude of persons. However large may be the auditorium, provided Rachel's voice can fill it, every spectator there receives the full impact of her inimitable rendition. This, we can see, forms the basis of a new arrangement. Three or four thousand persons sharing the same desire can settle upon a certain amount to be contributed by each one; and the sum total of their combined services represented by this contribution, which is offered as a tribute to the great tragic actress, exactly balances the unique services that she renders simultaneously to all her listeners. This is *value*.

Just as a great number of auditors may reach an agreement to listen, so a group of actors may reach an agreement to sing in an opera or present a play. Agents may be called in to spare the contracting parties countless petty details of production. Value is multiplied, is made more complex, is ramified, is distributed more widely; but its nature does not change.

Let us end with what are called exceptional cases. They are

the acid test of good theories. When a rule is correct, the exception does not weaken it, but confirms it.

Here is an old priest walking along, pensive, a staff in his hand, a breviary under his arm. How serene his features! How expressive his countenance! How rapt his look! Where is he going? Do you not see the church spire on the horizon? The young village vicar does not yet trust his own prowess; he has called the old missionary to his aid. But, before he could do so, a number of arrangements had to be made. The elderly preacher will indeed find bread and board at the rectory. But between one Lent and another, one has to live; it is the common law. Therefore the young vicar has taken up a collection, modest, but sufficient, from the rich of the village; for the old pastor was not demanding, and in response to the letter he had been written he replied: "My daily bread, that is my necessary expense; a sou to give as alms to the poor, that is my luxury."

Thus, the economic prerequisites are duly satisfied; for political economy insists on slipping in everywhere and is involved in everything, and I really believe that to it should be attributed the quotation: *Nil humani a me alienum puto.**

Let us pursue this illustration a little further, from the economic point of view, naturally.

This is a true exchange of services. On the one hand, an old man agrees to devote his time, his energies, his talents, his health, to bring some degree of enlightenment to the minds of a small number of villagers, to raise their moral level. On the other hand, bread for a few days, a superb bombazine cassock, and a new broad-brimmed hat are guaranteed the man who preaches the word of God.

But there is something else here. There is a veritable bombardment of sacrifices. The old priest refuses everything that is not absolutely indispensable to him. Of this poor pittance half is taken care of by the vicar; and the other half is raised by the Croesuses of the village, relieving the other villagers of the cost

* ["(I am a man); I consider none of the incidents that befall my fellow creatures to be a matter of unconcern to me." Terence, *The Self-Tormentor*, I, 1, 23.— TRANSLATOR.]

of providing their share, who nevertheless will be edified by the sermons.

Do these sacrifices invalidate our definition of value? Not in the least. Every man is free to render his services on his own terms. If the terms are extremely easy, or indeed gratis, what is the result? The *service* retains its utility, but loses its value. The old priest is convinced that his efforts will receive their reward in another world. He does not expect it here below. He knows, doubtless, that he renders his auditors a service by speaking to them; but he also thinks that they render him a service by listening to him. It follows that the transaction is made on a basis advantageous to one of the contracting parties, and with the consent of the other. That is all. In general, exchanges of services are motivated and evaluated by considerations of self-interest, but sometimes, thank Heaven, by the promptings of altruism. In such cases either we surrender to others satisfactions that we had the right to keep for ourselves, or we exert for them efforts that we could have devoted to ourselves. Generosity, loyalty, self-sacrifice are impulses of our nature that, like many other factors, influence the current *value* of a service contracted for, but do not change the general law of value.

In contrast to this reassuring example, I could introduce another of a quite different character. For a service to have value in the economic sense of the word, that is, actual value, it is not obligatory that the service be real, conscientiously rendered, or useful; all that is necessary is that it be accepted and paid for by a service in return. The world is full of people who foist upon the public and receive from it payment for services of highly questionable worth. Everything depends on the *judgment* passed on the services, and for that reason morality will always be the best auxiliary of political economy.

Some rogues succeed in spreading a false belief. They are, they say, the special emissaries of Heaven. They can open as they choose the gates of Paradise or of Hell. When this belief has taken root, they say, "Here are some little images to which we have given such power that they can make those who wear them happy through all eternity. Giving you one of these images is rendering you an immense *service;* give us, therefore, *services* in return."

This is a *created value*. It is based on an erroneous appraisal, you will say; that is true. The same can be said of many material things whose value is indisputable, for they would find purchasers if they were put up for auction. The science of economics would be impossible if it recognized as values only those values that are judiciously appraised. At every step it would be necessary to repeat a course in physics or the moral sciences. In the state of isolation, a man may, by reason of depraved desires or poor judgment, pursue with great effort an unreal satisfaction, a delusion. Similarly, in society, it happens, as a philosopher said, that sometimes we purchase our regrets at a very high price. If it is in the nature of human intelligence to be more disposed to truth than to error, all these frauds are destined to disappear, these false services to be refused, to lose their *value*. Civilization in the long run will put all things and all men in their proper place.

I must, however, terminate this overlengthy analysis. The wants of breathing, drinking, eating; the wants of vanity, of the mind, of the heart, of public opinion, of well-founded or groundless hopes—we have sought value in all of them, and we have discovered it wherever *services are exchanged*. We have found it to be everywhere of identical nature, based on a clear, simple, absolute principle, although affected by a multitude of varying circumstances. If we had passed all our other wants in review—if we had summoned the cabinetmaker, the mason, the manufacturer, the tailor, the doctor, the doorman, the lawyer, the businessman, the painter, the judge, the President of the Republic—we should have discovered nothing more: sometimes material things, sometimes forces furnished gratis by Nature, but always human services exchanged for other human services, being measured, estimated, appraised, *evaluated* by comparison with one another, and alone evidencing the result of this evaluation, that is, *value*.

There is, nevertheless, one of our wants of a very special nature, which binds our society together, which is both the cause and the effect of all our transactions and the perennial problem of political economy. I wish to say a few words about it. I mean the *want of exchanging.*

In the preceding chapter we described the marvelous effects of exchange. They are such that men are naturally disposed to facilitate exchange even at the price of great sacrifice. For that reason there are highways, canals, railroads, wagons, ships, businessmen, merchants, bankers; and it is impossible to believe that humanity, in order to facilitate exchange, would have subjected itself to such a tremendous levy on its energies if it had not found a large measure of compensation in the act of exchange.

We have also seen that simple *barter* could make possible nothing more than very inconvenient and limited transactions.

For this reason men thought of the idea of breaking up barter into two factors, *buying* and *selling*, through the medium of an intermediate commodity, easily divisible and, above all, possessing *value*, so that it would in its own right commend itself to the public's confidence. This commodity is money.

What I wish to note here is that what we call, by ellipsis or metonymy, the value of gold and silver, rests on the same principle as the value of air, water, the diamond, the sermons of our old missionary, or the trills of Mme. Malibran; that is, on services rendered or received.

Gold, which is widely distributed along the favored banks of the Sacramento, does indeed derive from Nature many of its desirable qualities: malleability, weight, beauty, brilliance, even utility, if you wish. But one thing Nature did not give gold, because Nature is not concerned with it, and that is value. A man knows that gold corresponds to a much felt want, that it is greatly desired. He goes to California to look for gold, just as my neighbor a little while ago went to the well to get water. He exerts strenuous efforts, he digs, he shovels, he washes away gravel, he melts the ore, and then comes to me and says, "I will do you the service of turning this gold over to you; what service will you render me in return?"

We discuss the matter; each one ponders over the factors that enter into the decision; at last we come to an agreement; and there we have value made manifest and definite. Deceived by the abbreviated expression, "Gold has value," we might well believe that gold contains value just as it does weight or malleability, and that Nature took the pains to place it there. I trust that the reader is now convinced that this is a misapprehension. He will become convinced later that it is a deplorable misapprehension.

There is also another error involving gold, or rather money. Since it is customarily the intermediate agent in all transactions, the mean term between the two extremes in *roundabout* or *indirect barter*, since its value is always the standard of comparison when two services are to be exchanged, it has become the *measure* of value. Practically, it cannot be otherwise. But our science should never lose sight of the fact that money, as far as value is concerned, is subject to the same fluctuations as any other product or service. Science does lose sight of this fact frequently, and it is not surprising. Everything seems to conspire to cause money to be considered the measure of value in the same sense that the litre is a measure of capacity. It plays an analogous role in transactions. We are not conscious of its fluctuations because the franc, along with its larger and smaller components, always retains the same denomination. And even arithmetical tables conspire to encourage the confusion by listing the franc, like a measure, alongside the metre, the litre, the are, the stere, the gramme, etc.

I have defined value, at least as I conceive it. I have subjected my definition to the test of various and sundry cases; no one of them, it seems to me, has disproved it. Finally, the scientific sense that I have given the word is in accord with common usage, a fact that constitutes no negligible advantage or trifling guarantee; for what is science except experience viewed in the light of reason? What is theory except the methodical presentation of universal practice?

The reader must permit me now to glance rapidly at the systems that have been accepted up to the present time. It is not in a spirit of controversy, and even less of criticism, that I undertake this survey, and I should gladly abandon it if I were not convinced that it can cast new light on the central thought of this book.

We have seen that writers on the subject have sought to locate the principle of value in one or more of the accidental phenomena that influence it greatly—physical composition (materiality), durability, utility, scarcity, labor, etc.—as a physiologist might seek to locate the principle of life in one or more of the external phenomena that encourage its development: air, water, sunlight, electricity, etc.

Physical Composition (Materiality) of Value

"Man," says M. de Bonald, "is an intellect served by bodily organs." If the economists of the materialistic school had merely tried to say that men can render one another services only through a physical medium, in order to conclude that there is always a material element in these services, and consequently in value, I should carry the matter no further, since I have always had a horror of those quibblings and subtleties in which our minds are only too prone to delight.

But this is not what they meant. They believed that value was communicated to matter, either by men's labor or by the action of Nature. In a word, deceived by the elliptical expressions, "Gold *is worth* so much," " wheat *is worth* so much," etc., they were led to see in matter a quality called *value,* as the physicist finds in it density and weight—and even these attributes have been questioned.

However that may be, I most positively question the attribution of value to it.

At the outset we must admit that matter and value are rarely separated. When we say to a man, "Deliver this letter," "Fetch me some water," "Teach me this science or that technique," "Give me advice on my illness or my lawsuit," "Guard my safety while I work or sleep," what we ask for is a service, and in this service we recognize, before the whole world, that there is value, since we willingly pay for it with an *equivalent* service. It would be strange if we should refuse to admit in theory what universal assent admits in practice.

It is true that our transactions often involve material objects;

but what does this prove? It proves that men, by exercising fore-sight, often get ready to render services that they know will be asked of them. Whether I buy a suit ready-made or bring in a tailor to work at my house by the day, in what respect does this change the principle of value, particularly to the extent of making it reside at one time in the suit and at another time in the service?

Here we could ask a subtle question: Must we see the principle of value in the material object, and therefore, by analogy, attribute it to the service? I maintain that it is just the contrary; we must recognize that it is in the services, and then attribute it, if you will, by metonymy, to the material object.

Besides, the numerous examples that I have presented to the reader relieve me of the necessity of carrying this discussion further. But I cannot refrain from trying to justify myself for having brought it up, by showing to what dangerous conclusions we can be led by an error, or, if you prefer, by a half-truth, that we encounter at the beginning of our scientific study.

The least of the drawbacks to the definition that I am assailing is that it has mutilated and stunted political economy. If value is attributed to matter, then, where there is no matter there is no value. Thus, the physiocrats used the term "sterile" classes to designate three-fourths of the population, while Adam Smith softened it to "unproductive" classes.

And yet, since in the last analysis facts are stronger than definitions, these classes simply had to be brought back, by some route or other, into the orbit of economic study. The materialists did it by way of analogy; but their scientific language, created for other data, was already so materialistic in tone that the analogies they used resulted in a shocking extension of the meaning of their terms. What do such phrases as these mean: *To consume an immaterial product? Man is accumulated capital? Security is a commodity?*

They not only made their language a materialistic jargon, but **they** were also reduced to overloading it with subtle distinctions in their attempt to reconcile ideas that they had erroneously separated. They invented *value in use* in contrast *to value in exchange.*

Finally, and this is a serious error indeed, the concepts of the two great social phenomena, *private property* and *the communal domain,* were so confused that the former could not be justified, and the latter could not be discerned.

In point of fact, if value resides in matter, then it is mixed with those other physical qualities of an object that constitute its usefulness to man. Now, these qualities are often placed in the object by Nature. Therefore, Nature helps to create *value,* and hence we must attribute value to those things that in essence are *free of charge* and *common to all.* Where, then, is the basis of property to be found? When the payment that I make to acquire a material product, wheat, for example, is distributed to all the workers who, in its production, have rendered me *services,* who should receive the share corresponding to the amount of value that is due to Nature and that man had nothing to do with? Should it be paid to God? Nobody supports this idea, and God has never been known to claim His wages. Should it be paid to a man? On what grounds, since, according to the hypothesis that value resides in matter, he has done nothing to earn it?

Let no one think that I am exaggerating, that in the interest of my own definition I am trying to force the economists' definition to its rigorously logical conclusions. On the contrary: they themselves very explicitly have drawn these conclusions under the pressure of logic.

Thus, Senior has gone so far as to say: "Those who have appropriated the resources of Nature receive compensation in the form of rent without having made any sacrifices. Their role consists merely of holding out their hands for contributions from the rest of the community." Scrope asserts: * "Ownership of land is an artificial restriction placed on the enjoyment of the gifts that God had intended to be used for the satisfaction of the wants of all men." Say affirms: "It would *seem* that arable land should be counted as natural wealth, since it is not of human creation but is given gratis to man by Nature. But as this wealth is not fugitive

* [George Poulett Scrope (1797–1876), English economist and geologist, prolific writer of pamphlets, particularly in refutation of the Malthusian theory.— TRANSLATOR.]

like air or water, since a field is a fixed and circumscribed area that *certain* men *have managed* to appropriate to themselves, excluding all other men who have given assent to the appropriation, land, which was a gratuitous asset of Nature, has *become* social wealth, which *must be* paid for if used."

Certainly, if this is true, Proudhon* was right in asking this terrible question, to which he gives an answer more terrible yet:

"To whom should the rent of the land be paid? To the one who produced the land, of course. Who made the land? God. In that case, landowner, withdraw."

Yes, through a faulty definition, political economy has put logic on the side of the socialists. It is a terrible weapon, but I shall break it in their hands, or rather, they shall gladly surrender it to me. Nothing will remain of their conclusions after I have destroyed their original principle. And I propose to prove that, while Nature combines with man's acts to produce wealth, yet what Nature does remains free of charge and common to all by its very essence, and only what man does represents *services, value;* it alone requires payment; it alone is the foundation, the explanation, and the justification of private property. In a word, I maintain that, in their relation to one another, men are owners only of the value of things; and that, as they pass products from hand to hand, what they bargain for is only value, that is, reciprocal services, adding as a gratuitous gift, into the bargain, all the qualities, properties, and utilities imparted to these products by Nature.

If political economists, by misunderstanding this fundamental consideration, have weakened the theoretical basis of the defense of the right to private property, representing it as an unnatural institution, necessary, but unjust, they have at the same time neglected and left completely unnoticed another admirable phenomenon, the most moving evidence of God's bountiful Provi-

---

* [Pierre-Joseph Proudhon (1809–1865), French social theorist and experimenter, a prolific writer on political and economic questions, for the most part radical or anarchistic in viewpoint. Bastiat and he had a fiery controversy over his proposal of loans without interest.—TRANSLATOR.]

dence toward His creature, man, namely, the phenomenon of the *progressive trend toward more and more gratuitous and common utility.*

Wealth (taking this word in its generally accepted sense) stems from the combination of two kinds of operations, those of Nature and those of man. The former are *free of charge* and *common to all,* by divine gift, and never cease to be so. The latter alone *possess value,* and consequently they alone can be *claimed as private property.* But in the course of the development of human intelligence and the progress of civilization, the action of Nature plays a larger and larger role in the creation of any given utility, and the action of man, a proportionately smaller one. Hence, it follows that the area of gratuitous and common utility constantly increases among men at the expense of the area of value and private property—a fruitful and reassuring observation that is entirely lost sight of as long as political economists attribute any value to the action of Nature.

In all religions God is thanked for His bounty. The father blesses the bread that he breaks and gives to his children—a moving tradition that would not be justified if the blessings of Providence were not given gratis.

Durability of Value

Durability, that so-called *sine qua non* of value, is connected with what I have just discussed. For value to exist, Adam Smith believed, it must be fixed in some object that can be exchanged, accumulated, preserved—consequently in something *material.*

"There is one kind of labor," he says, "that increases [1] the value of the object on which it is expended. There is another kind that does not have this effect."

"The labor that goes into manufactured goods," Smith adds, "is fixed and takes concrete form in some salable article of merchandise, which lasts *at least for some time* after the work is completed. The work of servants, on the contrary [and the author lists soldiers, magistrates, musicians, teachers, etc., under this heading] is not fixed in any salable merchandise. The services disappear as rapidly as they are performed and leave no trace of value behind them."

We see that it is implied here that value refers to the modification of things rather than to men's satisfactions. This is a colossal error; for if it is good that the form of things be modified, it is solely in order to attain the satisfaction that is the goal, the end, the *consummation* of all effort. If, then, we achieve the satisfaction by immediate and direct effort, the result is the same; if, moreover, the effort can be transferred, exchanged, evaluated, it contains the principle of *value*.

As for the time interval between the effort and the satisfaction, Smith gives it too much importance when he says that the existence or nonexistence of value depends on it. "The value of an article of salable merchandise," he says, *"lasts at least for some time."*

Yes, indubitably, it lasts until the article has fulfilled its function, i.e., to satisfy a want, which is exactly the case with a service. As long as this dish of strawberries stays on the side table, it will retain its value. But why? Because it is the result of a service I decided to render myself or that others rendered me in consideration of payment, and a service *of which I have not yet availed myself*. As soon as I avail myself of it, by eating the strawberries, the value will disappear. *The service will have vanished, leaving no trace of value behind it.* Exactly the same thing holds true of a personal service. The consumer causes the value to vanish, because it was created for this end. It makes little difference to the notion of value whether the pains taken today satisfy a want immediately or tomorrow or next year.

Suppose I am afflicted with a cataract. I call an oculist. The instrument he uses has *value,* because it is durable, but not the operation, although I pay for it, argue about the fee, and even compare it with the fees of other oculists! But such an assumption is contrary to the most ordinary facts, the most widely accepted notions; and what kind of theory is it that, when it cannot explain universal practice, dismisses it as of no account?

I beg the reader to believe that I am not allowing myself to be carried away by undue love of controversy. If I dwell on certain elementary ideas, I do so in order to prepare the way for most important conclusions that will be evident later. I do not know whether or not I am violating the laws of method by anticipating these conclusions, but in any case I permit myself this minor infraction for fear of trying the reader's patience. For this reason at an earlier point in my book I referred in an anticipatory way to *private property* and *common utility*. For the same reason I shall now say a word about *capital*.

Adam Smith, who made wealth an attribute of matter, could conceive of capital only as an accumulation of material objects. How, then, can value be assigned to services that cannot be accumulated or turned into capital?

Among those things called capital goods we place tools, machines, industrial equipment, at the head of the list. They serve to apply the forces of Nature to the work of production, and since the power of creating value was attributed to these forces, economists were led to believe that these tools of production, *in themselves,* possessed the same faculty, independently of any human service. Thus, the spade, the plow, the steam engine, were supposed to work together simultaneously with natural resources and human forces in creating not only utility, but value as well. But all value is paid for in exchange. Who, then, was to be paid for that part of value which is independent of human service?

It is for this reason that Proudhon's school, after questioning the legitimacy of *land rent,* is led to question *interest on capital* as well—a broader concept, since it embraces the first. I maintain that the Proudhon fallacy, from the scientific point of view, has its origins in Smith's. I shall show that capital, like natural resources, taken by itself and in reference to its own action, creates utility, but never value. Value, in its essence, is the product of a legitimate *service.* I shall show also that, in the social order, capital is not an accumulation of material objects, dependent on the durability of matter, but an accumulation of *values,* that is, of *services.* Hence, this recent attack on the idea of the productivity of capital will be repulsed—virtually at least, by destroying its foundation —and, moreover, in a way that should fully satisfy the very people who instigated it; for if I prove that the phenomenon of exchange is nothing but a *system of mutual services,* M. Proudhon must own himself beaten by the very triumph of his own principle.

Labor

Adam Smith and his disciples have ascribed value to labor under the condition of materiality. This is contradictory to their other theory that the forces of Nature have some share in the production of value. I have no need here to refute the contradictions that are evident in all their unfortunate conclusions when these authors speak of land rent or of interest on capital.

However this may be, in finding the principle of value in labor, they would be coming quite close to the truth if they did not make reference to manual labor. I said, in fact, at the beginning of this chapter that value must be related to effort, an expression that I preferred to "labor," since it is more general and includes the whole area of human activity. But I hastened to add that it could have its source only in efforts that were exchanged, or reciprocal services, because it is not something existing by itself, but solely as an expression of a relationship.

There are, then, strictly speaking, two flaws in Smith's definition. The first is that it does not take exchange into account, without which value can neither be created nor conceived of; the second, that it uses a word, "labor," which is too narrow in its meaning, unless that meaning is extended beyond its normal limits to include not only the degree of intensity and the length of time expended, but also the skill and sagacity of the worker, and even the good or bad fortune he happens to encounter.

Note that the word "service," which I substitute in the definition, eliminates these two flaws. It necessarily implies the idea of transmission, since a service cannot be rendered unless it is received; and it also implies the idea of an effort without assuming a corresponding amount of value.

Here is where the English economists' definition fails most seriously. To say that value resides in labor is to suggest that the two are in a reciprocal relation, that there is a direct proportion between them. In this respect, the definition is contrary to the facts, and a definition contrary to the facts is a faulty one.

Very frequently a piece of work that is considered insignificant in itself is accepted by the world as having tremendous *value* (examples: the diamond, a prima donna's singing, a few strokes of a banker's pen, a shipper's lucky speculation, the lines of a Raphael's brush, a papal bull of indulgence, the easy duties of a queen of England, etc.); even more frequently a slow, exhausting task ends in disappointment, in a nonvalue. If such is the case, how can we establish a correlation, a fixed ratio, between *value* and *labor?*

My definition eliminates the difficulty. It is obvious that there are circumstances under which one may render a great service that does not require great pains; others under which, after taking great pains, one finds that no *service* has been rendered to anyone, and therefore it is more exact, from this point of view also, to say that value resides in service rather than in labor, since it exists in direct proportion to the former and not to the latter.

I go further. I maintain that value is appraised at least as much in consideration of the labor it can spare the user as of the labor it has cost the producer. I ask the reader to be good enough to recall the dialogue between the two contracting parties in the negotiations over the diamond. It was not prompted by exceptional circumstances, and I venture to say that in substance it is at the heart of all transactions. It must not be forgotten that we are assuming that the two contracting parties have complete freedom to exercise their will and judgment. Each of them is induced to agree to the exchange for various reasons, first among them, certainly, being the difficulty that the recipient of the diamond would experience in obtaining directly the satisfaction that the other offers him. This difficulty is taken into account by both parties, making the one more or less conciliatory and the other more or less exacting. The pains that the one offering the diamond went to also influence the negotiation; it is one of the elements, but not the only one. Therefore, it is not exactly correct to say that value is determined by labor. Value is determined by a great many considerations, all included in the word "service."

It is very true that, under the influence of competition, values *tend* to be related efforts, or the rewards to the deserts. This is one of the beautiful harmonies of the social order. But, as far as value is concerned, this leveling tendency exerted by competition is entirely extraneous; and sound logic does not permit us to confuse the influence exerted on a phenomenon by an extraneous element with the phenomenon itself.[2]

Utility

Jean-Baptiste Say, unless I am mistaken, was the first writer to shake off the yoke of the concept of the *materiality* of value. Very explicitly he made value a *moral quality*—an expression that perhaps overshoots the mark, for value is neither physical nor moral; it is simply a relationship.

But the great French economist had himself said, "It is not granted to any man to arrive at the outermost limits of knowledge. Scholars climb upon one another's shoulders to explore a horizon that keeps on extending farther and farther." Perhaps Say's glory (as far as the present question is concerned, for in other respects his claims to fame are as numerous as they are imperishable) is to have passed on to his successors a fruitful insight into the subject.

Say's axiom was this: *The basis of value is utility.*

If it were a question here of utility as related to human services, I should have no argument with him. At the very most I could say that the axiom is so self-evident as to be superfluous. It is quite clear that no one consents to pay for a *service* unless, rightly or wrongly, he considers it useful. The word *service* is so completely included in the idea of *utility* that it is simply the translation, and even the literal carrying over, of the Latin word *uti*, to *serve.*

But, unfortunately, this is not the way Say meant it. He found the principle of value not only in human services rendered through the medium of things, but also in the *useful* qualities that Nature imparts to things. By so doing, he again placed upon his neck the yoke of materiality, and, we must add, he did nothing to tear away the harmful veil that the English economists had thrown over the question of private property.

Before discussing Say's axiom on its own merits, I must indicate what its logical implications are, so as to avoid the reproach that I involved myself and the reader in a tedious dissertation.

There can be no doubt that the utility Say speaks of is the utility that resides in material things. If wheat, wood, coal, cloth have value, it is because these products have qualities that fit them for our use, to satisfy our need to be fed, warmed, clothed.

This being the case, since Nature creates *utility,* it also creates *value*—a most harmful confusion of ideas that the enemies of private property have forged into a terrible weapon.

Suppose I buy a product—wheat, for example—at the market for sixteen francs. A large part of the sixteen francs is distributed, through countless ramifications, through an inestimable maze of advances and repayments, among all the men, far and near, who have helped to put the wheat at my disposal. There is something for the man who plowed the field, the man who sowed the seed, who reaped the crop, who threshed the grain, who carted it away, as well as for the smith and the wagoner who made the equipment. Up to this point there is no disagreement, whether one is an economist or a communist.

But I perceive that four of my sixteen francs go to the owner of the land, and I have every right to ask whether this man, like all the others, has rendered me a service assuring him, like all the others, an unquestioned right to compensation.

According to the doctrine that it is the purpose of this book to establish, the answer is categorical. It is a very emphatic *yes.* Yes, the owner has rendered me a service. What is it? It consists in the fact that he or his ancestor has cleared the land and fenced it off; he has cleared out the weeds and drained off the stagnant water; he has fertilized the vegetable garden; he has built a house, barns, and stables. All this represents long hours of labor that he has performed himself or, what amounts to the same thing, paid others to perform for him. These are certainly services for which, by virtue of the just law of reciprocity, he should be reimbursed. Now, this owner has never been remunerated, at least to the full extent. Nor could he be, since he could not charge the whole amount to the first man who came along and bought a bushel of wheat. What, then, is the arrangement that has been worked out? Truly, the most ingenious, the most legitimate, and the most equitable in the world. It is this: Whoever wishes to buy a sack of wheat will pay not only for the services of the workers we have just enumerated but also for a small part of the *services* rendered by the owner; in other words, the *value* of the owner's services will be distributed over all the sacks of wheat that come from this field.

Now, we may ask whether this remuneration, set here at four francs, is too much or too little. I reply: This question does not concern the science of political economy, which notes that the value of the services of the owner of real property is governed by exactly the same laws as all other services; and that is sufficient.

Some may object that this system of piecemeal reimbursement would eventually result in the complete amortization of the owner's outlay, and consequently should lead to the cancelation of his property rights. Those who make this objection are not aware that it is the nature of capital to produce perpetual income, as we shall learn later.

For the moment, however, I must not stray longer from the subject, and I shall observe (for this is the gist of the matter) that out of my sixteen francs there is not a centime that is not used to pay for human services, that there is not one that corresponds to the so-called *value* that Nature is supposed to have imparted to the wheat by giving it *utility*.

But, if, basing your argument on the axiom of Say and the English economists, you assert, "Out of the sixteen francs, twelve go to the plowmen, sowers, reapers, wagon-drivers, etc.; two to pay for the owner's personal services; then two others represent a value that has as its basis the *utility* created by God, by natural resources, without any human co-operation"; do you not see that you will at once be asked, "Who is to profit from this part of *value?* Who has a right to this remuneration? God does not come forward to claim it. Who will dare stand in His place?"

The more Say tries to explain private property according to this hypothesis, the more vulnerable his position becomes. First, quite properly, he compares the land to a laboratory where chemical experiments are conducted with results useful to mankind. "The land," he adds, "is therefore the *producer of a utility,* and when *it* [the land] exacts payment in the form of a profit or a rent for the *owner,* it has indeed given something to the consumer in return for what the consumer gives it. It has given him a utility that it has produced, and because it has produced this utility, *the land is just as productive as labor is.*"

Thus, the assertion is clear-cut. Here are two claimants who come forward to divide the payment the consumer owes for the wheat, namely, land and labor. They have identical rights, for the land, says Say, is just as productive as labor is. Labor demands payment for a *service,* the land for a *utility;* yet the land does not request the payment for itself (under what form could it be made?), but for *its owner.*

Whereupon Proudhon summons the owner, who calls himself the land's authorized agent, to produce his credentials.*

You tell me to pay you, in other words, to render you a service, says Proudhon, for receiving *utility* produced by natural resources, without assistance from man, who has already been paid separately.

But I insist on asking: Who will profit from my payment, that is, my services?

Will it be the producer of the utility, that is, the land? That is absurd, and I can bide my time quite easily until the land sends the bailiff after me.

Will it be a man? On what grounds? If it is for having rendered me a service, well and good. But in that case you share my point of view. Human service is the thing that *has value,* not Nature's; that is the conclusion to which I wished to lead you.

However, that is contrary to your own hypothesis. You say that the human services are paid fourteen francs, and that the two francs that complete the payment for the wheat correspond to the value created by Nature. In that case, I repeat my question:

* [Cf. chap. 9, p. 252.—TRANSLATOR.]

By what right can any man lay claim to them? And is it not unfortunately only too clear that, if you apply specifically the name of *landowner* to the man who claims the two francs, you are justifying that too-famous maxim: *Property is theft?*

And let no one think that this confusion between utility and value is limited to undermining the foundations of real property. After questioning the legitimacy of the idea of land rent, it leads also to questioning interest on capital.

Machines, tools of production, are, in fact, like the land, producers of *utility*. If this utility has *value,* it must be paid for; for the word "value" implies a right to payment. But to whom is it paid? To the owner of the machine, of course. Is it for a personal service? Then simply say that the value is in the service. But if you say that there must be first a payment for the service, and then a second for the utility produced by the machine, independently of any human action already paid for, we ask you to whom does this second payment go, and how can the man who has already been paid for all his services have the right to demand something more?

The truth is that the utility produced by Nature is *free of charge,* and therefore *common to all,* just like the utility produced by the tools of production. It is free of charge and common to all on one condition: that we take the pains, that we perform the service, of helping ourselves to it; or, if we ask someone else to take the pains or perform the service for us, that we render him an equivalent service in return. The value resides in these comparative services, and not at all in the natural utility. The pains can be great or small, a fact that changes the value, but not the utility. When we are near a gushing spring, the water is free to all, provided we are willing to stoop down to get it. If we commission a neighbor to go to this trouble for us, then I see an agreement, a bargain, a *value,* but the water remains free of charge, nevertheless. If we are an hour's distance from the spring, the terms of the bargain will be different in degree, but not in principle. Value will not on that account have passed into the water or into its utility. The water will continue to be *free of charge* on condition that we go and get it or pay those who, after free bargaining, consent to spare us this trouble by assuming it themselves.

The same holds true for everything. Utilities are everywhere about us, *but we have to stoop to pick them up.* This effort, sometimes very simple, is often very complicated. Nothing is easier, in most cases, than helping ourselves to water, whose utility has been prepared by Nature. It is not so easy to gather in wheat, whose utility has also been prepared by Nature. That is why the value of these two efforts differs in degree, but not in principle. The service is more or less exacting; consequently, it *is worth* more or less. The utility is and always remains *free of charge.*

Suppose a tool of production is introduced, what then is the result? The utility is more easily made available. Therefore, the service has less *value.* We certainly pay less for books since the invention of printing. An admirable and misunderstood phenomenon! You say that tools of production produce value. You are wrong. You should rather say that it is utility, and gratuitous utility, that they produce; as for value, far from producing any, they progressively destroy it.

It is true that the maker of the machine has rendered a service. He receives a remuneration that increases the value of the product. It is for this reason that we are inclined to think that we pay for the utility produced by the machine, but this is a delusion. We pay for the *services* contributed by all those who had a part in making it or operating it. So little value resides in the utility that has been produced that, even after we have paid for the new services, we obtain the utility on better terms than before.

Let us, then, learn to distinguish between utility and value. An understanding of the science of economics comes only at this price. I maintain, without fear of indulging in paradox, that the ideas of utility and value, far from being identical or even reconcilable, are opposites. Want, effort, satisfaction—this, we have said, is man from the economic point of view. Utility is related to want and satisfaction. Value is related to effort. Utility is the good that terminates want with satisfaction. Value is the evil, for it is born of the obstacle that intervenes between want and satisfaction. If it were not for obstacles, there would be no efforts to be made or exchanged; utility would be infinite, *unconditionally* free of charge and common to all, and the notion of value would never have been brought into the world. Because of the presence of obstacles, utility is free of charge only on condition that there be an exchange of efforts, which, when compared with one another, constitute value. The more obstacles are reduced by the bounty of Nature or the progress of science, the nearer utility comes to being absolutely free of charge and common to all; for the cost in terms of effort and, consequently, the value decrease along with the obstacles. I should consider myself fortunate indeed if, through all these dissertations, which may well appear unnecessarily subtle, which fill me with misgivings because of their length and at the same time because of their conciseness, I should succeed in gaining acceptance for this reassuring truth: *Private ownership of value is legitimate;* and this other comforting truth: *Utility tends constantly to become the gratuitous and common possession of all.*

Still another observation: Everything that *serves* us is *useful (uti,* "to serve"). Accordingly, it is highly doubtful whether anything exists in the universe, whether force or matter, that is not *useful* to man.

In any case, we can affirm, without fear of being mistaken, that countless things are useful to us without our being aware of the fact. If the moon were placed higher or lower in the heavens, it is quite possible that the mineral kingdom, consequently the vegetable kingdom, and consequently also the animal kingdom, would be profoundly modified. If it were not for this star shining so brightly in the sky as I write, perhaps the human race could not exist. Nature has surrounded us with utilities. We recognize this quality of being *useful* in many substances and phenomena; science and experience reveal it to us in others every day; in still others it exists, though completely and perhaps for all time unknown to us.

When these substances and these phenomena exert their useful action upon us, but *without our agency,* we have no interest in comparing the degree of utility they have for us; and, what is more to the point, we hardly have the means of doing so. We know that oxygen and nitrogen are useful to us, but we do not try, and should probably try in vain, to determine in what proportion. They do not furnish us with the elements necessary for evaluation, for value. I could say the same thing for the salts, the gases, the forces that abound throughout Nature. When all these agents move and combine so as to produce utility for us, but *without our contributing to it,* we enjoy this utility without *evaluating it.* When our co-operation is introduced and, above all, is exchanged, then and only then appraisal and value make their appearance, but they are applied to our co-operation, not to the utility of substances or phenomena of which we are frequently ignorant.

That is why I say: Value is the appraisal of services exchanged. These services may be very complex. They may have required vast amounts and various types of labor in times remote or recent. They may be transmitted from one hemisphere or generation to another hemisphere or generation, involving numerous contracting parties, necessitating credits, the advancing of funds, varied arrangements, before the general balance is arrived at. Yet the principle of *value* always resides in them, and not in the utility of which they are the vehicle, a utility which is essentially free of charge, which passes from hand to hand *into the bargain,* if I may be permitted the expression.

After all, if anyone persists in attributing the basis of value to utility, I have no quarrel with him; but let it be well understood that we do not mean that utility which is in things and phenomena by the gift of Providence or the power of science, but the utility of human services compared and exchanged.

Scarcity

According to Senior, of all the circumstances that influence value, scarcity is the most decisive. I have no objection to make to this remark, unless it is that by its form it assumes that value is inherent in things—an hypothesis that I will challenge if it is even hinted at. Fundamentally, the word "scarcity," as used in connection with the subject with which we are dealing, expresses in abridged form this idea: Other things being equal, a service has greater value according to the difficulty we should experience in performing it for ourselves, and consequently, according to the more exacting terms we encounter when we ask someone else to do it for us. Scarcity is one of these difficulties. It is one more *obstacle* to surmount. The greater it is, the more we pay those who surmount it for us. Scarcity often occasions very high remunerations; and that is why I refused to agree a little earlier in this work with the English economists' position that value is in direct proportion to labor. We must take into account Nature's miserliness toward us in certain respects. The word "service" embraces all these meanings and shades of meaning.

Judgment

Storch attributes *value* to the judgment that enables us to discern it. Of course, every time we are confronted with a question of the relation between two things, we must compare and *judge*. Nevertheless, the relation is one thing, and the judgment we pass on it is another. When we compare the height of two trees, their heights and the difference between their heights are distinct from our evaluation of them.

But in determining value, what is the relation that we are to judge? It is the relation between two services that are exchanged. It is a question of knowing, when services are rendered and received, what is the *value* of the one in respect to the other. It is a question of knowing, when services, involving the transfer of acts or the exchange of things, are rendered and received, what the one *is worth* in respect to the other, keeping in mind all the circumstances, rather than concerning ourselves with the amount of intrinsic utility these acts or these things may contain; for this utility may fall partially outside the realm of human activity and therefore outside the realm of *value*.

Storch is not aware of the fundamental error that I am attacking, when he says:

"Our judgment enables us to discern the relation that exists between our wants and the *utility* of things. The verdict that our judgment pronounces on the *utility of things* constitutes their value."

And, further on:

"In order to create value, three circumstances must coincide: (1) Man experiences, or conceives, a want. (2) Something exists that is capable of satisfying the want. (3) His judgment pronounces a favorable verdict on the utility of the thing. Hence, the value of things is their relative *utility*."

During the daylight hours I experience the want of seeing clearly. Something exists that is capable of satisfying the want, sunlight. My judgment pronounces a favorable verdict on this thing's utility, and . . . . it has no value. Why? Because I enjoy it without having to ask a service from anyone.

At night I experience the same want. Something exists that is capable of satisfying it very imperfectly, a candle. My judgment pronounces a verdict on the utility, but on the relatively slight utility of this thing, and it has *value*. Why? Because the person who took the pains to make the candle is unwilling to render me the service of letting me have it unless I render him an equivalent service.

What we must compare and judge, to determine value, is not, therefore, the *relative utility* of the things, but the relation between the two services.

Expressed in these terms, I do not reject Storch's definition.

Let us summarize briefly to show that my definition includes all that is true in my predecessors' definitions and corrects all that is erroneous through their inclusion of too much or too little.

The principle of value, as I have said, resides in a human service. It is derived from the appraisal and comparison of two services. Value must be connected to effort. Service implies an effort of some sort. It supposes a comparison of efforts that are exchanged, or at least exchangeable. Service implies the term *giving* and *receiving*.

In fact, however, it is not proportional to intensity of effort. *Service* does not necessarily imply such a proportion.

Many outside circumstances influence value without becoming

value themselves. The word "service" takes all these circumstances into account in their proper measure.

Materiality

When the service consists of the transfer of a material object, there is no reason for not saying, by metonymy, that the object *has value*. But we must not lose sight of the fact that this is a mere trope, or figure of speech, by which we attribute to the object the value arising from the services connected with it.

Durability

Whether having materiality or not, value lasts until the want is satisfied, and no longer. Its nature is not changed by any time gap, great or small, arising between the exerting of the effort and the satisfying of the want, nor by the kind of service, whether personal or including material commodities.

Accumulation

What can be accumulated by saving, in the social order, is not things, but value, or services.[3]

Utility

I agree with Say that utility is the basis of value, provided that we mean the relative utility of services, not the utility that resides in things.

Labor

I agree with Ricardo that labor is the basis of value, provided first that we take the word "labor" in its most general sense, and, second, that we do not give it a ratio to value out of keeping with all the facts; in other words, provided we substitute the word "service" for the word "labor."

Scarcity

I agree with Senior that scarcity influences *value*. But why? Because it makes *service* all the more valuable.

Judgment

I agree with Storch that value results from an act of judgment, provided that we mean the judgment that we pass on the utility of *services*, not on the utility of things.

Thus, economists of all persuasions should own themselves satisfied. I say that all are right, because all have glimpsed one side of the truth. Error, to be sure, lay on the other side. The reader must decide whether my definition takes into account the whole truth and rejects all the errors.

I must not conclude without saying a word about that economic equivalent of the squaring of a circle: *the measure of value;* and here I shall repeat, even more emphatically, the observation that ends the preceding chapters.

I said that our wants, our desires, our tastes, have no limits or exact measure.

I said that our means of satisfying them, the gifts of Nature, our faculties, our activity, foresight, discernment, have no exact measure. Each one of these elements is itself a variable quantity; it differs from man to man, and within each individual it differs from minute to minute, thus forming in its entirety what is the very essence of variability.

If, now, we consider what the circumstances are that influence value, such as utility, labor, scarcity, judgment, and if we realize that there is not one of these that does not vary infinitely, how can we stubbornly persist in seeking a fixed measure of value?

It would be strange indeed if we should find fixity in a mean term composed of variable elements, in a mean term that is merely a relation between two extremes more variable still!

Economists who seek *an absolute measure of value* are there-

fore pursuing a will-o'-the-wisp, and, not only that, something
entirely useless. By universal practice gold and silver have been
adopted as this measure, even though their variability has not
gone unrecognized. But of what importance is the variability
of the measure, if, since it affects in like manner the two objects
that are exchanged, it does not alter the fairness of the exchange?
It is a *mean proportional,* which can rise or fall, without on that
account failing in its purpose, which is to register exactly the
relation that exists between the two extremes.

The science of political economy does not, like exchange, have
as its goal the establishment of the *current ratio between two
services,* for in that case money would suffice. What it does seek
to establish is the *ratio of effort to satisfaction;* and, in this respect,
a measure of value, even if it existed, would tell us nothing; for
effort, in attaining its satisfaction, always employs a variable
amount of gratuitous utility that has no value. It is because this
element of social well-being has been lost sight of that writers have
deplored the absence of a measure of value. They have failed to
realize that the measure would in no wise answer the question
propounded: What is the relative wealth, or prosperity, of two
classes, two nations, two generations?

To solve this question, political economy needs a measure
capable of showing, not the *relation between two services,* which
can serve as the vehicle for transmitting greatly varying amounts
of gratuitous utility, but the *relation between effort and satisfaction;* and this measure could only be effort, or labor, itself.

But how can labor serve as a measure? Is it not itself one of
the most variable of elements? Is it not characterized by varying
degrees of skill, physical exertion, uncertainty, danger, distaste-
fulness? Does it not have to be complemented by certain intellectual faculties and moral virtues? Does it not, by reason of all
these circumstances, lead to infinitely varied amounts of
remuneration?

There is one kind of labor that in all times, in all places, is
identical with itself, and this is the one that must serve as the
norm. It is the simplest, the crudest, the most primitive, the most

muscular, the one most lacking in help from Nature's resources, the one every man can perform, which renders those services that each can render to himself, which requires neither exceptional strength nor skill nor apprenticeship—work of the kind performed by the first members of the human race, that, in a word, of the simple day laborer. This kind of work is always the most plentiful, the least specialized, the most uniform, and the least well paid. All wages are scaled and graded with this as a base; when circumstances are favorable to day labor, the rate of other wages increases also.

If, then, we wish to compare two societies, we must not turn to a *measure of value,* for two most logical reasons: first, because none exists; second, because if one did exist, it would give us only a wrong answer to our question, an answer that would ignore an important factor contributing to progress in human well-being: gratuitous utility.

What we must do, on the contrary, is to forget value completely, especially money, and ask: In a given country, at a given time, how much special utility of every category is there, and how does the sum total of all these utilities relate to a given amount of unskilled labor? In other words: How much comfort and well-being can the ordinary day laborer obtain in exchange for his services?

We may say that the natural social order is perfectible and harmonious if, on the one hand, the number of men engaged in unskilled labor and receiving the lowest possible wages is continually decreasing, and if, on the other, these wages, measured, not in value or in money, but in material satisfactions, are continually increasing.[4]

The ancients well described all the possible combinations of exchange: *Do ut des* (product exchanged for product), *do ut facias* (product for service), *facio ut des* (service for product), *facio ut facias* (service for service).*

* [These Latin phrases mean: "I give to you that you may give to me." "I give to you that you may do for me." "I do for you that you may give to me." "I do for you that you may do for me."—Translator.]

Since products and services are interchanged, they must necessarily have something in common, something against which they can be compared and appraised, namely, *value*.

But value is always identical with itself. Whether in a product or in a service, it has the same origin, the same cause.

This being the case, does value exist originally, essentially, in the *product,* and is the notion that it exists also in the *service* an extension, by analogy, of its meaning?

Or rather, on the contrary, does value reside in the service, and is it incorporated in the product solely and precisely because the service itself is incorporated in the product?

Some persons seem to think that this question is merely a quibble. We shall see about that presently. For the time being I shall say only that it would be strange if in political economy a good or a bad definition of value were a matter of indifference.

It appears indubitable that originally political economists believed that value resided in the product, and, more than that, in the *material* of the product. The physiocrats attributed value exclusively to the land and called all classes *sterile* that added nothing to matter; so closely in their eyes were *matter* and *value* linked together.

It would seem that Adam Smith should have refuted this notion, since he derived *value* from *labor.* Do not nonmaterial services require labor, and therefore do they not imply value? Though so near the truth, Smith did not grasp it; for, in addition to saying emphatically that, for labor to have value, it must be applied to matter, something physically tangible and capable of accumulation, we all know that, like the physiocrats, he puts on the unproductive list all those classes of society whose activity is limited to services.

Smith does, in fact, devote a great deal of attention to these classes in his treatise on wealth *(The Wealth of Nations).* But does this not merely prove that, after formulating his definition, he found it cramping, and, that consequently, his definition was wrong? Smith would not have won his great and just renown if he had not written his magnificent chapters on education, the clergy, public services, and if, in writing on wealth, he had confined himself within the limits of his definition. Happily he escaped, by being inconsistent, from the yoke of his own premises. This is the way it always happens. A man of genius, when he starts from a false premise, never escapes the charge of inconsistency; without it, his views would become increasingly absurd, and, far from being a man of genius, he would not even be a man of ordinary intelligence.

Just as Smith went a step beyond the physiocrats, so Say went a step farther than Smith. Little by little, Say came to recognize that value resides in services, but only by analogy, by extension. He attributed value in its true essence to products, and nothing proves this better than the bizarre heading under which he listed services: "nonmaterial products," two words that clash stridently when put together. Say started from Smith's premises, as is proved by the fact that the full theory of the master is found related in the first ten lines of the works of the disciple.[5] But he thought deeply, and his thinking progressed during the next thirty years. Thus, he came nearer the truth, but he never reached it.

Moreover, we could well believe that he fulfilled his mission as an economist, enlarging, as he did, the notion of value so as to include services as well as products, and tracing its transmission through services to products, if the socialists' propaganda, which was founded on his own deductions, had not come to reveal the shortcomings and dangers of his fundamental hypothesis.

Suppose, then, that I were asked this question: Since certain products have value, since certain services also have value, and since value, being always identical wherever found, can have only one origin, one cause, one identical explanation; is this origin, this explanation, to be found in products or in services?

I declare confidently, the answer is not for an instant doubtful, and for this irrefutable reason: for a product to have value, a service is implied; whereas a service does not necessarily imply a product.

This answer seems to me conclusive, as certain as a demonstration in mathematics.

Whether or not a service has material form, it has value, since it is a service.

If a material object renders a service for someone, it has value; if it renders no service, it has no value.

Hence, value is not transmitted from the material object to the service, but from the service to the material object.

Nor is this all. Nothing is more easily explained than this pre-eminence, this priority, where value is concerned, of services over products. We shall see that it is due to a circumstance which it was easy to observe, but which was not observed, for the very reason that it was so obvious. The circumstance is none other than man's natural foresight, which disposes him not to stop at performing the services that are asked of him, but to ready himself in advance to perform the services that he anticipates will be asked of him. Thus, while the *facio ut facias* type of exchange remains the key factor, the dominant factor, in any transaction, it tends to be transformed into the *do ut des* type.

John says to Peter, "I want a mug. I should make it; but if you are willing to make it for me, you will be doing me a service, and I will do you an equivalent service in return."

Peter accepts. He goes in search of the proper kinds of clay, he mixes them, he kneads them; in a word, he does what John would have had to do.

It is quite evident here that it is the service that determines the value. The key word in the transaction is *facio*. And if later value is incorporated in the product, it is only because it is the outcome of the service, which is the combination of the labor performed by Peter and of the labor that John has been spared.

Now, it can happen that John often makes the same proposal to Peter, and other persons may make it also, so that Peter may foresee that he is certain to be asked to perform services of this kind and may get ready to perform them. He can say to himself: I have acquired a certain skill in making mugs. Experience tells me that the mugs correspond to a want that craves satisfaction. I can therefore manufacture them in advance.

Henceforth John will have to say to Peter, not *facio ut facias*, but *facio ut des*. If he, likewise, has foreseen Peter's wants and has worked at providing them in advance, he will say, *do ut des*.

But, I ask, in what respect does this progress, which stems from man's foresight, change the origin and nature of value? Does not service still remain its cause and its measure? What difference does it make, as far as the true idea of value is concerned, whether Peter waits to be asked before he makes a mug, or whether he makes it ahead of time, anticipating that he will be asked?

Please bear this in mind: In the history of mankind, inexperience and improvidence precede experience and foresight. Only in the course of time have men come to anticipate their mutual wants fully enough to prepare for them. Logically, the *facio ut facias* pattern had to precede the *do ut des*. The latter is both the result and the outward sign of some growth of knowledge, of a certain amount of experience, of political security, of faith in the future—in a word, of some degree of civilization. This foresight on the part of society, this faith in the *demand* that induces men to prepare the *supply,* this kind of intuitive statistical sense, to be found in all men, which establishes such a surprising balance between wants and the means of satisfying them, is one of the most powerful stimulants to human progress. Thanks to it, we have the division of labor, or at least as far as trades and professions are concerned. Thanks to it, we have one of the blessings men most ardently desire: fixed rewards for services, in the form of *wages* for labor and *interest* on capital. Thanks to it, we have credit, long-range financing, projects involving shared risks, etc. It is surprising that *foresight,* that noble attribute of man, has been so much neglected by the economists. It is due, as Rousseau said, to the difficulty we have in observing the environment in which we are immersed and which forms our natural habitat. Only unusual phenomena strike us, and we allow to pass unnoticed those that, constantly at work around us, upon us, and within us, modify us and our society so profoundly.

To return to our subject: It may be that man's foresight, in its infinite ramifications, tends more and more to substitute the *do ut des* for the *facio ut facias;* but let us, nevertheless, remember that it is in the primitive and *necessary* form of exchange that the notion of value is first found, that this form is that of reciprocal service, and that, after all, from the point of view of exchange, a product is only *a service that has been anticipated.*

Having once established that value is not inherent in matter and cannot be classified among its attributes, I am far from denying that value passes from the *service* into the *product,* or *commodity,* in such a way as to become incorporated, so to speak, in it. I beg those who disagree with me to realize that I am not such a pedant that I would exclude from our language such familiar expressions as: "Gold has value," "Wheat has value," and "Land has value." I believe only that I am within my rights in asking for a scientific explanation; and if the answer is "Because gold, wheat, land, have an *intrinsic value,*" then I believe I have the right to say: "You are wrong, and your error is dangerous. You are wrong, because there is gold, and there is land, that is valueless—the gold and the land that has not yet been the occasion of any human service. Your error is dangerous because it leads to classifying as a usurpation of God's gratuitous gifts to men what is actually man's simple right to exchange his services with other men."

I am therefore ready to admit that products have value, provided others will admit with me that value has no necessary connection with products, that, on the contrary, it is related to and derived from services.

From this truth there follows a very important (in political economy a fundamentally important) conclusion, which heretofore has not been and could not be drawn, namely: *When value has passed from the service to the product, it still remains subject to all the vicissitudes that can affect the value of any service.* It is not fixed in the product, as would be the case if it were one of the product's intrinsic elements; no, it is essentially variable. It can keep rising indefinitely, or it can fall to zero, according to the type of service from which it originated.

The man who makes a mug now to be sold a year from now imparts value to it undoubtedly; and this value is determined by the value of the service—not by the present value of the service, but by the value it will have in a year. If, at the moment of sale, this kind of service is more in demand, the mug will be worth more; it will depreciate if the contrary is true.

That is why man is constantly stimulated to exercise foresight, to put it to good advantage. He always expects, through the appreciation or depreciation of his service, to be rewarded for what he has correctly anticipated and to be punished for his miscalculations. And note that his successes or his failures will coincide with the general prosperity. If he has calculated properly, he is prepared in advance to offer society services more sought after, more highly thought of, more efficient, which satisfy more keenly felt wants; he has contributed to reducing scarcity, to increasing the supply of services of this type, to placing them within the reach of a larger number of persons with less economic hardship. If, on the contrary, he is mistaken in his estimate of the future, he depresses still further the value of services for which the demand is already weak; he makes, at some cost to himself, a merely negative contribution, that of warning the public that services of a certain type do not at the present time require a great amount of its activity, that effort directed into this channel will yield poor returns.

This significant fact—that value *incorporated in a product,* if I may so describe it, continues to be identical with the value of the service to which it gives rise—is of the greatest importance, not only because it confirms the theory that the principle of value resides in the service, but also because it readily explains phenomena that other systems classify as abnormal.

Is there a general human tendency to *lower* rather than to raise the *value* of a product once it is placed on the world market? This is another way of asking whether the type of services that has created the particular value tends to receive better or poorer remuneration. Both are equally possible, and the fact that this is so offers limitless opportunities to men's foresight.

We may note, however, that for beings endowed with a capacity for experimenting, learning, and improving, progress is the general law. The probability is, therefore, that at a given moment in history a given expenditure of time and effort will obtain better results than at a previous moment in history; hence, we may conclude that the prevailing trend is toward a decrease in the value incorporated in a product. For example, if the mug that I just used as a symbol for products was made several years ago, it most probably has undergone depreciation. The fact is that today, for the production of an identical mug, we have more skill, more resources, better tools, more readily available capital, and

more highly specialized labor. Therefore, the prospective purchaser of the mug does not say to the seller, "Tell me what the
labor on this mug cost you in quantity and quality, and I will pay
accordingly." No. He says, "Today, thanks to the progress of this
art, I can make for myself or procure through exchange a similar
mug for a certain amount of labor of a certain quality, and that
is the limit that I will agree to pay you."

The end result of this is that all value attached to a commodity,
that is to say, all accumulated labor, all capital, tends to depreciate as it encounters services that are naturally perfectible and
increasingly productive; and that, in an exchange between current labor and previous labor, the advantage is generally on the
side of current labor, as it should be, since it renders the greater
services.

And this shows how empty are the tirades we constantly hear
against the value of real property. This value is no different from
any other in its origin or in its nature or in its obedience to the
general law of slow depreciation. It represents services performed
a long time ago: drainage, clearing, stonework, grading, fencing,
additions to vegetable gardens, building, etc.; and its function is
to collect payment for them. But the amount to be collected is not
determined out of consideration for the work that went into them.
The real-estate owner does not say, "Give me in exchange for this
land as much labor as went into its development." (This is how
he would have expressed himself if value came from labor, as
Adam Smith theorized, and were proportional to it.) Even less
does he say, as Ricardo and a number of other economists suppose,
"Give me first as much labor as went into this ground, then a
certain additional amount as the equivalent of all its natural
resources." No, the owner of the property, speaking for all the
previous owners, as far back as the one who originally cleared it,
is reduced to this humble statement:

"We have prepared services, and we ask to exchange them for
equivalent services. In times past we worked hard; for in our day
your powerful modern devices were unknown: there were no
highways; we were compelled to do everything with the strength
of our own arms. Beneath these furrows lie buried the toil per-

formed by the sweat of many brows, the effort of many human lives. But we do not demand toil for toil; we should have no means of obtaining such terms. We know that labor on the land as it is performed today, whether in France or elsewhere, is much more efficient and more productive. What we ask and what obviously cannot be denied us, is for our past labor to be exchanged for present labor on a basis proportional, not to their duration or their intensity, but to their results, so that we may receive the same remuneration for the same service. By this arrangement we are the losers from the point of view of our labor, since, to perform the same service, it takes two or perhaps three times as much of our labor as of yours. But it is an arrangement that perforce we must accept; for we no more have the means of imposing other terms than you do of refusing these."

And, in point of fact, this is the way things are done. If we could make an exact accounting of the amount of incessant effort, drudgery, toil, and sweat that were required to bring every acre of the soil of France to its present level of productivity, we should be thoroughly convinced that the purchaser does not pay at the rate of equivalent amounts of labor—at least in ninety-nine cases out of a hundred.

I add this reservation, for we must not lose sight of the fact that a service incorporated in a commodity can acquire value as well as lose it. And although the general trend is toward depreciation, yet the contrary phenomenon does occur occasionally, in exceptional circumstances, involving land as well as other things, without, however, doing violence to the laws of justice or warranting any hue and cry against monopoly.

In fact, services are always at hand to reveal the presence of value. It can generally be assumed that past labor renders less service than present labor; but this is not an absolute law. If past labor renders less service, which is almost always the case, than present labor, it takes more of the former than of the latter to establish a balance, since, I repeat, equivalence is determined by services. But, on the other hand, when it happens that it is the past labor that renders the greater service, then a greater amount of the present service will be required in payment.

6

Wealth

Thus, in everything that is calculated to satisfy our wants and desires, two things must be considered and differentiated: what Nature has done and what man has done, what is free of charge and what is acquired through effort, the gift of God and man's service, *utility* and *value*. In the same object one of them can be immense, and the other imperceptible. While utility may remain constant, value can and does decrease steadily as ingenious new devices enable us to achieve an identical result with less effort.

At this point, even as we begin the study of political economy, we can foresee one of the greatest difficulties, one of the most fertile sources of misunderstanding, controversy, and error.

What is *wealth?*

Are we *rich* in proportion to the utilities we have at our disposal, that is, according to the wants and desires that we can satisfy? "A man is rich or poor," wrote Adam Smith, "according to the number of *useful* things he is able to enjoy."

Are we *rich* in proportion to the *values* we possess, that is, the *services* we have at our disposal? "Wealth," said Jean-Baptiste Say, "exists in direct proportion to value. Wealth is great if the total value that it contains is considerable; it is small if the total value is small."

Uninformed people give two meanings to the word "wealth." Sometimes we hear them say: "The abundance of water in such and such a country is a source of wealth to it," when they are thinking only in terms of utility. But when someone of them tries to ascertain his own wealth, he prepares what is called an inventory, in which he reckons value only.

With all due respect for the experts, I believe that, in this instance, the uninformed are right. Wealth, in fact, can be either *real* or *relative*. From the former point of view, it is reckoned according to our satisfactions. Mankind's wealth is greater or less according to its level of prosperity, whatever may be the value of the objects that maintain it. But suppose we want to know each man's individual share in the general prosperity, in other words, his *relative wealth?* This is a simple ratio, which value alone reveals, because value is itself a relative term.

Political economy is a science that concerns itself with men's general prosperity and material comfort, with the ratio of their efforts to their satisfactions, a ratio that is improved by the increase in the amount of gratuitous utility available for the work of production. In political economy, therefore, we cannot exclude this factor from our idea of wealth. Scientifically speaking, real wealth is not to be found in the sum total of values, but in the sum of gratuitous utility or onerous utility contained in these values. From the point of view of our satisfactions, that is, as far as our real wealth is concerned, we are as much enriched by the value that we have lost through progress in the means of production as by the value that we still possess.

In the transactions of everyday life we no longer take utility into account, in so far as, through the decrease in value, it becomes *free of charge*. Why? Because what is free of charge is *common to all*, and what is a common possession has no effect on each person's individual share of the total real wealth. No exchange is made of what is held by all in common; and since, in business transactions, we need to know only that proportion which is constituted by value, that is all we concern ourselves with.

A debate arose between Ricardo and Jean-Baptiste Say on this question. Ricardo used "wealth" in the sense of utility; Say, in the sense of "value." Neither of them could possibly win a complete victory, because the word has both meanings, depending on whether one views wealth as real or relative.

But we must add a word of caution, all the more important

because Say's authority is so great in such matters; for if we identify wealth (meaning the real, effective level of our material comforts) with value, if, in particular, we affirm that wealth and value are in direct proportion to each other, we run the risk of putting our economic thinking on the wrong track. The works of second-rate economists and of the socialists prove this only too well. This is an unfortunate starting point, since it loses sight of what is, in fact, humanity's noblest heritage; for we must consider as nonexistent that part of our material well-being which, through progress, has been rendered common to all, and we expose our minds to the greatest of all dangers—that of becoming involved in a *petitio principii,* in which we assume as true what we are trying to prove, of looking at political economy backwards and constantly confusing the goal that we wish to reach with the obstacle that blocks our way.

In fact, without these obstacles there would be no value. Value is the sign, the symptom, the testimony, the proof of our natural infirmity. It constantly reminds us of the sentence originally pronounced upon us: "In the sweat of thy face shalt thou eat bread." For the Omnipotent the words *effort, service,* and, consequently, *value,* do not exist. As for us, however, we are placed in a world of *utilities,* of which many are free of charge, but others are to be had only at the price of our toil. Obstacles stand between these utilities and the wants that they can satisfy. We are condemned to doing without the utility or overcoming the obstacle by our efforts. Sweat must indeed fall from our brows, or from the brows of those who toil for our profit.

The more values a society possesses, therefore, the clearer the evidence that it has surmounted obstacles, but the clearer the evidence, also, that it had obstacles to surmount. Shall we go so far as to say that these obstacles create wealth, since without them the values would not exist?

We can imagine the case of two nations. One has more satisfactions than the other, but it has fewer values, because Nature has favored it and placed fewer obstacles in its way. Which nation is the richer?

We can carry this further: Let us take the same nation at two stages in its history. The obstacles to be overcome are the same.

But today it overcomes them with such ease, it has become so efficient in its transportation, agriculture, textile production, for example, that the values of these things have been considerably reduced. It has, therefore, been able to choose one of these two courses: either to be content with the same satisfactions as before, translating its improved methods into increased leisure (and in that case shall we say that its wealth has declined because it has fewer values?); or else it can choose to apply the surplus efforts newly made available to it to the task of increasing its satisfactions, and should we be justified in concluding that because its total values remain stationary, its wealth has also remained stationary? This is what comes of identifying value with wealth.

This is indeed a treacherous shoal for the political economist. Is wealth to be measured by the satisfactions achieved or by the values created?

If there were no obstacles between utilities and wants, there would be no efforts, services, values, any more than there are for God; and, while measuring wealth in terms of satisfactions, mankind would be in possession of infinite wealth; yet in terms of value, it would have no wealth at all. Thus, two economists, according to the definition they chose, might say: *Mankind is infinitely rich,* or *Mankind is infinitely poor.*

The infinite, it is true, is in no respect an attribute of humanity. But mankind is never static; it always moves in some direction; it exerts efforts; it exhibits tendencies; it gravitates toward steadily increasing wealth or steadily increasing poverty. Now, how can political economists come to a common understanding, if this successive reduction of effort in relation to satisfaction, of pains to be taken or rewarded, that is, value, is considered by some an advance toward wealth and by others a descent into poverty?

Yet if the difficulty merely concerned economists, we could say: Let them have their arguments. But legislators and governments are daily required to take measures that exercise a very real influence over human affairs. And what a plight we are in if these measures are taken in ignorance so complete that wealth cannot be distinguished from poverty!

So, I make this declaration: The theory that defines wealth in terms of value is, in the last analysis, a mere glorification of the role of obstacles. It rests on the following syllogism: Wealth is proportional to value, value to effort, effort to obstacles; therefore, wealth is proportional to obstacles.

I make this further declaration: Because of the division of labor, which assigns every man to a trade or a profession, this illusion is very difficult to destroy. We all live by the services that we render in overcoming obstacles, satisfying wants, or removing pain: the doctor by combatting disease; the farmer, hunger; the textile manufacturer, cold; the carriage-maker, distance; the lawyer, injustice; the soldier, danger to the country; and so complete is the list that there is not a single obstacle whose elimination would not seem most inopportune and most inconvenient to someone, and even disastrous to society at large, since it would appear that a source of services, value, and wealth was to be destroyed. Very few economists have completely resisted this false notion, and, if political economy ever succeeds in dispelling it, on that score alone its practical mission in the world will have been accomplished; for I now make this third declaration: Our public policy is steeped in this notion, and whenever governments feel obliged to make special concessions to some class, profession, or industry, they follow no other procedure than to erect obstacles designed to encourage the development of a certain type of efforts, in order to increase artificially the number of services society will be obliged to call for, and thus to increase value and, supposedly, wealth.

And, in fact, it is very true that this procedure is useful for the class receiving the special favor. We see the ensuing self-congratulation and applause, and what happens? The same special concessions are successively granted all other classes.

First identify utility with value, then value with wealth. What could be more natural? Political economists have never been taken more unawares. For what has happened? At every step along the path of progress, they have reasoned thus: "The obstacle is lessened; therefore, effort is reduced; therefore, value is lowered; therefore, utility is decreased; therefore, our wealth is diminished; therefore, we are the most unfortunate of men for ever having bethought ourselves of inventing and exchanging, for having five fingers instead of three, and two arms instead of one; hence, we must set the government, which has force at its disposal, at correcting these abuses."

This type of *political economy in reverse* supports a large number of newspapers and many sessions of our legislative assemblies. It misled the honest and philanthropic Sismondi; * it is expounded very logically in M. de Saint-Chamans' book.†

"A nation has two kinds of wealth," he says. "If we consider only *useful* commodities from the point of view of their quantity, their supply, we deal with wealth that procures society things that it can consume, and this I shall therefore term *consumers' wealth.*

"If we consider commodities from the point of view of their exchangeable value, or simply their value, we deal with wealth that brings society value, and this I therefore term *value wealth.*

"Political economy deals primarily with value wealth; and it is with it primarily that government may properly deal."

This being granted, what can political economy and government do? Political economy can indicate the means of increasing value wealth; and government can put these means into effect.

But value wealth is in proportion to efforts, and efforts are in proportion to obstacles. Political economy must therefore show the way, and government must employ all its resources to multiply the obstacles. This is the logical conclusion, and M. de Saint-Chamans faces it squarely.

Does exchange make it easier for men to acquire more *consumers' wealth* for less *value wealth?* Then we must restrain exchange.[1]

Is there any amount of gratuitous utility that we can replace with onerous utility—for example, by eliminating a tool or a machine? We must not neglect the opportunity, for it is obvious,

---

* [Jean Charles Léonard de Sismondi (1773–1842), Swiss historian and economist. —Translator.]

† [Auguste, Vicomte de Saint-Chamans (1777–1861), Deputy and Councillor of State under the Restoration, protectionist and upholder of the balance of trade. His celebrated stand on the "obstacle" here quoted by Bastiat comes from his *Nouvel essai sur la richesse des nations,* 1824. This work was later (1852) incorporated in his *Traité d'économie politique.*—Translator.]

he says, that if machines increase *consumers' wealth,* they decrease *value wealth.* "*Let us bless the obstacles* that the high cost of fuel in our country puts in the way of the multiplication of steam engines." [2]

Has Nature favored us in any way? It is our loss, for, by so doing, she has deprived us of a chance to work. "I admit that it is quite possible for me to desire to see done by hand, sweat and toil, and forced effort, what can be produced spontaneously and without pains." [3]

What a shame, therefore, that Nature has not obliged us to manufacture drinking water! It would have been a wonderful opportunity to produce *value wealth.* Most fortunately, we even the score with wine. "Find the secret of making wine flow as abundantly as water from springs in the earth, and you will discover that this fine system of things will bankrupt one quarter of France." [4]

Within the gamut of ideas that our economist so naively runs, there are innumerable means, all very simple, of reducing men to the level where they may create *value wealth.*

The first is to take it away from them as rapidly as they acquire it: "If taxes confiscate money from areas where it is plentiful, in order to allocate it to areas where it is scarce, they serve a useful purpose, and this action, far from representing a loss to the state, represents a *gain.*" [5]

The second is, after taking it, to throw it away. "Luxury and extravagance, so disastrous to the wealth of private individuals, are *advantageous* to the wealth of the nation. 'That's a fine moral doctrine you are preaching,' people will say to me. I make no such claims. We are dealing with political economy, not morals. We are seeking means of making nations richer, and I preach the gospel of luxury." [6]

An even faster means is to destroy it by a few good wars. "If you will admit with me that the extravagances of a spendthrift are as productive as any other expenditures; that government spending is equally productive, ... you will not be surprised at England's wealth, after this very costly war of hers." [7]

But all these means of encouraging the creation of *value wealth*

—taxes, luxury, war, etc.—must yield the palm to a much more effective device: conflagration.

"Construction is a great source of wealth, because it brings revenue to the sellers of builders' supplies, to workmen, and to various classes of artisans and artists. Melon * quotes Sir William Petty † who classes as *national profit* the work done for the rebuilding of London after the famous fire that destroyed two-thirds of the city, and he estimates it [this profit!] at a million pounds sterling (1866 value) per year for four years without injuring other businesses in any way. Without accepting this exact figure as a completely accurate estimate *of this profit,"* adds M. de Saint-Chamans, "we may be certain at least, that this event did not have an adverse effect on England's wealth at this period. . . . . Sir William Petty's estimate is not impossible, since the need to rebuild London must have created vast sources of new revenue." [8]

Economists who start from the premise that *wealth is value* would inevitably arrive at the same conclusions as M. de Saint-Chamans, if they were logical; but they are not logical, because on the road to absurdity all of us stop short of the final destination, some a little sooner, some a little later, according to the relative reasonableness of our minds. M. de Saint-Chamans himself seems to have drawn back just a shade from the full consequences of his theory when he finds that they lead to praise of conflagration as a road to wealth. We see him hesitate and content himself with perfunctory approval. Logically he should have carried his reasoning ·to its ultimate conclusion and stated openly what he clearly implies.

Of all economists, M. Sismondi is certainly the one who most distressingly falls afoul of this difficulty. Like M. de Saint-Chamans, he started with the idea that value is one of the component elements of wealth; like him he erected on this foundation a *political economy in reverse,* deploring everything that reduces

* [Jean François Melon (d. 1738), French lawyer and minor government official, and political theorist.—TRANSLATOR.]
† [Sir William Petty (1623–1687), English economist. Author of numerous works on trade and vital statistics.—TRANSLATOR.]

value. He too praises obstacles; bans machinery; anathematizes exchange, competition, and freedom; glorifies luxury and taxes; and finally reaches this conclusion, that the more abundantly men have everything, the more completely they have nothing.

Yet M. de Sismondi seems, from beginning to end, to have a subconscious feeling that he is mistaken, and that a veil that he cannot lift may have interposed itself between his mind and the truth. He does not quite dare to draw explicitly, like M. de Saint-Chamans, the ultimate conclusions inherent in his theories; he is disturbed, he hesitates. He wonders sometimes if it is possible for all men, since the beginning of the world, to have been in error and on the road to suicide, in seeking to decrease the ratio of effort to satisfaction, that is, in seeking to decrease *value*. A friend and yet an enemy of liberty, he fears it, since, by creating the abundance that reduces value, it leads to poverty; and, at the same time, he does not know how to go about destroying this fatal liberty. Thus, he reaches the outer limits of socialism and artificial social orders; he suggests that government and the social sciences must regulate and restrict everything; then he realizes the danger of his advice, retracts, and finally gives way to despair, saying: "Liberty leads to a bottomless pit; restraint is as impossible as it is ineffective; there is no way out." And there is none, indeed, if value constitutes wealth, that is, if obstacles to our well-being constitute our well-being, that is, if adversity is prosperity.

The latest writer, to my knowledge, to stir up this question is M. Proudhon. It was a windfall for his book, *Economic Contradictions*. Never was there a finer opportunity to seize an *antinomy,* a contradiction, by the hair and shout defiance at the science of political economy. Never was there a finer opportunity to ask, "Do you view increase in value as a good thing or as an evil? *Quidquid dixeris argumentabor.*" * I leave it to the reader to imagine what a fine time he must have had! [9]

"I call upon every responsible economist," he said, "to tell me, other than by rewording or repeating my question, for what reason value decreases as production increases, and vice versa.

* ["Whatever you say, I shall argue against it."—Translator.]

. . . . In technical terms, value in use and value in exchange, although necessary to each other, exist in inverse ratio to each other. . . . . Value in use and value in exchange always remain, then, inextricably linked to each other, although by their nature they always tend to be mutually exclusive.

"There is no assignable cause or possible explanation for this contradiction inherent in the notion of value. . . . . If we grant that man has need of a great variety of commodities that he must obtain through labor, we are necessarily faced with a conflict between value in use and value in exchange, and from this conflict a contradiction arises at the very outset of our study of political economy. No intelligence, no will, either divine or human, can prevent it. Thus, instead of seeking a useless explanation, let us be content to note the fact that the *contradiction is inevitable*."

We know that the great discovery with which we can credit M. Proudhon is that everything is both true and false, good and bad, legal and illegal; that there is no principle that is not self-contradictory; and that the *contradiction* is not in erroneous theories, but in the very essence of things and phenomena: "It is the expression of pure necessity, the inner law of being, etc."; consequently, it is inevitable, and it would be theoretically irremediable, but for the *series of contradictory elements,* and practically irremediable but for the *banque du peuple.** God, a contradiction; liberty, a contradiction; property, a contradiction; value, credit, monopoly, common ownership, contradiction on contradiction! When M. Proudhon made this tremendous discovery, his heart must surely have leaped for joy; for since contradiction is in all things, there is always something to contradict, which for

* [Bastiat here refers ironically to Proudhon's famous declaration: "The series is the antithesis of unity." Convinced that the various elements of society were inherently opposites, like the positive and negative poles of an electric battery, Proudhon advanced the theory that from their antithetical nature came the life and movement of society. Therefore, it was neither possible nor desirable to look for any unifying principle from which to formulate a synthesis of social phenomena.

The "People's Bank" was Proudhon's ill-fated effort at establishing a co-operative enterprise providing for the free exchange of goods and services, together with interest-free loans. The bank failed in 1849.—TRANSLATOR.]

him is the supreme happiness. He once said to me, "I'd be perfectly willing to go to heaven, but I'm afraid that everybody agrees up there, and I couldn't find anyone to argue with."

It must be admitted that the subject of value gave him an excellent opportunity to indulge in contradiction to his heart's content. But, begging his pardon, the contradictions and the conflicts that this word "value" suggests stem from erroneous theories, and not at all, as he asserts, from the nature of the phenomenon.

Theorists first began by confusing value with utility, that is, by confusing the ills with the benefits (for utility is the means to the end sought—the benefit—and value comes from the obstacle—the ill—that stands between the end and the desire). This was the initial error, and when they saw its consequences, they thought that they could save the situation by thinking up a distinction between value in use and value in exchange, a cumbersome tautology that involved the fallacy of applying the same word, "value," to two opposite phenomena.

But if, setting aside these subtleties, we keep to the facts, what do we see? Certainly, only something very natural and far from contradictory.

Suppose that a man works exclusively for himself. If he acquires skill, if his capacities and his intelligence develop, if Nature becomes more generous, or he learns to utilize it better for his needs, *he has more comforts and well-being and goes to fewer pains.* Where do you see any contradiction, and where do you find anything to make such protests about?

Now, instead of being alone, this man has contacts with other men. They exchange, and I repeat my observation: In proportion as they acquire skill, experience, capacity, intelligence, in proportion as Nature, becoming more generous, or being made more amenable, co-operates more effectively, *they have more comforts and well-being and go to fewer pains;* there is a greater amount of gratuitous utility at their disposal; in their transactions they offer one another a larger proportion of usable results for a given amount of labor. Where, then, is the contradiction?

Ah! if you make the error, like Adam Smith and all his successors, of applying the same term "value" both to results obtained and to trouble taken, then, the antinomy, or the contradiction, appears. But, you may be sure, it lies entirely in your erroneous explanation, and not at all in the facts.

M. Proudhon would, therefore, have had to formulate his proposition in this way: Granted man's need for a great variety of commodities and the necessity of providing them through his labor and his precious gift of learning and improving, nothing in the world is more natural than the steady increase of results in relation to efforts, and it is not at all contradictory that a given value transmits more in the way of available utilities.

For, once again, utility is, for man, the good side of the coin; value, the bad side. Utility relates only to our satisfactions; value, to the pains we take. Utility makes possible our satisfactions and is in proportion to them; value indicates our innate infirmity, is created by obstacles, and is in proportion to them.

By virtue of man's perfectibility, gratuitous utility tends more and more to replace the onerous utility denoted by the word "value." Such is the phenomenon, and it most certainly presents nothing contradictory.

But there still remains the question of determining whether the word "wealth" is to include both these utilities taken together or the second only.

If we could set up, once and for all, two classes of utility, put on one side all those that are gratuitous, and on the other all that are onerous, we should thus establish two classes of wealth that we should call, with M. Say, *natural wealth* and *social wealth;* or else, with M. de Saint-Chamans, *consumers' wealth* and *value wealth.* This done, we should, as these writers suggest, concern ourselves no further with the first class.

"The blessings available to all," says M. Say, "which all may enjoy as they will, without the necessity of procuring them, without fear of exhausting them, such as air, water, sunlight, etc., having been given us gratis by Nature, may be called *natural wealth.* Since they cannot be produced or distributed or consumed, *they do not fall within the scope of political economy.*

"That type of wealth which it is the function of political economy to study is composed of those things that we possess having a recognized value. We can call it social wealth, because it exists among men living together in society."

"It is with *value wealth*," says M. de Saint-Chamans, "that *political economy is primarily concerned,* and every time I shall speak in this book of wealth without specifying the type, it will be to this type only that I refer."

Almost all economists have considered the matter in this light.

"The most striking distinction that we encounter at the outset," says Storch, "is that there are some values that are capable of appropriation, and that there are others that are not.[10] *Only values of the first type belong to the study of political economy,* for analysis of the others would furnish no results worthy of the attention of a statesman."

For my own part, I believe that that portion of utility which, as a result of progress, ceases to be onerous, ceases to have value, but does not on that account cease to be utility, and falls eventually within the domain called *common to all* and *free of charge,* is the very one that must constantly attract the attention of the statesman and the economist. Otherwise, instead of viewing with deep and sympathetic understanding the great results of this process that so influence and elevate humanity, all that the political economist will see in it is a mere contingent phenomenon, unstable, tending to decrease, if not to disappear entirely, just a simple relation, or, in a word, nothing but another case of value. Without perceiving what is happening, he will permit himself to be carried along, content merely to consider effects, obstacles, the interests of the producer, and worse yet, to confuse those interests with the public interest. This, in fact, amounts to choosing the ills intsead of the benefits, and finally, under the leadership of men like Saint-Chamans and Sismondi, ending with a socialist utopia or in Proudhon's land of contradiction.

Furthermore, is not the line of demarcation between these two utilities entirely a fanciful, arbitrary, and impossible one? How do you propose to dissolve the union of Nature and man, when they are everywhere mingled, combined, fused, and, even more, when one of them tends constantly to replace the other, and in so

doing becomes the source of all progress? If the science of economics, so dry in some respects, can, in others, so inspire and
enchant our minds, it is precisely because it sets forth the laws
governing this association between man and Nature; because it
shows how gratuitous utility replaces onerous utility more and
more, how man's satisfactions increase as his toil and drudgery decrease, how obstacles are constantly reduced, along with value, how
the producer's losses are more than compensated by the consumer's increasing prosperity, how natural wealth, that is, wealth
free of charge and *common* to all, takes the place of wealth that is
individual and privately owned. Would you, then, exclude from
political economy the very element that constitutes its divine
harmony?

Air, water, sunlight are free of charge, you say. That is true, and
if we made use of them only in their natural forms, if we did not
harness them to any labor of our own, we could exclude them
from the domain of political economy, just as we exclude the
utility that may, quite possibly, exist in comets. But consider
where man started and how far he has come. Originally he had a
most imperfect notion of how to make air, water, sunlight,
and other natural resources work for him. His every satisfaction
was bought at the cost of great personal effort, required a great
amount of labor for the result obtained, could be surrendered
to another only as a great *service*—represented, in a word, a great
amount of *value.* Little by little these resources, water, air, light,
and others, like gravitation, elasticity, thermodynamics, electricity, the energy of plant life, have emerged from their relative
inertia. They have become incorporated more and more into
our industry. They have been substituted more and more for
human labor. They have accomplished gratis what once cost
much in terms of human toil. Without impairing our satisfactions, they have annihilated value. To express it in ordinary
terms, what used to cost ten days' work now requires one. All this
annihilated value has passed from the domain of private property
to the domain of what is free of charge and common to all. A
considerable amount of human effort has been freed and made
available for other enterprises. Thus, for equal pains, equal

services, equal value, mankind has enlarged prodigiously its circle of satisfactions, and you say that I should eliminate from political economy the study of this gratuitous and common utility, which alone can explain progress in all its height and breadth, if I may so express myself, in all it brings in prosperity and equality!

Let us state as a conclusion, then, that we may give, and give legitimately, two meanings to the word "wealth":

Effective Wealth, real wealth, which produces satisfactions, that is, the sum of the utilities that human labor, with Nature's help, puts at society's disposal.

Relative Wealth, that is, each individual's share in the general wealth, which share is determined by value.

Here, then, is the harmonious law that can be expressed thus:

Through labor the action of man is combined with the action of Nature.

From this co-operation utility results.

Each individual takes from the general store of utility in proportion to the services that he renders—in the last analysis, then, in proportion to the utility he himself represents.[11]

The Morality of Wealth

We have just studied wealth from the economic point of view. It may be useful also to say something about its moral effects.

In all ages wealth, from the moral standpoint, has been a subject of controversy. Certain philosophers, certain religions have decreed that it is to be despised; others have lauded moderation—*aurea mediocritas* ("the golden mean"). Very few, if any, have admitted that a burning ambition for the enjoyment of a large fortune is a proper moral attitude.

Who is wrong? Who is right? It does not behoove political economy to treat this subject of individual morality. I say only this: I am always inclined to believe that in matters of common, universal practice, the theorists, the scholars, the philosophers are much more prone to be mistaken than is common practice itself, especially when in this word "practice" we include not only the actions of the great majority of mankind, but their sentiments and their ideas as well.

Now, what does common practice show us? It shows us all men struggling to emerge from poverty, which is their starting point; all preferring the experience of satisfaction to that of want, wealth to privation—all of them, I say, including, with few exceptions, the very ones who declaim so eloquently to the contrary.

The desire for wealth is tremendous, constant, universal, overwhelming. In almost all parts of the world it has triumphed over our instinctive aversion to work. It takes the form, whatever one may say, of even baser greed among savages and barbarians than among civilized peoples. All the voyagers who left Europe imbued with the idea that Rousseau had made popular in the eighteenth century that in the antipodes they would encounter the natural man, the unselfish, generous, hospitable man, were struck with the rapacious avarice by which these primitive men were devoured. In our time, our soldiers have been able to testify as to the opinion we should hold of the much vaunted unselfishness of the Arab tribes.

On the other hand, all men, even those whose conduct is at variance with it, agree in principle that we should honor unselfishness, generosity, self-control, and should castigate that excessive love of wealth which leads us to stoop to any means to secure it. And yet with the same unanimity all men lavish their praise on the person who, whatever his walk of life, strives by honest and persevering toil to better his lot and his family's position in society. From this collection of facts, opinions, and attitudes, we must, it seems to me, arrive at the judgment we should pass on wealth as it affects individual morality.

First of all, we must recognize that the motivating force that drives us toward wealth comes from Nature; it is the creation of Providence and is therefore *moral*. It has its roots in that original and common state of destitution which would be the lot of all of us were it not for the desire that it creates in us to free ourselves from the chains of want. We must recognize, secondly, that the efforts that all men make to break these chains, provided they remain within the bounds of justice, are respectable and commendable, since they are everywhere commended and respected.

Furthermore, no one will deny that there is a moral side to labor itself. This is expressed in the proverb that belongs to all nations: "Idleness is the mother of all vices." ("Satan still finds work for idle hands to do.") And we should fall into shocking contradiction if we said, on the one hand, that labor is indispensable to men's morality, and, on the other, that men are immoral when they work to gain wealth.

In the third place, we must recognize that the desire for wealth becomes immoral when it goes beyond the bounds of justice and equity, and that the greater the wealth of the greedy, the more severely is greed itself censured.

Such is the judgment that is pronounced, not by a few philosophers or sects, but by the vast majority of mankind, and I accept it.

I must remark, however, that it is possible, without contradiction, for this judgment not to be the same today as it was in antiquity.

Both the Essenes and the Stoics lived in a society in which wealth was obtained at the price of oppression, pillage, and violence. It was immoral not only in itself, but, by virtue of the immorality of the means by which it was acquired, it revealed the immorality of the men who enjoyed it. A reaction against it, even an exaggerated one, was quite natural. Modern philosophers who declaim against wealth without taking into account the difference in the means of acquiring it liken themselves to Seneca or Christ. They are mere parrots repeating words that they do not understand.

But the question that political economy raises is this: Does wealth represent moral good or moral evil for mankind? Does the steady increase in wealth imply, from the point of view of morality, progress or decadence?

The reader can anticipate my answer, and he realizes that I have already had to say a few words about personal morality in order to avoid the following contradictory, or rather impossible, conclusion: What is immoral for the individual is moral for society at large.

Without having recourse to statistics, without consulting prison records, we may express our problem in these terms:

Does man degenerate in proportion as he gains greater control over material things and Nature, as he harnesses them to his needs, as he uses them to create greater leisure for himself, and as, freeing himself from the demands of his most pressing bodily needs, he is able to rescue from the inertia where they lay dormant moral and intellectual faculties that undoubtedly were not given him with the intent that he should let them remain in eternal lethargy?

Does man degenerate in proportion as he passes from the most inorganic state, so to speak, and rises toward the most spiritual state of which he is capable?

To pose the problem thus is to solve it.

I grant that when wealth is accumulated by immoral means, its influence is immoral, as was the case with the Romans.

I also agree that when it is amassed and distributed with great inequality, digging deeper and deeper chasms between the social classes, it has an immoral influence and gives rise to subversive passions.

But can the same thing be said for wealth that is the fruit of honest labor and of free transactions, when it is distributed in a uniform manner among all classes? Certainly such a position is not tenable.

Nevertheless, the books of the socialists are full of denunciations of the rich.

I cannot really understand how these schools of thought, so divergent in other respects, but so unanimous on this point, can fail to see the contradiction into which they fall.

On the one hand, wealth, according to the leaders of these schools, has a deleterious, demoralizing influence that withers the soul, hardens the heart, and leaves only a taste for depraved pleasures. The rich have all the vices. The poor have all the virtues. They are just, sensible, generous; such is the line adopted.

And, on the other hand, all the socialists' powers of imagination, all the systems that they invent, all the laws that they try to foist upon us, have the effect, if we are to believe them, of turning poverty into wealth. . . . .

The morality of wealth is proved by this maxim: the profit of one is the profit of the other. . . . .[12]

7

Capital

Economic laws act in accordance with the same principle, whether they apply to great masses of men, to two individuals, or even to a single individual condemned by circumstances to live in isolation.

An individual in isolation, provided he could survive for any length of time, would be at once capitalist, entrepreneur, workman, producer, and consumer. The entire economic cycle would run its course in him: want, effort, satisfaction, gratuitous and onerous utility. Observing each of these elements, he would have some notion of the workings of the whole mechanism, even though it would be reduced to its simplest form.

Now, if there is anything in the world that is clear, it is that he could never confuse what is gratis with what requires effort. That would imply a contradiction in terms. He would know full well when materials or forces were provided by Nature, without need for labor on his part, even in those cases where their addition made his own labor more productive.

An individual living in isolation would never dream of obtaining through his own labor something that he could get directly from Nature. He would not walk two miles for water if he had a spring beside his cabin. For the same reason, in every instance where his own labor might be called upon, he would try to substitute Nature's help as much as possible.

That is why, if he were building a boat, he would utilize the lightest wood in order to use to advantage the specific gravity of water. He would try to rig up a sail, so that the wind might spare him the trouble of rowing, etc.

In order thus to harness the forces of Nature, he needs tools and instruments.

At this point we perceive that our isolated man will have to do some calculating. He will ask himself this question: At present I obtain a certain satisfaction for a given amount of effort. When I have the proper tool, will I obtain the same satisfaction for less total effort, counting both the effort still to be exerted to obtain the satisfaction and the effort required to make the tool?

No man is willing to waste his strength for the mere pleasure of wasting it. Our Robinson Crusoe will not, therefore, set about making the tool unless he can foresee, when the work is done, a definite saving of his labor in relation to his satisfaction, or an increase in satisfactions for the same amount of labor.

A circumstance that will greatly influence his calculations is the number of products his tool will help him turn out and the number of times he will be called on to use it during its lifespan. Robinson Crusoe has a standard for his comparison, which is his present effort, the effort he must go to if he tries to obtain the satisfaction directly and without help of any kind. He estimates that the tool will save him effort each time he uses it; but it takes labor to make the tool, and he will mentally distribute this labor over the total number of occasions on which he may use it. The greater the number, the stronger will be his inclination to enlist the aid of the natural resource. It is here, in this distribution of an *advance outlay* over the total number of products to be made, that we find the principle and the basis of interest.

Once Robinson Crusoe has decided to make a tool, he discovers that his inclination to make it and the uses he can put it to are not enough. It takes tools to make tools; it takes iron to hammer iron, and so on, as he moves from one difficulty to another, until he reaches the first one, which seems to be insoluble. This cycle makes us aware of the extremely slow process by which capital must originally have been formed and of the tremendous amount of human effort that was required for every satisfaction.

Nor is this all. Even if the tools needed to make tools are

available, the *materials of production* are still required. Even though they are furnished gratis by Nature, like stone, they still have to be collected, which involves going to some trouble. But nearly always the possession of these materials presupposes long and complicated earlier labor, as for example, processing wool, linen, iron, lead, etc.

And even this is not all. While a man is working thus for the sole purpose of making his future work easier, he is doing nothing for his present needs. Now, these belong to an order of phenomena in which Nature brooks no interruption. Every day he must feed, clothe, and house himself. Robinson Crusoe will therefore perceive that he can do nothing about harnessing the forces of Nature until he has accumulated *provisions*. Every day he is hunting he must redouble his efforts; he must lay aside part of his game; then he must impose privations on himself so as to have time to make the tool he has in mind. Under these circumstances, it is more likely that he will content himself with making a very crude and imperfect tool, barely adequate for its intended use.

With time, all his means and facilities will improve. Reflection and experience will have taught our Robinson Crusoe, stranded on his island, better working methods; the first tool itself will furnish him with the means of making others and of gathering his supplies more quickly.

Tools, materials, provisions, all constitute what he will doubtless call his capital, and he will readily grant that the larger this capital, the better the control he will have over the forces of Nature, that the more he harnesses them to his labor, the greater, in a word, will be his satisfactions in relation to his efforts.

Let us pass now to the social order. Here, too, capital will be composed of the tools and instruments of production, of the materials and provisions without which no long-range undertaking is possible either in isolation or in society. The possessors of this capital have it only because they have created it either by their efforts or their privations; and they have exerted their efforts (over and beyond their current wants), they have undergone these privations, only for the sake of future advantage, in order, for example, to turn to their use a large number of natural resources. To surrender this capital would mean for them to give up the advantage they had sought to obtain. It would mean surrendering this advantage to others; it would be rendering a *service*. Consequently, we must either disregard the simplest considerations of reason and justice, or we must admit that they have a perfect right to turn over this capital only in exchange for some other service freely bargained for and voluntarily agreed to. I do not believe that there is a man on earth who will contest the equity of *reciprocity of services,* for reciprocity of services means equity in other terms. Will it be said that the transaction cannot possibly be *free,* because the one who has capital is in a position to impose his own terms on the one who does not? But how should the transaction be carried on? How can an equivalence of *services* be determined except by an exchange voluntarily agreed to? And is it not clear, moreover, that the borrower, being free to consent or not to consent, will refuse, unless it is to his advantage to accept, and unless the loan can improve his situation? It is clear that this is the question he will ask himself: Will the use of this capital afford me advantages that will more than compensate for the terms that are stipulated? Or else: Is the effort that I am now required to make for a given satisfaction greater or less than the sum total of the efforts to which I shall be obligated by the loan, first to render the *services* that are asked of me, and then to realize the satisfaction with the aid of the borrowed capital? If, all things considered, there is no advantage, he will not borrow; he will be content with his present situation; and in that case, how has he been wronged? He can be mistaken, someone will say. True enough. We can be mistaken in every imaginable transaction. Does this mean, then, that no transaction can ever be free? Assuming for the moment that such is the case, will someone kindly tell us what should be put in the place of free will and free consent? Shall it be coercion? For, apart from free will, I know of nothing but coercion. No, someone says, it will be the judgment of a third party. I am perfectly willing, on three conditions. First, that the decision of this person, whatever name he be given, not be executed by force. Second, that he be infallible, for it is not worth the trouble to replace one fallible person by another; and the fallible persons whom I distrust the least are the interested parties themselves. Finally, the third condition is that this person receive no pay; for it would be a strange way of showing one's good will toward the borrower to deprive him of his liberty and then place an added burden on his shoulders in compensation for this philanthropic service. But let us forget legal questions and return to political economy.

Capital, whether composed of materials, provisions, or tools, presents two aspects: utility and value. I have explained the theory of value very badly if the reader has not comprehended that the one who surrenders a certain amount of capital demands payment for its value only, that is, for the service he put into producing it, the pains he took, plus the effort saved the recipient. Capital, indeed, is a commodity like any other. It receives its name only from the fact that it is designed for future consumption. It is a great error to believe that capital is in itself a distinct entity. A sack of wheat is a sack of wheat, even though, depending on the point of view, it is revenue for the seller and it is capital for the buyer. Exchange works on this invariable principle: value for value, service for service; and all the gratuitous utility that goes into the transaction is given into the bargain, inasmuch as what is gratis has no value, and transactions are concerned only with value. In this respect, transactions involving capital are no different from any others.

There are some remarkable implications for the social order in all this, though I can refer to them only briefly here. Man in isolation has capital only when he has collected materials, provisions, and tools. Such is not the case with man in society. He needs only to have rendered *services* in order to have the means of receiving from society, through the mechanism of exchange, equivalent services. What I mean by the mechanism of exchange is money, promissory notes, bank notes, and even bankers themselves. Whoever has rendered a *service* and has not yet received the corresponding satisfaction is the bearer of a token, which either itself has value, like money, or is fiduciary, like bank notes. This token entitles him to collect from society, when and where he wills, and in whatever form he wills, an equivalent *service*. These circumstances do not in any way, in principle, in effect, in point of legality, alter the great law that I seek to elucidate: *Services are exchanged for services.* It is still barter in embryo—developed, grown, and become complex, but without losing its identity.

The bearer of the token may therefore collect from society, at his pleasure, either an immediate satisfaction or an object that, for him, has the character of capital. This is a matter with which the one who surrenders the token has no concern whatsoever. All that matters in any way is that the *services be equal.* Or, again, he may surrender his token to another person to use it as he pleases, subject to the double condition that it be returned to him along with a *service,* and at a given date. If we analyze this transaction carefully, we find that in this case the one who surrenders the token *deprives himself,* in favor of the borrower, either of an immediate satisfaction that he will postpone for a few years or of an instrument of production that would have increased his own resources, harnessed the forces of Nature, and improved the ratio of his efforts to his satisfactions. He deprives himself of these advantages in order to bestow them upon another. This is certainly rendering a *service,* and it is impossible to deny that in all justice this service is entitled to something in return. The mere return of the thing advanced, at the end of a year, cannot be considered a payment for the special service. Those who maintain such a view fail to understand that this transaction is not a sale, in which, since delivery is immediate, the payment is also immediate. Payment is deferred, and this deferment is itself a special service, since it imposes a sacrifice on the part of the one granting it, and bestows a favor on the one requesting it. There are, therefore, grounds for remuneration; otherwise we should have to negate this supreme law of society: *Service for service.* This remuneration is called by different names according to circumstances: *hire, rent, installments,* but its generic name is interest.[1]

Thus, thanks to the marvelous device of exchange, a remarkable thing takes place, for every *service* is, or may become, capital. If

workmen are to begin a railroad ten years hence, we cannot set
aside now the actual wheat that will feed them, the textiles that
will clothe them, and the wheelbarrows that they will use during
this long-range operation. But we can set aside and deliver to them
the equivalent *value* of these things. To do so, we need only
at the present time render society *services* and receive in return
tokens or certificates, which ten years from now we can convert
into wheat or textiles. And we are not even forced to let these
tokens lie idle and unproductive during this period. There
are businessmen and bankers, there is the necessary machinery in
society, to render the service, in exchange for services in return,
of assuming these sacrifices in our place.

What is still more amazing is that we can reverse this procedure,
impossible as this may seem at first glance. We can turn into
tools, railroads, and houses, capital that has not yet been produced, utilizing for this purpose *services* that will not be rendered
until the next century. There are bankers who will make the
necessary advances on the faith that workers and travelers of the
third or fourth generation to come will provide the payment; and
these checks drawn on the future are passed from hand to hand
and never remain unproductive. I do not believe, frankly, that
the inventors of artificial social orders, however numerous they
may be, could ever imagine a system at once so simple and so
complex, so ingenious, and so just. Surely, they would give up
their dull and stupid utopias if they did but know the beautiful
harmonies of the dynamic social mechanism instituted by God.
There was also once a king of Aragon who wondered what advice
he would have given Providence on the running of the celestial
mechanism if he had been called into consultation.* Such a presumptuous thought would not have occurred to Newton.

But, it must be emphasized, all transmission of services from
one point to another, in time or space, rests upon this assumption:
To grant a postponement of payment is to render a service; in
other words, on the assumption that it is legitimate to charge
interest. The man † who, in our day, tried to suppress interest

* [Cf. chap. 1, p. 9, note †.—TRANSLATOR.]
† [The reference is obviously to Proudhon.—TRANSLATOR.]

did not understand that he was proposing to take exchange back to its primitive, embryonic form of simple, direct barter with no provision for time past or time to come. He did not realize that, while considering himself the most forward-looking of men, he was actually the most backward, since he wished to rebuild society on the crudest and most primitive plan. He desired, so he said, *reciprocity of services.* But he proposed to begin by refusing to admit as *services* the very type of *services* that link, bind together, and unite all times and all places. Of all the socialists he is the one who, despite the boldness of his resounding aphorisms, has best understood and most respected the present social order. His reforms are limited to a single proposal, which is negative. It consists of removing from society the most powerful and most remarkable of its moving parts.

I have explained elsewhere the legitimacy and the perpetuity of interest. I shall limit myself here to reminding the reader that:

1) The legitimacy of interest is based on the fact that *the person who grants credit renders a service.* Hence, interest is legitimate, by virtue of the principle of *service for service.*

2) The perpetuity of interest is based on the additional fact that *the person who borrows must repay in full at the date of expiration.* Now, if the object or the value is returned to its owner, he can relend it. It will be returned a second time; he can lend it a third time; and so on *perpetually.* What one of the succeeding and voluntary borrowers can have any cause for complaint? But, since the legitimacy of interest has so frequently been contested in these times as to alarm capital and drive it away or into hiding, let me show how senseless all this strange uproar is.

Now, first of all, would it not be quite as absurd as it would be unjust if no interest were charged at all or if the interest payment were the same whether the terms agreed upon were for a period of one year, two years, or ten years? If, under the influence of the so-called *egalitarian* doctrine, our civil code should, unfortunately, so decree, it would mean the immediate suppression of an entire category of human transactions. There would still be *barter transactions* and *cash sales,* but there would no longer be *installment buying* or *loans.* The egalitarians would, in-

deed, lift from the borrowers the burden of interest, but by denying them the loan. On this analogy we can also relieve men of the
painful necessity of paying for what they purchase. We have only
to forbid them to buy, or, what amounts to the same thing, make
the law declare that *prices are illegal.*

The egalitarian principle does indeed have an egalitarian element in it. First, it would prevent the accumulation of capital;
for who would want to lay up savings from which no return
could be realized? Secondly, it would reduce wages to zero; for,
where there is no capital (tools, materials and provisions), there
can be no provision for future labor, and so, no wages. We
should therefore soon reach the state of perfect and absolute
equality: no one would have anything.

But can any man be so blind as not to see that deferment of
payment is *in itself* an *onerous act,* and, therefore, subject to
remuneration? But even aside from the question of loans, does
not everyone in all transactions try to shorten the delays he must
experience? It is, in fact, the object of our constant concern.
Every entrepreneur looks ahead to the time when the advances
he has made will bring a return. We sell at a higher or a lower
price with this in view. To be indifferent to this consideration,
we should have to be unaware of the fact that capital is a force;
for, if we do know it, we naturally desire to have it accomplish
as quickly as possible the task to which we have assigned it, so
that we may reassign it to still another.

They are poor economists indeed who believe that we pay
interest on capital only when we borrow. The general rule, and a
just one, is that he who enjoys the satisfaction must pay all that
it costs to produce it, *the inconveniences of delay* included,
whether he performs the service himself or has another perform
it for him. The man in isolation, who, of course, carries on no
transaction with anyone else, would consider as *onerous* any situation that would deprive him of his weapons for a year. Why,
therefore, would not a similar situation be considered onerous
in society? If one man voluntarily undergoes this privation for
the benefit of another man who voluntarily agrees to compensate
him, how can this compensation be considered illegitimate?

Nothing would be done in this world, no enterprise requiring advance outlays would be carried through to completion, men would not plant, sow, or plow, if delays and postponements were not *in themselves* considered as *onerous,* to be treated and paid for as such. General agreement is so unanimous on this point that there is no exchange in which it is not the guiding principle. Extensions of time and postponements enter into the appraisal of *services,* and, consequently, into the amount of *value* they possess.

Thus, in their crusade against interest, the egalitarians trample underfoot not only the most basic notions of justice, not only their own principle of *service for service,* but also all human precedent and universal practice. How dare they display, for all to see, such inordinate egotism and presumption? And is it not a strange and sorry sight to see these zealots implicitly and explicitly take as their motto: Since the world began all men have been wrong, except myself. *Omnes, ego non.**

I ask the reader to forgive me for having so much insisted on the legitimacy of interest, which is based on this axiom: *Since postponements cost something, they must be paid for, cost* and *payment* being correlative terms. The fault lies in the spirit of our age. We must, in the face of the attacks made by a few fanatical innovators, take our stand clearly on the side of those vital truths that all humanity accepts. For the writer who seeks to demonstrate the harmony of all economic phenomena, it is a most painful thing, believe me, to be compelled to stop at every step to explain the most elementary concepts. Would Laplace † have been able to explain the solar system in all its fundamental simplicity, if there had not been certain areas of common understanding among his readers, if, in order to prove that the earth rotates, he had first been obliged to teach them to count? Such is the cruel dilemma of the economist in our day. If he does not stop to present fully the rudiments of his subject, he is not understood; and if he does explain them, the beauty and simplicity of the whole is swallowed up in a torrent of details.

It is truly fortunate for mankind that *interest* is legitimate.

* ["All men, but not I."—TRANSLATOR.]

† [Pierre Simon, Marquis de Laplace (1749–1827), French mathematician and astronomer.—TRANSLATOR.]

Otherwise man too would face a difficult dilemma: either, by remaining just, to perish; or, through injustice, to prosper.

Every industry represents a union of efforts. But among these efforts there is an essential distinction to be made. Some are directed toward services that are to be performed immediately; others, toward an indefinite series of services of a similar nature. Let me explain.

The pains a watercarrier goes to in the course of a day must be paid for by those who are benefited by them; but the pains he took previously to make his cart and his waterbarrel must be distributed, as regards payment, among an indefinite number of users.

Similarly, weeding, plowing, harrowing, reaping, threshing concern only the present harvest; but fences, clearings, drainage, buildings and improvements concern and facilitate an indefinite number of future harvests.

According to the general law of *service for service,* those who receive the satisfaction must recompense the efforts exerted for them. In regard to the first type of effort, there is no difficulty. Bargaining and *evaluating* are carried on between the one who exerts the effort and the one who benefits from it. But how can services of the second type be *evaluated?* How can a fair proportion of the permanent outlay, general expenses, fixed capital, as the economists call it, be distributed over the entire series of satisfactions that these things are designed to effect? By what method can their weight be made to fall evenly on the shoulders of all those who use the water, until the cart is worn out; on those who consume the wheat, as long as the field remains productive?

I do not know how they would solve this problem in Icaria or in the phalanstery, but I am inclined to believe that the inventors of societies, who are so prolific in their artificial arrangements and so ready to have them foisted on the public by law—which means, whether they admit it or not, by *force*—could not imagine a more ingenious solution than the entirely natural procedure that men have discovered for themselves (how presumptuous of them!) since time immemorial, the procedure that it is now proposed to forbid them to use, namely, that derived from the law of *interest.*

Let us assume that a thousand francs have been spent in real property improvements; let us assume also an interest rate of five per cent and an average harvest of five thousand liters. By this reckoning one franc is to be charged against each hundred liters of wheat.

This franc is evidently the legitimate payment for an actual service rendered by the landowner (who could also be called the worker) just as much to the man who will receive a hundred liters of grain ten years from now as to the man who buys it today. Therefore, the law of strict justice is observed.

Suppose, now, that the property improvements or the cart or the waterbarrel has a lifespan that can be determined only within approximate limits; then, provision for a sinking fund is added to the interest, so that the owner will not suffer a loss but may continue to operate. This is still in accordance with justice.

We must not assume that this one-franc interest charged against each hundred liters of wheat is an invariable amount. On the contrary, it represents value and obeys the general law of value. It increases or decreases according to the fluctuations of supply and demand, that is, according to the particular pressures of the moment and the general prosperity of society.

We are usually inclined to believe that this type of remuneration tends to increase, if not for industrial improvements, at least for agricultural improvements. Even admitting that this rent was originally fair, it is said, it finally becomes exorbitant, for the landowner thereafter stands by in idleness while his rent continues to rise from year to year, simply because the population is increasing, and therefore the demand for wheat also.

This tendency exists, I agree, but it is not confined to land rent; it is common to all types of labor. The value of every kind of labor increases with the density of the population, and the common day laborer earns more in Paris than in Brittany.

But we must also bear in mind that this tendency is counterbalanced, as far as land rent is concerned, by an opposite trend, which is that of progress. Improvements made today by better methods, with less human labor, and at a time when the interest rate has fallen, prevent too high a rent from being asked for previous improvements. The landowner's fixed capital, like the manufacturer's, deteriorates in the long run as more and more efficient labor-saving devices appear. This is a remarkable law, which overturns Ricardo's gloomy theory; it will be analyzed more completely when we discuss real property.

Note that the problem of the distribution of services to be performed in payment for permanent improvements could not be solved without the law of *interest*. The owner could not distribute his actual capital over an indefinite number of successive users; for where would he stop, since the exact number cannot be determined? The earlier ones would have paid for the later ones, which is not just. Furthermore, a time would have come when the owner would have been in possession of both his capital outlay and his improvements, which is not just either. Let us acknowledge, then, that the natural machinery devised by society is ingenious enough so that we do not have to supplant it with any artificial device.

I have presented the phenomenon in its simplest form in order to give a clear idea of its nature. In practice things do not occur in quite this way.

The landowner does not himself work out the distribution, and he does not decide that a charge of one franc, more or less, will be placed on each hundred liters of wheat. He finds that men have already decided these matters, both the prevailing price of wheat and the rate of interest. On this information he decides how he will invest his capital. He will use it to improve his land if he estimates that the price of wheat will permit him to realize the normal rate of interest. If such is not the case, he will invest it in an industry that promises a better return, and is, fortunately for society, more likely to attract capital for that very reason. This is the way the process really operates in reaching the same result as sketched above, and it offers us still another harmony of economic law.

The reader will understand that I have confined myself to one particular case simply as a means of illustrating a general law that applies to all professions and occupations.

A lawyer, for example, cannot make the first client who comes his way reimburse him for all he has spent on his education, his probation, his law office—perhaps amounting to as much as twenty thousand francs. This would not only be unjust; it would be impossible. The first client would never put in his appearance, and our budding Cujas * would be reduced to imitating the host who, when he saw that no one had come to his first ball, declared: "Next year I shall begin by putting on my second ball."

The same thing applies to the businessman, the doctor, the shipowner, the artist. In every calling these two types of effort are to be found; the second type must, without fail, be distributed over an indeterminate number of consumers, and I defy anyone to contrive a method of distribution other than the mechanism of *interest*.

In recent times great pains have been taken to stir up public resentment against that infamous, that diabolical thing, capital. It is pictured to the masses as a ravenous and insatiable monster, more deadly than cholera, more terrifying than riots, as a vampire whose insatiable appetite is fed by more and more of the life-blood of the body politic. *Vires acquirit eundo.*† The tongue of this blood-sucking monster is called "rent," "usury," "hire," "service charges," "interest." A writer whose great talents could have made him famous had he not preferred to use them to coin the paradoxes that have brought him notoriety has seen fit to cast this paradox before a people already tormented by the fever of revolution. I too have an apparent paradox to offer the reader, and I beg him to decide whether it is not both a great and a reassuring truth.

But, before presenting it, I must say a word about the manner in which M. Proudhon and his school explain what they call the injustice of *interest*.

Capital goods are tools of production. Tools of production are designed to harness the *gratuitous* forces of Nature. Through the steam engine we utilize the pressure of volatile gases; through the watch spring, the elasticity of steel; through weights or water-

---

* [Jacques Cujas (1520–1590), a jurist from Toulouse.—Translator.]

† ["It gains momentum as it goes along." The description of slander in Virgil's *Aeneid*, IV, 1, 175.—Translator.]

falls, gravitation; through Volta's battery, the speed of the electric spark; through the soil, the chemical and physical combinations that we call vegetation; etc., etc. Now, confusing utility with value, they think of these natural resources as having an *inherent* value *of their own,* and consequently assume that those who appropriate these resources receive payment for the privilege of using them, for value implies payment. They assume that commodities are charged with one *item* for man's services, which is accepted as just, and with another *item* for Nature's services, which is rejected as unjust. Why, they say, require payment for gravitation, electricity, vegetation, elasticity, etc.?

The answer is found in the theory of *value*. That class of socialists who take the name of egalitarians confuse the legitimate *value* of the tool of production, which is produced by human service, with the useful result it accomplishes, which is in fact always gratis, once this legitimate value, or the interest on it, has been deducted. When I pay a farmer, a miller, a railroad company, I give nothing, absolutely nothing, for the properties of vegetation, gravitation, steam pressure. I pay for the human labor that has gone into the tools that have harnessed these forces; or, what is more advantageous for me, I pay the interest on this labor. I pay for service with service, and thereby the useful action of these forces is turned to my profit and without further cost. The whole transaction is like an exchange, like a simple act of barter. The presence of capital does not alter this law, for capital is merely accumulated value, or *services* whose special function is to enlist the co-operation of Nature.

And now for my paradox:

Of all the elements that make up the total value of any product, the one we should pay for most gladly is that very element called interest on advance outlays or on capital.

And why is that? Because wherever this element makes us pay *once,* it saves us from paying *twice.* Because, by its very presence, it serves notice that the forces of Nature have contributed to the final result and are not being paid for their contribution; because, as a result, the same general amount of utility has been made available to us, but with this difference, that, fortunately for us, a certain proportion of gratuitous utility has replaced onerous utility; and, in a word, because the price of the product has gone down. We obtain it for a smaller proportion of our own labor, and what happens to society as a whole is what would happen to a man in isolation if he produced some ingenious invention.

Consider the case of a workingman in modest circumstances who earns four francs per day. For two francs, that is, for a half-day's labor, he buys a pair of cotton socks. If he tried to obtain them directly and by his own labor, I truly believe that his whole life would not be long enough for him to do so. How does it happen, then, that his half-day's labor pays for all the *human services* that were rendered to him for this commodity? In keeping with the law of *service for service,* why was he not required to contribute several years of labor?

The reason is that in the making of this pair of socks the proportion of *human services* has been enormously reduced, thanks to capital, by the use of natural resources. Our workman, nevertheless, pays not only for all the labor now required to perform this task but also for the interest on the capital that enlisted the co-operation of Nature; and we must note that had this last item not been available, or had it been declared illegal, capital would not have been employed in conjunction with natural resources, the commodity would have been produced by onerous utility only, that is, exclusively by human labor, and our workman would still be just where he started, that is, with the choice of either going without the socks or else of paying for them with several years of toil.

If our workman has learned to analyze what he sees, he will certainly make his peace with capital when he perceives how much he owes it. Above all, he will be convinced that God's gratuitous gifts to him are still gratuitous, that they have even been lavished upon him with a generosity that is not due to his own merits, but to the excellent operation of the *natural* social order. Capital is not the vegetative force of Nature that makes the cotton germinate and bloom, but the *pains taken* by the planter; capital is not the wind that filled the sails of the ship, nor the magnetic force to which the compass reacted, but the *pains taken* by the sailmaker and compass-maker; capital is not the compression of the steam that turns the spindles of the mill, but the *pains taken* by the builder of the mill. Germination, the power of the winds, magnetic attraction, stream pressure—all these things are certainly free of charge, and that is why the value of the socks is so low. As for the combined pains taken by the planter, the sailmaker, the compass-maker, the shipbuilder, the sailor, the manufacturer, the business-man, they are distributed, or rather, in so far as capital is concerned in the operation, the interest on them is distributed, over countless purchasers of socks; and that is why the amount of labor performed by each one of them in return for the socks is so small.

Truly, modern reformers, when I see you trying to replace this admirable order by a contrivance of your own invention, there are two things (or rather two aspects of the same thing) that utterly confound me: your lack of faith in Providence and your great faith in yourselves; your ignorance and your arrogance.

It is clear from the foregoing analysis that the progress of humanity coincides with the rapid formation of capital; for, when new capital is created, obstacles that once were surmounted by labor, that is, onerously, are now overcome by Nature, without effort; and this is done, be it noted, not to the profit of the capitalists, but to the profit of the community.

This being the case, it is the paramount interest of all men (from the economic point of view, of course) that the rapid formation of capital be encouraged. But capital increases of its own accord, spontaneously, so to speak, under the triple influence of a dynamic society, frugality, and security. We can hardly exert direct action on the energy and frugality of our fellow men, except through public opinion, through an intelligent expression of our likes and our dislikes. But we can do a great deal for the creation of security, without which capital, far from expanding, goes into hiding, takes flight, or is destroyed; and consequently we see how almost suicidal is the ardor for disturbing the public peace that the working classes sometimes display. They must learn that capital has from the beginning of time worked to free men from the yoke of ignorance, want, and tyranny. To frighten away capital is to rivet a triple chain around the arms of the human race.

The *vires acquirit eundo* parallel is completely applicable to capital and the beneficial influence it exerts. The creation of new capital always and necessarily releases both labor and the resources for paying labor and makes them available for other enterprises. Capital, therefore, contains within itself a strong progressive tendency—something like the laws of momentum. And this is a further argument that can be used against the very different kind of progressive tendency that Malthus notes, although political economists, to my knowledge, have neglected it until now. But this is a harmony that cannot be developed here. We reserve it for the chapter on population.

I must arm the reader in advance against a specious objection. If the function of capital, it will be said, is to have Nature perform what was hitherto performed by human labor, regardless of the good it brings to humanity as a whole, it must be harmful to the working classes, especially those who live on wages; for anything that adds to the number of employable workers increases their competition for jobs, and this is doubtless the secret reason for the proletarians' hostility to capitalists. If this objection were well founded, there would indeed be a discordant note in the social harmony.

The misconception here involved consists in losing sight of this truth: *For every amount of human effort that capital releases as it extends its operations, it likewise makes available a corresponding amount of money for wages,* so that these two elements meet and complement each other. Labor is not made permanently idle; when replaced in one special category by gratuitous energy, it turns its attack against other obstacles on the main road to progress, all the more surely because its remuneration is already available within the community.

And therefore, returning to the illustration given above, we can readily see that the price of socks (like the price of books, transportation, and everything else) goes down, under the influence of capital, only by leaving a part of the former price in the hands of the purchaser. This is so obvious that even to state it is almost childishly redundant; the worker who now pays two francs for what used to cost six has, therefore, four francs left over. Now this is the exact proportion of human labor that has been replaced by the forces of Nature. These forces are, therefore, a pure and simple gain, and the ratio between labor and available remuneration has not been altered at all. I make bold to remind the reader that the answer to this objection was already given [2] when, as we were studying man in isolation, or else still dependent on the primitive law of barter, I put the reader on his guard against the widespread fallacy that I am now attempting to refute.

Let us, therefore, have no qualms about allowing capital to form and increase in accord with *its* own tendencies and those of the human heart. Let us not imagine that, when the rugged workman saves for his old age, when the father plans a career for his son or a dowry for his daughter, by thus exercising man's noble faculty of foresight they are jeopardizing the general welfare. Such would be the case, private virtues would indeed be antagonistic to the public weal, if the interests of capital and labor were incompatible.

We must realize that humanity is far from being subject to this contradiction, rather, this impossibility (for how can we conceive of the constant deterioration of the whole resulting from the constant improvement of all its parts?); that, on the contrary, Providence, in its justice and goodness, has assigned, along the path of progress, a finer role to labor than to capital, more effec tive incentives, more generous compensations to him who now contributes the sweat of his brow, than to him who lives by the sweat and toil of his fathers.

Therefore, having established that every increase in capital is necessarily accompanied by an increase in the general welfare, I venture to present as incontrovertible the following axiom relating to the distribution of this prosperity:

As capital increases, the capitalists' absolute share in the total production increases and their relative share decreases. On the other hand, the workers' share increases both relatively and absolutely.

I can express my thought more clearly with figures.

Let us represent society's total production at successive periods in its history by the numbers 1,000, 2,000, 3,000, 4,000, etc.

I state that capital's share will drop successively from 50% to 40%, to 35%, to 30%, and labor's share will consequently rise from 50% to 60%, to 65%, to 70%; but in such a way that capital's *absolute* share at each period will be larger, although its *relative* share will be smaller.

Thus, the distribution will be made in the following manner:

DISTRIBUTION OF SHARES OF INCREASED PRODUCTION

	TOTAL PRODUCTION	CAPITAL'S SHARE	LABOR'S SHARE
First period	1,000	500	500
Second period	2,000	800	1,200
Third period	3,000	1,050	1,950
Fourth period	4,000	1,200	2,800

Such is the great, admirable, reassuring, necessary, and *invariable* law of capital. By proving it, it seems to me, we can utterly discredit those rantings that have been dinned into our ears for so long against the *greed*, the *tyranny*, of the most powerful instrument for civilization and *equality* that has ever been conceived.

This proof is divided into two parts. First, we must prove that capital's *relative* share does constantly decrease.

This will not take long, for it amounts to saying: *The more plentiful capital is, the lower its interest rate.* Now, this point is not open to question, nor has it been questioned. It not only can be explained scientifically; it is self-evident. Even the most unorthodox schools of thought admit it; in fact, the school that has specifically set itself up as the enemy of what it calls *diabolical* capital makes this fact the basis of its theory; since, from the evident fact of the decline in the rate of interest, it concludes that capital is inevitably doomed. For, this school says, since its extinction is inevitable, since it is sure to happen within a certain period of time, since this day will usher in the reign of unalloyed bliss, we must hasten and encourage its coming. This is not the place to refute these theories and their implications. I call attention only to the fact that all schools of thought—economists, socialists, egalitarians, and others—admit that, in the *natural* order of society, interest rates do indeed go down as capital increases. And even if they chose not to admit it, the fact would not be the less certain; for it is supported by the authority of the whole of human experience, and the acquiescence, perhaps involuntary, of all the capitalists in the world. It is a fact that the interest rate is lower in Spain than in Mexico, in France than in Spain, in England than in France, and in Holland than in England. Now, when interest goes down from 20% to 15%, then to 10%, to 8%, to 6%, to 4½%, to 4%, to 3½%, to 3%, what does this fact have to do with the question before us? It means that capital, for its contribution, through industry, to the general prosperity, is content with, or if you prefer, is forced to be content with, a share that becomes increasingly smaller as more capital is accumulated. Did capital once receive a third of the value of wheat, homes, linen, ships, canals? In other words, when these things were sold, did one-third go to the capitalists and two-thirds to the workers? Little by little the capitalists receive only a fourth, a fifth, a sixth; their *relative* share is constantly decreasing; the workers' share is rising proportionately, and thus the first part of my demonstration is proved.

It remains for me to prove that capital's *absolute* share constantly increases. It is true enough that interest rates tend to go down. But when and why? When and because capital increases. It is, therefore, entirely possible for the total accumulation of capital to increase, but for the *percentage* to decrease. A man has more income with 200,000 francs at 4% than with 100,000 francs at 5%, even though, in the first case, he charges less for the use of his capital. The same thing holds true for a nation and for all humanity. Now, I maintain that the *percentage,* in its tendency to decline, cannot and must not be reduced so rapidly that the *sum total* of interest paid is smaller when capital is plentiful than when it is scarce. I readily admit that if the capital of mankind is represented by 100 and the interest rate at 5, this rate will not be more than 4 when capital reaches 200. Here we see that the two effects are produced simultaneously: a smaller *relative* share, a larger *absolute* share. But, on the same hypothesis, I refuse to admit that the increase in capital from 100 to 200 can cause the interest rate to fall from 5% to 2%, for example. For, if such were the case, the capitalist who had 5,000 francs of income on 100,000 francs of capital would now have only 4,000 francs of income on 200,000 francs—a contradictory and impossible result, a strange anomaly that would be corrected by the simplest and least painful remedy imaginable; for in order to raise his income, the capitalist would need only to waste half of his capital. Strange and happy age when we could become rich by pauperizing ourselves!

We must, therefore, not lose sight of the fact that the combined action of these two correlated phenomena—increase of capital, lowering of the rate of interest—takes place *necessarily* in such a way that the total product constantly rises.

And, it may be remarked in passing, this fact destroys utterly and absolutely the fallacy of those who imagine that, because the interest rate falls, it eventually will disappear entirely. The result of this would be that the time would come when capital would be accumulated in such quantities that it would yield no return to its owners. Let us reassure ourselves; before that time comes, the owners of capital will be quick to dissipate it in order to restore their income.

This, then, is the great law of capital and labor, in so far as it relates to their sharing of what they produce jointly. Each one has a larger and larger *absolute* share, but capital's *proportional* share constantly decreases as compared with that of labor.

Therefore, capitalists and workers, cease looking at one another with envy and distrust. Shut your ears to those absurd tirades, as vain as they are ignorant, which, under pretence of brotherly love in the future, begin by sowing the seeds of discord in the present. Recognize that your interests are common, identical; that, whatever may be said to the contrary, they merge, they work together for the common good; that the toil and sweat of our generation mingle with the toil and sweat of generations gone by. Recognize too, that some amount of remuneration must indeed go to all those who have participated in the task, and that the most intelligent as well as the most equitable system of distribution is in operation among you, thanks to the wisdom of the laws of Providence, in a system of free and voluntary transactions. Let no parasitical sentimentalists impose their decrees upon you to the peril of your physical well-being, your liberty, your security, and your *self-respect*.

Capital has its roots in three attributes of man: foresight, intelligence, and thrift. For him to resolve to lay aside capital funds, he must, in fact, anticipate the needs of the future, sacrifice the present for them, exercise control over himself and his appetites, resist not only the allurements of the pleasures of the moment, but also the prickings of his vanity and the whims of public opinion, which is always so indulgent toward the light-minded and the extravagant. He must also link cause and effect in order to know by what means and by what tools Nature will become docile and will submit to the work of production. Above all, he must be moved by a sense of family devotion, so that he will not draw back before the sacrifices whose benefits will be enjoyed by his loved ones when he is no more. To accumulate capital is to provide for the subsistence, the protection, the shelter, the leisure, the education, the independence, the dignity of generations to come. None of this can be done without putting into practice all our most social virtues, and, what is harder, without making them our daily habit.

It is quite common, however, to attribute to capital a kind of deadly efficiency that would implant selfishness, hardness, and Machiavellian duplicity in the hearts of those who possess it or aspire to possess it. But is this not confused thinking? There are countries where labor is mainly fruitless. The little that is earned must quickly go for taxes. In order to take from you the fruit of your labor, what is called the state loads you with fetters of all kinds. It interferes in all your activities; it meddles in all your dealings; it tyrannizes over your understanding and your faith; it deflects people from their natural pursuits and places them all in precarious and unnatural positions; it paralyzes the activities and the energies of the individual by taking upon itself the direction of all things; it places responsibility for what is done upon those who are not responsible, so that little by little the distinction between what is just and what is unjust becomes blurred; it embroils the nation, through its diplomacy, in all the petty quarrels of the world, and then it brings in the army and the navy; as much as it can, it perverts the intelligence of the masses on economic questions, for it needs to make them believe that its extravagances, its unjust aggressions, its conquests, its colonies, represent a source of wealth for them. In these countries it is difficult for capital to be accumulated in natural ways. Their aim, above all, is by force and by guile to wrest capital from those who have created it. The way to wealth there is through war, bureaucracy, gambling, government contracts, speculation, fraudulent transactions, risky enterprises, public sales, etc. The qualities needed to snatch capital violently from the hands of the men who create it are exactly the opposite of the qualities that are necessary for its creation. It is not surprising, therefore, that in these countries *capital* connotes ruthless *selfishness;* and this connotation becomes ineradicable if the moral judgments of the nation are derived from the history of antiquity and the Middle Ages.

But when we turn our attention, not to the violent and fraudulent seizure of capital, but to its creation by intelligence, foresight, and thrift, we cannot fail to see that its acquisition by these means is a benefit for society and an aid to morality.

No less beneficial, socially and morally, than the formation of capital is its action. Its effect is to harness Nature; to spare man all that is most physical, backbreaking, and brutish in the work of production; to make mind master over matter; to provide more and more, I do not say idleness, but leisure; to make our most purely physical wants less imperious by rendering their satisfaction easier; to replace them with pleasures of a higher order, more delicate, more refined, more aesthetic, more spiritual.

Thus, no matter what our point of view, whether we consider capital in its relation to our wants, which it ennobles; to our satisfactions, which it refines; to Nature, which it tames for us; to morality, which it makes habitual in us; to our social consciousness, which it develops; to equality, which it fosters; to liberty, which is its life-blood; to justice, which it guarantees by the most ingenious methods; we shall perceive always and everywhere (provided only that it be created and put to work in a social order that has not been diverted from its natural course) that capital bears that seal and hallmark of all the great laws of Providence: harmony.

8

Private Property
and Common Wealth

While freely granting to the land, to the forces of Nature, and to the tools of production what is their just due—the power of creating utility—I have taken pains to deprive them of what has been attributed erroneously to them—the faculty of creating value—since this faculty resides exclusively in the services that men perform for one another through exchange.

This simple correction will at one and the same time strengthen the role of property by redefining it according to its true character and will reveal to political economists a fact of the greatest importance, which, if I am not mistaken, they still have not noticed, namely, that of common ownership, constituting a real, essential, and progressively increasing communal domain, which develops providentially in any social order that is guided by the principles of liberty. Its manifest destiny is to lead all men, as brothers, from their state of original equality, the equality of privation, want, and ignorance, toward ultimate equality in the possession of prosperity and truth.

If this basic distinction between the utility of things and the value of services is sound in principle as well as in the consequences I have deduced from it, its significance cannot be misunderstood; for it means that the promise of utopia falls within the scope of political economy, and that all conflicting schools of thought will be reconciled in a common faith, to the complete satisfaction of all minds and of all hearts.

Men of property and of leisure, however high on the social scale your achievements, your honesty, your self-control, your thrift, may have carried you, you are still strangely disturbed. Why? Because the sweet-smelling but deadly perfume of utopia threatens your way of life. There are men who say, who rant, that the competency you have laid aside for the quiet of your old age, for your daily bread, for the education and the future of your children, has been acquired at the expense of your brethren. They say that you have stood between God and His gifts to the poor; that, like the greedy publicans of old, you have exacted a tribute on these gifts in the name of property, of interest, of rent, and hire. They call upon you to make restitution. To add to your dismay, only too often your own advocates make this implicit admission in coming to your defense: The usurpation is indeed flagrant, but it is necessary.

But I say, no, you have not misappropriated the gifts of God. You have received them gratis from the hand of Nature, it is true; but you have also passed them on gratis to your fellow men and have withheld nothing. They have acted similarly toward you, and all that has passed between you has been *compensation* for mental or physical effort, for sweat and toil expended, for dangers faced, for skills contributed, for sacrifices made, for pains taken, for *services rendered and received.* You thought only of yourselves, perhaps, but even your own self-interest has become in the hands of an infinitely wise and all-seeing Providence an instrument for making greater abundance available to all men; for, had it not been for your efforts, all the *useful effects* that Nature at your command has transmitted without payment among men would have remained eternally dormant. I say, *without payment;* for the payment you received was only the simple return to you of the efforts you had expended, and not at all a price levied on the gifts of God. Live, then, in peace, without fear and without qualms. You have no other property in the world save your claim to services due you for services that you have fairly rendered, and that your fellow men have voluntarily accepted. This property of yours is legitimate, unassailable; no utopia can prevail against it, for it is part and parcel of our very nature. No new ideology will ever shake its foundations or wither its roots.

Men of toil and hardship, you can never shut your eyes to this truth: that the starting point for the human race was a state of complete community, a perfect equality of poverty, want, and ignorance. By the sweat of its brow humanity is regenerated and directs its course toward another state of community, one in which the gifts of God are obtained and shared at the cost of less and less effort; toward equality of another kind, the equality of well-being, of enlightenment, of moral dignity. To be sure, men's steps along this road to a better and better life are not all of equal length, and to the degree that the rapid strides of the advance guard might impede your own, you would have just cause for complaint. But the contrary is the case. No spark of knowledge illumines another's mind without casting some small gleam of light upon your own; no progress is achieved by others, prompted by the desire for property, that does not contribute to your progress; no wealth is created that does not work for your liberation, no capital that does not increase your enjoyments and diminish your toil, no property acquired that does not make it easier for you to acquire property, no property created that is not destined to increase the abundance shared by all men. The social order has been so artfully designed by the Divine Artificer that those who have moved farthest ahead along the road to progress extend a helping hand, wittingly or unwittingly; for He has so contrived that no man can honestly work for himself without at the same time working for all. It is strictly accurate to say that any attack upon this marvelous order would be on your part not only an act of homicide, but of suicide as well. The whole of mankind constitutes a remarkable chain wherein, miraculously, motion imparted to the first link is communicated with ever increasing speed right up to the last.

Men of good will, lovers of equality, blind defenders and dangerous friends of all who suffer, who lag behind on the road to civilization, you who seek to establish the state of community in this world, why do you begin by unsettling men's minds and natural interests? Why, in your pride, do you aspire to bend all wills

to the yoke of your social inventions? Do you not see that this
community for which you yearn so ardently, and which is to
extend the kingdom of God over the whole world, has already
been conceived and provided for by God Himself; that He has
not awaited your coming to make it the heritage of His children;
that He does not need your inventions or your acts of violence;
that every day His admirable decrees make it more and more a
reality; that He has not turned for guidance to the uncertainties
of your childish makeshifts nor even to the increasing expression
of altruism manifested by acts of charity, but has entrusted the
accomplishment of His plans to the most active, the most personal, the most enduring of our energies, our own self-interest,
confident that it is ever alert? Study, therefore, the machinery of
society, as it came from the hands of the Great Artificer, and you
will be convinced that He evidences a concern for all men that
goes far beyond your dreams and fantasies. Then, perhaps,
instead of proposing to redo the divine handiwork, you will be
content to pay it homage.

This does not mean that there is no room in the world for
reforms or reformers. Nor does it mean that humanity must not
eagerly recruit and generously encourage devoted researchers and
scholars, loyal to the cause of democracy. They are still most
necessary, not to subvert the law of society, but, on the contrary,
to oppose the artificial obstacles that disturb and pervert its
natural action. Truly, it is difficult to understand how people can
continue to repeat such trite statements as this: "Political economy is very optimistic toward accomplished fact; it affirms that
whatever *is,* is right; whether confronted with evil or with good,
it is content to say *laissez faire."* Do they imply that we do not
know that humanity began in complete want and ignorance, and
under the rule of brute force, or that we are *optimists concerning
accomplished facts such as these?* Do they suggest that we do not
know that the motive force of human nature is aversion to all
pain, all drudgery; and that, since labor is drudgery, the first manifestation of self-interest was the effort to pass this painful burden along from one to another? Do they mean to say that the
words "cannibalism," "war," "slavery," "privilege," "monopoly,"

"fraud," "plunder," "imposture," have never reached our ears, or that we see in these abominations the inevitable rumblings of the machine on the road to progress? But are not they themselves to some extent willfully confusing the issue in order to accuse us of confused thinking? When we admire the providential laws that govern men's transactions, when we say that the self-interest of every man coincides with that of every other man, when we conclude that the natural direction of these coincident interests tends to achieve relative equality and general progress; obviously it is from the operation of these laws, not from interference with their operation, that we anticipate harmony. When we say, *laissez faire,* obviously we mean: *Allow these laws to operate;* and not: *Allow the operation of these laws to be interfered with.* According as these laws are conformed to or violated, good or evil is produced. In other words, men's interests are harmonious, provided every man remains within his rights, provided services are exchanged freely, voluntarily, for services. But does this mean that we are unaware of the perpetual struggle between the wrong and the right? Does this mean that we do not see, or that we approve, the efforts made in all past ages, and still made today, to upset, by force or by fraud, the natural equivalence of services? These are the very things that we reject as breaches of the social laws of Providence, as attacks against the principle of property; for, in our eyes, free exchange of services, justice, property, liberty, security, are all merely different aspects of the same basic concept. It is not the principle of property that must be attacked, but, on the contrary, the principle hostile to it, the principle of spoliation and plunder. Men of property of all ranks, reformers of all schools, this is the mission that must reconcile us and unite us.

It is time, it is high time, that this crusade should begin. The ideological war now being waged against property is neither the most bitter nor the most dangerous that it has had to contend with. Since the beginning of the world there has also been a real war of violence and conspiracy waged against it that gives no sign of abating. War, slavery, imposture, inequitable taxation, monopoly, privilege, unethical practices, colonialism, the right to employment, the right to credit, the right to education, the right to public aid, progressive taxation in direct or inverse ratio to the ability to pay—all are so many battering-rams pounding against the tottering column. Could anyone assure me whether there are many men in France, even among those who consider themselves conservatives, who do not, in one form or another, lend a hand to this work of destruction?

There are people in whose eyes property appears only in the form of a plot of land or a sack of coins. Provided only that the land's sacrosanct boundaries are not moved and that pockets are not literally picked, they are quite content. But is there not also property in men's labor, in their faculties, in their ideas—in a word, is there not property in services? When I throw a service into the social scale, is it not my right that it remain there, suspended, if I may so express myself, until, according to the laws of its own natural equivalence, it can be met and counterbalanced by another *service* that someone is willing to tender me in exchange? By common consent we have instituted forces of law and order to protect property, so understood. Where are we, then, if these very forces take it upon themselves to upset this natural balance, under the socialistic pretext that freedom begets monopoly, that *laissez faire* is hateful and merciless? When things reach such a pass, theft by an individual may be rare and severely dealt with, but plunder is organized, legalized, and systematized. Reformers, be of good cheer; your work is not yet done; only try to understand what it really is.

But, before we proceed to the analysis of plunder, public or private, legal or illegal, its role in the world, the extent to which it is a social problem, we must, if possible, come to a clear understanding of what the communal domain and private property are; for as we shall see, private property is bounded on one side by plunder even as it is bounded on the other by the communal domain.

From what has been said in previous chapters, notably the one on utility and value, we may deduce this formula:

Every man enjoys gratis all utilities furnished or produced by

Nature on condition that he take the pains to avail himself of them, or that he pay with an equivalent service those who render him the service of taking pains for him.

In this formula two elements are combined and fused together, although they are essentially distinct.

There are, first, the gifts of Nature: gratuitous raw materials and gratuitous forces; these constitute the communal domain.

In addition, there are the human efforts that go into making these materials available, into directing these forces—efforts that are exchanged, evaluated, and paid for; these constitute the domain of private property.

In other words, in our relations with one another, we are not owners of the utility of things, but of their value, and value is the appraisal made of reciprocal services.

Private property and the communal domain are two correlative ideas founded, respectively, on those of *effort* and *freedom from effort.*

What is *free of effort* is held in *common,* for all men enjoy it and are permitted to enjoy it unconditionally.

What is *acquired by effort* is *private property,* because taking pains is prerequisite to its satisfaction, just as the satisfaction is the reason for taking the pains.

If exchange intervenes, it is effected by the evaluation of two sets of pains taken, or two services rendered.

This recourse to pains implies the idea of an obstacle. We may then say that the result sought comes closer and closer to the condition of being gratis and common to all in proportion as the intervening obstacle is reduced, since, according to our premise, the complete absence of obstacles would imply a condition of being completely gratis and common to all.

Now, since human nature is dynamic in its drive toward progress and perfection, an obstacle can never be considered as a fixed and absolute quantity. It is reduced. Hence, the pains it entails are reduced along with it, and the service along with the pains, and the value along with the service, and the property with the value.

But the utility remains constant. Hence, what is free of charge and common to all is increased at the expense of what formerly required effort and was private property.

To set man to work, a motive is necessary; and that motive is the satisfaction aimed at, or utility. It cannot be denied that he tends always and irresistibly to achieve the greatest possible satisfaction with the least possible amount of work, that is, to make the greatest amount of utility correspond with the least amount of property; consequently, the function of property, or rather of the spirit of property, is continually to enlarge the communal domain.

Since the human race started from the point of greatest poverty, that is, from the point where there were the most obstacles to be overcome, it is clear that all that has been gained from one era to the next has been due to the spirit of property.

This being the case, can anyone be found anywhere in the world who is hostile to the idea of property? Does not everyone see that it is impossible to imagine a force in society that is at once more just and more democratic? The fundamental dogma of Proudhon himself is *mutuality of services*. On this point we are in agreement. The point on which we differ is this: I call this dogma *property*, not mutuality of services, because careful analysis assures me that men, if they are free, do not and cannot have any other property than the ownership of value, or their services. Proudhon, on the contrary, like most economists, thinks that certain natural resources have an *intrinsic value of their own*, and that they are consequently *appropriated*. But, as for the idea that services constitute property, far from opposing it, he makes it his main article of faith. Does anyone desire to go further yet? As far as to say that a man should not be the owner of the pains he himself takes, that, in exchange, it is not enough to turn over gratis the help received from natural resources, that he must also surrender gratis his own efforts? But let him take care! This would mean glorifying slavery; for, to say that certain men must render services that are not paid for means that other men must receive services that they do not pay for, which is certainly slavery. Now, if he says that this gratuitous gift must be reciprocal, he is merely quibbling; for, either the exchange will be made with a certain degree of justice, in which case the services will be in some way or other *evaluated* and paid for; or else they will not be evaluated and paid for, and, in that case, some will give much and others little, and we are back to slavery.

It is therefore impossible to argue against the idea that services exchanged on the basis of value for value constitute legitimate property. To explain that this property is legitimate, we do not need to have recourse to philosophy or jurisprudence or metaphysics. Socialists, economists, egalitarians, believers in brotherly love, I defy you one and all to raise even the shadow of an objection against the *legitimacy of a voluntary exchange of services,* and consequently against property, as I have defined it, and as it exists in the natural order of society.

Of course, I know that in practice the ideal principle of property is far from having full sway. Against it are conflicting factors: there are services that are not voluntary, whose remuneration is not arrived at by free bargaining; there are services whose equivalence is impaired by force or fraud; in a word, plunder exists. The legitimacy of the principle of property is not thereby weakened, but confirmed. The principle is violated; therefore, it exists. We must cease believing in anything in this world, in facts, in justice, in universal consent, in human language; or else we must admit that these two words, "property" and "plunder," express opposite, irreconcilable ideas that can no more be identified than yes and no, light and dark, good and evil, harmony and discord. Taken literally, the famous formula, *property is theft,** is therefore absurdity raised to the nth degree. It would be no less outlandish to say that *theft is property;* that what is legal is illegal; that what is, is not, etc. It is probable that the author of this bizarre aphorism merely desired to catch people's attention with a striking paradox, and that what he really meant to state was this: Certain men succeed in getting paid not only for the work that they do but also for the work that they do not do, appropriating to

* [This is the famous and controversial answer Proudhon gave to his own question, *What is Property?* which is the title of his first published work (1840). —TRANSLATOR.]

themselves alone God's gifts, gratuitous utility, the common possession of all. But in that case it would first be necessary to prove the statement, and then to say: *Theft is theft.*

To steal, in common usage, means to take by force or fraud something of value to the detriment and without the consent of the person who has created it. It is easy to understand how fallacious economic thinking was able to extend the meaning of this melancholy word, "steal." First, utility was confused with value. Then, since Nature plays a part in the creation of utility, it was concluded that Nature also contributed to the creation of value, and, it was said, since this part of value is the fruit of no one's labor, it belongs to everyone. Finally, noting that value is never surrendered without compensation, the economists added: He *steals* who exacts payment for value that has been created by Nature, which is not in any way a product of human labor, which is *inherent in the nature of things* and is, by providential design, one of the *intrinsic qualities* of material objects, like specific gravity or density, form or color.

A careful analysis of value overturns this elaborate structure of subtleties, from which economists sought to deduce a monstrous identification of plunder with private property.

God put raw materials and the forces of Nature at man's disposal. To gain possession of them, either one has to take pains, or one does not have to take pains. If no pains are required, no man will willingly consent to buy from another man at the cost of effort what he can pluck from the hands of Nature without effort. In this case, no services, exchange, value, or *property* are possible. If pains must be taken, it is incumbent on the one who would receive the satisfaction to take them; hence, the satisfaction must go to the one who has taken the pains. This is the principle of property. Accordingly, if a man takes pains for his own benefit, he becomes the owner of all the combined utility created by his pains and by Nature. If he takes the pains for the benefit of others, he stipulates that he be given in return a utility representing equal pains, and the resulting transaction presents us with two efforts, two utilities that have changed hands, and two satisfactions. But we must not forget the important fact that the transaction is carried out by the comparison, by the *evaluation,* not of two utilities (they cannot be evaluated), but of the two services that have been exchanged. It is therefore accurate to say that, from his own individual point of view, man by his labor becomes the owner of the natural utility (this is the only reason that he works), whatever may be the ratio (infinitely variable) of his labor to the utility. But from the social point of view, in regard to the relations of one man with another, men can never be owners of anything except value, which is based, not on the bounty of Nature, but on human services, pains taken, risks run, resourcefulness displayed in availing oneself of that bounty; in a word, as far as gratuitous and natural utility is concerned, the last person to acquire it, the one who ultimately receives the satisfaction, is placed, by way of exchange, in exactly the position of the first worker. The latter happened to come upon the gratuitous utility and went to the trouble of taking possession of it; the ultimate consumer remunerates him by taking an equivalent amount of pains for him in return and thus substitutes his right of possession for the original owner's; the utility becomes his under the same terms, that is to say, gratis, provided he takes the necessary pains. In all this there is neither in semblance nor in fact a usurpation of the gifts of God.

Hence, I confidently advance this proposition as incontrovertible:

In their relation to one another, men are owners only of value, and value represents only services that are compared and voluntarily rendered and received.

I have already shown that, on the one hand, this is the true meaning of the word *value;* and that, on the other, men never are, never can be, owners of anything except value, a conclusion to be drawn from logic as well as from experience. From logic: for why should I buy from a man, using my pains as payment, what I can obtain from Nature, either without pains or with fewer pains? From universal experience, which is a weighty argument, since nothing can give more support to a theory than the expressed and tacit consent of all men of all times and all places: now, I affirm that universal agreement accepts and approves the meaning that I give here to the word "property." When a public official makes an *inventory* following a death, or orders one to be made; when a businessman, a manufacturer, a farmer, makes a similar appraisal on his own initiative; or when the receivers in a bankruptcy case are requested to make one; what is inscribed on the stamped pages of the inventory as each item is presented? Is it the item's *utility*, its intrinsic worth? No, it is its *value;* that is, the equivalent amount of effort that any potential purchaser would have to exert in order to obtain a similar item. Do the appraisers concern themselves with deciding whether a given object is more useful than another? Do they take into account the satisfactions that these objects can give? Do they rate a hammer above a piece of bric-a-brac because the hammer can admirably turn the law of gravity to the advantage of its owner? Or do they rate a glass of water above a diamond, because, objectively speaking, the water can render more tangible service? Or a volume of Say above a volume of Fourier, because Say gives more lasting pleasure and solid instruction? No; they *evaluate,* they seek out the *value,* rigorously following, please note, my definition. Or rather, my definition follows their practice. They take into account, not the natural advantages, or the gratuitous utility, contained in each item, but the services that anyone acquiring it would have to perform himself or have another perform for him in order to obtain it. They do not appraise—please pardon the rather flip expression —the trouble God went to, but the pains that the purchaser would have to take to obtain it. And when the appraisal is finished, when the public knows the total amount of value listed in the inventory, all say with one voice: This is what the heir *owns.*

Since property includes only value, and since value indicates only relationships, it follows that property is itself a relation.

When people, on comparing two inventories, declare one man to be richer than another, they do not mean that this comparison applies necessarily to the amounts of absolute wealth or material well-being enjoyed by the two. In satisfactions, in absolute well-being, there is an element of *common utility* that can greatly affect this ratio. All men, in point of fact, are equal in their access to the light of day, the air they breathe, the warmth of the sun;

and any inequality between the two inventories—expressed by the difference in property or value—can apply only to the amount of *onerous utility*.

And so, as I have already said many times and shall doubtless say many times more (for it is the greatest, the most admirable, and perhaps the most misunderstood of all the social harmonies, since it encompasses all the others), it is characteristic of progress (and, indeed, this is what we mean by progress) to transform onerous utility into gratuitous utility; to decrease value without decreasing utility; and to enable all men, for fewer pains or at smaller cost, to obtain the same satisfactions. Thus, the total number of things owned in *common* is constantly increased; and their enjoyment, distributed more uniformly to all, gradually eliminates inequalities resulting from differences in the amount of property owned.

Let us never weary of analyzing the result of this social mechanism.

How many times, when considering the phenomena of the social order, have I not had cause to appreciate how profoundly right Rousseau was when he said, "It takes a great deal of scientific insight to observe what we see every day"! Thus it is that *habit*, that veil which is spread before the eyes of the ordinary man, which even the attentive observer does not always succeed in casting aside, prevents us from seeing the most marvelous of all social phenomena: real wealth constantly passing from the domain of private property into the communal domain.

Let us try, nevertheless, to establish the fact that this democratic evolution does take place, and, if possible, to plot its course.

I have said elsewhere that, if we wished to compare two different eras of a nation's history from the point of view of their actual prosperity, we should have to resort to man-hours of unskilled labor as our measure, asking ourselves this question: What is the difference in the amount of satisfaction that could be obtained in this society, at different stages of its progress, by a given amount, say one day, of unskilled labor?

This question implies two others:

What was, at the dawn of civilization, the ratio between satisfactions and the simplest kind of labor?

What is this ratio today?

The difference in the two will measure the increase in gratuitous utility in relation to the amount of onerous utility, i.e., the extent of the communal domain in relation to that of private property.

I do not believe that a man interested in public affairs can apply himself to any more interesting or instructive problem. I ask the reader's indulgence if I seem to cite a tediously long list of examples before reaching a satisfactory solution.

At the beginning of this book I made a kind of table of the most general human wants: breathing, food, clothing, shelter, transportation, education, amusement, etc.

Let us follow this list and see what satisfactions a common laborer could obtain for a certain number of days' work at the dawn of society and what he can obtain now.

Breathing

Here the satisfaction is gratis and common to all from the very beginning. Nature, having taken care of everything, leaves us nothing to do. No efforts, services, value, property, progress are possible. From the point of view of utility, Diogenes is as rich as Alexander; from the point of view of value, Alexander is as poor as Diogenes.

Food

In the present state of things, the value of a hundred liters of wheat is worth, in France, fifteen to twenty days of the most unskilled kind of labor. This is a fact and, whether known or not, is worth noting. We can state, therefore, that today humanity, as represented by its most backward element, the day laborer, obtains the satisfactions represented by a hundred liters of wheat for fifteen days of the most unskilled kind of labor. It is estimated that it takes three hundred liters of wheat to feed one man for a year. The unskilled laborer produces, therefore, if not his actual subsistence, at least (what amounts to the same thing) the value of his subsistence with forty-five to sixty days out of his year's labor. If we represent by *one* the standard of value (which for us is one day of unskilled labor), the value of a hundred liters of wheat is represented by 15, 18, or 20, depending on the yearly fluctuations. The ratio of these two values is *one to fifteen.*

In order to determine whether or not progress has been achieved and, if so, to measure it, we must ask ourselves what this same ratio was on the day that men first made their appearance. In truth, I would not dare hazard a figure; but there is a way of establishing the unknown *x* of this equation. When you hear someone declaiming against the social order, against private ownership of the land, against rent, against machines, take him to a virgin forest or confront him with a fetid swamp. Say to him: I wish to free you from the yoke that you complain of; I wish to rescue you from the atrocious struggles of anarchistic competition, from the conflicts of antagonistic interests, from the selfishness of wealth, from the tyranny of property, from the crushing rivalry of machines, from the stifling atmosphere of society. Here is land like that encountered by the men who first cleared the forests and drained the swamps. Take as much of it as you want by tens or hundreds of acres. Cultivate it yourself. All that you make it produce is yours. There is only one condition: you must have no recourse to society, which, you say, has victimized you.

This man, please note, would find himself in the same position, in respect to the land, as mankind itself was originally in. Now, I declare without fear of contradiction that he would not raise one hundred liters of wheat every two years. Therefore, the ratio is fifteen to six hundred.

Thus, progress can be measured. As far as wheat is concerned, and despite the fact that he is obliged to pay rent on his land, interest on capital, and the cost of hiring his tools—or rather, because he does pay for these things—a day laborer obtains for fifteen days' work what he could hardly have secured in six hundred days. The value of wheat, measured in terms of the most unskilled labor, has therefore fallen from six hundred to fifteen, or from forty to one. A hundred liters of wheat has for man exactly the same utility that it would have had the day after the Flood; it contains the same amount of nourishment; it satisfies the same want and to the same degree. It represents the same *absolute wealth;* it does not represent the same *relative wealth.* Its production has in large measure been *turned over to Nature.* It is obtained for *less expenditure of human effort; less service* is performed as it passes from hand to hand; it has *less value;* in a word, it has become *gratis,* not completely, but in the ratio of forty to one.

And it has not only become *gratis,* but *common* to all by the same ratio. It is not to the profit of the producer that thirty-nine fortieths of the total effort have been eliminated; but it is to the consumer's profit, whatever may be his own line of work.

Clothing

The same phenomenon occurs in the case of clothing. An ordinary day laborer goes into one of the Marais* warehouses and gets a suit that corresponds to twenty days of his work, assumed to be of the most unskilled variety. He could not make the suit himself even if he spent his whole life at it. In the time of Henry IV it would have cost him three or four hundred days' work to buy a similar suit. What has happened to the materials in these two suits to make such a difference in their *value* in terms of man-hours of unskilled labor? It has been annihilated, because *gratuitous* forces of Nature have taken over the job; and the annihilation is to the advantage of all mankind.

For we must never lose sight of this fact: every man owes to his fellows services equivalent to those that he receives. If the weaver's art had made no progress, if his work were not now done in part by *gratuitous* forces of Nature, it would take the weaver two or three hundred days to weave the cloth, and our laborer would have to contribute two or three hundred days of his own labor to obtain it. And, since the weaver cannot, however much he might like to do so, persuade society to pay him two or three hundred days'

* [An old quarter of Paris where low-priced goods are sold.—TRANSLATOR.]

labor for what is done for nothing by the forces of Nature, that is, to pay him for the progress that mankind has made, it is quite accurate to say that this progress has worked to the advantage of the purchaser, of the consumer, and to the better satisfaction of mankind as a whole.

Transportation

Before the time when any progress had been made, when the human race was still reduced, like our hypothetical day laborer, to primitive and unskilled labor, if a man wanted to have a hundred-pound load transported from Paris to Bayonne, he would have had only this choice: either to put it on his own shoulders and carry it over hill and dale to its destination, which would have taken over a year of slow plodding; or to get someone else to do this hard chore for him. Since, given the conditions we have outlined, the new carrier would have used the same means and required the same time, he would have demanded a year's labor in return. At this period in history, therefore, representing the value of unskilled labor as *one,* transportation was worth three hundred per hundred-pound weight carried a distance of four hundred fifty miles.

Things have certainly changed. In fact, there is no day laborer in Paris who could not obtain the same result at a cost of two days' labor. The choice is still the same. Either one must do the job oneself or have it done by others and pay them for it. If our laborer does it himself, it will still cost him a year of hard plodding; but if he turns to professional haulers, he will find twenty, any one of whom would be willing to do it for him for three or four francs, that is, for the equivalent of two days' worth of unskilled labor. Thus, the value of unskilled labor being represented as *one,* transportation that was worth three hundred is now worth only *two.*

How has this amazing revolution come about? It took many a century. Certain animals had to be tamed, mountains tunneled, valleys filled in, rivers spanned. First sledges were used, then wheels; obstacles that had represented labor, services, value, were lessened; in a word, man reached the point where he could do, for pains equal to two, what originally he could do only for pains equal to three hundred. All this progress was achieved by men who were concerned only with their own self-interest. And yet today who reaps the reward? Our poor day laborer and, along with him, everyone else.

Let no one say that this is not an example of common ownership. I maintain that this is common ownership in the strictest sense of the word. Originally this particular satisfaction was balanced on the scales of the general economy by three hundred days' worth of unskilled labor or by a smaller, but proportional, amount of more highly skilled labor. Now two hundred ninety-eight out of three hundred parts of this effort have been taken over by Nature, and humanity has been correspondingly relieved of it. Now, obviously, all men are equal as regards those obstacles that have been removed, the distance that has been annihilated, the toil that has been eliminated, the value that has been destroyed, since they all enjoy the result without paying for it. They pay only for the quantity of human effort still required, amounting to two, with unskilled labor as the measure. In other words, for the man who is unskilled and has only his physical strength to offer, two days of labor are still required to obtain the satisfaction desired. All other men obtain it for less work than that: a Paris lawyer, earning thirty thousand francs a year, for one twenty-fifth part of a day, etc. By this reasoning, then, we see that men are equal as regards the value that has been destroyed, and that what inequality remains falls within the domain of the surviving value, that is, within the domain of private property.

For political economy, proceeding by way of example can mean walking on dangerous ground. The reader is always inclined to believe that the general phenomenon that it is the author's intention to describe holds true only in the particular case cited. But it is clear that what has been said of wheat, clothing, transportation, is true of everything else. When the author generalizes, it is for the reader to make the concrete application; and when the author performs the dull and uninspiring task of analysis, it is asking little enough that the reader give himself the pleasure of making the synthesis for himself.

Essentially, the basic law can be stated thus:

Value, which is social property, is created by effort and obstacles.

As obstacles decrease, effort and value, or the domain of private property, decreases proportionally.

As satisfactions are achieved, the domain of private property constantly decreases and the communal domain steadily increases.

Must we conclude, as M. Proudhon does, that private property is destined to disappear? Granted that for each specific result obtained, each satisfaction achieved, its role grows less, as the extent of the communal domain increases; does this mean that private property will eventually be completely absorbed and destroyed?

To draw such a conclusion is to misunderstand entirely the very nature of man. We encounter here a fallacy similar to the one that we have already refuted concerning interest on capital. Interest rates tend to fall, it was said; hence, interest is ultimately bound to disappear altogether. Value and the domain of private property decrease, it is now said; therefore, they are ultimately bound to be eliminated entirely.

The whole fallacy consists in overlooking the significance of these three crucial words: for *each specific result.* Yes, it is quite true that men obtain *specific results* with less effort. It is because they have this faculty that they are perfectible and capable of progress; and because of this faculty we can state that the *relative* domain of private property grows smaller and smaller, if we consider its role in achieving a given satisfaction.

But it is not true that the *potential results* that are still to be obtained are ever exhausted, and therefore it is absurd to think that the absolute domain of private property is impaired by the laws of progress.

We have said many times and in every conceivable way: Every effort, in time, can lead to a greater total amount of gratuitous utility, without justifying us in concluding that men will ever stop making efforts. All that we have the right to conclude is that, as their energies are freed, they will be turned against new obstacles and will achieve, for the same effort, new and hitherto unheard-of satisfactions.

I emphasize this idea the more, in that we must, in times like the present, be permitted to leave no room for fallacious interpretations when we use the terrible words, "private property" and "the communal domain."

At any given moment in his life man in a state of isolation has only a limited amount of effort at his disposal. This is true also of society.

When man in a state of isolation achieves progress in some field by making the forces of Nature co-operate with his own labor, he reduces correspondingly the total amount of his efforts *in relation to the useful effect sought for.* He would also reduce his efforts in an *absolute* sense, if, content with his present lot, he converted his progress into increased leisure, refusing to apply his newly released energies toward procuring other satisfactions. But this assumes that ambition, desire, aspirations, are strictly limited forces; that the human heart is not infinitely capable of experiencing new impulses. Such, of course, is not the case. Hardly has Robinson Crusoe been able to make Nature do part of his work for him when he turns to new projects. The total amount of effort he expends remains the same; but he puts it to better, more fruitful, more productive use, because he avails himself of more of Nature's gratuitous collaboration; and the same thing occurs in society.

Because the plow, the harrow, the hammer, the saw, oxen and horses, the sail, water power, and steam have successively liberated man from a tremendous amount of effort he once had to expend, it does not necessarily follow that the energies thus made available are allowed to atrophy. Let us recall what was said about the indefinite elasticity of human wants and desires. Let us look about us, and we shall not hesitate to admit that every time man has succeeded in overcoming an obstacle by making use of the forces of Nature, he has turned his own powers against new obstacles. We print more easily now than we used to, but we do more printing. Every book represents less human effort, less value, less property; but there are more books, and, in the total reckoning, just as much effort and as much value and property. I could say the same thing for clothing, housing, railroads—for all human commodities. It is not a case of a decrease in the total value, but of an increase in the total utility. The *absolute* domain of private property has not shrunk, but the absolute domain of what is gratis and common to all has grown larger. Progress has not paralyzed labor; it has distributed prosperity more widely.

Things that are available without cost and are common to all constitute the domain of the forces of Nature, and this domain is steadily growing. This truth is supported by both reason and experience.

Value and private property constitute the domain of human efforts, of reciprocal services; and this domain is growing constantly smaller in relation to any particular satisfaction obtained, but not in relation to the sum total of all satisfactions, because the number of *potential* satisfactions open to mankind is limitless.

It is as true, therefore, to say that relative property constantly gives way before communal wealth as it is false to say that absolute property tends to disappear entirely. Property, like a pioneer, accomplishes its mission in one area, and then moves on to another. For it to disappear entirely, it would be necessary that there be no more obstacles to challenge human labor; that all effort become vain; that men no longer have need to exchange, to render one another services; that everything be produced spontaneously; that desire be immediately followed by satisfaction; that we all become the *equals of the gods.* Then, it is true, everything would be gratis and common to all. Effort, service, value, property—none of the things that bear witness to our innate infirmity would have any reason for existence.

But however high man may rise, he is still as far as ever from omnipotence. What does it matter what particular rung is his perch on the ladder of infinity? What characterizes God, so far as it is given us to understand Him, is that no barrier stands between

His will and its accomplishment: *Fiat lux, et lux facta est.** And even this is evidence of man's inability to understand God's omnipotence, for Moses could not avoid placing two words, which had to be pronounced, as an obstacle between the divine will and the coming of the light. But whatever progress is in store for man because of his perfectibility, we can affirm that his progress will never be so complete as to clear away every obstacle on the road to infinite prosperity and to render completely useless the work of his hands and his mind.

The reason is simple enough: as rapidly as certain obstacles are overcome, new desires appear that encounter new obstacles requiring new efforts. We shall always, then, have labor to perform, to exchange, to evaluate. Property will therefore exist until the end of time, always growing in its total amount, as men become more active and more numerous, although each effort, each service, each value, each unit of property, will, in passing from hand to hand, serve as the vehicle of an increasing proportion of gratuitous and common utility.

The reader will note that we use the word "property" in a very extended, but nonetheless exact, sense. *Property is the right to enjoy for oneself the fruits of one's own efforts or to surrender them to another only on the condition of equivalent efforts in return.* The distinction between property owner and proletarian is therefore fundamentally erroneous, unless we assert that there is a class of men who perform no work or have no rights over their own efforts or over the services that they render or over those that they receive in exchange.

It is erroneous to restrict the term "property" to one of its special forms, like capital or land, something that produces interest or rent; and it is this erroneous definition that is used to divide men into two hostile classes. Analysis shows that interest and rent are the fruit of services rendered and have the same origin, the same nature, and the same rights as manual labor.

The world is a vast workshop upon which Providence has

* ["And God said, Let there be light: and there was light." Genesis, I, 3.— TRANSLATOR.]

lavished raw materials and forces. Human labor applies itself to these materials and forces. Past efforts, present efforts, and even future efforts or promises of future efforts are exchanged. Their relative worth, established by exchange and independently of raw materials and the gratuitous forces of Nature, determines value; and every man is the owner of the value he has produced.

It may be objected: What difference does it make that a man is the owner, as you say, only of the value or of the acknowledged worth of his service? Ownership of the value carries with it ownership of its concomitant utility. John has two sacks of wheat; Peter, only one. John, you say, is twice as rich *in value*. Very well, then! He is also twice as rich in utility, and even in natural utility. He can eat twice as much.

True enough, but has he not performed double the amount of work?

But let us get at the roots of the objection.

Actual, absolute wealth, as we have already said, resides in utility. This is what the word itself means. Only *utility renders service (uti,* "to serve"). Only utility is related to our wants, and man has only utility in mind when he works. At least this is his specific goal; for things do not satisfy our hunger or our thirst because they contain value, but because they contain utility.

But note how this works in society.

In isolation man seeks to obtain utility, with never a thought for value, which, in fact, he could not even conceive of.

In society, on the other hand, man seeks to obtain value, with never a thought for utility. The thing he produces is not intended to satisfy his own wants. Hence, he has little concern with how useful it may be. The person desiring it must be the judge on that score. As far as he, the producer, is concerned, all that counts is that, when it is bargained for, as great a value as possible be assigned to it, for he is sure that the more value he is credited with contributing, the more utility he will receive in return.

The division of labor has brought about a situation in which each one produces what he will not consume and consumes what he has not produced. As producers we are concerned with value; as consumers, with utility. Such is the universal experience. The person who polishes a diamond, embroiders lace, distills brandy, or raises poppies, does not ask himself whether their consumption is reasonable or unreasonable. He does his work, and, provided his work brings him value in return, he is content.

And, we may note in passing, this state of affairs proves that morality or immorality resides not in the work of the producer of a commodity, but in the desire of the consumer; and that the improvement of society, therefore, depends on the morality of the consumer, not of the producer. How often have we cried out against the English for raising opium in India with the express purpose, it was said, of poisoning the Chinese! Such an accusation reveals an ignorance of the nature and scope of morality. Never shall we succeed in preventing the production of something that, since it is in demand, has value. It behooves the person seeking a satisfaction to reckon the effect it will have, and the attempt to separate foresight from responsibility will always be a vain one. Our winegrowers make wine and always will make it as long as it has value, without bothering to find out whether or not it makes people drunk in France or leads them to commit suicide in America. It is the judgment that men pass on their wants and their satisfactions that determines the direction of labor. This is true even in isolation; and if a foolish vanity had spoken more loudly to Robinson Crusoe than hunger, instead of spending his time in hunting, he would have spent it arranging feathers in his headdress. Similarly, a serious population encourages serious industries; and a frivolous population, frivolous industries.[1]

But, to return to our subject, I make this statement:

The man who works for himself has utility as his objective.

The man who works for others has value as his objective.

Now, property, as I have defined it, is based on value; and, since value is only a relative term, property itself is only a relative term.

If there were only one man on earth, the idea of property would never occur to him. Since he would be free to dispose as he wished of all the utilities about him and would never be confronted with others' rights limiting his own, how could it enter his mind to say: *This is mine?* These words presuppose the correlative: *This is*

not mine, or *This belongs to another. Mine* and *thine* are inseparable; and the word "property," or "ownership," necessarily
implies a relationship, since it indicates with equal clarity both
that a thing is *owned* by one person, and that it is not *owned* by
another.*

"The first man, who, having put a fence around a piece of
land," said Rousseau, "took it into his head to say, 'This is mine,'
was the true founder of civil society." †

What does this fencing off express except an idea of exclusion
and consequently of a relation existing between the owner and
others? If its sole purpose were to protect the land from animals,
it would be a precaution, not a sign of property; a boundary
marker, on the other hand, is a sign of property, and not of
precaution.

Thus, men are in reality owners only in relation to one another;
and, once this is granted, of what are they owners? Of value,
as is clearly evidenced in the exchanges they make with one
another.

Let us give, as is our custom, a very simple illustration.

Nature has been at work, through all eternity perhaps, in putting into spring water the qualities that enable it to quench our
thirst and, from our point of view, to give it *utility.* This is
certainly not my work, since the process has been completed
without my participation or knowledge. In this respect, I can
say that water, for me, is a gratuitous gift from God. What is *my
own* is the effort I exerted in order to provide myself with a day's
supply of water.

By this act of mine, of what have I become the owner?

In respect to myself, I am the owner, if I may use that term, of
all the utility that Nature has placed in this water. I can turn it
to my benefit in any way I see fit. It is, indeed, for no other reason
that I have gone to the trouble of going after it. To challenge
my right to it would be to say that, although men must drink to

* [In the original French: *propriété . . . exprime . . . qu'une chose est propre à
une personne . . . qu'elle n'est propre à aucune autre."*—TRANSLATOR.]
† [This famous statement is the opening sentence of the Second Part of the *Discourse on the Origin of the Inequality among Men.*—TRANSLATOR.]

live, they do not have the right to drink the water they have procured by their own labor. I do not believe that the communists, although they go very far, would go quite that far; and even under the system proposed by Cabet, the lambs of Icaria will be permitted, when they are thirsty, to drink from its streams of pure water.

But in respect to other men, presumably free to do as I have done, I am not, and cannot be, owner of anything more than what, by metonymy, is called the *value of the water,* that is, the value of the *service* I render by letting others have it. Since my right to drink it is recognized, it is impossible to contest my right to turn it over to someone else. And since his right to go to the spring to get it, as I did, is recognized, it is impossible to contest his right to accept the water that I fetched. If one man has the right to offer and another to accept, for a price that has been freely arrived at, the former is the *owner,* as far as the latter is concerned. It is truly discouraging to be writing in an age when it is impossible to take a step in the field of political economy without having to stop for such childishly obvious demonstrations.

But on what basis shall the arrangement be made? This is what, above everything else, we must know if we are to evaluate fully the social significance of this word "property," so distressing to the partisans of pseudodemocratic sentimentality.

But to continue my illustration: It is clear, since both I and the man who wishes to purchase the water I secured are free, that we shall take into consideration the trouble I went to and the trouble that he will be spared, as well as all other circumstances that create value. We shall haggle over the terms; and, if the bargain is concluded, it can be said without exaggeration or undue subtlety that my neighbor will have acquired *gratis,* or, if you will, *as nearly gratis as I did,* all the natural utility of the water. Is any further proof required that human effort, and not intrinsic utility, determines the degree to which the conditions of the transaction are onerous? It will be granted that the utility of this water remains constant, whether the spring be near at hand or far away. It is the pains taken or to be taken that constitute the variable, depending on the distance, and since the remuneration varies accordingly, it is in the pains, and not in the utility, that we find the principle of relative value, i.e., of property.

It is therefore certain that, in relation to others, I am not and cannot be owner of anything except my own efforts and my own services. These have nothing in common with the mysterious and unknown processes by which Nature has communicated utility to the things that I use to render my services. In spite of all further claims I might make, my property will never actually go beyond this limit; for, if I demand more for my service than its value, my neighbor will perform it for himself. This limit is absolute, definite, and impassable. It explains and completely justifies property, which is necessarily restricted to the very natural right of demanding a service in exchange for a service. It makes it evident that to speak of the enjoyment of natural utilities as "property" is to use the word in a very loose and purely nominal sense; that to use expressions like, "The property in an acre of land, in a hundredweight of iron, in a hundred liters of wheat, in a meter of cloth," is mere metonymy, like the "value" of water, iron, etc.; that, in so far as Nature has placed these things within men's reach, they are enjoyed gratis and by all; that, in a word, the idea of a gratuitous communal domain can be harmoniously reconciled with the idea of private property, since the gifts of God fall into the first category, and human services alone form the legitimate domain of the second.

Merely because I have chosen a very simple illustration to show the line of demarcation between the communal domain and that of private property, we should not hastily conclude that this line is blurred or effaced in more complex transactions. On the contrary; it remains clearly visible and is always to be observed in any free transaction. Going to the spring for water is admittedly a very simple act; but the act of growing wheat, if we consider it carefully, is no more complex, except that it includes a whole series of equally simple acts, in any one of which Nature's contribution and man's are combined. Therefore, the example I chose is completely typical. In the case of water, wheat, dry goods, books, transportation, painting, dance, music, certain circumstances, as we have admitted, can give great value to certain services, but no man can ever claim payment for anything else, and especially for Nature's aid, as long as one of the contracting parties can say to the other: If you ask me more than your service *is worth,* I shall look elsewhere, or I shall perform it for myself.

Not content with justifying the idea of private property, I should like to make it appealing even to the most rabid partisans of public ownership. To that end what must we do? We must describe its contribution to democracy, progress, and equality; we must make clear, not only that it does not give a monopoly on the gifts of God to a few individuals, but also that its special function is to increase steadily the extent of the communal domain. In this respect, it is far more ingenious than the plans thought up by Plato, More,* Fénelon, or Cabet.

That there are certain things that men avail themselves of gratis and on a footing of perfect equality, that there is in the social order, underlying private property, a very real communal domain, is a fact that no one disputes. Whether we are economists or socialists, we have only to open our eyes to see that this is so. In certain respects all of the children of God are treated alike. All are equal before the law of gravitation, which holds them to the earth, and in respect to the air they breathe, the light of day, the rushing water of the torrent. This vast and immeasurable store of common possessions, which has nothing to do with value or property, is called *natural wealth* by Say, in contrast to *social wealth;* by Proudhon, *natural possessions,* as against *acquired possessions;* by Considérant, *natural capital,* as against *created capital;* by Saint-Chamans, *consumers' wealth,* as against *value wealth;* we ourselves have called it *gratuitous utility,* as against *onerous utility.* Name it what you will, the important thing is that it exists, that we are justified in saying that there exists among men a common store of gratuitous and equal satisfactions.

---

* [Sir Thomas More (1478–1535), whose *Utopia,* published first in Latin in 1516 and later in English is a satire on the government and society of his day, which are compared with a fictitious island commonwealth, modeled on Platonic principles, where goods are owned in common.—Translator.]

And though *social wealth, acquired wealth, created wealth, onerous wealth, value wealth*—in a word, *property*—may be unevenly distributed, we cannot say that it is unjustly distributed, since every man's share of it is proportional to his own *services*, for it is based on them and receives its evaluation from them. Furthermore, it is evident that this inequality is lessened by the existence of the common store of gratuitous utility, in virtue of the following law of mathematics: The relative difference between two unequal numbers is lessened if the same number is added to each. If, then, our inventories show that one man is twice as rich as another, we cannot consider this proportion as accurate when we take into account both men's share of the common gratuitous utility; and even what inequality we do discover would steadily grow less if the common store steadily increased.

The question, therefore, is whether this *common store* is a fixed and invariable quantity, vouchsafed once and for all to man by Providence at the beginning of time, on which is superimposed a stratum of *private property*, in such a way that no connection or interaction exists between the two phenomena.

Economists have concluded that the social order has no influence on this natural and common fund of wealth and for that reason have excluded it from the study of political economy.

The socialists go further. They believe that the social order tends to transfer to the domain of private property what is rightfully part of the common store, that it sanctions the usurpation of what belongs to all for the profit of the few; and for that reason they attack political economists for being unaware of this disastrous tendency, and society for passively submitting to it.

In fact, the socialists tax the economists with being inconsistent on this point, and with some reason; for the economists, after declaring that there was no connection between the communal domain and that of private property, went on to weaken their own assertion and open the way for the socialists' grievances when, confusing value with utility, they declared that the forces of Nature, that is, the gifts of God, had intrinsic value, value on their own account, for value always and necessarily connotes private property. On the day the economists made this error they lost the right and the means to justify logically the right to private property.

What I now say, what I declare with conviction as an absolute certainty in my own mind, is this: Yes, there is constant interaction between private property and the communal domain; and in this respect the first assertion, that of the economists, is wrong. But the second assertion, amplified and exploited by the socialists, is even more dangerously erroneous; for this interaction does not cause any part of the communal domain to be appropriated into the domain of private property, but, on the contrary, constantly extends the former at the expense of the latter. Private property, inherently just and legitimate, because it always is proportional to services, tends to convert onerous utility into gratuitous utility. It is the spur that impels the human intellect to realize the latent potential of the forces of Nature. It attacks, to its own profit admittedly, the obstacles that stand in the way of gratuitous utility. And when the obstacle is surmounted to any degree, we find that it results in corresponding benefit to all. Then, tirelessly, property attacks new obstacles, and this process continues with never an interruption, steadily raising the standard of living, bringing the great family of man nearer and nearer the goals of community and equality.

In this consists the truly marvelous harmony of the natural social order. Unfortunately, I cannot describe this harmony without combatting old objections that are always cropping up or without becoming tiresomely repetitious. No matter; I shall set myself to the task, and I beg the reader also to exert himself to some degree.

We must grasp fully this fundamental idea: When no obstacle between desire and satisfaction exists for anyone (for example, there is no obstacle between our eyes and the light of day), there is no effort to be made, no service to be performed for oneself or for others; no value, no property is possible. But when an obstacle exists, the whole series is constituted. First, we find effort coming into play; then, the voluntary exchange of efforts and services; then, the comparative appraisal of services, or value; and finally, the right of each one to enjoy the utilities contained in these values, or property.

If, in this struggle against equal obstacles, the contribution made by Nature and by labor always remained in the same proportion, private property and the communal domain would follow parallel lines with no change in their relative proportions.

But such is not the case. The goal of all men, in all their activities, is to reduce the amount of effort in relation to the end desired and, in order to accomplish this end, to incorporate in their labor a constantly increasing proportion of the forces of Nature. This is the constant preoccupation of every farmer, manufacturer, businessman, workman, shipowner, and artist on earth. All their faculties are directed toward this end; for this reason they invent tools or machines, they enlist the chemical and mechanical forces of the elements, they divide their labors, and they unite their efforts. How to do more with less, is the eternal question asked in all times, in all places, in all situations, in all things. Certainly they are motivated by self-interest; who can deny it? What other stimulant would urge them forward with the same degree of energy? Since every man here below bears the responsibility for his own existence and progress, how could he possibly have within him any lasting motive force except self-interest? You cry out in protest; but bear with me until the end, and you will see that, though each man thinks of himself alone, God is mindful of all.

Our constant concern is, therefore, to decrease our effort in relation to the end we seek. But when effort is diminished— whether by the removal of the obstacle or by the use of machines, the division of labor, joint activity, the harnessing of a force of Nature, etc.—this decreased effort is assigned a proportionately lower rating in relation to other services. We render a smaller *service* when we perform it for someone else; it has less value, and it is quite accurate to say that the domain of private property has receded. Has the utility of the end result been lost on that account? No, nor can it be by the very nature of our hypothesis. What, then, has happened to the utility? It has passed into the communal domain. As for that part of human effort which is no longer required, it does not on that account become sterile; it is directed toward other conquests. Enough obstacles appear and always will appear to thwart the satisfaction of our ever new and increasing physical, intellectual, and moral wants, so that our labor, when freed in one area, will always find something to challenge it in another. And so, since the domain of private property always remains the same, the communal domain increases like a circle whose radius is constantly lengthened.

Otherwise how could we explain progress and civilization, however imperfect the latter may be? Let us look upon ourselves and consider our weakness; let us compare our strength and our knowledge with the vigor and the knowledge that are presupposed by the countless satisfactions we are privileged to derive from society. Certainly we shall be convinced that, if we were reduced to our own efforts, we should not enjoy one hundred thousandth part of these satisfactions, even though each one of us had millions of acres of uncultivated land at his disposal. It is therefore certain that a given amount of human effort achieves immeasurably greater results today than in the time of the Druids. If this were true of only one individual, the natural inference would be that he lives and prospers at others' expense. But since the same thing happens for all members of the human family, we are led to the comforting conclusion that something outside ourselves has come to our aid; that the gratuitous co-operation of Nature has been progressively added to our own efforts, and that, throughout all our transactions, it has remained gratuitous; for if it were not gratuitous, it would explain nothing.

From the preceding considerations we may deduce the following propositions:

All property is value; all value is property.

What has no value is gratuitous; what is gratuitous is common to all.

A decline in value implies a greater amount of gratuitous utility.

A greater amount of gratuitous utility implies a partial realization of common ownership.

There are times in our history when we cannot utter certain

words without running the risk of being misinterpreted. There will be no dearth of people ready to cry out, in praise or in condemnation, according to their economic persuasion: The author speaks of a communal domain; therefore he is a communist. I anticipate it, and I am resigned to it. But though resigned, I cannot refrain from seeking to avoid the imputation.

The reader must indeed have been inattentive (and it is for this reason that the readers most to be feared are those who do not read) if he has not discerned the great divide between the communal domain and communism. These two ideas are separated not only by the great expanse of private property but also by that of law, liberty, justice, and even of human personality.

By the communal domain is meant those things that we enjoy in common, by the design of Providence, without the need of any effort to apply them to our use. They can therefore give rise to no service, no transaction, no property. Property is based on our right to render services to ourselves or to render them to others for a remuneration. What the communist proposes to make common to all is not the gratuitous gifts of God, but human effort, or service. He proposes that each one turn over the fruit of his toil to the common fund and then make the authorities responsible for this fund's equitable distribution.

Now, one of two things will be done: either the distribution will be based on each man's contribution, or it will be made on some other basis.

In the first case, the communist hopes, as far as the result is concerned, to reproduce the existing order, contenting himself with substituting the arbitrary decision of a single individual for the free consent of all.

In the second case, on what basis will the distribution be made? Communism answers: On the basis of equality. What! Equality without reference to any difference in pains taken? We shall all have an equal *share,* whether we have worked six hours or twelve, mechanically or intellectually! But of all possible types of inequality this is the most shocking; and furthermore, it means the destruction of all initiative, liberty, dignity, and prudence.

You propose to kill competition, but take care; you are only redirecting it. Under present conditions we compete to see who works most and best. Under your regime we shall compete to see who works worst and least.

Communism fails to understand even man's nature. Effort is of itself painful. What disposes us to exert it? It can only be a sensation more painful still, a want to be satisfied, a suffering to be avoided, a good thing to be enjoyed. Our motive force is, therefore, self-interest. When we ask communism what it proposes as a substitute, it answers in the words of Louis Blanc: *honor,* and in the words of M. Cabet: *brotherhood.* In that case you must at least make me feel other people's sensations, so that I may know to what end I should direct my labor.

And then just what is this code of honor and this sense of brotherhood that is to be put to work in all mankind at the instigation and under the watchful eyes of Messrs. Louis Blanc and Cabet? But it is not necessary for me to refute communism here. All that I desire to state is that it is the exact opposite in every particular of the system that I have sought to establish.

We recognize the right of every man to perform services for himself or to serve others according to conditions arrived at through free bargaining. Communism denies this right, since it places all services in the hands of an arbitrary, central authority.

Our doctrine is based on private property. Communism is based on systematic plunder, since it consists in handing over to one man, without compensation, the labor of another. If it distributed to each one according to his labor, it would, in fact, recognize private property and would no longer be communism.

Our doctrine is based on liberty. In fact, private property and liberty, in our eyes are one and the same; for man is made the owner of his own services by his right and his ability to dispose of them as he sees fit. Communism destroys liberty, for it permits no one to dispose freely of his own labor.

Our doctrine is founded on justice; communism, on injustice. This is the necessary conclusion from what we have just said.

There is, therefore, only one point of contact between the

communists and ourselves: a certain similarity in the syllables composing the words "communism" and the "communal" domain.

But I trust that this similarity will not lead the reader astray. Whereas communism is the denial of private property, we see in our doctrine of the communal domain the most explicit affirmation and the most compelling demonstration that can be given in support of private property.

For, if the legitimacy of private property has appeared doubtful and inexplicable, even to those who were not communists, it seemed so because they felt that it concentrated in the hands of some, to the exclusion of others, the gifts of God originally belonging to all. We believe that we have completely dispelled this doubt by proving that what was, by decree of Providence, common to all, remains common in the course of all human transactions, since the domain of private property can never extend beyond the limits of value, beyond the rights laboriously acquired through services rendered.

And, when it is expressed in these terms, who can deny the right to private property? Who but a fool could assert that men have no rights over their own labor, that they may not rightfully receive voluntary services from those to whom they have rendered voluntary services?

There is another expression that requires explanation, for in recent times it has been strangely misused, viz., "gratuitous utility." Do I need to say that I mean by "gratuitous," not something that does not cost one man anything because he has taken it from another, but what does not cost anybody anything?

When Diogenes warmed himself in the sun, it could be said that he warmed himself gratis, for he received from the divine bounty a satisfaction that required no labor either from himself or from any of his contemporaries. I may add that this warmth from solar radiation remains gratuitous when a landowner uses it to ripen his wheat and his grapes, since, of course, when he sells his grapes and wheat, he is paid for his own services and not for the sun's. This interpretation may perhaps be fallacious (and if it is, there is nothing left to do but turn communist); but, in any case, such is the sense that the expression "gratuitous utility" obviously has and the sense in which I use it.

Since the establishment of the Republic* people have been talking a great deal about *interest-free* credit and education *free of charge*. But it is clear that they include a terrible fallacy in this word. Can the state make instruction shine down, like the light of day, on every corner of the land without requiring any effort from anybody? Can it cover France with schools and teachers who do not require payment in any form? All that the state can do is this: Instead of allowing each individual to seek out and pay for services of this type that he wants, the state can, by taxation, forcibly exact this remuneration from the citizens and then distribute the type of instruction it prefers without asking them for a second payment. In this case those who do not learn pay for those who do; those who learn little for those who learn much; those who are preparing for trades for those who will enter the professions. This is communism applied to one branch of human activity. Under this regime, on which I do not propose to pass judgment at this time, one may say, one must say: *Education is common to all;* but it would be ridiculous to say: *Education is free of charge.* Free of charge! Yes, for some of those who receive it, but not for those who pay out the money for it, if not to the teacher, at least to the tax collector.

There is nothing that the state cannot give *gratis* if we follow this line of reasoning; and if this word were not mere hocus-pocus, gratuitous education would not be the only thing we should ask of the state, but gratuitous food as well, and gratuitous clothing, and gratuitous housing, etc. Let us beware. The great mass of our citizens have almost reached this point; at least there is no dearth of agitators demanding, in the name of the common people, *interest-free* credit, *gratuitous* tools of production, etc., etc. Deceived by the meaning of a word, we have taken a step toward communism; why should we not take a second, then a third, until all liberty, all property, all justice have passed away? Will it be alleged that education is so universally necessary that we are

* [The reference here is to the Second Republic of 1848 (cf. chap. 3, p. 37).— TRANSLATOR.]

permitted for its sake to compromise with justice and our principles? But is not food even more important. *Primo vivere, deinde philosophari,** the common people will say, and, in all truth, I do not know what answer can be given them.

Who knows? Those inclined to accuse me of communistic leanings because I have noted the providential community of God's gifts will perhaps be the very ones to violate the right to learn and to teach, that is, to violate in its essence the right to property. These inconsistencies are more surprising than unusual.

---

* ["Let us concern ourselves first with gaining a living; afterwards we may philosophize." A common adage of antiquity.—TRANSLATOR.]

9

Landed Property

If the central thesis of this work is valid, we must conceive of mankind, in its relation to the world about it, along the lines that I shall now indicate.

God created the world. On the surface and in the bowels of the earth, He placed a host of things that are useful to man in that they are capable of satisfying his wants.

In addition, He imparted to matter various forces: gravitation, elasticity, density, compressibility, heat, light, electricity, crystallization, plant life.

He placed men in the midst of these raw materials and these forces and bestowed them upon him gratis. To them men applied their energies; and in so doing they performed services for themselves. They also worked for one another; and in so doing they rendered reciprocal services. These services, when compared for purposes of exchange, gave rise to the idea of value, and value to the idea of property.

Every man, therefore, became, in proportion to his services, a proprietor. But the forces and the raw materials, originally given gratis to man by God, remained, still are, and always will be, gratis, however much, in the course of human transactions, they may pass from hand to hand; for, in the appraisals that their exchange necessitates, it is *human* services, and not the *gifts of God,* that are *evaluated.*

From this it follows that there is not one among us who, provided only our transactions be carried out in freedom, ever ceases to enjoy these gifts. A single condition is attached: we must ourselves perform the labor necessary to make them available to us, or, if someone else takes this trouble for us, we must pay him the equivalent in other pains that we take for him.

If what I assert is true, then certainly the right to property is unassailable.

The universal instinct of mankind, which is more infallible than the lucubrations of any one individual could ever be, had been to adhere to this principle without analyzing it. Then the theorists came along and set themselves to scrutinizing the concepts underlying the idea of property.

Unfortunately, at the very beginning they made the error of confusing utility with value. They attributed inherent *value,* independent of any human service, to both raw materials and the forces of Nature. Once this error was made, the right to property could be neither understood nor justified.

For utility represents a relation between things and ourselves. No efforts, transactions, or comparisons are necessarily implied; it can be conceived of as an entity in itself and in relation to man in isolation. Value, on the contrary, represents a relation between one man and another; to exist at all it must exist in twofold form, since there is nothing with which an isolated thing can be compared. Value implies that its possessor surrenders it only for equal value in return. The theorists who confuse these two ideas therefore make the assumption that in exchange a man trades value supposedly created by Nature for value created by other men, that is, utility requiring no labor, for utility that does require labor—in other words, that he profits from the labor of others without contributing labor of his own. The theorists first characterized property so understood as a *necessary monopoly,* then merely as a *monopoly,* then as *injustice,* and finally as *theft.*

Landed property received the first brunt of this attack. It was inevitable. Not that all industry in its operation does not likewise use the forces of Nature; but in the eyes of the multitude these forces play a much more striking role in the phenomena of plant and animal life, in the production of food and what are improperly called *raw materials,* both of which are the special province of agriculture.

Moreover, if there is one monopoly more repugnant to human conscience than any other, it is undoubtedly a monopoly on the things most essential to human life.

This particular confusion—evidently quite scientifically plausible to begin with, since, so far as I know, no theorist avoided falling into it—was rendered even more plausible by existing conditions.

Quite frequently the landowner lived without working, and it was easy to draw the conclusion that he must indeed have found a means of being paid for something other than his labor. And what could this something be except the fertility, the productivity, of the land, the instrument that supplemented his own efforts? Hence, *land rent* was assailed by various epithets, depending on the times, such as "necessary monopoly," "privilege," "injustice," "theft."

And it must be admitted that the theorists were in part led astray by the fact that few areas of Europe have escaped conquest and all the abuses that conquest has brought with it. They understandably confused the phenomenon of landed property that had been seized by violence with the phenomenon of property as it would be formed naturally under normal conditions.

But we must not imagine that the erroneous definition of the word "value" did no more than undermine landed property. The power of logic is inexorable and indefatigable, whether it be based on a true or a false premise. Just as the land has light, heat, electricity, plant life, etc., to aid it in producing value, does not capital likewise call upon the wind, elasticity, gravitation to co-operate with it in the work of production? There are, therefore, other men, besides agriculturists, who receive payment for the use of the forces of Nature. This payment comes to them in the form of interest on capital, just as rent comes to the landowner. Therefore, declare war on interest as well as on rent!

Thus, property has been attacked with ever increasing force by economists and egalitarians alike, in the name of this principle, which I maintain is false: *The forces of Nature possess or create value.* For all schools are agreed that it is true and differ only in

the violence of their attack and in the relative timidity or boldness of their conclusions.

The economists have stated: *Landed property is a privilege,* but
it is necessary; it must be maintained.

The socialists: *Landed property is a privilege,* but it is necessary; it must be maintained, but required to make a reparation,
in the form of right-to-employment legislation.

The communists and the egalitarians: *Property in general is a
privilege;* it must be destroyed.

And *I* say, as emphatically as I know how: *Property is not a
privilege.* Your common premise is false; hence, your three conclusions, though conflicting, are also false. *Property is not a privilege;* therefore, you cannot say that it must be tolerated, that it
must be required to provide a reparation, or that it must be
destroyed.

Let us review briefly the opinions voiced on this serious
problem by the various schools of thought.

We know that the English economists have advanced this
principle, with apparent unanimity: *Value comes from labor.*
They may quite possibly be in agreement with one another, but
can their agreement be called consistent with their own reasoning? Let the reader judge for himself whether or not they have
attained this greatly-to-be-desired consistency. He will note
whether or not they constantly and invariably confuse gratuitous
utility, which cannot be paid for, which contains no value, with
onerous utility, which comes only from labor, and which alone, as
they themselves say, possesses value.

Adam Smith: "In agriculture, too, Nature labours along with
man; and *though her labour costs no expense,* its produce has
nonetheless its value, as well as that of the most expensive
workmen." *

Here, then, we have Nature producing *value.* And he who

* [*The Wealth of Nations* (Rogers edition), I, 367. The italics are Bastiat's, not
Smith's. The phrase "nonetheless" (*n'en a pas moins*") is added by Bastiat.—
TRANSLATOR.]

would purchase wheat must pay for this value, although it has not cost anybody anything, even in terms of labor. Who will dare step forward to claim this so-called *value?* But for this word "value" substitute "utility," and all becomes clear, and private property is vindicated and justice satisfied.

> This rent may be considered as the produce *of those powers of Nature,* the use of which the landlord lends to the farmer. . . . . It [the rent!] *is the work of Nature,* which remains after deducting or compensating *everything that can be regarded as the work of man.* It is seldom less than a fourth and often more than a third of the whole produce. No equal quantity of productive labour employed in manufactures can ever occasion so great a reproduction. In them Nature does nothing; man does all. . . . .*

Is it possible to assemble a greater number of dangerous errors in fewer words? On this reckoning, a fourth or a third of the *value* of food products must be attributed *exclusively* to the powers of Nature. And yet the landowner charges the tenant, and the tenant the proletarian, for this so-called value, which remains after payment is made for *the work of man.* And it is on this basis that you propose to justify the right to property! What, then, do you propose to do with the axiom: *All value comes from labor?*

Furthermore, we have the assertion that Nature *does nothing* in manufactures! So gravitation, volatile gases, animals do not aid the manufacturer! These forces do the same thing in the factories that they do on the land; they produce gratis, not value, but utility. Otherwise property in capital goods would be as much exposed to communist attacks as landed property.

Buchanan,† in his comment, while accepting the theory of the master on rent, is led by the logic of the facts to criticize him for declaring it advantageous.

Smith, in regarding as *advantageous* to society that portion of the soil's produce which represents profit on farm land [what language!]

* [*Ibid.,* I, 368.—Translator.]
† [David Buchanan, the younger (1779–1848), journalist, author on economic subjects, and editor of Adam Smith's works in 1814.—Translator.]

does not reflect that rent is only the effect of high price, and what the landlord gains in this way he gains only at the expense of the consumer. Society gains nothing by the reproduction of profit on land. It is one class profiting at the expense of the others.*

Here we find the logical deduction: rent is injustice.

Ricardo: "Rent is that portion of the produce of the earth *which is paid* to the landlord for possessing the right to exploit *the productive and indestructible powers of the soil.*" †

And, in order that there be no mistake, the author adds:

Rent is often confounded with the interest and profit of capital. . . . . It is evident that a portion only of the money . . . . represents the interest of the capital which had been employed in improving the land, and in erecting such buildings as were necessary, etc.; the *rest is paid for the use of the original and indestructible powers of the soil.* In the future pages of this work, then, whenever I speak of the rent of land, I wish to be understood as speaking of that compensation which the farmer pays to the owner of the land for the use of *the original and indestructible powers of the soil.*

McCulloch: ‡ "What is properly termed Rent is the sum paid for *the use of the natural and inherent powers of the soil.* It is entirely distinct from the sum paid for the use of buildings, enclo-

---

* [*The Wealth of Nations* (Buchanan edition), II, 55, note. Bastiat's translation, which has been given literally above, differs from the original in the long paraphrase used to render the English words "the reproduction of rent" as well as in the addition of the parenthesis that it elicits. Buchanan actually says: "In dwelling on the reproduction of rent as so great an advantage to society, Smith does not reflect that rent is the effect of high price, and that what the landlord gains in this way he gains at the expense of the community at large. There is no absolute gain to society by the reproduction of rent. It is only one class profiting at the expense of another class."—TRANSLATOR.]

† [*Political Works* (McCulloch's edition), pp. 34, 35. Bastiat has again for the sake of emphasis altered slightly the English text, which is as follows: "Rent is that portion of the produce of the earth which is paid to the landlord for the use of the original and indestructible powers of the soil."—TRANSLATOR.]

‡ [John Ramsay McCulloch (1789–1864), British economist and statistician, author of *Principles of Political Economy* (1825).—TRANSLATOR.]

sures, roads, or other improvements. *Rent is, then, always a monopoly."*

Scrope: "The value of land and its power of yielding Rent are due to two circumstances: first, the appropriation of *its natural powers;* second, the labor applied to its improvement."

The conclusion is not long in coming:

"Under the first of these relations *rent is a monopoly.* It restricts the usufruct of the gifts that God has given to men for the satisfaction of their wants. This restriction *is just only in so far as it is necessary* for the common good."

How great must be the perplexity of those good souls who refuse to admit that anything can be necessary which is not just!

Scrope concludes with these words:

"When it goes beyond this point, it must be modified on the same principle that caused it to be established."

The reader cannot fail to perceive that these authors have led us to the denial of the right to property, and have done so very logically by starting with this proposition: The landowner exacts payment for the gifts of God. Hence, land rent is an injustice that has been legalized under the pressure of necessity; it can be modified or abolished as other necessities dictate. This is what the communists have always said.

Senior: "The instruments of production are labour and natural agents. Natural agents having been appropriated, proprietors *charge for their use* under the form of Rent, which is the recompense of no sacrifice whatever, and is received by those who have neither laboured nor put by, but who merely hold out their hands to accept the offerings of the rest of the community."

Having dealt property this heavy blow, Senior explains that a portion of rent corresponds to interest on capital, and then adds:

The surplus is taken by the *proprietor of the natural agent,* and is his reward, not for having laboured or abstained, but simply for not having withheld when he was able to withhold; for having permitted the gifts of Nature to be accepted.

We see that this is still the same theory. The landowner is presumed to come between the hungry and the food God had intended for them, provided they were willing to work. The owner, who had a share in its production, charges for this labor, as is just, and then he charges a second time for Nature's labor, for the productive forces, for the indestructible powers of the soil, which is unjust.

We are sorry to find this theory, developed by John Stuart Mill, Malthus, *et al.,* also gaining acceptance on the Continent.

"When one franc's worth of seed," says Scialoja, "yields one hundred franc's worth of wheat, this great increase in value is due in large part to the land." *

This is confusing utility with value. One might as well say: When water, which costs only a sou ten yards from the spring, costs ten sous at a hundred yards, this increase in value is due in large part to the help of Nature.

Florez Estrada: † "Rent is that part of the product of agriculture which is left *after all the costs of its production have been met.*"

Hence, the landowner receives something for nothing.

All the English economists begin by asserting this principle: *Value comes from labor.* They are therefore merely inconsistent when they thereupon attribute *value to forces contained in the soil.*

The French economists, for the most part, assign value to utility; but, since they confuse gratuitous utility with onerous utility, the harm they do property is equally great.

Jean-Baptiste Say:

The land is not the only natural agent that is productive; but it is the only one, or almost the only one, that man has been able to appropriate. The waters of the sea and of the rivers, in being able to turn the wheels of our machines, to provide us with fish, to float our ships, likewise have productive power. The wind and even the sun's rays work for us; but, *fortunately,* no one has yet been able to say: The wind and the sun belong to me, and I must be paid for the service they render.

---

* [Antonio Scialoja (1817–1877), Italian economist and follower of the English school.—TRANSLATOR.]

† [Alvaro Florez Estrada (1765–1833), Spain's most distinguished economist of the first half of the nineteenth century.—TRANSLATOR.]

Say apparently deplores the fact that anyone can say: The land belongs to me, and I must be paid for its service. *Fortunately,* I maintain, the landowner can no more charge for the services of the land than for the wind's or the sun's.

The earth is a wondrous chemical workshop wherein many materials and elements are mixed together and worked on, and finally come forth as grain, fruit, flax, etc. Nature has presented this vast workshop to man as a *gratuitous* gift, and has divided it into many compartments suitable for many different kinds of production. But certain men have come forth, have laid hands on these things, and have declared: This compartment belongs to me; that one also; all that comes from it will be my exclusive property. And, amazingly enough, *this usurpation of privilege,* far from being disastrous to society, has turned out to be advantageous.

Of course, the arrangement has proved advantageous! And why? Because it is neither privilege nor usurpation; because the one who said, "This compartment is mine," could not add, "What comes from it will be my exclusive property," but instead, "What comes from it will be the exclusive property of anyone wishing to buy it, paying me in return for the pains I take, or that I spare him; what Nature did for me without charge will be without charge to him also."

Say, I beg the reader to note, distinguishes in the value of wheat the shares that belong, respectively, to property, to capital, and to labor. With the best of intentions he goes to great pains to justify this first portion of payment which goes to the landowner and which is not charged against any previous or present labor. But he fails, for, like Scrope, he falls back on the weakest and least satisfactory of all available arguments: *necessity.*

If it is impossible for production to be carried on not only without land and capital, but also without these means of production becoming *property,* can we not say that their owners perform a productive function, since without it production could not be carried on? It is, indeed, a convenient function, although in the present state of society it requires an accumulation of capital goods from previous production or savings, etc.

The confusion here is obvious. For the landowner to be a

capitalist, there must be an accumulation of capital goods—a fact that is neither questioned nor to the point. But what Say looks on as "convenient" is the role of the landowner as such, as someone charging for the gifts of God. This is the role that must be justified, and it entails neither accumulation nor savings.

If, therefore, property in land and in capital goods [why associate things that are different?] is created by production, I can fittingly liken property to a machine that works and produces while its owner stands idly by, charging for its hire.

Still the same confusion. The man who has made a machine owns *capital* goods, from which he derives legitimate payment, because he charges, not for the work of the machine, but for the labor he himself has performed in making it. But the *soil*, which is *landed* property, is not *the product of human labor*. On what grounds is a charge made for what it does? The author has here lumped together two different types of property in order to persuade us to exonerate the one for the same reasons that we exonerate the other.

Blanqui: *

The farmer who plows, fertilizes, sows, and harvests his field, provides labor without which there would be nothing to reap. But the action of the land in germinating the seed, and of the sun in ripening the crop, are independent of this labor and co-operate with it to form the *value* represented by the harvest. . . . . Smith and many other economists have asserted that human labor is the only source of value. This is certainly not the case. The farmer's industry is not the only thing that creates the *value* in a sack of wheat or a bushel of potatoes. His skill will never be so great as to produce germination, any more than the alchemist's patience has discovered the secret of making gold. This is obvious.

It is impossible to confuse more completely, first, utility with value, and, secondly, gratuitous utility with onerous utility.

Joseph Garnier: †

* [Jérôme Adolphe Blanqui (1798–1854), French economist and head of the Paris École de Commerce.—TRANSLATOR.]

† [Clement Joseph Garnier (1813–1881), commentator on Adam Smith and generally recognized as one of the ablest of the French economists. Professor in the Paris École supérieure de Commerce.— TRANSLATOR.]

Rent paid to the landowner is fundamentally different from the payments made to the workman for his labor or to the entrepreneur as profit on the outlays made by him, in that these two types of payment represent compensation, to the one for pains taken, to the other for sacrifices or risks he has borne, whereas the landowner receives rent more *gratuitously* and *merely by virtue of a legal convention* that guarantees to certain individuals the right to landed property.[1]

In other words, the workman and the entrepreneur are paid, in the name of justice, for services that they render; the landowner is paid, in the name of the law, for services that he does not render.

The most daring innovators do nothing more than propose to replace private ownership by collective ownership. . . . . *They have reason on their side, it seems to me, as regards human rights;* but, practically speaking, they are wrong until such time as they can demonstrate the advantages of a better economic system. . . . .[2]

But for a long time to come, even though admitting that *property is a privilege and a monopoly,* we must add that it is a useful and natural monopoly. . . . .

In short, it is apparently admitted by political economists [alas! yes, and herein lies the evil] that property does not stem from divine rights, or rights of demesne, or from any other theoretical rights, but simply from its practical advantages. *It is merely a monopoly that is tolerated in the interest of all,* etc.

This is the identical judgment passed by Scrope and repeated by Say in milder terms.

I believe that I have sufficiently proved that the economists, having started from the false assumption that *the forces of Nature possess or create value,* went on to the conclusion that private property (in so far as it appropriates and charges for this value that is independent of all human services) is a privilege, a monopoly, a usurpation, but a necessary privilege that must be maintained.

It remains for me to show that the socialists start from the same assumption but change their conclusion to this: Private property is a necessary privilege; it must be maintained, *but* we must require the property owner to furnish compensation in the form of a guarantee of employment for those who are without property.

After this, I shall summon the communists, who declare, still arguing from the same premise: Private property is a privilege; it must be abolished.

And finally, at the risk of repeating myself, I shall close by refuting, if possible, the common premise from which all three conclusions are derived: *The forces of Nature possess or create value.* If I succeed, if I demonstrate that the forces of Nature, even when converted into property, do not create value, but utility, which is passed on by the owner in its entirety, reaching the consumer without charge, then economists, socialists, communists will all have to agree to leave the world, in this respect, as it is.

M. Considérant writes: [3]

In order to see how and under what conditions *private property* can appear and develop legitimately, we must understand the *fundamental Principle of Property rights:* Every man OWNS LEGITIMATELY THE THING *which his labor, his intelligence,* or, more generally, HIS ACTIVITY HAS CREATED.

This principle is incontestable, and it is well to note that implicitly it recognizes the right of all men to the land. In fact, since the land was not created by men, it ensues from the fundamental Principle of Property that the land, the common fund presented to the species, can in no wise be legitimately the absolute and exclusive property of any particular individuals who have not created *this value.* Let us then formulate the true Theory of Property, establishing it exclusively on the unassailable principle which bases the *Legitimacy of Property* on the fact of the CREATION *of a thing or of the value possessed by it.* In order to do this, let us consider the creation of Industry, that is, the origin and development of agriculture, manufacture, the arts, etc., in human society.

Let us imagine that on the land of a remote island, on the soil of a nation, or over the whole earth (the area of the theater of operations changes in no way the significance of the facts), one generation of mankind devotes itself for the first time to industry, that is, for the first time it farms, manufactures, etc. Each generation, by its labor, by its intelligence, by its own industry, *creates commodities, develops values,* that did not previously exist on the unimproved land.

Is it not perfectly evident that in this first industrial generation the possession of Property will be in conformity with Justice, IF *the value and wealth produced by the industry of all* is distributed among their producers IN PROPORTION TO THE CONTRIBUTION of each one to the creation of the general wealth? This is incontestable.

Now, the results of this labor fall into two categories that must be carefully distinguished.

The *first category* includes those things coming from the soil that belonged to the first generation by right of use: products increased, refined, or manufactured by the labor and industry of this generation. These products, finished or unfinished, consist either of consumers' goods or of tools of production. It is clear that the products are fully and legitimately the property of those who by their industry have created them. Each one of these persons has, therefore, the right either to consume them immediately or to put them away to be disposed of according to his subsequent convenience, whether it be to use them, exchange them, or give them away or transfer them to whomsoever desired, without need of authorization from anyone. According to this hypothesis, this property is obviously legitimate, respectable, sacred. It cannot be attacked without attacking *Justice, Right, and individual Liberty*—in a word, without committing an act of plunder.

Second category. But not all the things created by the industrial activity of this first generation fall into the above category. Not only has this generation created the products that we have just designated (consumers' goods and tools of production), but it has also added an *additional value* to the *original value of the soil* by cultivating it, building upon it, and adding permanent improvements.

This additional value obviously constitutes a product, a value, due to the first generation's industry. Now, if, by some means or other (we are not concerned here with the question of means), the ownership of this extra value is distributed equitably, that is, in proportion to each one's labor in creating it, each one of these persons will possess *legitimately* the portion that falls to him. He will therefore be able to dispose of this legitimate private property as he sees fit, exchanging it, giving it away, transferring it, without any of the other individuals, in other words, society, ever having any right or authority whatsoever over these values.

We can understand perfectly well, therefore, that, when the second generation comes along, it will find upon the land capital of two different types:

A. *Original or Natural Capital,* which has not been created by men of the first generation—that is, the *value* of the unimproved land.

B. *Capital Created* by the first generation, including: first, the *products,* goods, and implements that have not been consumed or worn out by the first generation; second, the extra value that the labor of the first generation may have added to *the value of the unimproved land.*

It is therefore evident, and the clear and necessary consequence of the basic Principle of Property Rights, which has just been established, that every individual of the second generation has equal rights to the *Original or Natural Capital,* whereas he has no right to the other capital, the *Capital Created* by the labor of the first generation. Every individual member of this first generation can therefore dispose of his share of the *Created Capital* in favor of any person or persons of the second generation he chooses—children, friends, etc.—without any individual or even the State itself, as we have just said, having any claim (in the name of Property Rights) over such disposal made by the donor or testator.

Let us note that, following our hypothesis, a member of the second generation is already favored over a member of the first generation because, in addition to rights to the *Original Capital,* which have been preserved for him, he may be fortunate enough to receive a share of the Created Capital, that is, value that has been produced not by him, but by previous labor.

Let us assume that Society is so constituted:

1. That the Rights to *Original Capital,* that is, to the resources of the land in its unimproved form, are preserved or that EQUIVALENT RIGHTS are recognized for every person born into this world in any age whatsoever.

2. That *Created Capital* is continually distributed among men *as rapidly as it is created,* in proportion to each person's participation in its creation.

If the machinery of the social order meets these two conditions, PROPERTY, in such a regime, would be established under conditions of ABSOLUTE JUSTICE. *Fact* and *ideal* would then be in complete accord.[4]

We note that our socialist author makes a distinction here

between two kinds of value: *created value,* which can legitimately be converted into property, and *noncreated value,* also called the *value of unimproved land,* original capital, natural capital, which can become private property only by an act of usurpation. Now, according to the theory that I advance, the ideas expressed by the words "noncreated," "original," "natural," completely exclude the ideas of *value* and *capital.* This is the error in the premise that leads M. Considérant to the following melancholy conclusion:

Under the System by which Property is established in all civilized nations, the common fund, to whose complete enjoyment all humanity has full rights, has been raided: it is now taken over by a small minority, to the exclusion of the great majority. And truly, if only one man were in fact deprived of his rights to the enjoyment of the common fund, this one exclusion would in itself be a sufficient violation of Justice to brand the system of Property that sanctioned it as unjust and illegitimate.

Yet M. Considérant acknowledges that the land cannot be cultivated except under the system of private property. This is *necessary monopoly.* How can all these things be reconciled, and the rights of the proletariat to original, natural, noncreated capital, or the value of the unimproved land, be protected?

Very well, let an industrial Society, which has taken over the possession of the Land and has deprived man of the faculty of exercising freely and at will his four natural Rights; let such a Society, I say, grant the individual as reparation for the Rights that it has taken away, the RIGHT TO EMPLOYMENT.

If anything in the world is clear, it is that this theory, except for the conclusion, is exactly the one held by the economists. The person buying a farm product pays for three things: (1) current labor (nothing more legitimate); (2) the *additional value* imparted to the soil by previous labor (still completely legitimate); (3) finally, *original capital* or *natural* or *noncreated capital,* the gratuitous gift of God, called by Considérant the *value of the unimproved land;* by Smith, the *indestructible powers of the soil;* by

Ricardo, the *productive and indestructible powers of the land;* by Say, *natural agents.* This is what has been *usurped,* according to M. Considérant; this is what has been *usurped,* asserts Jean-Baptiste Say. This is what constitutes *injustice* and *plunder* in the eyes of the socialists; this is what constitutes *monopoly* and *privilege* in the eyes of the economists. They are further agreed as to the *necessity,* the usefulness, of this arrangement. Without it, the land would not produce, say the disciples of Smith; without it, we should return to the savage state, say the disciples of Fourier.

We see that in theory, at least as regards the great question of equity, there is much more of an *entente cordiale* between the two schools than might be imagined. They are divided only in regard to the conclusions to be drawn from the fact on which they agree and in regard to the legislative action to be taken. "Since property is tainted with injustice, inasmuch as it assigns to the landowners remuneration that is not their just due, and since, on the other hand, it is necessary, let us respect it but exact reparations from it."

"No," say the economists, "although it is a monopoly, let us respect it, since it is necessary, and leave it alone." Yet they offer even this feeble defense very half-heartedly, for one of their most recent spokesmen, M. Garnier, adds: "You are correct from the point of view of human rights, but you are wrong from the practical standpoint, until you can show what could be done by a better system."

To which the socialists do not fail to reply: "We have found it. It is the right to employment. Let us try it."

At this juncture M. Proudhon arrives on the scene. Do you imagine, perhaps, that this celebrated contradictor is going to contradict the fundamental premise of the socialists and the economists? Not at all. He has no need to do so in order to demolish the principle of property. On the contrary: he seizes hold of this premise; he embraces it; he presses it to his bosom, and squeezes from it its most logical conclusion. "Aha," he says, "you admit that the gifts of God have not only utility but *value;* you admit that the landowners usurp them and sell them. Therefore, property is theft. Therefore, it is not necessary to maintain it or to exact reparations from it, but to *abolish* it."

M. Proudhon has mustered many arguments against landed property. The one that carries the most weight, the only one that carries any weight, is the one furnished him by those authors who have confused utility with value.

"Who has the right," he asks,

to charge for the use of the soil, for wealth that was not made by man? To whom is due the rent on the land? To the producer of the land, of course. Who made it? God. In that case, landlord, you may withdraw.

. . . . But the Creator of the earth does not sell it. He gives it away without charge; and He gives to all alike. How, then, is it that among His children some are treated as eldest sons and others as bastards? How does it happen, if originally man's right was equality of inheritance, that it has posthumously become inequality of status?

Replying to Jean-Baptiste Say, who has compared the land to a tool of production, he says:

I agree that the land is a tool of production; but who wields it? Is it the landowner? Is he the one who by the magic of property rights imparts to it strength and fertility? His monopoly consists of just this, that, though he has not made the implement, he charges for the service it performs. Let its Maker appear and demand His rent, and we will settle with Him; or else let the landowner, who claims to have full title, produce his power of attorney from the Maker.

Evidently these three systems are in fact only one. Economists, socialists, egalitarians, all direct the *same reproach* against landed property, that of charging for something that it has no right to charge for. Some call this abuse *monopoly;* others, *injustice;* and still others, *theft.* These are merely different degrees of guilt in the same bill of complaint.

Now, I appeal to the attentive reader: Is this complaint well-grounded? Have I not demonstrated that only one thing stands between God's gifts and human hunger, viz., human service?

Economists, you declare: "Rent is what is paid to the landowner for the use of the productive and indestructible powers of the soil."

I answer: No. Rent is what is paid the water carrier for the pains he took to make his cart and his wheels, and the water would cost more if he carried it on his back. In the same manner, wheat, flax, wool, wood, meat, fruit would cost us more if the landowner had not improved the instrument that produces them.

Socialists, you say: "Originally the masses enjoyed their right to the land subject to their labor. Now they are excluded and robbed of their natural heritage."

I reply: No, they are not excluded or robbed; they do enjoy gratis the utility that the land has produced, subject to their labor, that is, on condition that they pay by their own labor those who spare them labor.

Egalitarians, you say: "The monopoly of the landowner consists in the fact that, while he did not make the means of production, he charges for its service."

I answer: No, the land as a means of production, in so far as it is the work of God, produces *utility,* and this utility is gratuitous; it is not within the owner's power to charge for it. The land, as a means of production, in so far as the landowner has prepared it, worked on it, enclosed it, drained it, improved it, added other necessary implements to it, produces *value,* which represents human *services* made available, and this is the only thing he charges for. Either you must recognize the justice of this demand, or you must reject your own principle of *reciprocal services.*

In order to learn what the real elements are that constitute the value of the land, let us observe how landed property is created, not through violence or conquest, but according to the laws of labor and exchange. Let us observe what conditions are like in this respect in the United States.

Brother Jonathan, an industrious water carrier in New York, left for the Far West, carrying in his wallet a thousand dollars, the fruit of his labor and thrift.

He passed through many fertile areas in which the soil, the sun, and the rain perform their miracles, yet, in the economic and *practical* sense, impart *no value* to them.

As he was something of a philosopher, he kept saying as he went along: "In spite of all that Smith and Ricardo say, value must be something else than the *productive, natural, and indestructible power of the soil.*"

Finally, he reached the State of Arkansas and saw before him a beautiful farm of about a hundred acres, which the government had put up for sale at a dollar an acre.

"A dollar an acre!" he said to himself. "That's very little, so little, in fact, that it's almost nothing. I'll buy this land, clear it, sell my crops, and, instead of being a water carrier as I once was, I too shall be a landowner!"

Brother Jonathan, who was a ruthlessly logical man, liked to have a reason for everything. He said to himself: "But why is this land worth even a dollar an acre? No one has ever laid a hand on it. It is virgin territory. Could Smith, Ricardo, and all the rest of the theorists down to Proudhon, possibly be right? Could it be that the land does have value independently of any labor, service, or other human intervention? Must it be admitted that the productive and indestructible powers of the soil are *worth* something? Why, then, are they not *valuable* in the areas I have just been through? And, besides, since these marvelous powers are so far superior to man's capacity, which will never be able to duplicate the phenomenon of growth, as M. Blanqui has so profoundly observed, why, then, are they *worth* only a dollar?"

But he was not long in realizing that this value, like all values, is an entirely human and social creation. The American Government did indeed ask the price of a dollar an acre, but, on the other hand, it guaranteed, at least to a certain degree, the safety of the purchaser; it had constructed a road of sorts in the vicinity; it had arranged for the delivery of letters and papers; etc.

"Service for service," said Jonathan. "The government charges me a dollar, but it fully renders me the equivalent. Henceforth, begging Ricardo's pardon, I shall explain the value of this land in human terms, and its value would be even greater if the highway were nearer, the mail service more convenient, my safety more assured."

While discoursing thus, Jonathan kept on working; for, in all fairness to him, it must be said that he was a doer as well as a thinker.

After he had invested the rest of his dollars in buildings, fences, clearings, trenchings, drainage, preparations, etc., after he had dug, plowed, harrowed, sowed, and harvested, came the moment for selling the crop. "Now at last I'll know," cried Jonathan, still obsessed with the problem of value, "whether in becoming a landowner I have turned into a monopolist, a privileged aristocrat, a despoiler of my fellow men, or a usurper of the divine bounty."

So he took his grain to market and held converse with a Yankee: "My friend," he said, "how much will you give me for this corn?"

"The current price," said the other.

"The current price? But will that give me something beyond the interest on my investment and the compensation for my labor?"

"I'm a merchant," said the Yankee, "and I have to be satisfied with payment for my past and present labor."

"And I was satisfied with that when I was a water carrier," replied Jonathan; "but now I'm an owner of landed property. The English and French economists have assured me that in that capacity, I should receive, in addition to payment for my past and present labor, a profit from *the productive and indestructible powers of the soil.* I should levy a special tribute on the gifts of God."

"The gifts of God belong to everyone," said the merchant. "I certainly use the *productive power* of the wind to sail my ships, but I don't charge for it."

"And I propose that you pay me something for these powers, so that Messrs. Senior, Considérant, and Proudhon will not for naught have called me a monopolist and a usurper. If I am to bear the shame, I should at least have the profit."

"In that case, my friend, I bid you farewell; I'll appeal to other landowners for my corn, and if I find that they feel as you do, I'll grow some for myself."

Thus, Jonathan learned that, under a system of liberty, not everyone who will may become a monopolist. "As long as there is land to be cleared in the Union," he said to himself, "I shall be only the one who puts these famous *natural and indestructible forces* to work. I shall be paid for the pains I take and nothing more, exactly as in the old days, when, as a water carrier, I was paid for the pains I took and not for those that Nature took. I see clearly that the one who enjoys the gifts of God is not the man who raises the grain, but the one who consumes it."

After several years Jonathan became interested in another venture and looked around for a tenant for his farm. The conversation between the two parties was very interesting and would shed much light on the question if I were to quote it in its entirety.

But we must be content with the following excerpt:

Jonathan: What! You don't want to pay me as rent anything more than the interest, at the current rate, on my capital outlay?

The tenant: Not a penny more.

Jonathan: And why, if you please?

The tenant: Because for that amount of capital I can put another farm in exactly the same condition as yours.

Jonathan: That seems to be a conclusive argument. But consider that, when you begin to farm my land, you will have not only my capital but also the *natural and indestructible powers of the soil* working for you. You will have at your disposal the marvelous effects of the sun and the moon, of natural affinity and electricity. Must I let you have all these for nothing?

The tenant: Why not, since you paid nothing for them, and derive nothing from them, any more than I shall?

Jonathan: Derive nothing from them? Goodness gracious, what do you mean? I derive everything from them. Without these wonderful phenomena all my industry wouldn't raise a single blade of grass.

The tenant: Of course. But remember the Yankee. He refused to give you a penny for all this help of Nature, just as the New York housewives refused to give you anything for the admirable process by which Nature feeds the spring.

Jonathan: But Ricardo and Proudhon . . . . .

The tenant: What do I care about Ricardo? Let us deal on

the terms I have laid down, or else I *shall go and clear some land* beside yours. The sun and the moon will work for me there for nothing.

It was the same old argument, and Jonathan began to understand that God has taken rather wise precautions so that His gifts should not be easily intercepted.

Having somewhat lost his taste for being a landowner, Jonathan decided to direct his energies elsewhere. He determined to put his farm up for *sale.*

Needless to say, no one was willing to give him more than he had himself paid. Despite his citation of Ricardo and his allusions to the so-called value inherent in the indestructible powers of the soil, everyone gave him the same answer: "There are other farms besides yours." And these few words silenced his demands even as they destroyed his illusions.

In this transaction there was, indeed, a fact of great economic importance that has not been sufficiently noted.

Everyone realizes that if a manufacturer wished, after ten or fifteen years, to sell his equipment, even if it were as good as new, the probability is that he would be compelled to suffer a loss. The reason is simple: Ten or fifteen years rarely go by without bringing some mechanical progress. For that reason the person who puts a fifteen-year-old piece of machinery up for sale can hardly expect to be paid for all the work that went into it; because now, thanks to progress, better machines can be obtained for the same amount of labor—and this, let me say in passing, is further proof that value is proportional, not to labor, but to service.

Hence, we can conclude that it is in the nature of tools of production to lose some of their value through the mere action of time, independently of any wear and tear, and we may express this fact in the following proposition: *One of the effects of progress is to decrease the value of existing tools of production.*

It is clear, of course, that the more rapid the progress, the greater the difficulty of existing implements in keeping pace with new ones.

I shall not stop here to point out the harmonies suggested by this law. All that I wish to call attention to is the fact that landed property is no exception to it.

Brother Jonathan made this discovery to his personal sorrow and loss. He had this conversation with his prospective buyer:

"The permanent improvements I have put into this land represent a thousand days of labor. I propose, first, that you pay me the equivalent of these thousand days, and then something additional for the inherent value of the soil, which is independent of any human labor."

The buyer answered:

"In the first place, I shall give you nothing for the value of the soil itself, since this is merely utility, which is as abundant in the surrounding farms as in yours. So, as far as this inherent, extrahuman utility goes, I can get it gratis, which proves that it has no value.

"In the second place, for the thousand days' labor that your accounts show you put into bringing your land to its present condition, I will give you eight hundred, and my reason is that today for eight hundred days' labor I can do on adjoining land what you in the past did on yours in a thousand days. Please bear in mind that in the past fifteen years progress has been made in draining, clearing, building, digging wells, constructing stables, and providing transportation. For every job less labor is needed, and I have no desire to pay you ten for what I can get for eight, especially since the price of grain has gone down proportionately, which is not to your profit or mine, but to that of all mankind."

Thus, Jonathan had no choice but to keep his land or sell at a loss.

Of course, the value of land is not subject to any one single circumstance. Other factors, like the construction of a canal or the founding of a town, can cause a rise in its value. But the factor that I have mentioned, progress, always works in the direction of a fall in its value.

The conclusion to be drawn from the foregoing observations is this: As long as there is in a country an abundance of land still to be cleared, the landowner, whether he farms it himself, rents it, or sells it, enjoys no privilege, no monopoly, no exceptional advantage, and, most notably, reaps no special windfall from the bounty of Nature. How could he, assuming that men are free? Does not everyone having any capital and the strength of his hands possess the right to follow the calling of his choice— agriculture, manufacturing, commerce, fishing, navigation, the arts, or the professions? And would not men with capital and capacity turn more eagerly toward the careers that offered exceptional returns? And would they not desert those likely to entail losses? Is not this inevitable distribution of human energies sufficient, granted our hypothesis, to maintain in equilibrium the returns yielded in all branches of enterprise? In the United States do we see farmers making their fortunes any more rapidly than businessmen, shipowners, bankers, or doctors, as would inevitably happen if they received both payment for their own labor and also, over and beyond what others receive, a payment, as has been alleged, for the incalculable labor of Nature?

Very well, then, do you really want to know how, even in the United States, a landowner could set up a monopoly for himself? I shall try to explain.

Let us imagine that Jonathan assembles all the landowners in the Union and speaks to them thus:

"I have tried to sell my crops, and I haven't been able to find anyone willing to give me a high enough price for them. I have tried to rent my land, and no one will meet my terms. I have tried to sell it and have met with the same disappointment. My demands have uniformly been cut short with the same answer: *There is other land nearby.* The result is, unfortunately, that my services in the community are rated, like those of everyone else, *at what they are worth*, despite all the sweet-sounding promises of the theorists. I am allotted nothing, absolutely nothing, for this productive and indestructible power of the soil, for those forces of Nature, solar and lunar radiations, rain, wind, dew, frost, which I believed were my property, but which, in reality, I own in name only. Is it not an iniquitous thing that I am paid only for my services, and even then only at the rate to which it has pleased my competitors to lower them? You all suffer from this same oppression; you are all victims of anarchistic competition. Things would not be in this state, as you can readily understand, if we were to *organize* landed property, if we were to act concertedly to prevent anyone from hereafter clearing a square inch of American soil. Then, when the population, because of its growth, would be clamoring for the limited supply of food to be had, we would be in a position to set our own prices and make great fortunes, which, in turn, would be a great boon to the other classes, for, being rich, we would provide them with employment."

If, on hearing this discourse, the united landlords seized control of the legislature and enacted a statute forbidding all further clearing of the land, they undoubtedly would, for a time, increase their profits. I say, for a time, because the natural laws of society would be lacking in harmony if the punishment did not spring from the crime itself. Out of respect for scientific accuracy, I shall not say that the new statute would impart value to the power of the soil or to the forces of Nature (if that were the case, the statute would work to the harm of no one); but I shall say: The balance of services would be violently upset; one class would exploit the other classes; a system of slavery would be introduced into the country.

Let us move on to another hypothesis, which, in fact, represents actual conditions in the civilized nations of Europe, where the land has already become private property.

We must now consider whether, in this case too, the great mass of consumers, or the *community,* continues to enjoy gratis the productive power of the soil and the forces of Nature; whether the holders of the land are owners of anything beyond its *value,* that is, of their honest services evaluated according to the laws of competition; and whether, when they charge for their services, they are not forced, like everybody else, to include gratis the gifts of God.

Suppose, then, the whole territory of Arkansas has been sold by the government, divided into private estates, and put under cultivation. When Jonathan offers his grain or even his land for sale, does he vaunt the productive power of the soil and try to include it as part of the land's value? He can no longer be stopped short, as in the previous case, by the crushing retort: "There are uncleared lands adjoining yours."

The new situation implies that the population has grown. It is divided into two classes: (1) the class that supplies the community with agricultural services; (2) the class that supplies industrial, intellectual, or other services.

What follows seems to me quite evident. Provided the workers (other than the landowners) who wish to get grain are perfectly free to appeal to Jonathan or to his neighbors or to landowners in neighboring States or even to clear uncultivated land outside of Arkansas, it is absolutely impossible for Jonathan to force an unjust law upon them. The mere existence somewhere of land without value is an insuperable barrier to privilege, and therefore this hypothetical case is the same as our preceding one: Agricultural services are subject to the law of general competition, and it is utterly impossible to charge more for them than they are *worth*. Let me add that they are worth no more *(ceteris paribus)* than services of any other kind. Just as the manufacturer, after charging for his time, his pains, his trouble, his risks, his outlay, his skill (all of which constitute human service and are represented by value), can charge nothing for the law of gravitation or the expansibility of steam, of whose aid he has availed himself; so Jonathan can reckon as the aggregate value of his grain only the sum total of his services, past and present, and can include nothing at all for the help he has received from the laws of vegetation. The balance of services is not impaired as long as they are freely exchanged on the market at a mutually agreeable price, and the gifts of God that transmit these services are exchanged gratis along with the services and stay in the communal domain.

It will undoubtedly be pointed out that, as a matter of fact, the value of the soil increases steadily. This is true. As the population increases and becomes richer, as the means of transportation improve, the landowner receives a better price for his services. Is this a special law applicable only to him, or does it not rather apply to all producers? For an equal amount of labor does not a doctor, a lawyer, a singer, a painter, or a day laborer obtain more satisfactions in the nineteenth century than in the fourth, in Paris than in Brittany, in France than in Morocco? But this increase in satisfaction is not obtained at anyone's expense. This much needs to be understood at least. Further discussion must wait until we analyze this law of the value (used here metonymically) of the soil in another part of this work when we reach Ricardo's theory.[5]

For the present, it is enough to note that Jonathan, under the conditions of this hypothesis, cannot oppress the industrial classes, provided the exchange of services is free, and that labor may, without any legal restraint, be distributed in Arkansas or elsewhere among all types of production. This freedom stands in the way of landowners who would divert to their profit the gratuitous benefits of Nature.

This would no longer be the case, however, if Jonathan and his colleagues took over the legislature and prohibited or hampered the freedom of exchange—if, for example, they decreed that not a kernel of foreign wheat could enter the territory of Arkansas. In that case the value of the services exchanged between landowners and nonlandowners would no longer be determined by justice. The nonlandowners would have no protection against the demands of the landowners. Such legislation would be as iniquitous as the other measure we just referred to. The effect would be precisely the same as if Jonathan, having offered for sale a sack of wheat that would otherwise sell for fifteen francs, drew a pistol from his pocket, pointed it at the buyer, and said, "Give me three francs more, or I will blow your brains out."

This procedure (which we must call by its right name) is *extortion*. Whether it be by the exercise of *private force* or by *law*, it does not change in character. If by the exercise of private force, as in the case of the pistol, it is an act against property. If by law, as in the case of the ban, it is still an act against property, and beyond that, a denial of the right to property. As we have seen, one has property rights only over values, and value is the estimation of two services that are freely exchanged.

Hence, it is not possible to conceive of anything more antagonistic to the fundamental right to property than an alteration, effected in the name of the law, in the equivalence of exchanged services.

It is perhaps not idle to point out that laws of this nature are iniquitous and disastrous, whatever may be the opinion of either oppressed or oppressor toward them. In some countries we see the working classes clamoring for such restraints because they bring wealth to the landowners. They do not perceive that it is at their expense, and, as I know by experience, it is not always prudent to tell them so.

It is indeed strange. The common people listen eagerly to the zealots who preach communism, which is slavery, since not to be master of one's own services is slavery; and yet they disdain those who on all occasions defend liberty, which is the common sharing of God's bounty to man.

We now reach the third hypothetical case, wherein the entire arable surface of the globe has become private property.

Here again we observe two classes: those who possess the soil and those who do not. Will those of the first class be able to oppress the members of the second? And will the second not be forever reduced to offering more and more labor for the same quantity of food?

If I answer this objection, it will be, obviously, for the sake of scientific completeness, for we are still hundreds of centuries away from the time when such a hypothesis could become a reality.

But the fact is that everything indicates that the time must come when the landowners' claims cannot be kept within bounds by the magic words: There is more land to be cleared.

I beg the reader to note that this hypothesis also implies that at that time the population will have reached the extreme limit of the earth's ability to provide sustenance.

This adds a new and important element to the question. It is almost as if I were asked: What will happen when there is not enough air left to fill all the extra lungs in the world?

Whatever theory we may hold on the problem of population, it is at least certain that the population can *increase,* and even that it *tends* to increase, since it does increase. The entire economic organization of society is such that it appears to anticipate this trend, with which it is in complete harmony. The landowner always hopes to charge for the use of the natural resources he has at his command, but he is always disappointed in his foolish and unjust demands by the great supply of similar natural resources that do not pass through his hands. Nature's relatively infinite prodigality with her forces keeps him from being anything more than a mere custodian over some of them. Now, what will happen when men will have reached the limits of this bounty? It will no longer be possible for anything more to be hoped for in that direction. Inevitably the trend toward increased population will then come to a halt. No economic system can prevent this from necessarily happening. In the hypothetical case we are considering, any increase in population would be checked by a corresponding rise in the death rate. No proponent of human betterment, however optimistic, can go so far as to assert that the number of human beings can continue to rise when there is no possible chance for a further increase in the supply of food.

Here, then, is a new order; and the laws of the social world would not be harmonious if they had not provided for this contingency, so different from the conditions under which we live today.

The difficulty we foresee can be illustrated in this manner: Imagine a ship in the middle of the ocean with a month to go before reaching land and with only enough food for two weeks. What must be done? Obviously each sailor's ration must be reduced. This is not being hardhearted; it is merely being prudent and just.

Similarly, when the population is extended to the extreme limit of what the earth, with all possible land under cultivation, can support, there will be nothing harsh or unjust about the law that takes the gentlest and most effective means of preventing further multiplication of the species. And once again the solution can be found in the principle of the private ownership of the land. The owner of landed property, under the spur of personal interest, will make the soil produce the most food of which it is capable. By the division of inheritances private ownership of land will make every family aware of the dangers of a rising birth rate. It is very clear that under any other system—communism, for example—there would be no equally strong incentive for greater production nor so firm a brake on increasing population.

In the final analysis, it seems to me that the political economists will have performed their task when they prove that the great and just law of the *reciprocity of services* works harmoniously as long as further progress is not ruled out for mankind. Is it not reassuring to reflect that, until that time and so long as liberty prevails, it is impossible for one class to oppress another? Are the economists obliged to answer this other question: Granted the tendency of the race to multiply, what will happen when there is no more room on the earth for new inhabitants? Is God holding back, for that epoch, some cataclysm of creation, some marvelous manifestation of His infinite power? Or, in keeping with Christian dogma, must we believe in the destruction of this world? Obviously these are no longer economic problems, but are analogous to the difficulties eventually reached by all sciences. The physicists are well aware that every moving body on earth goes downward and never rises again. Accordingly, the day must come when the mountains will have filled the valleys, when rivers will be as high at their mouth as at their source, when their waters will no longer flow, etc., etc. What will happen then? Should the physical sciences cease to observe and admire the harmony of the world as it now is, because they cannot foresee by what other harmony God will make provision for a state of things that is far in the future but nonetheless inevitable? It seems to me that this is indeed a case in which the economist, like the physicist, should respond by an act of faith, not by an act of idle curiosity. He who has so marvelously arranged the abode where we now dwell will surely be able to prepare a different one for different circumstances.

We judge the soil's fertility and man's skill by the facts that we observe. Is this a reasonable rule to follow? Then, adopting it, we could say: Since it has required six thousand years for a tenth of the surface of the globe to attain a sorry kind of agriculture, how many hundreds of centuries will elapse before its entire surface is turned into a great garden?

Even in this evaluation, already quite reassuring, we are merely making a supposition based on a scientific generalization, or rather, on our present state of agricultural ignorance. But, I repeat, is this an acceptable rule to follow; and does not analogy suggest that the true potentialities of this art, which are perhaps infinite, are beyond our present knowledge? The savage lives by hunting, and he requires five square miles of land. How great would be his surprise to learn that a pastoral people can support more than ten times that number in the same space! The nomadic shepherd, in turn, would be amazed to learn that ordinary agriculture would permit of a population ten times greater. Tell a peasant accustomed to this method that another tenfold increase would be possible by crop rotation, and he would not believe you. And is the rotation of crops, which is the last word for us, also the last word for the human race? Let us, therefore, stop worrying about the fate of mankind. Thousands of centuries lie ahead of it; and in any case, without asking political economists to settle problems that are out of their field, let us confidently leave the fate of future generations in the hands of Him who will call them into existence.

Let us summarize the central ideas of this chapter.

The two phenomena, utility and value, the contribution of Nature and the contribution of man, consequently communal wealth and private property, are to be found in agricultural enterprises as in all others.

In the production of the wheat that satisfies our hunger, something takes place that is quite analogous to the production of the water that quenches our thirst. Does not the sea, which inspires the poet, also stir us, the economists, to fruitful meditation? It is a vast reservoir intended to give drink to all human creatures. Yet they are so far removed from its cooling waters, which, worse still, are filled with brine! But the marvelous resourcefulness of Nature comes to the rescue. The sun warms and stirs this mass and subjects it to slow evaporation. It turns to vapor, and, freed from its salt, which rendered it unsuitable for use, rises to the upper regions of the air. Winds, moving in from all directions, waft it toward the inhabited continents, where the cold congeals it and attaches it in solid form to the mountainside. Soon the warmth of springtime melts it. Its weight carries it down the slopes, and, as it flows through beds of schist and gravel, it is filtered and purified; it spreads out in all directions, feeding the refreshing springs in all parts of the world. This is certainly an immense and ingenious industrial project that Nature carries out for the benefit of mankind. Conversion of materials from one form to another, transportation from one place to another, creation of utility—all the elements of industry are there. Yet where is *value?* It has not yet been created, and if the so-called labor of God could be charged for (and it would be charged for if it had *value*), who could say what a single drop of water *would be worth?*

Yet all men do not have a spring of living water flowing at their feet. To quench their thirst they must still go to some pains, make some effort, practice foresight, employ their skill. It is this supplementary human labor that gives rise to arrangements, transactions, *evaluations.* In it, then, we find the origin and the basis of value.

With man, ignorance comes before knowledge. Originally, therefore, he was reduced to going after the water he drank and to doing, with a maximum of pains, such additional work as Nature had left him to do. This was the period in the development of exchange when water had its greatest *value.* Little by little he invented the cart and the wheel, he trained horses, he devised pipes, he discovered the laws of the siphon; in a word, he put part of the burden of his labor on the gratuitous forces of Nature, and proportionally the value of the water, but not its utility, decreased.

And, in this process, something takes place that must be carefully noted and understood if we are to avoid seeing discord where there is actually harmony. The purchaser of the water obtains it on better terms; that is, he exchanges a smaller amount of his labor for any given amount of water at each step along the path of progress, even though, in this case, he is obliged to pay for the instrument by means of which Nature is put to work. Formerly he paid for the labor of going after the water; now he pays for this labor and also for the labor it took to construct the cart, the wheel, and the pipe. And yet, *everything included,* he pays less. This illustration shows how unfortunate and erroneous is the bias of those who believe that the compensation paid to capital represents an added burden to the consumer. Will these people never realize that capital, in any given case, eliminates more labor than it demands as payment?

The process that has just been described applies equally well to the production of wheat. In it too there exists, antedating human industry, a tremendous, immeasurable industry of Nature, much of which even yet is not understood by the most advanced scientific thinking. Gases and minerals are present in the soil and in the atmosphere. Electricity, chemical forces, wind, rain, light, heat, life are all successively busy, often without our knowledge, transporting, transforming, collecting, dividing, combining these elements; and this wonderful industry, whose activity and utility surpass our understanding and even our imagination, possesses no value. The latter makes its appearance at the first intervention of man, who, in this case, has more *supplementary* labor to perform than in the other.

In order to direct these forces of Nature, to remove the obstacles that hinder their action, man takes possession of an instrument, which is the soil, and he does so without harming anyone, for this instrument has no value. This is not a debatable matter, but a simple fact. Show me, in any part of the world whatsoever, a piece of land that has not directly or indirectly been the object of man's activity, and I will show you a piece of land totally lacking in value.

Yet the farmer, in order to produce wheat, with the help of Nature, performs two very distinct types of labor. One type is directly related to the yearly harvest, is related to it alone, and must be paid for by it alone: things like planting, weeding, harvesting, transplanting. The other, like constructing farm buildings, providing drainage, clearing, fencing, etc., spans an indefinite number of successive harvests; this cost must be distributed over a series of years, a process that is carried out accurately by the admirable device that we call the laws of interest and amortization. The crops furnish the farmer's payment if he consumes them himself. If he exchanges them, he receives in return services of a different type, and the appraisal of the services so exchanged constitutes their value.

Now, it is easy to understand that all this long-range labor that the farmer performs on the soil represents a *value* that has not yet been paid for, but that surely will be. He cannot be forced to relinquish it and to allow another person to take over his right to it without compensation. Value has been incorporated, implanted in the soil; for that reason we may well say, by metonymy: *The soil has value.* It has value, in fact, because no one may now acquire it without offering in exchange the equivalent of this labor. But I maintain that this land, to which Nature's productive power had not originally communicated any value, still does not possess any value the more on that account. This power of Nature, which was gratis, is still gratis, and always will be. We may indeed say: This land *has value;* but what really has value is the human labor that has improved it, the capital that has been expended on it. Consequently, it is completely accurate to say that its owner is, strictly speaking, owner only of the value that he has created, of the services that he has rendered. And what ownership could be more legitimate? It has not been created at anyone's expense; it neither intercepts nor lays a tax on any gift of heaven.

Nor is this all. The capital outlay and the interest on it, which must be spread over successive harvests, far from increasing costs and becoming an extra burden for the consumers, enables them to obtain agricultural products on better and better terms in proportion as the amount of capital increases, that is, as the value of the soil is enhanced. I have no doubt that this assertion will be taken for an overly optimistic paradox, so accustomed are people to looking on the value of the soil as a calamity, if not an injustice. Yet I declare that it is not enough to say that the value of the soil has been created at no one's expense, or to say that it is harmful to no one; it must be stated that, on the contrary, it is to the profit of all. It is not merely legitimate; it is advantageous, even to those who are not landowners.

So here again we have the same phenomenon we just witnessed in regard to drinking water. As we said, as soon as the water carrier invented the cart and the wheel, it is quite true that the consumer was forced to pay for two types of labor instead of one: (1) the labor of making the cart or the wheel, or rather the interest and amortization on this capital outlay; (2) the actual labor that the water carrier was still required to perform. But it is equally true that these two types of labor together do not equal the total amount of labor of one type only that mankind was previously required to perform. Why is this true? Because, thanks to the invention of these mechanical aids, a part of the work has been turned over to the gratuitous forces of Nature. Indeed, it was the prospect of decreased toil that prompted the invention and brought about its adoption.

Exactly the same phenomena are to be observed in the case of land and wheat. Unquestionably, every time the landowner invests capital in permanent improvements, the succeeding crops must be charged with the interest on this capital. But it is equally certain that the amount of labor belonging to the other category, that of unskilled labor that must be performed annually, is also reduced in far greater proportions; so that the landowner, and hence the consumer, obtains each succeeding crop for less and less effort, it being the special characteristic of capital to substitute the gratuitous action of Nature for man's labor, which must be paid for.

Consider the following example: To produce the best crops, a field must be cleared of excessive moisture. Let us suppose that labor for this has not progressed beyond the first, or unskilled, category. Let us assume that the farmer must go out every morning with a pail to drain off water standing in spots where it would do harm. It is evident that at the end of the year this act will not have added any *value* to the soil, but the price of the crop will have been tremendously increased. So will all the prices of all succeeding crops, as long as the science of agriculture does not advance beyond this primitive procedure. But if the farmer digs a ditch, the soil immediately acquires *value*, for this work belongs to the second category. Such work becomes a part of the soil; it must be paid for by the crops of succeeding years, and no one can expect to acquire the land without paying also for this operation. But is it not true that it nevertheless tends to reduce the value of the crops? Is it not true that, although it required, during the first year, an unusual expenditure of effort, it saves in the long run more than it occasions? Is it not true that henceforth the drainage will be carried out more economically through the application of the laws of hydraulics than it was previously by dint of physical labor? Is it not true that the purchasers of the wheat will profit from the operation? Will they not have reason to deem themselves fortunate that the soil has acquired this new value? And, to generalize, is it not true, then, that the value given the soil is a sign of progress, which is to the benefit not of the owner alone, but of all mankind? How absurd, then, it would be of mankind, and how hostile to its own best interests, to say: The amount added to the price of the wheat for interest and amortization on this ditch, or for what it represents in the total value of the soil, is a privilege, a monopoly, a theft! Reasoning in this wise, the owner, in order to be no longer a thief or a monopolist, would only have to fill in his ditch and go back to the pail. Would you who do not own land be any better off for that?

Enumerate all the permanent improvements that together make up the value of the soil, and you can make the same observation for each one of them. After you destroy the ditch, destroy the fences too, forcing the owner to go back to standing guard on his field; destroy the well, the barn, the road, the plow, the grading, the artificial mould; put back into it the stones, the weeds, the tree roots, and then you will have achieved utopian equality. The soil, and the human race along with it, will have returned to its original state: it will no longer have value. The crops will no longer be burdened with capital. Their price will be free of that cursed element called interest. Everything, absolutely everything, will be done by current labor, visible to the naked eye. Political economy will be greatly simplified. France will support one man for every five square miles of land. All the others will have starved to death; but it can no longer be said: Property is a monopoly; it is an injustice; it is theft.

Let us not, therefore, be insensible to those economic harmonies that pass before our eyes as we analyze the concepts of exchange, value, capital, interest, private property, public ownership. Need I present the entire cycle? But perhaps we have gone far enough to realize that the social world, no less than the material world, bears the impress of the divine hand, from which come wisdom and loving-kindness, and toward which we should raise our eyes in awe and gratitude.

I cannot refrain from returning to a remark of M. Considérant.

Taking as his premise the idea that the soil has value in itself, independent of man's activity, that it is *original and noncreated capital*, he concludes, logically from his premise, that *to convert it into private property is to usurp it*. This supposed iniquity moves him to declaim vehemently against modern society. On the other hand, he agrees that permanent improvements add an *extra value* to this original capital, as an additional element so completely fused with the rest as to be inseparable. What, then, is to be done? For we are confronted with a total value composed of two parts, one of which, having been produced by labor, is legitimate property, and the other, being the creation of God, is an iniquitous usurpation.

This is no small dilemma. M. Considérant solves it by the *right to employment*.

Humanity's progress on Earth obviously demands that the land not be left in a wild and uncultivated state. Our very Destiny, as Human Beings, therefore, is opposed to the idea that man's Right to the Earth should retain its *rude and original* FORM.

In his forests and savannas the savage enjoys his four natural Rights of Hunting, Fishing, Gathering wild fruits, and Grazing. Such is the original form of his Rights.

In all civilized societies, the man of the common people, the Proletarian, is purely and simply despoiled of these rights. We cannot, therefore, say that his original Rights have changed form, since they no longer exist. The form has disappeared along with the Substance.

Now, what would be the form under which his Rights could be reconciled with the conditions of an industrial Society? The answer is simple.

In the savage state man, to enjoy his Rights, is *obliged to act*. The *Labor* of Fishing, Hunting, Gathering, and Grazing is the condition placed upon the exercise of his Rights. His original Rights, therefore, are simply his *Right to perform these labors.*

Very well, then, since an industrial Society has taken possession of the Earth, and prevents men from exercising on the soil freely and at will their four natural Rights, let this Society grant to them, in compensation for the Rights it takes away, the RIGHT TO EMPLOYMENT: then, if principle and practice are properly understood and carried out, the individual will have no grounds for complaint.

The indispensable prerequisite for the Legality of Property is, therefore, that Society recognize the Common Man's RIGHT TO EMPLOYMENT, and that it *guarantee* him for a given amount of his activity at least as much in the way of subsistence as a similar amount of activity *would have* brought him in his original state of savagery.

I do not propose to argue the point in all its ramifications with M. Considérant, for I should become insufferably repetitious in the process. If I proved to him that what he calls *noncreated capital* is not capital at all; that what he terms the *additional value* of the soil is not *additional value,* but *total value;* he would have to admit that his whole argument breaks down, and with it all his complaints against the manner in which humanity has seen fit to organize itself and to live since the time of Adam. But this controversy would oblige me to restate what I have already said concerning the fact that the forces of Nature remain inherently and unalterably gratuitous. I shall confine myself to observing that if M. Considérant is the spokesman for the working classes, he does them such a disservice that they may well consider that they have been betrayed. He says that the landowners have usurped both the land and all the miracles of vegetation that take place on it. They have usurped the sun, the rain, the dew, oxygen, hydrogen, and nitrogen—at least to the extent that these contribute to the raising of agricultural products—and he asks them to assure the worker, as compensation, at least as much in the way of subsistence for a given amount of activity as a similar amount of activity would have brought him in the original or savage state.

But do you not perceive, M. Considérant, that landed property has not waited for you to issue your injunctions, that it has already been a million times more generous? For, after all, what does your proposal actually come to?

In the original state of savagery, your four rights of fishing, hunting, gathering wild fruits, and grazing supported—or rather, allowed to eke out an existence in all the horrors of privation—approximately one man per five square miles. The usurpation of the land will therefore be deemed legitimate, according to your theories, if the guilty parties support one man per five square miles, with the further requirement that he exert himself as greatly as a Huron or an Iroquois must. Please note that the area of France is only thirty thousand square leagues; that, consequently, provided it support thirty thousand inhabitants in that state of material well-being afforded by a life of savagery, you are content to ask nothing more, on behalf of the workers, from the owners of property. Now, this leaves thirty million Frenchmen who do not have a square inch of land; and among that number there are quite a few—the President of the Republic, cabinet ministers, magistrates, bankers, businessmen, notaries, lawyers, doctors, brokers, soldiers, sailors, teachers, journalists, etc.—who would surely not be disposed to change their way of life for that of an Iowa Indian. Landed property must, therefore, already do a great deal more than you require. You demand from it a right to employment that, within certain fixed limits, and only in return for a certain amount of effort, will provide the masses with a level of subsistence equal to that which a state of savagery could offer them. The system of landed property does much better than that. It offers more than the right to employment; it offers actual employment, and if it did no more than meet the taxes it now pays, that figure is still a hundred times more than you would demand.

Alas! I am sorry to say that I have not yet finished with landed property and its value. I still have to state, and refute in as few words as possible, a plausible and even significant objection.

People will say:

"The facts belie your theory. Undoubtedly, as long as there exists in a country a large amount of uncultivated land, its mere presence will prevent cultivated land from acquiring exorbitant value. Undoubtedly, also, even when all the land has been converted into private property, if adjoining nations have great tracts yet to be tilled, the right of free bargaining will hold the value of landed property within just limits. In these two cases land prices would not seem to represent more than the capital outlay, and rent more than the interest on it. From these facts one must conclude, as you do, that what is done by the soil itself and by the forces of Nature, since it does not figure in the costs and cannot be added to the price of crops, does remain gratis and therefore common to all. All this is plausible. We may well be at a loss to discover the flaw in this line of reasoning, and yet it is fallacious. To be convinced that this is so, we have only to note the fact that in France there is cultivated land ranging in price from a hundred to six thousand francs an acre, an enormous difference, which is to be explained more by reason of the variations in fertility than in previous improvements. Do not deny, therefore, that fertility has its own inherent value; every bill of sale attests to this fact. Anyone buying a piece of land determines its quality and pays accordingly. If two fields are placed side by side and have the same advantages of location, but differ in their soil, the one consisting of rich loam and the other of barren sand, surely the first will be worth more than the second, even though the same capital improvements have been made on both. And, in fact, this is a point about which the buyer is not at all concerned. His eyes are turned toward the future, not the past. He is interested, not in what the land has cost, but in what it will yield, and he knows that its yield will be in proportion to its fertility. Therefore, this fertility has its own specific, intrinsic value, which is independent of any human labor performed on it. To maintain the contrary is to attempt to find the justification for private property in ingenious quibblings, or rather in a paradox."

Let us, therefore, investigate what really gives value to the soil.

I ask the reader to remember that at the present time this question is a most vital one. Previously it could be either dismissed or treated superficially by economists, as a question of little more than passing interest. The legitimacy of private property was not then contested. Such is no longer the case. New theories, which have been only too successful, have cast doubt among even the best minds regarding the right to property. And on what do the authors of these theories base their complaint? On just the allegation contained in the objection I have presented above. On just this fact, which unfortunately has gained acceptance by all schools of thought, that the soil derives from its fertility, from Nature, an inherent value that has not been transmitted to it by any human agency. Now, value is not transferred gratis. Its very name excludes the idea that it is gratuitous. Therefore, we say to the landowner: You demand from me a value that is the fruit of my labor, and you offer me in exchange another value that is the fruit neither of your labor nor of anyone's labor, but of Nature's bounty.

And, make no mistake about it, this indictment would be a terrible one if it were based on fact. It did not originate with Messrs. Considérant and Proudhon. It is to be found in Smith, in Ricardo, in Senior, in all the economists without exception, not merely as a theory, but as an indictment. These authors have not stopped at attributing an extrahuman value to the soil; they have gone so far as to deduce clearly the consequences of this theory and to brand landed property as a privilege, a monopoly, a usurpation. To be sure, after thus blasting it, they have defended it in the name of *necessity*. But is such a defense anything more than a flaw in reasoning, which the logicians of communism have been quick to set right?

It is, therefore, not for the sake of yielding to an unfortunate proclivity for quibbling that I take up this delicate subject. I should have preferred to spare the reader and myself the tediousness that even now I feel is gathering over the final pages of this chapter.

The answer to the objection that I have just presented is to be found in my theory of value, which is set forth in chapter 5. There I stated: Value does not necessarily imply labor; even less is it necessarily proportional to labor. I showed that value is based less on the *pains taken* by the one who surrenders what is exchanged than on the *pains spared* the recipient, and for that reason I attributed it to something that includes both elements: *service*.

A great service can be rendered, I said, at the cost of very little effort, and a very minor service can be rendered with great effort. The only result, then, is that labor does not *necessarily receive a remuneration* that is always proportional to its intensity, either in the case of the man living in isolation or in that of the man living in society.

Value is determined after bargaining between two contracting parties. Each one brings to the bargaining his own point of view. You offer me wheat. Of what importance to me are the time and trouble it may have cost you? What I am concerned about is the time and trouble it would cost me to obtain it elsewhere. The knowledge you have of my situation may make you more or less demanding; the knowledge I have of yours may make me more or less ready to come to terms. Hence, there can be no necessary measure of the payment you are to receive for your labor. That depends on circumstances and the value they give to the two services being exchanged. Soon we shall take up an external factor, called competition, whose function it is to regularize values and to make them correspond more and more closely to effort. Yet this correspondence is not of the essence of value, since it is established only under the pressure of a contingent fact.

Keeping this in mind, I can say that the value of the soil is created, fluctuates, is set, like that of gold, iron, water, an attorney's advice, a doctor's consultation, the performance of a singer or of a dancer, or an artist's painting—like all values; that it obeys no special laws; that it constitutes property that is of the same origin, the same nature, and is as legitimate as any other property. But it does not at all follow—this must be clear by now—that, of two efforts applied to the soil, one may not be better remunerated than the other.

Let us revert to that most simple of all industries, the one best fitted to illustrate the tenuous dividing line between man's onerous labor and Nature's gratuitous collaboration. I refer to the humble labor of the water carrier.

A man fills a barrel with water and brings it home. Does he own a value that necessarily is proportional to his labor? In that case the value would be distinct from the service that the water can render. Furthermore, it could not fluctuate, for labor that has once been performed is not susceptible of increase or diminution.

Very well, then, the very day after the water barrel has been filled and delivered, it can lose all its value, if, for example, it rains during the night. In that case, everybody has his supply of water; the barrel of water can render no service; it is no longer wanted. In the language of economics, there is no demand for it.

On the other hand, it can acquire considerable value if exceptional, unforeseen, and urgent demand arises.

The result is that man, working with the future in mind, can never know in advance exactly what that future holds in store for his labor. The value incorporated in a material object will be greater or less according to the services it will render; or, rather, human labor, the source of this value, will receive, according to circumstances, a greater or a smaller remuneration. Such eventualities fall within the domain of foresight, and foresight, too, is entitled to its reward.

But, I ask, what do these fluctuations of value, the variations in the price paid labor, have to do with Nature's marvelous industrial achievement, with the wonderful laws of physics that, without help from us, transport the waters we drink from the ocean to the spring? Because the value of this barrel of water varies according to circumstances, must we conclude that Nature sometimes charges a great deal, sometimes very little, and sometimes not at all, for evaporation, for the transportation of clouds from the sea to the mountains, for freezing, for melting, and all the wonderful industrial activity that feeds the spring?

The same is true of agricultural products.

The value of the soil, or rather of the capital invested in the soil, is composed not of one element, but of two elements. It depends not only on the labor that has gone into the soil but also on society's capacity to reward that labor, on demand as well as on supply.

Take the case of a field. Not a year goes by in which some work of a permanent nature is not done on it, and, by the same token, its value is enhanced.

Furthermore, new roads are built, and others are improved;

law enforcement becomes more efficient; new markets are opened up; there are increases in population and in wealth; new careers are opened to intelligence and skill; and these changes in the physical environment and the general prosperity result in additional remuneration for labor past and present, and, concomitantly, greater value for the field.

In all this there is neither injustice nor special privilege for the landowner. Every line of work from banking to manual labor presents the same phenomenon. Each one finds its own remuneration enhanced through the mere fact of improvement in the surroundings in which it is carried on. This action and reaction of the prosperity of each one on the prosperity of all, and vice versa, is the very law of value. How completely erroneous it is to conclude from this evidence that the soil or its productive forces have a so-called value of their own can be seen from the fact that in intellectual work, in the professions and occupations in which material things and physical laws play no part, the same benefits are enjoyed. This is not exceptional, but the universal experience. The lawyer, the doctor, the teacher, the artist, the poet, are better paid, for the work they do, in proportion as their city or nation increases in prosperity, as the taste or the demand for their services grows, as the general public is both willing and able to remunerate them better. The simple sale of a doctor's or a lawyer's practice or of the good will of a business concern is carried out on this principle. Even the Basque Giant and Tom Thumb, who make their living by the mere display of their abnormal stature, exhibit themselves to their greater profit before the curious throngs of well-to-do city dwellers than before a few poor villagers. In this case demand does not merely contribute to value; it creates it entirely. Why should we feel that it is exceptional or unjust for demand also to have an influence on the value of land and of agricultural products?

Will it be alleged that the value of land can thereby rise exorbitantly? Those who say so have certainly never considered the enormous amount of labor that has gone into arable land. I venture to state that there is not a field in France that is *worth* as much as it cost, that can be exchanged for as great an amount of labor as has actually been expended on it to bring it to its present state of productivity. If this statement is well founded, it is conclusive. It does not permit of the least hint of injustice being charged against the principle of landed property. Therefore, I shall come back to this subject when I have occasion to consider Ricardo's theory of rent. I shall show that we must apply also to capital invested in land the general law that I have formulated in these terms: In proportion as capital increases, what it produces is distributed among the capitalists or landowners and the workers in such a way that the former's *relative* share constantly decreases, although their *absolute* share increases, while the latter's share increases in both respects.

The illusion that leads men to believe that productive forces have a value of their own because they have utility, has been responsible for many miscalculations and catastrophes. It has often involved them in premature efforts at colonization whose history reads like a lamentable chronicle of martyrs. They reasoned thus: In our country, we can acquire value only through labor; and when we work, we receive value only in proportion to our labor. If we went to Guiana, to the banks of the Mississippi, to Australia, or Africa, we could take possession of vast stretches of land, uncultivated, to be sure, but fertile. Our reward would be that we should become the owners both of the value that we should create and of the *intrinsic value* that is to be found in this land.

They set out, and harsh reality is not slow in confirming the truth of my theory. They work; they clear the land; they drive themselves to the point of exhaustion; they undergo hardship, suffering, sickness; and then, after they have made their land fit for production, they find, if they try to sell it, that they cannot get back what it cost them, and they are forced to acknowledge that value is of human creation. I defy anyone to cite an example of colonization that at the beginning was not a disaster.

Upwards of a thousand labourers were sent out to the Swan River Colony; but the extreme cheapness of the land [eighteen pence, or less than two francs, an acre] and the extravagant rate of labour, afforded them such facilities and inducements to become landowners, that capitalists could no longer get anyone to cultivate their lands. A capital of £200,000 [five million francs] was lost in consequence, and the colony became a scene of desolation. The labourers having left their employers from the delusive desire to become landowners, agricultural implements were allowed to rust, seeds rotted, and sheep, cattle, and horses perished from want of attention. A frightful famine cured the labourers of their infatuation, and they returned to ask employment from the capitalists; but it was too late.[6]

The Australian Association, attributing the disaster to the cheapness of the land, raised the price to twelve shillings. But, adds Carey,* from whom I take this quotation, the real cause was that the farm workers were convinced that the land had *intrinsic value,* apart from any work done on it, and were eager to appropriate this so-called *value,* which they assumed would virtually assure them a yearly rent.

The sequel provides me with an even more conclusive argument.

In 1836, the landed estates of the colony of Swan River were to be purchased from the original settlers at a shilling an acre.[7]

Thus, this soil, for which the company had charged twelve shillings—and on which the settlers had spent much time and money—was now resold for one shilling! What had happened to the value of the *productive and indestructible powers of Nature?* [8]

The vast and important subject of the value of land has not been exhaustively treated, I realize, in this chapter, which was written at intervals in the midst of constant interruptions: I shall return to it, but I cannot close without submitting one observation to my readers and particularly to economists.

Those illustrious scholars who have contributed so much to the

* [Henry Charles Carey (1793–1879), *Principles of Political Economy* (Philadelphia, 1837), Pt. I, pp. 49–50. Bastiat and Carey held very similar views on value, although they differed sharply on many other questions. Their lively discussions were printed in the *Journal des économistes* in 1851, the year after Bastiat's death.— TRANSLATOR.]

progress of political economy, whose lives and works breathe the spirit of benevolence and philanthropy, who, at least in certain respects and within the areas of their investigation, have discovered for us the true solution to the problems of society, men like Quesnay, Turgot, Smith, Malthus, Say, have not escaped, I do not say refutation, which is always in order, but slander, defamation, and the coarsest of insults. To attack their writings, and even their motives, has almost become the fashion. It will be said, perhaps, that in this chapter I myself furnish arms to their detractors, and, indeed, this is hardly the moment for me to turn against those whom, I most solemnly declare, I look upon as my first instructors, my guides, and my masters. But, in the last analysis, must not my highest allegiance be to truth, or to what I consider to be truth? Where in the world is there a book into which no error has crept? Now, in political economy, just one error, if we press it, if we torture it, if we insist upon drawing all its logical implications from it, will eventually be found to include all other errors; it will lead us to chaos. No book exists, therefore, from which an isolated proposition cannot be taken out of context and be declared incomplete, false, and consequently as involving a world of errors and confusions.

In all good conscience I believe that the definition that the economists have given of the word *value* is an error of this kind. We have just seen that this definition placed them in a position where they themselves cast grave doubt upon the legitimacy of landed property, and, by logical deduction, upon the whole system of capital; and only by an illogical chain of reasoning did they stop short of disaster along this road. Their inconsistency saved them. They redirected their steps toward the way of truth, and their error, if such it be, stands as the only blemish on their works. The socialists came along and laid hold of this definition, not to refute it, but to adopt it, to strengthen it, to make it the starting point for their propaganda, and to expatiate on all its implications. There has been in our time imminent danger to society in all this, and for that reason I felt it my duty to speak my mind completely, to trace this erroneous theory back to its very beginnings. Now, if one wished to conclude from my remarks that I have parted company with my masters, Smith and Say, with my friends Blanqui and Garnier, solely because they failed to grasp the full significance of one line out of all the many pages in their excellent and learned writings, and perhaps misused, as I believe, the word "value"; if one should conclude on that account that I no longer have faith in political economy and the economists; I can only protest—and that I do, most emphatically, as is evidenced by the very title of this book.

10

Competition

There is no word in all the vocabulary of political economy that has so aroused the angry denunciations of the modern reformers as the word "competition," to which, to add to the insult, they unfailingly apply the epithet "anarchistic."

What does "anarchistic competition" mean? I do not know. What can replace it? I do not know that either.

Of course, I hear the cries of "Organization! Association!" But what does that mean? Once and for all we must come to an understanding. I really must know what kind of authority these authors propose to exert over me and over all men living on this earth of ours; for, in truth, the only authority I can grant them is the authority of reason, provided they can enlist reason on their side. Do they really propose to deprive me of the right to use my own judgment in a matter where my very existence is at stake? Do they hope to take from me my power to compare the services that I render with those that I receive? Do they mean that I should act under restraints that they will impose rather than according to the dictates of my own intelligence? If they leave me my liberty, competition also remains. If they wrest it from me, I become only their slave. The association will be *free* and *voluntary*, they say. Very well! But in that case every group with its associated members will be pitted against every other group, just as individuals are pitted against one another today, and we shall have *competition*. The association will be all-embracing, it is replied. This ceases to be a joking matter. Do you mean to say that anarchistic competition is wrecking our society right now, and to cure this malady we shall have to wait until all mankind, the French, the English, the Chinese, the Japanese, the Kafirs, the Hottentots, the Lapps, the Cossacks, the Patagonians, persuaded by your arguments, agree to unite for all time to come in one of the forms of association that you have contrived? But beware! This is simply to acknowledge that competition is indestructible; and do you have the presumption to claim that an indestructible, and therefore providential, phenomenon of society can be mischievous?

After all, what is competition? Is it something that exists and has a life of its own, like cholera? No. Competition is merely the absence of oppression. In things that concern me, I want to make my own choice, and I do not want another to make it for me without regard for my wishes; that is all. And if someone proposes to substitute his judgment for mine in matters that concern me, I shall demand to substitute my judgment for his in matters that concern him. What guarantee is there that this will make things go any better? It is evident that competition is freedom. To destroy freedom of action is to destroy the possibility, and consequently the power, of choosing, of judging, of comparing; it amounts to destroying reason, to destroying thought, to destroying man himself. Whatever their starting point, this is the ultimate conclusion our modern reformers always reach; for the sake of improving society they begin by destroying the individual, on the pretext that all evils come from him, as if all good things did not likewise come from him.

We have seen that services are exchanged for services. In the last analysis, each one of us comes into the world with the responsibility of providing his own satisfactions through his own efforts. Hence, if a man spares us pains, we are obligated to save him pains in return. His effort brings us a satisfaction; we must do as much for him.

But who is to make the comparison? For it is absolutely necessary that these efforts, these pains, these services that are to be exchanged, be compared so that an equivalence, a just rate, may be arrived at, unless injustice, inequality, chance, is to be our norm—which is another way of throwing the testimony of human reason out of court. There must be, therefore, one or more judges. Who will it be? Is it not natural that, in every particular case, wants should be judged by those who experience them, satisfactions by those who seek them, efforts by those who exchange them? Is it proposed in all seriousness to substitute for this eternal vigilance by the interested parties a social authority (even if it should be the reformer himself) charged with determining the intricate conditions affecting countless acts of exchange in all parts of the world? Is it not obvious that this would mean the establishment of the most fallible, the most far-reaching, the most arbitrary, the most inquisitorial, the most unbearable, the most short-sighted, and, fortunately, let us add, the most impossible of all despotisms ever conceived in the brain of an Oriental potentate?

We need only know that competition is merely the absence of any arbitrary authority set up as a judge over exchange, to realize that it cannot be eliminated. Illegitimate coercion can indeed restrain, counteract, impede the freedom of exchange, as it can the freedom of walking; but it cannot eliminate either of them without eliminating man himself. This being so, the only question that remains is whether competition tends toward the happiness or the misery of mankind—a question that amounts to this: Is mankind naturally inclined toward progress or fatally marked for decadence?

I do not hesitate to say that competition, which, indeed, we could call freedom—despite the aversion it inspires and the tirades directed against it—is essentially the law of democracy. It is the most progressive, the most egalitarian, the most universally leveling of all the laws to which Providence has entrusted the progress of human society. It is this law of competition that brings one by one within *common* reach the enjoyment of all those advantages that Nature seemed to have bestowed gratis on certain countries only. It is this law, also, that brings within *common* reach all the conquests of Nature that men of genius in every century pass on as a heritage to succeeding generations, leaving still to be performed only supplementary labors, which they exchange without succeeding in being remunerated, as they would like to be, for the co-operation of natural resources. And if, as always happens at the beginning, the value of this labor is not proportional to its intensity, it is once again competition that, by its imperceptible but constant action, restores a fairer and more accurate balance than could be arrived at by the fallible wisdom of any human officialdom. The accusation that competition tends toward inequality is far from true. On the contrary, all *artificial* inequality is due to the absence of competition; and if the distance separating a Grand Lama from a pariah is greater than that between the President and an artisan in the United States, the reason is that competition (or liberty) is suppressed in Asia, and not in America. Therefore, while the socialists find in competition the source of all evil, it is actually the attacks upon competition that are the disruptive elements working against all that is good. Although this great law has been misunderstood by the socialists and their partisans, although it is often harsh in its operation, there is no law that is richer in social harmonies, more beneficial in its general results; no law attests more strikingly to the immeasurable superiority of God's plans over man's futile contrivances.

I must at this point remind the reader of that curious but indisputable effect of the social order to which I have already called his attention,[1] for too frequently the force of habit causes us to overlook it. It may be characterized thus: *The total number of satisfactions that each member of society enjoys is far greater than the number that he could secure by his own efforts.* In other words, there is an obvious disproportion between our consumption and our labor. This phenomenon, which we can all easily observe, if we merely look at our own situation for an instant, should, it seems to me, inspire in us some sense of gratitude toward the society to which we owe it.

We come into the world destitute in every way, tormented by countless wants, and provided with only our faculties to satisfy them. It would appear, a priori, that the most we could hope for would be to obtain satisfactions equal to our labors. If we possess more, infinitely more, to what do we owe the excess? Precisely to that natural order of society against which we are constantly railing, when we are not actually trying to destroy it.

The phenomenon, in itself, is truly extraordinary. It is quite understandable that certain men should consume more than they produce, if, in one way or another, they usurp the rights of others and receive services without rendering any in return. But how can this be true of all men simultaneously? How can it be that, after exchanging their services without coercion or plunder, on a footing of *value for value,* every man can truly say to himself: I use up in one day more than I could produce in a hundred years?

The reader realizes that the additional element that solves the problem is the increasingly effective participation of the forces of Nature in the work of production; it is the fact of more and more gratuitous utility coming within the *common* reach of all; it is the work of heat, of cold, of light, of gravitation, of natural affinity, of elasticity, progressively supplementing the labor of man and reducing the value of his services by making them easier to perform.

Certainly I must have explained the theory of value very badly indeed if the reader thinks that value declines immediately and automatically through the mere act of harnessing the forces of Nature and releasing the labor of man. No, such is not the case; for then we could say, as the English economists do: Value is in direct proportion to labor. The man who uses the help of a gratuitous force of Nature performs his services more easily; but he does not on that account voluntarily surrender any part whatsoever of what he has been accustomed to receive. To induce him to do so, some pressure from without—heavy, but not unjust—is necessary. This pressure is competition. As long as it does not intervene, as long as the man using a force of Nature remains master of his secret, that force of Nature is gratuitous, undoubtedly, but it is not yet *common to all;* the conquest of Nature has been achieved, but to the profit of only one man or one class. It is not yet of benefit to all mankind. Nothing has been changed in the world, except that one type of *services,* although partially relieved of its burden of pains, still brings the full price. We have, on the one hand, a man who asks the same amount of labor as before from his fellow men, while he offers them a reduced amount of his own labor; and, on the other, all mankind, still obliged to make the same sacrifices in time and toil to obtain a commodity that is now produced in part by Nature.

If things were to remain in this state, every new invention would bring into the world a further source of ever spreading inequality. Not only could we not say that value is proportional to labor, but we could not even say that value tends to become proportional to labor. All that we have said in earlier chapters concerning *gratuitous utility* and the *trend toward the enlargement of the communal domain* would be illusory. It would not be true that services are exchanged for services in such a way that God's gifts are transmitted, free of charge, from person to person until they reach the ultimate consumer. Everyone who had once managed to exploit any part of the forces of Nature would for all time to come charge for it along with the cost of his labor; in a word, mankind would be organized on the principle of universal monopoly, instead of the principle of an expanding domain of gratuitous and common utilities.

But such is not the case. God has lavished on His creatures the gifts of heat, light, gravitation, air, water, the soil, the marvels of plant life, electricity, and many other blessings too numerous to mention. And even as He has implanted in each man's heart a feeling of self-interest, which, like a magnet draws all things to it; so has He, in the social order, provided another mainspring whose function it is to preserve His gifts as they were originally intended to be: gratis and common to all. This mainspring is competition.

Thus, self-interest is that indomitable individualistic force within us that urges us on to progress and discovery, but at the same time disposes us to monopolize our discoveries. Competition is that no less indomitable humanitarian force that wrests progress, as fast as it is made, from the hands of the individual and places it at the disposal of all mankind. These two forces, which may well be deplored when considered individually, work together to create our social harmony.

And, we may remark in passing, it is not surprising that individualism, as it finds expression in a man's self-interest when he is a producer, has always revolted against the idea of competition, has decried it, and sought to destroy it, calling to its aid force, guile, privilege, sophistry, monopoly, restriction, government controls, etc. The immorality of its means discloses clearly enough the immorality of its end. But the amazing, and unfortunate, thing is that political economy—that is, false political economy—propagated with such ardor by the socialist schools, has, in the name of love of humanity, equality, and fraternity, espoused the cause of individualism in its narrowest form and has abandoned the cause of humanity.

Let us now see how competition works.

Man, under the influence of self-interest, always and inevitably seeks out the conditions that will give his services their greatest *value*. He is quick to realize that there are three ways in which he may use the gifts of God to his own special advantage:[2]

1. He may appropriate to his own exclusive use these gifts themselves.
2. Or he alone may know the *techniques* by which they may be put to use.
3. Or he may possess the only *implement* by which their co-operation can be secured.

In every one of these cases he gives little of his own labor in exchange for a *great deal* of others' labor. His services have great relative *value*, and we tend to assume that the excess value resides inherently in the natural resource. If this were so, this value could not be diminished. What proves that value is, instead, created by services is, as we shall see, the fact that competition simultaneously diminishes both value and services.

1. Natural resources, the gifts of God, are not uniformly distributed over the earth's surface. What an infinite range of plant life extends from the land of the pine to the land of the palm tree! Here the soil is more fertile, there the warmth of the sun more vivifying; stone is found in one place, lime in another; iron, copper, oil in yet others. Water power is not to be found every-

where; the action of the winds cannot everywhere be turned to our profit. The mere fact of the distance that separates us from things necessary to us can make an incalculable difference in the obstacles our efforts encounter; even man's faculties vary, to a certain extent, according to climate and race.

It is easy to see that, were it not for the law of competition, this inequality in the distribution of God's gifts would result in a corresponding difference in men's material prosperity.

Any person finding a natural advantage within reach would turn it to his own profit, but not to that of his fellow men. They would be allowed to share in what he possessed only as he distributed it and at an exorbitant price that he would set arbitrarily. He could place any value he pleased on his services. We have already seen that the two extremes between which value is set are the *pains taken* by the one performing the service and the *pains spared* the one receiving it. If it were not for competition, nothing would prevent the setting of the value at the upper limit. For example, the inhabitant of the tropics would say to the European: "Thanks to my sun, I can obtain a given amount of sugar, coffee, cocoa, or cotton for labor *equal to ten,* whereas you, who in your cold part of the world are obliged to resort to greenhouses, heaters, and storage barns, can produce them only for labor *equal to a hundred.* You ask me for my sugar, my coffee, my cotton, and you would not be at all disturbed if, in arriving at my price, I considered only the pains I took. But I, on the other hand, am particularly aware of the pains I save you, for I know they are what determine how much you will be willing to pay, and I set my demands accordingly. Since I can do for pains equal to ten what you in your country do for pains *equal to a hundred,* it is certain that you would refuse if I were to demand of you, in return for my sugar, a product that would cost you pains *equal to a hundred and one;* but I ask only for pains equal to *ninety-nine.* You may very well be upset about it for a while, but you will come around, for at that rate the exchange is still to your advantage. You find these terms unfair; but after all, it is to me, not you, that God has given a warm climate. I know that I am in a position where I can exploit this boon of Providence by refusing it to you unless you are willing to pay me a surcharge, for I have no competition. So, here are my sugar, my cocoa, my coffee, my cotton. Take them on my terms, produce them yourself, or go without them."

It is true that the European could in his turn speak in like fashion to the inhabitant of the tropics: "Excavate your land, dig mines, look for iron and coal, and count yourself fortunate if you find them; for, if you don't, I am determined to raise my demands to the limit. God has given us both of these precious gifts. First, we take as much of them as we need; then, we forbid others to take any unless they pay us a special levy on our windfall."

Even if transactions were carried on in this manner, it still would not be possible, from the strictly scientific point of view, to attribute to natural resources the value that resides essentially in *services*. But it would be understandable if this mistake were made, for the result would be the same. Services would still be exchanged for services, but would evidence no tendency to be measured by effort, by labor. The gifts of God would be *personal* privileges and not *common* blessings, and we could perhaps complain with some reason of having been treated by the Author of all things in so hopelessly unfair a manner. Would we, then, be brothers here below? Could we consider ourselves the children of a common Father? The absence of competition, that is, of liberty, would exclude any idea of fraternity. Nothing would be left of the republican motto of "Liberty, Equality, Fraternity."

But let competition appear on the scene, and there will be no more of these one-sided transactions, of these seizures of the gifts of God, of this revolting exorbitance in the evaluation of services, of these inequalities in the exchange of efforts.

And let us note, first of all, that competition must necessarily intervene, called into being, as it is, by the very fact of these inequalities. Labor instinctively moves in the direction that promises it the best returns, and thus unfailingly brings to an end the abnormal advantage it enjoyed; so that inequality is merely a spur that, in spite of ourselves, drives us on toward equality. This is one of the finest examples of *teleology* in the social machine.

Infinite goodness, which has distributed its blessings over the earth, has, it would seem, selected the greedy producer as its agent for effecting their equitable distribution among all mankind, and it certainly is a wonderful sight to see self-interest continually bringing about the very thing it always tries to prevent. Man, as a producer, is necessarily, irresistibly, attracted toward the largest possible rewards for his services, and by that very fact always brings them back into line. He pursues his own interest, and what does he promote, unwittingly, unwillingly, unintentionally? The general good.

Thus, to return to our example, the inhabitant of the tropics, by the very fact that he realizes exorbitant profits from exploiting the gifts of God, attracts competition. Human labor flocks there with an eagerness that, if I may so express myself, is proportional to the magnitude of the inequality, and is not content until the inequality has been eliminated. Through the effect of competition we see tropical labor *equal to ten* successively exchanged for European labor equal to eighty, then sixty, then fifty, then forty, then twenty, and finally ten. There is no reason, under the natural laws of society, why things should not reach this point, that is, why services exchanged should not be measured in terms of labor performed and pains taken, with the gifts of God being thrown in gratis by both parties. So, when things do reach this point, we must realize, with gratitude, how great a revolution has taken place. First, the pains taken by both parties are now equal, which should satisfy our desire for justice. Then, what has become of the gift of God? This deserves the reader's full attention. No one has been deprived of it. Let us not, in this matter, be taken in by the clamor raised by the tropical producer. In so far as he is himself a consumer of sugar, cotton, or coffee, the Brazilian still profits from the heat of the sun; for this beneficent body has not ceased to help him in the work of production. All that he has lost is his unfair power to levy a surcharge on the consumption of the inhabitants of Europe. The gift of Providence, because it was *free of charge,* had to, and did, become *common to all;* for what is *free of charge* and what is *common to all* are essentially one and the same.

God's gift has become—and I beg the reader not to forget that
I am using a particular case to illustrate a universal phenomenon
—common to all. This is not a flight of rhetoric, but the statement
of a mathematical truth. Why has this wonderful fact not been
understood? Because communal wealth is always achieved in the
form of *value* that has been *eliminated,* and our minds have great
difficulty in grasping what is expressed negatively. But, I ask,
when, in order to get a certain amount of sugar, coffee, or cotton,
I offer only a tenth of the pains I should have had to take in order
to produce them myself, and for the reason that in Brazil the
sun performs nine-tenths of the work, is it not true that I am
exchanging labor for labor? And do I not, in a positive sense,
receive, in addition to the Brazilian's labor, and into the bargain,
the help that the tropical climate has contributed? Can I not state
with complete accuracy that I, like all men, share in Nature's
bounty in producing these things on the same terms as an Indian
or a South American, that is, gratis?

England has an abundance of coal mines. This is, beyond
doubt, of great *local* advantage, particularly if we assume, as I
shall in order to simplify the illustration, that there is no coal on
the Continent. As long as no exchange takes place, the advantage
this gives to the English consists in the fact that they have more
fuel than other nations and have it for less pains, for less expenditure of valuable time. As soon as exchange is introduced, taking
no account of competition, their exclusive possession of the mines
enables them to demand large sums in payment and thus to set a
high price on their pains. Not being able to go to these pains
ourselves, or to appeal elsewhere, we shall be obliged to submit.
English labor engaged in this type of work will be very highly
paid; in other words, coal will be expensive, and Nature's bounty
can be considered to be lavished on one nation, and not on all
mankind.

But this state of things cannot last; a great natural and social
law is opposed to it, viz., competition. Precisely because this type
of labor is highly paid in England, it will be in great demand
there, for men are always in quest of high wages. The number of
miners will increase, both through new recruits transferring from

other industries and through the new generation of local miners' sons entering their fathers' trade. They will offer their services for less; they will be satisfied with a constantly decreasing rate, until it reaches the *normal* amount generally paid for similar work in the entire country. This means that the price of English coal will go down in France; that a given amount of French labor will obtain a greater and greater amount of English coal, or rather of English labor as it is represented in the coal; it means, in a word, and this is what I wish to point out, that the gift that Nature appeared to have conferred on England was in reality conferred on all mankind. Coal from Newcastle is bestowed gratis on all men. This is neither paradox nor exaggeration; the coal is bestowed *without cost,* like water from a rushing stream, provided only that men take the *pains* to get it or to compensate the pains of those who get it for them. When we buy coal, it is not the coal that we pay for, but the labor required to extract it and to transport it. All that we do is to offer what we consider as an equal amount of labor in wines or silks. So great has been Nature's bounty toward France that the amount of labor we offer in return is not more than we should have had to perform if the coal deposits had been located in France. Competition has put both nations on an equal footing as far as coal is concerned, except for the slight and unavoidable differences due to distance and transportation costs.

I have offered two illustrations, and, in order to make the phenomenon the more impressive by reason of its size, I have chosen international operations on a very large scale. For that reason I am afraid that I may have failed to make the reader realize that the same phenomenon constantly takes place all about us and in our most ordinary transactions. Let him, then, be good enough to pick out the most humble objects, a glass, a nail, a slice of bread, a piece of cloth, a book. I ask him to reflect a little on these unpretentious articles. Let him ask himself what an incalculable amount of gratuitous utility would, were it not for competition, have indeed remained free of charge for their producers, but would never have become free of charge for humanity; that is, would never have become *common to all.* He may well say to himself, as he buys his bread, that, thanks to competition, he pays nothing for what is done by the sun, the rain, the frost, the laws of vegetation, or even, despite all that is said, for what is done exclusively by the soil. He pays nothing for the law of gravitation set to work by the miller, nothing for the law of combustion set to work by the baker, nothing for the strength of the horses set to work by the deliveryman. Let him reflect that he pays only for services rendered, pains taken by human agents; that, were it not for competition, he would have had to pay an additional charge for all that is done by these natural resources; that this charge would have been limited only by the difficulty he would have experienced in producing the bread with his own hands; that, consequently, a whole lifetime of labor would not have been enough to meet the price he would have been asked to pay. Let him realize that there is not a single article he uses that might not give rise to the same reflection, and that this holds true for every person on the face of the earth; and then he will understand the flaw in the socialist theories, which, viewing only the surface of things, only society's outer shell, have so irresponsibly railed against competition, that is to say, against human freedom. Then he will understand that competition, which insures that the gifts of Nature so inequitably distributed over the globe will retain their double character of being free of charge and common to all, must be considered as the principle of a fair and natural equalization; that it must be admired as the force that holds in check selfish impulses, with which it combines so skillfully that competition serves as both a restraint on greed and a spur to the activity of self-interest. It deserves to be blessed as the most striking manifestation of God's impartial concern for all His creatures.

From the preceding discussion it is possible to arrive at the solution of one of the most controversial of questions: that of free trade among nations. If it is true, as seems to me incontestable, that the various nations of the world are led by competition to exchange with one another nothing but their labor, their efforts, which are gradually brought to a common level, and to include, *into the bargain,* the natural advantages each one enjoys; how blind and illogical, then, are those nations that by legislative action reject foreign goods on the grounds that they are cheap, that they have little value in proportion to their total utility, that is, for the very reason that they contain a high degree of gratuitous utility!

I have already said, and I repeat now, that a theory inspires me with confidence when I see that it agrees with universal practice. Now, it is certain that nations would carry on certain kinds of exchange with one another if they were not *forcibly* forbidden to do so. It takes the bayonet to prevent them; hence, it is wrong to prevent them.

2. Another factor that puts certain men in an exceptionally favorable position as regards remuneration is their exclusive knowledge of the techniques for utilizing *the forces of Nature.* What we call an invention is a conquest over Nature won by human genius. We must observe how these admirable and peaceful conquests, which originally are a source of wealth for those who make them, soon become, under the influence of competition, the *gratuitous and common* heritage of all mankind.

The forces of Nature do indeed belong to everyone. Gravitation, for example, is common property; it surrounds us, permeates us, rules over us. Nevertheless, if there were only one way to harness it for a given practical result, and if some man knew this way, he could set a very high price on his pains or refuse to take them at all unless a considerable amount were given in return. His demands in this respect would go as high as the point at which they would impose on the consumers a greater sacrifice than the old method would entail. He may have succeeded, for example, in eliminating nine-tenths of the labor required for producing article x. But at the present time x has a current market price that has been established by the pains it takes to produce it in the ordinary way. The inventor sells x at the market price; in other words, he is paid ten times more for his pains than are his competitors. This is the first phase of the invention.

Let us note, first of all, that this in no wise outrages justice. It is just that the man who reveals a new and useful process to the world should receive his reward: *to each according to his ability.*

Let us note further that up to this point mankind, the inventor excepted, has benefited only potentially, by anticipation so to speak, since, in order to obtain article *x*, everyone but him is still obliged to make the same sacrifices as before.

At this juncture, however, the invention enters its second phase, the phase of imitation. Excessive compensations by their very nature arouse covetousness. The new process spreads, the price of *x* steadily drops, and the remuneration also declines, more and more rapidly as the time interval between the invention and its imitations lengthens, that is, as it becomes easier and easier, and less and less risky, to copy the invention, and consequently less and less worth while. Certainly there is nothing in all this that could not be sanctioned by the most enlightened and impartial legislation.

At last the invention reaches its third and final phase, the phase of universal distribution, where it is *common property,* and *free of charge* to all. Its full cycle has been run once competition has brought the returns for the producers of article *x* into line with the prevailing and normal rate for similar types of labor. Then the nine-tenths of the pains that are eliminated by the hypothetical invention represent a conquest of Nature for the benefit of all mankind. The utility of article *x* remains the same; but nine-tenths of it have been supplied by gravitation, which was originally common to all in theory, and has now become common to all in fact in this special application. This is proved by the fact that all consumers on the face of the earth may now buy article *x* for one-tenth of what it once cost them. The rest of the cost has been eliminated by the new technique.

If the reader will stop to consider that every human invention has run this cycle, that *x* is here the algebraic sign for wheat, clothing, books, ships, for whose production an incalculable quantity of pains, or value, has been eliminated by the plow, the loom, the printing press, and the sail; that this observation applies to the humblest tool as well as to the most complex machinery, to the nail, the wedge, the lever, even as to the steam engine and the telegraph; he will understand, I hope, how this problem is solved within the human family, *how a steadily greater and more equitably distributed amount of utility or enjoyment becomes the return for a given amount of human labor.*

3. I have already shown how competition brings into the *gratuitous* and *common* domain both *the forces of Nature* and the *processes* by which they are harnessed. It remains for me to show that it performs the same function for the *implements* by means of which these forces are put to work.

It is not enough that there should exist in Nature forces like heat, light, gravitation, electricity; it is not enough that human intelligence should be able to conceive of a way of utilizing them. There is still need for *implements* to make these concepts of the mind a reality and for *provisions* to support men while they are occupied with this task.

Possession of *capital* is a third factor that, as respects remuneration, is favorable to a man or a class of men. He who has at his disposal the tool the worker needs, the raw materials on which the labor is to be performed, and the means of subsistence during the operation, is in a position to demand a remuneration; the principle involved is certainly just, for capital merely represents pains previously taken and not yet rewarded. The capitalist is in a good position to lay down the law, true enough; yet let us note that, even when he faces no competition, there is a limit beyond which he may not press his claims. This limit is the point at which his payment would eat up all the advantages that his service would provide. Hence, there is no excuse for talking, as people often do, about the *tyranny of capital,* since never, even in the most extreme cases, can its presence be more harmful to the worker's lot than its absence. The capitalist, like the man from the tropics who has at his disposal a certain degree of heat that Nature has denied other men, like the inventor who possesses the secret of a *process* unknown to his fellow men, can do no more than say: "Do you desire the use of my labor? I set a given price on it. If you find it too high, do as you have done heretofore: go without it."

But competition intervenes among the capitalists. Implements, raw materials, and provisions can help to create utility only if they are put to work; hence, there is rivalry among capitalists to find a use for their capital. Since the amount by which this rivalry forces them to reduce their claims below the maximum limits that I have just determined brings about a reduction in the price of the product, this amount represents, therefore, a net profit, a *gratuitous* gain for the consumer, that is, for mankind!

It is evident here that cost can never be completely eliminated; since all capital represents some pains that have been taken, the principle of remuneration is always implied.

Transactions involving capital are subject to the universal law of all exchange, which is never carried out unless it is to the mutual advantage of the two contracting parties. This advantage, although it tends to be equal on both sides, may accidentally be greater for one than for the other. The return on capital is subject to a limit beyond which no one will consent to borrow; this limit is *zero service* for the borrower. Likewise, there is a limit below which no one will consent to make a loan; this limit is *zero return* for the lender. This is self-evident. If the demands of either party are raised to the point of *zero* advantage for the other, the loan becomes impossible. The return on capital fluctuates between these two extremes, raised toward the upper limit by competition among borrowers, brought back toward the lower limit by competition among lenders; so that, through a necessity that is in harmony with justice, it rises when capital is scarce and falls when capital is abundant.

Many economists believe that the number of borrowers increases more rapidly than capital can be formed, and hence that the natural trend of interest is upwards. The *facts* are conclusive in favor of the contrary opinion, and we observe that the effect of civilization everywhere is to lower the rate on the hire of capital. This rate, it is said, was 30 or 40 per cent in Rome; it is still 20 per cent in Brazil, 10 per cent in Algiers, 8 per cent in Spain, 6 per cent in Italy, 5 per cent in Germany, 4 per cent in France, 3 per cent in England, and even less in Holland. Now, all this amount by which, through progress, the interest on capital has been reduced, though lost to the capitalist, is not lost to mankind. If the rate of interest, starting at 40, falls to 2 per cent, it means a drop of 38 out of 40 parts for this item in the cost of production of all commodities. They will reach the consumer freed from this charge in the proportion of nineteen-twentieths; this force, then, like *the forces of Nature,* like more efficient *techniques,* results in *abundance, equalization,* and, ultimately, a general rise in the standard of living for the human race.

I still have to say a few words about the competition that labor creates for itself, a subject that has recently inspired so much sentimental rhetoric. But is it really necessary? Has the subject not been exhaustively treated, for the careful reader, by all that has already been said? I have proved that, thanks to competition, men cannot for long receive an abnormal return for the co-operation of *the forces of Nature,* for knowing special *techniques,* or for possessing the *instruments* whereby these forces are put to work. To do this is to prove that efforts tend to be exchanged on an equal footing, or, in other words, that value tends to be proportional to labor. This being so, I do not really understand what is meant by competition among workers. I understand even less how it could be harmful to their situation, since, in this respect workers are also consumers; the laboring class includes everybody, and in fact itself comprises the great community that in the last analysis reaps the rewards of competition and the benefits accruing from the steady elimination of value resulting from progress.

The course of development is as follows: Services are exchanged for services, or value for value. When a man (or a group of men) appropriates a natural resource or acquires a new technique, he bases his charges, not on the pains he takes, but on those he spares others. He raises his demands to the highest possible limit, without ever being able thereby to injure the welfare of others. He assigns the greatest possible value to his services. But gradually, through the effect of competition, this value tends to correspond to the pains he has taken; so that the full course has been run when his pains are exchanged for equal pains, every one of which represents the means of transmitting a growing amount of gratuitous utility, beneficial to the entire community. Such being the case, it would be a glaring inconsistency to say that competition hurts the workers.

And yet this is constantly being said, and it is even widely accepted. Why? Because this word "worker" is used to mean one particular class, not the great community of all those who work. This community is divided into two groups. On one side are placed all those who have capital, who live entirely or in part on previous labor or on intellectual labor or on the proceeds of taxation; on the other are placed those who have only their hands and their wages, those who, to use the time-honored expression, form the proletariat. The relations of these two classes with each other are observed, and the question is asked whether, in view of the nature of these relations, the competition carried on by the wage earners among themselves is not harmful to their interests.

The situation of these men, it is said, is essentially precarious. Since they receive their wages daily, they live from day to day. During the bargaining that, in every free system, goes on before terms are reached, they are unable to wait; they must, no matter what, find work for the morrow or die. If this is not entirely true of all of them, it is at least true of many of them, of enough of them to depress the entire class; for the most hard-pressed, the most wretchedly poor, are the ones who capitulate first, and they set the general wage scale. In consequence, wages tend to be set at the lowest rate compatible with bare subsistence; and in this state of things the least bit of added competition among the workers is a veritable calamity, since for them it is not a question of a lower standard of living, but of not being able to live at all.

Certainly there is much truth, too much truth, *in actual fact*, in this allegation. To deny the sufferings and the miserable conditions prevailing among this class of men who perform the physical labor of the work of production would be shutting our eyes to the truth. The fact is that what we rightly term the *social problem* is related to the deplorable state of a great number of our fellow men, for, although other classes of society are not immune to many anxieties, many sufferings, economic reverses, crises, and upheavals, it is, nevertheless, true that *freedom* would be considered as the solution to the problem, if freedom did not appear helpless in curing this running sore that we call pauperism.

And since it is with this question that the social problem is most concerned, the reader will understand that I cannot analyze it here. Would to God that its solution might be the outcome of this whole book of mine, but obviously it cannot come from a single chapter!

I am now concerned with setting forth certain general laws that I believe to be harmonious, and I am confident that the reader also has become aware that these laws exist, that they tend toward the common sharing of all things and consequently toward equality. But I have not tried to deny that their action has been greatly hindered by disturbing factors. If, then, at the present moment we encounter any shocking *fact* of inequality, how can we interpret it until we know both the normal laws of the social order and the disturbing factors?

On the other hand, I have not sought to deny the existence of evil or its mission. I have felt entitled to state that, since man has been given *free will,* the term "harmony" need not be confined to a total system from which evil would be excluded; for free will implies error, at least as a possibility, and error is evil. Social harmony, like everything else that involves man, is relative; evil constitutes a necessary part of the machinery designed to conquer error, ignorance, and injustice, by bringing into play two great laws of our nature; responsibility and solidarity.

Since pauperism is an existing fact, must its existence be imputed to the natural laws that govern the social order or rather to human institutions that perhaps work contrary to these laws or, finally, to the victims themselves, who by their own errors and mistakes must have called down upon their heads so severe a punishment?

In other words: Does pauperism exist by divine plan or, on the contrary, because of some artificial element still remaining in our political order or as individual retribution? Fate, injustice, individual responsibility? To which of these three causes must this frightful sore be attributed?

I do not hesitate to say that it cannot be the result of the natural laws that have been the object of our study throughout this book, since these laws all tend toward equality under improved conditions, that is, toward bringing all men closer together in their enjoyment of a constantly rising standard of living. Hence, this is not the place to delve into the problem of poverty.

For the moment, if we wish to consider separately that class of workers who carry out the more physical part of the work of production, and who, without sharing, generally speaking, in its profits, live on fixed earnings that we call "wages," the question that we must ask is this: Without taking into account either the goodness or the badness of our economic institutions or the woes that the members of the proletariat may have brought upon themselves, what is, as far as they are concerned, the effect of competition?

For this class of people, as for all others, the effect of competition is twofold. They are aware of it both as buyers and as sellers of services. The error of all those who write on this subject is that they never see more than one side of the question, like physicists who, if they understood only the law of centrifugal force, would believe and constantly predict that all is lost. Provide them with incorrect data, and you will see with what flawless logic they will lead you to their conclusions of doom. The same may be said of the lamentations that the socialists base on their exclusive preoccupation with the phenomenon of centrifugal competition, if I may use such an expression. They forget that there is also centripetal competition, and that is enough to reduce their theories to childish rantings. They forget that the worker, when he goes to market with the wages he has earned, is the center toward which countless industries are directed, and that he then profits from the universal competition of which the industries all complain in their turn.

It is true that the members of the proletariat, when they consider themselves as producers, as suppliers of labor or services, also complain of competition. Let us admit, then, that competition is to their advantage on the one hand, and to their disadvantage on the other; the question is to determine whether the balance is favorable or unfavorable, or whether there are compensating factors.

Unless I have expressed myself very badly, the reader now realizes that in this wonderful mechanism the interplay of various aspects of competition, apparently so antagonistic, brings about, as its singular and reassuring result, a balance that is favorable to all simultaneously, because of the gratuitous utility that steadily enlarges the circle of production and constantly falls within the communal domain. Now, what becomes free of charge and common to all is advantageous to all and harmful to none; we can even add, and with mathematical certainty, that it is advantageous to everyone in direct proportion to his previous state of poverty. This part of gratuitous utility, which competition has forced to become *common to all,* makes value tend to correspond to labor, to the obvious benefit of the worker. This, too, provides the basis for the solution of the social problem that I have tried to keep constantly before the reader, and which only the veil of misconceptions born of habit can prevent him from seeing, namely, that for a given amount of labor each one receives a sum of satisfactions whose tendency is to increase and to be distributed equally.

Furthermore, the condition of the worker is the result, not of one economic law, but of all of them. To understand his condition, to discover what is in store for him, what his future holds, is the one and only function of political economy; for, from its point of view, what else can there be in the world except workers? I am wrong, for there are also plunderers. What gives services their just value? Freedom. What deprives them of their just value? Oppression. Such is the cycle that we have still to traverse.

As for the fate of the working class, which carries out the more immediate work of production, we can evaluate it only when we are in a position to know how the law of competition combines with those of wages and of population and also the disrupting effects of unjust taxation and monopoly.

I shall add only a few more words on competition. It is quite clear that a decrease in the sum total of satisfactions distributed among men is a result that would be foreign to the nature of competition. Does it tend to make this distribution unequal? Nothing on earth is clearer than that competition, after attaching, so to speak, a greater proportion of utility to every service, to every value, works unceasingly to level the services themselves, to make them proportional to efforts. Is competition not the spur that turns men toward productive and away from unproductive careers? Its natural action is, therefore, to assure greater equality and at the same time a higher and higher social level.

Let us, however, understand what we mean by equality. It does not imply identical rewards for all men, but rewards in keeping with the quantity and quality of their efforts.

A host of circumstances contributes to making the remuneration of labor unequal (I am speaking now of free labor subject to the laws of competition). On close examination we discover that this alleged inequality, nearly always just and necessary, is in reality nothing else than actual equality.

All other things being equal, more profit can be had from dangerous labor than from labor that is not; from trades that require a long apprenticeship and outlays that remain unproductive for a long time, implying on the part of the family the long-sustained exercise of certain virtues, than from those in which physical strength alone is necessary; from the professions that demand trained minds and refined tastes, than from trades where nothing is needed beyond one's two hands. Is all this not just? Now, *competition* necessarily establishes these distinctions; society does not need Fourier or M. Louis Blanc to decide the matter.

Among these various factors the one most generally decisive is inequality of training; and here, as everywhere else, we see competition exerting its twofold influence, leveling classes and raising the general standard of society.

If we think of society as being composed of two strata placed one above the other, with intelligence predominant in the one, and brute force predominant in the other, and if we study the natural relations of these two strata with each other, we shall readily notice that the first one possesses a power of attraction, while in the second there is a force of aspiration, and these two work together to form the two strata into one. The very inequality of rewards inspires the lower stratum with a burning desire to reach the higher regions of well-being and leisure, and this desire is encouraged by gleams from the light that illuminates the upper classes. Teaching methods are improved; books cost less;

instruction is acquired more rapidly and cheaply; learning, which had been monopolized by a single class or even caste, veiled in a dead language or in hieroglyphics, is written and printed in the vernacular, permeates the atmosphere, so to speak, and is breathed in like the air.

Nor is this all. Even while more universal and more equal education is working to bring the two social strata together, very important economic factors that are connected with the great law of competition accelerate their fusion. Progress in the knowledge of the laws of mechanics constantly decreases the proportion of brute labor in any operation. The division of labor, by simplifying and isolating each one of the operations that contribute to turning out the finished product, places within the reach of all new industries that previously were open only to a few. Moreover, a complex of various types of labor that originally required highly diversified skills becomes, with the mere passing of time, simple *routine* and is performed by the least skillful, as has happened in agriculture. Agricultural techniques, which, in antiquity, earned for their discoverers honors approaching deification, are today so completely the heritage and almost the monopoly of the most brutish sort of men, that this most important branch of human industry has become almost taboo, so to speak, for the well-bred. It is possible to draw false conclusions from all this and to say: "We do indeed observe that competition lowers remunerations in all countries, in all trades and professions, in all ranks of society, that it levels them downwards; but this means that the wages for unskilled labor, for mere physical exertion, will become the norm, the standard for all remuneration."

The reader has misunderstood me if he does not perceive that *competition,* which tends to bring all excessive remunerations into line with a more or less uniform average, *necessarily* raises this average. This is galling, I admit, to men in their capacity as producers; but it results in improving the general lot of the human race in the only respects in which improvement may reasonably be expected: in well-being, in financial security, in increased leisure, in moral and intellectual development, and, in a word, in respect to all that relates to *consumption.*

Will the objection be made that mankind has not made the progress that this theory would seem to imply?

I shall reply, in the first place, that competition in modern society is far from playing its natural role. Our laws inhibit it at least as much as they encourage it; and to answer the question whether inequality is due to the presence or the absence of competition, we need only observe who the men are who occupy the limelight and dazzle us with their scandalous fortunes, to assure ourselves that inequality, in so far as it is artificial and unjust, is based on conquest, monopolies, restrictions, privileged positions, high government posts and influence, administrative deals, loans from the public funds—with all of which competition has no connection.

Secondly, I believe that we fail to appreciate the very real progress that has been made since the very recent times from which we must date the partial emancipation of labor. It has been said with much truth that it takes a great deal of scientific insight to observe the facts that are constantly before our eyes. The present level of consumption enjoyed by an honest and industrious working-class family does not surprise us because habit has familiarized us with this strange situation. If, however, we were to compare the standard of living that this family has attained with the one that would be its lot in a hypothetical social order from which competition had been excluded; if statisticians could measure with precision instruments, as with a dynamometer, its labor in relation to its satisfactions at two different periods; we should realize that freedom, despite all still-existing restrictions on it, has wrought a miracle so enduring that for that very reason we fail to be aware of it. The total proportion of human effort that has been eliminated in achieving any given result is truly incalculable. There was a time when the day's work of an artisan would not have bought him the crudest sort of almanac. Today for five centimes, or the fiftieth part of his daily wage, he can buy a paper containing enough printed matter for a volume. I could say the same thing for clothing, transportation, shipping, illumination, and a host of satisfactions. To what are these results due? To the fact that a tremendous proportion of human labor, which must be paid for, has been replaced by the gratuitous forces of Nature. This represents value that has been eliminated, that no longer requires payment. It has been replaced, through the action of competition, by gratuitous and common utility; and, let us note, when, through progress, the cost of a given commodity happens to drop, the labor required to pay for it that is saved the poor man is always proportionately greater than that saved the wealthy man, as can be demonstrated mathematically.

Finally, this constantly growing flood of utility, poured forth by labor and pumped through all the veins of the social body by competition, is not to be measured entirely in terms of present material comforts. Much of it is absorbed into the rising tide of ever increasing new generations; it is diffused over an increased population, in accordance with the laws, closely related to our present subject, which will be set forth in another chapter.

Let us pause a moment to look back over the road we have just traveled.

Man has wants that know no limits; he experiences desires that are insatiable. To satisfy them he has raw materials and forces that are supplied him by Nature, faculties, implements—all the things that his *labor* can put into operation. Labor is the resource most widely distributed among all men. Every man seeks instinctively, inevitably, to bring to his aid all the forces of Nature, all the natural or acquired talent, all the capital that he can, in order that all this co-operation may bring him more utility or, what amounts to the same thing, more satisfactions. Thus, the more and more active participation of natural resources, the constant development of his intellectual faculties, the progressive increase of capital, all give rise to this phenomenon, surprising, at first sight: that a given amount of labor furnishes a constantly growing sum of utility, and that everyone may, without taking away from anyone else, enjoy a number of consumers' satisfactions far out of proportion to the ability of his own efforts to produce them.

But this phenomenon, the result of the divine harmony that Providence has implanted in the social structure, would have turned against society itself, by introducing the seeds of constantly increasing inequality, if it were not combined with another and no less admirable harmony, competition, which is one of the branches of the great law of human *solidarity*.

In fact, if it were possible for the individual, family, class, or nation that finds certain natural advantages within reach or makes an important discovery in industry or acquires through thrift instruments of production, to be permanently exempt from the law of competition, it is obvious that this individual, family, or nation would retain the monopoly of its exceptional remuneration for all time to come, at the expense of mankind. Where would we be if the inhabitants of the tropics, free from all competition among themselves, were able, in exchange for their sugar, coffee, cotton, and spices, to demand from us, not amounts of labor equal to theirs, but pains equal to those we ourselves would have to take in order to raise these commodities in our rugged climate? By what an immeasurable distance would the various social strata of mankind be separated if only the race of Cadmus * could read; if no one could handle a plow unless he could prove that he was a direct descendant of Triptolemus; † if only Gutenberg's descendants could print, Arkwright's sons could operate a loom, Watt's progeny could set the funnel of a locomotive to smoking? But Providence has not willed that these things should be, for it has placed within the social machinery a spring as amazingly powerful as it is simple. Thanks to its action every productive force, every improved technique, every advantage, in a word, other than one's own *labor*, slips through the hands of its producer, remaining there only long enough to excite his zeal with a brief taste of exceptional returns, and then moves on ultimately to swell the gratuitous and common heritage of all mankind. All these discoveries and advantages are diffused into larger and larger portions of individual satisfactions, which are more and more equally distributed. Such is the action of *competition*. We have already noted its economic effects; it remains for us to glance

---

* [Legendary founder of Thebes, supposed to have brought the Phoenician alphabet to Greece. He is best known to mythology, of course, as the famous sower of the dragon's teeth.—TRANSLATOR.]

† [Legendary king of Eleusis, supposed to have invented the plow and to have taught agriculture to Attica.—TRANSLATOR.]

at a few of its political and moral consequences. I shall confine myself to pointing out the most important.

Some superficial commentators have accused competition of creating *antagonisms* among men. This is true and inevitable as long as men are considered solely as producers; but consider them as consumers, and you will see that competition binds individuals, families, classes, nations, and races together in the bonds of universal brotherhood.

Since the riches that originally appear to be the exclusive possession of a few become, through the admirable decree of divine bounty, the common patrimony of all; since the *natural advantages* resulting from location, fertility, temperature, mineral deposits, and even industrial aptitude, merely slip through the hands of their producers because of the competition they engage in with one another, and turn exclusively to the profit of the consumer; it follows that there is no country that does not have a selfish interest in the advancement of every other country. Every step of progress that is made in the Orient represents potential wealth for the Occident. Fuel discovered in the south of France means warmer homes for the men of the north. Let Great Britain make all the progress she can with her spinning mills. Her capitalists will not be the ones to reap the benefit, for the interest on money will not rise; nor will it be her workers, for their wages will remain the same; but, in the long run, the Russian, the Frenchman, the Spaniard, all mankind, in a word, will obtain equal satisfactions for less pains, or, what amounts to the same thing, greater satisfactions for equal pains.

I have spoken only of the benefits; I could have said as much for the ills that afflict certain peoples or certain regions. The peculiar action of competition is to make general what was once particular. It acts on exactly the same principle as insurance. If a scourge of Nature ravages the farmers' lands, the consumers of bread are the ones who suffer. If an unjust tax is levied on the vineyards of France, it is translated into high wine prices for all the wine-drinkers on earth. Thus, both advantages and disadvantages of any degree of permanence merely slip through the hands of individuals, classes, and peoples; their ultimate destiny, as ordained by Providence, is to affect all humanity and to raise or lower its standard of living. Hence, to envy any people whatsoever the fertility of its soil or the beauty of its ports and its rivers or the warmth of its sun is to fail to understand the benefis that we are invited to share. It is to disdain the abundance that is offered us; it is to deplore the *toil* that we are spared. Hence, national jealousies are not only perverse sentiments; they are absurd. To harm others is to harm ourselves; to spread obstacles, tariffs, coalitions, or wars along the path of others is to obstruct our own progress. Consequently, evil passions have their punishment even as noble sentiments have their reward. With all the moral authority that it commands, the principle of complete justice for all speaks to our self-interest, enlightens public opinion, proclaims and must eventually make prevail among men this eternally true proposition: The useful is one of the aspects of justice; liberty is the most beautiful of social harmonies; equity is the best policy.

Christianity gave to the world the great principle of the brotherhood of man. It speaks to our hearts, to our sentiments, to our noblest instincts. Political economy proclaims the same principle in the name of cold reason, and, by showing the interrelation of cause and effect, reconciles, in reassuring accord, the calculations of the most wary self-interest with the inspiration of the most sublime morality.

A second conclusion to be derived from this doctrine is that society is a true *common* association. Messrs. Owen and Cabet may save themselves the trouble of seeking the solution to the great *communist* problem; it has already been found. It is derived, not from their despotic contrivances, but from the organization that God has given to man and to society. The forces of Nature, efficient techniques, tools of production—everything is available in common to all men or tends to become so, everything, I say, *except the individual's pains,* labor, and effort. There is, there can be, among men, only one *inequality,* which even the most uncompromising communists admit: the inequality that comes from that of men's efforts.

Efforts alone are exchanged for other efforts according to terms discussed and agreed upon. All the utility imparted to commodities by Nature, by the genius of past centuries, and by human foresight are obtained *gratis, into the bargain.* The reciprocal remunerations established are related only to respective efforts, whether performed in the present under the name of labor or prepared in the past under the name of capital. The system is therefore a *commonwealth* in the most literal and rigorously accurate sense of the word, unless one wishes to assert that each person's share in the satisfactions should be equal, although his participation in the labor is not, a situation that certainly would produce the most unjust and monstrous of inequalities—and the most disastrous, for it would not destroy competition, but would merely reverse its direction: men would still compete, but they would compete to excel in idleness, stupidity, and improvidence.

Finally, this doctrine that we have just elaborated, so simple, and yet, as we believe, so true, lifts the great principle of human *perfectibility* out of the realm of mere oratory and establishes it as a demonstrable fact. From this inner drive, which never rests within man's heart and always prompts him to improve his lot, is born progress in the arts, which is nothing more nor less than the co-operation of forces that are by their very nature incompatible with any remuneration. From competition comes the process that transfers into the communal realm advantages originally held by certain individuals only. The amount of effort once required for a given result grows constantly less, to the benefit of the entire human race, which thus finds that its circle of satisfactions and leisure grows larger from generation to generation, and that its physical, intellectual, and moral level rises. By virtue of this arrangement, so deserving of our study and everlasting admiration, we clearly discern mankind moving upward from the state to which it had fallen.

Let no one misconstrue my words. I do not say that brotherhood, community, and perfectibility are contained in their entirety in the idea of competition. I do say that it is allied and combined with these three great social dogmas, that it is part of them, that it reveals them, and that it is one of the most powerful agents for effecting their realization.

I have set myself the task of describing the general and, consequently, beneficial effects of competition, for it would be sacrilege to assume that any great law of Nature could be permanently harmful in its effect, but I am far from denying that its action may be accompanied by much hardship and suffering. It even seems to me that the theory that I have just advanced explains both this suffering and the inevitable complaints to which it gives rise. Since the function of competition is to *level*, it must necessarily work against anyone who raises his proud head above the level. We understand how every producer, in order to set the highest price on his labor, tries to hold on for as long as possible to the exclusive use of a *resource*, a *technique*, or a *tool* of production. Now, since competition quite properly has as its mission and result the taking away from the individual of this exclusive enjoyment and making it *common* property, it is inevitable that all men, in so far as they are producers, should join in a chorus of imprecations against *competition*. They can become reconciled to it only when they take into account their interests as consumers; when they look upon themselves, not as members of a special group or corporation, but as men.

Political economy, it must be admitted, has not yet done enough to dispel this disastrous fallacy, which has been the source of so many hatreds, calamities, resentments, and wars. Instead, it has expended its efforts, with little scientific justification, in analyzing the phenomena of production. Even its terminology, convenient as it is, is not in keeping with its object of study. "Agriculture," "manufacture," "commerce," make excellent classifications, perhaps, when the intention is to describe the techniques followed in these arts; but this description, though ideally suited for technology, hardly contributes to an understanding of social economy. I may add that it is positively dangerous. When we have classified men as farmers, manufacturers, and businessmen, what can we talk to them about except their special class interests, which are made antagonistic by competition and are in conflict with the general welfare? Agriculture does not exist for the sake of the farmers, manufacturing for the manufacturers, or trade for the businessmen, but in order that all men may have at their disposal the greatest possible number of commodities of all descriptions. The laws of *consumption,* what is good for it and makes it equitable and moral—these are the really important matters from the social and humanitarian point of view; these are the real objects of the science of political economy; these are the questions on which the clear light of its understanding needs to be focused, for therein lies the bond between classes, nations, and races, the principle and the explanation of the brotherhood of man. It is, therefore, with regret that we see economists expending their great talents and lavishing their wisdom on the problem of production, while they reserve a little space at the end of their books, in the supplementary chapters, for a few brief commonplaces on the phenomena of consumption. Recently a justly celebrated professor was known to have entirely suppressed this aspect of our science, to have concerned himself with the *means* to the exclusion of the *ends,* and to have banished from his course all reference to the *consumption of wealth,* on the ground, he said, that this was a subject that belonged to ethics and not to political economy! Can we be surprised that the general public is more concerned with the disadvantages of competition than with its advantages, since the former affect the public from the particular point of view of *production,* which is always being talked about, and the latter only from the general point of view of consumption, which is never mentioned?

As for the rest—I repeat—I do not deny, I recognize and deplore as much as others, the suffering that competition has inflicted on men; but is this a reason for shutting our eyes to the good that it accomplishes? It is all the more reassuring to perceive this good because I believe that competition, like the other great laws of Nature, can never be eliminated. If it could be destroyed, it undoubtedly would have succumbed in the face of the universal opposition of all men who ever competed in the production of any commodity since the beginning of the world, and particularly under the impact of the *mass uprising* of all the modern reformers. But if they have been mad enough to try to destroy it, they have not been strong enough to do so.

And what element of progress is there in the world whose beneficial action has not been marred, particularly at the beginning, by much suffering and hardship? Our great urban masses of human beings stimulate bold flights of thought, but they often deprive individuals in their private life of the corrective of public opinion and serve to shelter debauchery and crime. Wealth combined with leisure favors the cultivation of the mind, but it also nurtures ostentation and snobbishness among the great and resentment and envy among the lowly. Printing brings enlightenment and truth to all strata of society, but it also brings nagging doubt and subversive error. Political liberty has let loose enough tempests and revolutions upon the earth and has sufficiently modified the simple and naive customs of primitive peoples to make serious thinkers wonder whether they would not prefer tranquillity under the shadow of despotism. Christianity itself has sown the great seed of love and charity upon ground soaked in the blood of the martyrs.

Why has it entered into the plans of infinite Goodness and Justice that the happiness of one region or one age should be purchased by the sufferings of another age or another region? What is the divine purpose hidden under this great and irrefutable law of *solidarity*, of which *competition* is merely one of the mysterious aspects? Human wisdom does not know the answer, but human wisdom does know that good is constantly spreading and evil diminishing. Beginning with the social order as it had been made by conquest, where there were only masters and slaves, and where the inequality within society was extreme, the work of *competition* in bringing ever closer together men of different rank, fortune, and intelligence could not be accomplished without inflicting individual hardships that, as the work has progressed, have continually become less, like the vibrations of a sound or the oscillations of a pendulum. Against the sufferings still in store for it, humanity is daily learning how to oppose two powerful remedies, *foresight*, born of experience and enlightenment, and *social co-operation*, which is organized foresight.

Conclusion to the Original Edition

In the first part of this work—alas, all too hastily written!—
I have tried to fix the reader's attention on the line of demarcation, always shifting, but always distinct, that separates the two
regions of the economic world: Nature's collaboration and man's
labor, the liberality of God and the handiwork of man, what is
gratuitous and what is onerous, what is paid for in exchange
and what is donated without charge, total utility and the partial
and supplementary utility that constitutes value, absolute wealth
and relative wealth, the contribution of chemical or mechanical
forces brought to the aid of production by the instruments that
render them serviceable and the just returns due the labor that
has created these instruments, common wealth and private
property.

It was not enough to point out these two orders of phenomena,
so fundamentally different in nature; it was also necessary to
describe their relations, and, if I may so express it, their harmonious evolution. I have tried to explain how it was the function of
private property to seize hold of utility for the human race, to
transfer it to the communal domain, and then to fly away to new
conquests, so that each given effort (and, consequently, the sum
total of all efforts) constantly renders available to mankind an
increasing number of satisfactions. Progress consists in the fact that
human services, when exchanged, while keeping their relative
value, act as a vehicle to convey a larger and larger proportion of
utility which is free of charge, and therefore common to all.
Thus, the possessors of value, of any kind whatsoever, far from
usurping and monopolizing God's gifts, actually multiply them,
but do not on that account make them any the less gratuitous
to all—which was the intent of Providence.

In proportion as satisfactions (for which progress makes Nature

317

foot the bill) fall, by reason of that very fact, within the communal domain, they become *equal,* since inequality can be conceived only in the realm of men's services, which are compared, appraised, and evaluated for exchange. Hence, it follows that equality is necessarily progressive. It is also progressive in another respect, for the inevitable result of competition is to equalize services themselves and to make their rewards correspond more and more closely with their true worth.

Let us now glance over the ground remaining for us to cover.

In the light of the theory that we have set forth in this volume, we still have to examine more closely the following subjects:

Man's relations, both as producer and as consumer, with economic phenomena.

The law of rent on landed property.

The law of wages.

The law of credit.

The law of taxation, which, introducing us to what is, strictly speaking, the subject of government, will lead us to the comparison of private and voluntary services with public and compulsory services.

The law of population.

We shall then be in a position to solve a number of practical problems that are still subjects of controversy: free trade, automation, luxury, leisure, association, organization of labor, etc.

Anticipating our findings in this study, I do not hesitate to say that they may be expressed in the following terms: *A steady approach by all men toward a continually rising standard of living* —in other words: *improvement and equalization*—in a single word: HARMONY.

Such is the final result of the providential plan, of the great laws of Nature, when they act without impediment, when we consider them in themselves, apart from the disturbance to which their action has been subjected by error and violence. At the sight of this harmony the economist may well cry out, as does the astronomer on beholding the movement of the planets, or the physiologist when he contemplates the structure of our human organs: *Digitus Dei est hic!* *

* ["The hand (literally, the finger) of God is here."—TRANSLATOR.]

But man is a free agent, and consequently fallible. He is subject to ignorance and passion. His will, which can err, enters as an element into the workings of economic laws; he can misunderstand them, he can nullify them, he can divert them from their purpose. Just as the physiologist, after admiring the infinite wisdom that has gone into the creation and arrangement of each one of our organs and vital parts, also studies them in their abnormal state, when they are sickly and diseased; so we too shall have to enter a new world, the world of social disturbances.

We shall introduce this new study with a few observations on man himself. It would be impossible for us to evaluate the ills of society, their origin, their effects, their function, the ever narrowing limits within which their own action compresses them (a phenomenon that constitutes what I would almost dare to call a harmonious discord), if we did not examine the necessary consequences of free will, the aberrations due to self-interest, which always entail retribution, and the great laws of human responsibility and solidarity.

We have seen that all the *social harmonies* are contained in germ in these two principles: PROPERTY and LIBERTY. We shall see that all the social discords are merely the extension of these two contrary principles: PLUNDER and OPPRESSION.

And, indeed, the words "property" and "liberty" merely express two aspects of the same fundamental notion. From the economic point of view, liberty is connected with the act of production, property with the thing produced. And, since value has its origin in human activity, we can say that liberty implies and includes property. The same holds true of oppresson as related to plunder.

Liberty! Therein, in the last analysis, lies the source of harmony. Oppression! Therein lies the source of discord. The struggle between these two forces fills the annals of history.

And since oppression has as its aim the unjust seizure of property, since it is transformed into and merges its identity with plunder, it is plunder that I shall show in action.

Man comes into this world bound to the yoke of want, which is pain.

He can escape only by subjecting himself to the yoke of toil, which is also pain.

He has, then, only a choice between two kinds of pain, and he hates pain.

For this reason he looks about him, and if he sees that his fellow man has accumulated wealth, he conceives the idea of making it his own. Hence, property unjustly acquired, or plunder!

Plunder! Here is a new element in the economy of society.

From the day when plunder first appeared on earth, until that day, if it ever comes, when plunder will have completely disappeared, this element has had and will have a profound effect on the entire social mechanism; it will disturb, to the point of making them unrecognizable, the operation of the harmonious laws that we have worked to discover and describe.

Our task, then, will not be done until we have given a complete account of plunder.

Perhaps it will be thought that it is only an accidental, abnormal phenomenon, a sore that will soon heal, unworthy of scientific investigation.

But let us beware. Plunder occupies, in the traditions of families, in the history of nations, in the occupations of individuals, in the physical and intellectual energies of all classes, in the arrangements of society, in the precautions of governments, almost as important a place as property itself.

No, plunder is not a passing scourge, accidentally affecting the social mechanism, and the science of economics may not exclude it from consideration.

In the beginning this sentence was pronounced on man: In the sweat of thy face shalt thou eat bread. Hence, it appears that effort and satisfaction are indissolubly joined, and that the one can never exist unless paid for by the other. Yet everywhere we see man revolting against this law, and saying to his brother: Yours be the toil; mine, the fruit of that toil.

Enter the hut of the savage hunter or the tent of the nomadic shepherd. What sight meets your eyes? The wife, thin, disfigured, terrified, faded before her time, bears all the burden of the household chores, while the husband lolls in idleness. What idea can we form here of family harmony? It has disappeared, because force has laid upon the defenceless the burden of toil. And how many centuries of civilization will it take before woman will be raised from this frightful degradation?

Plunder, in its most brutal form, brandishing torch and sword, fills the annals of history. What are the names that make up history? Cyrus, Sesostris,* Alexander, Scipio, Caesar, Attila, Tamerlane, Mohammed, Pizarro, William the Conqueror—outright plunder by means of conquest. To it go the laurel wreaths, the monuments, the statues, the triumphal arches, the songs of the poets, the heady admiration of women!

Soon the conqueror thinks of a better way of dealing with the conquered than to kill them, and slavery covers the earth. Almost down to our own day, all over the world, it was the accepted way of life, leaving in its wake hatred, resistance, civil strife, and revolution. And what is slavery except organized oppression with plunder as its object?

If plunder arms the strong against the weak, it no less lets loose the intelligent upon the credulous. What industrious peoples are there on earth who have escaped exploitation at the hand of sacerdotal theocracies, Egyptian priests, Greek oracles, Roman augurs, Gallic druids, brahmins, muftis, ulemas,† bonzes, monks, ministers, mountebanks, sorcerers, soothsayers, plunderers of all garbs and denominations? It is the genius of plunderers of this ilk to place their fulcrum in heaven and to glory in a sacrilegious complicity with God! They put in chains, not men's bodies alone, but their minds as well. They put the brand of servitude as much upon the conscience of a Seid ‡ as upon the brow of a Spartacus, thus achieving what would seem to be impossible: the enslavement of the mind.

Enslavement of the mind! What a frightful association of words! O liberty! We have seen thee hunted from country to country, crushed by conquest, nigh unto death in servitude,

* [Mythical king of Egypt, often confused with Rameses and other pharaohs of his dynasty.—TRANSLATOR.]

† [A body composed of the hierarchy of the Moslems.—TRANSLATOR.]

‡ [The slave of Mohammed, the first person to accept Mohammed's declaration that he was the special Prophet of Allah. Voltaire uses Seid (Gallicized to *Séïde*) as the symbol of blind fanatical devotion in his tragedy, *Mahomet, ou le fanatisme.*—TRANSLATOR.]

jeered at in the courts of the mighty, driven from the schools, mocked in the drawing room, misinterpreted in the studio, anathematized in the temple. It would seem that in thought thou shouldst find an inviolable refuge. But if thou shouldst surrender in this last haven, what becomes of the hope of the ages and of the dignity of man?

Yet in the long run (so man's forward-looking nature wills it) plunder generates, in the very places where it holds sway, opposition that paralyzes its power, and knowledge that unmasks its impostures. It does not yield on that account, however; it merely becomes more cunning, and wrapping itself in forms of government and alignments, playing one faction against another, turns to political scheming, so long a fertile source of illicit power. Then we see plunder usurping the citizens' liberty in order the more readily to exploit their wealth, and draining off their substance the better to conquer their liberty. Private enterprise becomes public enterprise. Everything is done by government functionaries; a stupid and vexatious bureaucracy swarms over the land. The public treasury becomes a vast reservoir into which those who work pour their earnings, so that the henchmen of the government may tap them as they will. Transactions are no longer regulated by free bargaining, and nothing can establish or preserve the principle of *service for service*.

In this state of things the true notion of property is effaced, and every man appeals to the law to give his services an artificial and arbitrary value.

Thus, we enter the era of privilege. Plunder, becoming more and more subtle, establishes itself in monopolies and hides behind restrictions; it diverts the natural course of exchange and forces capital, and after it, labor and the whole population, into artificial channels. It produces laboriously in the north what could be produced easily in the south; it creates precarious industries and livelihoods; it substitutes for the gratuitous forces of Nature the onerous drudgery of human labor; it supports business concerns that cannot survive against competition, and then invokes the use of force against their competitors; it arouses international jealousies, encourages nationalistic sentiments, and invents ingenious theories that make allies of its own dupes; it always has impending industrial panics and bankruptcies; it undermines in the minds of the citizens all confidence in the future, all faith in liberty, and even their sense of justice. And then, when science exposes these misdeeds, Plunder stirs up even its victims against science, with the battle cry: Onward to utopia! Indeed, it repudiates not only the science that stands in its way, but even the idea that science can be applied to these areas, declaring with crowning cynicism: There are no absolute principles!

Nevertheless, spurred on by their suffering, the working-class masses revolt and topple over everything above them. Government, taxation, legislation, everything is at their mercy, and you believe perhaps that Plunder's reign is at an end; you believe that the principle of service for service will be established on the only foundation possible or imaginable, that of liberty. Undeceive yourself. Alas! This pernicious idea has infiltrated the masses: property has no origin, sanction, legitimacy, or justification other than the law, and thereupon the masses institute legislation to plunder one another. Suffering from the wounds inflicted upon them, they undertake to heal everyone of their number by giving to each the right to oppress his neighbor. This is called solidarity, brotherhood: "You have produced; I have not; we are comrades; let us share." "You own something; I own nothing; we are brothers; let us share."

We must therefore examine the abuses perpetrated in recent years in the name of "association," "organization of labor," "interest-free credit," etc. We shall have to subject them to this acid test: Are they in harmony with the principle of liberty or of oppression? In other words: Are they in conformity with the great economic laws, or do they constitute a disturbance of their operation? *

Plunder is too universal, too persistent, to be considered a purely accidental phenomenon. In this case, as in so many others, it is impossible to separate the study of natural laws from the study of the things that disturb their operation.

* [Bastiat here refers to the ill-fated projects like the national workshops, interest-free credit, and the unemployment compensation laws set up by the socialists after the 1848 Revolution. Designed to aid the industrial workers, their costs were met by increased taxation, which fell heavily upon the rest of the nation, particularly the peasants.—TRANSLATOR.]

But, it will be said, if plunder necessarily enters into the workings of the social mechanism as a *discord,* how do you dare affirm the harmony of economic laws?

I shall repeat here what I have said elsewhere: In everything that concerns man, a being who is *perfectible* only because he is *imperfect,* harmony does not consist in the complete absence of *evil,* but in its gradual reduction. The social body, like the physical body, is possessed of a curative force, *vis medicatrix,* whose laws and unfailing power cannot be studied without again eliciting the words: *Digitus Dei est hic.*[1]

11

Producer and Consumer

If the standard of living of the human race is not constantly on the rise, man is not perfectible.

If the tendency of society is not continually to raise all men to this ever upward-moving standard of living, economic laws are not harmonious.

Now, how can the standard of living rise unless a given amount of labor yields increasing satisfactions, a phenomenon that can be explained only by the transforming of onerous utility into gratuitous utility?

And, on the other hand, how can this utility, when it has become gratuitous, raise all men to a common standard unless it at the same time becomes common wealth?

This, then is the essential law of social harmony.

I very much wish that the language of economics could supply me with two words to indicate services rendered and received other than the words "production" and "consumption," which connote too much an exchange of materials. Obviously, there are services, like those of the priest, the teacher, the soldier, the artist, which promote morality, education, security, the enjoyment of the beautiful, and yet have nothing in common with industry, in the strict sense of the word, except in so far as their ultimate aim is *satisfaction*.

The words are in accepted usage, and I have no desire to indulge in neologisms. But at least let it be understood that by "production" I mean that which imparts utility, and by "consumption," I mean the enjoyments that utility imparts.

Let the protectionist school—which is really a variety of communism—believe me when I say that in using the words "producer" and "consumer," I am not so illogical as to imagine, as I have been accused of doing, that the human race is divided into two distinct classes, the one concerned only with producing and the other only with consuming. Just as the biologist may divide the human race into whites and blacks, men and women, so the economist may divide it into producers and consumers, because, as our esteemed friends the protectionists observe with great penetration, *producer and consumer are one and the same person.*

But precisely because they are one and same person, every man must be considered by the science of political economy in this double capacity. It is not a matter of dividing the human race into two parts, but of studying two very different aspects of man. If the protectionists were to forbid grammar to use *thee* and *me* on the ground that each one of us is in turn *the one speaking* and *the one spoken to,* we could remind them that, while it is perfectly true that we cannot put all the tongues on one side and all the ears on the other simply because we all have ears and a tongue, yet it does not follow that, as each phrase of a conversation is uttered, the tongue does not belong to one man and the ears to the other. Similarly, *as each service is performed,* the one rendering it is perfectly distinct from the one receiving it. Producer and consumer confront each other from opposite sides, so opposed, indeed, that they are constantly in dispute.

The same people who are unwilling for us to study man's self-interest from the double point of view of consumer and producer have no qualms about making this distinction when they speak to the legislative assembly. Then we see them demanding monopoly or free trade, depending on whether they are selling or buying the commodity in question.

Without, therefore, paying heed to the pleas of the protectionists that the case be thrown out of court, let us recognize that in the social order the division of labor has created for every person two roles so distinct from each other that their interplay merits our careful study.

In general, we devote ourselves to a trade, a profession, or career from which we do not expect to receive our satisfactions directly. We render and we receive services; we offer and we demand value; we make purchases and sales; we work for others, and others work for us; in a word, we are *producers* and *consumers*.

When we go to the market place, we have different, even opposite, points of view, depending on whether we go as consumers or producers. In the case of wheat, for example, the same man does not desire the same thing when he goes as a buyer as when he goes as a seller. As a buyer he hopes for abundance; as a seller, for scarcity. These hopes stem from the same source, self-interest; but as buying or selling, giving or receiving, supplying or demanding, are completely opposite actions, they cannot fail, though they have the same motivation, to give rise to conflicting desires.

Desires that clash cannot both simultaneously coincide with the general welfare. In another work [1] I have tried to show that men's desires as consumers are the ones that are in harmony with the public interest, and it cannot be otherwise. Since satisfaction is the end and purpose of labor, since the amount of labor depends solely upon the obstacles it encounters, it is clear that labor is the *evil*, and that everything should be done to lessen it, while satisfaction is the *boon*, and that everything should be done to increase it.

Here we encounter the great, eternal, and deplorable fallacy that arises from the false definition of *value* and its confusion with *utility*.

Since value is merely the expression of a relation, the greater its importance for the individual, the less is its importance for all men collectively.

For all men collectively only utility matters; and value in no wise serves as its measure.

For the individual also, only utility matters. But value is its measure; since for each determinate value he contributes, he can obtain from society an equivalent measure of the utility of his choice.

If we consider man in isolation, it becomes as clear as day that consumption is the essential thing, and not production; consumption quite clearly implies labor, but labor does not imply consumption.

The division of labor led certain economists to measure the general welfare, not in terms of consumption, but in terms of labor. And by following their example, we have come to this strange reversal of principles, that we favor labor at the expense of its results.

This is the reasoning that has been followed:

The more obstacles that are overcome, the more value for us. Hence, let us multiply the obstacles that are in our way.

The flaw in this reasoning is very obvious.

Yes, undoubtedly, granted a given number of obstacles, it is a good thing for a given quantity of labor to be able to surmount as many of them as possible. But it is simply monstrous to decrease the effectiveness of labor or to increase the difficulties in its way in order to obtain more value.

The individual member of society wants to see his services, even though retaining the same degree of utility, increase in value. If his wishes are granted, it is easy to see what will happen. He will enjoy a better living, but his fellows will have less, since the total utility has not been increased.

We cannot, therefore, pass from the particular case to the general rule and say: Let us take such measures as will satisfy the desire of every individual for an increase in the value of his services.

Since value is purely relative, we should have accomplished nothing if the increase remained in every instance in proportion to previous value; if it were set arbitrarily and unequally for different services, we should do nothing but introduce injustice into our distribution of utilities.

It is characteristic of every commercial transaction to give rise to *argument* and *discussion*. Good heavens! What have I just said? Have I not called down on my head the wrath of all the sentimentalist schools, which are so numerous these days? *Argument* implies *antagonism,* they will say to me. You therefore admit that antagonism is the natural state of society.

Once again I must stop to enter the lists against them. In our country the science of economics is so poorly understood that it is impossible to say a word without raising up an opponent.

I have been reproached, with reason, for having written this sentence: "Between buyer and seller there exists a fundamental antagonism." The word "antagonism," especially reinforced by the word "fundamental," goes far beyond my intention. It appears to indicate a permanent hostility of interests, and consequently an ineradicable social discord, whereas I was merely referring to that short-lived argument, or discussion, which takes place before any bargain is made, and which is inherent in the very idea of a transaction.

As long as there remains, to the great chagrin of the sentimental utopian, the least vestige of liberty in this world, the seller and the buyer will argue for their interests, will haggle over their prices, will *bargain,* as the saying goes, and the laws governing the social order will not become the less harmonious on that account. Can we imagine that the one *supplying* a service and the one *demanding* it can come together without having momentarily divergent views on its *value?* And do we think that this is any world-shaking calamity? Either we must banish every transaction, every exchange, every act of barter, every vestige of liberty, from this earth, or we must recognize the right of each one of the contracting parties to defend his position, to *make the most* of his side of the argument. Indeed, this free debate, so often deplored, is in fact the means of establishing an equivalence of services and equity in transactions. How else will the social planners arrive at that equity that they desire so much? Will they shackle with their laws the freedom of one of the contracting parties? In that case he will be at the mercy of the other. Will they strip both parties of the power to determine their own interests on the pretext that henceforth they must sell and buy on the principle of brotherly love? But in that case I must say that what the socialists are proposing is nonsense, for in some way or other the respective interests of the parties to the transaction have to be determined. Will the bargaining take place in reverse, with the buyer presenting the seller's case, and vice versa? Such transactions would be highly entertaining, we must admit.

"Sir, pay me only ten francs for this piece of cloth."

"What do you mean? I want to give you twenty francs."

"But, sir, it's worthless; it's out of style; in two weeks it will be worn out," says the merchant.

"It's of the best quality and will last two winters," replies the customer.

"Very well, sir, just to make you happy, I'll add five francs to the price; that's the most brotherly love will let me do for you."

"It goes against my socialist principles to pay less than twenty francs; but we all have to make sacrifices, and I accept."

Thus, the weird transaction will come out in exactly the ordinary way, and the social planners will observe with regret that accursed liberty still surviving, although moving in the wrong direction and creating antagonisms in reverse.

"This is not what we want," say the social planners; "this would be individualistic freedom."

"What do you want, then? For services still have to be exchanged and their conditions determined."

"We propose that their control be entrusted to us."

"I thought so."

Brotherhood! Sacred tie that joins soul to soul, divine spark come down from heaven into the hearts of men, how can thy name be thus taken in vain? In thy name it is proposed to stifle all freedom. In thy name it is proposed to erect a new despotism such as the world has never seen; and we may well fear that after serving as a protection for so many incompetents, as a cloak for so many ambitious schemers, as a bauble for so many who haughtily scorn human dignity, it will at last, discredited and with sullied name, lose its great and noble meaning.

Let us, therefore, not have the presumption to overthrow everything, to regulate everything, to seek to exempt all, men and things alike, from the operation of the laws to which they are naturally subject. Let us be content to leave the world as God made it. Let us not imagine that we, poor scribblers, are anything but more or less accurate observers. Let us not make ourselves ridiculous by proposing to change humanity, as if we stood apart from it and from its errors and shortcomings. Let us permit producer and consumer to have their respective interests, to discuss, debate, and settle their differences through fair and peaceful arrangements. Let us limit ourselves to observing their relations and the ensuing results. This is what I propose to do, and always in keeping with what I proclaim is the great law of human society: the gradual equalization of individuals and classes concomitant with general progress.

A line no more resembles a force or a velocity than it does a value or a utility. Nevertheless, the mathematician finds lines and diagrams helpful. Why should not the economist also?

There are values that are equal to each other; there are values that have known ratios to each other of a half, a fourth, double, triple. There is no reason for not representing these differences by lines of varying lengths.

Such is not the case with utility. Utility, in general, as we have seen, can be broken down into gratuitous utility and onerous utility—into utility due to the action of Nature, and utility created by human labor. The latter, since it can be assigned value and be measured, may be represented by a line of fixed length; the former cannot be measured or assigned any value. It is certain that Nature contributes much toward the production of a hundredweight of wheat, a cask of wine, a side of beef, a pound of wool, a ton of coal, a cord of wood. But we have no way of measuring Nature's aid contributed by a great multitude of forces, most of which are unknown and have been in operation since Creation. Nor is there anything to be gained from so doing. Gratuitous utility, then, must be represented by a dotted line of indeterminate length.

Two products, then, the one *worth* twice the other, may be represented by these lines:

IB, *ID*, represent the total product, general utility, the thing that satisfies the want, absolute wealth.

IA, IC, represent the co-operation of Nature, gratuitous utility, the part that is common wealth.

AB, CD, represent the human service, onerous utility, *value,* relative wealth, the part that is private property.

I do not need to say that *AB,* in whose place you may put, in your imagination, whatever you wish—a house, a piece of furniture, a book, an aria sung by Jenny Lind, a horse, a piece of cloth, a doctor's appointment, etc.—can be exchanged for twice *CD,* and that the two parties to the transaction will give each other, into the bargain, and without even realizing that they are doing so, the one, *IA,* the other, twice *IC.*

Man is so constituted that his constant concern is to lessen the ratio of effort to result, to substitute the action of Nature for his own action—in a word, to do more with less. His skill, his intelligence, his industry are always directed toward this end.

Let us suppose, then, that John, the producer of *IB,* discovers a process whereby he can complete his task with half the labor it previously took, everything included, even the cost of making the implement used to harness the forces of Nature.

As long as he keeps his secret, there will be no change in the figures given above. *AB* and *CD* will represent the same values, the same ratios; for since John is the only one in the world who knows the formula, he will turn it to his own exclusive advantage. Either he will rest half the day, or else he will make two *IB's* rather than one per day; his labor will be better paid. The conquest over Nature will be to the benefit of mankind, but mankind as represented, in this case, by one man.

The reader should note, in passing, how treacherous is the axiom of the English economists: *Value comes from labor,* if its intent is to assume that *value* and *labor* are proportional. In our illustration we have a case in which labor has been reduced by half, and yet there is no change in value, and this happens every minute of the day. Why? Because the service is the same. The person furnishing *IB* performs the same service before as after the invention. This will no longer be the case when Peter, the producer of *ID,* can say to John: "You ask me for two hours of my labor in exchange for one of yours; but I am familiar with your process, and if you place such a high price on your service, I shall do it for myself."

Now this day comes inevitably. When a new process is invented, it does not remain a secret for long. Then the value of product *IB* will fall by one-half, and we shall have these two figures:

I		*A*	*A'*	*B*
I			*C*	*D*

AA' represents value eliminated, relative wealth that has disappeared, private property made public, utility previously onerous, now gratuitous.

This has taken place because John, used here as the symbol of the producer, is put back in his original position. He now can make *IB* twice for the amount of effort that it used to take him to make it once. In order to have two *ID*'s, he must give two *IB*'s, whether *IB* represents furniture, books, houses, or anything else.

Who gains by all this? It is obviously Peter, the producer of *ID*, used here as the symbol of all consumers, including John himself. If, in fact, John wishes to use his own product, he will save himself the time represented by the elimination of *AA.'* As for Peter, that is, all the consumers on earth, they can now purchase *IB* for half the time, effort, labor, value, required before the natural resource was introduced. Hence, this resource is free of charge and, besides, common to all.

Since I have ventured to use geometric figures, let me employ them once again in the hope that this method, admittedly a little irregular in economics, will aid the reader in understanding the phenomenon to be described.

Every man, as producer or as consumer, is a center from which radiate the services he renders and to which are directed the services he receives in exchange.

Let us then place at *A* (Fig. 1) a producer, for example, a copyist, as the symbol of all producers or of production in general. He presents society with four manuscripts. If, at the moment at which we are making our observation, the *value* of each of the manuscripts is fifteen, he is performing *services* equal to sixty, and he receives an equal sum of value, variously distributed over many services. For the sake of simplification I show only the four points *BCDE* along the circumference.

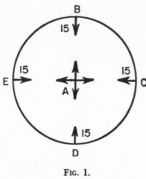

Fig. 1.

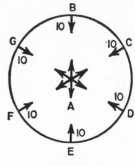

Fig. 2.

Value produced = 60	Value produced = 60
Value received = 60	Value received = 60
Utility produced = 4	Utility produced = 6

Now suppose this copyist discovers the art of printing. He thereafter does in forty hours what used to take him sixty. Let us assume that competition has forced him to reduce the price of his books in the same ratio; they are now worth only ten, instead of fifteen. But it also happens that our worker can produce, not four, but six books. On the other hand, the amount received as payment, starting from the circumference, which was sixty, has not changed. There is, therefore, as much remuneration for six books, worth ten each, as there was previously for four when each manuscript was worth fifteen.

This, I may briefly remark, is what is always lost sight of in discussions concerning the question of machinery, free trade, and progress in general. We observe that labor is laid off by more efficient techniques, and we become alarmed. We fail to note that a corresponding proportion of the cost is likewise placed at our disposal at the same time.

The new transactions, then, are represented by Fig. 2, where we see radiating from center *A* a total value of sixty, spread over six books instead of four manuscripts. The lines extending inward from the circumference continue to represent a total value of sixty, which is necessary now, as formerly, to balance the services rendered.

Who, then, has gained by the change? From the point of view of *value*, nobody. From the point of view of real wealth, actual satisfactions, the countless number of consumers located on the circumference. Each one of them can now purchase a book for a third less labor. But the consumers are all mankind. For notice that A himself, if he gains nothing as producer, if he is still obliged, as formerly, to put in sixty hours of work to receive the old pay, nevertheless gains, as a user of books, that is, on the same basis as other men. Like all of them, if he desires to read, he obtains this satisfaction at a saving of one-third of his labor.

What if, in his capacity as producer, he sees the profit from his own discovery eventually slip through his hands because of competition? Where in that case, is there compensation for him?

First, it consists in the fact that, as long as he was able to keep his secret, he continued to sell for fifteen what cost him only ten.

Second, his compensation consists in the fact that he obtains books for his own use at less cost and thus shares in the advantages he has contributed to society.

But third, his greatest compensation consists in this fact: even as he was forced to benefit mankind by his progress, so he benefits from the progress of mankind.

Just as the progress made by A was of profit to B, C, D, E, so the progress realized by B, C, D, E, will be to the profit of A. A finds himself alternately at the center and at the circumference of world-wide industry, for he is alternately producer and consumer. If B, for example, is a cotton spinner who substitutes the bobbin for the spindle, the profit will go to A as well as to C and D. If C is a sailor who replaces the oar with the sail, the saving will profit B, A, E.

In the final analysis, the whole system rests on this law:

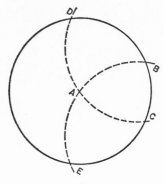

FIG. 3.

Progress is of benefit to the producer, as such, only long enough to reward him for his skill. It soon brings about a fall in value, which gives the early imitators a fair, though smaller, recompense. Finally, the value levels off in proportion to the reduction in labor, and the entire saving accrues to mankind.

Thus, all profit from the progress of each, and each profits from the progress of all. The *one for all, and all for one* motto advanced by the socialists and proclaimed to the world as something new to be found in budding form in their social orders based on oppression and coercion has actually been provided by God Himself; and He derived it from liberty.

God, I say, provided it; and He did not establish His law in a model community under the direction of M. Considérant, or in a phalanstery of six hundred *harmoniens,** or in an experimental Icaria, on condition that a few fanatics submit to the arbitrary power of a monomaniac, and that the unbelievers pay for the believers. No, God has provided it on a general, world-wide basis, through a marvelous mechanism in which justice, liberty, utility, and social consciousness are combined and reconciled to a degree

* [The individual members of Fourier's phalanstery, or "harmonious" community, were called *harmoniens,* a term that he himself invented.—TRANSLATOR.]

that should dampen the ardor of the planners and builders of artificial social orders.

Note that this great law—*one for all, and all for one*—is much more universal than my description of it would suggest. Words are cumbersome, and the pen is even more so. The writer is reduced to showing successively, one after another, with discouraging slowness, phenomena that stir our admiration only when we view them collectively.

Thus, I have just spoken of *inventions*. One might conclude from what I have said that they represent the only case in which progress, when once achieved, slips out of the producer's hands and finds its way into the common treasury of all mankind. This is not so. It is a general law that any advantage whatsoever created by special circumstances of location, climate, or any other liberality of Nature, quickly slips through the hands of the one who first discovers it and lays hold of it, yet is not on that account lost, for it moves on to feed the immense reservoir from which flow the satisfactions that men enjoy in common. Only one proviso is attached to this result: labor and exchange must be free. To go against liberty is to go against the will of Providence; it amounts to suspending the action of God's law, to restricting progress in the two directions it takes.

What I have just said concerning the blessings of life is true also of its evils. Nothing stops with the producer, whether advantage or disadvantage. Both tend to be distributed over the whole of society.

We have just seen with what eagerness the producer seeks out whatever will make his task easier, and we have assured ourselves that very shortly his profit will elude him. He appears to be, in the hands of a superior intelligence, only the blind and docile instrument of general progress.

With the same eagerness he avoids everything that would impede his activity; and this is a fortunate thing for mankind, since in the long run it is mankind that is harmed by these impediments. Let us assume, for example, that A, a book producer, has had a heavy tax levied upon him. He must add it to the price of his books. It will become an integral part of the books' value, which means that B, C, D, E, will have to offer more of their labor for the same satisfaction. What compensation they receive for this loss will depend upon the use the government makes of the tax. If it puts it to good use, they perhaps will not lose; they may even gain by the arrangement. If it is used to oppress them, their vexation will be doubly galling. But as far as A is concerned, he is relieved of the burden of the tax, even though he advances the money for it.

This does not mean that the producer does not often suffer greatly from obstacles of all sorts, taxes included. Sometimes taxes burden him to the breaking point, and it is precisely for this reason that their incidence tends to be shifted so that they fall ultimately on the masses.

Thus, wine in France was once the object of a multitude of taxes and controls. Then a system was contrived for restricting its sale outside the country. This case illustrates how the evils that arise tend to ricochet from producer to consumer. As soon as the tax and the restrictions are put into effect, the producer strives to make up for his losses. But since both the consumer *demand* and the supply of wine remain unchanged, he cannot increase his price. At first his income is no more after the imposition of the tax than it was before. And since, prior to the tax, he received only a normal return, determined by the value of the services freely exchanged, he discovers that he is out the amount of the tax. In order for prices to be raised, there must be a decrease in the amount of wine produced.[2]

The consumer, or the public, is, therefore, in relation to the loss or gain that is first experienced by a given class of producers, what the earth is to electricity: the great common reservoir. Everything comes from it; and everything, after making more or less lengthy detours, after producing more or less varied phenomena, returns to it.

We have just noted that economic effects merely slip away from the producer, so to speak, and ultimately come to rest at the consumer's door, and, therefore, that all the great economic questions must be studied from the consumer's point of view if we wish to grasp their general and lasting consequences.

This subordination of the producer's role to that of the consumer, which we have deduced from our consideration of *utility,* is fully confirmed by considerations of *morality.*

Now, the fact is that responsibility always rests where the initiative is. And where is the initiative? In *demand.*

Demand (which implies the ability to pay) determines everything: the allocation of capital and labor, the distribution of population, the morality of the various occupations, etc. It is *demand* that corresponds to wants, whereas *supply* corresponds to effort. Wants are reasonable or unreasonable, moral or immoral. Effort, which is merely an effect, is amoral or else has only a reflected morality.

Demand, or consumption, says to the producer: "Do this for me," and the producer obeys. This would be obvious in every case if the producer always and everywhere followed the lead of the consumer and waited for the demand.

But in reality things do not happen this way at all.

Whether exchange brought about the division of labor, or the division of labor introduced exchange, is a subtle and idle question. Let us say that men exchange because, being intelligent and sociable creatures, they understand that exchange is a means of improving the ratio of effort to result. What is brought about solely by the division of labor and by foresight is that a man does not wait for a formal order from others before he sets to work. Experience teaches him that such an order is tacit in human relations and that the demand exists.

He exerts the effort to satisfy it in advance, and this gives rise to the trades and professions. Hats and shoes are made in advance; men prepare themselves to sing, to teach, to plead cases, to cure diseases, etc. But in these cases does supply really precede demand and create it?

No. Men prepare themselves because they are reasonably certain that these different services will be in demand, although they may not always know by whom. And the proof that this is the case consists in the fact that the relations among these services are well enough known, that their *value* has been well enough established, so that one may with some confidence devote himself to making a given article or embark on a given career.

The impetus of demand, then, comes first, since it has been possible to estimate its range so accurately.

Therefore, when a man enters a trade or a profession, when he becomes a producer, what is his first concern? Is it the *utility* of the thing he produces, its good or bad, moral or immoral results? Not at all; he thinks only of its *value*. It is the demander who considers its *utility*. Its utility corresponds to his want, his desire, his whim. *Value,* on the contrary, corresponds only to effort expended, to service transmitted. Only when, through exchange, the supplier becomes in his turn a demander, does he care about utility. When I decide to make shoes rather than hats, it is not because I have asked myself whether it is more to men's advantage that their feet be warm than their heads. No, this question concerns the demander and determines the demand. Demand, in turn, determines value, or the regard in which the public holds the service. Value, in a word, determines effort, or supply.

The moral results of this fact are quite noteworthy. Two nations may be equally provided with values, that is, with relative wealth,[3] and yet be very unequal in their real utilities, that is, their absolute wealth. This happens when one of the nations has more unreasonable desires than the other, is concerned with artificial or immoral wants, while the other is mindful of its real wants.

In the one country a taste for learning may predominate, in the other a desire for good eating. In this case one renders a service to the first country by teaching it something; in the second, by tickling its palate.

Now, men reward services according to the importance they attach to them. If they did not exchange, they would perform the service for themselves; and what would be the determining factor if not the nature and intensity of their desires? In one of these nations, therefore, there will be many teachers; in the other, many cooks.

In both countries the services exchanged may be equal in amount and may therefore represent equal value, the same relative wealth, but not the same absolute wealth. This means nothing more nor less than that the one country puts its labor to good use, the other to bad.

And the result, as regards satisfactions, will be this: One of the countries will have much learning; the other will eat well. The ultimate consequences of this diversity of tastes will have a great influence not only on real wealth but also on relative wealth; for learning, for example, can develop new ways of performing services, a thing that good meals cannot do.

We observe among the nations a prodigious diversity of tastes, the result of their past traditions, their character, their beliefs, their vanity, etc.

Undoubtedly, there are wants so immediate and so pressing, for example drinking and eating, that they may almost be considered fixed quantities. Yet it is not unusual to see one man go without eating as well as he would like in order to have clean clothing, while another man considers the cleanliness of his clothing only after he has satisfied his appetites. The same is true of nations.

But once these pressing wants are met, everything else depends much more on the will; it is a matter of taste, and in this area the role of morality and good sense is enormous.

The intensity of a nation's various desires always determines the quantity of labor, out of the sum total of all its efforts, that it sees fit to devote to the satisfaction of each particular desire. The Englishman wants above all else to be well fed. Therefore, he devotes an enormous quantity of his labor to producing foodstuffs; and if he produces other things, it is for the purpose of exchanging them abroad for food. The total amount of wheat, meat, butter, milk, sugar, etc., consumed in England reaches terrifying proportions. The Frenchman wants to be amused. He likes what catches the eye, and he enjoys change. The direction taken by his labor is fully in accord with his desires. In France there are many singers, comedians, milliners, coffeehouses, smart shops, etc. In China, the desire is to provide oneself with pleasurable dreams through the use of opium. For this reason a great amount of the national effort goes into obtaining this precious narcotic, either directly through production or indirectly through exchange. In Spain, where people are inclined toward the pomp and ceremony of religious ritual, their efforts are directed toward the decoration of churches, etc.

I will not go so far as to say that there is never any immorality in effort that has as its goal the rendering of services related to immoral or depraved desires. But it is evident that what is essentially immoral in such cases is the desire itself.

There could be no possible doubt on this question if man lived in a state of isolation, nor can there be any in regard to man in society, for society is simply the individual enlarged.

Who would dream of blaming our workers in the south of France for producing brandy? They respond to a *demand*. They dig their vineyards, they dress their vines, they harvest and distill the grapes, without concerning themselves about what will be done with the product. It behooves the one who seeks the satisfaction to determine whether it is respectable, moral, reasonable, beneficial. The responsibility rests with him. Otherwise the business of the world could not be carried on. Where would we be if the tailor were to say to himself: "I will not make a suit in the style that has been ordered, because it is much too elegant and ostentatious, or because it hampers breathing, etc., etc.?"

And what concern of our poor winegrowers is it whether the rich *bons vivants* of London get drunk on the wines of France? And can the English seriously be accused of raising opium in India with the deliberate intention of poisoning the Chinese?

No, a frivolous people always encourages frivolous industries, just as a serious people creates serious industries. If mankind is improving, this moral growth is due, not to the producer, but to the consumer.

Religion understood this perfectly when it severely admonished the rich man—the great *consumer*—in regard to his tremendous responsibility. From a different point of view and in different language political economy arrives at the same conclusion. It affirms that we cannot prevent *supplying* what is *demanded;* that the product for the producer is merely a *value*, a kind of currency, which no more represents evil than good, whereas in the mind of the consumer it is *utility*, an enjoyment that is either moral or immoral; that, therefore, it behooves the one who voices the desire and makes the demand to accept the consequences, whether beneficial or disastrous, and to answer before the justice of God, as before the opinion of mankind, for the good or evil end to which he has directed the labor of his fellow men.

Thus, from whatever point of view we consider it, we perceive that consumption is the great end and purpose of political economy; that good and evil, morality and immorality, harmony and discord, everything finds its meaning in the consumer, for he represents mankind.[4]

12

The Two Mottoes

Modern moralists who hold up the axiom: *One for all, all for one,* against the ancient proverb: *Every man for himself, every man by himself,* have a very incomplete notion of society, and, for that reason, a quite false one. I shall even add, to their surprise, a very gloomy one.

Let us first eliminate the superfluous elements from these two famous mottoes. *All for one* is a redundancy, added for the sake of antithesis, since its meaning is necessarily included in *one for all. Every man by himself* is an idea that has no direct bearing on the other three, but as it is very important for political economy, we shall examine its implications later.

There remains, then, the conflicting sense of these two fragments of proverbs: *One for all—every man for himself.* The first one, it is said, expresses the principle of altruism; the second, the principle of individualism. The one unites; the other divides.

If we refer solely to the motive that prompts any effort, the conflict is undeniable. But I maintain that this is not the case if we consider the final outcome achieved by all human efforts taken collectively. Examine society as it actually is, obeying the individualistic impulse where remunerable services are concerned, and you will be convinced that *every* man, while working *for himself,* is in fact working *for all.* This cannot, indeed, be contested. If the reader of these lines follows a profession or a trade, I have only to ask him to consider his own case. I ask him whether all his labors do not have satisfactions for other persons as their object,

and whether, on the other hand, he does not owe all his own satisfactions to the labor of others.

Obviously those who say that *every man for himself* and *one for
all* are mutually exclusive believe that individualism and association are incompatible. They think that *every man for himself*
implies isolation or a tendency in that direction; that personal
interest divides men instead of uniting them, and results in a
situation in which *every man is by himself,* that is, the absence of
all social relations.

In this respect, I repeat, they have a quite false notion of
society, because it is an incomplete one. Men, even when moved
only by their own self-interest, seek to unite with others, to combine their efforts, to join forces, to work and to perform for one
another, to *be sociable,* or to associate. It would not be correct to
say that they act in this way in spite of self-interest; on the
contrary, they act in this way because of self-interest. They are
sociable because they benefit from association. If they were to
lose by it, they would not associate. Individualism, then, accomplishes the task that the sentimentalists of our day would entrust
to brotherhood, to self-sacrifice, or to some other motive opposed
to self-love. And this fact proves (this is the conclusion we are
always reaching) that Providence has known much better how to
take care of the organization of society than do its self-styled
prophets. For either society is harmful to individuality, or else
it is advantageous. If harmful, how and why in all good reason
are our socialist friends to introduce something that hurts everyone? If, on the contrary, association is an advantage, it will be
achieved by virtue of self-interest, the strongest, the most lasting,
the most uniform, the most universal of all motives, whatever
may be said.

Let us take a concrete example. A squatter goes and clears some
land in the Far West. Not a day goes by that he does not realize
how many inconveniences isolation causes him. Soon a second
squatter also moves out to the wilderness. Where will he pitch his
tent? Does he *spontaneously* move away from the first squatter?
No. He *spontaneously* moves near him. Why? Because he is aware
of the advantages men enjoy, for equal efforts, from the mere

fact of being near each other. He knows that in countless instances they can lend and borrow tools, unite their action, overcome obstacles that would be too much for them individually, make exchanges, communicate their ideas and opinions, provide for their common defense. A third, a fourth, a fifth squatter come into the wilderness, and invariably they are attracted by the presence of the firstcomers. Then others with more capital may arrive on the scene, certain that they will find hands waiting to be put to work. A colony is formed. They may vary the crops somewhat; cut a road through to the main highway where the stagecoach passes; begin to trade with the outside world; plan construction of a church, a schoolhouse, etc. In a word, the settlers become stronger, by the very fact of being together, infinitely stronger than would be their total strength if each were living alone. This is the reason that they were drawn together.

But, it will be said, *every man for himself* is a very gloomy and cold-blooded maxim. All the arguments, all the paradoxes in the world will not keep it from arousing our resentment, from reeking with *selfishness;* and is not selfishness worse than an evil, is it not the source of all the ills of society?

Let us understand one another, please.

If the motto *every man for himself* is understood in the sense that it must direct all our thoughts, all our actions, all our relations, that it must underlie all our affections, as fathers, sons, brothers, husbands, wives, friends, and citizens, or rather, that it must stifle these affections, it is frightful, horrible, and I do not believe that there is a single man on earth who, even if he did make it the guiding rule of his life, would dare to proclaim it as such.

But will the socialists always refuse to admit, despite the evidence of the facts everywhere, that there are two kinds of human relations: those springing from altruism, which we leave to the realm of morality; and those that are actuated by self-interest, which exist among people who do not know one another, who owe one another nothing but justice, and which are regulated by agreements voluntarily arrived at after free debate? This is precisely the type of agreements that constitute the domain of political economy. Now, it is no more possible to found transactions of this nature on the principle of altruism than it would be reasonable to base the ties of family and friendship upon self-interest. I shall never cease telling the socialists: You wish to combine two things that cannot be combined. If you are mad enough to try, you will never be strong enough to succeed. The blacksmith, the carpenter, the farmer, who exhaust their strength in rough toil, may be excellent fathers, admirable sons; they may have a high moral sense and affectionate hearts. Nevertheless, you will never persuade them to labor from dawn to dusk, to strain and sweat, to impose upon themselves hard privations, in the name of disinterested devotion to their fellow men. Your sentimental sermonizing is and always will be unavailing. If, unfortunately, a small number of workers should be led astray by your words, they would be just so many dupes. Let a merchant begin to sell his goods on the principle of brotherly love, and I do not give him even a month before his children will be reduced to beggary.

Providence has therefore wisely given our predilection for social relations quite other guarantees than these. Granted man's nature as a being whose feelings are inseparable from his personality, it is impossible to hope, to desire, to imagine that self-interest could be *universally* eradicated. And yet nothing less than this would be necessary to establish a just balance in human relations; for if you eliminate this motive force only in the case of some superior individuals, you will be creating two classes: the evil ones on the alert for victims, and the virtuous, for whom the role of victim is ready-made.

Since, in matters of labor and exchange, the principle of *every man for himself* was the motive bound to prevail, what is admirable, what is marvelous is that the Author of all things has made it work within the social order to achieve the ideal of brotherhood expressed in the motto, *one for all;* that His deft hand has made the obstacle the instrument of His will; that the general interest has been entrusted to self-interest and is eternally safeguarded by the very fact that self-interest is indestructible. It seems to me that, confronted with these facts, the communists and other inventors of artificial social orders might well admit—and without too much sense of humiliation, after all—that when it comes to organization, their divine rival is definitely their superior.

And note well that in the natural order of society, the principle of *one for all*, which developed from that of *every man for himself*, is much more complete, much more absolute, much more personal, than would be the case under communism or socialism. Not only do we work for all, but we cannot make any kind of progress whatsoever without sharing its benefits with the entire human community.[1] Things are arranged in such a marvelous way that when we have developed a technique or discovered a gift of Nature, some new fertility in the soil, or some new application of the laws of the physical universe, the profit goes to us momentarily, fleetingly, as is our just recompense, useful to spur us on to further efforts. Then our advantage slips through our hands, despite our attempts to retain it; it ceases to be personal, becomes social, and eventually comes to rest for all time within the realm of what is free of charge and common to all. And, even while we contribute to the enjoyment of mankind the progress we have made, we ourselves enjoy the progress that other men have made.

In the last analysis, by the application of the principle of *every man for himself*, all the efforts of the most intense individualism act in the direction of a situation that could be characterized by the expression, *one for all*, and everything that represents a step on the road to progress is worth to society in gratuitous utility millions of times more than the profits it brings its inventor.

On the principle of *one for all*, no one would act even *for himself*. What producer would consider doubling his labor in order to receive one thirty-millionth more in wages?

Someone may, perhaps, ask me why I go to the trouble to refute this socialist axiom. What harm can it do? Undoubtedly, it will not penetrate into the workshops, the countinghouses, the stores; it will not establish the principle of self-sacrifice in the fairs and the markets. Either it will come to nothing, and you can let it rest in peace; or else it will soften somewhat the unyielding principle of self-interest, which, since it brooks no feeling of sympathy for others, has no claim on ours.

What is false is always dangerous. It is always dangerous to represent as reprehensible and damnable a universal, eternal principle that God has clearly ordained for the preservation and improvement of mankind, a principle, I admit, that as a motive does not appeal to our hearts, but does, by its results, astonish and satisfy our minds. It is a principle, furthermore, that leaves the way completely open for the action of motives of a higher order that God has also implanted in men's hearts.

But what happens is that the socialist public accepts only half of their motto, the second half: *All for one.* People continue to work, as before, *every man for himself,* but to demand in addition that all also work for *every man.*

And this was inevitable. When the dreamers decided to change the great mainspring of human activity in order to replace individualism with brotherhood, what did they think up? A contradiction that is at the same time also pure hypocrisy. They began to cry out to the masses: "Stifle self-interest in your hearts, and follow us; and your reward shall be all the good things and all the pleasures of this world." When people try thus to parody the tone of the Gospel, they must conclude as the Gospel does. The self-denial of brotherhood implies sacrifice and suffering. "Dedicate yourselves," means: "Take the humblest place; be ye poor, and gladly endure hardship." But, under the pretext of self-sacrifice, to promise enjoyment; to exhibit, behind the so-called renunciation, material comforts and wealth; to combat the passion that is scathingly called *selfishness* by appealing to the crassest materialism—all this was not merely to testify to the indestructible vitality of the very principle that they proposed to overthrow; it meant exalting it to the highest possible point, even while declaiming against it; reinforcing the enemy, instead of vanquishing him; substituting unjust covetousness for legitimate individualism; and, despite the sham of a vague mystic jargon, actually stirring up the grossest kind of sensuality. Greed was bound to respond to this appeal.[2]

And is not this the point that we have now reached? What is the cry going up everywhere, from all ranks and classes? *All for one!* When we say the word *one,* we think of ourselves, and what we demand is to receive an unearned share in the fruits of the labor of all. In other words, we are creating an organized system of plunder. Unquestionably, simple out-and-out plunder is so clearly unjust as to be repugnant to us; but, thanks to the motto, *all for one,* we can allay our qualms of conscience. We impose on others the *duty* of working for us. Then, we arrogate to ourselves the *right* to enjoy the fruits of other men's labor. We call upon the state, the law, to enforce our so-called *duty,* to protect our so-called *right,* and we end in the fantastic situation of robbing one another in the name of brotherhood. We live at other men's expense, and then call ourselves heroically self-sacrificing for so doing. Oh, the unaccountable folly of the human mind! Oh, the deviousness of greed! It is not enough that each of us tries to increase our share at the expense of others; it is not enough that we want to profit from labor that we have not performed. We even convince ourselves that in the process we are sublime examples of self-sacrifice; we almost go so far as to call our unselfishness Christlike. We have become so blind that we do not see that the sacrifices that cause us to weep with admiration as we contemplate ourselves are not made by us at all, but are exacted by us of others.[3]

The manner in which this great hocus-pocus is carried out is worth observing.

"Stealing! For shame! How base! Besides, it can put you in prison; it's against the law."

"But suppose the law prescribed it and sanctioned it; wouldn't that be nice?"

"What a brilliant idea!"

Forthwith they ask the law for some trifling privilege, just a small monopoly, and since, to give it proper authority will cost somebody a few francs, they ask the state to take over the responsibility. Then the state and the law connive to bring about the very thing that it was their mandate to prevent or to punish. Little by little the taste for monopoly spreads. There is no class that does not demand its own special privilege. *All for one,* they cry. We too want to show that we are philanthropic and understand what solidarity is.

The result is that the classes granted the privileges steal from one another and lose at least as much by the demands made on them as they gain by the demands they make on others. Furthermore, the great masses of workers, to whom it has been impossible to grant any privileges, suffer until they can endure it no longer. They revolt, they cover the streets with barricades and bloodshed, and now it is they who must be reckoned with.

What will they demand? An end to the abuses, privileges, monopolies, and restrictions by which they have been engulfed? Not at all. The masses, too, have been imbued with the spirit of philanthropy. They have been told that the famous principle of *all for one* was the solution to the social problem; they have been shown by countless examples that privilege (which is only theft) is nevertheless highly moral if it has the sanction of the law. Therefore, we see the people demand. . . . What? . . . . Privileges! They, too, call upon the state to provide them with education, employment, credit, assistance, at the people's expense. Oh, what a strange illusion! How long can it last? We can well understand how all the upper classes, beginning with the highest, can come, one after the other, to demand favors and privileges. Beneath them are the great masses of the people for the burden to fall upon. But how the people, once they have won their battle, can imagine that they too can enter as a body into the ranks of the privileged, create monopolies for themselves and over themselves, extend abuses widely enough to provide for their livelihood; how they can fail to see that there is nobody below them to support these injustices, is one of the most amazing phenomena of this or any age.

What has happened? Society had followed this course to general shipwreck and quite properly grew alarmed. The people soon lost their power, and now the old order of abuses has temporarily regained its footing.*

Yet the lesson has not been entirely lost on the upper classes.

* [In this way Bastiat, of course, briefly summarizes the events of the Revolution of 1848.—TRANSLATOR.]

They realize that the workers must be given justice. They are eager to do so, not only because their own security depends upon it, but also, it must be admitted, out of a sense of equity. Yes, I state with great conviction that the wealthy classes ask nothing better than to find the solution to this great problem. I am sure that if they were asked to give up a considerable portion of their wealth in order to assure the future happiness and contentment of the common people, they would gladly make the sacrifice. They therefore earnestly seek to come, to use the time-honored phrase, *to the aid of the laboring classes*. But to that end what do they propose? Still a communistic system, the communism of privilege, though mitigated and held, they trust, within the bounds of prudence. That is all; they go no further. . . . .

13

Rent[1]

If, when there is an increase in the value of land, there were a corresponding increase in the prices of agricultural products, I could understand the objections raised against the theory presented in chapter 9 of this book. It could then be said: As civilization advances, the worker's situation becomes less favorable in relation to the landowner's; this is perhaps a necessary development, but it is certainly not a law of harmony.

Fortunately, this is not the case. In general, the circumstances that increase the value of land decrease at the same time the prices of what is raised on it. Let me explain this by an illustration.

Let us suppose that there is a farm located twenty miles from the city and worth one hundred francs. A highway is constructed that runs close to this farm. It opens up a market for the crops, and at once the value of the farm rises to one hundred and fifty francs. The landowner, now having the means to make improvements or to raise a greater variety of crops, improves his property, and its value increases to two hundred francs.

Thus, the farm's value has been doubled. Let us examine this additional value, first from the standpoint of justice, then from the standpoint of the utility enjoyed, not by the proprietor, but by the consumers in the city.

As for the increase in value coming from the improvements made by the landowner at his own expense, there is no question. This is a capital investment and follows the law of all capital investments.

The same is true, I venture to say, for the highway. The operation follows a more circuitous course, but the result is the same.

In fact, the owner, by reason of his farm, pays his share of the public expense. For many years he contributed to the general utility by doing work on outlying areas. Finally, a road has been constructed that runs in a direction that is helpful to him. All the taxes he has paid can be compared to stocks he might have bought in government enterprises; and the yearly rent, which now comes to him because of the new highway, may be regarded as their *dividend*.

Will it be said that a landowner may pay taxes forever and never receive anything in return for them? This case, then, is analogous to the other; and the improvements, although effected through the complicated and more or less questionable medium of the tax, may be considered as having been carried out by the landowner and at his expense in proportion to the partial advantage that he realizes.

I spoke of a highway, but I could have cited any other example of government intervention. Police protection, for example, gives value to land as well as to capital and labor. But who pays for police protection? The landowner, the capitalist, the worker.

If the state spends its revenue wisely, equivalent value must in some form or other find its way back to the landowner, the capitalist, and the worker. For the landowner it can only be in the form of an increased price for his land. If the state spends its revenue unwisely, it is unfortunate. The tax money is lost; the taxpayers should have been more alert. In that case the land does not rise in value, but certainly that is not the fault of the landowner.

But, now that the land has thus increased in value through government action and private initiative, do the crops raised on it bring a higher price from the city dwellers? In other words, is the interest on these hundred francs added as a surcharge on every hundredweight of grain that comes from this land? If the grain previously cost fifteen francs, does it now cost fifteen and a fraction? This is a most interesting question, since justice and the universal harmony of men's interests depend on its answer.

I reply confidently: *No*.

No doubt the landowner will now get a return of five francs more (I am assuming a profit rate of five per cent), but he will not get them at a cost to anyone. Quite the contrary; the buyer, in his turn, will profit even more.

The fact is that the farm we have chosen as an illustration was originally remote from any markets, and little was produced on it. Because of transportation difficulties the products that reached the market were expensive. Today production has been stepped up; transportation is economical; a greater amount of grain reaches the market, costs less to get there, and is sold at a better price. So even though he yields the landowner a total profit of five francs, the buyer profits even more.

In a word, an economy of effort has been effected. To whose profit? To the profit of the two contracting parties. According to what law is a gain of this kind shared? The law that we have often cited in reference to capital, since this increase in value represents a capital gain.

When there is a capital gain, the landowner's (or capitalist's) share increases in absolute value and diminishes in relative value; the worker's (or consumer's) share rises in both absolute and relative value.

Observe how this occurs. As civilization develops, the lands nearest the centers of population increase in value. Inferior crops give way to superior ones. First, pasture lands give way to cereal crops; then, cereals are replaced by truck gardens. Foodstuffs come from greater distances at less cost, so that—and this is an unquestionable fact—meat, bread, vegetables, even flowers, cost less than in more backward countries, although labor is better paid than elsewhere.

The Clos-Vougeot*

Services are exchanged for services. Often services prepared in advance are exchanged for present or future services.

* [The famous Burgundy vineyard possessing a particular quality of soil enabling it to produce correspondingly superior grapes (and wine). Bastiat uses it, along with the diamond, as an illustration of a commodity having—apparently, but not actually—value derived from "the gratuitous gifts of Nature."—TRANSLATOR.]

Services have value, not according to the labor they demand or have demanded, but according to the labor they save.

Now, it is a fact that human labor is becoming more efficient.

From these two premises is deduced a very important phenomenon for social economy: In general, labor previously performed loses value when exchanged for current labor.[2]

Twenty years ago, let us say, I made something that cost me a hundred days' work. I propose an exchange and say to my prospective buyer: Give me something that costs you likewise a hundred days. Probably he will be able to reply: In the last twenty years great progress has been made. What cost you a hundred days can now be made with seventy days' labor. Now, I measure your service, not by the time it cost you, but by the service it renders me. This service of yours is worth seventy days, since with that amount of time I can perform it for myself or find someone to perform it for me.

Consequently, the value of capital falls constantly, and capital, or previous labor, is not in as favorable a position as superficial economists believe.

There is no machine not completely new that has not lost some of its value, exclusive of deterioration resulting from use, from the very fact that better ones are made now.

This is true also of land. There are very few farms that have not cost more labor to bring them to their present state of fertility than it would cost today with the more efficient means we have at our disposal.

Such is the *general*, but not *inevitable, trend*.

Labor performed in the past may render greater service today than it did previously. This is rare, but it does happen. For example, I have kept some wine that represents twenty days' labor. If I had sold it immediately, my labor would have received a certain remuneration. I have kept my wine; it has improved; the next crop was a failure; in short, the price has gone up, and my return is greater. Why? Because I render *more* service, because the buyer would have to take *more pains* to get this wine than I took, because I satisfy a want that has become greater, of higher value, etc.

This is the question that must always be considered.

There are a thousand of us. We each have our acre of land, which we clear. Time goes by, and we sell it. Now, it happens that out of the thousand of us nine hundred and ninety-eight do not receive, or never will receive, as many days of current labor for our land as it has cost us; and that is because our past labor, which was less skillful, performs relatively less service than current labor. But there are two landowners whose labor has been more intelligent or, if you will, more successful. When they offer it for sale, it is found to represent inimitable services. Everyone says: It would cost me much more to perform this service for myself; hence, I shall pay a high price; and, provided I am not coerced, I am still very sure that it will not cost me as much as if I performed this service by any other means.

This is the story of the Clos-Vougeot. It is the same as the case of the man who finds a diamond or who has a beautiful voice or a figure to exhibit for five sous, etc.

In my native province there is much uncultivated land. The stranger never fails to ask: Why do you not cultivate this land? The answer is: Because the soil is poor. But, it may be objected, right beside it is absolutely similar land, and it is cultivated. To this objection the native finds no reply.

Is it because he was wrong to answer in the first place: *The soil is poor?*

No, the reason why new land is not cleared is not that the soil is poor; for some of it is excellent, and still it is not cleared. This is the reason: to bring this uncultivated land to a state of fertility equal to that of the adjacent cultivated land would cost more than to buy the adjacent land itself.

Now, to any man capable of reflection this proves incontestably that the land has no value in itself.

(Develop all the implications of this idea.) [3]

Money[4]

. . . .
. . . .

Credit[5]

. . . .
. . . .
. . . .

14

Wages

All men eagerly long for security. We do indeed find a few restless, adventurous individuals in the world for whom the thrill of the unknown is a kind of emotional necessity. Nevertheless, we can affirm that men, taken as a whole, want to be free of fear for their future, to know what to count on, to arrange their lives in advance. To understand what store they set by security, we need only to observe how eagerly they rush into government employment. Let no one say that they do so because of the prestige of public service. There are certainly civil service positions in which the work involved is far from being of a high order. It consists, for example, in spying on one's fellow citizens, prying into their affairs, annoying them. Yet such positions are nonetheless sought after. Why? Because they represent security. Who has not heard a father say of his son: "I'm trying to get him on the list for a temporary appointment in such and such a government bureau. Naturally, it's irritating that they require such a costly education. It's also true that with that kind of education, he might have gone into some more brilliant career. As a government functionary he will never get rich, but he will be sure of his living. He will always have enough to eat. In four or five years he will be getting a salary of eight hundred francs; then he will go up, step by step, to three or four thousand. After thirty years of service, he can retire on his pension. His livelihood is therefore assured. It's up to him to learn to live moderately and humbly, etc."

Security, then, has an all-powerful appeal.

And yet, when we consider the nature of man and of his labors, security seems incompatible with it.

Anyone looking back in his mind's eye to the hazards faced by human society at its inception will have difficulty in understanding how a great multitude of men can possibly obtain from the social order any fixed, assured, and constant means of existence. That they do so is another of those phenomena that fail to impress us as strikingly as they should for the very reason that our eyes are accustomed to them. Here are functionaries who receive fixed salaries, property owners who know in advance what income they will have, investors who can exactly calculate their returns, workmen who earn the same wages every day. If we exclude money, which is introduced simply to facilitate evaluation and exchange, we shall perceive that what remains stable is the quantity of the means of existence, the value of the satisfactions received by these various categories of workers. Now, I maintain that this stability, which little by little is spreading to all mankind, to all kinds of labor, is a miracle of civilization, a prodigious accomplishment of the social order that is so foolishly denounced in our day.

Let us go back, then, to a primitive social order. Let us imagine that we say to a hunting, fishing, pastoral, warrior, or agricultural people: "As your society progresses, you will be able to tell further and further in advance exactly what will be your total enjoyments for every year."

These good people would not believe us. They would reply: "That will always depend on something that eludes all calculation—the uncertainty of the seasons, for example, etc." They would never be able to understand the ingenious efforts by which men have succeeded in establishing a kind of insurance bridging all times and all places.

Now, this mutual insurance against the vicissitudes of the future is entirely dependent on a field of human knowledge that I shall call *experimental statistics*. And since there is continual progress in this field, based as it is on experience, it follows that security also can be progressively extended. It is favored by two permanent factors: first, men long for security; second, every day they acquire more means of attaining it.

Before I demonstrate how security is established in those human transactions in which at first sight it would not seem to be an important concern, let us see how it is obtained in a transaction in which it is of special concern. The reader will thus understand what I mean by experimental statistics.

Consider a group of men who are all homeowners. One house happens to burn, and its owner is ruined. At once alarm spreads among all the others. Each one says to himself: "The same thing could happen to me." It is not surprising, therefore, that the owners meet and make provision to share possible loss by forming a mutual fire-insurance association. Their agreement is very simple. It is expressed in these terms: If the house of one of us burns, the rest of us will take up a collection to help him.

By this device each owner can be sure of two things: first, that he will have a small share in all misfortunes of this type; second, that he will never have to bear the full brunt of any one misfortune.

In reality, if we extend the calculation over a great number of years, we see that the homeowner makes, so to speak, an arrangement with himself. He lays up savings with which to pay for the disasters that may strike.

This is *association*. Indeed, the socialists give the name *association* exclusively to arrangements of this kind. As soon as speculation is introduced, they say, association disappears. I say that it is improved, as we shall see.

The motive that prompted our homeowners to form an association, to provide for mutual insurance, was a love of stability, of security. They prefer known risks to unknown risks, a great number of possible small losses to one large one.

Nevertheless, their objective has not been completely accomplished, and there is still much uncertainty in their situation. Each one of them may say: "Suppose disasters multiply. Will my assessment not become exorbitant? In any case, I should like to know in advance what it will be, and also to insure my household goods, my merchandise, etc., in the same manner."

These difficulties appear to be in the nature of things and beyond man's power to avoid. We are always tempted to believe, after every advance, that everything possible has been done. How, indeed, can we eliminate this *hazard* contingent on misfortunes still in a realm beyond our ken?

But mutual insurance has, through experience, gradually acquired in society an important piece of statistical information, namely, the ratio, in terms of yearly averages, between values destroyed by disasters and values covered by insurance.

Armed with this information, an individual or a company, having made all the necessary calculations, goes to the homeowners and says: "By providing for mutual insurance, you have tried to purchase your peace of mind. The price this precious asset costs you is the indeterminate assessment you set aside annually to cover your losses. But you never know in advance what this price will be; and, on the other hand, your peace of mind is never complete. Well, I am here to propose a different procedure. In consideration of *a fixed annual premium* that you will pay me, I will assume the risk for all losses. I will insure all of you, and here is the capital to guarantee my promises."

The homeowners are quick to accept, even though this premium would cost a little more than the average assessment under the mutual insurance agreement; for the most important thing in their eyes is not the saving of a few francs, but the assurance of complete peace of mind.

At this point the socialists contend that the association is destroyed. I maintain that it is improved and on the way to still further improvement.

But, say the socialists, now the insured no longer have any common tie! They no longer see one another; they no longer have to reach a common understanding. Parasitical middlemen have intruded themselves among them, and the fact that the homeowners now pay more than is necessary to cover their losses is proof that the insurers are reaping outrageous profits.

It is easy to answer this criticism.

First of all, the association now exists under another form. The premium contributed by the insured still provides the fund to pay for the losses. The insured have found the means of remaining in the association without the bother of running it. Obviously, this is an advantage to every one of them, inasmuch as the end in view is nonetheless attained; and the opportunity of remaining in the association and still retaining independence of movement and the free use of one's faculties is precisely what characterizes social progress.

As for the middleman's profit, it is explainable and completely justified. The insured remain members of the association for the recovery of their losses. But a company has stepped in that offers them the following advantages: first, it removes the element of risk to which they were still exposed; second, it frees them from all trouble or labor that their losses might entail. These are *services*. Now, service for service. The fact that the proposal is willingly accepted and paid for is proof that the company is performing a service of definite value. The socialists are merely being ridiculous when they rant against the middleman. Does he impose his services by force? Has he other means at his disposal than to say: "I shall cost you something in the way of pains, but I shall save you more"? How, then, can he be called a parasite, or even a middleman?

Therefore, I declare that the association thus transformed is in a position to improve in every way.

In fact, the companies, in the hope of realizing profits proportional to the extent of their business, try constantly for new accounts. They have agents everywhere, they extend credit, they invent countless new coverages in order to increase the number of policyholders, that is, of *associated parties*. They insure many, many risks that were not covered by the original mutual association. In short, the association steadily increases so as to include more people and more things. As this expansion continues, it allows the companies to lower their rates; they are, in fact, forced to do so by competition. And here again we encounter the great law: the benefit soon slips through the hands of the producer and ultimately comes to rest with the consumer.

Nor is this all. The companies take out insurance on one another in the form of reinsurance; so that, as far as recovery of losses is concerned, which is the heart of the matter, a thousand different companies, operating in England, France, Germany, and America, form a single great corporation. And what is the result? If a house happens to burn in Bordeaux, Paris, or any-where else, homeowners from all over the world—Englishmen, Belgians, Germans, Spaniards—have their assessment ready and are prepared to make good the loss.

This is an example of the power, the scope, the perfection, that a free and voluntary association can attain. But in order to do so, it must be free to choose its own methods. Now, what happened when the socialists, those great devotees of association, were in power? They found nothing more urgent to do than to browbeat associations of every description, and insurance associations in particular. And why? For the very reason that in order to operate on a world-wide basis, insurance companies follow the procedure of allowing every one of their members to remain independent. How little these poor socialists understand the social mechanism! They want to take us back to the first uncertain steps taken by society in its infancy, to the primitive and almost savage forms of association. They would suppress all progress on the ground that it has departed from these forms.

We shall see that, because of these same prejudices, this same ignorance, they rail constantly against *interest,* or else against *wages,* which are *fixed* forms, and therefore highly developed, for the payment of what is due capital and labor.

The wage system particularly has been the object of the social-ists' attack. They have almost gone so far as to present it as some-thing hardly less cruel than slavery or serfdom. In any case, they have viewed it as an oppressive and one-sided arrangement having only the semblance of liberty, as exploitation of the weak by the strong, as tyranny exercised by capital over labor.

Though everlastingly wrangling with one another over the new institutions they would like to establish, they evince a striking unanimity in their common hatred of existing institutions, and the wage system most of all; for, if they cannot reach agreement on the social order of their choice, we must at least give them their due in that they always see eye to eye in abusing, deploring, slandering, hating, and generating hatred for anything that actually exists. I have stated elsewhere the reasons for this attitude.[1]

Unfortunately, all this did not remain a purely academic question; for socialist propaganda, aided and abetted by a weak and ignorant press, which, without admitting its socialist sympathies, nevertheless sought to curry popular favor by its sensational tirades, has succeeded in inspiring hatred for the wage system even among the wage earners. The workers have become dissatisfied with this form of remuneration. It appears to them unjust, humiliating, odious. They feel that it brands them with the mark of servitude. They desire to share by other means in the distribution of wealth. From this point to becoming infatuated with the most extravagant utopias is only a step, and this step has been taken. In the February Revolution the great preoccupation of the workers was to get rid of the wage system. For the means of doing so they consulted their gods; but on the occasions when the gods did not remain silent, their oracular utterances were, as is customary, anything but clear, though the great word "association" did predominate, as if *association* and *wages* were mutually exclusive. Then the workers proposed to try all the forms of this association that was supposed to bring them liberty, and, to make it the more attractive, they invested it with all the charms of "solidarity" and attributed to it all the merits of "brotherhood." For the moment, one would have thought that the human heart itself was about to undergo a great transformation and, shaking off the yoke of self-interest, would henceforth be guided by nothing less than the purest forms of self-sacrifice. Strange contradiction! People hoped to receive, by way of association, at once the glory of self-sacrifice and the enjoyment of profits hitherto unknown. While they raced madly after fortune, they demanded that they be awarded, or rather they awarded themselves, the palm of martyrdom. Apparently these misguided workers, on the verge of being swept along on the path of injustice, felt the need of deluding themselves, of glossing over with idealism the lessons in plunder that their apostles had taught them, and of covering them with a veil before offering them up in the sanctuary of a new revelation. Perhaps never before had so many dangerous errors, such gross contradictions, taken such a hold upon the human mind.

Let us see, then, what *wages* are. Let us look at their origin, their form, and their effects. Let us recognize why they were created; let us determine whether in the development of humanity they represent a step backward or forward. Let us ascertain whether or not they are essentially humiliating, degrading, brutalizing; and whether it is possible to discern their alleged connection with slavery.

Services are exchanged for services. What is offered and accepted in exchange is labor, effort, pains, trouble, natural or acquired skills; what is transmitted are satisfactions; what determines the exchange is mutual advantage; and what measures it is the free evaluation of reciprocal services. The various arrangements to which human transactions have given rise have necessitated a very large economic vocabulary, but the words "profit," "interest," "wages," although they express different shades of meaning, do not change the real nature of things. It is always the *do ut des,* or rather the *facio ut facias* * which, as far as the science of economics is concerned, forms the basis of all human evolution.

Wage earners are no exception to this law. Consider carefully. Do they perform services? Undoubtedly. Do they receive services? They do indeed. Are these services exchanged freely, voluntarily? Do we perceive fraud or violence in this type of transaction? It is at this point, perhaps, that the complaints of the workers begin. They do not go so far as to contend that they have been deprived of their freedom, but they declare that this freedom is purely nominal and even a mockery, for the person whose decisions are determined by necessity is not free in fact. It remains to be seen whether the lack of freedom thus understood is not the result of the worker's situation rather than of the manner in which he is paid.

When a man contributes the strength and skill of his hands to another's service, his payment may consist of a share in the thing produced or else in a fixed wage. In the one case as in the other, he must bargain over this share—for it may be larger or smaller—or for this wage—for it may be higher or lower.

* [See chap. 5, p. 147.—TRANSLATOR.]

And if the man is in absolute want, if he cannot wait, if he is under the spur of urgent necessity, he will submit to its law; he will not be able to resist the conditions laid down by the man for whom he is to work. But it must be noted that it is not the form of his payment that puts him in this state of dependency. Whether he runs the risk of being paid according to the outcome of the enterprise, or whether he contracts for a fixed wage, it is his precarious situation that has put him at a disadvantage in the bargaining. The innovators who have presented the workers with the idea of *association* as an infallible cure have therefore deceived them and themselves as well. They can convince themselves of this fact by observing carefully situations in which the impoverished worker receives a share of the produce rather than a wage. Certainly there are no men in France more wretchedly poor than the fishermen and the vineyard workers in my native province of Bearn, although they have the honor of enjoying all the benefits of what the socialists exclusively term *association*.

But before inquiring into the influences that determine the rate at which wages are set, I must define, or rather describe, the nature of this transaction.

Men have a natural tendency—and consequently one that is beneficial, moral, universal, and indestructible—to desire security in regard to their means of existence, to seek stability, and to avoid risk and uncertainty.

Nevertheless, in the earliest stages of society risk and uncertainty held, so to speak, absolute sway; and I have often been amazed that political economy has failed to point out the great progress that has been achieved in constantly lessening their influence on human affairs.

For example, in a small community of hunters, in a nomadic tribe, or a newly established colony, who can predict with certainty what one's labor will be worth tomorrow? Does there not even seem to be a fundamental conflict between these two ideas, for could there be anything more uncertain than the results of labor devoted to hunting, fishing, and agriculture?

Therefore, it would be difficult to find, in the early period of any society, anything resembling salaries, retainers, stipends, wages, incomes, rents, interest payments, insurance premiums, etc., all of which are things invented to give more stability to the status of the individual, to remove from mankind as much as possible that painful sense of uncertainty and anxiety in regard to the means of existence.

The progress that has been made in this direction is truly remarkable, even though custom has so familiarized us with the fact that we fail to notice it. And yet, since the results obtained by labor, and consequently the consumption of products by mankind, can be so profoundly modified by the course of events, by unexpected circumstances, like Nature's whims, inclement weather, and disasters of all kinds, how does it happen that so many men find that, thanks to fixed wages, rents, salaries, pensions, they are exempt, for a time, and some for life, from that *uncertainty* which seems to form a part of our very nature?

The cause, the motive power, of this wonderful evolution by mankind is to be found in the tendency of all men to strive toward the attainment of their well-being, to which stability is so essential. The means consists in the substitution of the *fixed contractual payment* covering calculable risks for the earlier form of association wherein all members are liable for all risks of the enterprise—in other words, the creation of a more efficient association. It is curious, to say the least, that our great modern reformers would have us believe that association is dissolved by the presence of the very element that actually improves it.

For certain men to be willing to bind themselves by contract to assume certain risks that naturally fall on others, some degree of progress must have been made in a special field of knowledge that I have called *experimental statistics;* for they must be able through experience to appraise, at least approximately, these risks, and consequently the *value of the services* they render those for whom they take this responsibility. That is why the transactions and associations of primitive and ignorant peoples do not permit of provisions of this nature, and why, therefore, risk and uncertainty, as I have said, hold full sway over them. If a savage who is getting along in years and has a certain supply of game laid up engages a young hunter to help him, he will pay him, not with fixed wages, but with a certain share in the kill. How, in fact, could either of them draw inferences from the known to the unknown? The lessons of the past are not sufficiently available to them to permit them to insure themselves against the future beforehand.

In an age of ignorance and barbarism men undoubtedly *associate, enter into associations,* since otherwise, as we have shown, they cannot live; but association among them can assume only that primitive, elementary form which the socialists represent as the law and the salvation of the future.

Later on, in the case of two men who have long worked together sharing common risks, there comes a time when it is possible for them to calculate their risks in advance, and one of them may assume all the risks in consideration of a stipulated payment.

This arrangement certainly represents progress. To be assured of this, we need only to know that the arrangement is made freely, by mutual consent, which would not happen unless it were to the advantage of both parties. But it is easy to understand in what respects it is to their advantage. One party, by assuming all the risks of the undertaking, gains the advantage of having it completely under his control; the other gains that stability of position so dear to men's hearts. And society in general cannot fail to gain, because now an enterprise that was once subject to the conflicting pressures of two minds and two wills enjoys a unified policy and direction.

But, because the form of the association has been changed, can we say that it has been dissolved, as long as the two men continue to participate in it and nothing has been altered except the manner of distributing what they produce? Above all, can we say that the association has been vitiated as long as the new policy is freely agreed to and it satisfies all parties?

In order to create new means of satisfaction, it is almost always —I could say, always—necessary to have both current labor and the fruits of previous labor available. At the outset capital and labor, when they join forces in a common project, are each obliged to share its risks. This stage continues until these risks can be calculated experimentally. Then two tendencies, equally natural to the human heart, are to be observed: I mean the tendencies toward *unified control* and *fixed responsibilities.* Capital then says to Labor: "Experience teaches us that your eventual profit will amount to an average return of so much. If you are willing, I will guarantee you this amount and will run the enterprise, assuming, for better or for worse, all its risks."

Labor may perhaps reply: "This proposal suits me. Sometimes in a year I receive only three hundred francs; at other times I receive nine hundred. These fluctuations cause me great inconvenience; they prevent me from regulating my expenses and those of my family in a systematic way. It is an advantage for me to be relieved of this continual uncertainty and to receive a fixed return of six hundred francs."

When this reply is given, the terms of the contract will be changed. They will indeed continue to *unite their efforts,* to *share the proceeds,* and consequently the association will not be dissolved; but its form will be altered in that one of the parties, Capital, will take all the risks and all the extraordinary profits, while the other party, Labor, will enjoy all the advantages of stability. Such is the origin of wages.

Sometimes the procedure of reaching an agreement is reversed. Often it is the entrepreneur who says to the capitalist: "We have worked hitherto on the basis of a common sharing of the risks. Now that we have a better knowledge of our expectations, I propose that we draw up a contract. You have twenty thousand francs invested in the enterprise, for which one year you received five hundred francs, and another year fifteen hundred. If you are willing, I will give you a thousand francs a year, or five per cent, and will free you of all risk, on condition that I direct the enterprise as I wish."

Probably the capitalist will reply: "Since, with considerable and vexatious ups and downs, I receive on the average no more than a thousand francs per year, I prefer to be assured of this sum regularly. Therefore, I shall continue the association by keeping my capital invested in the business, but without assuming any of the risks. My activity and my intelligence can now be more freely turned in other directions."

From the point of view of society as well as that of the individual, this represents a gain.

Evidently there is in mankind a longing for stability that is constantly working to restrict and circumscribe the role of chance and uncertainty. When two persons share a risk, they cannot eliminate the risk itself, but there is a tendency for one of the two to assume it on a contractual basis. If capital takes the responsibility, then labor receives a fixed return, which is called *wages*. If labor chooses to accept the risk, for better or for worse, then the return on capital is set aside and fixed under the name of *interest*.

And since capital consists exclusively of human services, we may say that *capital* and *labor* are two words that express the same fundamental idea; consequently, the same may be said of *interest* and *wages*. Hence, at this point, where false economic theory never fails to find a conflict, true economic theory always finds identity.

Thus, in their origin, nature, and form, *wages* are in no way essentially degrading or humiliating, any more than *interest* is. Both represent the returns due to current and to previous labor as their respective shares of the results of a common enterprise. But, in the long run, it nearly always happens that the two parties provide for a fixed payment for one of these shares. If it is current labor that wants a uniform return, it gives up its share in further but risky profits for the sake of *wages*. If it is previous labor that wants a uniform return, it sacrifices its hope of extra but uncertain profits in return for *interest*.

Personally, I am convinced that this new stipulation, representing a later addition to the original association, far from dissolving it, actually improves it. I have no doubts on this score when I reflect that the new arrangement arises from a keenly felt need, from the natural desire of all men for stability, and that, besides, it satisfies all parties without harming—indeed, on the contrary, by improving—the general welfare.

The modern reformers who, alleging that they invented the principle of association, would like to take us back to the days of its most rudimentary forms, ought surely to tell us in what respect *contracts stipulating fixed payments* contravene justice or equity, in what ways they retard progress, and by virtue of what principle they propose to ban such arrangements. They should also tell us how, if such stipulations are so barbarous, they reconcile the increasing presence and influence of these contracts in modern society with what the reformers themselves proclaim about the perfectibility of mankind.

For my part, I am convinced that these stipulations are one of the most marvelous signs of progress and one of the most potent factors in the development of society. They are at once the fulfillment and the reward of a past and very ancient civilization and the promise of endless progress for the future. If society had been content with that primitive form of association which makes all parties subject to the risks of an enterprise, ninety-nine per cent of human transactions could not have been carried on. The man who today has a part in twenty enterprises would have been bound for all time to a single one. All operations would have lacked unity of policy and direction. In a word, man would never have enjoyed stability, that precious asset which may well be the source of genius.

The *wage system*, then, is derived from a natural and indestructible human tendency. Let us note, however, that this system is but an imperfect answer to men's longings. It makes the workers' pay more uniform and equal, more in line with an average figure; but there is one thing that it cannot do, any more than a pooling of risks could, and that is to guarantee them employment.

And at this point I cannot refrain from commenting on the power of a feeling to which I have referred in the course of this discussion, a feeling that the modern reformers do not appear to be at all aware of: I mean man's aversion to uncertainty. It is precisely this feeling that has so favored the socialist ranters in their efforts to foster a hatred for the wage system in the minds of the workers.

We can think of three stages in the progress of the worker's status: the stage in which risk and uncertainty predominate; the stage in which stability predominates; and an intermediate stage in which risk and uncertainty, though partially eliminated, still militate against complete stability.

What the workers have not understood is that the kind of association preached by the socialists represents the infancy of society, the period of the first faltering steps, of sudden ups and downs, of alternating plenty and want—in a word, the absolute reign of risk and uncertainty. The wage system, on the contrary, represents the intermediate stage that separates risk and uncertainty from stability.

Now, the workers, not yet having attained—far from it—a stable condition, placed their hopes, like all men suffering from economic woes, in some kind of change in their status. That is why the socialists found it very easy to dazzle them with the great word "association." The workers felt that they were being carried forward, whereas in reality they were being swept backward.

Yes, the unfortunate workers were being swept back toward the first uncertain steps in the evolution of society; for was the kind of association being preached to them anything other than the system in which all members are held liable for all the risks? This arrangement is inevitable in times of complete ignorance, since contracts stipulating fixed payments presuppose at least a rudimentary knowledge of experimental statistics. Is the socialists' proposal anything more or less than a pure and simple return to the reign of risk and uncertainty?

Therefore, the workers, who had been so enthusiastic for association as long as it had remained a mere theory, changed their minds as soon as the February Revolution made it appear a real possibility.

At that time many employers, whether under the spell of the universal enthusiasm for association, or out of fear, offered to replace the payment of wages with a profit-sharing arrangement. But the workers drew back from common sharing of this kind— the sharing of the risks. They understood that in reality what they were being offered, in case the enterprise should fail, was the absence of any kind of payment whatsoever, which for them meant death.

Then we observed a phenomenon that would reflect little honor on our country's working class were it not that the blame should be placed on the so-called reformers, in whom the working class, unfortunately, had placed its trust. The workers clamored for a hybrid association providing for a retention of wages and at the same time for their participation in the profits, without, however, involving them in the risks.

It is very unlikely that the workers would ever on their own have thought of putting forward such demands. There is in human nature a fund of good sense and justice to which obvious unfairness is repugnant. In order to deprave man's heart, it is first necessary to corrupt his mind.

This is what the leaders of the socialist school did not fail to do, and, in this regard, I have often wondered whether their motives were not deliberately perverse. I have always been inclined to respect men's motives as something inviolate, but in this case it is difficult to find them above reproach.

After stirring up the working classes against their employers by the persistent and unfair tirades with which socialist books are filled; after convincing the workers that they were involved in a war, and that in war all is fair against the enemy; the leaders of the socialists then clothed the workers' ultimatum, in order to gain it wider acceptance, in scientific subtleties and went so far as to give it colorings of mysticism. They even personified society as an abstract being owing to every individual a certain *minimum*, namely, a guarantee of livelihood. "You have the right, then," they told the workers, "to demand a fixed wage." Thus, they began by satisfying man's natural inclination for stability. Then, they proclaimed that, apart from wages, the worker was entitled to a share in the profits; and, when asked if he should also have a share in the losses, they replied that, by virtue of government intervention and guarantees from the taxpayer, they had invented a system of universal industry and full employment exempt from any possibility of loss. This was the means of allaying the last remaining scruples of the unfortunate workers, who were therefore, as I have said, quite disposed at the time of the February Revolution to demand the adoption for their benefit of these three provisions:

1. Continuation of their wages.
2. A share in the profits.
3. Exemption from any share in the losses.

It will be said, perhaps, that these demands are not as unfair or as impossible as they appear, since they have been introduced and maintained in many newspaper concerns, in the railroads, etc.

I say in reply that there is something very childish about deceiving oneself by giving high-sounding names to very trivial things. If one will only be open-minded about the matter, one will doubtless be convinced that this type of profit-sharing, which a few concerns make available to their wage earners, does not constitute association or deserve to be so called, nor does it represent a great revolution in the relations between two classes of society. It is an ingenious bonus system, a useful incentive for the wage earners, offered in a form that is not exactly new, despite the efforts to present it as an endorsement of socialism. The employers who, in adopting this practice, set aside a tenth or a twentieth or a hundredth part of their profits, when they have any, may make a great show of this act of generosity and proclaim themselves noble regenerators of the social order; but the matter really does not deserve our notice, and so I return to my subject.

The establishment of the wage system, then, marked a forward step for society. Originally, past labor (capital) united with current labor (the workers), in sharing the risk, to undertake joint enterprises that, under such terms, must have had very limited scope. If society had not discovered other systems, no large-scale operation would ever have been carried out in this world. Mankind would still be back in the era of hunting and fishing, and a few primitive attempts at agriculture.

Later, obeying the double impulse that leads us both to seek stability and to desire to be in charge of operations for which we have to bear the risks, the two associates, without in any way dissolving their association, established the system by which it was agreed that one party would pay the other a fixed amount and would himself assume all the risks along with the direction of the enterprise. When this fixed sum goes to previously performed labor, to capital, it is called *interest;* when it goes to current labor, it is called *wages.*

But, as I have observed, wages are only partially successful in obtaining, for a certain class of men, a state of stability, or security, as regards their means of livelihood. The wage system represents a step—a very definite step, and one so difficult to make that at first sight one might think it impossible—toward the attainment of this wonderful goal; but it does not represent its complete attainment.

In passing, it is perhaps not idle to state that security resembles all the other great objectives that mankind pursues. They are all constantly approached, but never perfectly attained. For the very reason that security is so great a blessing, we shall always strive to extend its benefits among us; but it is not within our power ever to enjoy it completely. We can even go so far as to say that such a state of things is not desirable, at least for man as he now is. An absolute degree of any good thing whatsoever would mean the extinction of all desire, all effort, all planning, all thought, all foresight, all virtue; perfection excludes perfectibility.

The laboring classes, having risen with the passage of time, and thanks to the progress of civilization, to the level represented by the wage system, have not therefore ended their quest for security.

Of course, wages can be counted upon at the end of a day's work; but when circumstances, a crisis in industry, or simply illness, have forced hands to stop working, wages likewise stop coming in. Should the worker then turn to enforced idleness for his daily bread and that of his family? His only recourse is to save up, during his working days, against the time when he will be old or ill.

But who can reckon in advance, for any individual, the number of days when he can help himself, compared to the days when he will need help?

What is impossible for one person becomes more feasible for many by virtue of *the law of large numbers.* That is why this assessment, paid in during periods of employment against periods of unemployment, attains its goal much more efficiently, more regularly, more surely, when it is centralized in the association rather than left to the risks incurred by the individual.

Hence the various *mutual-aid societies,** admirable institutions

* [These are the mutual insurance associations best exemplified in Bastiat's time by the English Friendly Societies.—TRANSLATOR.]

that came into being within society long before even the name of socialism existed. It would be difficult to say to what impulse the invention of such arrangements should be credited. I believe, in truth, that they sprang from the very fact that the need was there, from man's longing for stability, from that ever restless, ever active instinct that prompts us to bridge the gaps that civilization encounters in its progress toward security for all ranks of society.

In any case, I saw mutual-aid societies spring up spontaneously more than twenty years ago among the destitute day laborers and artisans in the poorest villages in the Department of Landes.

The intention of these societies is obviously to secure a stable level of satisfactions, to distribute over all periods of life the wages earned during periods of employment. In all the localities where the societies exist, they have done a great deal of good. The members of the association feel sustained by a sense of security, one of the most precious and comforting feelings that man can experience in his journey through life. In addition, all members feel their mutual dependence, their contribution to one another's needs; they understand to how great an extent the individual's good or bad fortune becomes the good or bad fortune of all; they meet together to observe a few religious ceremonies that their statutes provide for; in a word, they are called upon to cultivate that alert concern for one another's activities so calculated to inspire both self-respect and an appreciation of the dignity of others, which is the first and most difficult step on the road to any kind of civilization.

The secret of the success of these societies—a success that has indeed come slowly, as does everything that involves the masses—is liberty, and this is readily explicable.

The natural danger that threatens such associations consists in the removal of the sense of responsibility. No individual can ever be relieved of responsibility for his own actions without incurring grave perils and difficulties for the future.[2] If the day should ever come when all our citizens say, "We shall assess ourselves in order to aid those who cannot work or cannot find work," there would be reason to fear that man's natural inclination toward idleness would assert itself, and that in short order the industrious would be made the dupes of the lazy. Mutual aid therefore implies mutual supervision, without which the benefit funds would soon be exhausted. This mutual supervision, which is for the association a guarantee of continued existence, and for each individual an assurance that he will not be victimized, is also the source of the moral influence it, as an institution, exercises. Thanks to it, drunkenness and debauchery are gradually disappearing, for by what right could a man claim help from the common fund when it could be proved that he had brought sickness and unemployment on himself through his own fault, by his own bad habits? This supervision restores the sense of responsibility that association, left to itself, would tend to relax.

Now, in order that such supervision may bear its full fruit, the mutual-aid societies must be free, must have certain well-defined prerogatives and be in complete control of their own funds. They must be allowed sufficient flexibility to adapt their regulations to fit local needs.

Suppose that the government interferes. It is easy to imagine the role it will assign itself. Its first concern will be to take over all funds on the pretext of centralizing them; and, in order to make this measure more palatable, it will promsie to increase them out of resources taken from the taxpayer.[3] "For," it will say, "is it not entirely natural and just that the state should contribute to so great, so generous, so philanthropic, so humanitarian a work as this?" The first unjust act will be to force into the society, through taxation, citizens who have no right to share in the benefits. The second unjust act will be to propose, in the name of unity, of solidarity (call it what you will), that all associations be merged into one, subject to uniform regulations.

But, I ask, what will happen to the morality of the institution when its treasury is fed by taxes; when no one, except possibly some bureaucrat, finds it to his interest to defend the common fund; when every member, instead of making it his duty to prevent abuses, delights in encouraging them; when all mutual supervision has stopped, and malingering becomes merely a good trick played on the government? The government, to give it its just due, will be disposed to defend itself; but, no longer being able to count on private action, will have to resort to official action. It will appoint various agents, examiners, controllers, and inspectors. It will set up countless formalities as barriers between the workers' claims and his relief payments. In a word, an admirable institution will, from its very inception, be turned into a branch of the police force.

The state will perceive, first of all, the advantages to be gained from adding to the vast throng of its appointees, from multiplying the number of jobs at its disposal, from extending its patronage and electoral influence. It will not realize that, in arrogating to itself a new function, it has also placed upon itself a new, and, indeed, a frightening responsibility. For what must the immediate consequence be? The workers will no longer look upon their common treasury as property to be administered and maintained by themselves, with their own claims on it limited by the extent of its resources. Little by little they will become accustomed to considering unemployment benefits, not as something provided by the limited funds that they have accumulated by their own foresight, but as a debt that society owes them. They will never admit that society cannot pay and will never be satisfied with the benefits they receive. The state will constantly be obliged to ask for new additions to the budget. At this point, encountering opposition from the treasury officials, it will find itself in inextricable difficulties. Abuses will increase all the time, and the government will shrink, as it always does, from rectifying them until there comes the day of explosion. But when this happens, the government will discover that it has to reckon with a population that has lost the ability to act for itself, that looks to a cabinet minister or an official for everything, even its livelihood, a population whose thinking has become so warped as to have lost any notion of right, property, liberty, or justice.

These were some of the reasons for my alarm, I admit, when I discovered that a commission of the legislative assembly had been instructed to prepare a bill on mutual-aid societies. I felt that the knell of doom had rung for them, and I was the more distressed because I am convinced that a great future is in store for them provided they continue to be allowed to breathe the bracing air of freedom. And, indeed, is it so difficult to permit men to experiment, to feel their way, to choose, to make mistakes, to correct them, to learn, to work together, to manage their own property and their own interests, to act for themselves, at their own risk and peril, on their own responsibility? Do we not see that this is what makes them men? Must we always start with the fatal premise that all those who govern are guardians and all the governed are wards?

I maintain that, left to the care and supervision of those concerned, the mutual-aid societies have a most promising future before them, and I need no further proof of my statement than to cite what is taking place across the Channel.

In England individual initiative has not waited for the government to organize a powerful mutual-assistance association among the working classes. For a long time *free* and self-administered associations have existed in the principal towns of Great Britain etc. . . . .

The total number of these associations, for the United Kingdom, amounts to 33,223, including no less than three million fifty-two thousand individuals, which is half the adult population of Great Britain. . . . .

This great confederation of the laboring classes, this institution which provides a practical and effective outlet for the impulse of brotherly love, rests on the most solid foundations. The combined revenue is five million pounds sterling, and the accumulated capital amounts to eleven million two hundred thousand pounds.

Needy cases are paid out of this fund when employment declines or stops. We are sometimes amazed at England's ability to withstand the repercussions of the tremendous and far-reaching upheavals that her gigantic industrial machine from time to time, and almost periodically, experiences. This ability is to be explained, in large part, by the fact that we have just mentioned.

Mr. Roebuck [4] proposed that, in view of the vastness of the problem, the government, *acting paternalistically,* and *on its own initiative,* should take the responsibility for solving it. . . . . The Chancellor of the Exchequer refused.

In cases where private individuals are capable of managing their own affairs, the government, in England, deems it unnecessary to interfere. It watches from above to make sure that there are no irregularities; but it permits every man to receive the reward of his own efforts and to run his own business according to his own lights and his own convenience. Certainly England owes a part of her greatness as a nation to this independence of her citizens.[5]

The author could have added: It is also to this independence that the citizens owe their experience and their personal worth. It is to this independence that the government owes its relative freedom from responsibility, and consequently its stability.

Among the institutions that can arise from the *mutual-aid societies,* once they have completed the evolution that they have now barely begun, I give first place, because of its social importance, to *old-age pensions* for the workers.

There are persons who call such an institution a flight of fancy. These persons, no doubt, profess to know the farthermost limits of security beyond which humanity may not go. I shall ask them these simple questions: If they had never been familiar with any social condition except that of primitive tribes that live by hunting or fishing, would they ever have foreseen, I do not go so far as to say returns on landed property, government securities, or fixed salaries, but even the wage system, that first step toward stability in the condition of the poorest classes? And later, if they had known only of the wage system such as it exists in countries where the spirit of association has not yet appeared, would they have ventured to predict the role that was destined to be played by *mutual-aid societies* such as we have seen in operation in England? Or do they have some good reason to believe that it was easier for the laboring classes to progress first to a wage system, and then to mutual-aid societies, than it is to go on to establishing old-age pensions? Would this third step be more difficult than the other two?

As for myself, I observe that humanity thirsts for security; I see that, from age to age, it fills in the gaps where its achievements have been incomplete, for the benefit of one class or another, by marvelous methods that appear well beyond the inventive powers of any one individual, and I certainly would not venture to predict at what point it will cease its progress along this road.

What is certain is that old-age pensions are universally, unanimously, eagerly, ardently longed for by all the workers, and quite naturally so.

I have often questioned them, and I have always found that the great torment of their lives is not the burden of their toil or the smallness of their wages or even the resentment that the sight of inequality could understandably kindle within them. No; the cause of their concern, their discouragement, their anxiety, their anguish, is the uncertainty of the future. Whatever profession we may belong to, whether we be civil servants, capitalists, owners of property, businessmen, doctors, lawyers, soldiers, magistrates, we have reaped so many benefits, without realizing it and therefore without any sense of gratitude, from the progress that society has made that we no longer understand this torture of uncertainty. But let us put ourselves in the place of a worker or an artisan who, on awakening every morning, is haunted by this thought: "I am young and strong; I am working, and indeed, it seems to me that I have less leisure and more heavy toil than most of my fellow men. Yet I barely succeed in providing for my own needs and those of my wife and children. But what will become of me, what will become of them, when age or illness have sapped my strength? I must exercise superhuman self-control and prudence if I am to save out of my wages enough to meet these misfortunes. As for illness, to be sure, there is always the chance that I may be lucky, and, besides, there are the mutual-aid societies. But old age is not something to be avoided by good luck; it is sure to come. Every day I can feel it coming nearer; it is bound to catch up with me; and then, after a blameless life of honest toil, what prospects do I face? The poorhouse, the prison, or a hovel for myself; for my wife, beggary; for my daughter, still worse. Oh, why isn't there some social institution that could wrest from me, even by force, during my younger days enough to provide for my old age?"

We must, indeed, bear in mind that this thought, which I have just expressed so inadequately, is tormenting, even at the moment that I am writing these words, and every day and every night, and every hour of the day and night, the terrified imaginations of a vast number of our brethren. And when mankind is faced with a problem in such terms as these, we can rest assured that it is not insoluble.

If, in their efforts to gain greater security for themselves, the workers have spread alarm among the other classes of society, it is because they have turned their efforts in a wrong, unjust, and dangerous direction. Their first thought—as is always the practice in France—was to raid the public treasury, to finance their old-age pensions through taxation, to appeal to the state or the law; that is, to enjoy the profits of plunder without incurring either the dangers or the public disapproval attached to it.

It is not from this quarter of the social horizon that the institution so ardently desired by the workers can come. Old-age pensions, if they are to be useful, sound, praiseworthy, if the means of obtaining them is to be in harmony with the end in view, must be the fruit of the workers' own efforts, energy, wisdom, experience, and foresight. They must be fed by their sacrifices, watered by the sweat of their brows. They have no claims on the government except for freedom of action and the suppression of fraud.

But has the time come when it is possible to set up old-age pensions for the workers? I do not dare affirm it; indeed, I do not believe it is so. In order to establish an institution that may achieve a new degree of security for any class in society, it is necessary that a certain amount of progress, a certain advance in civilization, be achieved in the social milieu in which the institution is to exist. An atmosphere congenial to its survival must be prepared. If I am not mistaken, it must be the responsibility of the *mutual-aid societies,* with the material resources they have built up, with their spirit of association, experience, foresight, and the sense of self-respect that they can instil in the working classes, to set up the old-age pensions.

For if you will observe what has happened in England, you will be convinced that such things are intricately interrelated, and for progress to be made in one area, progress must first be made in certain others.

In England all adults so desiring have over a period of time joined the *mutual-aid societies* of their own accord, and this is a most important point to bear in mind when we are dealing with operations that must be carried out on a large scale if they are to have any statistical validity.

These societies have tremendous capital funds and in addition receive considerable annual income.

It can be assumed—otherwise we should have to deny the progress of civilization—that a smaller and smaller percentage of these prodigious funds will be required for sick and unemployment benefits.

Better public health is one of the contributions of civilization. Hygiene and medical science are making progress; machines are taking over the most backbreaking jobs; and longevity is increasing. In all these areas the demands on the mutual-aid associations tend to diminish.

Even more decisive and inevitable is the gradual elimination of great industrial crises in England. They were caused sometimes by those sudden enthusiasms that the English periodically experience for rash enterprises that dissipate vast amounts of capital, and sometimes by the great increase in food costs resulting from protective tariffs; for it is quite clear that when meat and bread are very high, and it takes all the people's resources to procure them, other commodities are not bought, and shut-downs in the factories become inevitable.

Public discussion and the lessons learned in the hard school of experience are eliminating the first of these causes; and we can already predict that this nation, which rushed with such sheeplike credulity into American loans, Mexican mine speculations, and railroad schemes, will be more wary than others of the California gold mirage.

What shall I say of free trade? Its triumph is due to Cobden,* [6] not to Sir Robert Peel; † for the apostle would always have found a statesman, whereas the statesman could never have done without the apostle. Here is a new force in the world and one that will, I

---

* [Richard Cobden (1804–1865), English manufacturer, member of Parliament, and champion of free trade, known personally to Bastiat and much admired by him.—Translator.]

† [Sir Robert Peel (1788–1850), English statesman, member of the Conservative Party, and Prime Minister in the 1840's.—Translator.]

trust, deal heavy blows to the monster called *unemployment*. Restriction of trade has the undeniable tendency and effect of placing some of the country's industries, and consequently a part of its population, in a precarious situation. Just as great waves, which are momentarily held above the level of the surrounding sea by some temporary force, constantly threaten to break loose, so these artificially established industries, hemmed in on all sides by successful competitors, are always on the point of toppling down. What is needed to start their collapse? A mere modification of an article in one of the world's innumerable tariff laws. The change is made, and a panic results. Furthermore, the narrower the circle of competition, the greater the variations in the price of a given commodity. If a department of France, a district, or a town had its own customs regulations, the fluctuations in prices would be considerable. Liberty acts on the same principle as insurance. In different parts of the world and in different years it compensates the bad harvests by the good ones. It keeps prices close to an average figure. It is therefore a leveling and balancing force. It contributes to stability; hence, it combats instability, that great cause of panics and unemployment. It is no exaggeration to say that the first fruit of Cobden's work will be greatly to lessen the dangers that in England led to the formation of the mutual-aid societies.

Cobden has undertaken another task (and it will succeed, for truth well served always triumphs), which will be no less important for the security of the workers. I mean the abolition of war, or rather (what amounts to the same thing), the fostering of the spirit of peace in public opinion, which decides the question of war or peace. War is always the greatest of the upheavals that a people can suffer in its industry, the conduct of its business, the investment of its capital, and even its tastes. Consequently, it is a powerful factor in creating disruption and misery among the classes who have the least control over the course their labor is to take. The more remote the danger from this source, the less burdensome will be the responsibilities of the mutual-aid societies.

And, on the other hand, through the force of progress, with the mere passing of time, their resources will become greater and greater. The day will then come when they can win a new and decisive victory over the insecurity that is inherent in human affairs by expanding their functions and setting up old-age pensions; and this they will undoubtedly do, for such is the ardent and unanimous desire of the workers.

It should be noted that even while material circumstances are paving the way for such action, moral circumstances also are favorable, thanks to the influence exerted by the societies themselves. These societies are developing among the workers habits, qualities, virtues, whose possession and dissemination are a necessary preliminary to old-age pensions. On close examination we realize that this institution presupposes a very advanced type of civilization, of which it is both the effect and the reward. How would it be possible if men were not accustomed to meeting, working together, and managing their common affairs, or, on the contrary, if they were addicted to vices that aged them before their time, or if they had come to think that anything is permissible against the public, and that the common interest is fair game for any kind of fraud?

If the establishment of old-age pension funds is not to be a source of disturbance and discord, the workers must understand that they are to depend on no one but themselves, that the common fund must be voluntarily created by those who expect to share in it, that it is wholly unfair and antisocial to make the classes that will not share in the disbursements contribute to the fund by way of taxes, that is, by force. Now, we are far from having reached that point, and the frequent appeals to the state show only too clearly what the workers' hopes and demands are. They feel that their retirement fund must be fed by state appropriations like those for government functionaries. Thus, one abuse always gives rise to another.

But if we agree that old-age pension funds are to be maintained exclusively by those who have a personal stake in them, can we not say that the system already exists, since life insurance companies offer policies that permit every worker to make provision for the future through some sacrifice of the present?

I have written at considerable length about *mutual-aid societies* and *old-age pensions,* although these institutions are only indirectly connected with the subject of this chapter. I have yielded to my desire to show mankind gradually proceeding toward the attainment of security, or rather (since security implies something static), emerging victorious in its battle against risk and uncertainty, that ever present threat to all the enjoyments of life, that sword of Damocles that appears to hang unavoidably over human destiny. The gradual elimination of this threat by its reduction to the average level of the risks that all men at all times and in all places must run is certainly one of the most admirable social harmonies that the political economist can contemplate.

And we must not think that ultimate victory over risk and uncertainty will depend upon the fate of these two institutions of more or less accidental origin. On the contrary: even if experience should prove them unfeasible, mankind would still make its way toward stability. The very fact that uncertainty is considered an evil is sufficient guarantee that it will be continually and, sooner or later, successfully attacked, for such is the law of our nature.

If, as we have seen, the wage system represents, from the point of view of security, an advance over previous forms of association between capital and labor, it still leaves too much to chance and uncertainty. Of course, the worker knows what to count on as long as he has a job, but how long will he have a job, and how long will he have the strength to do it? This is what he does not know; this is the frightful question that hangs over his future. The uncertainty that faces the capitalist is quite different. It is not a question of life or death. His problem may be stated thus: "I shall in any case get some interest on my principal, but will it be more or less?" This is the question that is asked concerning labor that has already been performed.

The philanthropic sentimentalists who see in this situation a shocking case of inequality that they would like to destroy by artificial—and, I might add, unjust and violent—means do not stop to consider that, after all, we cannot change the nature of things. Labor already performed cannot fail to enjoy greater security than labor still to be performed, because finished products cannot fail to be surer resources than products still to be made; because services already rendered, received, and evaluated are on a sounder footing than services that are still up for sale in the open market. If you are not surprised that, of two fishermen, the one who, having worked and saved for a long time, owns lines, nets, boats, and a supply of fish, has less fear for the future than the one who has absolutely nothing except a willingness to go fishing, why are you surprised that, to a certain extent, the same differences are to be seen in the social order? In order to justify the envy, jealousy, and sheer spitefulness with which the worker regards the capitalist, the latter's security would have to be one of the causes of the worker's insecurity. But the contrary is the case, and the very fact that capital is available to one man means that the other man is guaranteed his wages, however inadequate these wages may appear to you to be. Certainly if it were not for capital, the worker's risk and uncertainty would be much more imminent and ruthless. And if the hardships of risk and uncertainty were made worse so that they might be made equal and common to all, would the worker in any way be better off?

Two men have run risks equal, for each one, to an amount that we may represent as 40. One of them by his labor and foresight succeeds in reducing his risks to 10. At the same time his companion's risks, through the mysterious effects of association, have gone down, not to 10, but to 20. What could be fairer than that the one who has earned it should get the larger share of the reward? What could be more surprising and gratifying than that the other should profit from his brother's virtues? Now, this is just what the philanthropists reject, on the ground that it is contrary to the ideal of equality.

The old fisherman said to his companion one day:

"You don't have a boat or nets or any other implement for fishing except your two hands, and you run a great risk of having a poor catch. Besides, you don't have any provisions, and yet you can't work on an empty stomach. Come and join me; it's to your interest as well as mine. It's to your interest, for I will give you a part of our catch, and however much or little it may be, it will still be better than what you could do on your own. It's also to my interest, for the additional amount that I will get with your help will be more than what I shall have to give you. In a word, your labor, my labor, and my capital combined will bring us a *surplus* over what these would bring us separately, and the sharing of this surplus explains how the association can be profitable to both of us."

And thus the agreement was made. Later the younger fisherman preferred to receive a fixed number of fish every day. Thus, his variable and uncertain profit was turned into wages, but without endangering the advantages of the association and most certainly without dissolving it.

And it is in such circumstances that the socialists, in the name of their so-called philanthropy, rant against the tyranny of boats and nets, against the fact that the situation is naturally less precarious for the man who owns boats and nets, because he has made them for the very purpose of having some degree of certainty! It is in such circumstances that they try to persuade the destitute fisherman that he is the victim of his *voluntary* arrangement with the older fisherman, and that he should hasten to return to his isolation!

Yes, the capitalist's future is less precarious than the worker's; which is equivalent to saying that he who already owns something is better off than he who does not yet own anything. Such is the way things are, and such is the way things should be, and that is why every man aspires to become an owner.

Men tend, therefore, to emerge from the status of wage earners to become capitalists. This is a tendency that conforms to the nature of the human heart. What worker does not desire to have his own tools, his own working capital, his own store or workshop or farm or house? What workman does not desire to become the boss? Who is not happy to give orders after having long taken them? It remains to be determined whether the great laws of the economic world, whether the natural play of the social machinery, encourage or militate against this tendency. This is the final question we shall consider on the subject of wages.

And who can have any doubts on this score?

Let us recall how production always and inevitably develops:

gratuitous utility constantly replacing onerous utility; human efforts constantly becoming less in comparison with the results they obtain, and, as they are freed from one task, embarking upon new enterprises; every hour's labor corresponding to a steadily increasing quantity of satisfactions. From these premises how can we fail to deduce that there is a constant increase in *usable goods and services* ready to be distributed, and, consequently, continual improvement in the workers' condition, and, consequently also, a steady advance within the frame of their relative improvement?

For here, the effect having become a cause, we not only see progress continuing, but accelerating as it gathers momentum. In fact, from age to age saving becomes easier, since labor's compensation becomes greater. Now, saving increases capital, stimulates the demand for more hands, and raises wages. The rise in wages in turn encourages saving and the transformation of the wage earner into the capitalist. There is a constant action and reaction, therefore, between wages and saving, and this is always favorable to the working classes, always a factor in relieving them from the yoke of pressing need.

It will be said, perhaps, that I present here everything that can bring a gleam of hope to the workers' eyes and that I hide everything that can plunge them into discouragement. If there are tendencies toward equality, I may be told, there are also tendencies toward inequality. Why do you not analyze them all, in order to explain the workers' true situation and thus bring the science of political economy into accord with the melancholy facts that it seemingly refuses to see? You show us gratuitous utility taking the place of onerous utility, the gifts of God falling more and more into the common domain, and, by that very token, man's labor receiving a steadily increasing compensation. From this increased compensation you conclude that saving becomes easier and easier; and from the increased ease of saving you deduce a new increase in compensation, bringing still further increases in savings, and so on through all time to come. It may be that this order of things is as logical as it is optimistic; it may be that we are not able to refute it scientifically. But where are the actual facts to support it? Where may we actually see the emancipation of the proletariat being carried out? In the great manufacturing centers? Among the agricultural workers? And, if the predictions of your theory do not prove true, are there not perhaps, in addition to those economic laws that you cite, other laws, working in an opposite direction, that you fail to mention? For example, why do you say nothing about the competition that takes place among laborers, forcing them to accept lower wages; about the urgent need to gain a livelihood, which exerts a constant pressure on the worker and compels him to accept the capitalist's terms, so that the most destitute, the hungriest, the most isolated worker, and consequently the one least able to refuse any offer, sets the wage scale for all the others? And if, despite all these obstacles, the status of our unfortunate brothers does happen to improve, why do you not show us how the law of population interposes its disastrous operation, multiplying the already teeming multitudes, intensifying competition, increasing the supply of labor, winning the day for capital, and constraining the worker to accept, for a twelve- or sixteen-hour day, only the *irreducible minimum* (such is the classic phrase) *for subsistence?*

If I have not taken up all these aspects of this problem, it is because it is impossible to put everything into a single chapter. I have already set forth the general law of competition, and we have seen how far it is from giving any class, especially the least fortunate one, serious reason for discouragement. Later, when I explain the law of population, it will be evident, I hope, that, in its general effects, it is not at all ruthless. It is not my fault that the solution of every great problem—for example, the fate of a large percentage of the human race—is to be found, not in the operation of a single, isolated economic law, and consequently, in a single chapter of this book, but in the operation of the sum total of all these laws, that is, in the entire book.

Then too—and I call the reader's attention to this distinction, which most certainly is not a mere quibble—when we are confronted with a certain phenomenon, we must be careful not to attribute it to general and providential laws if on the contrary it is produced by the violation of those laws.

I certainly do not deny the existence of the calamities of all possible types—drudgery, insufficient wages, insecurity, the sense of inferiority—that assail those of our fellow men who have not yet been able to rise, by the acquisition of property, to a more comfortable condition. But we must recognize that insecurity, want, and ignorance constituted the starting point for the entire human race. That being the case, the question is, it seems to me, whether: (1) the general laws of Providence do not tend to lighten this triple yoke for all classes; (2) the achievements of the most advanced classes do not ease the way for the more backward. If the answer to these questions is in the affirmative, we may say that the fact of social harmony is established, and that the ways of Providence are justified, if indeed Providence stands in need of justification.

Furthermore, since man is endowed with initiative and free will, it is certain that the beneficent laws of Providence are of service to him only in so far as he conforms to them; and although I affirm that he is perfectible by nature, I certainly do not mean that he advances even when he misunderstands or violates them. Thus, I say that transactions that are carried out among the parties concerned freely, voluntarily, without fraud or violence, promote progress for everyone. But this is far from saying that progress is inevitable, and that it will be achieved through war, monopoly, and fraud. I say that wages tend to rise, that this rise encourages saving, and that saving, in turn, raises wages. But if the wage earner, through habits of debauchery and dissipation, prevents this progress from being initiated, I do not say that its results will still be evident, for the contrary is implied by my statement.

In order to put the scientific theory to the test of actual fact we must compare two different eras: for example, 1750 and 1850.

First, we must ascertain the proportion of proletarians to property owners on the two dates. We should find, I expect, that during the last century the number of those who have some working capital has grown greatly in comparison with those who have none.

Next, it would be necessary to determine the exact status of each of these two classes, which can be done only by observing the satisfactions they enjoy. Most likely we shall find that in our times both classes derive far more real satisfactions, the one from its accumulated labor, the other from the labor it is still performing, than was possible in the days of the Regency.

If this twofold progress has not been respectively or relatively all that could be desired, especially for the working class, we must ask whether its course has not been more or less retarded by error, injustice, violence, misunderstandings, passions—in a word, by some fault on the part of man, by accidental causes that must not be confused with what I call the great and constant laws of social economy. For example, have there not been wars and revolutions that could have been avoided? Have not these atrocities first drained off, then dissipated, incalculable amounts of capital, thereby diminishing the funds available for wages and postponing for many workers' families the hour of emancipation? Have they not also diverted labor from its natural end, demanding of it, not satisfactions, but destruction? Have we not had monopolies, privileges, discriminatory taxation? Have there not been absurd expenditures, ridiculous fashions, wasted efforts, which can be attributed only to childish impulses and prejudices?

And what does all this prove? That there are general laws that men may either obey or disobey.

It cannot be denied that the French in the last hundred years have often run counter to the natural and orderly evolution of society; nor can we fail to hold continual warfare, periodic revolutions, injustice, privilege, dissipation, and all manner of folly, responsible for a frightful waste of our energies, our capital, and our labor.

Yet, on the other hand, despite all these facts that are only too evident, we observe something else, namely, that during this same hundred-year period the property-owning class has been recruited from the proletariat, and that both classes now have respectively available to them a greater number of satisfactions.

If we follow, then, a rigorously logical line of reasoning, we arrive at this conclusion: *The general laws of the social world are harmonious, and they tend in all respects toward the improvement of mankind.*

For, in the final analysis, if after a period of a hundred years during which these laws have been so frequently and so flagrantly violated, mankind has moved ahead, we must conclude that their action is beneficent enough to more than counterbalance the effects of disturbing factors.

And how could it be otherwise? Is there not something equivocal or, rather, redundant in the expression "beneficent general laws"? How can they fail to be beneficent? When God implanted in every man an irresistible impulse to achieve the good, and, in order to enable him to discern it, an inner light capable of correcting his errors, from that very moment He decreed that mankind was perfectible, and that, despite all gropings, errors, miscalculations, oppressions, and waverings, mankind would ever advance toward the endless promise of a better world. This advance, with the errors, miscalculations, and oppressions eliminated, is what we mean by the general laws of the social order. The errors and the oppressions are what I call the violations of these laws and the disturbing factors that work against them. Hence, the laws cannot fail to be beneficent, and the disturbing factors to be baneful, unless we go so far as to question whether the disturbing factors may not have more lasting effects than the general laws. Now, this is contrary to our premise that our intelligence, though fallible, is capable of correcting its errors. It is clear that, the social world being constituted as it is, sooner or later error is held in bounds by responsibility, and that oppression sooner or later is broken against the rock of solidarity; hence, it follows that the disturbing factors are not permanent by nature, and that only those phenomena whose action is disturbed by them merit the name of general laws.

In order to conform our actions to general laws, we must know what they are. Let me, therefore, dwell somewhat upon the relations, so poorly understood, that exist between capitalist and worker.

Capital and Labor cannot get along without each other. In constant mutual confrontation, they enter into arrangements that are among the most important and interesting that the economist can observe. And—make no mistake about it—observations on this subject that are poorly made, if they become widely accepted, can give rise to inveterate animosities, bitter conflicts, crimes, and bloodshed on a vast scale.

Now, I declare with the firmest conviction that for some years the public mind has been saturated with the most completely false theories on this subject. It has been alleged that free and voluntary transactions between capital and labor must give rise, not accidentally, but necessarily, to monopoly for the capitalist and oppression for the worker. Consequently, it was boldly concluded that freedom must everywhere be stifled; for, I repeat, when such theorists accused freedom of creating monopoly, they professed, not to be merely observing a fact, but rather to be formulating a law. In support of this theory they cited the effect of the machine and of competition. M. de Sismondi was, I believe, the originator, and M. Buret * the propagator, of these gloomy doctrines, although the latter is most timid in his conclusions, and the former has not ventured to draw any conclusions at all. But others have come along who were bolder. After stirring up hatred for the words "capitalism" and "landlordism," after persuading the masses of the absolute truth of the so-called discovery that *liberty leads inevitably to monopoly,* deliberately or not, they stirred up the people to lay violent hands on this accursed liberty.[7] After four days of bloody rioting, liberty was rescued but is still not secure, for do we not see the state, in compliance with popular prejudice, ready at every moment to interfere in the relations of capital and labor?

The role of competition has already been deduced from our theory of value. We shall do the same in showing the effects of the machine. Here we must limit ourselves to setting forth a few general ideas on the relations between capitalist and worker.

The fact that first forcibly strikes our gloomy reformers is that the capitalists are richer than the workers. They obtain more satisfactions; hence, they allot themselves a larger, and consequently unfair, portion of the commodities produced by the joint efforts of both. This is the conclusion suggested by the more or

* [Antoine Eugène Buret (1810–1842), brilliant and, as Bastiat implies, pessimistic precursor of French socialism. Author of *De la misère des classes laborieuses en Angleterre et en France,* 1840.—TRANSLATOR.]

less intelligently and impartially prepared statistics that present
the situation of the working classes.

These gentlemen forget that *absolute poverty* is the inevitable
starting point for all men, and it inevitably persists as long as they
have acquired nothing, or nobody has acquired anything for
them. To make the blanket observation that capitalists are better
off than simple day laborers is merely to note the fact that those
who have something have more than those who have nothing.

The questions for the worker to ask himself are not: Does my
labor bring me a great deal? Does it bring me very little? Does it
bring me as much as it brings another? Does it bring me what I
should like?

Rather, he should ask: Does my labor bring me less because I
have put it at the service of the capitalist? Would it bring me
more if I performed it on my own, or if I joined my labor with
that of others as destitute as I am? My situation is bad. Would I
be better off if there were no capital on earth? If the share that I
receive as a result of my arrangement with capital is larger than
my share would be without it, what grounds do I have for complaint? And then, if transactions are free and voluntary, what are
the laws determining whether there is to be a rise or a fall in the
amount of our respective shares? If the nature of these transactions is such that, as the total to be distributed increases, my share
in the increase becomes steadily larger,[8] then, instead of vowing
eternal hatred against the capitalist, ought I not to look upon
him as a good brother? If it is well established that the presence
of capital is advantageous to me, and that its absence would mean
my death, am I very wise or prudent in abusing it, intimidating
it, requiring it to be frittered away or forcing it into hiding?

It is constantly alleged that, in the bargaining that precedes the
contract, the situations of the two parties are not equal, since
capital can wait while labor cannot. The needier party, it is said,
must always be the one to give in, with the result that the capitalist is able to dictate the wage rates.

Undoubtedly, if we look at things only superficially, the one
who has laid up provisions and, by reason of his foresight, can
bide his time has the advantage in the bargaining. If only an

isolated transaction is considered, the one who says: *Do ut facias,* is not so hard pressed to reach a conclusion as the one who responds: *Facio ut des.* For when one can say *do,* one owns something, and when one owns something, one can wait.

We must not, however, lose sight of the fact that the principle of value is the same whether it is related to a service or to a product. If one of the parties says *do,* instead of *facio,* it is for the reason that he has had the foresight to perform the *facio* in anticipation of the want. Essentially, service is in both instances the measure of value. Now, if every delay means suffering for current labor, it means a loss for labor previously performed. We must not think, therefore, that the one who says *do,* the capitalist, will take any great delight in delaying the bargain, particularly if we take into account all his other transactions as well. As a matter of fact, do we see much capital lying idle for this reason? Are there very many manufacturers who stop production, shipowners who cancel their sailings, farmers who delay harvesting their crops, solely to depress wages, by subjecting their workers to the pressure of hunger?

But, without denying that in this respect the capitalist's position is more advantageous than the worker's, do we not have something else to consider in regard to their arrangements? Is there not an advantage for *current labor* in the fact that *accumulated labor* loses value through the mere lapse of time? I have already referred to this phenomenon. However, it is important in this connection to call it again to the reader's attention, for it has a great influence on the pay that current labor receives.

What, in my opinion, renders Smith's theory that *value comes from labor* false, or at least incomplete, is the fact that it assigns only one element to value; whereas value, being merely the expression of a relationship, necessarily has two elements. Besides, if value came solely from labor and represented only it, value would be proportional to labor, which is contrary to all the facts.

No, value comes from service rendered and received; and service depends as much, if not more, upon the pains it spares the one who receives it as upon the pains taken by the one who performs it. The most commonplace facts confirm this reasoning.

When I buy an article, I may well ask myself: "How long did it take to make it?" And this is undoubtedly one of the factors that figure in my evaluation; but also and above all else I ask: "How long would it take me to make it? How long did it take me to make the thing asked of me in exchange?" When I buy a service, I ask not only how much it will cost the seller to perform it for me, but also how much it will cost me to perform it for myself.

These personal questions and the answers they elicit are so essential a part of the evaluation as to be usually the determining factor in it.

Try to buy a diamond that someone has happened to find. You will be asked to pay for little or no labor, but the price will be high. Why will you consent? Because you will take into account the labor you will be spared, the labor that otherwise you would be obliged to perform, in order to satisfy your desire to own a diamond.

When, therefore, *previously performed labor* and *current labor* are exchanged, the amount of time or effort they require is not considered, but rather what is considered is their value, that is, their mutual service, the utility each offers the other. If the capitalist were to say, "Here is a product that cost me ten hours of labor," and if the worker were in a position to reply, "I can make the same product in five hours," the capitalist would be forced to yield the difference. For, once again, it matters very little to the present purchaser to know how much labor the product used to cost; what he cares about is how much labor the service he anticipates from the product will save him today.

The capitalist, in a very general sense, is the man who, having foreseen that a given service will be in demand, has prepared it in advance and has incorporated its fluctuating value in a commodity.

When labor has thus been performed by way of anticipation, with a view to future remuneration, there is nothing to assure us that at a particular future date it will perform exactly the same service, spare the same pains, and, consequently, retain a uniform value. Such a situation would, indeed, be most unlikely. It may be very much in demand, very difficult to replace by any other means; it may render services that are more highly or more widely appreciated and acquire an increasing value with the passing years; in other words, it may be exchanged for a steadily increasing amount of current labor. Thus, it is not impossible that a given product, like a diamond, a Stradivarius violin, a painting by Raphael, a vineyard in Château-Lafite,* may be exchanged for a thousand times more days' labor than it originally required. This means nothing more nor less than that previous labor is very well remunerated in this case because it renders great service.

The opposite is also possible. It can happen that what once required four hours' labor is now sold for only three hours of equally strenuous labor.

But—and this seems to me most important from the standpoint and in the interest of the laboring classes, which so ardently and understandably long to emerge from the present precarious situation that so fills them with dread—although both alternatives are possible and do successively occur, although accumulated labor may sometimes gain and sometimes lose value as compared with current labor, yet the first case is rare enough so that it may be considered as accidental and exceptional, whereas the second is the result of a general law that has its origin in the very nature of man.

There is no gainsaying the fact that man, with his capacity to learn through reason and experience, is by nature capable of progress, at least in industrial matters (for, from the moral point of view, my assertion may be open to challenge from some quarters). There is certainly no question that, thanks to new and improved machinery, to increased use of the gratuitous forces of Nature, most things are today accomplished with less labor than they used to require; and we may confidently assert that in any ten-year period, for example, a given amount of labor will, in most cases, produce greater results than the same amount of labor could produce in the previous decade.

And what is the conclusion to be drawn from this? That previously performed labor is constantly depreciating in relation to

* [Located in Pauillac, renowned for its vineyards producing Bordeaux wine.— TRANSLATOR.]

current labor; that, in exchange, without any injustice and in order to achieve parity of services, the former must offer more hours than it receives in return. This is an inevitable result of progress.

You say to me: "Here is a machine; it is ten years old, but it is still new. It cost one thousand days of labor to make it. I will let you have it for the same number of days' labor."

I answer: "In the last ten years new tools have been invented, new techniques have been discovered, so that today I can make, or have made (which amounts to the same thing), the same kind of machine for six hundred days' labor; therefore, I will pay you no more."

"But I shall be losing four hundred days' labor."

"No, for six days of today's labor are worth ten of yesterday's. In any case what you offer me for one thousand I can get elsewhere for six hundred."

Here the debate ends. If time has depressed the value of your labor, why should I bear this loss?

You say to me: "Here is a piece of land. To bring it to its present state of fertility, my ancestors and I spent one thousand days' labor on it. In fact, my ancestors knew nothing of axes, saws, or spades and did it all with their own bare hands. Nevertheless, give me first one thousand of your days' labor to match the one thousand I give you, then add three hundred for the productive powers of the soil, and the land is yours."

I answer: "I will not give you one thousand three hundred days' labor for it or even one thousand, and here are my reasons: There are on the surface of the earth an indefinite number of productive powers that are valueless. And besides, today we do know about spades, axes, saws, plows, and many other ways of making labor easier and more productive; so that with six hundred days' labor I can either put uncultivated land into the same state as yours or else (which amounts to absolutely the same thing for me) *obtain through exchange all the advantages you derive from your land.* Hence, I will give you six hundred days and not one hour more."

"In that case," you answer, "not only do I fail to benefit from the alleged value of the productive powers of this soil, but I do not even get back the actual number of days of labor my ancestors and I devoted to its improvement. Is it not strange that I should be accused by Ricardo of selling the productive powers of Nature; by Senior of engrossing the gifts of God; by all the economists of being a monopolist; by Proudhon of being a thief; while in fact I am merely a dupe?"

"You are no more dupe than monopolist. You receive the equivalent of what you give. Now, it is neither natural nor just nor possible that hard labor done by hand centuries ago should be exchanged on an equal day-for-day basis for the more intelligent and productive labor done nowadays."

Thus, we see that, through the admirable working of the social mechanism, when previous labor and current labor are brought together for comparison, when it is a question of determining their relative shares in the product of their joint efforts, the specific superiority of each is taken into account: they share in this distribution according to the comparative services they render. Now, it may well happen sometimes, under exceptional circumstances, that this superiority is on the side of previous labor. But man's nature and the laws of progress cause it to fall, in the vast majority of cases, on the side of current labor. Progress comes to the aid of labor; capital deteriorates.

Aside from this result, which shows how empty and vain are the rantings inspired in our modern reformers by the so-called *tyranny of capital,* there is another consideration still more fitted to extinguish in the workers' hearts that deplorable and unnatural hatred against the other classes that people have tried with some success to kindle.

The consideration I refer to is this:

Capital, no matter how high it sets its claims and whatever its success in realizing them, can never put labor in a worse position than would be its lot in isolation. In other words, the presence of capital is always more favorable to labor than would be its absence.

Let us recall the illustration I used a little while ago.

Two men are reduced to gaining their livelihood by fishing.

One of them has some nets, a line, a boat, and a few provisions to last him until he brings in his next catch. The other has only his two hands. It is to their mutual interest to associate.[9] Whatever may be the terms on which they agree to share the catch, neither the richer nor the poorer man will find them detrimental to his own situation; for the instant either one of them finds the association less to his advantage than isolation, he may return to isolation.

In the life of the savage, as in the life of a pastoral, an agricultural, or an industrial society, the relations between capital and labor always conform to this pattern.

Thus, doing without capital is always a final way out for labor. If the demands of capital were to go so far as to make joint action less profitable for labor than isolated action, labor would be free to turn to isolation as a refuge, always available (except in slavery) against a voluntary association that seems disadvantageous; for labor can always say to capital: "I prefer going it alone to the terms you offer."

Someone objects that this refuge is an illusion and a mockery, that, for the worker, going it alone is completely impossible, and that without equipment he would die.

This is true, but it confirms the truth of my statement to the effect that even if capital carries its demands to the most extreme limits, it still is beneficial to labor by the very fact of their joint association. Labor enters a condition worse than the worst joint association only at the moment when the association terminates, that is, when capital withdraws. Cease, then, apostles of doom, to cry out against the tyranny of capital, since you agree that its action is always—to a greater or lesser extent, no doubt, but always—beneficial. A singular tyrant indeed, whose power is a help to all who turn to it and is harmful only when withheld!

But, the objector may insist, although this might have been true at the beginning when society was first formed, today capital has invaded everything; it occupies all the positions; it has taken possession of all the land. The worker no longer has air to breathe, room or land on which to set foot, or a stone on which to lay his head without the permission of capital. He is therefore subject to the dictates of capital. You give him as a refuge only isolation, which, as you admit, is death!

This statement reveals complete ignorance of economic law and deplorable confusion.

If, as is said, capital has taken over all the forces of Nature, all the land, all the space on earth, I ask: For whose profit? For its own profit, of course. But how is it, then, that a simple laborer, with only his two hands, can procure in France, in England, in Belgium, a thousand, a million times more satisfactions than he could obtain in isolation—not on the social hypothesis that you find so revolting, but on that other hypothesis, so dear to you, of a society in which capital has not yet been guilty of any usurpation?

I shall keep returning to this fact in our debate, until you, with your new scientific theories, can find some other explanation for it, for, as far as I am concerned, I feel that I have already accounted for it.[10]

Yes, take the first workingman that comes along in Paris. Ascertain what he earns and what satisfactions he enjoys. When you have both properly railed against the curse of capital, I shall step in and address this workingman in the following terms:

"We are going to destroy capital and all its works. I am going to put you down in the middle of a hundred million acres of the most fertile land, and I shall give you full and complete ownership of everything in it both above and below ground. You will be elbowed by no capitalist. You will enjoy unrestrictedly your four natural rights of hunting, fishing, gathering fruits, and grazing. It is true that you will have no capital; for, if you did, you would be in exactly the same position that you criticize in the case of others. But, after all, you will not have to complain of landlordism, of capitalism, of individualism, of usurers, of speculators, of bankers, of profiteers. The land will be entirely yours. Decide if you wish to accept."

At first, the workingman will dream of a life as monarch of all he surveys. Yet, as he reflects, he will probably say to himself: "Let's see. Even when you have a hundred million acres of good land, you still have to live. First, let's calculate the *bread* supply in the two situations. At present I earn three francs a day. With wheat at fifteen francs I can have a hundredweight of it every five days. That's the same as sowing and reaping it myself. When I am the owner of a hundred million acres of land, the most I can have, without capital, is a hundredweight of wheat in two years, and in the meanwhile I can starve to death a hundred times. Therefore, I'll settle for my wages."

The truth is, we do not pay enough attention to the progress humanity has had to make even to assure the poor pittance our workers now live on.[11]

Improvement in the workers' status is to be found in the wage system itself and in the natural laws that govern wages.

1. The worker tends to rise to the rank of an entrepreneur having capital resources.

2. Wages tend to rise.

Corollary: Moving from the status of wage earner to entrepreneur becomes increasingly less desirable and easier.

15

Saving

Saving is not the accumulation of quarters of game, kernels of wheat, or pieces of money. The storing up of materials and consumers' goods of this kind, which is necessarily confined within very narrow limits, represents *saving* only for man in isolation. All that we have already said about value, services, and relative wealth shows us that, socially speaking, saving, though of kindred origin, follows a different course and assumes a different character.

Saving is voluntarily postponing until a later date our payment from society, in the form of equivalent services, for services previously rendered it. For example, a man may every day, from the time he is twenty until he is sixty, perform for his fellow men business and professional services equal, let us say, to four, while asking in return services equal only to three. In that case he is in the position of being able, in his old age, when he can no longer work, to receive from society payment for one-fourth of all his labor over the previous forty years.

The fact that his tokens of acknowledgment, which he has received and accumulated through the years, take the form of bills of exchange, promissory notes, bank notes, and specie, is an entirely secondary and nonessential consideration. It has reference only to the means of execution. It can change neither the nature nor the consequences of saving. The illusion created by the fact that money is involved is none the less an illusion, although nearly all of us fall victim to it.

Indeed, it is very difficult for us to resist the error of believing that the saver takes values out of circulation and, consequently, does a certain degree of harm to society.

In this matter we are confronted with one of those seeming contradictions that run counter to logic, one of those barriers that appear to be an insurmountable obstacle to progress, one of those painful discords that lead us to doubt either the omnipotence or the loving-kindness of the Author of all things.

On the one hand, we know that humanity cannot prosper, improve, achieve for itself greater leisure and stability, and consequently intellectual and moral progress, unless it constantly adds great amounts to its existing store of capital. On the rapid increase in capital also depend the demand for labor, the raising of wage rates, and consequently progress toward equality.

But, on the other hand, is not *saving* the opposite of *spending,* and if he who spends encourages and stimulates labor, does not he who saves do the contrary? If everybody began to economize as much as possible, employment would fall off correspondingly and would become completely nonexistent if one-hundred-percent saving were possible.

What advice can we therefore give to mankind? And what valid moral precepts can political economy offer, when apparently it can conclude with nothing better than this contradictory and disastrous alternative: *If you do not save,* new capital will not be formed, and capital will be used up. There will be an increasing supply of workers, but the fund out of which they are to be paid will remain unchanged. The workers will enter into competition with one another; they will offer their services at lower rates; wages will be depressed; and mankind will suffer a decline in these respects. There will be a decline in another respect as well, for if you do not save, you will have no bread for your old age; you will not be able to provide for a more rewarding career for your son, a dowry for your daughter, or any expansion for your business, etc. *If you save,* you reduce the funds available for wages, you injure a great number of your fellow men, you deal a heavy blow to labor, which is everywhere the source of human satisfactions; consequently, you reduce mankind's standard of living.

These disturbing contradictions disappear when we view them

in the light of the explanation that I have given of saving—an explanation based on the theories to which our study of value has led us.

Services are exchanged for services.

Value is the appraisal of two services compared with each other.

Accordingly, saving is permitting some period of time to intervene between the rendering of a service and the receiving of an equivalent service, or, in more general terms, interposing an interval of time between the service rendered and the service received.

Now, in what way does an individual harm society or injure labor when he postpones demanding from society a service to which he is entitled? I shall demand a year from now a value that I could demand now. Thus, I give society an extra year in which to pay. During that time labor can continue to be performed and services to be exchanged just as if I did not exist. I have not disrupted anything. On the contrary: I have added one more satisfaction to those my fellow men enjoy, and for a year they enjoy it gratis.

Gratis is not the word, for I must complete my description of the phenomenon.

The time interval between the two services is itself the subject of bargaining and exchange, for it possesses value. Herein lie the origin and the explanation of *interest*.

For example, a man performs a service now, but he proposes to receive the equivalent service ten years from now. This represents a value whose immediate enjoyment he forgoes. Now, it is characteristic of value to be able to assume all possible forms. In return for a given value, one may be sure of obtaining any imaginable service, whether productive or unproductive, of equal value. The person who defers for ten years his demand for the payment of an account due him defers not only the enjoyment of a satisfaction but the possibility of turning this value to productive use. For this reason he will find people in the world who are interested in negotiating with him for this deferment. Someone will say to our thrifty friend: "You have the right to receive immediate payment for a certain value, and it suits your convenience not to collect it until ten years from now. Very well, for these ten years transfer your claim to me; let me act in your place and stead. I shall collect the value which is owed you; I shall put it to productive use for ten years, and repay you when the debt falls due. In this way you will be doing me a *service,* and since a service has a value that is arrived at by comparing it with another service, it remains only for us to appraise the service that I seek from you and to set its *value.* Once this point has been discussed and settled, I shall be required to return to you, when the debt falls due, not only the value of the service owed you but also the value of the service you are going to do me."

The value of this temporary transfer of values previously saved is called *interest.*

For the same reason that a third party may desire that, in *return for a service,* a given value previously saved be transferred to him, so the original debtor may also request the same transfer. In either case this is called *asking for credit.* Granting credit is allowing time for the repayment of a value; it is surrendering in favor of another person one's own enjoyment of the value; it is rendering a service; it is acquiring the right to an equivalent service in return.

But to revert to the economic effects of saving: Now that we know all the details of this phenomenon, it is very evident that it in no wise harms industry in general or human labor. Even if the person making the saving received cash in exchange for the services he had rendered, and hoarded it, he would be doing society no harm, since he was able to collect these values from it only by contributing equal values to it. I must add that this kind of hoarding is unlikely, exceptional, abnormal, for it is contrary to the self-interest of those who indulge in it. Pieces of money in a man's hand mean: He who possesses us has rendered services to society and has not yet been paid for them. Society has placed us in his hands as a token. We are at one and the same time an acknowledgment, a promise, and a guarantee. On the day he chooses, he may, by producing and surrendering us, receive from society the services to which he is entitled.

Now, this man is not pressed by any urgent need. Does it

follow that he will hoard his money? No, since, as we have seen, the time interval between the two services exchanged is itself negotiable. If our thrifty friend proposes to go for ten years without claiming from society the services due him, it is to his interest to name a substitute in order to increase the original value owed him by the value of this special service. Saving, therefore, in no way implies actual hoarding.

Let moralists no longer be dismayed by this consideration.

16

Population

I have been anxious to reach this chapter if only to vindicate Malthus after the violent attacks that have been directed against him. It is almost incredible that authors of no consequence, of no standing, so uninformed that they display their ignorance on every page they write, should have succeeded, by dint of echoing one another's words, in discrediting in the public mind a serious, conscientious, and philanthropic author and in representing as absurd a carefully developed theory that, at the very least, is worthy of close study and attention.

It may be that I do not entirely share Malthus' opinions. There are two sides to every question, and I feel that Malthus kept his attention fixed too much on the dark side. For my part, I admit, I have so often in my study of economics had occasion to come to the conclusion that *what God does, He does well,* that, when logic leads me to a different view, I cannot help but mistrust my logic. I know that this faith in a providential design can be intellectually dangerous. The reader will subsequently be able to judge whether or not my personal bias in this respect has led me astray. But it will never prevent me from acknowledging that there is a great deal of truth in Malthus' admirable work nor from paying homage to the ardent love of mankind that inspired every line he wrote.

Malthus, who had a profound and thorough understanding of economics, clearly understood as well all the ingenious forces with which Nature has provided mankind in order to assure its progress. At the same time, he believed that human progress could be completely paralyzed by virtue of the operation of one law, the law of population. As he contemplated the world, he said sadly to himself: "God appears to have taken great care of the species, but to have shown very little concern for the individual. In fact, whatever species of animal we consider, we find its fecundity so overwhelming, its power of reproduction so extraordinary, its generative capacity so superabundant, as indeed to assure the survival of the species, but to leave the individual in a most precarious position; for all the reproductive cells cannot be given life; some must fail to be born or must die prematurely. Man is no exception to this law. (And it is surprising that this shocks the socialists, who are always declaring that the rights of the whole of society must take precedence over the rights of the individual.) God has certainly assured the continuation of the human race by providing it with great powers of reproduction. The numbers of mankind would then naturally come to exceed what the soil could maintain, if foresight were not exercised. But man is endowed with foresight, and hence his reason and his will are alone able to halt this disastrous trend."

Starting from these premises, which Malthus held as incontestable, though others may challenge them if they will, he necessarily had to place the greatest possible stress on the exercise of foresight. For there was no middle course: either man must voluntarily curb his excessive reproduction, or else, like all other species, become subject to the operation of repressive checks.

Malthus, therefore, never felt that he could go too far in exhorting men to exercise foresight; the greater his love for them, the more he felt obliged to hold up to them the disastrous consequences of unwise reproduction, so that they might the better avoid them. He said: If you reproduce irresponsibly, you will never be able to escape the punishment that awaits you, in various and sundry, but always horrible, forms: famine, war, pestilence, etc. Asceticism, charity, social and economic justice can never be more than ineffectual remedies.

In his ardor Malthus allowed an expression to escape him that, when separated from the context and spirit of his work, may seem harsh and unfeeling. It appeared in the first edition of his book, which was then only in pamphlet form and not yet a work in four volumes. It was pointed out to him that in the form in which this passage was couched his thought could be misinterpreted. He hastened to delete it, and it never reappeared in the subsequent numerous editions of the *Essay on Population.*

But one of his opponents, Mr. Godwin,* had picked it up, and M. de Sismondi (one of those men who, with the best intentions in the world, do the most harm) reproduced the unfortunate words. Immediately all the socialists seized upon it, and that was all they needed to try, condemn, and execute Malthus on the spot. Certainly they must thank Sismondi for his erudition; for they themselves had never read either Malthus or Godwin.

Thus, they represented as the basis of his system the passage that Malthus himself later deleted. They repeat it *ad nauseam.* In a little 18mo volume M. Pierre Leroux † repeats it at least forty times; it forms the stock in trade of all the second-rate reformers' tirades.

One day, after he had written a chapter against Malthus, I was talking with the most celebrated and articulate member of this school. I quoted some of the opinions expressed in the *Essay on Population,* and I received the impression that he had no knowledge of the work. I said to him, "You have refuted Malthus, but have you by any chance read him through from one end to the other?"

"I have not read him at all," he replied. "His whole system is set forth on one page and can be summed up in his famous arithmetical and geometrical ratios. That's enough for me."

"Apparently," I said to him, "you care nothing for the public, for Malthus, for the truth, for conscience, or for yourself."

* [William Godwin (1756–1836), known as the author of *The Adventures of Caleb Williams* as well as of the essays in *The Enquirer* (1797), "Avarice and Profusion," "Riches and Poverty," and "Beggars," which dealt with "the general question of the future improvement of society." It was, of course, in answer to these that Malthus was first prompted to write his *Essay on Population* the following year. —Translator.]

† [Pierre Leroux (1797–1871), French philosopher, publisher, and encyclopedist, a disciple of Saint-Simon. Editor of *Le Globe.*—Translator.]

This is the way an opinion gains acceptance in France. Fifty ignoramuses repeat in chorus some absurd libel that has been thought up by an even bigger ignoramus; and, if only it happens to coincide to some slight degree with prevailing attitudes and passions, it becomes a self-evident truth.

We must recognize, however, that science cannot approach a problem with the deliberate intention of arriving at an optimistic conclusion. What would we think of a man who began his study of physiology already committed to the proposition that God could not have willed that men should be afflicted with disease? If the physiologist advancing such a hypothesis were challenged by another who pointed to the facts, he probably would become angry and might even accuse his colleague of *irreverence;* but it is difficult to imagine that he would go so far as to accuse him of being the creator of disease.

Yet this is what has happened in Malthus' case. In a work well supported with facts and figures, he set forth a law that runs counter to the idea of many optimists. Men who refused to accept this law have attacked Malthus spitefully and bitterly, with flagrant bad faith, as if he himself had deliberately thrown in the way of the human race obstacles that, according to him, stem from the law of population. It would have been more scientific simply to prove that Malthus was wrong, and that his so-called law is not in fact a law at all.

Population, it must be emphasized, is one of those all too numerous subjects that remind us that man often has little more open to him than a choice between two evils. Whatever may have been God's intent, suffering has entered into His plan. Let us not seek for harmony in the absence of evil, but in the tendency of evil to lead us back to the good and to become less and less prevalent. God has given us free will. First we have to *learn*—which is a long and difficult task; then we have to *act* in conformity with what we have learned, which is hardly easier. In this way, we shall gradually free ourselves from some of our suffering, without ever altogether escaping from it; for even when we succeed completely in avoiding punishment, we do so only by increased exercise of the painful virtue of foresight. The more we succeed in securing ourselves from the repressive hand of retribution, the more we must incur the inconveniences of prevention.

It does no good to rebel against this situation; it is the human condition; it is the atmosphere in which we live and breathe. If we face the facts courageously, we shall see that a large area has been left open for the exercise of our initiative. Here, as everywhere else, man can choose between two possibilities: either the pain that he imposes upon himself—foresight, labor, virtue, the effort of will needed to act in conformity with universal law, deliberate co-operation with the will of God, an act of sacrifice that becomes a joy, a struggle with himself that raises him above his finite nature—or the pain that is imposed upon him, the punishment he suffers, in a position of passivity in relation to beings of a lower order, a lesson forced upon the intelligent creature by inanimate or unconscious agents, a consciously felt fall from his position of eminence that places him on the downward path which leads to a degradation still more profound.

It is by accepting the inescapable condition of man, by never losing sight of his wretchedness as well as of his sublimity, that we shall approach, with Malthus, the problem of population. On this great question we shall first play the role, to some extent, of a mere reporter; then, we shall present our own views. If the laws of population can be reduced to a single concise formula, it will certainly be fortunate for the advancement and dissemination of the science of political economy. But if, by reason of the number and complexity of the data relating to the problem, we discover that these laws do not permit of brief and exact definition, we shall have the wisdom to abandon the attempt. Accuracy, even at the risk of being excessively long, is preferable to oversimplification.

We have seen that progress consists in making the forces of Nature serve more and more as means for the satisfaction of our wants, so that in each successive age the same amount of utility is obtained at the cost of less effort, leaving at the disposal of society either increased leisure or a greater supply of labor for providing new satisfactions.

We have further shown how each advance over Nature, after first rewarding the initiative of a few men, soon becomes, by the operation of the law of competition, the gratuitous and common heritage of all mankind.

From these premises, it would appear to be a likely conclusion that human well-being would surely have increased and at the same time would have rapidly become more equitably distributed.

But, in point of fact, such has not been the case. There are in the world great multitudes of men who are in wretched circumstances, and their wretchedness is not of their own making. What are the causes of this situation?

I believe that there are several. The first is called *plunder*, or, if you will, *injustice*. Economists have referred to it only incidentally and only in so far as it implies some error, some false scientific notion. Since they were setting forth general laws, they did not feel that it behooved them to concern themselves with the effect of these laws when they were not in operation, when they were being violated. But plunder has played, and continues to play, too important a role in the world for us, even as economists, to be able to ignore it. It is not alone a question of haphazard thefts, cases of petty larceny, isolated crimes. War, slavery, pious frauds, privilege, monopoly, restrictions, tax abuses—these are the most striking manifestations of plunder. We can realize, by noting their presence or the deep imprints they have left, what a great influence disturbing forces of such vast proportions must have exerted or still do exert on social and economic inequality; later we shall attempt to measure their scope and range.

But another factor that has delayed progress and, more particularly, has stood in the way of its equitable distribution among all men has been, according to certain authors, that of population.

Obviously, if, even as wealth increases, the number of men among whom it must be distributed increases even more rapidly, absolute wealth may become greater, and at the same time individual wealth may become less.

If, in addition, there are certain types of services that can be performed by anyone, like those that require only physical strength, and if the class that performs these functions, which is the most poorly paid, is the very one that multiplies most rapidly, then the workers will create a disastrous competition within their own ranks. The lowest social stratum, if it multiplies more rapidly than progress develops, will never share in its benefits.

We thus see how fundamentally important the law of population is.

Malthus formulated it in these terms:

Population tends to remain on a level with the means of subsistence.

In passing, let me observe that it is surprising that Malthus has been assigned the honor, or the responsibility, of formulating this law, whether it is true or false. There has not been a single writer on such subjects, since the days of Aristotle, who has not proclaimed it, and often in the same terms.

We need only glance at the whole of animate creation to perceive—beyond the shadow of a doubt—that Nature is much more concerned with the species than with the individual.

Her precautions for the survival of the species are tremendous, and among these precautions the copious fecundity of the powers of reproduction figures prominently. This superabundance appears everywhere to exist in inverse ratio to the degree of sensitivity, intelligence, and strength with which each species resists destruction.

Thus, in the vegetable kingdom the means of reproduction, by seeds, sprouts, etc., that can be supplied by a single individual are incalculable. I should not be surprised if a single elm tree, provided all its seeds sprouted, could produce a million trees a year. Why does this not happen? Because not all these seeds find the conditions necessary to life, namely, space and nourishment. They are destroyed, and since plants do not have sensitivity, Nature has spared neither the means of reproduction nor those of destruction.

Animals that exist on barely more than the level of vegetable life likewise reproduce in immense numbers. Who has not wondered how oysters can multiply rapidly enough to withstand the amazing toll that is taken of them for human consumption?

As we move up the scale of animate creatures, we find that

Nature becomes less lavish with the means of reproduction she supplies.

Vertebrates cannot multiply as rapidly as the others, especially among the larger species. After nine months of gestation, the cow gives birth to only one calf and must suckle it for a considerable time. Nevertheless, it is obvious that the reproductive powers of the bovine species are more than sufficient. In rich countries, like England, France, and Switzerland, cattle are on the increase, despite the very heavy toll taken of them; and if we had unlimited pasture lands, there is no doubt that we could attain both a higher rate of consumption and more rapid reproduction. I suggest that, if land and feed were ample, we could in a few years time have ten times our present number of steers and cows and still eat ten times our present amount of beef. The reproductive capabilities of cattle are, therefore, far from having shown us the full measure of their power, aside from any extraneous limitations arising from lack of land or feed.

It is certain that man's reproductive capability is less powerful than that of any other species, and inevitably so. Man was not designed to be as exposed to annihilation as the animals, in view of the superior capacity for feeling, intelligence, and sympathy with which Nature has endowed him. But is he *physically* exempt from that law by virtue of which all species are capable of multiplying more rapidly than space or food permit? It is impossible to suppose so.

I say *physically,* for I am speaking here only of the physiological law.

There is a fundamental difference between the *physiological capacity* for reproduction and *actual* reproduction.

The one is the absolute organic potential, freed from every obstacle and every external limitation. The other is what actually remains after all the adverse factors that restrict and limit this potential have run their course. Thus, the reproductive potential of the poppy can well be one million per year, and yet in a given poppy field the actual reproduction may remain stationary or even decrease.

It is this physiological law that Malthus tried to formulate. He sought to determine in what period of time a certain number of men could double *if their space and food were unlimited*.

We can see at once that, since this hypothesis of *complete satisfaction of all wants* is never realized, the *theoretical* period is necessarily shorter than any observable period of *actual* doubling could ever be.

In fact, cases observed yield widely varying figures. According to the studies made by M. Moreau de Jonnès,* using current population trends as his basis, the doubling would require: 555 years in Turkey, 227 in Switzerland, 138 in France, 106 in Spain, 100 in Holland, 76 in Germany, 43 in Russia and England, 25 in the United States, deducting the numbers due to immigration.

Why these tremendous differences? We have no reason for believing that they stem from physiological causes. Swiss women are as robust and as fertile as American women.

It must be that the absolute physiological potential of reproduction is held in bounds by external checks. And this is proved beyond question as soon as some circumstance or other happens to remove these checks. Thus, an improvement in agriculture, a new industry, some new source of local wealth, is invariably accompanied by a rise in the birth rate. In the same way, when a scourge like a plague, a famine, or a war destroys a large part of the population, immediately the rate of reproduction is accelerated.

When, then, the rate slows down or comes to a halt, it is because land and food either are, or are likely to be, deficient; it is because it encounters an obstacle, or, seeing an obstacle in its path, falls back.

This phenomenon, the exposition of which raised such a clamor against Malthus, seems to me to be really incontestable.

If we put a thousand mice in a cage with only enough food to keep them alive from day to day, their number, despite their well-known fertility, could never exceed a thousand; or if it did, there would be privation and suffering, both of which would tend to decrease the number. In this case, it would certainly be correct

* [Alexandre Moreau de Jonnès (1778–1870), French statistician. Director of statistics for the French government (1834–1852).—TRANSLATOR.]

to say that an external cause imposes a limit, not on their fertility, but on the result of their fertility. There would certainly be a conflict between the physiological tendency and the limiting factor; hence, the population would remain constant. This is easily proved, for if we were gradually to raise the daily ration until we had doubled it, we should soon see two thousand mice in the cage.

And how do his opponents try to answer Malthus? Against his theory they cite the *facts*. They say to him: The proof that man's reproductive capabilities are not without definite limits is to be found in the fact that in certain countries the population is stationary. If the law of constant increase were true, if population doubled every twenty-five years, France, which had thirty million inhabitants in 1820, would today have more than sixty million.

Is this logical?

Of course not!

I first note that the population in France has increased only one-fifth in twenty-five years, whereas elsewhere it has doubled. I seek the reason. I find it in the lack of space and sustenance. I perceive that, under the conditions existing today in agriculture, population, and mode of life, it is difficult to create the means of subsistence with sufficient rapidity for all *potential* births to become *actual* births or, if they do, for those *born* to survive. Now, I declare that the means of subsistence cannot double—or at lease they do not double—in France every twenty-five years. It is precisely the combined action of all these negative forces that, in my opinion, holds in check the physiological potential; and to argue against me, you cite the slowness of reproduction as proof that the physiological potential does not exist! Such a line of reasoning cannot be advanced seriously.

Has the geometric progression indicated by Malthus been challenged on any more reasonable grounds? Malthus never advanced the fatuous premise that "mankind, in *actual fact*, multiplies in geometrical ratio." He says, on the contrary, that this is not in fact the case, since he is investigating the obstacles that prevent it from being so, and he offers this ratio merely as a formula to show the physiological potential of reproduction.

Seeking to discover in what period of time a given population could double, *assuming that all wants were satisfied* and *no obstacles were encountered at any time,* he set the figure at twenty-five years. He arrived at this figure after direct observation of the people that, though falling infinitely short of meeting the conditions of his hypothesis, came nearest to them—the American people. Once this period had been arrived at, and because the matter under consideration was the *potential* rate of reproduction, he declared that population *tended to increase* in geometrical ratio.

This is denied, but, in all truth, to do so is to go against the evidence. It may well be that the period necessary to double the population is not twenty-five, but thirty, or forty, or fifty years; it may vary from race to race. All this is more or less debatable; but it most assuredly cannot be alleged that, on this hypothesis, the progression would not be geometrical. If in fact one hundred couples produced two hundred offspring in a given period, why would two hundred couples not produce four hundred in an equal period?

Because, it is said, their reproduction would be held in check.

This is just what Malthus says.

But by what will it be held in check?

Malthus assigns two general checks to man's unlimited increase: he calls them the *preventive check* and the *positive check.**

Since population can be kept below its physiological tendencies only by a decrease in births or an increase in deaths, there is no doubt that Malthus' classification is complete.

Besides, when conditions of space and sustenance are such that population cannot go beyond a certain figure, there is no doubt that the action of the positive check is more powerful in the same degree to which the action of the preventive check is less powerful. To say that births can increase without an increase in deaths while the food supply remains stationary is to fall into an obvious contradiction.

It is no less evident, a priori, and apart from other extremely

* [Bastiat prefers to call Malthus' "positive" check the "repressive" check (*l'obstacle répressif*). His preference is respected in the following pages.—Translator.]

grave economic considerations, that in this situation voluntary self-restraint is preferable to restraints imposed from without.

Up to this point, then, Malthus' theory cannot be challenged in any detail.

Perhaps Malthus was wrong in setting this twenty-five-year period, which he had observed in the United States, as the limit of human fertility. I know very well that he felt that by this means he was avoiding any possible reproach of exaggerating or of being too theoretical. How can anyone dare claim, he said to himself, that I am allowing too much latitude for the *possible* when I am basing my conclusions on the *actual facts?* He was not aware that in thus combining the *possible* with the *actual,* and in setting up as the measure for *the law of reproduction,* with no reference to *the law of limitation,* a period arrived at through observation of data subject to both these laws, he ran the risk of not being understood. But this is precisely what happened. People laughed at his geometrical and arithmetical ratios; they reproached him for using the United States as the type for the rest of the world; in a word, they used against him his failure to distinguish between two very different laws and contested his findings by using each of them to refute the other.

When we try to determine what is, theoretically, the reproductive power of the human race, we must forget for the moment all physical or moral checks resulting from lack of space, food, or creature comforts. But, once the question is couched in these terms, it is really superfluous to find an exact answer. In the human species, as in all living organisms, this power surpasses by a tremendous margin all instances of rapid reproduction observable in the past or to be observed in the future. In the case of wheat, for example, assuming that every seed sprouts five stalks, and each stalk produces twenty grains, each grain can then theoretically produce ten million grains in five years. Or take the canine race. Calculating in the same way, with four puppies per litter and six years of fecundity, we find that a pair of dogs can in twelve years produce eight million offspring.

In the human race, setting puberty at sixteen and the end of fertility at thirty, each couple could bring eight children into the world. We reduce this number by half to allow for premature deaths, which would be a great deal since we are assuming the satisfaction of all wants, a hypothesis that would greatly lower the death rate, and we still find these figures for a twenty-five-year period: 2 – 4 – 8 – 16 – 32 – 64 – 128 – 256 – 512; etc., or two million in two centuries.

If we make the calculation on the basis adopted by Euler, the period of doubling will be twelve years and a half; eight periods will make just a century, and the increase in this period of time will be as 512:2.

At no time, in no country, has the number of men ever been known to increase with such frightening rapidity. According to *Genesis,* the Hebrews entering Egypt numbered seventy couples; in the *Book of Numbers,* two centuries later, we find that the census taken by Moses listed six hundred thousand men twenty-one years of age and over; hence, a total population of at least two million. We may thus reckon that the population had doubled every fourteen years. The statistical tables of the Bureau of Standards are hardly applicable to Biblical matters. Shall we say that the figure of six hundred thousand men of military age implies a total population in excess of two million, and shall we conclude from this that the population doubled in a shorter period than Euler calculated? We are free to challenge either Moses' census or Euler's estimates; but we certainly will not contend that the Hebrews multiplied more rapidly than it is possible to multiply. That is all I ask.

After this example, which appears to be the one in which *actual* fecundity most nearly approximated *potential* fecundity, we have that of the United States. Here we know that the doubling takes place in less than twenty-five years.

It is unnecessary to carry these inquiries further; it is enough to recognize that in our species, as in all species, the physiological potential of reproduction is greater than the actual reproduction. Furthermore, it would be a logical absurdity for the actual to be greater than the potential.

Along with this absolute force, which we have no need to

measure more accurately, and which we may quite well consider as uniform, there exists, as we have said, another force, which, to a degree, limits, restrains, and arrests the action of the first and places in its way certain obstacles that vary greatly according to time and place, and according to the occupations, manners and customs, laws, and religions of various peoples.

This second force I call the *law of limitation,* and it is clear that the rise and fall of population, in every country, is the result of the combined action of this law with the other.

But what is this law of limitation? We may say, in a very general way, that the propagation of life is restricted or impeded by the difficulty of sustaining life. This idea, which we have already expressed in Malthus' formula, requires further development. It constitutes the most essential part of our subject.[1]

Organisms endowed with life but not with feeling are strictly passive in this struggle between the two forces. For plant life, it is entirely accurate to say that in every species the existing numbers are kept within the limits imposed by the means of subsistence. The reproductive power of their seeds is infinite, but their resources in terms of land and its fertility are not. The seeds harm and destroy one another; they fail to germinate; and, in the last analysis, only as many grow as the soil can nourish. Animals are sentient, but they appear, for the most part, to be lacking in foresight; they propagate, they multiply rapidly, without any concern for the fate of their posterity. Only death, a premature death, can limit their reproduction and maintain the balance between their number and their means of subsistence.

M. de Lamennais,* speaking to the people in his inimitable style, declared: "There is room for all on earth, and God has made the earth rich enough to provide abundantly for the wants of all." And farther on: "The Author of the universe has not caused man's condition to be worse than that of the animals; and are they not all invited to Nature's rich feast? Is a single one of them turned away?" And again: "The plants of the fields thrust

* [Félicité de Lamennais (1782–1854), French philosopher, Catholic priest, reformer, and ardent champion of the working classes.—TRANSLATOR.]

out their roots beside each other into the earth, and it feeds them all, and all grow in peace; no one of them absorbs the other's life-giving sap."

We may be permitted to take these utterances as mere hollow declamations serving to encourage dangerous conclusions and may well regret that such wonderful oratory has been expended on the popularization of the most disastrous of errors.

It is certainly not true that one plant does not steal another's sap, and that all thrust out their roots into the soil without doing harm to one another. Millions of seeds fall each year upon the ground, draw from it a beginning of life, then die, strangled by stronger and hardier plants. It is not true that all the animals that come into the world are invited to Nature's rich feast, and that not one of them is turned away. Wild species destroy one another, and among the domesticated species man cuts off an incalculable number. Nothing serves better to prove the existence and the interrelation of these two laws of reproduction and limitation. Why are there so many cattle and sheep in France despite the toll that is taken of them? Why are there so few wolves and bears, although far fewer are killed, and they are designed by Nature to multiply far faster? The reason is that man furnishes the first with food and denies it to the other; he so applies the law of limitation to them that he leaves more or less latitude for the operation of the law of reproduction.

Thus, for both plants and animals, the limiting force seems to take only one form, that of *destruction*. But man is endowed with reason, with foresight; and this new factor alters the manner in which this force affects him.

Undoubtedly, in so far as man has physical organs, in so far as, to speak bluntly, he is an animal, the *law of limitation,* in the form of destruction, applies to him. It is impossible for the number of men on earth to exceed their means of subsistence: that would be equivalent to saying that more men exist than can exist, which is an absurdity. If, therefore, man's reason and foresight become dormant, he falls to the level of plants or animals; he becomes a mere brute. Then, inevitably he multiplies in accordance with the great physiological law that governs all species; and it is also inevitable that he should be destroyed by reason of the law of limitation, to whose action, in this case, he has remained indifferent.

But, if he exercises foresight, this second law comes within the orbit of his will. He alters it; he directs it; indeed, it is no longer the same law; it is no longer a blind force, but an intelligent force; no longer merely a natural law, it becomes a social law also. Man is the meeting point where these two principles, mind and matter, merge and become one; he is not entirely under the dominion of either the one or the other. Hence, the *law of limitation* is evidenced in the human race under two forms and maintains population at a necessary level through the double action of foresight and destruction.

These two forces are not uniform in their operation. On the contrary: the greater the action of the one, the less the action of the other. There is one objective that must be realized—limitation. It is attained by greater or lesser degrees of either *repression* or *prevention*, depending upon whether man is brutish or spiritual, whether he is more mind or more matter, whether he lives in the vegetable kingdom or in the moral sphere. The law operates in varying degrees from within or without, but one way or the other it always operates.

We in France do not fully appreciate how great the domain of foresight is, for Malthus' translator, by retaining the vague and inadequate literal words "moral restraint," * has put into general circulation a most imperfect idea of what the concept includes. He further weakens Malthus' meaning by appending this definition: "Moral restraint is the virtue of not marrying when one does not have the means to support a family, and yet living in chastity." The obstacles that society wisely puts in the way of mankind's *possible* increase in population take many other forms than that of moral restraint as just defined. For example, why the blessed ignorance of the earliest years, doubtless the only ignorance that it would be criminal to dispel, which is respected by all and guarded by the zealous mother like a treasure? Why is the age of ignorance followed by that seemly and mysterious

---

* [In French, *la contrainte morale.*—TRANSLATOR.]

modesty with which the maiden awes and enchants her lover, lengthening and beautifying the days of innocent courtship? How marvelous, and yet under any other circumstances how absurd, are the veils that are drawn between ignorance and knowledge, and, later, the obstacles that are placed between knowledge and bliss. Why does public opinion, with all its power, impose such strict laws upon the relations between the sexes, brand with shame their least infraction, and pursue relentlessly those who succumb to weakness and their unfortunate offspring, even unto the fourth and fifth generation? And then the punctilious code of honor, the rigid reserve, so universally admired even by those who do not practice it, the standards, the exacting conventions, the precautions of all kinds—what are all these except manifestations of the law of limitation operating on the moral, intelligent, and *preventive* level, the level, in a word, that is man's and man's alone?

Allow these bars to be let down, allow the human race, in matters that relate to the union of the sexes, to lose its concern for the conventions, for fortune, for the future, for public opinion, for good conduct, let it descend to the plane of plant or animal life; and can there be any doubt that man's power of reproduction, like that of the plants and animals, will function so overwhelmingly as soon to necessitate the intervention of the *law of limitation,* operating this time on the physical, brutish, and *repressive* level, that is, through the instrumentality of poverty, disease, and death?

Can anyone deny that, but for foresight or moral considerations, sexual impulses would be too strong to be resisted, in our species as in all others, from the age of puberty on? If we set this age at sixteen, and if the civil records show that, in a given country, marriage is not contracted before the age of twenty-four, this means that the moral and preventive aspects of the *law of limitation* have subtracted eight years from the period that the law of reproduction would otherwise be in operation; and if to this figure we add those who practice complete celibacy, we shall recognize that the Creator has not dealt with intelligent man as He has with the unreasoning beasts, and that man has it within his power to turn *repressive* limitation into *preventive* limitation.

It is quite curious that in regard to this great question the idealistic and the materialistic schools have, so to speak, exchanged roles. The idealists thunder against the use of foresight, insisting that brute instincts be obeyed; while the materialists exalt man's moral nature and urge that reason curb passion and appetite.

The difficulty lies in a failure to see the problem in its true light. Let the father of a family consult the most orthodox priest concerning the guidance of his children, and he will surely get from him, for the particular case, advice that is actually in complete agreement with scientific *principles;* yet this same priest rejects them when they are given the name of principles. "Protect your daughter," the old priest will say; "expose her the least you can to the temptations of the world. Cultivate like a precious flower the blessed ignorance and the heavenly modesty that are at once her charm and her defense. Wait until a fit and worthy suitor comes along. In the meanwhile, labor to provide a suitable future for her. Consider that in poverty marriage brings many hardships and even more dangers. Remember those old proverbs, which embody the wisdom of nations, and which assure us that financial security is the surest guarantee of marital peace and harmony. Why should you be hasty? Do you want your daughter to be burdened at twenty-five with a family that she cannot raise and educate in keeping with your own rank and station? Do you want her husband, feeling the insufficiency of his income, to give way to worry, to despair, and perhaps at last to demoralization? The problem you face is the most serious of all those to which you can turn your attention. Weigh it carefully. Think it over calmly. Avoid undue haste, etc."

Suppose that the father answered in the words of M. de Lamennais: "In the beginning God gave this commandment to all men: 'Be fruitful, and multiply, and replenish the earth, and subdue it.' And yet you say to a girl: 'Give up hope of a family, the blameless delights of marriage, the holy joys of motherhood. Deprive yourself; live alone. In what way can you be fruitful save in multiplying your woes?' " Do you think that the old priest would have nothing to say in answer to this line of reasoning?

"God," he would say, "has not bidden men to be fruitful like the beasts of the field, without measure, without discernment, without heed for the future. He has not endowed his chosen creatures with reason only to forbid them to use it in meeting the most crucial problems of their lives. He has indeed bidden man to be fruitful; but, to be fruitful, man must live, and to live, he must have the means of supporting life; and in God's commandment that man multiply is implied the commandment that he provide for his young ones the means of existence. Religion has not classed virginity as a crime. Far from it: religion has made it a virtue, has honored, sanctified, and glorified it. We must not, therefore, feel that we are violating one of God's commandments when we take steps to obey it with prudence, and with a view to the prosperity, the happiness, and the dignity of our families."

Well, now, do we not hear reasoning of this kind, which is the voice of experience, repeated daily, and do we not see it used by every moral and enlightened family as a guide to conduct? And what is it except the application of a general theory to a particular case? Or rather, what is this theory except a generalization drawn from particular cases? The idealist who, on principle, rejects recourse to preventive limitation is like a physicist who would say to people: Always act in the particular case as if bodies had mass, but do not admit in theory that mass exists.

Up to this point we have confined ourselves entirely to the theory of Malthus; but it seems to me that there is one attribute of man to which he, like most authors, has not attached the importance it deserves. It plays a very great role in the phenomena of population, it solves a number of the problems that this great question raises, and it renews in the soul of him who loves mankind the assurance and confidence that an incomplete understanding of political economy might have shaken. This attribute, which, moreover, is included in our notions of reason and foresight, is *perfectibility*. Man is perfectible. He is capable of improvement or degeneration. If, in a strict sense, he is capable of remaining stationary, he is also capable of moving up or down the endless ladder of civilization. This is true of individuals, of families, of nations, and of races.

Malthus did not fully appreciate this capacity for progress and was consequently led to pessimistic conclusions, and these in turn have aroused public opinion against him. And, indeed, since he envisaged the *preventive check* in something of an ascetic form and therefore, we must admit, one not likely to be widely accepted, he could not expect that it would have much effect. Hence, it was his belief that the *repressive* (or, as he called it, the positive) *check* would be the decisive one; in other words, vice, poverty, war, crime, etc.

In my opinion, there is a fallacy in this reasoning; for, as we shall see, the action of the preventive force is not confined solely to the practice of chastity, an act of self-denial, but also and above all, it finds expression in a state of well-being, in an instinctive tendency towards self-preservation and the protection of one's family.

Population, it has been said, tends to keep at the level of the means of subsistence. Let me note that for this term, the *means of subsistence,* once universally accepted, J. B. Say has substituted another term that is much more accurate: *the means of existence.* At first glance it would appear that *subsistence* alone is involved in this question. Such is not the case. *Man does not live by bread alone,* and a study of the facts shows clearly that population stops increasing or declines when the sum total of all the means of existence, including clothing, housing, and the other things that climate or even habit render necessary, becomes insufficient.

We must say, therefore: Population tends to keep at the level of the *means of existence.*

But are these means a fixed, absolute, uniform quantity? Certainly not. As civilization improves, man's wants become greater, even for his mere subsistence. Considered from the point of view of man as a perfectible being, the means of existence, among which must be included the satisfaction of moral, intellectual, and physical wants, permit of as many varying degrees as there are in civilization itself, that is, an infinite number. Undoubtedly, there is a lower limit: the satisfaction of hunger and a certain amount of protecton against cold are basic necessities for the maintenance of life; and we can observe life at this level among the Indians in America and the poverty-stricken in Europe. But as for an upper limit, I know of none; there is none. Once natural wants are satisfied, others arise that are artificial at the beginning, if you will, but which in their turn become natural through the force of habit, and, when they are satisfied, others arise, and still others, with no discernible end.

Hence, with every step that man takes along the road of civilization, his wants become more extensive, and his means of existence, which we may call the point at which the great *laws of increase* and *limitation* meet, keep pace with his wants. For, although man is capable of degeneration as well as improvement, he naturally turns away from the one and aspires toward the other. His efforts tend to keep him from falling back from the heights that he has already won and to raise him even higher; and *habit,* which has so well been called second nature, acts like a valve in our arteries to block any backward movement. It is therefore quite natural that man's habitually progressive tendency should manifest itself also in the control he exercises over his own multiplication and impel him to apply to this problem his best moral and intellectual efforts.

The consequences of man's being thus constituted are many; we shall confine ourselves to mentioning just a few of them. First, we readily admit with the economists that population and the means of existence reach an equilibrium; but since the means of existence are capable of infinite fluctuation and vary with the civilization and the habits of life that produce them, we cannot agree, as we compare different peoples and classes, that population is proportional to *production,* as stated by J. B. Say,[2] or to income, as affirmed by M. de Sismondi. Furthermore, since every step up the ladder of culture implies a higher degree of foresight, the moral and preventive check must more and more neutralize the action of the brutish and repressive check, according as progress is achieved in society or in any of its segments. It follows that any social progress contains within itself the seed of still further progress. *Vires acquirit eundo,* since improved standards of living and greater foresight engender one another in indefinite succession. Similarly, when, for whatever reason, mankind retrogresses, want and improvidence exert a cause-and-effect action upon each other, and the decline would never be halted if society had not been provided with that self-healing faculty, the *vis medicatrix,* which Providence has implanted in all living organisms. We may observe, in fact, that during every stage of a period of decline the action of the law of limitation in its destructive form becomes progressively more painful and more readily discernible. At first there is merely a backward movement, a decline in the standard of living; later come poverty, hunger, disorders, war, death— painful but unfailing methods of instruction.

We should like to pause here long enough to demonstrate how this theory explains the facts, and how, in turn, the facts support the theory. When, in the case of a nation or a class, the means of existence fall to that lower level at which they become one with the means of mere subsistence, as in China, in Ireland, and among the poorest classes in all countries, the least fluctuation in popula- tion or food supply is recorded in the mortality rate. The facts in this instance confirm the inferences of science. For a long time now Europe has not experienced a famine, and the elimination of this scourge has been attributed to a multitude of causes. A number of them do exist, undoubtedly, but the one most generally responsible is that the *means of existence* have risen, by reason of social progress, far above the means of subsistence. When years of scarcity come, many satisfactions can be sacrificed before any curtailment of food is rendered necessary. Such is not the case in China or in Ireland. When men have nothing except a little rice or a few potatoes, with what will they buy other foods if the rice or the potatoes happen to fail them?

And finally, there is a third consequence of man's perfectibility, which we must point out here because it refutes the pessimistic side of Malthus' theory. We have attributed to him the formula: Population tends to keep at the level of the means of subsistence. We should have said that he went far beyond this, and that his real formula, the one from which he derived such distressing conclu- sions, is this: Population tends to *increase faster than* the means of subsistence. If Malthus had merely meant by this statement that in the human race the power to beget life is greater than the power to sustain it, there could have been no possible argument. But

this is not what he meant. He declares that, taking into consideration absolute fertility, on the one hand, and, on the other, the
means of limiting it in the form of either repression or prevention,
we find that the result is nonetheless a tendency for population to
increase faster than the means of subsistence.[3] This is true of all
living species, except man. Man is an intelligent being and can
make unlimited use of the preventive check. He is perfectible; he
seeks to improve his situation; he finds decadence repugnant.
Progress is his normal state; progress implies an increasingly enlightened use of the preventive check; hence, *the means of existence increase more rapidly than population.* This result is not only
to be deduced from the theory of perfectibility, but is also confirmed by the *facts,* since everywhere we find the range of man's
satisfactions widening. If it were true, as Malthus says, that for
each increase in the means of existence there is a corresponding
and greater increase in population, the poverty of our race would
necessarily be constantly on the increase, and civilization would
stand at the beginning of time, and barbarism at the end. Just the
opposite takes place. Hence, it follows that the law of limitation
has been powerful enough to hold the rising tide of population
below the rate at which goods and services are produced.

We can see from the foregoing how vast and difficult the
question of population is. It is no doubt regrettable that a precisely formulated answer has not yet been given to it, and naturally I regret even more that I myself cannot be the one to give it.
But do we not see how incompatible the subject is with the
narrow limitations of any dogmatic axiom? And is it not a vain
and idle thing to try to express in the form of a set equation the
relations of data that are essentially variable? Let us recall what
these data are.

1. *The law of increase,* i.e., the absolute, potential, physiological capacity of the human race to propagate life, without reference
to the difficulties of sustaining life. This first datum, which alone
can be measured at all accurately, is the only one in which
accuracy is unnecessary; for of what importance is the theoretical
upper limit of population increase, if it can never be reached

under the actual conditions of human existence, which require man to live by the sweat of his brow?

2. There is, therefore, a *limit* to the law of increase. What is it? The means of existence, it is said. But what are these means? An indeterminate sum total of satisfactions. They are variable, and therefore the limit we are seeking to determine varies with them according to place, time, race, social rank, manners, public opinion, and habit.

3. Finally, what is the force that holds population within these constantly changing bounds? As far as man is concerned, it has two components: the *repressive* check and the *preventive* check. Now, the action of the first of these, to which, by its very nature, no exact measurement can be applied, is, furthermore, entirely subordinate to the action of the second, which, in turn, is dependent on the degree of civilization attained, habits, religious and political traditions, property and labor relations, family arrangements, etc., etc. It is therefore impossible to establish between the law of increase and the law of limitation an equation by which the actual population can be deduced. In algebra a and b represent known quantities that are numbered, measured, and of fixed proportions; but *means of existence, self-control,* and the *mortality rate*—three key data in the problem of population—are themselves variable and are made even more so by the amazing variability of the subject to whom they refer, man, that creature who, according to Montaigne, is so marvelously inconstant and diverse. It is therefore not surprising that in seeking to make of this equation something more exact than its nature permits of, economists have managed to create more disagreement than unity of opinion, for there is not one term in the formulas they employ that is not open to a host of objections, based both on theory and on fact.

Let us now proceed to consider a few practical applications, for in practical application we find both the clearest explanation of the theory and the true fruit of the tree of economic knowledge.

Labor, we have said, is the sole article of exchange. In order to secure a utility (unless Nature gives it to us gratis), we must go to the pains of producing it or repay with equivalent pains the persons who have taken the pains for us. Man creates absolutely nothing. He can merely arrange, reorder, or transport for a useful end things already existing. He performs none of these acts without taking pains, and the fruit of his pains is his property. If he surrenders it to another, he has the right to receive in return a service judged to be equivalent after free bargaining. This is the principle of value, of compensation, of exchange; and simple though it is, it is nonetheless true. In what we call *commodities* there exist varying degrees of *natural utility* and of *man-made utility*. The latter, in which alone the idea of labor is implicit, is the sole subject of human transactions; and, without in any way taking exception to the famous and useful formula of J. B. Say: "Products are exchanged for products," I accept the following as being more scientifically accurate: *Labor is exchanged for labor,* or rather, *services are exchanged for services.*

This does not mean that a given amount of labor is exchanged for another on the basis of the time or effort required to perform it, or that he who offers an hour's pains or expends a quantity of effort sufficient to register one hundred degrees on the dynamometer can always demand that a like amount of effort be expended for him in return. *Time spent* and *effort exerted* are two of the elements that have a bearing on the appraisal of labor, but they are not the only ones. There are also the questions of how disagreeable the work is, how dangerous, how difficult, how much it requires in the way of intelligence and foresight, and even how successfully it has been performed. Where free and voluntary transactions are the rule, where property rights are completely assured, every man has complete control over his own labor, and is therefore free to exchange it at his own price. His willingness to accept the demands of the other party to the transaction ends at the point where it is more to his advantage to retain possession of the product of his own labor. There is also a limit to his demands. This is the point at which the other party to the transaction finds it to his interest not to make the exchange.

There are in society as many economic strata, so to speak, as there are gradations in the established rates of compensation. The

most poorly paid of all types of labor is that which least rises above
the purely mechanical, animal level. This is in accord with providential intent and is at once just, useful, and inevitable. The
unskilled laborer soon reaches that *limit to his demands* to which
I have just referred, for there is no one who cannot perform this
purely mechanical type of labor; and he himself is soon pushed to
the *limit where he must accept others' demands,* for he is incapable of performing for himself the intelligent labor that his wants
require. The *time spent* and the *muscular strength expended,*
which are attributes of matter, are the only bases for determining
the remuneration due this kind of physical labor, and that is why
it is usually paid *by the day.* All industrial progress consists in
replacing, in every product, a certain amount of *man-made,* and
consequently *onerous, utility* by the same amount of *natural,* and
consequently *gratuitous, utility.* It follows that, if there is any one
class in society whom free competition is more likely to benefit
than any other, it is the laboring class. What would be its lot if the
forces of Nature and the techniques and tools of production were
not constantly employed, thanks to competition, in making available to all *gratis* the results of their combined action? The mere
day laborer is not capable of putting heat, gravitation, and elasticity to his own use. He does not invent the techniques, nor does
he possess the tools, by which these forces are exploited. When
these discoveries are first made, their inventors are very well paid
for their labor, which requires a high degree of intelligence. In
other words, this labor of theirs is rated as equal to a tremendous
amount of unskilled labor; that is, the thing they produce is
expensive. But competition intervenes; the price of the product
falls; the harnessing of the services of Nature benefits no longer
the producer, but the consumer; and the pay for the labor involved approximates that of labor whose pay is reckoned in terms
of its duration. Thus, the common store of gratuitous utility
steadily increases. Products of all kinds tend to assume, and do in
fact assume, more and more every day, that form of *gratuitous
utility* under which we enjoy water, air, and light. Thus, the
general standard of living tends to rise, and inequalities tend to
diminish; therefore, apart from the action of the law of popula-

tion, the lowest class of society is the one that, potentially, should improve most rapidly. But we have said, "apart from the action of the law of population," and thus we return to our subject.

Let us imagine a basin into which an inlet, which keeps growing in size, pours an increasingly large stream of water. If no other factors are involved, the level of water in the basin will steadily rise; but if the sides of the basin are flexible, so that they can expand or contract, it is obvious that the water level will depend upon the combined action of these two factors. The level will fall, no matter how much larger a volume of water the inlet pours into the basin, if the basin's capacity increases even more rapidly; it will rise if the circumference of this reservoir widens at a relatively slower rate, and it will rise even more rapidly if the sides of the reservoir remain the same, and still more if they contract.

This illustration aptly depicts the stratum of society to which, admittedly, the great mass of humanity belongs, and gives us an indication of the probable fate in store for it. Its remuneration, that is, the objects that can satisfy its wants and provide its sustenance, is represented by the water flowing through the variable inlet. The flexible sides of the reservoir represent the increase or decrease of population. It is certain [4] that the means of existence reach it in constantly increasing amount, but it is also certain that its circumference can expand even more rapidly. Consequently, the way of life which this class enjoys will be more or less favorable, on a higher or a lower plane, in proportion as the law of limitation, morally and intelligently applied as a preventive check, holds within bounds the maximum physiologically potential reproduction. There is a limit beyond which the numbers of the working class cannot rise: the point at which the sums available for their remuneration are not sufficient to support them. But there is no limit to their possible progress, which depends upon only two factors, and one of these, wealth, is steadily increasing, while the other, population, can be controlled at will.

All that we have just said about the lowest stratum of society, which performs the hardest and most unskilled type of labor, applies as well to all the higher strata, whose relative status is in inverse ratio, so to speak, to the degree of physical and unskilled labor that their work requires them to do. Considering each class apart from the others, we find that the same general laws apply to all. In every one of them there is the same conflict between the physiological power of reproduction and the moral power of self-restraint. The only variable from one class to another is the point at which these two forces meet, the height at which the scale of remuneration and the mores of each particular class fix that limit on population which we call the *means of existence.*

But if we consider the various social strata, no longer individually, but collectively and in their mutual relations, I believe that we can discern that the two forces have precisely the opposite tendency, and this is certainly the explanation of the actual situation of mankind. We have demonstrated how all economic phenomena, and especially the law of competition, tend to level all classes. Theoretically this seems to us incontestable. Since no special advantage of Nature, no ingenious technique, none of the implements by which these techniques are put to use, can remain the permanent monopoly of their producers as such; since the product of their labor, by an inevitable dispensation of Providence, tends to become the common, gratuitous, and consequently equal heritage of all mankind; it is clear that the most impoverished class is the one that derives the greatest *relative* advantage from the admirable operation of the laws of social economy. Just as the poor man is treated as generously in regard to the air he breathes as the rich man, so he becomes the rich man's equal in regard to all that part of the value of commodities which is constantly being eliminated by progress. There is, then, in mankind a basic tendency toward *equality.* I do not mean here a tendency to desire equality, but a tendency to achieve it. Nevertheless, equality has not been achieved or else is being achieved so slowly that when we compare two widely separated ages we can hardly discern that any forward steps have been taken at all. They are, indeed, so little in evidence that many observers refuse to admit their existence, although mistakenly, to be sure. What stands in the way of this intermingling of classes at a common and steadily rising level?

I do not believe that we need look elsewhere for the answer

than at the various degrees of *foresight* that each class of society evidences in respect to the question of population. The law of limitation, as we have said, is available to all men in its *moral* and *preventive aspects.* Man, as we have also said, is perfectible, and, as he progresses, he makes more intelligent use of this law. It is therefore natural that the more enlightened a class, the more effective the measures it adopts, the more considerable the sacrifices it imposes upon itself, in order to maintain its own population at a level in keeping with its *means of existence.*

If the science of statistics were sufficiently advanced, it would probably turn this theoretical conjecture of mine into a certainty by showing that early marriages are less frequent in the upper than in the lower strata of society. Now, if such is the case, it is easy to understand how, in the great market place of society where all classes offer their respective services to the highest bidder, where all types of labor are exchanged, unskilled labor is always in greater supply than skilled, intelligent labor. And this explains the persistence of that social inequality which so many other powerful forces constantly tend to eliminate.

The theory that we have just expounded in this brief fashion leads to this practical observation, namely, that the best forms of philanthropy, the best social institutions, are those that, working in accord with the providential plan as the social harmonies reveal it to us—which is equality along with constant progress—succeed in distributing among all ranks of humanity, and especially the lowest, the gifts of knowledge, reason, morality, and foresight.

We say "institutions," because the fact is that foresight springs as much from the necessities of one's situation as from purely intellectual considerations. There are certain systems of property or, rather, of production, that encourage, more than others, the acquisition of what the economists call a knowledge of the market, and consequently of *foresight.* It seems certain, for example, that sharecropping,* much more than the system of renting land at a fixed rate,[5] encourages the lower classes to apply the preventive check to the rising tide of population. A family of sharecroppers

---

* [In French, *le métayage,* as distinguished from *le fermage.* Cf. chap. 1, p. 18.— TRANSLATOR.]

is in a far better position than a family of day laborers to realize the inconveniences of early marriage and of excessive reproduction.

We speak, too, of "forms of philanthropy." For indeed, charity, while it can be of immediate and local benefit, can have only a very limited effect, if not, in fact, a bad effect, upon the permanent well-being of the working class; for it does not develop, may indeed paralyze, the very virtue most able to improve working-class conditions, namely, the virtue of *foresight*. The encouragement of wholesome attitudes, and above all of habits that indicate a certain amount of self-respect, is the greatest and most lasting service that can be rendered the lower classes.

The *means of existence*, we cannot repeat too often, are not a fixed quantity; they depend upon one's way of life, on public opinion, on *habits*. On every rung of the social ladder there is the same repugnance to moving a step down from the position to which one has become accustomed as can be felt by those on the lowest rung. Perhaps, indeed, the anguish experienced by the titled nobility at the sight of their scions' being lost among the bourgeoisie is keener than that felt by the bourgeois whose sons become manual laborers, or by the manual laborers whose children are reduced to beggary. The *habit* of certain comforts, of a certain dignity in one's way of life, is therefore one of the strongest of incentives for the exercise of foresight; and if the working class once rises to a certain level of satisfactions, it will be unwilling to descend, even though, in order to preserve its position and to maintain a wage scale in keeping with its new habits, it must resort to the infallible means of preventive limitation.

It is for this reason that I regard as one of the most admirable examples of real philanthropy the decision apparently made by many manufacturers and landowners in England to pull down their mud and thatch cottages and to erect in their place brick houses that are clean, spacious, well-lighted, well-ventilated, and appropriately furnished. If this measure were to be generally adopted, it would raise the tone of the working class and turn into real wants what are now only items of relative luxury; it would raise that limit which we call the *means of existence*, and, consequently, the *wage scale* at its lower level. Why not? The poorest class in civilized countries is far above the poorest class among savage peoples. It has risen so far; why should it not rise even higher?

Yet we must entertain no illusions. Progress can be made only slowly, for it must be, to some degree, *general*. We might imagine that it could be achieved rapidly in one part of the world, if different peoples did not influence one another. But such is not the case. There exists for the human race a great law of *solidarity*, which applies to progress as well as to decline. If in England, for example, the condition of the workers were to be noticeably improved as a result of a general rise in wages, French industry would have a better chance of outstripping its rival, and by its success would slow down the trend toward improved conditions on the other side of the Channel. It would seem that Providence is unwilling that one people should rise beyond certain limits above another. Thus, in the great whole of human society, as in its most minute details, we always find that there are admirable and unyielding forces that tend, in the last analysis, to turn over to the masses what were once individual or group advantages, and to bring all such special cases down to a common level, which, like the ocean when the tide is running, is both everywhere even and yet constantly rising.

In summary, given perfectibility, which is man's distinctive characteristic, and the action of competition and the law of limitation being known, the destiny of the human race, at least here on earth, may, it seems to us, be predicted in these terms: (1) a simultaneous rise in the level of all classes of society, or in the general level of mankind; (2) a gradual elimination of all class differences, as far as is consistent with absolute justice; (3) a reduction in the relative size of the highest and the lowest social strata, and an increase in the middle classes. One might say that these laws must bring about absolute equality. But they will not, any more than an asymptote, infinitely extended, would ever meet the curve which it constantly approaches. . . . .[6]

17

Private and Public Services

Services are exchanged for *services.*

The *equivalence* of services results from voluntary exchange and the free bargaining that precedes it.

In other words, every service tendered society *is worth* as much as any other service to which society attaches equal importance, provided that all *bids* and all *asking prices* are made, compared, and discussed in complete *freedom.*

There is no use in quibbling or making subtle distinctions. It is impossible to conceive of the idea of value without associating with it the idea of freedom.

When no violence, no coercion, no fraud is introduced to impair the equivalence of services, it may be said that *justice* prevails.

This does not mean that mankind will then have reached a state of perfection, for freedom always leaves room for errors in individual judgment. Man is often the dupe of his own opinions and passions, nor does he always rank his desires in their most reasonable order. We have seen that a service may be assigned a value that has no reasonable relation to its utility; we need only give certain desires priority over others. Only as our intelligence, our good sense, and our standards improve, shall we strike the ideal balance, putting every service in its proper moral place, if I may so express myself. A worthless article, a childish show, an immoral pleasure may command a high price in one country and be scorned and frowned upon in another. The equivalence of services is therefore something other than a just appraisal of their utility. Nevertheless, in this regard, it is freedom and a sense of responsibility that correct and improve our tastes, our desires, our satisfactions, and our judgment.

In every country in the world there is a class of services that, in the manner in which they are performed, distributed, and paid for, develop in a way quite different from that of private or voluntary services. These are *public services*.

When a want assumes a sufficiently general and widespread character to be called a *public want,* it may appear fitting to all those belonging to a given group (municipality, province, or nation) to provide for the satisfaction of this want through joint action or delegation of authority. In this case the citizens appoint functionaries to perform and make available throughout the community the particular service in question, and they provide for its payment through an assessment that, at least in principle, is commensurate with the means of each member.

Basically, the original elements of the social economy are not necessarily altered by this particular form of exchange, especially when the free consent of all parties is assumed. It is still an exchange of efforts, of services. The functionaries labor to satisfy the wants of the taxpayers; and the taxpayers labor to satisfy the wants of the functionaries. The relative value of these reciprocal services is determined by a procedure that we shall have occasion to examine; but the essential elements of exchange, at least theoretically, remain intact.

Therefore, certain writers, whose opinion has been biased by the sight of crushing and abusive taxation, have been wrong in considering as *lost* all values allocated to public services.[1] This sweeping condemnation will not bear analysis. In so far as *loss* or *gain* is concerned, *public service* does not in any way differ, scientifically considered, from *private service.* Whether I guard my land myself or pay a man to guard it or pay the state to have it guarded for me, does not alter the fact that I make a sacrifice for the sake of an advantage. One way or another, to be sure, I give up something that has cost me effort, but I receive protection in return. This is not a loss, but an exchange.

Will someone object that I surrender a physical object and in return receive nothing that has either body or form? This would be falling back into the erroneous notion of value. As long as value was attributed to matter, not to services, it was necessarily believed that all public services were without value, that is, that they represented an actual loss. Later, when political economists wavered between true and false notions of value, they also necessarily wavered between true and false notions of taxation.

If taxation does not necessarily constitute a loss, even less does it necessarily constitute an act of plunder.[2] In modern societies plunder by taxation is undoubtedly practiced on an exceedingly large scale; and, as we shall see, it is one of the most active of all the elements that upset the equivalence of services and disturb the harmony of interests. But the best way to combat and destroy the abuses of taxation is to avoid the extreme position that represents it as being *inherently* spoliative and extortionate.

Thus, considered in themselves, in their own nature, in their normal state, and apart from all abuses, *public services* are, like *private services,* purely and simply acts of exchange.

But the procedures by which, in these two forms of exchange, services are compared, bargained for, transmitted, balanced, and evaluated are so different in themselves and in their effects that the reader will permit me, I am sure, to treat this difficult subject in some detail, since it is one of the most interesting that can be presented for the consideration of economists and statesmen. Indeed, this is the connecting link between economics and government. It is here that we find the origin and the import of that most grievous error ever to infect the science of political economy, the error of identifying society with government—*society,* the *whole* that includes both private services and public services, and *government,* that mere fraction of the whole which includes only public services.

When, unfortunately, following the teaching of Rousseau and of all his faithful disciples, the French republicans, we use interchangeably the words "government" and "society," we are deciding by implication, a priori, and without study of the facts, that the state can and must absorb all private activity, all individual liberty and responsibility; we are deciding that all private services must be converted into public services, that the social order is a mere convention that owes its existence to the law; we are declaring ourselves in favor of the omnipotence of the lawgiver and the downfall of humanity.

But what we actually observe is that public services or government action increases or decreases according to time, place, or circumstances, from the communism of Sparta or the Paraguay missions to the individualism of the United States, with French centralization as a midpoint along the way.

The first question to be asked, then, as we begin the study of political science is this:

What are the services that should remain in the realm of private activity? What are those that should fall within the domain of public or collective activity?

That question amounts to this:

Within the great circle that we call "society," what should be the circumference of the smaller circle we call "government"?

It is evident that this question is connected with political economy, since it requires the comparative study of two very different forms of exchange.

Once this problem is solved, there still remains another: How can public services best be organized? We shall not consider this question, since it falls entirely within the field of government.

Let us examine the essential differences between *private services* and *public services,* since this is a necessary preliminary to determining what should be the logical line of demarcation between them.

This entire book up to the present chapter has been devoted to showing the evolution of *private services.* We have seen that it is, implicitly or explicitly, based on this formula: *You do this for me, and I will do that for you;* which implies a double and mutual consent regarding what is given and what is received. The notions of barter, exchange, appraisal, value, cannot, therefore, be conceived of without *freedom,* nor freedom without *responsibility.* Each party to an exchange consults, at his own risk and peril, his wants, his needs, his tastes, his desires, his means, his attitudes, his convenience—all the elements of his situation; and nowhere have we denied that in the exercise of free will there is the possibility of error, the possibility of an unreasonable or a foolish choice. The fault is imputable, not to the principle of exchange, but to the imperfection of human nature; and the remedy is to be found only in *responsibility* itself (that is, in freedom), since it is the source of all experience. To introduce coercion into exchange, to destroy free will on the pretext that men may make mistakes, would not improve things, unless it can be proved that the agent empowered to apply the coercion is exempt from the imperfection of our nature, is not subject to passion or error, does not belong to humanity. Is it not evident, on the contrary, that this would be tantamount not only to putting responsibility in the wrong place, but, even worse, to destroying it, at least in so far as its most precious attribute is concerned, that is, as a rewarding, retributive, experimental, corrective, and, consequently, progressive force? We have also seen that free exchange, or services voluntarily received and voluntarily rendered, constantly increases, thanks to the effect of competition, the relative proportion of gratuitous utility to onerous utility, the domain of common wealth in relation to the domain of private property; and we have thus come to recognize in freedom the power that in every way promotes equality, or social harmony.

As for the forms of free exchange, there is no need to describe them, for, if coercion assumes endless forms, freedom has only one. Once again, the free and voluntary transfer of services from one person to another can be defined in these simple words: Give me this, and I will give you that. Do this for me, and I will do that for you. *Do ut des; facio ut facias.*

This is not the way that *public services* are exchanged. In their case, coercion is to some degree inevitable; and we must expect to find infinite varieties, from the most complete despotism to the most widespread and direct participation by all the citizens.

Although this political ideal has never been fully realized anywhere, and perhaps never will be except in imagination, we shall nevertheless assume that it has been. For what do we seek to discover? The modifications that *services* undergo when they enter the public domain; and, for scientific purposes, we must abstract from all local and particular acts of injustice, in order to consider public service in its essence and under the most legitimate conditions. In a word, we must study the transformation it undergoes by the very fact of becoming public, apart from the causes that have made it public and the abuses that may enter into its administration.

The procedure is as follows:

The citizens appoint representatives. These representatives meet and decide by majority vote that a certain kind of want—education, for example—can no longer be satisfied by the citizens' own free efforts or free exchange, but is to be provided for by a class of functionaries specially assigned to this task. This is the procedure for *rendering* the service. As for the service *received,* since the state has availed itself of the time and talents of a new group of functionaries for the benefit of the citizens, it must also take from the citizens what is needed to support the functionaries. This is accomplished by means of a general tax or assessment.

In every civilized country this tax is paid in the form of money. It is hardly necessary to remark that behind this money there is labor. In the last analysis, it is a payment in kind. Ultimately, the citizens work for the functionaries, and the functionaries for the citizens, even as in their voluntary services the citizens work for one another.

We make this observation to guard against a very commonly accepted monetary fallacy. We often hear it said that the money functionaries receive falls back, like a refreshing rain, on the citizens, and the inference is drawn that this so-called rain is an additional benefit accruing to the service. This reasoning has been used to justify the most parasitical activities. Those who reason thus do not realize that if the service had remained a private one, the money, instead of going first to the state treasury and from there to the functionaries, would have gone directly from those receiving the service to those performing it voluntarily and from them would likewise have fallen, like a gentle rain, upon the entire community. The fallacy in this kind of reasoning becomes evident when we look beyond the circulation of currency to the fundamental fact of labor exchanged for labor, of services exchanged for services. In the realm of government operation it may happen that functionaries receive services from the citizens without rendering services in return; in that case the taxpayer suffers a loss, no matter what illusion the circulation of bank notes may create.

In any case, let us return to our analysis.

This, then, is exchange under a new form. Exchange implies ultimately two activities: *giving* and *receiving*. Let us see how the change from private to public status affects the transaction from the twofold point of view of services *rendered* and services *received*.

In the first place, we note that always or nearly always public service eliminates, in law or in fact, private services of the same nature. When the state undertakes a service, it generally takes pains to decree that no one except itself shall render it, especially if it anticipates revenue from the venture. In France the postal service, tobacco, playing cards, gunpowder, etc., etc., are cases in point. But even if the state did not take this precaution, the end result would be the same. What industry can undertake the rendering of a service to the public that the state performs for nothing? We rarely find anyone seeking a means of livelihood in the private teaching of law or medicine, the construction of highways, the breeding of thoroughbred horses, the founding of schools for the arts and crafts, the clearing of Algerian land, the establishment of museums, etc., etc. The reason is that the public will not buy what the state offers it for nothing. As M. Cormenin* said, the shoe industry would fail very quickly, even though the first article of the Constitution declared it inviolate, if the government were to decide to give everyone shoes free of charge.

The truth is, the word "gratuitous" as applied to public services contains the grossest, and, I may add, the most childish of fallacies. I marvel at the public's extreme gullibility in being taken in by this word. People ask us, "Are you against *gratuitous* education? *Gratuitous* stud farms?"

* [Louis Marie de la Haye, Vicomte de Cormenin (1788–1868), French jurist and political pamphleteer.—Translator.]

Quite the contrary! I'm for them and I would also be for gratuitous food and gratuitous housing. . . . if these were possible.

But the only thing that is really gratuitous is what does not cost anyone anything. Now, public services cost everybody something; the reason they cost the receiver nothing is that everybody has paid for them in advance. The person who has already paid his share of the general assessment will certainly not pay again in order to have the same service performed for him by private industry.

Thus, public service replaces private service. It adds nothing to the nation's general industry nor to its wealth. It has functionaries do what private industry would have done. It remains for us to determine which of the two systems will involve the greater incidental inconvenience. The purpose of this chapter is to answer these questions.

When the satisfaction of a want becomes the object of a public service, it is in large part removed from the sphere of individual freedom and responsibility. The individual is no longer free to buy what he wishes, when he wishes, to consult his means, his convenience, his situation, his tastes, his moral standards, any more than he can determine the relative order in which it seems reasonable to him to provide for his wants. Willy-nilly, he must accept from society, not the amount of service that he deems useful, as he does with private services, but the amount that the government has seen fit to prepare for him, whatever be its quantity and quality. Perhaps he does not have enough bread to satisfy his hunger, and yet the government takes from him a part of this bread, which would be indispensable to him, in order to give him instruction or public spectacles that he neither needs nor desires. He ceases to exercise free control over the satisfaction of his own wants, and, no longer having any responsibility for satisfying them, he naturally ceases to concern himself with doing so. Foresight becomes as useless to him as experience. He becomes less his own master; he has lost, to some extent, his free will; he has less initiative for self-improvement; he is less of a man. Not only does he no longer judge for himself in a given case, but he loses the habit of judging for himself. This moral torpor, which takes possession of him, likewise takes possession of his fellow citizens, and we have seen entire nations fall in this way into disastrous inertia.[3]

As long as a set of wants and corresponding satisfactions remains in the realm of free choice, every man is a law unto himself in this regard and does as he sees fit. This seems natural and just, since no two men find themselves in identical circumstances, nor is there any one man whose circumstances do not vary from day to day. As long as there is free choice, all the human faculties—comparison, judgment, foresight—continue to be exercised. As long as there is free choice, every good decision brings its reward; every error, its punishment; and experience, that harsh complement of foresight, fulfills its mission, so that society cannot fail to improve.

But when the service becomes public, all individual rules of conduct cease to exist and become merged and generalized in a single written law, which is coercive, which is the same for everyone, which makes no provision for special situations, and which atrophies the noblest faculties of human nature.

If state intervention takes from us our control over ourselves in respect to the services we receive, it does so even more completely in respect to the services we perform for the state in return. This counterpart, this second element of exchange, is likewise withdrawn from the domain of freedom and is, instead, regulated without reference to particular cases by a law enacted in advance, carried out by force, and from which no one is exempt. In a word, as the services rendered us by the state are imposed upon us, those it demands from us in return are also imposed upon us, and, indeed, in all languages bear the name of *imposts*.

At this point countless difficulties and inconveniences present themselves in theory; for in practice the state surmounts all obstacles by means of armed force, which is the inevitable corollary of every law. But (to remain in the realm of theory) the conversion of a private service into a public one raises the following serious questions:

Will the state under all circumstances demand of every citizen a tax *equivalent* to the services it renders? This would be justice, and this, very definitely, is the *equivalence* that almost unfailingly manifests itself in free and voluntary transactions and in the price arrived at in the *bargaining* that precedes them. If the state, therefore, were desirous of achieving this kind of *equivalence,* which is justice in the most exact sense, it would not be worth while to remove any given type of services from the domain of private enterprise. But the state does not care about this and cannot care about it. One cannot *haggle* with functionaries. The law follows a uniform pattern and cannot stipulate conditions for each particular case. At the very most, that is, where it is conceived in the spirit of justice, it seeks to establish a kind of average and approximate equivalence between the two types of services exchanged. Two principles of taxation, the one proportional and the other progressive, have seemed, on different grounds, to carry this approximation to its ultimate limits. But the most superficial reflection will be enough to show that proportional taxation cannot, any more than progressive taxation, bring about a rigorously accurate equivalence of services exchanged. Public services, therefore, not only doubly deprive the private citizen of his freedom in regard to both services received and services rendered, but also commit the wrong of distorting the value of these services.

A far more than minor drawback to public services is that they destroy the principle of responsibility or at the very least misdirect it. But, for man, responsibility is everything! It is his motive force, his teacher, his rewarder and punisher. Without responsibility man no longer has free will, he is no longer perfectible, he is no longer a moral being, he learns nothing, he is nothing. He falls into inertia and no longer counts except as a unit of the herd.

If it is a misfortune when the sense of responsibility is extinguished in the individual, it is an even more serious misfortune when the state develops an exaggerated sense of its own responsibility. Man, however degraded, is always sufficiently enlightened to perceive the source of the good and the evil that come to him; and when the state takes charge of everything, it becomes responsible for everything. When subjected to these artificial arrangements, a people in distress can only blame its government; and its only remedy, its only political recourse, is to overthrow it. Hence an inevitable succession of revolutions. I say "inevitable," for under this regime the people necessarily must suffer; and the reason is that the system of public services, over and beyond the fact that it distorts values, which is an injustice, also brings about an inevitable loss of wealth, which is ruination and injustice and the cause of suffering and resentment—four disastrous incitements of social disorder that, combined with loss of responsibility, can not fail to produce those political convulsions of which we have been the unfortunate witnesses for more than fifty years.

I would prefer not to digress from my subject. Yet I cannot refrain from observing that, when things are organized in this way, when the government, by turning one free and voluntary transaction after another into a public service, has come to assume gigantic proportions, there is reason to fear that revolutions, which are in themselves so great an evil, will cease even to have the advantage of being a remedy, except by dint of repeated experience. The loss of responsibility has perverted public opinion. The people, accustomed to calling upon the state for everything, accuse the government, not of doing too much, but of not doing enough. They overthrow it and replace it by another, to which they do not say: *Do less,* but: *Do more;* and thus the abyss that yawns before us becomes ever deeper.

Does the moment finally come when men's eyes are opened? Do they feel that they must set about reducing the prerogatives and responsibilities of the state? Then they are stopped by other difficulties. On the one hand, *vested interests* are aroused and unite; and the citizens hesitate to disturb all those functionaries who have been enjoying an artificial livelihood. On the other hand, the citizens have lost their capacity for initiative. At the very instant that they are about to regain the liberty that they have so ardently pursued, they become frightened; they reject it. Do you offer them the freedom to provide their own education? [4] They fear that all learning will be lost. Do you offer them freedom of worship? They fear that atheism will make inroads everywhere. They have been told so many times that all religion, all wisdom, all knowledge, all enlightenment, all morality reside in the state or are derived from the state!

But I shall come back to these considerations later and shall now return to my subject.

We have investigated the true role of competition in the formation of wealth. We have seen that it consists in passing its beneficial results on from the producer to the rest of mankind, in turning the progress it makes to the profit of the commonwealth, in steadily increasing the domain of gratuitous utility and consequently in bringing about a higher degree of equality.

But when private services become public, they are exempt from competition, and this admirable harmony is no longer manifested. The public official, in fact, is deprived of the stimulus that urges us on to progress. And how can progress work for the common good when it is nonexistent? The civil servant acts, not under the spur of self-interest, but under the shadow of the law. The law says to him: "You will render the public a certain fixed service, and you will receive from the public a certain other fixed service in return." A little more or a little less zeal changes nothing in these fixed terms. Self-interest, on the other hand, whispers these words into the ear of the free worker: "The more you do for others, the more others will do for you." In this case the remuneration depends entirely on how great and how intelligent is the effort made. Undoubtedly, group morale, the desire for advancement, a sense of duty can serve as active stimuli for the government official. But never can they replace the irresistible drive of self-interest. All experience confirms this line of reasoning. Everything that falls within the realm of bureaucracy is more or less static; it is doubtful whether teaching is better today than in the time of Francis I, and I do not think that anyone would propose comparing the activity that goes on in a government bureau with that of a private industry.

In proportion, then, as private services enter the category of public services, they lose momentum, at least to some degree, and become sterile, not to the detriment of those rendering the services (their pay does not change), but to the detriment of the whole community.

While these disadvantages, which I have merely sketched briefly, trusting to the reader's ingenuity to work out the details, are tremendous from the moral, political, and economic point of view, nevertheless, there is sometimes an advantage in substituting collective action for individual action. There are certain types of services of which the principal merit consists in regularity and uniformity. It is even possible, under certain conditions, for this change to public status to effect an economy of resources and, for a given satisfaction, to spare the community a certain amount of effort. The question to be answered, therefore, is this: What services are to remain in the realm of private initiative? What services are to be provided by collective or public activity? The study that we have just made of the essential differences between these two types of services will make easier the solution of this important problem.

First of all, is there some principle by which we may distinguish between what can legitimately be put within the sphere of collective activity and what should remain within the sphere of private activity?

I shall begin by stating that I call *collective activity* that great organization which finds its rule in the *law* and its means of execution in *force*, in other words, *government*. Let me not be told that free and voluntary associations also involve collective activity. Let it not be supposed that I give to the words *private activity* the sense of *isolated activity*. On the contrary: I assert that free and voluntary association still belongs in the domain of private activity, for it is one of the most powerful forms of exchange. It does not impair the equivalence of services; it does not affect the free appraisal of value; it does not destroy free will; it does not eliminate competition or the effects of competition; in a word, it does not have coercion as its principle.

But government action involves coercion by its very nature. It necessarily invokes the doctrine of *compelle intrare*.* It proceeds

* [Luke XIV, 23: "And the lord said unto the servant, Go out into the highways and hedges, and *constrain them to come in*." These words from the Parable of the Great Supper have historically been used as a pretext to force someone to do a thing against his will on the ground that it is to his ultimate good. Its greatest abuse was as a justification for the persecution of the heretics.—TRANSLATOR.]

by virtue of a *law*, and all men must submit, for law implies *punishment*. I do not believe that anyone can challenge these premises; for they have the support of the most impressive of all authorities, the authority of universal practice. Everywhere there are laws and the physical force to bring the recalcitrant into line.

And this, doubtless, is the origin of the axiom invoked by those who, identifying *government* with *society*, believe that the latter is, like the former, a mere convention: "Men, by joining together in society, have sacrificed a part of their liberty in order to preserve the rest."

Obviously this axiom is false when it is applied to free and voluntary transactions. When two men, with a view to their personal advantage, exchange their services or unite their efforts in preference to working alone, where can one see a sacrifice of their liberty in such an arrangement? Is it sacrificing one's liberty to put it to better use?

At the very most one could say: Men sacrifice a part of their liberty in order to preserve the rest, not at all when they unite in a society, but when they place themselves under a government, since the necessary mode of action of a government is force.

Now, even with this modification, the so-called axiom is still a fallacy, as long as the government stays within its legitimate prerogatives.

But what are these prerogatives?

Their scope and their limits are indicated to us by this special characteristic of having force as a necessary adjunct. I therefore declare: *Government acts only by the intervention of force; hence, its action is legitimate only where the intervention of force is itself legitimate.*

Now, force may be used legitimately, not in order to sacrifice liberty, but to safeguard it.

Consequently, the axiom, once alleged to be the basis of political science, which we have already proved to be fallacious for society, is also fallacious when applied to government. It is always with a sense of joy that I see these dismal theoretical discords disappear when subjected to careful analysis.

In what case is the use of force legitimate? There is one, and, I believe, only one: *the case of legitimate defense.* If this is so, the justification of government has been found, as well as the rational limit of its prerogatives.[5]

What is the right of the individual? The right to carry on free and voluntary transactions with his fellow men, who consequently have the same right. When is this right violated? When one of the parties encroaches upon the other's liberty. In that case it is incorrect to say, as is often done: "These are excesses; these are abuses of liberty!" We must say: "Liberty is lacking; liberty has been destroyed." There has been excessive use of liberty, undoubtedly, if we consider only the aggressor; but destruction of liberty if we consider the victim, or even if we consider, as we should, the phenomenon in its entirety.

The right of the man whose liberty is attacked, or, what is tantamount to the same thing, whose property, capabilities, or labor is attacked, is to defend them, *even by force;* and this is what is done by all men everywhere, whenever they can.

This is the origin of the right of any number of men whatsoever to join together, to associate, in order to defend, *even by their joint force,* the individual's liberty and property.

But the individual has no right to use force for any other end. I cannot legitimately *force* my fellow men to be industrious, sober, thrifty, generous, learned, or pious; but I can force them to be just.

For the same reason, the collective force cannot be legitimately employed to foster the love of labor, sobriety, thrift, generosity, learning, religious faith; but it can be legitimately employed to further the rule of justice, to defend every man's rights.

For where can we find the origin of collective rights except in the rights of the individual?

It is the unfortunate obsession of our age to wish to give pure abstractions a life of their own, to imagine a city apart from the people who live in it, mankind independently of the individual men who constitute it, a whole aside from its component parts, collective life without the individual units that comprise it. One might just as well say: "Here is a man. Imagine his limbs, his vital organs, his body and his soul, all the elements of which he is formed, to be destroyed. He still remains a man."

If a right does not exist for any one of the individuals whom collectively we designate, for the sake of brevity, as a *nation,* how can it exist for that fraction of the nation having merely delegated rights, which is the government? How can individuals delegate rights that they do not possess?

We must therefore consider this incontestable truth as the fundamental principle of political science:

Among individuals the intervention of force is legitimate only in the case of legitimate defense. A collective body of individuals can legally have recourse to force only within the same limitations.

Now, it is in the very nature of government to act upon its citizens by way of force. Hence, it can have no rationally justifiable functions other than the legitimate defense of the rights of the individual; it can be called upon only to safeguard the liberty and the property of all the citizens.

Note that, when a government goes beyond these limits, it sets out upon an endless course and can never escape the consequences, i.e., that it not only goes beyond its proper function, but also destroys it, which is the most monstrous of contradictions.

In fact, when the state has enforced respect for that fixed, invariable line which separates the rights of one citizen from those of another, when it has maintained justice for all, what more can it do without itself overstepping the boundary it has been called upon to protect, without destroying with its own hands, and by force, the liberty and the property entrusted to its keeping? Beyond the upholding of justice, I defy anyone to imagine a case in which government intervention would not be an act of injustice. Protest as much as you like that its acts are inspired by the purest philanthropy, are designed as incentives to virtue and industry, are bonuses, favors, direct protection, so-called gratuitous gifts, alleged acts of generosity; behind these fine appearances, or if you will, these fine realities, I will show you other less gratifying realities: the rights of some violated for the advantage of others, liberties sacrificed, property rights usurped, capabilities curtailed, acts of plunder perpetrated. And can the world witness a more sorry, a more lamentable spectacle than the sight of the public forces of law and order engaged in committing the very crimes that it was their duty to suppress?

In theory, it is enough that the government have the necessary instrumentality of *force* at hand for us to know what private services can legitimately be converted into *public services*. They are those services whose object is the maintenance of liberty, property, and individual rights, the prevention of crime—in a word, all that relates to the *public safety*.

Governments also have another function.

In all countries there is a certain amount of public property, some goods used collectively by all the citizens, like rivers, forests, and highways. On the other hand, there are also, unfortunately, debts. It is the government's duty to administer these active and passive parts of the public domain.

Finally, from these two functions stems a third: that of levying the taxes necessary for the efficient administration of *public services*.

Thus, it must watch over the public safety, administer public property, and levy taxes.

Such are, I believe, the reasonable limits within which government functions must be kept or to which they must be reduced.

This opinion, I know, conflicts with many widely accepted ideas.

"What!" people will say; "you propose to reduce the government to the role of judge and policeman? You would deprive it of all initiative? You forbid it to promote and encourage literature, the arts, commerce, navigation, agriculture, moral and religious ideas; you would strip it of its noblest prerogative, that of opening up to the people the road to progress!"

To those who express this opinion, I should like to address several questions.

Where has God implanted the motivating impulse of human actions and the longing for progress? In all men, or only in those men who have received or usurped a legislator's mandate or a bureaucrat's authority? Does not everyone of us carry within himself, within his very being, that indefatigable and boundless motive force which we call *desire?* As our more basic and material wants are satisfied, are not new desires of a higher order constantly forming, overlapping, expanding within us? Does love of the arts, of literature, of science, of moral and religious truth, does the thirst to know the answers to the problems involving our present or future existence, descend from society to the individual, that is, from the abstract to the real, from the merely verbal symbol to sentient and living beings?

If you start with the already absurd assumption that the government is the morally active force and that the nation is passive, are you not putting morals, doctrines, opinions, wealth, everything that makes up the life of the individual, at the mercy of the men who one after another come to power?

Besides, does the state have any resources of its own to perform the tremendous task that you propose to assign to it? Is it not obliged to take everything it spends, down to the last centime, from the citizens themselves? If the state, therefore, asks the individual citizens for the means to carry out its projects, it is because the individual citizens have already produced these means. It is, therefore, a contradiction to allege that the individual citizens are passive and inert. To what end had they created resources? To provide for satisfactions of their own choosing. What, then, is the state doing when it lays its hands on these resources? It does not create satisfactions; it *reallocates* them. It takes them away from the man who has earned them in order to give them to the man who has no right to them. Injustice, which it had a mandate to punish, it organizes into a system.

Will it be said that by reallocating satisfactions, it purifies and elevates them morally, that the wealth which individuals would have squandered on wants of a low order is redirected by the state to highly moral ends? But who will dare affirm that it is advantageous to interfere violently, *by force,* by plunder, with the natural order in which man's wants and desires develop, that it is moral to take a morsel of bread from the hungry peasant in order to provide the city dweller with the dubious morality of a theatrical performance?

Furthermore, wealth is not redistributed without a redistribution of industry and population. Such an arrangement is always, therefore, an artificial and precarious substitute for the solid and normal order that rests upon the immutable laws of Nature.

There are those who believe that a government whose authority is strictly circumscribed is the weaker on that account. It appears to them that numerous functions and numerous agencies give the state the stability of a broader base. But this is purely an illusion. If the state cannot go beyond certain definitely established limits without becoming an instrument of injustice, ruination, and plunder, without upsetting the natural distribution of industry, satisfactions, capital, and manpower, without creating potent causes of unemployment, industrial crises, and poverty, without increasing crime, without having recourse to ever more stringent repressive measures, without stirring up discontent and resentment, how will it derive any guarantee of stability from these accumulated elements of civil disorder?

People complain of men's proneness to revolution. Surely those who make this complaint do not stop to think. When we see private services raided and turned into public services, a third of the wealth that the citizens produce seized by the government, the law made into a weapon of plunder wielded by the citizens themselves, because its object is to impair the equivalence of services on the pretext of stabilizing it; when we see population and industry dislocated by legislative act, an ever deeper abyss yawning between the wealthy and the poor, capital reserves incapable of being formed in sufficient amounts to provide employment for the increasing population, whole classes condemned to the harshest privations; when we see governments, in order to be able to take credit for what little good is done, proclaiming themselves the initiators of every enterprise, and thus accepting responsibility for all that is bad; we wonder only that revolutions are not more frequent and are moved to admiration at the sacrifices that the people are capable of making for the sake of public order and tranquillity.

If only laws and the governments that are the instruments of their enforcement and administration were kept within the limits I have indicated, I wonder from what source revolutions could come. If every citizen were free, he undoubtedly would suffer less; and if, at the same time, the feeling of his own responsibility were brought to bear on him from all sides, how could it occur to him to place the blame for his sufferings upon a legal system, a government, that intervened in his affairs only to the extent of stopping him from committing acts of injustice and protecting him from the unjust acts of others. Have we ever seen a village rise in revolt against its justice of the peace?

The influence of liberty on law and order can be clearly seen in the United States. There, except for the administration of justice and of public property, everything is left to men's free and voluntary transactions, and we instinctively feel that it is the one country in the world where revolutions would have the least reason or opportunity. What advantage, even a seeming one, could the citizens expect to gain by changing the established order by violence, when, on the one hand, that order harms no one, and, on the other, can legally be amended, if the need arises, with the greatest of ease?

I am wrong. There are two potential causes of revolution in the United States: slavery and the high protective tariff. Everyone knows that these two questions are a constant threat to the public peace and to the Union. Now, please note carefully, can any more cogent argument be advanced in favor of my thesis? Do we not see that in these two cases the law is working against its proper purpose? Do we not see that in these instances law and the agents of its enforcement, whose mission should be the protection of liberty and property, are sanctioning, supporting, perpetuating, systematizing, and protecting oppression and plunder? In regard to the question of slavery, the law says: "I shall create an armed force, at the citizens' expense, not to maintain each one in his rights, but to destroy, in the case of some, all rights." In regard to the tariff question the law says: "I shall create an armed force, at the citizens' expense, not to make sure that their transactions are free, but to make sure that they are not free, to impair the equivalence of services, so that one citizen may have the liberty of two, and that another may have none at all. I take it upon myself to perpetrate these injustices, but I shall punish them most severely if the citizens make bold to perpetrate them without my consent."

It is not, therefore, because of a scarcity of laws or civil servants —in other words, of public services—that revolutions are to be feared. On the contrary: it is because of a multiplicity of laws, bureaucrats, and public services. For, by their very nature, public services, the law that regulates them, the force that carries them out, are never impartial. They can and they may be extended without danger, even advantageously, as far as is necessary to assure absolute justice for all; beyond that point they become so many instruments of legalized oppression and plunder, so many causes of disorder, so many incitements to revolution.

Shall I speak of the corrupting immorality that seeps into the veins of the whole body politic when, in principle, the law puts itself at the service of every spoliative impulse? Attend a meeting of the National Assembly when bonuses, subsidies, bounties, restrictions are on the agenda. See with what shameless rapacity everyone tries to make sure of his share of the plunder—plunder to which he would blush to stoop as a private individual. A man who would consider himself a bandit if, pistol in hand, he prevented me from carrying out at the border a transaction that was in conformity with my interests has no scruples in working and voting for a law that replaces his private force with the public force and subjects me, at my own expense, to the same unjust restriction. In this respect, what a sorry sight France presents at the present time! All classes are suffering; yet instead of demanding the abolition, for all time to come, of every act of legal plunder, every class turns to the law and says: "You who can do everything, you who have force at your command, you who turn wrong into right, despoil the other classes to my profit. Force them to buy from me or to pay me a subsidy or to give my children a gratuitous education or to lend me money without interest, etc., etc. . . . . ."

Thus, the law becomes a great school for demoralization; and if anything should surprise us, it is that private theft does not increase more rapidly than it does, when the nation's moral sense is thus perverted even by its own legislation.

What is most deplorable is that plunder, when thus aided

and abetted by the law, with no individual's scruples to stand in its way, eventually becomes quite a learned doctrine which has its professors, its journalists, its eminent authorities, its legislators, its sophisms, and its subtleties. Among the time-honored specious arguments advanced in its favor, this one is worth noting: Other things being equal, an increase in 'demand is advantageous to those supplying a service, since this new ratio between a more active demand and a static supply is what increases the *value* of the service. We therefore draw this conclusion: Plunder is good for everybody. The plundering class is benefited directly; the other classes, by the indirect effect of increased spending. In fact, the plundering class, having become richer, is in a position to enlarge the circle of its satisfactions. It cannot do this without *demanding,* in greater quantity, the *services* of the classes it has plundered. Now, for any service, an increase in demand is an increase in value. Consequently, the classes that have been legally robbed are only too happy to be robbed, since the product of the theft contributes to their employment.

As long as the law did not go beyond plundering the great majority to the profit of a small minority, this argument appeared very plausible and was always invoked with considerable success. "Let us turn over to the rich the taxes levied against the poor," it was said; "in this way we shall add to the capital of the rich. The rich will indulge in luxury, and luxury will provide work for the poor." And everybody, the poor man included, agreed that the recipe was infallible. Because I tried to point out the flaw in it, I was for long regarded, and still am regarded, as an enemy of the working classes.

But since the February Revolution, the poor have had a voice in making the laws. Have they demanded an end to legalized plunder? Not at all. The specious argument of the indirect effect of spending was too deeply implanted in their minds. What, then, have they demanded? That the law, playing no favorites, should now in its turn consent to plunder the rich. They have demanded gratuitous education, interest-free capital advances, state pension funds, progressive taxation, etc., etc. . . . . The rich have begun to cry out: "How scandalous! All is lost! New barbarian hordes have overrun society!" They have put up a desperate resistance to the demands of the poor. At first they fought at the barricades; now they are fighting the battle at the ballot box. But have the rich on that account renounced the policy of plunder? It has never occurred to them. The argument of the indirect beneficial effects of spending continues to serve as their pretext.*

We could, however, point out to them that if, instead of perpetrating plunder through the instrumentality of the law, they perpetrated it directly, their specious argument would lose its force. If, on your own personal authority, you stole a franc from a worker's pocket to help to pay for your admission to the theater, would you perchance have said to this worker, "My friend, this franc is being put into circulation and will provide work for you and your fellow workers"?

And would not the worker have had good reason to reply, "This franc will certainly go into circulation whether you steal it from me or not; it will go to the baker rather than to the stagehand; it will provide me with bread rather than you with a theatrical performance"?

It must be observed, furthermore, that the sophism of the indirect effect of spending could be equally well invoked by the poor. They could say to the rich, "Let the law help us steal from you. We shall consume more cloth, and that will help your factories. We shall consume more meat, and that will help your farms. We shall consume more sugar, and that will help your shipping."

Unhappy, thrice unhappy the nation in which such questions are asked; where it occurs to no one to make the law the rule of justice; where each one seeks only an instrument of theft to use to his own advantage; where all one's intellectual faculties are devoted to finding excuses for plunder in its remote and indirect consequences!

In support of the foregoing reflections, it will perhaps not be without value to quote an extract from the discussion that took place at the meeting of the General Council of Manufacturing, Agriculture, and Commerce on Saturday, April 27, 1850.[6]

---

* [This description of the aftermath of the February Revolution should be compared with the similar passage in chap. 4, pp. 87 ff.—TRANSLATOR.]

18

Disturbing Factors

Where would humanity now be if violence, guile, oppression, and fraud had never at any time or in any form left their ugly mark on man's transactions?

Would justice and liberty have inevitably given rise to inequality and monopoly?

To learn the answer to these questions, it was necessary, it seemed to me, to study the essential nature of human transactions, their origin, their reason, their effects, and the effects arising from these effects on down to the final result; and, for the study to be valid, it was necessary to exclude the contingent disturbances that are produced by injustice, for it will be admitted that injustice does not form an integral part of free and voluntary transactions.

It can well be maintained that it was inevitable that injustice should come into the world, that society could not have escaped it; and, granted man's nature, with his passions, his selfishness, his original ignorance and improvidence, I believe it. Hence, we shall also have to study the nature, origin, and effects of injustice.

But it is nonetheless true that the science of economics must begin by expounding the theory of human transactions on the assumption that they are completely free and voluntary, even as the physiologist expounds the nature and interrelation of our bodily organs without regard for the disturbing factors that modify these interrelations.

We believe that services are exchanged for services; we believe that the great desideratum is the equivalence of the services exchanged.

We believe that this equivalence is most likely to be established when transactions are voluntary and every man is allowed to judge for himself.

We know that men can be mistaken, but we also know that they can correct their errors; and we believe that the longer an error has persisted, the sooner we may expect to see it corrected.

We believe that whatever restricts liberty disturbs the equivalence of services, and that whatever disturbs the equivalence of services produces excessive inequality, the unmerited wealth of some, the no less undeserved poverty of others, a concomitant decrease in the general wealth, as well as hatred, discord, strife, and revolution.

We shall not go so far as to say that liberty—or the equivalence of services—produces absolute equality, for we do not believe in absolutes where man is concerned. But we do believe that liberty tends to bring all men closer together and to provide them with a constantly rising standard of living.

We believe that what inequality may remain, under a free system, is the result of fortuitous circumstances or the consequence of faults or vices, or is compensated for by nonmonetary advantages, and consequently cannot give rise to resentment.

In brief, we believe that *freedom* is *harmony*.

But in order to ascertain whether this harmony exists in reality or is a figment of our imagination, whether we actually observe it or merely long for it, it was necessary to subject free and voluntary transactions to the test of scientific inquiry; it was necessary to study the facts, their interrelations, and their consequences.

This is what we have done.

We have seen that, although countless obstacles stood between man's wants and his satisfactions, so that in isolation he could not have survived, yet, by joint effort, by the division of labor—in a word, by exchange—he has been able to develop enough resources to overcome the first obstacles, to assault the second set and overcome them also, and so on, in ascending scale and more and more rapidly as increased population facilitated exchange.

We have seen that his intelligence places at his disposal means of action that are increasingly numerous, powerful and efficient; that, as capital is accumulated, its absolute share in production rises, but that its relative share falls, whereas for labor both the absolute and the relative shares rise constantly. This is the first, and a most potent, factor in our progress toward equality.

We have seen that the admirable instrument which we call land, that marvelous laboratory in which is prepared everything that serves to feed, clothe, and shelter men, was given them gratis by the Creator; that although nominally it was transformed into private property, yet its productive action could not be appropriated and has remained gratuitous throughout the whole range of human transactions.

We have seen that private property not only has the negative virtue of not encroaching on mankind's common store of goods, but works positively and ceaselessly to increase it. This is the second source of equality, since the more abundant the common store, the more the inequality of private property is eliminated.

We have seen that under the influence of liberty services tend to acquire their normal value, that is, a value proportionate to labor. This is the third source of equality.

We have thus become convinced that a natural level tends to establish itself among men, not by pushing them back toward a lower state, or by keeping them stationary, but by inviting them to a constantly improving way of life.

Finally, we have seen that neither the laws of value, nor those of interest, nor those of rent, nor those of population, nor any other great natural law, can introduce, as has been alleged by those imperfectly grounded in the science of economics, an element of discord into the admirable order of a free society, since, on the contrary, harmony results from the operation of these laws.

On reaching this point, I seem to hear the reader cry out: "This is a good sample of the economists' optimism! Despite the all too obvious presence of hardship, poverty, the condition of the working class, pauperism, deserted children, malnutrition, delinquency, rebellion, inequality, they keep on merrily singing of the harmony of social laws, and turn away their eyes so that the sight of the horrible reality may not disturb the pleasure they take in their system. They, too, like the utopians they censure, run away from the world of reality to take refuge in a dream-world. More illogical than the socialists or even the communists —who see the evil, feel it, decry it, abhor it, and are at fault only in that they propose ineffective, impractical, or visionary remedies—the economists either deny that the evil exists or are insensible of it, if indeed they do not cause it by crying out to our sick society: *'Laissez faire, laissez passer;* everything is for the best in the best of all possible worlds.' "

In the name of the science of political economy, I reject with all my strength such reproaches and such interpretations of our words. We perceive the evil as well as our adversaries. Like them we deplore it; like them we seek to understand the causes; like them we stand ready to combat them. But we formulate the question differently. Society, they say, such as it has been made by the system of free labor and free exchange, that is to say, by the free play of natural laws, is detestable. Hence, we must tear from the machine the offending cog, which is liberty (called by the socialists "competition" and even "anarchistic competition"), and substitute for it by force artificial cogs of our own invention.

Thereupon, millions of social inventions are put forward. This is only natural, for there is endless room for imagination to run its course.

But what we, after studying the providential laws that govern the social order, declare is this: These laws are harmonious. They admit of the existence of evil, for they are set in operation by men, that is, by beings subject to error and pain. But in this mechanism evil too has its mission, which brings about its own limitation and eventual elimination by furnishing man warnings, corrections, experience, enlightenment—all things which can be summed up in the word "progress."

We add: It is not true that freedom prevails among men; it is not true that the laws of Providence operate to their fullest extent, or at least if they do act, their action has been limited to repairing gradually, painfully, the disturbing effects of ignorance and error. Do not accuse us, therefore, when we say *laissez faire;* for we do not mean by this to let men do as they will, even when they do wrong. We mean: Study the laws of Providence, marvel at them, and *allow them to operate*. Remove the obstacles that they meet in the form of abuses arising from violence and fraud, and you will discern among mankind this double mark of progress: greater equality and better living conditions.

For, in the end, it is one thing or the other: either men's interests are harmonious, or they are fundamentally antagonistic to one another. Men gravitate toward their own self-interest irresistibly; otherwise it would not be self-interest. And if they gravitated toward something else, this something else would have to be self-interest. Therefore, if men's interests are harmonious, they need only be understood, and harmony and the good life will be achieved, for men naturally pursue their own interest. This is what we maintain, and that is why we say: Make men understand, and *laissez faire,* i.e., let them alone. If men's interests are mutually antagonistic by nature, then you are right; there is no other means of achieving harmony than by forcing, frustrating, and thwarting the interests of all men. Yet it is a strange kind of harmony that can be achieved only by an external and despotic act that runs contrary to the interests of all! For you can well realize that men will not passively submit to being frustrated; and, in order to make them submit to your plans and arrangements, you must first be stronger than all of them together, or else you must succeed in deceiving them regarding their true interests. In fact, if men's interests are indeed mutually antagonistic by nature, the happiest solution would be for men to be in error on this point.

Force and fraud, then, are your two resources. I defy you to find any others, except to agree that men's interests are harmonious; and if you agree, you belong with us, and like us you must say: Permit the laws of Providence to act.

Now, you do not want that. Then we must repeat: You start with the idea that men's interests are mutually antagonistic; that is why you are unwilling to permit them to reach any mutual understanding or agreement; that is why you want nothing to do with freedom, why you desire arbitrary arrangements. You are consistent.

But take care. The battle lines will not be drawn solely between you and humanity. That conflict you accept, since your avowed aim is to thwart men's interests. But the conflict will also be waged among yourselves—you, the inventors, the organizers of societies; for you are a thousand, and will soon be ten thousand, all with different views. What will you do? I see exactly what you will try to do. You will try to seize control of the government, for it possesses the only force capable of overcoming all resistance. Will one of you succeed? While he is busy frustrating the desires of the governed, he will find himself attacked by all the other social planners, as eager as he is to seize the apparatus of government. Their chances of success will be all the better because the public's disaffection will come to their aid, since—let us not forget—the man in power will have injured everybody's interests. Here we are, then, launched upon a sea of never-ending revolution, all to answer this question: How and by whom will the interests of mankind be thwarted?

Do not accuse me of exaggeration. All this is inevitable if men's interests are mutually antagonistic; for on that hypothesis you will never find your way out of this dilemma: either men's interests must be left to their own devices, and disorder will ensue; or there must be found someone strong enough to thwart them, and in that case there will still be disorder.

It is true that there is a third way, which I have already indicated. It consists in deceiving men as to their true interests; and, since this is no easy thing for a mere mortal to do, the quickest course is to make oneself God. This is a role the utopians do not fail to play, when they dare, while biding their time until they can become ministers of state. Mystical language always predominates in their writings; it is a trial balloon to test the public's credulity. Unfortunately, this method can hardly be expected to work in the nineteenth century.

Let us, then, admit it frankly: in order to avoid inextricable difficulties, it is preferable for us, after studying human interests, to conclude that they are harmonious. Then the task of writers, like that of governments, becomes reasonable and easy.

Since man is often mistaken regarding his own interests, our role as writers is to explain them, to describe them, to make them understandable, for we may be sure that, once man comprehends them, he will follow them. Since the man who errs in regard to his own interests hurts the general interest (for this is a consequence of the harmony of men's interests), the government will be responsible for bringing the minority of dissidents, the violators of the providential laws, back to the path of justice and the common good. In other words, the sole mission of government will be to promote the reign of justice. True harmony springs spontaneously from man's nature and will persist unless destroyed by government action. To achieve it, government is not required to strain painfully or to spend great sums, encroaching the while on individual liberty.

It is evident from what we have said here that we are not such fanatical admirers of social harmony as to refuse to admit that it can be and often is disturbed. I must even say that, in my opinion, the disturbances that are introduced into this admirable order by blind passions, by ignorance and error, are infinitely greater and more prolonged than might be imagined. These are the disturbing factors that we are about to study.

Man is cast upon this earth. He is irresistibly drawn toward happiness and repelled by suffering. Since his actions are determined by these impulses, it cannot be denied that self-interest is his great motive force as an individual, as it is of all individuals, and consequently of society. Since self-interest, in the economic sphere, is the motive force of human actions and the mainspring of society, evil can come from it as well as good; in it we must find both harmony and that which disturbs harmony.

The eternal goal of self-interest is to silence the voice of want, or, more generally, of desire, by satisfaction. Between these two extremes, want and satisfaction, which are essentially personal and intransmissible, intervenes the transmissible and exchangeable mean, effort.

And above the whole mechanism rises the faculty of judgment and comparison, i.e., intelligence. But the human intellect is fallible. We can err. This fact cannot be gainsaid; for if someone said to us: Man cannot be mistaken, we should reply: You are not the one to whom to demonstrate social harmony.

We can be mistaken in a number of ways. We can misjudge the relative importance of our wants. In that case, if we live in a state of isolation, we turn our efforts in a direction that is not in conformity with our best interests properly understood. If we live in society and under the law of exchange, the result is the same: we create a demand and offer remuneration for services of a trivial or harmful nature, and direct human labor into these channels.

We can also be mistaken by failing to realize that some ardently desired satisfaction will remove one pain only by becoming the source of greater pains. There is hardly any effect that does not, in its turn, become a cause. Foresight was given us so that we might grasp the relation of cause and effect, so that we might not sacrifice the future for the present; but foresight is often lacking.

Error due to the weakness of our judgment or the strength of our passions is the primary source of evil. It belongs principally to the moral realm. Since in these cases the error and the passion are individual, the evil is also, to a certain extent, individual. Reflection, experience, and acceptance of responsibility are its proper correctives.

Yet errors of this nature may assume a social character and give rise to widespread suffering when they are erected into a system. There are countries, for example, whose rulers are firmly convinced that the prosperity of nations is measured, not by the number of wants that are satisfied, but by the amount of effort that is expended, no matter what the results. The division of labor encourages this illusion. Since it is observed that every profession is directed against some obstacle, it is imagined that the obstacle is a source of wealth. In these countries, when vanity, frivolity, and vainglory are the dominant passions, provoking like desires, and turning a part of the nation's industry in that direction, the rulers believe that all would be lost if those they govern should happen to reform and set a higher moral standard for themselves. What would happen, they say, to the hairdressers, the cooks, the grooms, the embroiderers, the dancers, the lacemakers, etc.? They do not realize that the human heart will always contain enough worthy, reasonable, and legitimate desires to give an outlet to labor; that it will never be a question of suppressing tastes, but of educating and transforming them; that, consequently, labor, by following the same evolution, will be reallocated, but not brought to an end. In the countries where these unfortunate doctrines hold sway, it is often said: "It is too bad that morals and industry cannot advance together. We should prefer that the citizens were moral, but we cannot let them become idle and poor. That is why we continue to enact laws encouraging luxury. If need be, we shall impose taxes on the people; and in their own best interest, to assure them of employment, we shall require our kings, magistrates, diplomats, and ministers to *indulge in ostentation*." This is said with all the good faith on earth. Even the people acquiesce in it with good grace. It is clear that, when luxury and frivolity thus become a matter for legislation, regulated, controlled, imposed, erected into a system, by the public police force, the law of responsibility loses its moral power. . . . .[1]

19

War

Among all the circumstances that have some part in giving to a people its distinctive features, its moral tone, its character, its habits, laws, and peculiar spirit, the one that overshadows all others, because it includes virtually all of them, is its manner of providing its means of existence. We owe this observation to Charles Comte,* and it is surprising that it has not had greater influence on the social and political sciences.

In fact, this circumstance affects the human race in two equally powerful ways: by being a constant concern, and by being the concern of everyone. Earning a living, supporting oneself, improving one's condition, raising a family—these are not matters of taste, opinion, or choice, involving one time or one locality only; these are the daily, lifelong, inescapable preoccupations of all men at all times and in all places.

Everywhere the major part of men's physical, intellectual, and moral forces is devoted directly or indirectly to creating and replenishing their means of subsistence. The hunter, the fisherman, the sheep raiser, the farmer, the manufacturer, the businessman, the laborer, the artisan, the capitalist, all think, first of all, in terms of keeping soul and body together (however prosaic this admission may be) and, secondly, of living better and better, if possible. That this is so is proved by the fact that it is for no other reason that they are hunters, manufacturers, farmers, etc. Similarly, the civil servant, the soldier, the magistrate enter upon these

* [Charles Comte (1782–1837), French economist, son-in-law of J. B. Say. Co-editor, with Charles Dunoyer, of *Le Censeur européen*.—TRANSLATOR.]

475

careers only in order to ensure the satisfaction of their wants. Nor should we hold it against the man who follows a vocation calling for disinterestedness and self-sacrifice if he, too, invokes the proverb: To the priest the altar is a livelihood; for before he became a priest, he was a man. And if at this very moment such an individual is writing a book against the vulgarity of this observation of mine, or rather against the vulgarity of the human condition, the sale of his book will argue against his own thesis.

God forbid that I should deny the existence of self-sacrifice. But it will be admitted that examples of it are exceptional, and this is what makes them meritorious and worthy of our admiration. For, if we consider mankind as a whole, unless we have made a pact with the demon of sentimentality, we must admit that disinterested acts cannot be compared, numerically speaking, with those that are dictated by the hard necessities of our nature. And it is because these acts, which make up the sum total of our labors, occupy so large a part of the lives of each one of us, that they cannot fail to influence greatly the phenomena of our national life.

M. Saint-Marc Girardin* says somewhere that he came to realize that political forms are relatively unimportant compared with the great general laws that are imposed upon people by their wants and by the labor they do. "Do you desire to know what any nation really is?" he asked. "Ask not how it is governed, but what it does for a living."

As a general judgment this is correct. But the author soon gives it a false sense by turning it into a system. The importance of political forms has been exaggerated; so what does he do? He reduces it to nothing, he denies it completely, or he recognizes its existence only to laugh at it. Political forms, he says, interest us only on election day or during the hour we set aside for reading the newspaper. Monarchy or republic, aristocracy or democracy, what difference does it make? And so we must look at the conclusion he reaches. Maintaining that *young* nations resemble one

---

* [Saint-Marc Girardin (1801–1873), literary critic and scholar, professor of literature in the Sorbonne, member of the French Academy, also active in political life.— TRANSLATOR.]

another, regardless of their political organization, he likens the United States to ancient Egypt, because both have carried out enterprises of gigantic proportions. But I protest. When the Americans clear vast tracts of land, dig canals, build railroads, they do it all for themselves, because they are a democracy and are their own masters! The Egyptians erected temples, pyramids, obelisks, and palaces for their kings and their priests, because they were slaves! And this is only a slight difference, a mere matter of form, hardly worth noticing, or, if we do notice it, deserving only to be laughed at! Oh, the deadly contagion of the veneration for things classic! How it corrupts its superstitious devotees!

Soon after, M. Saint-Marc Girardin, still pursuing the same point, that the principal occupations of a people determine its national character, goes on to say: In the past, nations concerned themselves with war and religion; today, their chief preoccupation is with commerce and industry. For this reason the generations that preceded us had a warlike and religious character.

Rousseau had earlier declared that concern with one's mere existence was the dominant interest of only a few nations, and those of a most unimaginative kind; that other nations, more worthy of the name, had devoted themselves to nobler pursuits.

Were not M. Saint-Marc Girardin and Rousseau perhaps the victims of one of the illusions of history? May they not have mistaken the amusements and the diversions, that is, the devices and instruments of despotism, in which some of the citizens indulged, for the occupations of the entire nation? And may not this illusion be due to the fact that historians are always talking about the class that does not work and never about the classes that do, so that eventually we come to identify the entire nation with the leisure class?

I cannot help thinking that among the Greeks, as among the Romans and in the Middle Ages, men were just as they are today, that is, subject to wants so strong, so recurrent, that it was necessary to provide for them on pain of death. Therefore, I cannot help concluding, that then, as now, these wants were the chief and most absorbing preoccupation of the great majority of the human race.

What does appear certain is that a very small number of men managed to live without working, supported by the labor of the oppressed masses. This small leisured group made their slaves construct sumptuous palaces, vast castles, or somber fortresses. They loved to surround themselves with all the sensuous pleasures of life and with all the monuments of art. They delighted in discoursing on philosophy and cosmogony; and, above all, they carefully cultivated the two sciences to which they owed their supremacy and their enjoyments: the science of force and the science of fraud.

For beneath this aristocracy were the countless multitudes occupied in creating, for themselves, the means of sustaining life and, for their oppressors, the means of surfeiting them with pleasures. Since the historians never make the slightest mention of these multitudes, we forget their existence; they do not count for us at all. We have eyes only for the aristocracy. It is this class that we call *ancient society* or *feudal society*. We imagine that such societies were self-sustaining, that they never had recourse to anything so mundane as commerce, industry, or labor; we admire their unselfishness, their generosity, their love of the arts, their spiritual qualities, their disdain for servile occupations, their lofty thoughts and sentiments; we declare, with a certain quaver in the voice, that at one time the nations cared only for glory, at another only for the arts, at another only for philosophy, at another only for religion, at another only for virtue; we very sincerely weep over our own sorry state; we speak of our age with sarcasm because, unable to rise to the sublime heights attained by such paragons, we are reduced to according to labor and to all the prosaic virtues associated with it so important a place in our modern life.

Let us console ourselves with the thought that it played a no less important role in ancient life. The only difference was that the labor that a few men had managed to escape fell crushingly on the oppressed masses, to the great detriment of justice, liberty, property, wealth, equality, and progress; and this is the first of the disturbing factors to which I must call the reader's attention.

The ways by which men provide their means of existence cannot fail to exert a great influence on their physical, moral, intellectual, economic, and political condition.

If we could observe a number of primitive tribes, one of which had devoted itself exclusively to hunting, another to fishing, a third to agriculture, and a fourth to navigation, who could doubt that these tribes would present considerable differences in their ideas, opinions, habits, customs, manners, laws, and religion? No doubt we should find human nature basically the same everywhere. Therefore, their laws, habits, and religions would have many points in common, which, I believe, could well be called the general laws of human society.

However, in our great modern societies all or nearly all the processes of production—fishing, agriculture, industry, commerce, the sciences, and the arts—are at work simultaneously, although in varying proportions in different countries. For this reason the differences among nations are not and cannot be as great as they would be if each nation devoted itself exclusively to one occupation.

But if the nature of a people's occupations greatly influences its morality, it is also true that its desires, its tastes, and its morality exert in their turn a great influence on the nature of its occupations, or at least on their relative importance. I shall not add anything more to this observation, which has already been presented elsewhere in this work,[1] and thus I reach the main subject of this chapter.

A man (and the same may be said of a people) can secure the means of existence in two ways: by creating them or by stealing them.

Each of these two main means of procurement includes a variety of procedures.

We can *create* means of existence by hunting, fishing, farming, etc.

We can *steal* them by bad faith, violence, force, fraud, war, etc.

If, remaining within the limits of either one of these two main categories, we observe that the predominance of one or another of the procedures appropriate to it is sufficient to give rise to considerable differences among the nations, how much greater must not this difference be between a people that lives by producing and a people that lives by plundering!

For there is not one of our faculties, of whatever order, that is not called into use by our need to provide for our existence; and what can we conceive of that is more likely to modify the social condition of a nation than that which modifies all the human faculties?

This consideration, in spite of its importance, has received so little attention that I must pause to comment on it for a moment.

In order for man to obtain a satisfaction, he must have performed a certain amount of labor; hence, it follows that plunder, in all its varieties, far from excluding the act of production, presupposes it.

And this thought, it seems to me, is such as to moderate somewhat the infatuation of the historians, the poets, and the novelists for those heroic ages past when, according to them, what they call *industrialism* did not yet dominate society. In those days, as in our own, people had to live; then, as now, labor performed its hard task. But some nations, some classes, some individuals had succeeded in loading off onto other nations, other classes, other individuals, their portion of the general toil and drudgery.

The characteristic feature of production is, so to speak, to create out of nothing the satisfactions that sustain and beautify life, so that an individual or a people is enabled to multiply these satisfactions indefinitely without inflicting privation of any kind on other men or other peoples; quite the contrary: for careful study of the economic mechanism of a free society has shown us that the success of one man in his work improves the chances of success for others in their work.

The characteristic feature of plunder is its inability to provide any satisfaction without a corresponding privation, for it does not create; it diverts to its own ends what has already been created by the labor of others. It entails the absolute loss of all the effort it itself costs the two parties concerned. Far from adding to the enjoyments of mankind, it decreases them, and, moreover, it allots them to those who have not deserved them.

In order to produce, we must direct all our faculties toward the conquest of Nature; for it is Nature that must be fought, mastered, and subjugated. That is why iron beaten into a plowshare is the emblem of production.

In order to plunder, we must direct all our faculties toward the conquest of men; for they are the ones we must fight, kill, or enslave. That is why iron beaten into a sword is the emblem of plunder.

As great as is the difference between the plowshare that feeds and the sword that kills, so great must be the difference between a nation of workers and a nation of plunderers. It is not possible for there to be any common ground between these two. They cannot have the same ideas, the same standards, the same tastes, the same character, the same customs, the same laws, the same morality, or the same religion.

And surely one of the saddest sights that can present itself to anyone who loves mankind is that of a productive age bending all its efforts to infect itself—by way of education—with the thoughts, the sentiments, the errors, the prejudices, and the vices of a nation of plunderers. Our age is often accused of a lack of consistency, of a failure to show any correlation between the ideals it professes and the way of life it pursues. The criticism is just, and I believe that I have here indicated the principal reason why this situation prevails.

Plunder by way of war, that is, rudimentary plunder, simple and undisguised, has its roots in the human heart, in man's nature, in the universal motive force that actuates the social world—his attraction toward satisfactions and his aversion to pain; in a word, in that motivating force that we all have within us: self-interest.

And I am not distressed at now being the one to indict self-interest. Until now the reader may well have believed that my veneration of this principle amounted to idolatry, that I attributed to it only happy consequences for humanity, perhaps that I even placed it above altruism, devotion, self-sacrifice. No, I have not passed any judgment on it; I have merely noted that it exists and that it is all-powerful. I should poorly appreciate its all-powerful nature and I should be guilty of contradicting myself in calling self-interest the universal motive force of mankind, if I did not now point it out as a source of discord, just as I previously indicated that it was the source of the laws that govern the harmony of the social order.

Man, as we have said, strives irresistibly to assure his own preservation, to improve his lot, and to attain, or at least to come as near as possible to attaining, happiness as he conceives it. For the same reason he shuns pain and suffering.

Now, labor, the operation that he must perform upon Nature in order to produce anything, is itself pain and drudgery. For this reason he is averse to labor and resigns himself to it only when it is the means of avoiding an even greater evil. Taking the philosophical point of view, there are those who say that labor is a boon. They are right if we consider its results. Relatively speaking, it is a boon; in other words, it is an evil that spares us greater evils. And that is precisely why men have such a great tendency to avoid labor, when, without recourse to it, they believe they can reap its rewards.

Others say that labor is in itself a boon; that apart from the results it brings in terms of production, it strengthens man morally and physically and is a source of happiness and health. All this is very true, and reveals once again the marvelous fecundity of God's providential design so abundantly evident in all His handiwork. Yes, even apart from its results in terms of production, labor promises man, as its supplementary rewards, strength of body and joy of soul; and since we have said that idleness is the mother of all vices, we must also recognize that labor is the father of many virtues.

But while all this is very true, it in no way changes the natural and irresistible bent of the human heart nor the attitude that causes us not to seek work for its own sake. We always compare our labor with its results. We do not devote more effort to a given task if we can accomplish it with less; nor, when confronted with two toilsome tasks, do we choose the greater. We are more inclined to diminish the ratio of effort to result, and if, in so doing, we gain a little leisure, nothing will stop us from using it, for the sake of additional benefits, in enterprises more in keeping with our tastes.

Man's universal practice, indeed, is conclusive in this regard. Always and everywhere, we find that he looks upon toil as the disagreeable aspect, and on satisfaction as the compensatory aspect, of his condition. Always and everywhere, we find that, as far as he is able, he places the burden of his toil upon animals, the wind, steam, or other forces of Nature, or, alas! upon his fellow men, if he can gain mastery over them. In this last case, let me repeat, for it is too often forgotten, the labor has not been lessened; it has merely been shifted to other shoulders.[2]

Man, thus confronted with a choice of pains, the pains of want and the pains of toil, and driven by self-interest, seeks a means of avoiding them both in so far as possible. And it is then that plunder presents itself as the solution to his problem.

He says to himself: It is true that I have no means of procuring the things necessary for my preservation and my enjoyment—food, clothing, and shelter—unless these things have previously been produced by labor. But they need not necessarily be produced by *my* labor. They need only have been produced by *someone*, provided I am the stronger.

Such is the origin of war.

I shall not dwell long on the consequences.

When things come to this pass, when one man or one nation labors while another man or another nation lies in wait, ready to spring and to seize the fruits when the labor is completed, the reader can appreciate at a glance what a loss of human energy is entailed.

On the one hand, the plunderer has not been able, as he had hoped, to avoid every kind of labor. Armed plunder itself requires effort and sometimes tremendous effort. Thus, while the producer devotes his time to creating the objects fitted to yield satisfactions, the plunderer uses his time in preparing the means of stealing them. But when the work of violence has been consummated or attempted, the objects of satisfaction are neither more nor less plentiful. They may satisfy the wants of different persons, but they cannot satisfy a greater number of wants. Thus, all the efforts that the plunderer has expended for plunder, and in addition those that he has not expended for production, are entirely lost, if not for him, at least for mankind.

Nor is this all. In the majority of cases a similar loss is involved for the producer. It is not at all likely that he will passively await, without taking precautionary measures, the event that threatens him; and all his precautions, weapons, fortifications, munitions, drill, are labor, and labor forever lost, not only for him who looks to it for his security, but for the human race.

But, if the producer does not feel that, by thus undergoing double labor, he will be strong enough to resist the threatened invasion, the situation is much worse, and the waste of human energies is on an even larger scale; for in that case his work stops altogether, since no man is disposed to produce merely to be plundered.

As for the moral consequences, the manner in which both parties are affected, the result is no less disastrous. God decreed that man should wage war only against Nature, peacefully, and should reap directly from her the fruits of victory. When he gains dominion over Nature only through the indirect means of dominion over his fellow men, his mission has been perverted; he has turned his faculties in a wrong direction. Just consider, for example, the virtue of *foresight,* the anticipatory view of the future, which in a certain manner elevates us to the realm of *Providence,* for to *foresee,* to look ahead, is also to *provide,* to *look out for;** consider how differently it is employed by the producer and by the plunderer.

The producer must learn the relation between cause and effect. To this end, he studies the laws of the physical universe and seeks to bring them more and more to his aid. If he observes his fellow men, it is for the purpose of foreseeing their desires and providing for them, in the hope of a return.

The plunderer does not observe Nature. And if he observes his fellow men, it is as a hawk spies out its prey, seeking a way to weaken it, to take it unawares.

* [In French, *prévoir* and *pourvoir.*—TRANSLATOR.]

The same differences are to be observed in the other faculties and extend to men's ways of thinking.[3]

Plunder by means of war is not an accidental, isolated, temporary phenomenon; it is a very widespread and constant fact. Only labor is more permanent.

Show me, then, a place on the globe where two races of men, one a race of conquerors, and the other a race of conquered, are not superimposed. Show me in Europe or in Asia or in the islands of the sea a favored spot still occupied by its original inhabitants. If the migrations of peoples have spared no land, it is because war has been a universal phenomenon.

The traces war has left are equally widespread. Apart from the blood it has spilled, the booty it has captured, the minds it has warped, the faculties it has perverted, it has everywhere left scars, and among them must be listed slavery and aristocracy.

Man has not been content to plunder wealth as rapidly as it is produced; he has seized upon wealth already created, capital in all its forms. He has especially cast his eyes upon its most stable form, landed property. And finally, he has seized upon man himself. For since human faculties are a means of production, he has found it quicker to seize them than to seize their products.

What powerful disturbing factors these great events have been, what obstacles to the natural progress destined for mankind! If we take into account the extent to which labor has been wasted by war, if we consider the extent to which what remained of the product of labor has been concentrated in the hands of a few conquerors, we can well understand why the masses are destitute, for their destitution cannot be explained in our day on the hypothesis of liberty.

How the Warlike Spirit Is Fostered

Aggressor nations are subject to reprisals. They often attack; sometimes they have to defend themselves. When they are on the defensive, they feel that justice is on their side, and that their cause is holy. Then they laud courage, devotion, patriotism. But, alas! They carry these ideas over into their wars of aggression. And in that case what is patriotism?

When two races, one victorious and idle, the other conquered and humiliated, occupy the same land, everything that arouses likes and desires is the portion of the former. To it belong the leisure, gala affairs, love of the arts, wealth, military pomp and parades, grace, elegance, literature, poetry. To the conquered belong calloused hands, desolate hovels, repulsive clothing.

The consequence is that the ideas and attitudes of the dominant race, always associated with its military ascendancy, determine public opinion. Men, women, children, all place the soldier's way of life above that of the worker, war above labor, plunder above production. The conquered race itself shares this sentiment, and when it overcomes its oppressors, it shows itself in its process of readjustment disposed to imitate them—more than disposed, indeed, for this imitation becomes a frenzy.

How War Ends

Since the spirit of plunder, like the urge to produce, has its origin in the human heart, the laws of the social world would never be harmonious, even in the limited sense that I have indicated, if in the long run the urge to produce were not destined to overcome the spirit of plunder.

20

Responsibility

In this book there is a central, dominant thought; it pervades every page, it gives life and meaning to every line. It is the thought that begins the Christian's creed: *I believe in God.*

Indeed, if this work differs from the writings of some economists, the difference consists in the fact that they seem to say: "We have little faith in God, for we see that the natural laws lead to disaster, and yet we say: *Laissez faire!* because we have even less faith in ourselves, and we realize that all human efforts to halt the operation of these laws merely hasten the day of catastrophe."

If it differs from the works of the socialists, it is because they say: "We do indeed pretend to believe in God, but in reality we believe only in ourselves, since we want nothing to do with *laissez faire,* and each and every one of us offers his social plan as infinitely superior to that of Providence."

I say: *Laissez faire;* in other words: Respect freedom, human initiative.[1]

Responsibility, solidarity, mysterious laws whose origins are unfathomable to us, aside from divine revelation, yet whose effects and unfailing influence on the progress of society it is given us to discern! For the very reason that man is a social being, these laws are interrelated, they overlap, they work together, even when on occasion they appear to be in conflict. Ideally they should be viewed as a whole, in their common action, were it not that science, with its feeble vision and uncertain step, is reduced to its scientific method, that unfortunate crutch which constitutes its strength even as it betrays its weakness.

Nosce te ipsum—"Know thyself"—is, as the oracle says, the beginning, the middle, and the end of the moral and political sciences.

We have stated elsewhere that, in regard to man or human society, harmony cannot mean perfection, but progress toward perfection. Now, progress toward perfection always implies some degree of imperfection in the future as well as in the past. If man could ever enter the promised land of *absolute good*, he would have no further need of his intelligence or of his senses; he would no longer be man.

Evil exists. It is inherent in human frailty; it evidences itself in the moral order as in the physical order, in the mass as in the individual, in the whole as in its parts. Because our eyes may hurt and our sight grow dim, will the physiologist ignore the harmonious mechanism of these wonderful organs? Will he deny the ingenious structure of the human body because that body is subject to pain, illness, and death, because Job once cried out in his despair: "I have said to corruption, Thou art my father, to the worm, Thou art my mother and my sister!" * In the same manner, because the social order will never bring mankind safely to port in the fantastic dreamland of absolute good, must the economist refuse to recognize the marvelous structure of the social order, which is so constituted as to diffuse more and more enlightenment, morality, and happiness among more and more people?

It is indeed strange that the natural scientist is allowed the right to admire Nature's handiwork, but that the political economist is

* [Job XII, 14. Bastiat's exact words for this passage are: "*O tombe, vous êtes ma mère: Vers du Sépulcre, vous êtes mes frères et mes sœurs!*" The actual words of the French Bible are closer to the English version given above. "*J'ai crié à la fosse: Tu es mon frère, et aux vers: Vous êtes ma mère et ma sœur.*" These slight differences, as well as the fact that Bastiat attributes the words to "the psalmist" rather than to Job, suggest that he may have quoted from memory.—TRANSLATOR.]

not. For, after all, what difference is there, as regards the harmony of final causes, between the structure of the individual body and the structure of the collective body? As we know, the individual is born, grows, develops, and, as life unfolds, acquires bodily grace and strength, until the moment comes when he kindles the flame of new life. At this moment he radiates beauty; his every movement bespeaks joy and grace; he emanates kindliness, affection, good will, harmony. Then, for yet some time his intelligence grows and deepens, as if to guide over the tortuous road of life those whom he has summoned into existence. But soon his beauty dims, his grace disappears, his senses grow dull, his body fails, his memory becomes uncertain, his thoughts grow less clear, and, alas! even his affections—save for a few choice souls —seem filled with selfishness, lose the charm, the freshness, the sincerity and simple naturalness, the depth, the idealism, the disinterestedness, the poetic imagination, and the indefinable aura that belonged to his earlier years. And despite the ingenious precautions taken by Nature to retard the process of dissolution— precautions termed by physiologists the *vis medicatrix,* the sole and melancholy harmony with which this science must be content— the cycle of his attainments is now run in reverse; one after another along the downward road the acquisitions of the past are abandoned, the loss of one faculty is followed by the loss of another, until at last is reached the inevitable loss of all. Even the genius of complete optimism can find nothing consoling or harmonious in this slow and relentless disintegration, in the sight of this being, once so proud and fair, on his melancholy descent to the tomb. The tomb! But is not the tomb the door to another abode? Thus it is that, when science can go no further, religion links together anew,[2] even for the individual, in another and fairer land, the harmonious notes interrupted here below.[3]

Despite this inevitable end, does the physiologist cease to consider the human body as the most perfect masterpiece to come from the hands of the Creator?

But if the body politic is subject to suffering, if indeed it may suffer unto death, yet society is not inevitably doomed. Whatever people may have said, we have no reason for anticipating that, after reaching its peak, it will of necessity decline. Even the crumbling of empires does not mean a retrogression for humanity, and the old molds of civilization are broken only to give way to a civilization more advanced. Dynasties may come to an end; forms of government may change; but the human race keeps on advancing nevertheless. The fall of a regime is like the falling of leaves in autumn. It fertilizes the soil, makes ready for the return of spring, and promises to future generations richer growth and more abundant harvests. I may go even further. Even from the purely national viewpoint, this theory of necessary decadence is as false as it is outmoded. It is impossible to see in a nation's mode of life any cause of inevitable decline. The analogy that has so often compared a nation to an individual and has attributed to both a childhood and an old age is nothing but a false metaphor. A community is continually being renewed. Provided its institutions are kept elastic and flexible, provided that, instead of colliding head on with new forces invented by the human mind, they are so organized as to permit of this expansion of intellectual energy and to adapt themselves to it, there is no discernible reason why a society should not flourish with the vigor of eternal youth. But, whatever we may think of the instability and collapse of empires, it remains true nonetheless that society, which in its entirety includes the whole of mankind, is built on more solid foundations. The more we study it, the more we remain convinced that it, too, has been provided, like the human body, with a *self-curing power* that saves it from its ills, and that, in addition, it has within itself a *forward drive,* which urges it on toward endless progress.

If then, the infirmities to which the individual is subject do not impair his physiological harmony, even less do collective ills impair the harmony of the social world.

But how can we reconcile the existence of evil with God's infinite goodness? It is not for me to explain what I do not understand. I shall merely observe that political economy is no more required to answer this question than is anatomy. Both these sciences, which are based entirely on objective observation, study man as he is, and do not require of God that He reveal to them His impenetrable secrets.

Thus, I repeat, in this book, harmony does not mean the idea of absolute perfection, but the idea of unlimited progress. It has pleased God to attach suffering to our nature, since He has willed that we move from weakness to strength, from ignorance to knowledge, from want to satisfaction, from effort to result, from acquisition to possession, from privation to wealth, from error to truth, from experience to foresight. I bow without murmur before this decree, for I cannot imagine how else our lives could have been ordered. If, then, by means of a mechanism as simple as it is ingenious, He has arranged that *all men should be brought closer together on the way toward a constantly rising standard of living,* if He thus guarantees them—through the very action of what we call evil—lasting and more widely distributed progress, then, not content with bowing before this generous and powerful hand, I bless it, I marvel at it, and I adore it.

We have seen schools of thought arise that have profited by the insolubility, humanly speaking, of this question to confuse all other questions, as if it were given to our finite minds to understand and reconcile the infinite. Placing over the portal of social science the sentence: *God cannot will evil,* they reach this series of conclusions: "There is evil in society; hence, society is not organized according to God's plan. Let us change and rechange and change still again the social order; let us keep on trying, let us go on experimenting, until we have found a form that removes every trace of suffering from this world. By this sign we shall know that the kingdom of God has come."

Nor is this all. These schools have been led to exclude freedom from their social planning on the same grounds as suffering, for freedom implies the possibility of error, and consequently the possibility of evil. "Allow us to organize you," they tell men; "do not take any active part yourselves; do not compare, judge, decide anything by yourselves or for yourselves; we hold *laissez faire* in abomination, but we demand that you let yourselves remain passive and that you let us act. If we lead you to perfect bliss, God's infinite bounty will be vindicated."

Contradiction, irrelevancy, overweening pride—it is hard to say which predominates in language of this kind.

One sect, among others, very unscientific, but very noisy, promises mankind unalloyed bliss. Only let the governing of mankind be given over to these gentlemen, and they confidently guarantee to rid it of every painful sensation.

But, if you refuse to place blind faith in their promises, they immediately raise that formidable and insoluble problem which has been the philosopher's despair since the beginning of the world, and they command you to reconcile the existence of evil with the infinite goodness of God. Do you hesitate? They accuse you of impiety.

Fourier exhausts all the combinations and permutations of this theme.

Either God was not able to give us a body of social law providing cohesion, justice, truth, and unity; in which case He is unjust in that He has created within us a want that we have no means of satisfying: *or He did not wish to do so;* in which case He is deliberately cruel, capriciously creating in us wants that it is impossible to satisfy: *or He was able and He did not wish to do so;* in which case He is the devil's rival, since He knows the right and prefers the reign of evil: *or He wished to do so and was not able;* in which case He is incapable of ruling us, since He knows and desires the good that He cannot do: *or He neither was able nor wished to do so;* in which case He is inferior to the devil, who is evil, but not stupid: *or He was able and He did wish to do so;* in which case the body of social law exists; He must have revealed it, etc.

And Fourier is the prophet. Let us surrender ourselves to him and his disciples, and Providence will be justified, our five senses will be transformed, and pain will disappear from the earth.

But why is it that these apostles of absolute good, these daring logicians who keep saying, "God being perfect, His handiwork must be perfect," and who accuse us of impiety because we resign ourselves to human imperfection—why is it, I ask, that they fail to realize that, even on the most favorable hypothesis, they would be just as irreverent as we? I devoutly hope that, under the reign of Messrs. Considérant, Hennequin,* etc., no one on the face of the earth should ever lose his mother or have a toothache —in which case he, too, could chant the litany: *Either God was not able or did not wish,* etc. I do indeed hope that evil returns to the infernal regions on the dawn of the great day of the socialist revelation; that one of their plans, the phalanstery, interest-free credit, anarchy, the *triade*,† the social workshop, etc., has the power to banish all future ills. Would it also have the power to take away all past suffering? Now, infinity has no limits; and if there has ever been a single unhappy person on the earth since the Creation, that is enough to render the problem of God's infinite goodness insoluble from their point of view.

Let us not, therefore, connect finite science with the mysteries of the infinite. Let us apply to the one observation and reason; let us leave the other to revelation and faith.

In all respects, from every point of view, man is imperfect. On this earth, at least, he encounters limitations in every direction and touches on the finite at every point. His strength, his intelligence, his affections, his life are not absolutes, but depend upon a material instrument subject to fatigue, change, and death.

Not only is this true, but our imperfection is so thoroughgoing that we cannot even conceive of perfection within ourselves or outside of ourselves. This idea is so completely alien to the human mind that every effort to grasp it must necessarily be futile. The more we attempt to lay hold of it, the more it eludes us and loses itself in inextricable contradictions. Show me a man who is perfect, and you will show me a man who cannot suffer, and who consequently has no wants, desires, sensations, sensibility,

---

* [Victor-Antoine Hennequin (1816–1854), disciple of Fourier, active political supporter of his ideas, and ally of Considérant.—TRANSLATOR.]
† [One of the divisions of Fourier's *phalanges*.—TRANSLATOR.]

nerves, or muscles; to whom nothing is unknown, who consequently does not have the power of attention, judgment, reasoning, memory, imagination, or a brain. In a word, you will show me a being who does not exist.

Thus, from whatever point of view we consider man, we must see him as a being subject to pain. We must admit that evil comes into the providential plan as a kind of force; and, instead of seeking illusive means of eliminating it, it behooves us instead to study its role and mission.

When God saw fit to create a being composed of wants and of faculties with which to satisfy them, he at the same time decreed that that being should be subject to pain and suffering; for without pain and suffering we can experience no wants, and without wants we cannot understand either the uses or the reasons for any of our faculties. Everything that makes for our greatness has its roots in everything that makes for our frailty.

Driven by countless impulses, endowed with an intelligence that enlightens our efforts and appraises their results, we also have *free will* to make our choice.

Free will implies the possibility of error, and error in turn implies pain and suffering as its inevitable consequences. I defy anyone to tell me what it means to *choose freely* if not to run the risk of making a bad choice; and what it means to make a bad choice if not to expose ourselves to pain and suffering.

And this is undoubtedly why all the schools that will be satisfied with nothing less for mankind than absolute good are without exception materialistic and deterministic. They cannot accept free will. They realize that freedom of action comes from freedom to choose; that free choice presupposes the possibility of error; that the possibility of error means also the possibility of evil. Now, in an artificial social order of the kind invented by the planners, evil cannot appear. For this reason men must not be exposed to the possibility of error; and the surest way to do this is to deprive them of their freedom to act and choose, that is, of their free will. It has been truly said that socialism is despotism incarnate.

In the presence of these follies one wonders by what right the planner of such a social order dares to think, act, and choose, not only for himself, but for everybody else; for, after all, he too is part of mankind, and by that very fact is fallible. And the further he proposes to extend the sphere of his knowledge and will, the more fallible he shows himself to be.

No doubt he feels that this objection of mine is fundamentally mistaken, because it includes him with the rest of mankind. Since he has pointed out the flaws in the divine handiwork and has undertaken to redo it, he is not a man; he is God and more than God.

Socialism has two elements: the madness of inconsistency and the madness of rampant self-pride.

But when the existence of free will, which is the starting point of my entire study, is denied, should I not take the time to prove that it does exist? I shall do nothing of the kind. Everyone knows in his heart that it does, and that is sufficient. I feel that it exists, not vaguely, but with an inner certainty a hundred times stronger than any demonstration by Aristotle or Euclid could make it. I feel it in the joy of my conscience when I have made a choice that does me credit, and in my remorse when I have made a choice that degrades me. Furthermore, I observe that all men affirm the existence of free will by their conduct, even though a few deny it in their writings. All men compare motives, deliberate, decide, retract, try to foresee the future; all offer advice, grow angry at injustice, applaud acts of unselfishness. Therefore, all recognize in themselves and in others the presence of free will, without which choice, counsel, foresight, morality, and virtue are all impossible. Let us avoid trying to demonstrate what general practice recognizes as true. Absolute fatalists or determinists are no more to be found in the world today, even in Constantinople, than there were once absolute skeptics, even in Alexandria.* Those who profess to be may well be foolish enough

---

* [Bastiat's reference here is obviously to the Constantinople of his day as a center of Mohammedanism, with its emphasis on fate (kismet), even as ancient Alexandria was a center of the Stoic philosophers.—TRANSLATOR.]

to try to convince others, but they are not adroit enough to convince even themselves. They prove with highly subtle arguments that they have no free will; but since they act as if they did have, let us not argue with them.

We find ourselves, then, surrounded by Nature, living with our fellow men; driven by impulses, wants, appetites, desires; provided with various faculties that enable us to work either with things or with men; moved to action by our free will; endowed with an intelligence that is perfectible, and therefore not perfect, and, if capable of enlightening us, capable also of leading us astray regarding the consequences of our acts.

Every human action—setting in motion a series of good or bad consequences that fall in part on the doer of the act and in part on his family, his neighbors, his fellow citizens and sometimes on all mankind—sets to vibrating, so to speak, two chords that give forth utterances of oracular importance for us: responsibility and solidarity.

Responsibility, as it relates to the person performing an act, is the natural connection between the act and its consequences. It is a complete system of *inevitable* rewards and penalties that was invented by no man, that acts with the uniformity of all the great natural laws, and that therefore we may consider to be divinely instituted. Its purpose is evidently to limit the number of our harmful actions and to increase the number of our useful actions.

This device, which is at once corrective and progressive, rewarding and punitive, is so simple, so near us, so closely identified with our whole being, so constantly at work, that not only must we admit its existence, but we must recognize that, like evil, it is one of the phenomena without which our whole life would be meaningless.

Genesis relates how, when the first man had been driven from the earthly paradise because he had learned to distinguish right from wrong—*to know good and evil*—God pronounced this sentence upon him: *In sorrow shalt thou eat of it* [the fruit of the earth] *all the days of thy life. Thorns and thistles shall it bring forth to thee . . . . . In the sweat of thy face shalt thou eat bread, till thou return unto the ground, for out of it wast thou taken; for dust thou art and unto dust shalt thou return.**

Here, then, we have good and evil—or human nature. Here we have acts and habits producing good or bad consequences—or human nature. Here are toil, sweat, thorns, tribulation, and death—or human nature.

Human nature, I say: for to choose, to err, to suffer, to correct one's errors—in a word, all the elements that make up the idea of responsibility—are so much a part of our sentient, intelligent, and free nature, they are so much one with this nature, that I defy the most fertile imagination to conceive of any other kind of existence for man.

That man once lived in an Eden, *in paradiso voluptatis,†* not knowing good and evil, *scientiam boni et mali,‡* is something that we may well believe, but we cannot understand it, so completely has our nature been transformed.

It is impossible for us to separate the idea of *life* from the idea of *sensation,* of sensation from *pleasure* and *pain,* of pleasure and pain from *reward* and *punishment,* of *intelligence* from *free will* and *choice,* and all of these ideas from the idea of responsibility; for it is the sum total of all of these ideas that gives us the concept of existence, so that, when we think of God, though our reason tells us that He cannot experience pain, our reason remains confused, so inseparable for us are the ideas of *existence* and sensation.

And that is doubtless why *faith* is the necessary complement of our lot. It is the only possible link between the creature and the Creator, who is, and will always be, for our reason, God the unknowable, *Deus absconditus.*

---

* [As would most Frenchmen of his time, Bastiat quotes this passage (Gen. 3: 17–19) from the Vulgate: *sciens bonum et malum . . . . . In laboribus comedes ex terra cunctis diebus vitae tuae. Spinas et tribulos germinabit tibi. In sudore vultus tui vesceris pane, donec revertaris in terram de qua sumptus es: quia pulvis es et in pulverem reverteris.*—TRANSLATOR.]

† ["In a paradise of delight."—TRANSLATOR.]

‡ ["Knowledge of good and evil."—TRANSLATOR.]

In order to know how intimately responsibility affects us and how ubiquitous its influence on us is, we need only observe the simplest facts.

Fire burns us; a blow on the body causes a bruise. If we were devoid of sensation, or if our senses were not painfully affected by exposure to fire or rough bodily contact, we should be in danger of death every instant of our lives.

From earliest childhood to extreme old age, life is a long apprenticeship. We learn to walk by repeated falls; we learn by hard and repeated experiences to avoid heat, cold, hunger, thirst, excesses. We complain that experience is a hard teacher; but if it were not, we should never learn anything.

The same is true of the moral order. The awful consequences of cruelty, injustice, terror, violence, fraud, and idleness, are what teach us to be kind, just, brave, temperate, honest, and industrious. Experience takes a long time; it will, indeed, always be at work but it is effective.

Since such is man's nature, it is impossible not to recognize in responsibility the mainspring of social progress. It is the crucible of experience. Those who believe in the superiority of former times, like those who despair of the future, fall into the most obvious inconsistency. Without realizing it, they commend error and censure enlightenment. It is as if they said, "The more I learn, the less I know; the more clearly I see what can hurt me, the more I will expose myself to it." If mankind had been imbued with such an idea, it would long since have ceased to exist.

Man's starting point is ignorance and inexperience; the farther back we go through the ages, the more we find him lacking in the knowledge of how to direct his choice, for such knowledge is acquired in only one of two ways: reflection or experience.

Now, it so happens that every human act includes, not one consequence, but a series of consequences. Sometimes the first is good, and the others are bad; sometimes the first is bad, and the others are good. From a given human decision may come combinations of good and evil in varying proportions. Let us call *vicious* those acts that produce more evil than good, and *virtuous* those acts that produce more good than evil.

When one of our acts produces a first result that is pleasurable, followed by a number of others that are harmful, so that the sum of the bad is greater than the good, this act tends to be done less frequently and to disappear as we acquire more foresight.

Men naturally perceive immediate consequences more quickly than remote consequences. Hence, it follows that what we call vicious acts are more common in times of ignorance. Now, the repetition of the same acts develops habits. The centuries of ignorance are therefore marked by the reign of bad habits.

Consequently, these are also the times of the reign of bad laws, for repeated acts and general habits determine the customs on which laws are modeled, and of which they are, so to speak, the official expression.

How is this ignorance brought to an end? How do men come to know the second, the third, and ultimately the final consequences of their acts and habits?

Their first means is to use the faculty of discerning and reasoning given them by Providence.

But there is a surer, more effective way, which is through experience. When the act is performed, the consequences necessarily follow. It is known that the first consequence will be good; it was precisely to obtain this result that the act was performed. But the second entails suffering, the third greater suffering, and so on.

Then people's eyes are opened, and the light dawns. The act is not repeated; the benefit of the first consequence is forgone through dread of the greater harm brought about by the others. If the act has become a habit, and one does not have the strength to give it up, at least one yields to it only with hesitation and repugnance, after an inner struggle. It is not recommended; it is censured; one's children are advised against it. Certainly this is the road to progress.

If, on the contrary, we leave a useful act undone—because its first result, the only one known, is painful, and the eventual, favorable results are unknown—we then experience the effects of our sins of omission. For example, a savage has eaten his fill. He does not foresee that he will be hungry tomorrow. Why should he work today? As far as the present is concerned, work represents pain; it requires no foresight to realize that. Hence, he remains idle. But the day flits by, another follows, and with it comes hunger. Under this spur he must go to work. This is a lesson that, often repeated, cannot fail to develop the virtue of foresight. Little by little idleness is seen for what it is. It is deplored; the young are admonished against it. Industriousness is backed by the authority of public opinion.

But for experience to become a real teacher and to fulfill its mission in the world, developing foresight, revealing the true nature of cause and effect, encouraging good habits and curbing bad ones—in a word, for it to become a fit instrument of progress and moral improvement—the law of responsibility must function. The results of bad actions must be brought home, and, let us admit it frankly, *evil* must, for the moment, exact its severe penalty.

Of course, it would be better if evil did not exist at all, and that would perhaps be the case if man were made according to a different plan. But, given man as he is, with his wants, his desires, his sensations, his free will, his power to choose and to err, his faculty of putting into operation a cause that necessarily entails effects that cannot be eliminated as long as the cause exists; the only way to eliminate the cause is to enlighten his free will, correct his choice, suppress the vicious act or habit; and these things can be done only by virtue of the law of responsibility.

We can therefore declare that, man being what he is, evil is not only necessary but useful. It has a mission; it enters into the universal harmony. It has the mission of destroying its own cause, of being self-limiting, of helping to achieve the good, of stimulating progress.

Let us illustrate this point with a few examples taken from our particular subject, which is political economy.

Thrift, Extravagance
Monopolies
Population. . . . .[4]

Three sanctions enforce the law of responsibility:

1. *Natural sanctions,* which I have just described, the punishments or rewards that inevitably stem from our acts or habits.

2. *Religious sanctions,* which comprise the punishments and rewards that in the next world will be meted out to our acts and habits, whether vicious or virtuous.

3. *Legal sanctions,* the punishments and rewards prepared in advance by society.

Of these three kinds of sanctions, I admit that it is the first that seems to me to be fundamental. In saying this, I cannot avoid coming into conflict with opinions that I respect; but I beg the Christians to allow me to present my views.

It will probably be a subject of eternal debate between the philosophically minded and the religiously minded to determine whether an act is vicious because supernatural revelation has declared it to be so regardless of its consequences, or whether revelation has declared it to be vicious because it brings about bad consequences.

I believe that Christianity can take its stand in favor of this second opinion. Christianity itself declares that it came, not to destroy the natural law, but to fulfill it.* It can hardly be admitted that God, who is the supreme principle of order, made an arbitrary classification of human acts and promised that some should be punished and others rewarded without any reference to their effects, that is, whether discordant or in tune with the universal harmony.

When He said: "Thou shalt not kill. Thou shalt not steal," surely it was His intention to forbid certain acts because they are harmful to man and society, which are His handiwork.

A regard for consequences is so powerful an influence on man that, if he belonged to a religion that forbade acts proved useful by universal experience or that sanctioned acts of an obviously harmful nature, I believe that eventually this religion would be unable to maintain itself and would fall before the advance of

---

* [Cf. Matt. 5: 17–48.—Translator.]

progress. Men would not for long attribute to God the deliberate design of encouraging evil and forbidding the good.

The question which I touch upon here does not, perhaps, have any great importance as far as Christianity is concerned, since it is a religion that commands what is inherently good and forbids only what is bad.

But what I am now considering is whether, in principle, religious sanctions merely serve to reinforce natural sanctions, or whether natural sanctions are of no importance compared to religious sanctions and must give way before them when the two come into conflict.

Now, unless I am mistaken, the tendency of the ministers of religion is to concern themselves very little with natural sanctions. They have an unanswerable reason for this: "God has commanded this; God has forbidden that." There is no room left for reasoning, for God is infallible and omnipotent. Even though the act should bring about the destruction of the world, you must march blindly ahead, just as you would if God spoke directly to you and showed you heaven and hell.

It can happen, even in the true religion, that innocent acts are forbidden by the citation of divine authority. For example, to charge interest on money has been declared a sin. If mankind had obeyed this prohibition, the human race would long since have disappeared from the face of the earth. For, without interest, no capital is possible; without capital, there can be no co-operation between past labor and present labor; without this co-operation, there can be no society; and without society, man cannot exist.

On the other hand, if we look closely at the question of interest, we may rest assured not only that it is useful in its general effects, but also that there is nothing in it that is contrary either to charity or to truth—any more than in a priest's or a pastor's stipend, and certainly less so than in certain of their perquisites.

Therefore, all the power and authority of the Church has not for a moment been able, in this matter, to disregard the nature of things. At the very most, the Church has barely been able, in a number of extremely insignificant cases, to disguise one, and that the least common, of the forms in which interest is charged.

The same thing is true of moral precepts. When the Gospel says: "But whosoever shall smite thee on the right cheek, turn to him the other also," * it gives us a precept that, if taken literally, would destroy the right to legitimate self-defense for the individual, and consequently for society. Now, without this right, the existence of the human race is impossible.

And therefore what has happened? For the last eighteen hundred years this admonition has been given merely lip service.

But, what is more serious, there are false religions in the world. These necessarily include precepts and prohibitions that are contradictory to the natural sanctions that authorize certain acts. Now, of all the means that have been given us to distinguish, in so important a matter, between what is true and what is false, what comes from God and what from imposture, nothing is more certain or more decisive than an examination of the consequences, good or bad, that a given doctrine may have for the progress of humanity: *Ye shall know them by their fruits.*

Legal Sanctions

Since Nature has prepared a whole system of punishments and rewards in the form of the effects that flow from every action and every habit, what must be done by human law? Only three courses are open: allow the law of responsibility to act alone, actively support it, or contravene it.

It appears to me beyond doubt that, when a legal sanction is applied, it must be only for the sake of giving greater power, regularity, certainty, and efficacy to natural sanctions. These two forces must work together, not in conflict with each other.

For example, if fraud is initially profitable to the person practicing it, in the long run it is more often disastrous for him; for it is harmful to his credit, his reputation, his honor. It creates mistrust and suspicion around him. Besides, it is always harmful to its victim. And finally, it alarms society and forces it to expend a part of its energies on onerous precautions. Thus, the combined evils resulting from fraud are far greater than its advantages. This

* [Matt. 5:39.—TRANSLATOR.]

is what we mean by the law of responsibility, which acts continually as a deterrent and a preventative. We can well understand, however, why the community does not leave the problem entirely to the slow, albeit relentless, action of responsibility, and sees fit to add a legal sanction to the natural sanction. In this case we can say that the legal sanction is merely the natural sanction regularized and formalized. It makes the punishment more immediate and certain; it gives greater publicity and significance to the facts; it surrounds the accused with certain safeguards, gives him the opportunity to clear himself, if he can, protects him against errors of public opinion and, by substituting the due penalty of the law, quiets the impulse to take personal vengeance. Finally, and this is perhaps the essential point, it does not nullify the lessons taught by experience.

Thus, we cannot say that legal sanctions are wrong in principle when they are in line with natural sanctions and work to accomplish the same ends.

It does not follow, however, that legal sanctions must in every case be substituted for natural sanctions, or that human laws may be justified by the mere fact that their action is in accord with that of the law of responsibility.

The artificial meting out of rewards and punishments entails for the community a number of inconveniences that must be taken into account. The machinery for applying legal sanctions is created by men, is run by men, and is costly in time and effort.

Before forbidding an act or a practice by legal authority, we must always ask this question: Does the extra benefit obtained by the addition of legal sanctions to natural sanctions compensate for the disadvantages necessarily involved in the apparatus of repression?

Or, in other words, are the disadvantages of artificial repressive measures greater or less than the dangers involved in impunity?

In the case of theft, murder, and most crimes and felonies, there is no doubt as to the answer. Therefore, all nations use the force of the law to suppress them.

But in the case of a practice on which it is difficult to pass an objective judgment, which may stem from moral causes requiring a very delicate weighing of values, a different question arises; and it may very well happen that, although this practice is everywhere held to be harmful and vicious, human law should remain neutral and abdicate its authority in favor of the law of natural responsibility.

Let us say first of all that the law must take this stand whenever it is dealing with a debatable act or practice, when one part of the population approves of something of which the other part disapproves. You contend that I am wrong to practice Catholicism; and I contend that you are wrong to practice Lutheranism. Let us leave it to God to judge. Why should I strike at you, or why should you strike at me? If it is not good that one of us should strike at the other, how can it be good that we should delegate to a third party, who controls the public police force, the authority to strike at one of us in order to please the other?

You contend that I am wrong to teach my son science and philosophy; I believe that you are wrong to teach yours Greek and Latin. Let us both follow the dictates of our conscience. Let us allow the law of responsibility to operate for our families. It will punish the one who is wrong. Let us not call in human law; it could well punish the one who is not wrong.

You say that I would do better to follow a given career, to work in a given way, to use a steel plow instead of a wooden one, to sow sparsely rather than thickly, to buy from the East rather than from the West. I maintain the contrary. I have made my calculations; after all, I am more vitally concerned than you in not making a mistake in matters that will decide my own well-being, the happiness of my family, matters that can concern you only as they touch your vanity or your systems. Advise me, but do not force your opinion on me. I shall decide at my *peril and risk;* that is enough, and for the law to interfere would be tyranny.

We see, then, that in almost all of the important actions of life we must respect men's free will, defer to their own good judgment, to that inner light that God has given them to use, and beyond this to let the law of responsibility take its course.

The interference of statute law in such cases, over and beyond the great disadvantage of being as likely to be wrong as to be right, would also involve the even greater risk of paralyzing our very intelligence, that guiding light which is our glory and the guarantee of all our progress.

But even when an act, a habit, or a practice is recognized by common judgment to be bad, vicious, immoral; when no doubt exists; when those who succumb to it are the first to deplore it; even then the interference of human law is not justified. We still have to know, as I have just said, whether, by adding to the bad effects of the vice the bad effects inherent in all legal machinery, we are not in the long run producing a sum of evils in excess of the good that the legal sanction can add to the natural sanction.

We might well consider at this point the good and bad results that can be obtained by the application of legal sanctions for the suppression of idleness, prodigality, avarice, selfishness, cupidity, ambition.

Let us take idleness as an example.

It is a very natural inclination of mankind, and there are many who echo the Italians in hailing the *dolce far niente* * and Rousseau's declaration: I am delightfully lazy. Undoubtedly, then, idleness has its satisfactions, for otherwise there would be no idle men in the world.

Nevertheless, so many evils come from idleness that it is proverbially known as the *mother of all vices.*

Its evils far outnumber its advantages; and surely the law of responsibility has operated with some effectiveness in this matter, either as a teacher or as a spur to action, since it is by labor that the world has reached the state of civilization in which we find it today.

Now, what could a legal sanction add to the providential sanction either as a teacher or as a spur to action? Suppose there is a law punishing idleness. Just how much would this add to the existing activity of the nation?

If it could be determined, we should know exactly how useful such a law would be. I admit that I have no idea. But we must ask ourselves how dearly we would have to pay for such benefits; and

* ["The sweet state of doing nothing."—TRANSLATOR.]

even a little reflection will incline us to the belief that the inevitable disadvantages arising from legal suppression would greatly outweigh its problematical advantages.

In the first place, France has thirty-six million inhabitants. All of them would have to be strictly supervised, to be followed into the fields, their workshops, their homes. I leave it to the reader to calculate how many extra civil servants, how much of an increase in taxes, etc., this would require.

Secondly, those who are already industrious—and, thank Heaven, their number is great—would be subjected no less than the idle to this unbearable inquisition. It is terribly cumbersome and ill-advised to subject a hundred innocent people to degrading measures for the sake of punishing one guilty person whom Nature, left to herself, will properly punish anyway.

And then, where does idleness begin? In every case brought to trial, a most minute and exacting investigation would have to be conducted. Was the accused really idle, or was he taking necessary rest? Was he sick, meditating, praying, etc.? How can all these delicate matters be weighed? Had he worked especially hard in the morning in order to enjoy a little leisure during the rest of the day? Think of all the witnesses, experts, judges, policemen that would be needed, and of all the opposition, the secret accusations, and the hatreds that would be incited!

Then there is the question of the miscarriage of justice. How many idlers would escape, and, on the other hand, how many industrious persons would be put into prison to pay for one day's idleness by a whole month of idleness!

In view of these and many other consequences, people said to themselves: Let us allow the natural law of responsibility to operate without interference. And they were right.

The socialists, who are never deterred from their goal by fear of acting despotically—for they have proclaimed the supremacy of the end over the means—have branded responsibility as *individualism* and have attempted to eliminate it or to absorb it within the scope of *solidarity* extended beyond its natural limits.

The results of this perversion of the two great motive forces of human perfectibility are disastrous. Man is left without dignity, without freedom. For, as soon as the person who acts is no longer personally responsible for the good or bad consequences of his act, his right to act as an individual no longer exists. If everything the individual does sets in motion a series of consequences involving society as a whole, the initiative for each act can no longer be left to the individual; it belongs to society. Only the community has the right to decide everything, to regulate everything: education, food, wages, amusements, travel, love, family, etc., etc. Now, society finds its expression in the law, and the law is simply the will of the lawgiver. Hence, we have a flock and a shepherd; even less than that, we have a workman and his inert raw material. We see, therefore, what the suppression of responsibility and individualism leads to.

In order to conceal this frightful objective from the common people, the socialists had to pander to their most selfish passions even while they ranted against the principle of selfishness. They said to these poor people: "Do not ask yourselves whether the hardships that you suffer are to be ascribed to the action of the law of responsibility. There are people in the world who are happy and prosperous, and in virtue of the law of solidarity they owe you a share of their prosperity." And in order to reach this stultifying level of factitious, legalized, official, forced, and unnatural solidarity, they raised plunder to the status of an economic system, distorted every notion of justice, and elevated that individualistic impulse, which they supposedly outlawed, to the highest point of power and perversity. Thus, everything in their system holds together: denial of the harmonies that spring from liberty, as its principle; despotism and slavery, as its result; immorality, as its means.

———————

Every attempt to divert responsibility from its natural course is an attack upon justice, freedom, order, civilization, or progress.

The good or bad consequences of a given act or habit follow it necessarily. If it were only possible to eliminate these consequences, there would undoubtedly be some advantage in suspending the natural law of responsibility. But the only result to be gained by a written law would be to make the good consequences of a bad act fall upon the doer, while its bad consequences would fall upon a third party or upon the community—which is certainly the characteristic feature of injustice.

Thus, modern societies are constituted on the principle that the father of a family is obliged to rear and care for the children he has brought into the world. And it is this principle that has kept and distributed the population within proper limits, every person being aware of his own responsibility. All men are not endowed with the same degree of foresight, and,[5] in the large cities, immorality is added to improvidence. Now, there are public funds and administrative agencies for taking care of children abandoned by their parents; no investigations are made of these shameful desertions, and a steadily growing wave of foundlings floods our poorer farm areas.

Here, then, we have a peasant who has married late in life, in order to avoid being overburdened with children, forced to care for other people's offspring. He will not advise his son to exercise foresight. And another who has always practiced continence, we find is taxed to pay for the support of bastards. From the religious point of view, his conscience is clear, but humanly speaking, he must say to himself that he is a fool. . . . .

We do not propose here to go into the grave question of public charity. We merely wish to make the essential observation that the more the state becomes centralized, and the more it turns natural responsibility into artificial solidarity, the more it deprives the consequences of an act—which will then affect parties not connected with it—of their providential character as agents of justice and retribution, and as preventive checks.

When the government cannot avoid assuming responsibility for a service that should remain in the realm of private activity, it must at least keep the burden of responsibility as much as possible upon the shoulders of the one to whom it naturally belongs. Thus, in the case of foundlings, the principle being that the father and the mother must raise the child, the law must exhaust every means to see that this is done. If the parents cannot be found, it must be the local community's responsibility; if not the local community, it must fall to the department. Do you wish to multiply to infinity the number of foundlings? Just declare that the state must take charge of them. It would be even worse if France were to provide for Chinese children, or vice versa. . . . .

It is indeed a singular thing that people wish to pass laws to nullify the disagreeable consequences that the law of responsibility entails. Will they never realize that they do not eliminate these consequencs, but merely pass them along to other people? The result is one injustice the more and one moral lesson the less. . . . .

How can the world be expected to improve except as everyone performs his duty? And will not everyone the better perform his duty if he will have to suffer should he neglect it? If social action is to be concerned with the operation of the law of responsibility, it should be to reinforce, not to divert, to concentrate, not to diffuse haphazardly, the consequences that this law exacts.

It has been said that public opinion is sovereign. Certainly if it is to rule well, it must be enlightened; and the better each and every man who contributes to creating it understands the relation of cause and effect, the more enlightened public opinion will be. Now, nothing makes us better appreciate this cause-and-effect relationship than experience, and experience, as we well know, is altogether a personal matter; it is the fruit of responsibility.

There is, then, in the operation of this law, a most valuable system of education with which it is very imprudent to tamper.

If by ill-advised measures you free men from the responsibility of their acts, they could still be taught by theory—but no longer by experience. And I am not certain that instruction that is not reinforced and backed by experience is not more dangerous than ignorance itself. . . . .

The *sense of responsibility* is a faculty that can be highly developed.

It is one of the most estimable of moral phenomena. There is nothing that we more admire in a man, a class, or a nation than responsibility; it reveals a high moral standard and a keen sensitivity to the decrees of public opinion. But the sense of responsibility can be highly developed in one direction and be very lacking in another. In France among the upper classes a man would die of shame if he were caught cheating at cards or indulging in solitary drinking. These things are laughed at among the peasants. But to traffic in political rights, to use our vote for ignoble ends, to compromise with our own integrity, to cry out, by turns, "Long live the King!" "Long live the League!" * according to the expediency of the moment—these are things that in our present society carry no opprobrium.

Women have much to contribute in developing the sense of responsibility.

They are extremely receptive to it. It devolves upon them to foster among men this force for moral improvement; for it is their role to mete out effectively blame and praise. . . . . Why do they not do so? Because they are not sufficiently aware of the connection between cause and effect in moral matters. . . . .

Moral knowledge concerns all mankind, but women particularly, for they shape the moral tone of a nation. . . . .

---

* [The Holy League, organized in 1576 by the Duc de Guise, had as its secret objective the overthrow of King Henry III of France.—TRANSLATOR.]

21

Solidarity

If man were perfect, if he were infallible, society would present a very different kind of harmony from that which we may actually expect it to offer us. Our idea of harmony is not Fourier's. It does not exclude the existence of evil; it leaves room for discord; and yet we shall recognize that harmony nonetheless exists, provided that discord serves to prepare the way and to lead us back to harmony.

This is our starting point: man is fallible, and God has given him free will and, with his ability to choose, also the ability to err, to mistake the false for the true, to sacrifice the future for the present, to yield to the unreasonable desires of his own heart, etc.

Man makes mistakes. But every act and habit has its consequences.

In virtue of the law of responsibility, as we have seen, these consequences fall upon the doer of the act; a natural concatenation of rewards or punishments therefore leads him toward what is good and away from what is bad.

If man had been designed by Nature for a solitary way of life and for solitary labor, responsibility would be his only law.

But he is by Nature's *design* a social creature. Contrary to what Rousseau said, man is not naturally a *complete and self-sufficient entity*, who has had to be transformed by the lawgiver's will into a component part of a greater *whole*. The family, the community, the nation, the human race, are collective units with which man has *necessary* relations. It follows that the acts and habits of the

512

individual bring about, in addition to the consequences that fall directly upon him, others, good or bad, that extend to his fellow men. This is what is called the *law of solidarity,* which is a kind of *collective responsibility.*

This idea of Rousseau that the lawgiver invented society—which is false in itself—has been disastrous in that it has led to the belief that solidarity is a mere creature of legislation; and we shall soon see that modern lawgivers use this doctrine as a basis for imposing upon society an *artificial solidarity,* which directly contravenes the action of *natural solidarity.* In all things the guiding principle of these great manipulators of the human race is to put their own creation in the place of God's creation, which they misunderstand.

Let us establish, first of all, the fact that the law of *solidarity* does exist in Nature.

In the eighteenth century people did not believe this; they refused to go beyond the doctrine of personal responsibility for one's faults. This age, which was engaged above all in reacting against Catholicism, apparently feared that, by admitting the principle of *solidarity,* it would open the door to the doctrine of *original sin.* Whenever Voltaire noted in the Bible a case of one man's bearing another's burdens, he would say ironically, "This is horrible, but God's justice is not man's."

This is not the place to discuss the question of original sin. But what Voltaire was deriding is, nevertheless, a fact, as incontestable as it is mysterious. The law of solidarity manifests itself in so many striking ways both in the individual and in the mass, both separately and collectively, in specific incidents and in general cases, that to fail to recognize it, one must possess all the blindness of sectarian bias or a burning zeal for bitter controversy.

The first rule of human justice is to concentrate the full punishment of an act upon its author, in accordance with the principle that misdeeds are personal. But this law, sacred as regards individuals, is not God's law, nor even society's.

Why is this man rich? Because his father was active, honest, industrious, and thrifty. The father practiced virtue; the son has reaped the reward.

Why is this other man always ailing, sickly, feeble, fearful, and wretched? Because his father, endowed with a strong constitution, abused it by debauchery and excess. The guilty man enjoyed the pleasurable consequences of his misdeeds; the innocent son has suffered their disastrous consequences.

There is not a man on earth whose lot has not been determined by billions of facts over which he himself had no control; that which I complain of today is perhaps due to some whim of my great grandfather's, etc.

Solidarity manifests itself on a still larger scale and at an even more incalculable range when we consider the interrelations among different peoples or different generations of the same people.

Is it not strange that the eighteenth century concerned itself so greatly with the intellectual or material labors whose fruits we enjoy today? Is it not amazing that we ourselves go to such pains to cover the country with railroads on which not one of us, perhaps, will ever travel? Who can fail to realize the profound influence that our old revolutions have on what is happening today? Who can foresee the heritage of peace or discord that our present debates will pass on to our children?

Consider the public debt. We make war on one another; we obey barbarous passions; in the process we destroy precious resources; and we find the means of shunting the burden of this destruction upon our children, who perhaps will hold war in abomination and will not be able to understand our passionate hatreds.

Cast your eyes upon Europe. Consider the events that keep France, Germany, Italy, and Poland in turmoil, and tell me whether the law of solidarity is a figment of the imagination.

It is unnecessary to carry this enumeration further. Besides, it takes the action of only one man, one nation, one generation, exerting some influence upon another man, another nation, another generation, to establish the law. The whole of society is simply a network of various interconnected manifestations of solidarity. This results from the communicable nature of our intelligence. The force of example, speech, literature, inventions, science, morals, etc.—all the unnoticed spiritual currents that unite men, all the apparently unconnected efforts that in the aggregate nevertheless impel mankind toward stability, toward a constantly rising standard of living, all that vast store of resources and knowledge upon which each of us can draw without lessening its supply, to which each of us adds without knowing it, all that exchange of ideas, of goods, of services, of labor, of evils and benefits, of virtues and vices, which makes the human family one great whole, and gives all these billions of brief existences a single common, universal, and continuous life—all this is *solidarity*.

There is, then, in the nature of things a certain incontestable measure of solidarity among men. In other words, responsibility is not entirely personal; it is shared with others. The action starts with the individual; the consequences extend to the community.

Now, we must realize that it is natural for every man to *desire to be happy and prosperous*. People may say, if they will, that I am praising selfishness. I am not praising anything; I am merely calling attention to a fact, the fact that this innate, universal impulse exists and cannot fail to exist—self-interest, the desire for well-being, the aversion to pain.

For this reason the individual is disposed to see to it that the good consequences of his acts redound to his own benefit and that the bad ones fall upon others; as much as possible he tries to distribute them over a large number of men so that they may be less noticeable and provoke less of a reaction.

But public opinion, the *queen of the world* and the daughter of solidarity, brings together all these scattered grievances, unites all these injured interests, into a formidable, solid core of resistance. When a man's habits are injurious to those about him, a hostile reaction is clearly evidenced. Such habits are judged severely, they are criticized, they are sternly reprobated; he who yields to them becomes an object of suspicion, contempt, and abhorrence. Whatever advantages he once found in such conduct are soon more than offset by the pains heaped upon him by public disapproval; to the unpleasant consequences that a bad habit always brings about, by virtue of the law of *responsibility,* there are added, by virtue of the law of *solidarity,* other consequences even more vexatious.

Contempt for the man soon extends to the habit or vice; and since the need for others' good opinion is one of our strongest motives, it is evident that the law of solidarity tends, by the reaction that it inspires against vicious acts, to restrain and to eliminate them.

Solidarity is, therefore, like responsibility, a *progressive force;* and we see that, as far as the doer of the act is concerned, it resolves itself into a kind of *refracted responsibility,* if I may so express myself. It is another system of reciprocal penalties and rewards admirably calculated to curtail what is bad, to encourage what is good, and to carry mankind forward along the road to progress.

But for solidarity to have this effect—for those who gain or lose by an act that they have not committed to influence the doer by their approval or disapproval, their gratitude or opposition, their esteem, affection, praise or scorn, hatred, and vengeance— one condition is indispensable: the connection between an act and all its effects must be known and understood.

When the public is in error on this subject, the law fails in its aim.

An act is harmful to the masses; but the masses are convinced that it is advantageous to them. Then what happens? Instead of reacting against it, condemning it, and thus suppressing it, the public extols it, honors it, and does it all the more.

Nothing happens more frequently, and here is the reason:

An act does not produce on the masses only one effect, but a series of effects. Now, it often happens that the first effect, which is beneficial, is quite local and completely visible, whereas the more remote effects spread through the body politic an evil that it is difficult to discern or to trace back to its cause.

War is an example. In the early stages of society not all the consequences of war are perceived. And indeed, in a civilization where the fruits of past labor are less exposed to destruction, where science and money have not been so much sacrificed to the war machine, etc., these consequences are less disastrous than in later stages. People see only the first campaign, the booty that follows triumph, the intoxication of victory; then war and the warrior are very popular. Later they will see the enemy, victorious in his turn, burning crops and harvests, imposing taxes and laws. With the changing tides of victory and defeat, they will see generations wiped out, agriculture destroyed, the two peoples impoverished. They will see the most vital part of the nation despising the arts of peace, turning their arms against the peaceful institutions of the country, serving as the instrument of despotism, expending their restless energy in sedition and civil discord, bringing barbarism and desolation to their own land even as they have already brought them to their neighbors'. Will people then say that war is banditry on a larger scale? No. They will see its effects without wishing to understand its cause; and as this nation in its decadence will in its turn have been invaded by a swarm of conquerors, many centuries after the catastrophe sober historians will write: This nation fell because during times of peace it became enervated, because it forgot the art of war and the fierce virtues of its ancestors.

I could point to the same false notions about slavery. . . . .

This is likewise true of religious errors. . . . .

In our day the protectionist system gives rise to the same mistake. . . . .

By the dissemination of knowledge, by enlightened discussion of cause and effect, to bring public opinion back to the intelligent attitude that condemns bad tendencies and resists the adoption of harmful measures, is to render a great service to one's country. When misguided public opinion honors what is despicable and despises what is honorable, punishes virtue and rewards vice, encourages what is harmful and discourages what is useful, applauds falsehood and smothers truth under indifference or insult, a nation turns its back on progress and can be restored only by the terrible lessons of catastrophe.

We have indicated elsewhere the gross abuse of the word "solidarity" of which certain socialist schools have been guilty.

Let us now consider in what spirit man-made law should be conceived.

It seems to me that there can be no doubt on this subject. Man-made law should be in accord with the natural law: it should hasten and assure just retribution for men's acts; in other words, limit the area of solidarity and bring home to the author of the act his own responsibility. The law can have no other objective than to restrain vicious acts and to encourage virtuous acts, and to this end it must facilitate the just distribution of rewards and punishments, so that the bad consequences of an act fall as much as possible upon the person who commits it. . . . .

Acting in this manner, the law conforms to the nature of things: solidarity initiates a reaction against the vicious act; the law merely regularizes this reaction.

Thus, the law contributes to progress; the more rapidly it brings home to the doer the bad effect of an act, the more surely it restrains the act itself.

Let us take an example. Violence has disastrous consequences. Among savage peoples its suppression is left to the natural course of events. What happens? It provokes a terrible reaction. When a man has committed an act of violence against another man, an inextinguishable thirst for vengeance is kindled in the victim's family and is passed on from generation to generation. The law intervenes. What should it do? Will it be content merely to stifle, suppress, punish the spirit of vengeance? It is evident that this would encourage violence by protecting it from all reprisals. This is not, therefore, what the law should do. It should take the role, so to speak, of the spirit of vengeance by organizing in its place the reaction against violence. It should say to the family that has been wronged: I assume responsibility for the suppression of the act of which you complain. Then the entire tribe shares with the family the feeling of being wronged and threatened. It investigates the charge, it interrogates the guilty man, it makes sure that there has been no error as to the fact or the person, and thus represses surely and with due regularity an act that otherwise would have been punished in an irregular way. . . . .[1]

22

The Motive Force of Society

It is not within the province of any branch of human knowledge to give the ultimate reason for things.

Man suffers; society suffers. We ask why. This is equivalent to asking why God has given man feeling and free will. We know on this subject only what is revealed to us by the faith in which we believe.

But whatever may have been God's plan, what we do know as a positive fact, what human knowledge can take as a starting point, is that man was created a *sentient being* endowed with *free will*.

This is so true that I defy anyone who may be astonished at it to conceive of a living, thinking, desiring, loving, acting being—of anything, in a word, resembling man—yet lacking in sensibility or free will.

Could God have done differently? Of course, our reason says yes, but our imagination will forever say no; so radically impossible is it for us to think of man as being without this double attribute. Now, to be *sentient* is to be capable of receiving identifiable sensations, that is, sensations that are pleasant or painful. Hence well-being and suffering. By the very fact of creating sensibility, God permitted evil or the possibility of evil.

In giving us free will, He has endowed us with the faculty, at least to a certain extent, of avoiding what is evil and seeking after what is good. Free will presupposes intelligence and is associated with it. What good would it be to have the power to choose, if the power to examine, to compare, and to judge were not joined to it? Thus, every man born into the world possesses a *motive force* and an *intellect*.

The motive force is that inner, irresistible drive, the very essence of all our energy, which impels us to shun evil and to seek after the good. We call it the instinct of self-preservation, personal interest, or self-interest.

This impulse has sometimes been decried, sometimes misunderstood, but there can be no question as to its existence. We seek indefeasibly everything that to our mind can improve our lot; we avoid everything that is likely to impair it. This fact is at least as certain as that every molecule of matter possesses centripetal and centrifugal force. And even as this double movement of attraction and repulsion is the great motive force of the physical universe, so the double impulse of human attraction toward happiness and human aversion to pain is the great motive force of the social machine.

But it is not enough that man should be irresistibly disposed to prefer good to evil; it is also necessary for him to distinguish between them. And this God has provided for by giving man the complex and marvelous mechanism called intelligence. To direct our attention, to compare, to judge, to reason, to relate cause and effect, to remember, to foresee—such are, if I may so express myself, the moving cogs of this wonderful machine.

The driving force that is in each of us moves at the direction of our intellect. But our intellect is imperfect. It is subject to error. We compare, we judge, we act accordingly; but we can be wrong, make a bad choice, turn toward evil, mistaking it for the good, or we may shun the good, mistaking it for evil. This is the first source of social *discord;* it is inevitable for the very reason that the mainspring of human nature, self-interest, is not, like attraction in the material world, a blind force, but one guided by an imperfect intellect. Let us therefore clearly realize that we shall find harmony only with this restriction attached to it. God has seen fit to establish the social order, or harmony, not upon the basis of perfection, but upon that of man's perfectibility. Yes, if our intellect is imperfect, it is also perfectible. It develops, enlarges, corrects its errors; it repeats and verifies its operations;

at every instant experience sets it right, and responsibility holds over our heads a whole system of punishments and rewards. Every step that we take toward error plunges us more deeply into suffering, so that the warning signal does not fail to make itself heard, and our decisions, and consequently our acts, are sooner or later inevitably set aright.

Under the impulse that actuates him, man, eager to pursue happiness, quick to seize hold of it, is quite likely to seek his own good in another's harm. This is a second and fertile source of discordant social relations. But their field is limited; they are inevitably eliminated by the law of solidarity. The activity of one individual thus misdirected provokes the opposition of all other individuals, who, being hostile to evil by their nature, reject injustice and punish it.

In this way progress is achieved, and it is nonetheless progress for being dearly bought. It is the result of a natural, universal drive that is innate, directed by an intellect that often errs, and subject to a will that is often perverse. Halted in its course by error and injustice, it surmounts these obstacles with the all-powerful aid of responsibility and solidarity—a help that is ever present, since it stems from the obstacles themselves.

This inner, indestructible, universal motive force that resides in every individual and makes of him an active being, this tendency of every man to seek happiness and to shun misery, this product, this effect, this necessary complement of sensibility, without which the latter would be merely a meaningless burden, this primordial phenomenon which is the origin of all human action, this attracting and repelling force which we have called the mainspring of the social machine, has been disparaged by most social philosophers and political theorists; and this is certainly one of the strangest aberrations to be found in the annals of science.

It is true that self-interest is the cause of all the evils, as well as all the benefits, that can fall to the lot of man. This cannot fail to be the case, since self-interest determines all our actions. Certain political theorists, seeing this, have conceived of no better way to cut off evil at its roots than to stifle *self-interest*. But, since by this act they would also destroy the very motive force of our activity, they thought it best to endow us with a different motive

force: *devotion* and *self-sacrifice*. They hoped that henceforth all
social transactions and arrangements would be carried out, at
their bidding, on the principle of self-abnegation. People are no
longer to seek their own good but others'; the admonitions of
pain and pleasure are no longer to count for anything, any more
than the punishments and rewards of responsibility. All the laws
of nature are to be overturned; the spirit of self-sacrifice is to take
the place of the instinct of self-preservation; in a word, no one is
ever to consider his own personality except to hasten to sacrifice it to the common good. It is from this complete transformation of the human heart that certain political theorists, who
believe themselves to be very religious, expect the coming of
perfect social harmony. They forget to tell us how they propose
to carry out the indispensable preliminary, the transformation of
the human heart.

If they are mad enough to undertake it, they will certainly not
be strong enough to achieve it. Do they desire the proof? Let them
try the experiment on themselves; let them try to stifle self-interest
in their own hearts so that it is no longer evidenced in the most
ordinary acts of their lives. They will not be long in admitting
their own inability to do so. How, then, do they presume to impose
upon all men, without exception, a doctrine to which they
themselves cannot submit?

I confess that it is impossible for me to find anything religious,
except in outward appearance and at the very most in intention,
in these affected theories, these impracticable maxims, to which
their authors give lip service while they continue to act like the
common run of humanity. Is it true religion that inspires in these
Catholic economists the presumptuous thought that God has done
His work badly and that they must set it right? Bossuet * was not

* [Jacques Bénigne Bossuet (1627–1704), bishop of Condom and of Meaux, was the
outstanding pulpit orator of his day, his funeral orations for members of the royal
family ranking as brilliant examples of French classical style and power. As tutor
to the heir apparent, the son of Louis XIV, he wrote his *Histoire universelle*, one
of the classics on which French school children were raised for generations. His
vigorous stand against Protestantism and his successful leadership of the Gallican
movement, which brought increased independence to the Catholic Church in France,
reveal him as an important ecclesiastical, as well as literary, figure.—TRANSLATOR.]

of this opinion when he said, "Man aspires to happiness; he cannot do otherwise."

Tirades against self-interest will never have great scientific significance; for by its very nature it is indestructible, or at least it cannot be destroyed within man without destroying man himself. All that religion, morality, and political economy can do is to enlighten us regarding this impulse, to show us not only the immediate but also the ultimate consequences of the acts that it prompts within us. Greater and constantly increasing satisfaction following a momentary sensation of pain; long and constantly aggravated suffering following a momentary pleasure: this, in the last analysis, is moral good and evil. What determines man's choice in favor of virtue must be his higher, enlightened self-interest, but basically self-interest it will always be.

If it is strange that people have decried self-interest, not only in its immoral abuses, but also as the providential motive force of all human activity, it is even more strange that they have not taken it into account and have felt that they could work in the social sciences without reference to it.

With the unaccountable folly of self-pride, political theorists have, in general, considered themselves the guardians and directors of this motive force. For every one of them the point of departure is always the same: Assuming that humanity is a flock of sheep and that I am the shepherd, how shall I set about making humanity happy? Or else: Given, on the one hand, a certain quantity of clay, and on the other, a potter, what must the potter do to make the best possible use of the clay?

Our political theorists may differ on how to decide who is the best potter, or who can mold the clay most effectively; but they agree on this point, that their function is to mold the human clay, just as it is the role of the clay to be molded by them. They establish between themselves, in their capacity as the lawgivers, and the rest of mankind a relationship analogous to that of guardian and ward. It never occurs to them that man is a living body, feeling, willing, acting in obedience to laws that it is not their province to invent, since these laws already exist, even less to impose, but rather to study. It does not occur to them that mankind is composed of a great host of beings in every way similar to themselves, in no way their inferiors or subject to them; that their fellow men are endowed both with an impulse to act and with intelligence to choose; that in everything men do they are affected by the promptings of responsibility and solidarity; and that, finally, from all these phenomena there results a pattern of already existing relations that it is not the province of the social sciences to create, as these theorists imagine, but to observe.

Rousseau was, I believe, the political theorist who most naively exhumed from antiquity this idea, which had already been resurrected by the Greeks, of the omnipotence of the lawgiver. Convinced that the social order is a human invention, he compares it to a machine. Men are the cogs; the prince makes it run. The lawgiver invents it at the bidding of the political theorist, who thus, in the last analysis, activates and controls the human race. That is why the political theorist never fails to address the lawgiver in the imperative mood; he orders him to give the orders: "Establish your nation on such and such a principle; give it good manners and customs; make it bow to the authority of religion; orient it toward war or commerce or agriculture or virtue, etc., etc." The more modest among them hide behind the anonymity of the passive voice. "Idlers *will not be* tolerated in the republic; the population *will be* suitably distributed between the cities and the country; steps *will be* taken so that there will be neither rich nor poor; etc., etc."

These formulas attest to the inordinate presumption of those who use them. Implicit in them is a conception of man that leaves the human race not one shred of self-respect.

I know of no doctrine more false in theory or more disastrous in practice. On both scores it leads to lamentable consequences.

It gives rise to the view that the social economy is an artificial arrangement that has sprung from the brain of an inventor. Every political theorist, therefore, constitutes himself an inventor forthwith. His greatest desire is to win acceptance for the machine he has invented; his greatest preoccupation is to represent all other proposed social orders as detestable and especially that which springs spontaneously from the nature of man and the nature of things. Books conceived according to this plan are and can be only a long tirade against society.

This false science does not study the concatenation of cause and effect. It does not investigate the good and the evil that acts produce, leaving it afterwards to the motive force of society to select the course to be followed. No, it enjoins, it restrains, it imposes, and if it does not have the power to do these things, at least it gives advice; like a physicist who would say to a stone, "There is nothing to hold you up; therefore I order you to fall, or at least I advise you to fall." It is on this principle that M. Droz * has said, "The aim of political economy is to make prosperity as general as possible"; a definition very favorably received by the socialists because it opens the door to every utopian scheme and leads to regimentation. What would people think of M. Arago † if he began his course of lectures in this fashion: "The aim of astronomy is to make gravitation as general as possible"? It is true that men are animate beings, endowed with will power and enjoying freedom of choice. But there is also a kind of inner force in them, a kind of gravitation; the question is to know toward what they gravitate. If it is inevitably toward evil, then there is no remedy, and certainly none will come from the political theorist, who as a man is subject to the same unfortunate tendency as the rest of mankind. If it is toward the good, the motive force is ready-made; science has no need of replacing it with coercion or advice. Its role is to enlighten men's free will, to show the relation between cause and effect, confident that, under the influence of truth, "prosperity tends to become as general as possible."

In practice, the doctrine that places the motive force of society, not in all mankind and in the nature of man, but in lawgivers and in governments, has even more unfortunate consequences. It tends to weigh down the government with a crushing responsibility

* [Joseph Droz (1773–1850), French philosopher and economist, member of the French Academy.—TRANSLATOR.]

† [Dominique François Arago (1786–1853), famous French scientist and statesman, member of the provisional government of 1848, and the Minister of War and the Navy.—TRANSLATOR.]

that does not belong to it. If there is suffering, it is the fault of the government; if there is poverty, the government is to blame. For is not the government the universal motive force? If this motive force is not good, we must destroy it and choose another. Or else the blame is placed on political economy itself, and in recent times we have heard it repeated *ad nauseam*: "All the suffering of society can be attributed to political economy." [1] Why not, when it is presented as having for its goal the securing of men's happiness without any effort on their part? When such ideas are current, the last thing that occurs to men is to turn their gaze upon themselves, and to see whether the real cause of their woes is not their own ignorance and injustice—their ignorance, which exposes them to the law of responsibility; their injustice, which brings down upon them the action of the law of solidarity. How could men dream of blaming themselves for their woes when they have been persuaded that by nature they are inert, that the source of all action, and consequently of all responsibility, lies outside themselves, in the will of the sovereign and of the lawgiver?

If I had to point out the characteristic trait that differentiates socialism from the science of economics, I should find it here. Socialism includes a countless number of sects. Each one has its own utopia, and we may well say that they are so far from agreement that they wage bitter war upon one another. Between M. Blanc's *organized social workshops* and M. Proudhon's *anarchy,* between Fourier's association and M. Cabet's communism, there is certainly all the difference between night and day. What, then, is the common denominator to which all forms of socialism are reducible, and what is the bond that unites them against natural society, or society as planned by Providence? There is none except this: *They do not want natural society.* What they do want is an artificial society, which has come forth full-grown from the brain of its inventor. It is true that each one desires to play Jupiter to this Minerva; it is true that each one fondly caresses his own invention and dreams of his own social order. But what they have in common is their refusal to recognize in mankind either the motive force that impels men toward the good or the *self-healing* power that delivers them from evil. They quarrel over who will mold the human clay, but they agree that there is human clay to mold. Mankind is not in their eyes a living and harmonious being endowed by God Himself with the power to progress and to survive, but an inert mass that has been waiting for them to give it feeling and life; human nature is not a subject to be studied, but matter on which to perform experiments.

Political economy, on the contrary, after first establishing the fact that within every man are the forces of impulsion and repulsion that together constitute the motive power of society, after making certain that this motive force tends toward what is good, does not propose to destroy it and to replace it with another of its own creation. Political economy studies the highly varied and complex social phenomena to which this motive force gives rise.

Does this mean that political economy has no more to do with social progress than the study of astronomy has to do with the actual movement of the heavenly bodies? Certainly not. Political economy deals with beings who possess intelligence and free will and as such—let us never forget it—are subject to error. Their tendency is toward the good; but they can be mistaken. The utilitarian function of science, therefore, is not to create causes and effects, not to change man's natural bent, not to foist upon him social orders, injunctions, or even advice, but to show him the good and the evil that results from his own decisions.

Thus, political economy is a science concerned exclusively with the observation and description of phenomena. It does not say to men: "I urge you, I advise you, not to get too close to the fire"; or: "I have thought up a social order; the gods have inspired me to create institutions that will keep you far enough away from the fire." No; political economy notes that fire burns, announces the fact, proves it, and does the same for all similar phenomena of the moral or economic order, convinced that this is all that is necessary. It assumes that an unwillingness to be burned to death is a basic, innate attitude that it did not create and that it cannot alter.

Political economists cannot always be in agreement, but it is easy to see that their differences are of quite another kind from those that divide the socialists. Two men who devote themselves to observing the same phenomenon and its effects, like rent, for example, or exchange or competition, may not arrive at the same conclusion; but this proves nothing except that one of the two, at least, has observed badly. The work will have to be done over. With the help of other investigators the chances are that the truth will finally be discovered. That is why—provided only that every economist, like every astronomer, keeps himself informed on the advances his predecessors have made—this science cannot fail to contribute to progress and consequently to be ever more useful, constantly correcting past errors in observation, and continually adding new observations to those already made.

But the socialists—isolating themselves from one another, so that they may concoct, each one on his own, artificial contrivances out of their own imaginations—could go on pursuing their investigations in this way through all eternity without ever coming to an agreement and without one man's work ever in any way helping another's. Say profited from Smith's investigations; Rossi, from Say's; Blanqui and Joseph Garnier, from those of all their predecessors. But Plato, Sir Thomas More, Harrington,* Fénelon, Fourier may revel to their heart's delight in drawing up their Republics, their Utopias, their Oceanas, their Salentes, their Phalansteries, without there ever being any connection between any one of these flights of fancy and the others. These dreamers draw it all, men and things alike, out of their own heads. They dream up a social order not connected with the human heart; then they invent a new human heart to go with their social order. . . . .

---

* [James Harrington (1611–1677), English political philosopher, whose work on the ideal state, entitled *Commonwealth of Oceana* (1656), advocating a written constitution, rotation of magistrates and legislators, indirect election of the president, the secret ballot, and agrarian reforms, is believed to have influenced political thought in the United States and other democracies.—TRANSLATOR.]

23

Evil

In recent years the science of political economy has been set back, has been given a false direction, by those who have sought to force it to deny the existence of evil or risk being convicted of denying the existence of God.

Writers who were doubtless eager to make a show of their exquisitely delicate feelings, their boundless love for their fellow man, and their matchless religious ardor, began to declare: "Evil cannot enter into the providential plan. Suffering was decreed neither by God nor by Nature; it comes from human institutions."

Since this doctrine was in full accord with the passions and prejudices that these writers wished to encourage, it soon became a popular one. Books and newspapers were filled with tirades against society. Political economy was no longer permitted to study the facts objectively. Whoever dared to warn mankind that a given vice, a given habit, necessarily involved dire consequences was branded as heartless, as an unbeliever, an atheist, a Malthusian, or an economist.

Meanwhile, socialism has carried its folly so far as to announce the end of all the ills of society, though not of all the ills of the individual. It has not yet dared to predict that man will reach the point where suffering, old age, and death will be eliminated.

Now, I ask, can the idea of the infinite goodness of God be reconciled more easily with the idea that evil strikes every individual coming into the world than with the idea that evil falls upon society as a whole? And is it not indulging in a contradiction so obvious as to be childish, to deny that pain and suffering exist for society as a whole and yet admit that they exist for every individual in society?

Man is subject to suffering and always will be. Therefore, society suffers and always will suffer. Those who speak to society must have the courage to declare this truth. Mankind is not a pampered little darling, with oversensitive nerves, who must be kept in ignorance of the coming struggle, particularly since, to emerge triumphant, men need to be alerted against it. In this respect all the books that have flooded France since the time of Sismondi and Buret seem to me to be lacking in courage. They do not dare to tell the truth. What is more, they do not dare even to study the truth for fear of discovering that absolute poverty, far from being attributable to the social order, is the necessary starting point for the human race, and, consequently, it is to the social order that are to be attributed all the conquests that have been achieved in the struggle against poverty. But after such a confession they would no longer be able to pose as the defenders of the people and the avengers of the masses whom civilization has oppressed.

After all, science simply presents the facts, shows how they are related, and draws inferences from them. It does not create the facts; it is not responsible for them. It is strange indeed that anyone should have gone to the length of giving expression and even wide circulation to this paradox: If mankind suffers, it is the fault of political economy! Thus, after being blamed for taking note of the woes of society, it is accused, precisely because it has noted them, of having caused them.

I have said that science can only observe and establish the facts. Even if it were to discover that mankind is retrogressive, not progressive, and that laws too strong to be resisted inevitably impel it toward irremediable decadence; even if it were to confirm the laws of Malthus and Ricardo in their most melancholy signification; even if it were unable to deny the tyranny of capital or the fundamental conflict between labor and the machine or any of the contradictory alternatives that, according to Chateaubriand * and de Tocqueville, confront the human race; science should still, albeit dolefully, declare the fact and declare it for all to hear.

Does it serve any good purpose to shut our eyes so as not to see the abyss, when the abyss is there, yawning at our feet? Do we demand that the biologist or the physiologist treat the individual human being as if his organs were immune to pain or destruction? *"Dust art thou, and to dust thou shalt return."* That is what the science of anatomy declares, supported by the experience of all mankind. Certainly this truth sounds harsh in our ears, at least as harsh as the questionable propositions of Malthus and Ricardo. Must we, then, to spare the delicate sensibilities that have suddenly developed among modern political theorists and that have given rise to socialism, deny the existence of evil? And must medical science boldly affirm our eternal rejuvenation and immortality? Or, if it refuses to stoop to such mummery, must people cry out, frothing at the mouth, as they do to the social scientists: "Medical scientists admit pain and death. Therefore, they are heartless misanthropists; they accuse God of malevolence or impotence. They are irreverent; they are atheists. What is even worse, they create the evil that they stubbornly refuse to deny."

I have never doubted that the socialists have led astray many generous hearts and sincere minds. God forbid that I should wish to humiliate anyone! But the truth is that the general character of socialism is very strange, and I wonder how long so childish a fabric of absurdities can remain in vogue.

Everything about socialism is sham and affectation.

It affects the form and language of science, and we have seen where it stands as a science.

It affects in its writings such delicately feminine sensibilities that it cannot bear to hear of the sufferings of society. At the same

* [Vicomte François René de Chateaubriand (1768–1848), a forerunner of the romantic movement in French literature, and a royalist in politics. He served the restored Bourbon monarchy, after the fall of Napoleon, as ambassador to England and Germany and as Minister of Foreign Affairs. His most famous works are *The Genius of Christianity* and *Memoirs from beyond the Tomb.*—TRANSLATOR.]

time that it has introduced into literature the current fashion for sickly sentimentality, it has brought into the arts the taste for the trivial and the horrible; in dress, the scarecrow style, the long beard, the scowling face, the airs of a village Titan or Prometheus; and in politics (in which such childishness is less innocent), the doctrine of bold measures *during the period of transition,* the violence of revolution, the sacrifice of men's lives and welfare en masse to an *idea.* But the greatest affectation of socialism is its religiosity! It is only a stratagem, true enough, but stratagems are always shameful for a school of thought when they lead to hypocrisy.

The socialists are always talking of Christ; but I ask them how they can accept the fact that Christ, the blameless one, was allowed to suffer and to cry out in his anguish, "Father, remove this cup from me; nevertheless not my will, but thine, be done," and why they find it strange that all mankind should have to perform this same act of resignation.

No doubt, if God had had other plans for mankind, He could have arranged things in such a way that, just as the individual advances toward certain death, so the human race would move toward inevitable destruction. Mankind would have had to submit; and science, with a curse or a benediction on its lips, would have been forced to acknowledge the tragic ending of the social drama, even as it acknowledges the melancholy end of individual man.

Happily, such is not the case.

There is redemption for both the individual man and the human race.

For the individual it is his immortal soul. For the human race it is its limitless perfectibility. . . . .

24

Perfectibility

Mankind is perfectible. It is progressing toward a better and better standard of living; its wealth is on the increase and is being more equitably distributed; its ideas are becoming sounder and more widely disseminated; its errors are disappearing, and with them the unjust acts that they serve to support; its learning shines ever brighter; its morality is improving; by way of reason or experience it is learning, in conformity with the law of responsibility, to secure greater rewards and to suffer fewer penalties; consequently, there is less and less evil and more and more good within society. These are propositions that cannot be doubted when we consider the nature of man and of his intellect, his distinctive characteristic, which was breathed into him along with the breath of life, and by virtue of which the revelation of Moses could declare that man was created in the image of God.

For man, as we know only too well, is not perfect. If he were perfect, he would not be a pale reflection of God; he would be God. He is, therefore, imperfect, subject to error and pain; and were he, in addition, static, by what right could he claim the ineffable privilege of bearing the image of the Perfect Being?

Furthermore, if intellect, which is the faculty of comparing, of judging, of correcting errors, of learning, does not constitute a kind of individual perfectibility, what then is it?

And if, in a society of beings capable of transmitting to others what they have learned, the uniting of each individual's capacity for perfection with that of all others does not insure collective perfectibility, then we must abandon all faith in philosophy and in moral and political science.

What makes for man's perfectibility is his intellect, or the capacity that is given him to pass from error, the source of evil, to truth, the source of the good.

What causes man to abandon, in his mind, error for truth, and later, in his conduct, evil for good, is knowledge and experience; it is the discovery he makes that there are in phenomena and in acts effects that he had not before dreamed of.

But, for him to gain this knowledge, it must be to his advantage to do so. For him to profit from this experience, it must be to his interest to profit from it. Therefore, in the last analysis, we must look to the law of responsibility to find the means to achieve human perfectibility.

And since responsibility cannot be conceived of without free will; since acts, if not voluntary, could not furnish valid instruction or experience; since beings whose improvement or deterioration would be entirely due to outside causes without any act of will, reflection, or choice on their part, as happens in the case of inert matter, could not be called perfectible in the moral sense of the word; we must conclude that freedom is the very essence of man's progress. To tamper with man's freedom is not only to injure him, to degrade him; it is to change his nature, to render him, in so far as such oppression is exercised, incapable of improvement; it is to strip him of his resemblance to the Creator, to stifle within him the noble breath of life with which he was endowed at his creation.

But because we proclaim to the world that our most unshakably held article of faith is our belief in man's perfectibility, in his inevitable progress in all areas of his life, which are so marvelously linked that the faster his progress in one of them, the faster it is in all the others, does this mean that we are utopians, or even that we are optimists, believing that all is for the best in the best of all possible worlds, and that we expect that one of these fine mornings the millennium will arrive?

Alas! When we look at the real world about us and see great masses of suffering, groaning humanity, wallowing in shame and degradation, in vice and crime; when we seek to gauge the moral effect exerted on society by the classes that should point out to the backward masses the road to the New Jerusalem; when we ask ourselves what use the rich make of their wealth, the poets of the divine spark of genius that Nature has kindled in them, the philosophers of the fruit of their long vigils, the journalists of the sacred mission entrusted to them, the dignitaries and ministers of state, the representatives of the people, and the kings, of the power that fate has placed in their hands; when we witness revolutions like the one that has lately shaken Europe, with every faction apparently seeking what must, in the long run, be most disastrous to itself and mankind; when we see greed assuming all possible forms and permeating all ranks, the constant sacrificing of others to one's own advantage and of the future to the present, and self-interest, the great and necessary motive force of humanity, manifesting itself only in its most materialistic and improvident forms; when we see the working classes, robbed of their well-being and self-respect by parasitical public functionaries, turning, in revolutionary paroxysms, not against the parasites who drain their substance, but against those who have earned the wealth they possess, that is, against the very element in society able to assure their emancipation and guarantee their rights and powers; when such sights meet our eyes in every country toward which we look, we become fearful of ourselves, and we tremble for our faith, which seems to us but a flickering light about to be extinguished, leaving us in the horrible night of pessimism.

But no, there is no reason to despair. Whatever may be the impression made upon us by events too close to us, mankind does move forward. We are victims of an illusion because we measure the life of the human race by our own; and because for us a few years are a long time, it seems to us that they are a long time for mankind as well. Nevertheless, even by this measure it seems to me that there are many respects in which the progress of society is discernible. I need hardly point out certain striking material achievements, such as the sanitation of our cities, our means of transportation and communication, etc. As regards politics, has not the French nation acquired some experience? Would anyone dare assert that, if all the difficulties through which France has recently gone had presented themselves half a century ago or earlier, she would have overcome them with equal skill, prudence, and wisdom and at so little sacrifice to her citizens? I am writing these lines in a country that has been wracked with revolutions. Every five years there was an insurrection in Florence, and each time half of the citizens plundered and massacred the other half. If we only had a little more imagination—not the imagination that creates, invents, and conjectures, but the imagination that re-creates the past—we should be more just toward our own age and our contemporaries. But what remains true, and true in a way that no one understands better than the economist, is that man's progress, particularly at its dawn, is exceedingly slow, slow enough to be the despair of anyone who loves his fellow man.

Men whose genius has won them that sacred trust which is the voice of the press ought, it seems to me, to be very slow in pronouncing upon society, in the midst of its ferment, any of those disheartening sentences that imply for mankind nothing but a choice between two forms of degradation.

We have seen several examples of this in connection with such subjects as population, rent, machinery, the breaking up of inherited estates, etc.

Here is another taken from M. de Chateaubriand who, by the way, merely gives expression to a very prevalent attitude: "The corruption of manners goes hand in hand with civilization. If the latter offers the means of liberty, the former is an inexhaustible source of slavery."

It cannot be doubted that civilization offers the means of liberty. It is no less indubitable that corruption is the source of slavery. But what is doubtful, more than doubtful—and personally I emphatically deny it—is that civilization and corruption go hand in hand. If this were the case, inevitably the *means of liberty* would counterbalance the *sources of slavery*, and stagnation would be the fate of the human race.

Furthermore, I do not think that a sadder, more discouraging, more hopeless thought, or one more conducive to despair, irreligion, impiety, and blasphemy, can enter the human heart than this: Every human creature, willingly or unwillingly, wittingly or unwittingly, moves in the direction of civilization, and . . . . civilization is corruption!

Then, too, if all civilization is corruption, in what do its advantages consist? For to aver that civilization has no material, intellectual, or moral advantage is an impossibility; such a thing would no longer be civilization. According to Chateaubriand, civilization means material progress, an increase in population, in wealth, in the standard of living, intellectual development, scientific knowledge; and all this progress implies and necessitates a corresponding decline in moral values.

All this would be enough to drive men to mass suicide; but no, I repeat, material and intellectual progress has not been designed and devised by man. God Himself decreed it in giving us ever increasing wants and perfectible faculties. We all move in this direction without willing it, without knowing it, Chateaubriand and those like him, if any, even more than the rest of us. And this progress is to drive us more and more deeply into immorality and slavery by virtue of its attendant corruption!

At first I thought that Chateaubriand had merely tossed off a phrase, as poets often do, without weighing it carefully. With writers of this class, form takes precedence over content. Provided the antithesis be neatly balanced, what does it matter if the thought be false and abominable? As long as the metaphor is effective, as long as it has an air of inspiration and profundity, as long as it wrings applause from the public, as long as it gives the author an oracular turn of expression, what does he care for accuracy and truth?

I thought, then, that Chateaubriand, giving way to a momentary burst of misanthropy, had allowed himself to indulge in a cliché, a commonplace to be heard on every street corner. "Civilization and corruption go hand in hand" has been repeated since the time of Heraclitus, but it is not, for all that, any the less false.

However, after a lapse of many years, the same great writer has repeated the same thought in what is apparently intended as a didactic form, which proves that this was one of his settled convictions. It is well to refute it, not because it comes from Chateaubriand, but because it is widespread.

Material conditions improve, intellectual progress is made, and the nations, instead of benefiting, lose ground. This is how the decline of society and the rise of the individual are to be explained. If the moral sense developed in the same ratio as the intellect, there would be a counterbalance, and mankind would flourish without danger. But the exact opposite happens. Our perception of good and evil becomes dim in proportion as our intellect is enlightened; our conscience becomes narrower in proportion as our knowledge grows.[1] *

---

* [This relatively long digression on Chateaubriand is to be explained by the fact that his *Mémoires d'outre-tombe* (1848–50), anticipated by public and critics as a world-shaking literary event, had just appeared as Bastiat was preparing these notes.—TRANSLATOR.]

25

Relations of Political Economy with Ethics, Politics, Legislation, and Religion[1]

Any given phenomenon is always found set between two other phenomena. One of these is its *efficient* cause, and the other its *final* cause; and science has not finished with it as long as either of these relations is not clear.

I believe that the human mind usually begins by discovering the final causes, because they concern us more directly. Furthermore, no other kind of knowledge turns us so strongly toward religious ideas, or is as likely to inspire deep within our hearts a lively sense of gratitude for God's inexhaustible bounty.

Habit, it is true, has made us so familiar with a great number of these *providential purposes* that we enjoy them without thinking about them. We see and we hear, without a thought for the ingenious mechanism of the eye and of the ear; the sun's rays, the drops of dew or rain lavish upon us their practical benefits or their pleasant sensations without eliciting our wonder or our gratitude. This comes about solely because these wonderful phenomena are always with us. For, let even a comparatively insignificant final cause happen to be called to our attention, let the botanist show us why one plant assumes a certain form, why another has a certain color, and at once we sense the ineffable enchantment unfailingly communicated to our hearts by new proofs of God's power and of His goodness and wisdom.

The domain of final causes is therefore, for man's imagination, like an atmosphere filled with religious thoughts.

But, after we have perceived or glimpsed this aspect of the phenomenon, we still must study it from the other side; that is, we must investigate its efficient cause.

Strangely enough, it sometimes happens that, after we have become fully familiar with this cause, we discover that it so inevitably entails the effect which at first had filled us with wonder that we are no longer willing to see in it the character of a final cause, and we say: I was very naive to believe that God had provided for such an arrangement with such a design; I see now that, given the cause that I discovered (and it is inevitable), this arrangement had to follow necessarily, apart from any so-called providential design.

In this way superficial science, with its scalpel and its analyses, sometimes destroys in our soul the religious sentiment that the simple spectacle of Nature had inspired.

This is often seen in the case of the anatomist or the astronomer. What a marvelous thing, says the layman, that, when a foreign body enters our flesh, where its presence would cause serious injury, an inflammation and a secretion of pus occur that tend to expel the object! No, says the anatomist; there is nothing intentional about this expulsion. It is the *necessary* effect of the suppuration, and the latter in turn is the *necessary* effect of the presence of a foreign body in our flesh. If you wish, I will explain the mechanism to you, and you can see for yourself that the effect follows the cause, but that the cause has not been arranged intentionally to produce the effect, since it is itself the necessary effect of a previous cause.

How I marvel, says the layman, at God's foresight in preventing rain from falling on the ground in sheets, providing, instead, for it to fall in gentle drops, as if from the gardener's sprinkler! Without this, all vegetation would be impossible. You are wasting your wonder, replies the learned physicist. A cloud is not a sheet of water; it cannot be held suspended in the atmosphere. It is a mass of microscopic vesicules much like soap bubbles. When their density increases, or when they burst under pressure, these billions of tiny drops fall, increasing on the way down from the water vapor that they precipitate, etc. If vegetation is helped by this, it is accidental; but you must not think that God amuses himself by pouring water on you through the nozzle of an immense sprinkler.

What lends a certain plausibility to science when it thus analyzes relations of cause and effect is, we must admit, the fact that through ignorance people very often attribute a phenomenon to a nonexistent final cause that evaporates in the light of reason.

Thus, in the beginning, before there was any knowledge of electricity, primitive peoples, frightened by the roar of thunder, could identify this awesome voice reverberating through the clouds only as a sign of divine wrath. Many an association of this kind has been exploded by the progress of the physical sciences.

This is the way man is constituted. When a phenomenon affects him, he seeks its cause, and, when he finds it, he gives it a name. Then he sets about finding the cause of this cause, and so on, until, being unable to go any farther, he stops and says: *This is God; this is the will of God.* Here is our *ultima ratio.** Yet man pauses only momentarily. Science advances, and soon the second, third, or fourth cause that had remained hidden is exposed to his view. Then the scientist says: This effect was not due, as people believed, to the immediate will of God, but to this natural cause that I have just discovered. And mankind takes possession of this discovery, and then, content with having moved back by one notch, so to speak, the line where its faith begins, asks itself: What is the cause of this cause? And, not discovering it, man persists in the tried and true explanation: *It is the will of God.* And so on for unnumbered centuries, in an endless progression of scientific revelations and acts of faith.

This onward march of mankind must seem to superficial minds to be destructive of every religious idea; for is its result not that, as science advances, God retreats? And do we not clearly perceive that the domain of final causes grows smaller as the domain of natural causes grows larger?

* [Our "final reason."—TRANSLATOR.]

Unhappy are those who give so narrow a solution to this fine problem. No, it is not true that, as science advances, the idea of God is pushed back. Quite the contrary; the truth is that this idea grows, broadens, and is exalted in our minds. When we discover a natural cause where we thought we had seen an immediate, spontaneous, supernatural act of the divine will, does this mean that that will is absent or indifferent? By no means. All it proves is that the processes involved are different from those we had imagined; that the phenomenon that we had looked upon as an accident in creation has its own special place in the universal order of things; and that everything, down to the most particular effects, has been foreseen from all eternity by the divine mind. Now, in what way is the idea that we form of the power of God diminished when we come to see that every one of the countless results that we discern or fail to discern in our investigations not only has its own natural cause, but is also connected with an infinite series of causes; so that there is not even the slightest movement, force, form, or life that is not a product of the whole and that can be accounted for apart from the whole?

Now, why this dissertation, so foreign, it would seem, to the object of our investigation? The reason is that the phenomena of political economy also have their efficient cause and their providential purpose; that in this body of concepts, as in physics, anatomy, or astronomy, the final cause has often been denied precisely because the efficient cause appeared to operate with the force of absolute necessity.

The social world is rich in harmonies that we do not fully perceive until our minds have gone back to their causes, in order to find their explanation, and have then gone forward to their effects, in order to know the ultimate purpose of the phenomena they exhibit. . . . .

Appendix

A Tentative Preface
to the *Harmonies*[1]

My dear Frédéric:

So you have done it: you have left our village. You have said
good-bye to the countryside you loved so well, to your father's
house within whose walls you enjoyed such complete independence, to your old books which still cannot get used to sleeping
in neglect on their dusty shelves, to the garden where on our
lengthy strolls we used to talk endlessly *de omni re scibili et
quibusdam aliis.** You have bade farewell to that little plot of
ground, the last resting place of so many dear ones with whom
we associate our fondest hopes and our tenderest memories. Do
you remember how the sight of their cherished graves renewed
our faith and quickened our thoughts?† But nothing could
prevent your departure. You could even bring yourself to leave
the good farmers who looked to you not so much because you
were their justice of the peace or because of your knowledge of
the law, but rather for your native sense of fair play; you could
even leave your circle of close friends whose quick repartee,
spilling over into two languages, and whose long-standing and
intimate affection you held far more precious than fine manners.
You have turned a deaf ear upon your double bass—which

---

* ["Of everything knowable, and a few other things too," a proverbial parody of
the pretentious motto of the philosopher Pico della Mirandola—"to know
everything knowable," the title of his "Nine Hundred Propositions."—TRANSLATOR.]
† [The French text has been somewhat simplified here.—TRANSLATOR.]

seemed to have the power to stimulate your mind endlessly to new thoughts. My friendship could not deter you, nor even that complete freedom you enjoyed, the most precious of privileges, in regard to your activities, your hours, your studies. You have left our village, and now you are in Paris, that seething whirlpool where, as Victor Hugo says * . . . . .

Frédéric, it is our custom to speak to each other with complete candor. Well! I must say that I'm amazed at your decision. I'll go further: I can't approve. You have allowed yourself to be carried away by illusions, I won't say of glory, but at least of public acclaim. Glory, as you well know, and as we have said many a time, can no longer be the portion of any save those endowed with strikingly superior intellectual gifts. It is no longer enough to be able to write with purity, grace, and warmth; ten thousand men in France can write like that. It is not enough to have wit; wit is found on every street corner. Don't you remember, when we would read even the most trivial paperbacks, so often devoid of good sense and logic, but nearly always rich in verve and imagination, that we would say, "Writing well is soon going to be a characteristic of the species, like good posture in walking or sitting." How can anyone dream of glory after seeing what has happened to Benjamin Constant,† or Manuel? ‡ Who gives them a thought today? What has become of their brilliant reputations, which once seemed destined to live forever?

Would you compare yourself to these great minds? Have you their erudition? Have you their great talent? Have you, like

---

* [Although Victor Hugo does refer more than once to the teeming population of Paris, the exact comparison that Bastiat probably had in mind here (and apparently could not remember well enough to quote) is to be found in another popular contemporary work, the satirical novel *Jérôme Paturot* (1843) by Louis Reybaud: ". . . . in this whirlpool of Paris, where so many lives are so intricately enmeshed, a single turn of the wheel can disperse them and break their contact." —Translator.]

† [Benjamin Constant de Rebecque (1767–1830), liberal politician and author. Today he is remembered chiefly as the author of the romantic novel *Adolphe* and as the lover of Mme. de Staël.—Translator.]

‡ [Jacques Antoine Manuel (1775–1827), a noted orator and member of the opposition during the Restoration.—Translator.]

them, spent your life in the most brilliant social circles? Have you the same opportunities of making yourself known or heard? Can you, if need be, call upon the same influential friends? You will say to me perhaps that if you fail to shine by your writings, you will achieve distinction by your deeds. Well, what about the fame of Lafayette? Will you, like him, make your name echo and re-echo throughout the New World as well as the Old and for three quarters of a century? Will your life be lived in times as momentous as his? Will you emerge as a key figure in three revolutions? Will it be your lot to make and unmake kings? Will you be viewed as a martyr at Olmütz and a demigod at the Hôtel de Ville? Will you become commander-in-chief of the National Guard? And even if such a brilliant destiny were in store for you, consider where it leads: to casting before the nations a blameless name to which, in their indifference, they pay no heed; to lavishing upon them noble examples and distinguished services which they are quick to forget.*

Oh, no! I cannot believe that your head has been so turned by vanity that you would sacrifice your real happiness for a public acclaim which you know full well is not for you, and which in any case would be short-lived indeed. You would never aspire to being "in the papers of the day the big man of the month." Such a course would be going counter to all that you have stood for in the past. If you had been led astray by any such vain glory, you would have bent every effort to winning your election to the Chamber of Deputies. Yet many times, when you were a candidate, I saw how you always refused to stoop to the things that get a man elected. You kept saying, "These days people have some concern for public affairs; they read, and they talk about

---

* [Bastiat here summarizes very briefly and accurately the high points in the legendary career of Lafayette: his participation in the American Revolution, the French Revolution of 1789, which drove out the Bourbon kings, and the Revolution of 1830; his "martyrdom" as prisoner of war in the infamous Austrian prison camp at Olmütz (1794); and his presentation before the city of Paris, at the Hôtel de Ville, as Commander-in-chief of the National Guard (1830). Bastiat also correctly refers to the disfavor into which Lafayette's name had fallen by 1845. The novelist Balzac, for example, speaks of Lafayette as an "old idol worshiped out of habit and fit only to be labeled and put into a museum for having viewed the world through rose-colored glasses."—TRANSLATOR.]

what they have read. I will use this opportunity, under the pretext of being a candidate, to disseminate a few useful truths." And beyond that you took no serious steps to win your election.

It is, therefore, not due to the promptings of vanity that you have turned your steps toward Paris. But what did induce you to go? Was it a desire to do something for mankind? I have a few remarks to make to you on that score.

Like you I cherish all forms of freedom, and first among them that freedom which is the most universally beneficial to all men, which they enjoy every minute of the day and under all circumstances of their lives—freedom of labor and freedom of exchange. I realize that the right to possess the fruits of one's toil is the keystone of society and even of human life. I realize that exchange is implicit in the idea of property, and that restrictions on exchange shake the foundations of our right to own anything. I approve of your devotion to the defense of this freedom, whose triumph will usher in justice among all nations and consequently will eliminate international hatreds and prejudices and the wars that follow in their train.

But are the arms that you propose to carry into the lists the proper ones with which to win acclaim, if such is your dream, or to gain victory for your cause? What is your concern, your sole concern? A demonstration, a series of calculations, the solution of a single problem, to wit: Does legal coercion add to the profit or the loss column in a nation's ledger? This is the subject to which you have given all the powers of your mind. These are the limits into which you have compressed this great question. Pamphlets, books, monographs, articles, speeches, have all been directed toward isolating this unknown element: Will the nation under freedom have a hundred thousand francs more or a hundred thousand francs less? You apparently are intent on putting under a bushel every light that does not turn its full beam upon this theorem, on stamping out in your heart all those sparks of the sacred fire that the love of mankind has kindled.

Are you not afraid that your mind will wither and shrink through constant exposure to this work of analysis, this never-ending concentration on an algebraic equation?

Remember that we have often said that unless a person proposes to work for progress in only one isolated branch of human knowledge, or, rather, unless nature has given him a cranium distinguished by only one dominant protuberance, it is better, especially if he is like us, merely a scientific amateur, to let his mind travel over the whole realm of intellectual activity than to limit himself to the solution of a single problem. It is better to seek out the connections between the various fields of knowledge and the harmony of the laws that govern the social order than to exhaust one's faculties in the elucidation of a single doubtful point at the risk of losing one's sense of the grandeur and majesty of the whole.

It was for this very reason that our reading was so capricious, and that we were so careful to shake off the yoke of conventional judgments. Sometimes we would read Plato, not to admire him on the authority of the ages, but to reassure ourselves of the utter inferiority of ancient society; and we would say: "Since that is as high as the finest genius of the ancient world could rise, let us take courage; man *is* perfectible, and our faith in his destiny is not misplaced." Sometimes in our long walks we brought along with us Bacon, Lamartine, Bossuet, Fox,* Lamennais, and even Fourier. Political economy was merely one stone in the social edifice that we were seeking to build in our minds, and we would say: "It is fortunate for society that men of genius like Say have patiently and tirelessly applied themselves to observing, classifying, and setting down methodically all the facts that constitute this excellent science. Henceforth the human mind can move forward from this firm base toward new horizons." How we marveled, therefore, at Dunoyer and Comte, who, though never deviating from the strictly scientific lines traced by Say, apply so happily the truths they learned from him to morals and legislation! I will admit that sometimes, as I listened to you, it seemed to me that you too might be able to take this same torch from the hands of your predecessors and turn its light upon some of the dark recesses of the social sciences, and particularly upon

* [Charles James Fox (1749–1806), British statesman, chief of the Whig party, and advocate of friendship with France.—Translator.]

those that have recently been plunged into darkness by the dissemination of mad doctrines.

Instead of this, you are totally absorbed in trying to clear up a problem that Smith and Say have already expounded a hundred times better than you could. Here you are, analyzing, defining, making your calculations and your distinctions, and, scalpel in hand, trying to cut through to find out just what, in the last analysis, is the exact meaning of the terms *price, value, utility, low cost, high cost, imports, exports.*

But finally, setting personal considerations aside, if you do not fear dulling your mind at such a task, do you think that, for the sake of the cause, you have chosen the best course to follow? The peoples of the world are not governed by algebraic *x's*, but by noble instincts, sentiments, common sympathies. What you needed to give them was a picture of the successive falling away of the barriers that divide men into mutually hostile communities, jealous provinces, warring nations. There was need to show them the fusion of races, interests, tongues, ideas, and to demonstrate how truth triumphs over error as mind meets mind in debate and discussion, how progressive institutions are substituted for the reign of absolute despotism and hereditary castes, how war is abolished, armies are demobilized, moral power replaces brute force, and the human race prepares to meet the high destiny to which it is called. These are the things that would have set the hearts of the masses afire, not your dry demonstrations.

And so, why restrict yourself? Why hold your mind a prisoner? It seems to me that you have subjected it to a monk's regimen, with the unvarying crust of dry bread as your sole diet, for you are constantly gnawing away morning, noon, and night at a mere monetary question. As much as you, I long for commerce to be free. But is all human progress dependent upon this one freedom? In times past your heart quickened at the idea of freedom of thought and speech, still held prisoner by the censor and the laws against free assembly. Your burning desire was for parliamentary reform and for the thoroughgoing separation of the delegating and controlling powers from the executive powers in all these branches. All forms of freedom are interrelated. Together they all constitute a systematic and harmonious whole; there is not one of them that, when proved true, would not help to prove the truth of the others. But you are acting like a mechanic who is taking the utmost pains to explain an isolated piece of machinery down to its most minute detail, omitting nothing. One is tempted to cry out: "Show me the other pieces; make them move together; the action of one is explained by the action of all the others." . . . .

Notes

1. I can illustrate this law more clearly by figures. Let us take three periods during which capital increases while labor remains constant, and let us represent total production in each of the three periods as: 80–100–120. The distribution will be as follows:

	Capital's Share	Labor's Share	Total
First period	45	35	80
Second period	50	50	100
Third period	55	65	120

Of course, these ratios are intended to serve only as an illustration.

NOTES TO CHAPTER 1

1. [This chapter was published for the first time in the *Journal des économistes,* in the January, 1848, issue.—EDITOR.]
2. It is alleged that our system of free competition, advocated by ignorant political economists and adopted as a means of getting rid of monopolies, results, in fact, in the general establishment of monster monopolies in all categories." (*Principes du socialisme,* by M. Considérant, page 15.) *

NOTES TO CHAPTER 2

1. [This chapter and the next were inserted in September and December, 1818, in the *Journal des économistes.*—EDITOR.]
2. "Our industrial system, based on irresponsible and unorganized competition, is nothing but a social hell, in which vast numbers of men suffer all the torments and all the agonies of ancient Taenarus; with one difference, however: the victims." (V. Considérant.)
3. [See chap. 2 of the second series of *Economic Sophisms.*—EDITOR.]

NOTES TO CHAPTER 3

1. This is a very common mathematical law, but one little understood in political economy.

* [Victor Considérant (1808–1893), as a socialist of the Fourier school, is the frequent object of Bastiat's criticism.—TRANSLATOR.]

2. One of the secondary aims of this book is to combat those modern sentimentalist schools which, despite the facts, refuse to accept the idea that suffering, in any degree whatsoever, has a providential purpose. As these schools profess to stem from Rousseau, I must quote them this passage from the master: "The evil that we see is not an absolute evil; and, far from being in direct conflict with the good, it co-operates with the good for the universal harmony."

NOTES TO CHAPTER 4

1. Even more, this slave, because of his superiority, eventually reduces the cost of other slaves and sets them at liberty. This is a *harmony* whose implications I leave to the reader.

2. [What follows is a note found among the author's papers. Had he lived, he would have incorporated it among his theories on exchange. Our function must be limited to including it at the end of the present chapter.—EDITOR.]

3. [See, for the refutation of this fallacy, the chapter "Producer and Consumer," which follows in this volume, and also chapters 2 and 3 of *Economic Sophisms,* First Series.—EDITOR.]

NOTES TO CHAPTER 5

1. *Increases!* The object, then, had value in itself before any human labor was performed upon it. It could have received it only from Nature. Therefore, the action of Nature is not gratuitous. Who, then, has the audacity to demand payment for the *extrahuman* part of value?

2. Because, under a regime of liberty, individual services enter into competition with one another, their remuneration tends to become approximately proportionate to the intensity of the labor involved. But, I repeat, this balance, this proportionality, is not inherent in the notion of value. Proof of this can be found in the fact that where there is no competition, there is no proportionality either. In this case no relationship is to be observed between the nature of the labor and the amount of its remuneration.

   The absence of competition can arise from the nature of things or from the perversity of mankind.

   If it arises from the nature of things, we may see a relatively modest expenditure of effort producing great *value* without anyone's having just cause for complaint. This is the case of the person finding a diamond; this is also the case of Rubini,* of Malibran, of Taglioni,† of the fashionable tailor of the moment, of the proprietor of the Clos-Vougeot,‡ etc., etc. Circumstances have given them extraordinary means of rendering service; they have no rivals, and their prices are high. The

* [Jean-Baptiste Rubini (1795–1854), an Italian tenor much admired in Paris.—TRANSLATOR.]

† [Maria Taglioni (1804–1884), a famous dancer.—TRANSLATOR.]

‡ [A famous Burgundy winery. Cf. chap. 13, p. 355.—TRANSLATOR.]

very fact of the extreme scarcity of the service is proof that it is not essential to the well-being and progress of mankind. It is, therefore, a luxury item, an object of ostentation available to the wealthy. Is it not natural that every man, before indulging in satisfactions of this nature, should wait until he is able to provide for his more basic and reasonable wants?

If competition is absent because some human agency has done violence to the natural balance, the same effects are produced, but with this tremendous difference, that they are produced in places and at times where and when they should not be produced. Then we see a relatively minor piece of work creating great value; but how? By stifling violently the competition whose function it is to relate remuneration to service. Then, even as Rubini can say to a music-lover, "I want a very high honorarium, or I will not sing for your guests"—acting on the principle that the service here is one that only he can render—so can a baker, a butcher, a landlord, a banker say, "I want exorbitant payment, or else you will not receive my wheat, my bread, my meat, my gold; and I have taken precautions: I have lined up rows of bayonets so that you cannot procure these things elsewhere, so that no one else may render you services analogous to mine."

People who class together artificial monopoly and what they call natural monopoly, because both have in common the power of increasing the value of labor, are either quite blind or quite superficial. .

Artificial monopoly is downright plunder. It produces evils that otherwise would not exist. It inflicts hardship on a considerable part of society, because it often includes the most vital articles. In addition it gives rise to resentments, hatred, reprisals, all the fruits of injustice.

The favors bestowed by Nature do no harm to society. At the very most we could say that they bring to light an evil that already existed and can in no way be imputed to them. It is too bad, perhaps, that tokay wine is not as plentiful, and therefore not as cheap, as ordinary red wine. But this is not a social evil; it was imposed on us by Nature. There is, then, between the favors bestowed by Nature and artificial monopoly this profound difference: the former are the result of pre-existent and inevitable scarcity; the latter is the cause of artificial and unnatural scarcity.

In the first case it is not the absence of competition that creates the scarcity; it is the scarcity that explains the absence of competition. Mankind would be childish indeed if it became upset, or if it rebelled, because there is only one Jenny Lind, one Clos-Vougeot, or one Regent.

In the second case quite the contrary is true. It is not because of a providentially created scarcity that competition is impossible, but because force has stifled competition, because a scarcity has been created that should never have been. [Note taken from the author's manuscripts.— EDITOR.]

3. See chap. 15. *Accumulation* is a circumstance of no consequence in political economy. Whether satisfaction is immediate or delayed, whether it can be postponed or separated from the effort that produces it, in no way changes the nature of things.

I am disposed to make a sacrifice for the pleasure of hearing a beautiful voice. I go to the theater and I pay; the satisfaction is immediate. If I had used my money to buy a dish of strawberries, I should have been able to postpone my satisfaction until the next day; that is all.

It can be said, of course, that the strawberries represent wealth, because I can still exchange them. That is true. Once the effort has been exerted, as long as the satisfaction remains unfulfilled, the wealth still exists. It is the satisfaction that destroys the wealth. When the dish of strawberries is eaten, this satisfaction will go the way of the other that brought me Alboni's* voice.

Service received, service rendered; such is political economy. [Note taken from the author's manuscript.—EDITOR.]

4. [What follows was intended by the author to be included in the present chapter.—EDITOR.]

5. *Treatise on Political Economy*, p. 1.

NOTES TO CHAPTER 6

1. *Nouvel essai sur la richesse des nations*, p. 438.
2. *Ibid.*, p. 263.
3. *Ibid.*, p. 456.
4. *Ibid.*, p. 456.
5. *Ibid.*, p. 161.
6. *Ibid.*, p. 168.
7. *Ibid.*, p. 168.
8. *Ibid.*, p. 63.
9. "If you take a stand in favor of competition, you will be wrong; if you take a stand against it, you will still be wrong: which means that either way you will be right." (P. J. Proudhon, *Economic Contradictions*, page 182.)
10. Always this eternal and hateful confusion between value and utility. I can easily show you utilities that belong to no one, but I defy you to show me anywhere in the world a single value that has no owner.
11. [What follows is the beginning of a supplementary note found among the author's papers.—EDITOR.]
12. [This last entry of the author is accompanied by no further comment. But other chapters in this volume supply it. Note particularly "Private Property and Common Wealth," "Relations between Political Economy and Ethics," and "Solidarity."—EDITOR.]

NOTES TO CHAPTER 7

1. See my monograph *Capital and Rent*.
2. Chap. 3, pp. 64 ff.

NOTE TO CHAPTER 8

1. See chap. 11.

* [Marietta Alboni (1823–1894), celebrated Italian singer.—TRANSLATOR.]

NOTES TO CHAPTER 9

1. *Éléments de l'économie politique,* 2nd ed., p. 293.
2. *Ibid.,* pp. 377–378.
3. [The words in italics and capitals are printed thus in the original text. —EDITOR.]
4. *Théorie du droit de propriété et du droit au travail,* 3rd ed., p. 15.
5. [See Vol. II (of the French edition), *Discours du 29 septembre, 1846.*— EDITOR.]
6. *Proceedings of the South Australian Association.*
7. *New Monthly Magazine.*
8. Ricardo.

NOTES TO CHAPTER 10

1. Chap. 1, pp. 3 ff.
2. See chap. 5, note 1.

NOTE TO CONCLUSION TO THE ORIGINAL EDITION

1. [Here ends the original edition of *Economic Harmonies.* We reproduce here the list of chapters, found in the author's handwriting, intended to complete the book. It indicates the writings he had planned and also the order that we have followed for the chapters, fragments, and outlines that were entrusted to us. The asterisks indicate subjects on which we have found no material.—EDITOR.]

Normal Phenomena
    1. Producer and Consumer
    2. The Two Mottoes
    3. Theory of Rent
    4. Money*
    5. Credit*
    6. Wages
    7. Saving
    8. Population
    9. Private and Public Services
    10. Taxation*

Corollaries
    11. Machinery*
    12. Free Trade*
    13. Middlemen*
    14. Raw Materials and Finished Goods*
    15. Luxury*

Disturbing Factors
    16. Plunder
    17. War
    18. Slavery*

19. Theocracy*
20. Monopoly*
21. Government Exploitation*
22. False Brotherhood or Communism*

General Observations
23. Responsibility and Solidarity
24. Self-Interest or Social Motivation
25. Perfectibility
26. Public Opinion*
27. Relation between Political Economy and Ethics*
28. Relation between Political Economy and Politics*
29. Relation between Political Economy and Legislation*
30. Relation between Political Economy and Religion*

NOTES TO CHAPTER 11

1. [*Economic Sophisms,* chap. 1 (First Series), p. 5.—EDITOR.]
2. [See the author's address on "Taxation on Beverages," Vol. V (of the French edition), p. 468.—EDITOR.]
3. See chap. 6.
4. [See Vol. IV (of the French edition), p. 72.—EDITOR.]

NOTES TO CHAPTER 12

1. See chaps. 10 and 11.
2. When the vanguard of the Icarian expedition left Le Havre, I questioned a number of these foolish men in order to find out what was at the back of their minds. *An easy life* was their hope and their motive. One of them said to me, "I am leaving now, and my brother is to go on the next trip. He has eight children, and you can understand what a help it will be to him not to have to feed and care for them any more."

   "I understand completely," I said; "but other people will have to accept this heavy burden."

   To load one's burdens onto the shoulders of others—such was the interpretation that these poor wretches gave to the fraternal motto, *all for one.*
3. [See the pamphlet "Plunder and Law" (*Selected Essays on Political Economy,* chap. 8).—EDITOR.]

NOTES TO CHAPTER 13

1. [The author has left only two or three short fragments on this important chapter. The reason is that he intended, as he said, to rely principally on the works of Mr. Carey of Philadelphia to refute Ricardo's theory. —EDITOR.]
2. [The same idea is presented at the end of the supplement to chap. 5. —EDITOR.]

3. [Of these proposed developments not one, unfortunately, exists; but we may be permitted to present here, in brief form, the two main conclusions to be drawn from the phenomenon that the author describes: 1. Suppose two fields, one, *A,* cultivated; the other, *B,* uncultivated. Assuming them to be of identical quality, the amount of labor previously required to clear *A* may be taken as the amount necessary to clear *B.* We can even say that because of our better knowledge, implements, means of communication, etc., it would take *fewer* days to put *B* into cultivation than it took for *A.* If the land had value in itself, *A* would be worth all that it cost to put it into cultivation, *plus something for its natural productive powers;* that is, much more than the sum now necessary to put *B* into comparable condition. Now, the opposite is true: *A* is worth less, since people buy it rather than cultivate *B.* When they buy *A,* they therefore pay nothing for its natural productive powers, since they do not pay even as much for the labor of cultivating it as this originally cost.

2. If field *A* yields 1,000 measures of wheat per year, field *B* when cultivated would yield the same quantity: *A* has been cultivated because, in the past, 1,000 measures of wheat fully compensated for the labor required both for its original clearance and its annual cultivation. *B* is not under cultivation because now 1,000 measures of wheat would not pay for an identical amount of labor—or even less, as we noted above.

What does this mean? Obviously that the value of *human labor* has risen as compared with the value of *wheat;* that a day's labor of a worker is worth more and receives more wheat in wages. In other words, wheat is produced for less effort and is exchanged for less labor, and the theory of the *rising costs of foodstuffs* is false. See, in Vol. I (of the French edition), the postscript of the letter addressed to the *Journal des économistes,* dated Dec. 8, 1850. See also on the subject the work of a disciple of Bastiat, *Du revenu foncier (Income from the Land)* by R. de Fontenay.—EDITOR.]

4. [See "Accursed Money!" Vol. V (of the French edition), p. 64.—EDITOR.]

5. [See "Interest-free Credit," Vol. V (of the French edition), p. 94.—EDITOR.]

NOTES TO CHAPTER 14

1. [Chap. 1, p. 7, and chap. 2, pp. 20–21.—EDITOR.]

2. [See the later chapter on "Responsibility."—EDITOR.]

3. [See, in Vol. IV (of the French edition), "The Law," and particularly, pp. 360 ff. (*Selected Essays on Political Economy,* chap. 2).—EDITOR.]

4. It is to be noted that Mr. Roebuck belongs to the *extreme Left* in the House of Commons. In this capacity he is the natural enemy of all imaginable governments; yet at the same time he advocates absorption by the government of all rights and all functions. The proverb is therefore false that says, "Never the twain shall meet."

5. Quoted from *La Presse,* June 22, 1850.

6. [See Vol. III (of the French edition), pp. 442–445.—EDITOR.]

7. The riots of June, 1848.
8. Chap. 7, p. 193.
9. [See chap. 4.—EDITOR.]
10. Chap. 7.
11. [The manuscript brought from Rome ends here. The short note that follows was found among the papers that the author had left in Paris. It indicates how he had proposed to end and sum up this chapter.—EDITOR.]

Improvement in the workers' status consists in wages themselves and in the natural laws that govern them.

1. The worker tends to rise to the rank of an entrepreneur having capital resources.

2. Wages tend to rise.

Corollary: Passing from the status of wage earner to entrepreneur becomes increasingly less desirable and easier.

NOTES TO CHAPTER 16

1. [What follows was written in 1846.—EDITOR.]
2. It is only fair to mention that Say recognized the means of existence as a variable quantity.
3. There are few countries whose populations do not tend to increase beyond the means of subsistence. So constant an increase as this must *necessarily* create distress among the lower classes and prevent *any permanent amelioration in their condition*. . . . . The principle of population. . . . will increase the number of people *before* the means of subsistence are increased. —Malthus, quoted by Rossi.*
4. [See chap. 11, pp. 336 ff.—EDITOR.]
5. Which creates a need for the day laborer.
6. [The beginning of the preceding chapter is of recent date; the rest is an article that appeared in 1846 in the *Journal des économistes*. After

---

* [This quotation, apparently taken from chap. 2 of the *Essay on the Principle of Population*, is not entirely faithful either to the letter or to the spirit of the original. The first sentence does not occur verbatim in Malthus, and appears to be simply a summary. The second and third sentences do appear, but the omissions alter their meaning somewhat. For purposes of comparison the original text follows, with the omission indicated by brackets: "[Yet in all societies, even those that are most vicious, the tendency to a virtuous attachment is so strong, that there is a constant effort toward an increase of population.] This [constant effort] as constantly tends to subject the lower classes of the society to distress, and to prevent any great permanent amelioration of their condition.

"[The way in which these effects are produced seems to be this:

"We will suppose the means of subsistence in any country just equal to the easy support of its inhabitants.] The constant effort towards population, [which is found to act even in the most vicious societies,] increases the number of people before the means of subsistence are increased." (Macmillan edition, 1909, p. 14.) —TRANSLATOR.]

this date the author's ideas on this important subject became more precise, and I hope I may be pardoned for undertaking, following certain notes, to complete the exposition of the doctrine.

At first, Bastiat recognized as the only check on the increase of population the action of the law so forcefully formulated by Malthus, according to which the immutable will of God and the free will of his intelligent creature enter, so to speak, to an equal extent, where man is *active* by virtue of his foresight, and *passive* only when he is punished for not choosing to exercise foresight or for not knowing how. For Bastiat, as well as for Malthus, what counteracts the physiological tendency to reproduction is the motive of individual responsibility: responsibility for labor, or *property;* and responsibility for procreation, or *patrimony* and *family.*

One could even say that in this respect Bastiat is more truly an economist than his predecessor; for, instead of placing the *preventive check* purely in the domain of morality, as the latter did, Bastiat established it scientifically on the basis of the feeling of self-interest, the progressive ambition for an improvement in one's well-being—in a word, on *individualism*—the foundation of a *society of property owners,* in irreconcilable opposition to socialism.

In the absence of this primary prerequisite of the social order, and with any arrangement that would suppress or weaken the feeling of personal responsibility by way of an artificial extension of social solidarity, the principle of the *preventive check* is destroyed, man falls back into a condition in which his destiny is governed by the fatal operation of the *repressive check,* and he finds himself enmeshed in that series of inevitable phenomena, that chain of crushing consequences, which Malthus triumphantly opposed to the communist systems of his time and of all time.*

As we live in an age when it is more than ever necessary to disarm one truth in order to arm another, we were anxious to establish, above all, the respects in which these two masters are in agreement against those who desire "the community of evil, the blame laid on society for all the faults of individual men, a common share in all the crimes committed by each one." †

But from this common premise, namely, *the moral effort by which man governs himself,* each of the two economists has drawn quite different conclusions. For, according to the first, that effort reduces itself to nothing more than virtuous self-restraint, and he does not venture to place much hope in the imperfect morality of the human race. The second sees it above all in foresight, in that control over one's conduct which is developed by the desire for well-being and by the fear of losing what one has already gained, and which determines and supports the social customs, duties, and moral sentiments prevailing in the environ-

* *Essay on Population,* Bk. III, chap. ii.
† Proudhon's definition of socialism (*Contradict. Économ.,* Vol. II, chap. xii, p. 381, Guillaumin edit.).

ment in which one lives. According to him, consequently, every step taken on the way toward well-being tends, by the need to go farther, to encourage this prudent self-control. Man, as life becomes easier for him, becomes more difficult and demanding in what he expects from life. Thus, the vicious circle in which Malthus seems to enclose mankind, Bastiat, by a hardly noticeable correction, opens up, so to speak, into a spiral of indefinite progress; and the problem of population, over which the sinister shadow of death appeared to have fallen, becomes, from his point of view, a law of social harmony and human perfectibility, like all other sociological laws.

There are in Bastiat's theory on this question two quite distinct parts.

In the first, he shows that Malthus failed to give sufficient significance to the preventive check in calling it *moral restraint,* and that the limit of the *means of existence,* which seems to present itself at first glance as a fatal and inflexible minimum, is, on the contrary, both in theory and in fact, a movable barrier that progress keeps constantly advancing—at least in every society founded on justice and liberty.

It would be pointless to reiterate here Bastiat's argument demonstrating this thesis, and, besides, it coincides with the admirable studies that Rossi has carried out on the same subject. In full agreement with Malthus that, "in view of the imperfect way in which the precept of *moral restraint* has hitherto been observed, it would be visionary to hope for *any important improvement* in this respect," one may be permitted, without being regarded as in any way *visionary,* to recognize and point out that men, once enjoying a condition of well-being, are very eager to avoid doing anything that might impair it, and that this principle of self-restraint manifests itself, quite unnoticed, to a great extent in the habits, ideas, and social customs of the upper classes. Of course, a young man of twenty-four beginning his career or just out of a school where he has received specialized training for his profession never gives a moment's thought to Malthus' law; all he is thinking of is *making a place* for himself before burdening himself with a family. A ship's captain who spends the whole year in the long voyage from Le Havre or Nantes to the Indies would laugh in your face if you complimented him on his virtue and will tell you that, having a good education, but little money, he is looking for a wife he can love, that is to say, one well brought up, like himself, with a certain refinement of mind and manners, etc. But for this he needs to attain some degree of affluence, and he proposes to devote five or six years of his youth to laboriously laying a foundation for his future happiness. Instead of five or six years only, it could well be ten or a dozen, and perhaps, taking a fancy to life at sea, he will end by remaining single. All this is hardly contestable.

But Bastiat goes farther than Rossi. The latter, although attributing to the upper classes a preponderant concern with the preventive check, thinks nevertheless that among the working classes the repressive check is virtually the only one that operates.

This distinction is too sharp. No doubt the proletariat is, by and large, less prudent than the bourgeoisie. But, in fact, it is easy to demonstrate, as Bastiat does, a progressive diminution in that part of the proletariat which is thriftless and improvident and a constant improvement in the well-being of the poorest classes. Now, in order for this twofold effect to be produced among a multitude which not only has an inherent tendency to increase, but which, besides, receives into its ranks those of the upper strata who fall from their superior social position, and which serves in some sort as an outlet for their vices, the preventive check must necessarily have operated on the proletariat far more powerfully than appears at first sight. How does this come about? It is simply that the proletariat encounters, in the very conditions of labor open to it, a multiplicity of obstacles already established that keep its numbers within bounds without its even being aware of them. I may cite, for example, domestic service—the whole business of working as *wet nurses,* which seems destined to absorb a good part of the exuberant fecundity of country women, and, for the men, military service and life in the army camp and the barracks; the great emigration of workers, which, in breaking their natural ties with family and neighbors, keeps them isolated, because of differences in the customs and sometimes in the language of the country to which they go in search of employment; the crowding of workmen in great centers of industry, around factories, foundries, mines, etc., with the concomitant substitution of the comradeship of the workshop for the intimacy of the family; migratory labor among field hands; the nomadic existence of traveling salesmen and others engaged in commerce properly so called; etc., etc.

To these one might well add the years of apprenticeship and the ever more demanding conditions imposed by progress. "To attain the high standard of living of modern society," says Proudhon, "a prodigious scientific, aesthetic, and industrial development is required. . . . . Twenty-five years of education no longer suffices to secure a position among the privileged classes. What will it be in the future? . . . ." * Obviously the preventive check is imposed on the proletariat in countless unnoticed ways.

No great effort, then, either of analysis or of observation is required to establish the fact that the *repressive check* operates with continually diminishing force—a conclusion that becomes evidently and incontestably apparent from an examination of the statistics concerning population trends in Europe. The capital point brought out by these figures is the increase in the *average span of life* that has taken place within the last hundred years. In England, M. Finlaison has established that the general death rate, which in 1805 was 1/42, is at present 1/46. According to M. Farr, the probable life expectancy of a person at the age of 20, which in 1698 was only 29, is now 40. In France, Messrs. Moreau de Jonnès, Bienaymé, etc., have drawn analogous conclusions.

Now, *an increase in the average span of life* and *a decrease in the*

* This whole passage from Proudhon is magnificent. (*Contrad. Écon.,* chap. xii, pp. 463–467, 474–496.)

operation of the repressive check are simply two ways of expressing one and the same economic fact.

Is it possible to say in specific terms what share each of the social classes enjoys in this common conquest over death? I do not know, but it is impossible that all should not have participated in it; and, in view of everything that has been accomplished for many years in France, and especially in England, to improve the hygienic conditions of the poor, to provide them with medical care and facilities, to do away with insanitary housing, to effect changes in unwholesome industries, to regulate child labor, to provide a special institution to minister to men's needs in every kind of danger, etc., etc., I think we are entitled to presume that this decrease in the death rate has manifested itself in the lower classes to a greater extent, perhaps, proportionately, than in any other.

The number of years of active life that a man can expect to enjoy has increased, on the average, by five or ten. I should like to demonstrate statistically, as I easily could, the enormous value of this magnificent achievement. I venture to say that of all the conquests that can be credited to the advance of civilization it is this that deserves, in the highest degree, the careful attention of economists. It is, indeed, a kind of epitome, a summation, of all the progress that has been made, as it is also the sure sign, the infallible source, of every new advance—both cause and effect operating in a never-ending cycle.

But we must resist the temptation to embark upon such a study, which would throw a vivid light on the basic question with which we are here concerned. Let us return to Bastiat.

In the first part, he has relied on *facts* to prove that progress is the dominant tendency. In the second, he resorts to *a priori reasoning* and theoretical laws to establish the same conclusion.

In this altogether new part of his system, Bastiat shows—or rather, alas! was to have shown—that the increase in population (provided always that it is contained within the natural limits imposed upon it by individual responsibility), is, in itself, a cause of progress, a stimulus to production. This is how he formulates this admirable law, in the chapter on exchange:

"Other things being equal, an increase in the density of the population means an increase in productive capacity."

This principle, which has appeared paradoxical to some overhasty economists, is really an unquestionable truth, a fundamental axiom already accepted in economics in another form, as can be seen from the following considerations.

Imagine a society consisting of a number of groups of people spread over a vast area and having no exchange relations with one another, and suppose, further, that the doubling of the population places between each of these isolated groups of people others equal in numbers and wealth, having no more relations among themselves than with the first groups. Certainly, then, the increase in what could be called the total population and the general wealth (mere "wealth" and "population" would be meaningless here in the absence of *unity*) would in no way change the relative affluence or individual well-being of each producer. But things are quite different in reality; exchange, communication, mutual relations exist within a nation between man and man, village and village, town and country, province and province, etc.

Now, suppose that in such an already existing network we have a proportional increase in population and capital, that we interpolate, so to speak, a second population altogether equal in number, with other tools, other houses, other cultivated fields, or the same fields yielding twice as much in the way of crops, etc. (which is what we mean by *other things being equal*). Is it to be believed that, because the population and the means of production stand in the same numerical relation as before, the absolute well-being of each of the workers will not have changed? To draw this conclusion would be a very serious error. I affirm, on the contrary, that, by virtue of the very density of the population, production is facilitated, that is to say, well-being and real wealth are increased in considerable proportion.

Even from the very outset, before any change takes place in the division of labor, "the sole fact of proximity immediately renders more advantageous the same apparatus of exchange." *

It is as clear as day, for example, that much of the cost of transportation and cartage is diminished by half. And certainly this in itself is already an enormous benefit to all concerned, for to what purpose do we expend such immense efforts to lay out roads, dig canals, construct railways, etc., if not to bring things and men closer together—to effect, in a word, *an artificial density of population*?

Consider, for example, a peddler who, in the course of a day's work, travels with his pack on his back a distance of some six or eight leagues among a number of small, isolated dairy farms. He sells some thread, ribbons, cotton goods, sweetmeats, and hardware. By the end of the day he will have made about a dozen separate trips. Now, suppose twice the population occupies the same area. One or the other of the following consequences will occur: either he will be satisfied to serve the same clientele, in which case he will find his twelve buyers in a circuit reduced to from three to four leagues and will have half the day remaining to him *to do something else;* or, within the same area, he will sell twice as much. On either hypothesis, the same pains will procure him double the profit; or, if you will, by retaining the same absolute profit, he can diminish by half the relative profit that he gets from each object he sells.

I lived in a town where a tailor, in order to make me a pair of duck trousers, and a poor shoemaker, in order to produce a pair of hunting shoes, were obliged to make a round trip of some three leagues and to lose a good third of their working day in the process. If the population doubled, there would be a tailor and a shoemaker in each of the two towns. I would have mine at my door, and the other would

* Bastiat, "Exchange."

find within the radius of a kilometer the same clientele that he had formerly served. The worker would gain a third of a day, and I would gain the value of the bottle of poor wine that I had to pay for his pains—*other things being equal.*

Distance plays an important—indeed, an enormous—role in all the details of production. I know of a number of fields situated as far as three or four kilometers from the farm to which they are attached. Fields are cultivated with the help of oxen, plodding beasts that would require two hours to make the trip. Here, then, are four hours that would be lost from each day's labor—four hours a day for seeding, four hours a day for harvesting, etc. Needless to say, one would not dream of transporting cattle this distance, and these fields lie idle for five or six years. But if the population doubles, some farms will be situated close to these tracts of land, they will be cultivated without difficulty, they will be kept fertile, and, in saying that they will easily yield three, four, five times more under these conditions, I think that no agriculturist will contradict me. I could multiply such proofs indefinitely.

But this is not all. "The density of the population not only results in a better use of the existing apparatus of exchange; it permits this apparatus itself to increase and improve by virtue of the division of labor." *

What is the effect of isolation? The impossibility of achieving a division of labor. In a primitive society, a settler on the land cuts the trees in the forest, carts them off, saws them into logs, fashions them into doors, ax handles, sabots, etc.

Yet we have to take account not only of the time lost and expenses incurred, but also of all the tools, all the incompletely mastered skills involved in these different kinds of labor. If, instead of isolated settlements or cabins, a village springs up, woodcutters will establish themselves in the forest, carters will devote their full time to transporting the wood, sawyers will cut it up, and there will be wheelwrights, carpenters, sabot-makers, etc. The whole process will be continuous, regular, without loss of time or energy; it will involve a minimum number of tools and a better and shorter period of apprenticeship, and it will be carried on with the dexterity and skill that come of long habit—all of which constitutes an enormous saving.

I speak of *isolation;* I could have spoken of *association.* To come to grips with Nature, man has need of a power and a continuity of action that numbers alone make possible. Five workers could not put up a jetty in three hundred years; set five hundred to work on the job, and within six months you will have an entire pier. Men differ more or less in their abilities according to circumstances. The more they combine their efforts in an irresistible union, the more they are able to deploy their different aptitudes in a common attack on the details of every problem. And there is no limit to the benefits to be derived from this kind of co-operation. Virtually every year, if one takes the

* Bastiat, "Exchange."

trouble to observe it, our capital is increased, by virtue of a further intensification of the division of labor or of a vast concentration of forces in a particular industry.

But, however unquestionable may be the benefits derived from the division of labor, whether on a limited or on a massive scale, the great—indeed, the supreme advantage—consists in technological progress, in the invention of tools and machines. Now, this improvement is possible only through the division of labor, and the division of labor is possible only by virtue of the density of the population.

How would the isolated settler of whom we have just spoken have, I do not say the possibility, but even the idea, of finding a way to improve the primitive means he employs to make himself a tool, a door, or a pair or shoes? But once the job is divided up, with one person doing nothing but cut boards, another hammering the nails, still another curing hides, etc., with twenty times less inventive ingenuity than that of the half-savage individual who was obliged to shift entirely for himself, each of the co-operating workers, intent exclusively on the accomplishment of a single, limited task fully within his capacity and command, brings to it all his skill and knowledge and gradually improves his techniques and his tools of production. He will invent the saw, the adze, the plane, the auger, the forge, the bellows, etc., and later machines driven by water power or steam, gigantic furnaces, and rotary shears and saws that cut iron bars or trees the way a knife slices fruit.

All this labor is sustained, accelerated, co-ordinated in an endless movement, involving continual contact between man and man, kept in a constant state of tension by competition, and enlightened by the interaction and convergence of the discoveries of science, that great common hearth to whose radiant light every isolated glimmer of experience makes its contribution. But we need go no further in our description, for—I admit it quite readily—we are simply repeating platitudes. The fact is that Bastiat's statement is nothing but a reformulation of the famous axiom of the division of labor: *The productive power of the human race is due to the density of the population.* This is, indeed, the definition of civilization itself.

Yes, to the end of time there will be a necessary, reciprocal relation between the two terms of God's great commandment: *Multiplicamini et subjicite universam terram.* Wherever man multiplies (in the desired conditions of his social development), his power to subdue Nature to his will must multiply even more rapidly.

If two adjacent provinces are separated for a long time by an insuperable obstacle and finally succeed in breaking through the barrier at two or three points, will the well-being of each be increased by the resulting communication between them? Every economist will agree that it will. Would not the mutual advantages be notably increased if, instead of two or three points of contact, ten or twenty were created, or if the two provinces were to envelop and interpenetrate each other? Would they not reap the maximum advantage if it were possible to superpose them, to join them together, so that communication, even in regard to the smallest details, would be established between town and town, house and house, and man and man? Now, this hypothetical super-position is precisely what is accomplished by the increasing density of the population, *all other things being equal.*

We may remark, in passing, that this diminution in the natural difficulties of labor brought about by an increase in the proximity and numbers of the workers not only profoundly modifies the pessimistic conclusion of Malthus but also suffices to upset Ricardo's dismal theory of rent. There can be no doubt that the errors or the terrors of these two contemporaneous economists reinforced each other. While Ricardo, concerned with the *pressure of population on the means of subsistence,* assumed a progressing increase in the value of food which nothing in fact justifies, Malthus, for his part, found in Ricardo's theory of rent, which he took seriously, a vindication of his own exaggerated apprehensions.

I believe that a better insight into these matters will lead us to quite opposite conclusions, and that the two collateral laws of population and of rent (or, more generally, of capital) will be seen for what they really are: the expression of mankind's constant approach toward the gratuitous enjoyment of goods and the improvement of well-being through the employment of ever more readily available and more powerful natural resources and forces of Nature.

When the science of statistics is in a position to make the necessary measurements, it will verify in all its details this conclusion of Bastiat: *that a necessary concomitant of any increase in a nation's population is an infinitely superior development in its productive capacity.* And, to cite only one proof of this proposition, M. Moreau de Jonnès has established that, as the population of France doubled after 1700, the per capita consumption of wheat rose from 472 to 541 litres, to which must be added around 240 litres of potatoes and cereals. And surely, if the consumption of *food,* which is least susceptible to increase in weight and volume, has nonetheless risen to such a notable extent, how prodigious must have been the rise in the consumption of *industrial* products, in the use and enjoyment of goods above the level of mere animal satisfaction!

England would furnish us with proofs even more powerful in the enormous increase, within half a century, that has taken place in its consumption of cereals, coal, metals, manufactured products, etc. But what we have said so far must suffice; it is but the echo of a loftier thought, and it is not our function to add anything further to it.

In summary, then, in opposition to the alleged population explosion, we have to take into account, first, the motive of self-interest, which impels each individual to improve his own well-being and that of his family; secondly, habit, which converts every already acquired improve-ment in his well-being into a need and a necessity of life, prevents him from falling back to a lower standard of living, and induces him, with-out his even being aware of it, to progress, if only because he remains in an environment that is itself progressive; thirdly, and finally, the indefinite increase in the capacity of each producer consequent upon the very increase in their total number.

Bastiat does indeed emphasize the unnoticed and naturally preventive role played by the motive of self-interest and individual responsibility—the increasing desire for a higher standard of living, the ambition for something better. He also shows how habit, which for every man turns each newly acquired luxury into a positive want, becomes a *lower limit to the means of existence,* below which no man is willing to allow his family to be reduced. But this, in a way, is only the negative side of the law; it merely shows that, in any society based on private property and family, *population cannot be a danger.*

It remained for him to show that *population can in itself be a positive force,* to demonstrate the inevitable increase in the power of production that results from the density of population. This, as the author himself says, is the important point that Malthus neglects, and the point that, if understood, will reveal to us harmony, and not the discord Malthus had seen.

We present below the completely anti-Malthusian conclusions that Bastiat drew from the premises he indicated in the chapter on "Exchange," pp. 59–98, and which he proposed to treat more fully in his discussion of population. The following are among the last notes that he wrote, and he stressed their importance:

"In the chapter on exchange we demonstrated that in isolation man's wants exceed his productive capacities, that in society his productive capacities exceed his wants.

"This excess of productive capacities over wants results from exchange, that is, the union of efforts, the division of labor.

"Hence the action and reaction of cause and effect in an endless cycle of progress.

"The excess of productive capacity over wants, creating for each generation a surplus of wealth, allows it to rear a new generation more numerous than itself. And a larger oncoming generation is in itself a better and more basic kind of division of labor; it represents a new degree of the excess of productive capacities over wants.

"This is an admirable harmony!

"Thus, at any given time, if the sum total of general wants is represented by 100, and the sum total of productive capacities at 110, the excess ten is distributed, for example, five to improve living conditions, to stimulate wants of a higher order, to foster the sense of human dignity, etc., and five to increase the population.

"For the second generation, the wants are 110: five more directed toward quantity, and five toward quality.

"But because of this very fact (both fuller physical, intellectual, and moral development and greater density of population, which facilitates production) the means of production have also increased their potential. They are now represented, for example, by the figures 120 or 130.

"A new excess, a new distribution, etc.

"And let us not fear an overabundance; a higher order of wants, which remedy and its bitter end. Thus, evil constantly combats evil, even as good constantly inspires good. And we might say that, when seen from a higher point of view, the deviations of free will are confined to a few oscillations of fixed amplitude, while the general course remains unchanged and unchangeable, every counter-movement of any intensity succeeding only in destroying itself, without in any way disturbing the orbit.

This force of action and reaction, which, by reward and pain, controls the orbit, which is at once voluntary and predestined, of the human race, this *law of gravitation for beings endowed with free will* (of which evil is the necessary half) expresses itself in two great principles— responsibility and solidarity—one of which brings home to the individual, while the other distributes over the body politic, the good or bad consequences of any act. The one speaks to the individual as though isolated and autonomous; the other brings him within the common fold, sharing unavoidably in the good or bad that befalls others, as an incomplete element, a dependent member, of a composite, imperishable whole, which is mankind. *Responsibility* is the sanction of individual liberty, the justification of the *rights* of man. *Solidarity* is the proof of his social dependence and the origin of his duties.

(A page was missing from Bastiat's manuscript. The reader will pardon me for attempting to continue the thought of this religious introduction.) —Editor.]

Religion *(religare, to rebind),* that which connects our present life with the life to come, the living with the dead, time with eternity, the finite with the infinite, man with God.

ould we not say that divine justice, which seems so incomprehensible hen we consider the fate of individuals, becomes strikingly clear when reflect on the destiny of nations? The life of every man is a drama ose action is begun on one stage and is completed on another; but is not the case with the life of nations. That instructive tragedy ns and ends on earth. That is why history is a part of Holy Writ; it ls the justice of Providence. (De Custines, *La Russie.*)

rtunately the author did not live to deal with the interesting ations of this idea, which he had proposed to present here by of concrete illustrations, although he did indicate what their character was to be. The reader will be able to compensate for their loss by referring to chapter 16 of this book, and to 7 and 11 of the pamphlet "What Is Seen and What Is Not Seen" *ssays on Political Economy,* chap. 1).—Editor.]

of this chapter is little more than a series of notes thrown thout transitions or development.—Editor.]

ER 21

notes come to an abrupt end at this point; the *economic* aw of solidarity is not indicated. We refer the reader to 11, "Competition," and "Producer and Consumer."

is merely an expression of the sense of human dignity, constitutes in itself a natural limit on population."

In conclusion,·then, we may say that, wherever institutions are based on the natural prerequisites of social order: the family—which presupposes the ownership of property; private property—which presupposes liberty; and liberty, which is inseparable from individual responsibility; a numerical increase in the population will always be accompanied by a more rapid increase in well-being and productive capacity.

All that God does, he does well; and social science reveals one and the same pervasive harmony throughout its domain.—Editor.]

NOTES TO CHAPTER 17

1. "As soon as this value is paid by the taxpayer, it is lost to him; as soon as it is consumed by the government, it is lost to everybody and does not revert to society." (Say, *Traité d'économie politique,* Bk. III, chap. 9, p. 504.)

   Undoubtedly, but society receives in return the service that is rendered —protection, for example. Besides, Say reverts to the correct doctrine a few lines farther on, in these terms:

   "To levy a tax is to do society a wrong, a wrong that is compensated for by no advantage, *whenever no service is rendered in return." (Ibid.)*

2. "Public taxes, even with the nation's consent, are a violation of property rights, since they can be levied only on values that have been produced by the land, the capital, or the industry of private individuals. Thus, *whenever they exceed the indispensable minimum necessary for the preservation of society,* they may justly be considered as an act of plunder." *(Ibid.)*

   Here again the qualifying clause corrects what would otherwise have been too sweeping a statement. The doctrine that *services are exchanged for services* greatly simplifies both the problem and its solution.

3. The effects of this transformation are given concrete meaning by an example cited by M. d'Hautpoul, the Minister of War. "Each soldier," he said, "receives sixteen centimes a day for his food. The government takes these sixteen centimes from him and agrees to feed him. The result is that every soldier has precisely the same ration, whether it fits his individual needs or not. One has too much bread and throws it away. Another does not have enough meat, etc. We have tried an experiment: We allow the soldiers to spend the sixteen centimes for whatever they wish, and we are happy to find a perceptible improvement in their condition. Each one consults his own taste, his inclinations, and current prices. Generally speaking, they have, of their own accord, partially substituted meat for bread. Here they buy more bread, there more meat, elsewhere more vegetables, in another place more fish. Their health has benefited; they are more content, and the state has been freed of a great responsibility."

   The reader will understand that we are not here considering this experiment from the military point of view. I cite it as illustrating a primary difference between public service and private service, between regimentation and freedom. Would it be better for the state to take from us the resources whereby we provide ourselves with food and to assume the responsibility of feeding us, or to leave us both the resources and the responsibility for providing our own sustenance? The same question may be raised in regard to every one of our wants.

4. [See the pamphlet entitled "Academic Degrees and Socialism" (*Selected Essays on Political Economy*, chap. 9).—EDITOR.]

5. [The author in one of his previous works proposed to answer this same question. He investigated the subject of the legitimate domain of the law. All the arguments contained in the pamphlet entitled "The Law" (*Selected Essays on Political Economy*, chap. 2) apply to his present thesis. We refer the reader to it.—EDITOR.]

6. [The manuscript ends here. We refer our readers to the pamphlet entitled "Plunder and Law" (*Selected Essays on Political Economy*, chap. 8), in the second part of which the author gives their just due to the sophisms pronounced at this meeting of the General Council.

In regard to the six chapters which were to follow, under the titles of Taxation, Machinery, Free Trade, Middlemen, Raw Materials, Luxury, we refer the reader to: (1) the discourse on the tax on beverages inserted in the second edition of the pamphlet "Parliamentary Inconsistencies"; (2) the pamphlet entitled "What Is Seen and What Is Not Seen" (*Selected Essays on Political Economy*, chap. 1); (3) *Economic Sophisms*.—EDITOR.]

NOTE TO CHAPTER 18

1. [The author was unable to continue this study of the errors that are, for those led astray by them, a cause of almost immediate suffering, nor was he able to describe another class of errors, characterized by violence and fraud, whose first effects fall most severely on others. His notes contain nothing relating to *disturbing factors*, except the preceding fragment and the one that follows. We also refer the reader to chapter 1 of the second series of the *Sophisms*, entitled "The Physiology of Plunder."—EDITOR.]

NOTES TO CHAPTER 19

1. [See the end of chapter 11.—EDITOR.]
2. We forget this when we ask: Is slave labor cheaper or more expensive than free labor?
3. [See "Academic Degrees and Socialism" (*Selected Essays on Political Economy*, chap. 9).—EDITOR.]

NOTES TO CHAPTER 20

1. [. . . . because I believe that a higher Power directs it, because, since God can intervene in the moral order only through the instrumentality of each man's self-interest and will, the resulting action of various interests and wills cannot lead to ultimate evil; for otherwise it would not be man or the human race alone that is on the road to error, b God Himself who, in virtue of His impotence or cruelty, would leading His imperfect creature on to evil.

We therefore believe in liberty because we believe in the ha of the universe, that is, in God. Proclaiming in the name of fa mulating in the name of science, the divine laws, flexible a of our dynamic moral order, we utterly reject the narrow, unv static institutions that some men in their blindness woul introduce into this admirable mechanism. It would be a atheist to say: *Laissez faire!* Leave it to chance! But we, wh have the right to cry: *Laissez passer!* Let God's or prevail! Let human initiative, the marvelous and un of all man's motive power, function freely! And fr stood, is no longer an anarchistic deification of in worship, above and beyond man's activity, is God

We are well aware that man may err; indeed is as great as the distance separating well-f truth still only vaguely, intuitively sensed. to seek, it is his destiny to find. Truth, let relation, an inevitable affinity, not only w standing and the instincts of his heart, and moral conditions of his life; so th intellectual comprehension as *absolute* *just*, or his aesthetic sense as *beaut* acceptance by the practical and ir

We know that free will can lea God surely did not haphazardly set it, as it were, on either sid order that man, striking ag back to the good.

Our wills, like inert m —whereas inanimate thir —for beings endowed w and repulsion does no tion of the will and itself, and it then r of co-operation o pleasure or pain if the act is go a state of wel it is *bad*, its p

And, after all, what is, at bottom, the whole operation of the laws of social harmony, what are the consonance of men's interests and the great maxims: *The prosperity of each is the prosperity of all; the prosperity of all is the prosperity of each,* etc.; what is the congruity between *private property* and *common wealth,* the services of capital, the increase of gratuitous utility, etc.; except the development from the utilitarian viewpoint of the very title of this chapter: Solidarity?—EDITOR.]

NOTE TO CHAPTER 22

1. "Poverty is political economy's doing. . . . . Political economy has to have death come to its aid. . . . . It is the theory of instability and theft." (Proudhon, *Economic Contradictions,* Vol. II, p. 214.)

"If the people lack the means of subsistence. . . . it is the fault of political economy." *(Ibid.,* p. 430.)

NOTE TO CHAPTER 24

1. *Mémoires d'outre-tombe,* Vol. XI.

NOTE TO CHAPTER 25

1. [The author unfortunately left no material on the four chapters indicated here, and which he had included in the plan of his work, except the introduction to the last one.—EDITOR.]

NOTE TO THE APPENDIX

1. [Bastiat wrote this rough draft of a tentative preface, in the form of a letter addressed to himself, toward the end of 1847.—EDITOR.]

Index of Names

Prepared by Vernelia A. Crawford

NOTE: This index includes titles of chapters listed under the appropriate subject classification. With the exception of these specific page references, which are hyphenated, the numbers in each instance refer to the *first* page of a discussion. A page number followed by the letter "n" or a figure in parentheses indicates a footnote reference. Translator's notes are at the bottom of the page; all other notes are at the end of the text. Explanation of a name or term is given in its initial entry.

Index of Subjects